THE WORLD

IN THE TWENTIETH CENTURY

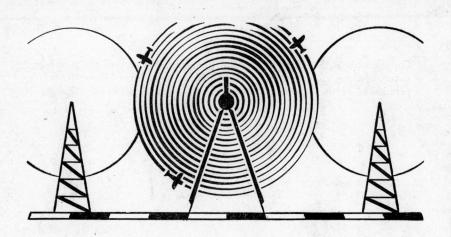

THE WORLD
in the Twentieth Century

BY GEOFFREY BRUUN

BOSTON

D. C. HEATH AND COMPANY

8115

Maps by Theodore R. Miller

Offices: BOSTON   NEW YORK   CHICAGO   ATLANTA
          SAN FRANCISCO   DALLAS   LONDON

Statistics are history standing still, and history is statistics put in motion.

LUDWIG AUGUST SCHLÖZER

FOREWORD

A TEXTBOOK on contemporary times must surmount grave limitations. It does not deal with closed chapters of history, episodes on which the returns are in and the results have been recorded and rationalized. It criticizes dramas still upon the stage, dramas for which the dénouement is often unresolved. The pageants of earlier centuries have hardened into conventional patterns, and long ago "high-piled books, in charactery," allotted the chief actors their historic roles. But for recent events the writer can offer only a provisional analysis, a temporary verdict. Truth is the daughter of time.

These considerations are chiefly responsible for the mode of treatment adopted in this text. Twentieth century history is still fluid, its values unverified, its trends unfulfilled. In these circumstances the historian must lean heavily upon such readily authenticated data as birth and death rates and industrial output. The bureau of statistics has become the cave of oracles, and students who would wrestle with contemporary problems must learn this arithmetic of power.

A second feature that may be noted here is the emphasis upon economics and geography. So many political forms and formulas have gone masked and hooded in recent decades that a people's destiny is most easily to be read in terms of its basic needs and resources. Though factions conspire and institutions crumble, the seas are not dried up nor the mountains removed. Fields and factories continue to shape historical movements even when the voices of the forum grow confused or silent. Vehement ideologies cannot safely defy the indices of industrial production. For this reason the geographic stage upon which the dramas of the twentieth century must be played out is worth attentive study; it offers surer clues to the meaning of events than political shibboleths and slogans.

Since this geographic stage has recently been expanded to global dimensions, the quest for a better global focus is a third characteristic of this text. "There are no islands any more." The local vicissitudes which have affected each people and each region during the past fifty years have always been contingent upon great events which happened elsewhere. This interdependence of the nations cannot be stressed too insistently. The twentieth century has already produced

two world wars and a world-wide economic depression. The interlocking interests and economies which expanded these disasters to
global proportions are still very imperfectly understood. If this survey
leaves its readers satisfied with what they know about global politics
and patterns of power, it will have failed in its major purpose.

A textbook is such a broad collective enterprise that it is impossible
to thank all the collaborators individually. My first acknowledgment
is due to Allan Nevins, De Witt Clinton Professor of American History at Columbia University, whose advice throughout the inception,
drafting, and revising of these chapters was a vital stimulus. The
flaws and limitations which persist are the measure of my inability to
profit more fully from his spacious and specific criticisms. To the
members of the College Department at D. C. Heath and Company,
and the staff at The Plimpton Press, who designed, set, corrected, and
clarified this volume, it is a special pleasure to record my pride at being associated for several months in their unsparing labors. To Mr.
Ted R. Miller, who executed all the maps, the reader is indebted for
the most illuminating pages which follow, and I am indebted for
convivial shoptalk and a deepened respect for cartography. Mrs.
Olive Brose earned my lasting gratitude for the many thoughtful cor-
rections she suggested when reading the galley proofs. Finally, for
the numerous acts of courtesy and cooperation which each permission
to quote and each credit line recalls, I want to repeat my formal acknowledgment and sincere appreciation.

GEOFFREY BRUUN

TABLE OF CONTENTS

PART VI THE ASIATIC AND PACIFIC WORLD

LIST OF ILLUSTRATIONS

LIST OF MAPS

LIST OF GRAPHS

PART I

Europe : 1900–1914

INTRODUCTION

1. ORIGINS

TODAY, for the first time in the annals of mankind, all parts of the world are in communication, all peoples are members of an interdependent society. There is no nation so remote or isolated that it can remain untouched by events on other continents. This contiguity and interdependence of the nations is a consequence of the hegemony established by the Europeans, for it is European conquest, culture, and technology which has knit the continents together. To understand how this dynamic European civilization won such worldwide influence it will be helpful to recall briefly how it arose in Europe itself.

Europe is not, in a geographical sense, one of the major continents; it is a peninsula jutting westward from the Eurasian land mass. The first European cultures were dependent and derivative, introduced by traders and colonists from the older civilizations which had arisen in the Nile and Euphrates Valleys. The barbaric aborigines of those regions now known as Spain, France, and England were raised to civilized status by the Romans some two thousand years ago. When the Roman Empire declined after the third century of our era, all Europe, including Italy, seemed destined to lapse again into timeless barbarism. But vestiges of Roman and Greek culture survived and the church preserved the memory and the ideal of that unity of language, law, and custom which had held the Roman world together. For nearly one thousand years, the period of the Middle Ages, the peoples of Christian Europe had only the bond of religious faith to unite them. Politically and economically, society broke down, disintegrating into smaller and smaller units until it became fragmentary and parochial. What little coherence remained was chiefly the product of a common faith and a common religious culture: Christendom was a community of the faithful. As trade and communications failed and towns decayed, the civilization of Roman times perished. The social unit became the hamlet or manor, where a few score or a few hundred families lived largely to themselves, raising their own supplies and depending upon an overlord and his armed retainers for administration and protection. ·

In this harsh era, poverty and hardship discouraged new experiments and daunted initiative. Society became and tended to remain static. Learning and even literacy were limited almost exclusively to the clergy. It was not lack of intelligence but lack of leisure and lack of opportunity which kept medieval communities backward. Even in the darkest centuries, between the sixth and the eleventh, some progress was achieved. Better methods of ploughing, of rotating crops, of harnessing horses and oxen, of constructing water and wind mills had been introduced before A.D. 1100. The canals, castles, and cathedrals constructed after that date all testify to the energy and will to collective activity which was developing in the later medieval period. But such collaboration suffered from rude practical limitations. It was limited by lack of political order, by absence of adequate means of transportation and communication, by deficiency of capital reserves for many large-scale projects, and by confusion resulting from haphazard scales of measurement and inadequate tools. The localism, poverty, and social inertia which overtook society after the collapse of the Roman power deepened for five centuries and then required another five to dissipate.

No prophetic observer contemplating the frugal life, the backward economy, the chaotic political institutions of Europe in the year 1000 could have foreseen that before another thousand years had passed Europe would lead the world. Such an imperial destiny seemed much more likely to descend upon the peoples of Asia. During those centuries when Europe was a decentralized patchwork of minute, autonomous fragments, great empires arose and waned beyond the frontiers of Christendom. The eastern half of the Roman Empire survived the fall of the West, and Constantinople remained the capital of a sophisticated and luxurious civilization. Because the European peoples, isolated in their scattered parishes, ignored developments outside their narrow world, modern historians have too often treated European society during the Middle Ages as if it existed in a vacuum. This narrow view still influences the thought of many European peoples when they think about Europe and its cultural origins.

The contrast between the civilized East and the barbarous West in

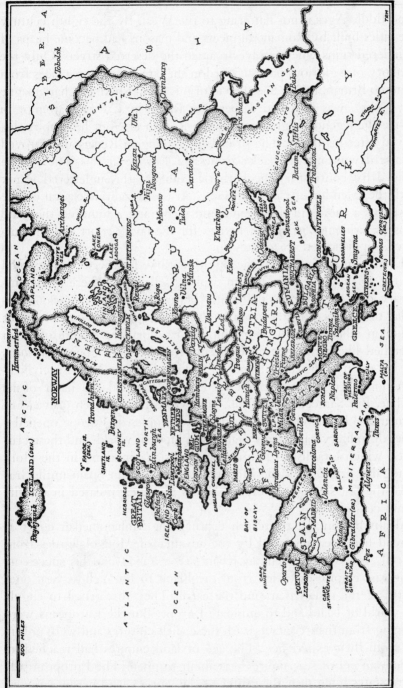

EUROPE, 1900

the Middle Ages is not flattering to the West. By the eighth century the cities built by Roman engineers and masons had become heaps of plundered ruins where wolves roamed the deserted streets. Only the memory of a glorious past survived in the late Roman provinces from Spain to Britain. In A.D. 800 the victorious Frankish king, Charlemagne (771–814), was crowned emperor at Rome in a wistful attempt to revive the legendary greatness of the Roman era, but his empire dissolved after his death. The so-called Carolingian Renaissance proved a false dawn, and the backwardness of Europe at this time can be gauged by contrasting the barbaric court of this unlettered Frank with the splendor of Constantinople. At the Byzantine capital on the Bosporus a thousand ships came and went, and a hundred thousand artisans fashioned articles of luxury for the lavish court and the cultured, sophisticated aristocracy.

Even Constantinople in the ninth century, however, was eclipsed by the splendor of the Moslem capital at Bagdad. There a contemporary of Charlemagne, the caliph Harun-al-Rashid (786–809), familiar to readers of the *Arabian Nights*, ruled a fabulous city of almost a million inhabitants. At the zenith of its glory the empire of Islam stretched like a threatening crescent from Syria to Spain, its horns closing upon Christian Europe. In Spain a brilliant Moorish civilization flourished while the rest of Europe touched the nadir of its decline. But Saracen civilization, however brilliant, often proved impermanent. In the eleventh century the peoples of Europe opened a series of military campaigns against the Moslem world; and these crusades, which established temporary Christian kingdoms in the Holy Land, also drove back the Mohammedan power in Spain until Granada, the last stronghold of the Moors there, capitulated in the fifteenth century.

Meanwhile in the thirteenth century the Mohammedan court at Bagdad had been menaced by the advance of Mongol hordes from central Asia. Under Genghis Khan (1162–1227) and his successors their vast empire extended from the Black to the Yellow Sea, onefourth of the distance around the earth. They threatened to engulf the world of Islam and to inundate Europe. But the Europeans were learning from their contacts with these alien cultures and were profiting from their experience. The age of land empires had reached its period; an era of sea empires was about to open. The European seaboard states lying near the center of the world's land masses enjoyed enviable advantages which predestined them to leadership in the new age. For Europe possessed a favorable climate, fertile soil, and a vigorous, rising population. It also possessed an indented coast, sheltered harbors, and navigable rivers which encouraged navigation, as well as hardy sailors and abundant wood for ships. Finally, it had begun by the close of the Middle Ages to evolve political and economic institutions favorable to expansion. After A.D. 1400 the stage was set for the great historic drama of the next five centuries, a drama without parallel in previous history. The Europeans were about to "inherit the earth."

2. THE OCEANIC AGE

The geographical discoveries of the fifteenth century, especially the voyage of Columbus to America (1492) and of Vasco da Gama to India (1498), were bold feats of navigation. But they were epoch-making and opened a new age only because the peoples on the Atlantic seaboard of Europe were ready to exploit the new opportunities. Leif Ericson with his Vikings had visited America about A.D. 1000 and had founded nothing more substantial than a saga. In the five centuries between Leif and Columbus, however, a notable change transformed European society. The best proof of this change is the rise in population, testifying to a more adequate food supply and greater security of life and property. After A.D. 1200 there was a marked revival of town life and signs of quickening trade. In politics, the extension of royal power in Spain, Portugal, France, and England curbed the disruptive forces of feudalism and ushered in the age of the national state. The monarchs with the aid of the townsmen checked the warfare and depredations of the barons and created centralized governments strong and wealthy enough to undertake the conquest and colonization of empires overseas. Without these conditions there could have been no voyages of discovery, no European conquest of the Americas, no exploitation of trade with the East Indies.

The first European states to profit by the opening of the Oceanic Age were Spain and Portugal. Both were newly forged kingdoms, both had Atlantic harbors, in both the population responded readily to the twin urges of crusading ardor and commercial enterprise which impelled the early explorers. The sixteenth century was the great century of Iberian conquest, during which the Spaniards ferried tons of gold and silver from America and the Portuguese tons of spices (worth their weight in gold) from the East Indies. The future culture and language patterns of Central and South America and the destinies of millions of native peoples from the Philippines to Ceylon were largely decided in that significant century. Spain and Portugal led the van and set the tempo of expansion and conquest.

Ocean communications are tenuous threads upon which to string the jewels of a maritime empire, for once the thread is severed the jewels are likely to be lost. In the seventeenth century the Netherlanders, the French, and the English challenged Spain and Portugal for control of the sea. The Dutch took over most of the Portuguese posts and trading monopolies in the East. The British between 1600 and 1800 captured the trade of the Spanish and Portuguese colonies in Latin America, and after 1800 they helped these colonies to achieve political as well as economic emancipation from the control of Madrid and Lisbon. The French, who likewise entered the colonial race in the seventeenth century, established colonies in Canada, Louisiana, and the West Indies and acquired trading posts in India. But the wars of the eighteenth century swept most of these French dependencies into the control of the British. The Spaniards under Philip II (1556–1598) and the French under Louis XIV (1643–1715) and Napoleon (1799–1814) learned the same bitter lesson that even the most powerful state could not maintain a military hegemony in Europe and naval supremacy on the sea at the same time. By the opening of the nineteenth century Great Britain was the leading colonial, naval, and maritime power of the world, and the rapid mechanization of British industry was making her the leading industrial power also. Free from invasion and from the burden of a large military force, she diverted her energies to the sea and benefited prodigiously from the vast opportunities of the Oceanic Age. The insecurity, destruction, and indemnities which crippled her chief commercial competitors, Spain, Portugal, the Netherlands, and France, as a result of European wars, redounded to the advantage of England. While European states exhausted themselves waging long campaigns to decide the fate of a few towns in Flanders, the English secured continental areas overseas.

Until 1750 colonial expansion was conditioned by two main factors: commercial profit and naval power. After the middle of the eighteenth century the British added a third element to the program of imperialism, the factory system. In the nineteenth century an overseas empire was to become the concrete expression of armed might, a territorial conquest financed by commercial profits, which produced raw materials for the mechanized industry of the mother country. The Industrial Revolution, gathering momentum in the late eighteenth century, transformed modern society, multiplied the products and profits of manufacture, and injected a new dynamism into the drama of imperial expansion. Colonies took on a new, a peremptory significance as sources of supply and as markets for factory output. Britain, the first state to feel the new industrial impulse powerfully, became in a few generations "the workshop of the world."

In a few decades the output of the British textile weaver was multiplied twentyfold. From 1820 to 1860 the number of weavers in England remained approximately the same. But when this number, roughly 250,000, worked in factories instead of laboring over a handloom in their homes, they produced fabrics which 5,000,000 handworkers could not have equaled under the domestic system. Spinning and weaving were the first crafts to be mechanized in this total fashion, but throughout the nineteenth century other processes once performed by hand were steadily transferred to more and more ingenious machines.

The lives of the workers as well as their output were transformed by the factory system. Within a century, so swift was the migration to the industrial towns, localities of 5000 or 10,000 inhabitants grew into cities of 50,000, or 100,000, or even 500,000 dwellers. The population of Great Britain rose from 10,000,000 in 1800 to 37,000,000 in 1900. Industry, commerce, and mining came to employ three-fourths of the working class, while agriculture sank into a neglected activity of minor importance. Four Englishmen out of five became city or town dwellers, treading pavements instead of ploughlands, more familiar with gas fumes than the reek of burning leaves; many millions of them crowded in tenements overshadowed by a pall of factory smoke under which grass withered and shade trees died. But such was the environment in which the machines were most readily accommodated and the machines were becoming the arbiters of the factory worker's fate. Political constitutions and legislative acts, the milestones on the political highway of man's advance, seemed but superficial markers in comparison with technological innovations which could change the direction in which a whole society was moving and reshape the life of millions in a few years.

3. THE TRIUMPHS OF MODERN TECHNOLOGY

Man has been described as "the animal that uses tools" and it is true that the successive stages in his climb to civilization are each marked by his acquisition and mastery of a new instrument or source of power. For eons the rate of progress must have been incomprehensibly slow.

The Paleolithic or Old Stone Age, when man's principal tool was a fist hatchet, is thought to have lasted 1,000,000 years. Then, perhaps 50,000 to 30,000 years ago, man began to make improvements in his implements; and for the last 10,000 years his inventiveness has grown at a surprising pace. But it is the last century which brought the most radical innovation of all, the "invention of invention." So bewildering have recent technical devices become in their cumulative effects that philosophers, politicians, and militarists hold their judgments in suspense while they wait the latest revelation from the scientists' laboratories.

This triumphant progress of technology is introducing a new emphasis and time scheme into historical writing. Political annalists long dated their records by the reigns of kings or the rise and fall of empires. Parallel to this political chronology, however, there must always have been a second ledger of human achievements, a calendar in which new eras opened not with a conquest or a coronation but with a discovery or invention. The conquest of fire, the domestication of animals, the cultivation of plants, the baking of pottery, weaving of cloth, smelting of metals, the invention of the wheel, the development of writing — these were triumphs less immediate and less dramatic than battles but much more enduring in their benefits.

A better method of basketmaking or boatbuilding might be preserved from generation to generation by tradition or transmitted from tribe to tribe by diffusion. The transmission of a technique is not possible, however, unless there is contact between peoples of differing cultural levels. So long as tribes and cultures remained local and segregated and discovery was the result of chance, progress was spasmodic and there must often have been regressive periods when skills painfully mastered were lost and forgotten. Before Europeans arrived in America the Aztecs and Incas did not know of the horse or the wheel; in these omissions they were at the level of the Egyptians or Babylonians before 3000 B.C. But once the Oceanic Age opened, the isolation of all cultures was at an end. Peoples at all levels of development, from the Indians of Patagonia who did not know the use of fire to the subtle artists of China with traditions and techniques perfected through the centuries, were laid open to the scrutiny of the exploring European. This contact with new ideas, methods, products, and customs could not fail to stimulate inventive minds.

European man had the will to conquer before he found the means: he could not have expanded his dominion without the improved sailing vessels which enabled him to cross wide oceans, the compass and charts which made navigation a science, the cannon which overawed and conquered. These early instruments of his imperialism are significant because they were instruments of precision and of power. The past five hundred years have been unique in human history not because of the political concepts evolved, the achievements in art or architecture, or the colonization of new lands. The characteristic which has raised modern man above his forebears and distinguishes contemporary civilization from all previous cultures is the superiority and complexity of the machines, and the most remarkable of these machines are the most recent.

But to operate machines requires energy, human, animal, or mechanical. Man's progress has been determined very largely by the forms of energy which he found it possible to harness when he wanted to get work done. The earliest sources of energy (aside from their own muscles) which men learned to employ were domesticated animals, oxen, elephants, horses. The forms of natural energy which they first utilized deliberately were wind and water. The sailing ship released galley slaves from a life of killing labor; the windmill pumped water for irrigation or to drain swamps; and the water mill ground flour. But wind was a capricious agent which often failed when most needed; and water power, though more dependable, could be harnessed only in moderate amounts at a fixed location.

It was the advent of steam power in the late eighteenth and early nineteenth century that opened the modern age of the machine and brought undreamed of advances in technological development. The steam engine could be applied to almost any task demanding vast and manageable power — to pumps in mines and ships, to mills and factories, to winches, derricks, and other stationary engines, and to steamships and locomotives for rapid travel. The nineteenth century was the "age of steam."

For some purposes, however, steam power was not well suited. Steam-driven buses were developed but they did not operate easily on the highways. Steam-driven tractors failed to solve the power problem of the ploughman and the reaper. By 1900 inventors had devised a lighter and more effective type of engine and applied it to these and many other purposes. The internal combustion engine was not radically different from the steam engine; it, too, utilized the expansive energy of hot gases in closed cylinders to produce a rotary motion. But it provided a more efficient power plant for automobiles, farm tractors, trucks, and small boats, and it made possible an engine light but powerful enough to lift a flying machine into the air and sustain it in flight. It appeared as if the century of steam was to be followed by a "century of petroleum" but within a generation after 1900 a still newer form of energy had relegated both steam-driven and gasoline-driven engines to a secondary place.

The twentieth century, it became evident almost at once, was to be predominantly an age of electricity. In electricity man had at last found the almost perfect form of power, measurable, transformable, instantaneously conductible, and available in almost incalculable amounts.[1] Used first for the electric telegraph, telephone, and incandescent lamp, then for the street railway and other traction engines, electricity speedily proved itself the ideal form of energy in home and factory. In 1900 less than 5 per cent of the power used in American industry was electrical. By 1914 the ratio had risen to 37 per cent, and by 1930 to 80 per cent. The energy locked in coal could now be converted through steam-driven generators and the resulting electric power carried on wires to towns or factories scores or hundreds of miles away. A multitude of electrically driven devices, from telephones to tabulators and arc welders to milking machines transformed ancient tasks and reduced toil in home and office, factory and farm. If for any reason its electric power supply fails, the heart of a modern city stops beating. Every year increases civilized man's dependence upon this cheap power.

All advanced nations felt the social and economic stimulus of the new forms of power and the new inventions. New requirements, new appetites, developed overnight. Electrical communication, lighting, and transmission called for extraordinary supplies of copper wiring, insulation, tungsten, and other materials. The gasoline engine devoured rivers of petroleum. As civilized man became more and more dependent upon his machines, he became more exigent in seeking and securing the raw materials, the minerals and metals and fuels which the machines required. Girded with a panoply of amazing instruments and goaded by the economic pressures which the operation of these instruments intensified, he became more enterprising and more ag-

---

[1] One kilowatt hour is considered equivalent to ten man-hours of work. At this ratio the 230,736,488,000 kw. hrs. of electrical energy used by the American people in 1944 was a substitute for the labor of 100,000,-000,000 slaves working twenty-four hours a day — a labor force fifty times the world population.

gressive in satisfying his needs. Progress based on an advancing technology led to a swifter use of all natural resources. When these were lacking within its political boundaries, each nation looked abroad. In the resulting race those countries still geared to an agrarian economy were at a disadvantage, for the race was to the swift, and the swift, in this case, were the nations equipped with modern machines.

Economic competition grew more intense, for an industrialized state is an expanding state with an expanding economy. In the late nineteenth century, when Germany, France, and the United States were energized by the forces of industrialism, they began to compete more vigorously with Great Britain and with one another for supplies, markets, and spheres of influence. This reaching and jostling made the world suddenly seem small. The steamship, railway, and electric telegraph had shrunk the planet; the oceans had become a highway linking all lands. The last unclaimed areas were seized after 1880 as the powers sought control of markets, protectorates, and sources of raw material. The last virgin areas were visited and scrutinized by keen-eyed surveyors who represented syndicates in London, Berlin, Paris, or New York. Expanding industries create their own demands. The foundries and factories of Manchester and Mannheim, Paris and Pittsburgh, Turin and Tokyo were growing hungry and the whole world was becoming too small a field to satisfy their potential appetites.

The New Industrial Revolution or Technological Revolution of the late nineteenth century shaped the contemporary world. It unlocked vast resources of power, magnified the wealth, expanded the production, multiplied the population of all the leading nations at an accelerating pace. A series of economic "explosions" shook the European continent and, passing beyond Europe, unbalanced the world equilibrium. The drives for empire, pressed by the dynamic, industrialized nation-states, will be studied in later chapters. As a prelude, it may be helpful to pause at the close of the nineteenth century to note world conditions in the years before 1900. A number of minor crises and international disputes, in the decade 1890–1899, call for analysis. They were signs on the road as humanity swung around a corner; they prefigured the future and were in a sense rehearsals of the great dramas of the twentieth century.

4. A DECADE OF THE NEW IMPERIALISM, 1890–1899

The last years of the nineteenth century were marked by an epidemic of minor imperialistic wars which left no continent or country unstirred. These wars were in most cases remote "colonial" wars. But their number, frequency, and seeming inevitability was a proof of the quickening tempo of the New Industrialism which fostered the New Imperialism. A list of these conflicts will reveal how global European or western civilization had become in its activities and aggressions.

The British were particularly enterprising during the 1890's, especially in Africa. They fought the desert tribes of the Sudan (1896–1898) to extend Anglo-Egyptian influence up the Nile Valley; and they conquered the Transvaal and Orange Free State between 1899 and 1902, although these Boer republics, organized by the descendants of seventeenth century Dutch settlers in South Africa, resisted long and bravely. In 1896 an Italian army attempted the conquest of Ethiopia (Abyssinia) but was defeated at Adowa. French forces in the same years conquered Madagascar (1894–1896) and also extended French control in West Africa. The Germans subdued three segments of the Dark Continent to which they laid claim, German East Africa, South West Africa, and the Cameroons. A map of Africa in 1870 and in 1900 suggests how swiftly this partitioning of the continent was carried out by the powers.

What the map does not reveal is the futile resistance offered by the native peoples, the foredoomed struggles of the Sudanese, Berbers, Riffs, Senegalese, Senussi, Hovas, Tuaregs, Ashantis, Basutos, Zulus, Matabeles, Bantus, and a score of other groups. Nor does the map reveal the heroism of the missionaries and explorers, the rivalries of aggressive trading companies, the long, obscure campaigns in desert and jungle, the pacification of fierce and primitive peoples. Wars with the aboriginal inhabitants were unequal contests in which the Europeans held all the advantages. More than once, however, the competition for territory led the great powers to the brink of war themselves. In the division of Africa the most critical incident of this kind came in 1898. An encounter between a French and a British expedition at Fashoda on the Upper Nile brought the two governments so close to hostilities that only adroit diplomacy averted war.

In Asia likewise the late nineteenth century found the powers competing for concessions and conquests. Before 1900 all India, Burma, and the Malay States were under British protection, and British influence was expanding in Afghanistan and Tibet. The French organized four conquered provinces, Cochin China, Cambodia, Annam, and Tonkin, as an Indo-Chinese Union under French protection (1887) and then went on to annex Laos (1893). In northern China

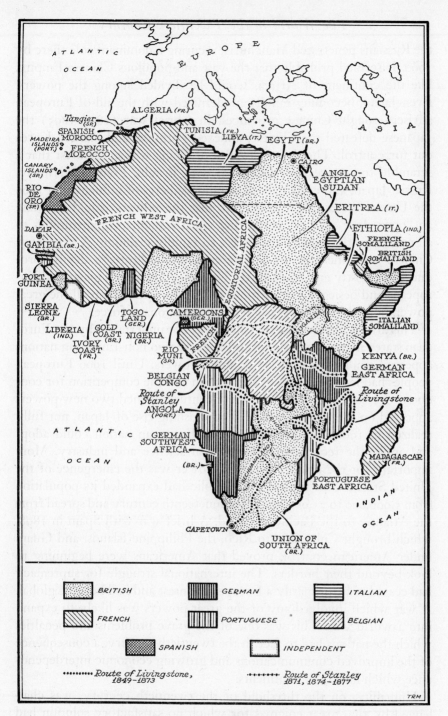

ATLANTIC
OCEAN

EUROPE

ASIA

Tangier
(SP.)
SPANISH MOROCCO
MADEIRA ISLANDS (PORT.)
FRENCH MOROCCO
CANARY ISLANDS (SP.)
RIO DE ORO (SP.)

ALGERIA (FR.)

TUNISIA (FR.)
LIBYA (IT.)
EGYPT (BR.)

CAIRO

ANGLO-EGYPTIAN SUDAN

ERITREA (IT.)

ETHIOPIA (IND.)
FRENCH SOMALILAND
BRITISH SOMALILAND

DAKAR
GAMBIA (BR.)

FRENCH WEST AFRICA

EQUATORIAL AFRICA

PORT. GUINEA

SIERRA LEONE (BR.)
LIBERIA (IND.)
IVORY COAST (FR.)
GOLD COAST (BR.)
TOGO-LAND (GER.)
NIGERIA (BR.)
CAMEROONS (GER.)
RIO MUNI (SP.)

ITALIAN SOMALILAND

UGANDA

KENYA (BR.)
GERMAN EAST AFRICA

FRENCH

BELGIAN CONGO

Route of Stanley

ANGOLA (PORT.)

Route of Livingstone

ATLANTIC
OCEAN

GERMAN SOUTHWEST AFRICA
(BR.)

BECHUANALAND

MADAGASCAR (FR.)

PORTUGUESE EAST AFRICA

INDIAN
OCEAN

CAPETOWN

UNION OF SOUTH AFRICA (BR.)

BRITISH	GERMAN	ITALIAN
FRENCH	PORTUGUESE	BELGIAN
SPANISH	INDEPENDENT	

·········· *Route of Livingstone,*
1849–1873

·········· *Route of Stanley*
1871, 1874–1877

TRM

THE PARTITIONING OF AFRICA TO 1914

the Russians penetrated Manchuria, securing a dominant role there by 1900. It seemed probable that the vast and populous Chinese Empire, like the continent of Africa, would be divided among the powers. Even Japan, becoming rapidly modernized with the aid of European advisers, sought Chinese provinces. In a brief war (1894–1895) the Japanese defeated the Chinese, annexed Formosa, and marked Korea out for control. The defenselessness of China was so manifest that a scramble for concessions followed, with Britain, France, Germany, Russia, Japan, and even Italy demanding spheres of influence. In 1899 the United States asked assurances that the powers would maintain an "open door" policy, permitting equal economic opportunities to all nations in the spheres they were so rapidly claiming. A year later, Chinese resentment at the interference of the "foreign devils" produced the costly and futile Boxer Uprising. The rebels massacred Europeans and besieged the legations in Peking, whereupon all the great powers joined in sending a punitive expeditionary force.

This armed intervention in China was not undertaken by the European states alone; it was significant because two non-European nations appeared among the concert of great powers. Until 1900 European peoples had led the march of civilization and the competition for conquests overseas. But as the twentieth century opened two new powers appeared on the world stage. The astonishing rise of Japan, not fully realized in 1900, indicated that a non-European nation could adopt and apply the techniques of European science and industry. More important for the balance of world power was the emergence of the United States. This formidable republic had expanded its population from 5,000,000 to 75,000,000 in the nineteenth century and spread from the Atlantic to the Pacific seaboard. A brief war with Spain in 1898, which brought Cuba, Puerto Rico, the Philippine Islands, and Guam under American control, proved that Americans were beginning to look beyond their borders. The international struggle for supremacy had ceased to be primarily a European contest and had become global. A war which involved any of the great powers was likely to expand into a world war. This was one of the grave problems and penalties which the nations had to face in the twentieth century, a consequence of the improved communications and growing economic interdependence which linked all continents.

Humanity, on the threshold of the twentieth century, was challenged by two great enigmas for which no satisfactory solution had been found. The first was the constant threat of war. Tension was mounting in Europe; the menace of an armed conflict deepened yearly. Austrian and Russian interests conflicted in the Balkans. Britain, France, Germany, and Italy were rivals for North African spheres. The Germans were increasing their army to meet the threat of the Franco-Russian alliance, and their fleet to overtake the British naval expansion. This condition of armed peace strained the resources and the nerves of the European peoples, creating a state of tension which was itself provocative of war.

All attempts to relieve the tension and to limit armaments by mutual agreement failed. In 1898 Czar Nicholas II of Russia issued a call for a peace conference to discuss the arbitration of disputes and reduction of arms. When the conference met at The Hague in 1899 some humane principles were affirmed and a court of international arbitration established. But it was evident that there was little real willingness to disarm and the results were a profound disappointment to lovers of peace. War remained a constant threat, its prophetic horrors magnified yearly as new weapons of destruction were invented.

The second great problem which confronted all civilized nations at the opening of the century was the problem of class conflict. Despite the amazing material progress of the preceding generations, the multiplication of wealth, the richer food supplies, the rise of trade and expansion of industry, in every country opulent classes flourished while indigent masses lived in want. The riddle of social justice, the problem of distributing goods and services more equitably, still defied solution. The threat of armed conflict among the industrialized states was matched by the menace of a class war within the industrialized states. To reduce grievances, to satisfy legitimate ambitions, to adjust the tensions between nations and classes without open hostilities, these were the major issues for which the statesmen of the twentieth century would have to seek a solution.

In the chapters which follow it will be seen how persistently these issues have dominated contemporary politics. All the leading states, regardless of their alliances or form of government, may be appraised under three heads: (1) The Problem of Resources, (2) The Problem of Defense, and (3) The Problem of Social Justice.

GREAT BRITAIN

The weary titan staggers beneath the too vast orb of its fate.
JOSEPH CHAMBERLAIN

1. RESOURCES: THE PROBLEM OF SUPPLY

NATURE endowed Great Britain with many of the advantages which helped to make it a leading power. As an island it was relatively secure from invasion and the people could dispense with a large army. Good harbors and a position near the center of the world's land masses were primary assets in the Oceanic Age. The moist but healthy climate, homogeneous population, and liberal political institutions permitted a steady expansion of the national energy and the national initiative. Spared the march of foreign armies and (save in the seventeenth century) the destruction of civil war, modern Britain has grown stronger and richer with each generation.

In the eighteenth century these and other advantages made Britain the predestined home of the Industrial Revolution. In England the rise of the factory system was favored by conditions that could be matched nowhere else. The capital required for experiment and for the construction of costly machinery had been accumulated in the hands of enterprising men. A supply of cheap labor became available opportunely because the enclosure movement in agriculture drove many farm hands and free tenants to the city. The wars of the French Revolution (1793–1814) kept Britain's rivals, especially France, occupied and blockaded during a critical quarter of a century, leaving British manufacturers a monopoly of ocean trade and the world for a market. Finally, iron to build machines and coal to run the steam engines were both available in England. The annual production of these two essentials rose prodigiously in the nineteenth century, coal from some 10,000,000 tons in 1800 to 300,000,000 in 1914, iron from 500,000 tons to 10,000,000 yearly in the same period.

One notable result of the mechanization of British industry and the rise of the factory system was a phenomenal expansion of the manufacturing cities. In 1800 nine out of ten people in England lived in the country or in small villages. By 1914 this ratio had almost been reversed: seven people out of ten lived in urban communities. This inevitable increase in the urban population is an index of industrialization, and it will be noted in other states as the methods of machine production spread to the Continent. In England one result of this overwhelming migration to the cities was the decline of agriculture. The island kingdom had been largely self-sustaining in 1800 but as it became the workshop of the world the population learned to rely more and more extensively upon imported food. Here again statistics tell the story vividly as a few figures will illustrate.

By 1914, when World War I commenced, the British were importing annually some 300,000,000 bushels of wheat, oats, and barley, 1,000,000,000 pounds of dairy products, 1,000,000,000 pounds of beef, 2,000,000,000 pounds of ham, pork, and mutton, 3,000,000,000 pounds of sugar. There is no need to extend the list to make the lesson clear. England, like a vast city, lived on the food delivered daily. Some of the imports came from nearby sources, from Ireland, Denmark, Holland; but most of it had to be shipped thousands of miles across the oceans, from Australia, India, the Argentine Republic, Canada, and the United States. Every working day of the year, 33,000,000 pounds of wheat, 10,000,000 pounds of sugar, 3,000,000 pounds of dairy foods, 1,000,000 pounds of tea, and many other items of food had to be landed safely on British docks. The average Englishman accepted this unparalleled achievement in transportation as a matter of fact. Yet it was a startling thought that he could enjoy his five o'clock tea, muffin, and marmalade for a few pennies although the ingredients might have come half way around the world. Those who paused to ponder the problem could hardly fail to realize how vulnerable Britain would become if a hostile power disrupted the sea lanes and cut off this daily stream of sea-borne supplies.

To feed 35,000,000 people, largely on imported food, was a problem difficult enough, but to feed the factory machines which consumed raw materials not by the pound but by the shipload was a staggering task. British textile mills required 1,000,000 tons of cotton annually, imported chiefly from the United States. The cloth produced for markets all over the world was valued at $500,000,000. In 1914, 50,000 tons of rubber (largely from the East Indies), 100,000 tons of copper, 300,000 tons of nickel (mostly from Canada), were annual requirements of British industry. The total import and export trade was valued at $7,000,000,000 a year when the First World War disrupted international economy.

To transport this great overseas trade Britain possessed a mercantile marine rated (1914) at over 18,000,000 tons, almost one-half the mercantile ocean tonnage of the world. These ships did not serve British needs alone; they conveyed goods for many nations and their operations were linked with the services provided by British bankers, insurance brokers, and commercial agents in all parts of the world. From their vast network of financial, maritime, mail, cable, and passenger services, as well as from their great investments of capital in foreign countries, British firms derived an invisible income which helped to equalize the trade balance of the nation. This added income from services was important because the cost of imports, including food, outran the value of exports. In 1913 this deficit in the trade balance rose to over $500,000,000.

By concentrating their activities upon the rewards of trade, industry, and finance, the British had grown wealthy and powerful. But they had also grown vulnerable. With three out of four wage earners dependent upon industry, commerce, shipping, or mining, it was evident that any serious disruption of the delicate balance of world trade would bring them swift and critical losses. When electricity, or "white coal," began to replace the steam engine, when oil and gasoline afforded new sources of fuel and energy, British coal miners by the hundred thousand were thrown out of work. When other nations, France, Germany, Italy, Russia, and the United States developed their own factory machines, British industrial prosperity was shaken. With the merchant ships of rival powers competing for passengers and cargoes, the profits of the British mercantile marine declined. As foreign markets were lost to rival manufacturers and the export trade fell off, the British found it more difficult to pay for the food and raw materials they had to import. Because business was expanding everywhere the total value of British trade continued to increase but the British share was falling.

Even in peacetime, therefore, Britain in the twentieth century faced the danger of an economic decline. If war or foreign blockade halted the shuttling of the ships which wove the fabric of British greatness, the nation might be paralyzed and impoverished in a few months. The supplies of food and materials on hand were seldom sufficient for more than a season. Prolonged interruption of trade would mean hunger for millions of the population and idle factories starved for raw stuffs. To safeguard the nation against such a contingency was the primary duty of the government, a responsibility which dominated the calculations of all leading British statesmen. The question of imperial defense and the influence it exerted on politics requires a section to itself.

2. DEFENSE: THE PROBLEM OF NAVAL SUPREMACY

Throughout most of the nineteenth century Britain's naval power had no serious rival. On all the oceans the ships of other nations dipped their ensigns in acknowledgment of her might. Her far-cruising battleships were never out of range of the innumerable islands, treaty ports, coaling stations, and other bases acquired in earlier years, where the units of the fleet could refit, take on supplies, and so maintain their distant circuits. Naval squadrons have only a limited range of effectiveness; like a beam of light a battleship loses power the farther it moves from its base. But British bases dotted all the oceans and they possessed added value because many of them were strategically located where the lines of maritime commerce converged at geographical bottlenecks. The map on page 34 reveals why control of such points as Gibraltar, Suez, Aden, and Singapore enabled the British to police the world commerce routes and why supplementary stations such as Halifax, Bermuda, Cape Town (at the southern tip of Africa), the Falkland Islands (at the southern point of South America), and a score of lesser stations permitted the British ships to remain at sea and perform their vital service of protecting British maritime interests.

To assure this naval supremacy the admiralty found it advisable after 1889 to adopt the principle of the "two-power standard." New navies were in process of construction, and the British decided that their security demanded the maintenance of a fleet equal to any two other navies of the world combined. It had been relatively easy to hold this preponderance without emphasizing it during the halcyon days of the mid-nineteenth century British ascendency. After 1889 the principle was openly avowed because it was more openly challenged. By 1900 naval competition had become a tense and dangerous rivalry. The French, the Russians, the Americans, the Italians, and the Japanese began to construct impressive fleets. But the threat which really alarmed the British was the German naval program. A German law of 1898 outlined plans for a powerful high seas fleet, and a second law of 1900 defined the aims still more clearly and ominously. Unless checked, Germany would soon possess a navy which approached that of Britain in strength. As the German forces could all be concentrated in the North Sea, whereas the British squadrons were normally dispersed throughout the world, this situation might easily result in relative German superiority in the waters around the British Isles.

The Lords of the Admiralty decided that Britain must maintain the two-power standard even if this meant building two warships for every one laid down in German shipyards. They also adopted plans for a new type of superbattleship. The first model, the *Dreadnought*, launched in 1906, was so heavily gunned and armored that it made all existing capital ships second rate. This achievement proved, ironically, not a gain but a setback for the British, for it opened a new phase in naval construction. All first line ships had to be revalued, and Britain's rivals began to build a new fleet of dreadnoughts from an even start. The Germans voted new and extravagant naval appropriations; British attempts to reach an agreement with them on naval limitation had no success. By 1908 the British government in a state of near panic was laying the keels of eight new dreadnoughts and was designing still larger and more expensive craft, the superdreadnoughts.

The jealousy engendered by this naval race was intensified, especially in Britain, by Anglo-German trade rivalry. By 1900 German steel production had risen to double the British; by 1914 it had trebled it. The value of German foreign trade climbed to two-thirds the British total, and some German wares outsold British products even in British markets. The psychological effects of such a trade war will be considered later in connection with subsequent trade crises. In this case there can be little doubt that after 1900 the combination of naval and business rivalry helped to increase Anglo-German hostility. In the 1890's the two countries had been on fairly friendly terms and proposals for an alliance were discussed in Berlin and in London. But after 1900 an estrangement grew and became official. The death of Queen Victoria (1901) brought a change of mood in court circles, for her son and successor, Edward VII (1901–1910), disliked his nephew, Kaiser William II, and showed a marked preference for the French. At the height of power Britain had avoided entangling alliances and maintained a position of "splendid isolation." But the balance was shifting and as the twentieth century opened Britain stood at the parting of the ways. The choices made by British diplomats in the next three years were decisive; they set the course of European history.

The first proof that the British were forsaking their policy of isolation came in 1902. An accord with Japan reached in that year safe-guarded British interests in the Far East. In 1904 an entente with France, supplemented by a naval agreement, relegated the major role in policing the Mediterranean to the French fleet, while the British concentrated their heaviest battleships in the North Sea. This move was a direct answer to the German naval challenge. It was not Russian threats that called the British fleet to home waters, especially as the Russian sea power sank with most of the Russian navy in the Russo-Japanese struggle of 1904–1905. With the most efficient army and the second largest navy in the world, Germany had become a threat to the balance of power in Europe and the British were facing the threat in their own fashion.

By 1907 the lines were forming for a titanic conflict. In that year Britain joined the Franco-Russian Alliance, which thus became a Triple Entente to match the Triple Alliance of Germany, Austria-Hungary, and Italy. Actually the Triple Alliance was less of a threat than it appeared, for Italy was an undependable partner and Austria was weakened by internal feuds. Germany formed the core of this *bloc*, and it was the rapid rise of German power, economic, military, and naval, which determined the British course of action.

In their policies after 1900 British leaders pursued a principle which had governed British diplomacy for three hundred years. Since the sixteenth century Britain had never failed to join a European coalition when any too-powerful state threatened to establish a hegemony on the Continent. The British had supported coalitions against Philip II of Spain, against Louis XIV of France, and against Napoleon, with the same resolution which they showed when German preponderance became a potential threat after 1900. In 1906 British officials discussed with the French staff the possibility of landing an expeditionary force in Europe if war came. The tension in international affairs and the heavy cost of armaments for which the British held German expansionists to blame, increased the strain. The British were planning to introduce an overdue program of social reforms at home but the burden of armaments compelled the government to curtail this liberal project. The national revenue would not cover the costs of social benefits and naval expansion at the same time. This budgetary dilemma was shared by all leading nations. Discontent among the working classes, the danger of social war within the state (mentioned at the close of the first chapter), could be reduced by improving the national health, public education, and living standards. But such measures could not be carried through without revenue. In the mood which gripped Europe under the "armed peace" the need for national defense seemed more urgent to most statesmen than the need for social reform. In all the European states the threat of war crippled the liberal projects of the reformers.

3. SOCIAL JUSTICE: THE PROBLEM OF THE LAISSEZ-FAIRE TRADITION

In the seventeenth and eighteenth centuries when most of the European states were still ruled by absolute monarchs, the British people evolved a parliamentary form of government. Their kings became "constitutional monarchs" with strictly limited powers, and the real authority passed to a committee or cabinet of ministers. As this cabinet came to be responsible to the party which held a majority of seats in the House of Commons and the members of the House were chosen by a vote of the electors, the statesmen who ruled England exercised powers delegated to them by the people or at least by that portion of the populace which enjoyed the right to vote. It was the first great European country to develop a working system of representative government, with a ministry responsible not to the monarch but to an elected assembly. As a consequence of its success the experiment, studied and imitated in many parts of the modern world, has earned for the government at Westminster the proud title "Mother of Parliaments."

During the nineteenth century the British steadily enlarged their system of political democracy. Successive reform bills redistributing seats in parliament and extending the franchise were passed in 1832, 1867, and 1884–1885, so that by the close of the century four out of five adult men could vote. This extension of the franchise made parliament more responsive to the wishes of the common people, and both political parties, the Liberals (or Whigs) and the Conservatives (or Tories), learned to formulate programs which would attract popular support.

Plans to assure a richer life and wider opportunities for members of the lower classes thus became important issues in all election campaigns. Broadly considered, there were two major methods whereby the status of the worker might be improved. One was to assure him a more adequate wage so that he could live more comfortably. The alternative was to reduce the cost of living so that he could buy more with the wage he received. In general, the Conservative Party, which represented the landowners with their agricultural interests, the Church of England, and some members of the wealthier classes, favored the first course. The Conservatives took a paternal attitude towards most social problems. They were willing to have the government regulate wages, hours, and working conditions, to assure a fair wage, and to check the exploitation of labor. But they were opposed to the trade unions and labor unions which the workers organized on their own initiative in order to extract better terms from their employers.

The Liberals in general were likewise unfriendly towards the unions. But they were even more strongly opposed to government regulation of business. They argued that Britain had grown rich and powerful under a laissez-faire policy, that workers and employers ought to be left free to settle terms among themselves, and that free trade, which allowed foodstuffs to enter England without hindrance, assured the worker the lowest possible world price on his bread. This, the Liberals submitted, was the surest way to promote the workers' welfare. These political arguments stemmed from economic conditions. Many Liberals were members of the new industrial classes, factory owners, businessmen, traders, or ship owners. What they desired was cheap food for the workers and the command of foreign markets. Trade is a reciprocal affair. Unless agrarian countries could sell their produce to England and thereby establish credits, they could not pay for British factory wares. The Liberals were not willing to protect British farmers by taxing importations of wheat; the Corn Laws which had protected agriculturists were repealed in 1846. The business classes, knowing England was too far ahead of all rivals to fear competition, favored a free-trade policy, and for a century commerce flowed in and out of English ports without tariff checks. Such unfettered trade, optimists averred, would draw the nations of the world together, permitting each people to produce whatever crops or manufactures they found most profitable. Tariff discrimination and tariff barriers not only constricted the natural arteries of trade but bred hostility and war. This philosophy under which England prospered in the nineteenth century persisted into the twentieth when conditions had changed. The British people did not bring themselves to abandon it until after the First World War.

In foreign as well as domestic policies the Liberals and Conservatives held divergent views. The Conservatives were less afraid of war than the Liberals, who dreaded a disruption of their trade; and Conservative cabinets were likely to be more imperialistic than Liberal regimes. The Conservatives believed that the government should make its power respected by subject peoples and by rival nations; when its authority had been duly vindicated Britain could then prove that "the strong can afford to be generous." This imperial policy led the Conservatives to oppose home rule for the Irish and helped to involve Britain in a bitter war with the Boer republics of South Africa. The embattled Boer farmers held out from 1899 to 1902 and inflicted some stinging defeats upon their mighty adversary. The conflict brought home to the British their unpopularity, their unpreparedness, and their imperial responsibilities. They realized that a policy which exposed troops to defeat in Africa at a time when discontented workers were striking at home, was a policy of conflicts and contradictions. When the resistance of the Boers was finally broken, the much criticized Conservative government promised South Africa self-rule within a few years, voted millions of pounds to restore the ruined farms, and then turned to placate the working classes at home.

It was time to heed the demands of the workers for they were preparing for political action. The conflict between capital and labor in Britain had taken a new turn after 1900. During the Boer War the unions suffered a sharp reverse when the Tory-minded House of Lords ruled that labor unions might be held legally and financially responsible for losses caused an employer through a strike (Taff Vale Decision, 1901). This ruling placed in jeopardy all the union funds, accumulated penny by penny from the workers' wages. Many workingmen had given scant attention to politics, believing that under a laissez-faire regime they could best improve their lot by dealing directly with their employers. After the Taff Vale Decision an increasing number came to feel that they had made a mistake in neglecting politics, that they should strive to elect more representatives to parliament and fight for their rights and their class interests by introducing remedial legislation. One result of this change in attitude was the rapid growth of a third party in British politics, the Labor Party. In the elections of 1906 the new group won twenty-nine seats.

The demand for social legislation and the need for a more powerful army and navy made it necessary for the government to raise a larger national revenue. The Liberals and the Conservatives differed on the wisest method of raising it. Joseph Chamberlain, a Liberal who had joined the Conservative Party, advocated a closer federation of the states of the empire with "imperial preference" for goods produced within the limits of Britain and the Dominions, and a tariff on foreign products entering British ports. A protective tariff would increase the national revenue and help British industries to compete against foreign rivals. Chamberlain's opponents were quick to point out that import duties would raise the price of many commodities favored by the British consumer and that the poor would feel the rise more sharply than the rich. The proposal for imperial preference and import duties aroused heated debates and was rejected largely because it seemed to make too many contribute for the benefit of too few.

In the election of 1906 the Conservatives were beaten and the Liberals assumed office. For the next eight years a Liberal-Labor combination controlled parliament and pressed a double program: to promote the welfare of the lower classes and to arm Great Britain against the growing threat of war. The two aims were often in conflict, for both involved heavy expenditures and one or the other had to be curtailed. As the Liberals were the free trade party they could not well resort to a tariff and had to increase the revenue by additional taxation. In drafting new fiscal measures the question most difficult to settle was the incidence of the proposed taxation, that is, the manner in which it should bear upon the various classes.

With the support of the Labor members and the Irish Nationalists (a group seeking home rule for Ireland) the Liberals could count upon 514 seats to 156 for the Conservatives. This strong majority was an assurance that far-reaching reforms would be attempted. Under prime ministers Sir Henry Campbell-Bannerman (1905–1908) and Herbert Asquith (1908–1916) the Liberal cabinet attacked the social questions which had grown acute during the previous decade of Conservative rule. Although government interference in matters of hours, wages, health, and employment rules meant a frank abandonment of laissez-faire ideals in domestic politics, the Liberals were prepared to abandon some of their ancient principles in return for Labor support. The prompt enactment of a Trade Disputes Bill (1906) made peaceful picketing legal and nullified the effect of the Taff Vale Decision by declaring that a union was not liable for damages resulting from illegal acts of its members. A Workingman's Compensation Act, passed the same year, decreed that employers must compensate workers for injuries incurred at their trade. An Old Age Pension Law (1909) promised annuities for all citizens over seventy whose annual income was less than £31 10s. Stricter provisions to safeguard the health of the young followed, a Trade Boards Act created commissions to judge wage rates and investigate sweatshop conditions, and government employment agencies freely assisted able-bodied workers to find occupations suited to their skill. The climax to the ambitious program of reform came with the National Insurance Act of 1911, which planned to institute medical supervision and sickness insurance for the whole working population of the British Isles and to provide unemployment insurance for over 2,000,000 workers whose type of work exposed them to frequent lapses of employment. Funds for these services were to be created from contributions made by employees, employers, and the state.

To administer these Acts would clearly impose a heavy responsibility and a heavy expense upon the government. The social services and naval expansion together caused a sharp increase in the budget. To meet it the energetic Chancellor of the Exchequer, David Lloyd George, proposed (1909) increased taxation on estates and incomes. His "war budget" in the fight against poverty was aimed at the rich; it taxed parks, game preserves, and other "idle" land and established special levies on various forms of unearned income. Producers and consumers were spared, while the possessors of wealth and those who received large incomes without making an adequate return to society were adjudged fair objects of taxation. All luxuries were likewise subject to taxes, from the rich man's automobile to the poor man's beer.

When the House of Lords, where the Conservatives were still entrenched, rejected the Lloyd George budget, the Liberals appealed to the nation and were returned to office with a reduced majority (1910). Insisting that the upper chamber was thwarting the expressed will of the people, the Liberals prepared to curtail its powers. As an institution the House of Lords seemed anomalous; its 620 members were made up of the peers of England, sixteen Scottish noblemen, twenty-eight Irish peers, and twenty-six bishops or archbishops of the Anglican Church. In addition there were four "Law Lords" (later seven) who decided legal cases referred to the House of Lords as a final court of appeal. To change the status of this chamber was equivalent to a constitutional amendment. As drawn up by the Liberals the Act embodying the proposed reform provided that the Lords should not veto money bills; that, despite their opposition, other measures would become law two years after their first introduction into the Commons if three successive sessions of the Commons approved them; and that a general election must be held at least once in five years. When the Lords rejected this Act, Asquith appealed to the electorate for the second time within a year (November, 1910). Once more the Liberals were returned to power, and Asquith threatened to ask the king, George V (1910–1935), to create enough new peers of Liberal persuasion to assure a majority for the bill. As in 1832, when they were faced by the same dilemma, the Lords yielded and the Parliament Act of 1911 was passed abridging their ancient prerogatives. But the Liberal drive had been weakened by the protracted maneuvering, and a secondary item on their program, the disestablishment of the Anglican Church in Wales, though finally passed under the new parliamentary regulations despite the veto of the Lords, was not put into force.

The outbreak of World War I in 1914 put a halt to social experiments and ended the eight-year period of Liberal reforms. This was especially tragic for the Irish nationalists, whose hopes of winning home rule once more miscarried. The troubled relationship between England and Ireland, however, can be considered more logically in the following section.

4. GREAT BRITAIN AND THE DOMINIONS

In one important respect Britain differed from the other great powers of Europe. London was not only the capital of a leading European state, it was also the political and financial heart of a world empire. Some 6,000,000 people of British birth or descent lived in the British overseas Dominions in 1900. As the population of Great Britain was then about 37,000,000, this meant that one Englishman in seven dwelt across the ocean but still remained under the British flag. This dispersion affected the international power and prestige of Britain very definitely because the British population in the colonies remained in general remarkably loyal to the motherland and the Dominions were growing so rapidly that within a few decades they might come to boast a total population approaching that of Great Britain itself. The rapid growth, the sound public order and credit, and the economic prosperity that distinguished the Dominions, made them with Britain and the United States outstanding examples of sanely governed democracies under Anglo-Saxon institutions.

The British record of colonization and conquest had not been one of uninterrupted success, however. They were forced to admit two signal failures in the difficult art of colonial government. Between 1775 and 1783 the thirteen American colonies broke away and achieved complete political independence as the United States of

America. Ireland, which had been the object of the earliest British overseas expansion, proved a second failure, for it remained for centuries an unreconciled and unassimilable conquest. After the loss of the American colonies the British granted Ireland a local parliament (1782) but the privilege was cancelled in 1801 when Britain was struggling against Napoleon and a French invasion of Ireland was a persistent danger. Throughout the nineteenth century Irish discontent led to persistent strife, with famine and emigration so reducing the population of that "most distressful country" that the total fell over a million between 1800 and 1914.

An evil fate seemed to attend all efforts to solve the Anglo-Irish problem. The great Liberal leader, William Ewart Gladstone (1809–1898), introduced a bill for Irish home rule in 1886 but was defeated in parliament. His second Home Rule Bill (1893) passed the Commons but was rejected in the House of Lords. Nothing less than home rule, however, would pacify the Irish Nationalists who were not satisfied merely to see Ireland represented in the British parliament. Their eighty members in the House of Commons kept up a constant agitation for a new home rule bill, and in 1912 the Liberal cabinet of Herbert Asquith introduced a measure providing for a parliament at Dublin. But the Irish people themselves were divided on the issue of independence. Fierce opposition developed in Ulster where the population, predominantly Protestant and distrustful of a settlement which would make them a minority in a Catholic state, threatened to resort to civil war. By 1913 an army of 100,000 Ulstermen was training openly and the Home Rule Bill was amended to exclude Ulster from its provisions indefinitely. This unresolved conflict was destined to grow more acute during World War I and culminated after 1918 in a savage struggle which is described in Chapter XXVI, section 1.

Despite their persistent failure to reconcile the Irish, in their other Dominions the British showed unusual gifts of statecraft by which they transformed conquered subjects into loyal citizens. When Canada passed under British control in 1763, the population of about 300,000 was almost exclusively French and Catholic. To reassure the *Canadiens* the government at London adopted the Quebec Act (1774) which guaranteed them the free exercise of their religion and the right to maintain their language and customs. Some friction inevitably developed as more British settlers moved into Canada and minor outbreaks and revolts occurred in the century after 1763, but the colony grew steadily. By 1860 the population had multiplied tenfold to an estimated 3,200,000, and in 1867 the four provinces — Quebec, Ontario, Nova Scotia, and New Brunswick — were federated by the British North America Act and proclaimed the Dominion of Canada. The Act further provided that the Dominion government should be modeled on that of Britain, with a Governor-General to represent the sovereign and a bicameral parliament consisting of a Senate and a House of Commons. Each province retained a provincial legislature similarly organized under a Lieutenant Governor as executive. As outlying territories were settled, new provinces were admitted until the original four became nine, the five additional being, in order of admission, Manitoba (1870), British Columbia (1871), Prince Edward Island (1873), and Alberta and Saskatchewan (1905).

With the bestowal of self-government, some skeptics predicted that the tie with the crown would not by itself keep Canadians loyal to the empire and that the Dominion would become entirely independent or unite with the United States. But the tie endured and the remarkable progress of the Canadian people demonstrated anew the benefits of British protection and British institutions.

The opening decade of the twentieth century brought three more self-governing Dominions into being, all of which owed much to the successful Canadian experiment. In Australia the six provinces or colonies known as New South Wales, Victoria, Queensland, South Australia, Western Australia, and Tasmania were united to form the Commonwealth of Australia which was proclaimed January 1, 1901. Like the Dominion of Canada, Australia acquired a federal parliament of two chambers, a Senate and a House of Representatives, under a Governor-General appointed by the British crown. The six constituent states, like the Canadian provinces, each retained its own local legislative assembly. In 1911 a federal capital was located at Canberra in New South Wales in an enclave to be known as the Capital Territory. By 1947 Canberra had become a city of 15,000.

The islands of New Zealand, which had a population of less than one million in 1901 when Australia became a self-governing Commonwealth, speedily advanced to the same independent status. In 1907 a British Order in Council changed the Colony of New Zealand into the Dominion of New Zealand, with a Governor-General and a bicameral legislature. Australia and New Zealand, which were geographically the most remote from London of all the possessions settled by the British, were paradoxically the most predominantly British in population, speech, and habit and the most active in supporting the programs for imperial defense.

The fourth British colony to emerge as a Dominion was the Union of South Africa. The British captured Cape Colony from the Dutch during the Napoleonic Wars (1806) and as in French Canada, which they had acquired half a century earlier, they had to deal with a conservative agrarian folk who desired to be let alone. Unfortunately for the Boers, as the Dutch settlers were called, increasing British pressure brought increasing strain. The Boers had enslaved the native African peoples and resented the measures the British took to abolish slavery in 1833. During the following decade thousands of Boer families migrated northward into virgin country in the valleys of the Orange and Vaal Rivers. This "Great Trek," however, solved their problem only temporarily, for the British followed. An agreement drawn up in 1852 (the Sand River Convention) recognized the Transvaal as Boer territory and it was organized as the South African Republic. In the same mood of appeasement the British withdrew from the Orange River area (Convention of Bloemfontein, 1854) and the Boers organized it as the Orange Free State. But the settlements did not last. In 1877, to protect the native Africans from exploitation, the British annexed the Transvaal. When the Boers resisted and defeated a British force at Majuba Hill, the South African Republic (Transvaal) was again declared independent. But time was on the side of the British, who had penetrated beyond the unprogressive Boer states to proclaim a protectorate over the vast Bechuanaland region to the east and were exploring the lands north of the Limpopo River which were later named Rhodesia in honor of the most ambitious imperialist of the time, Cecil John Rhodes (1853–1902). The British granted self-government to the Europeans of Cape Colony as early as 1852 and to the colony of Natal in 1893 in order to encourage development. The discovery of diamond mines near Kimberley (1867) and rich gold deposits in the southern Transvaal (1886) brought an invasion of fortune seekers. Rhodes, who believed ardently in the benefits of British rule and confessed, "I would annex the planets if I could," became prime minister of Cape Colony in 1890. He was not the man to tolerate opposition. The efforts made by the Boers to keep control of their republics and exclude newcomers or *Uitlanders* from citizenship stood in the way of progress and profit. With Rhodes's knowledge, British adventurers planned to break the Boer control by revolt and an armed uprising, a plan which culminated in an abortive raid on Johannesburg by a force of over six hundred men led by Dr. Leander S. Jameson (1895). Jameson was captured by the Boers and turned over to the British, who let him off with a light sentence. Four years later the increasing disputes between British and Boers brought on the South African (Boer) War (1899–1902).

The British were ill-prepared and underestimated the courage, skill, and resolution of their antagonists. Although they captured the Boer capital at Pretoria in the Transvaal and overran the Orange Free State (1900), their hardy and elusive adversaries refused to accept defeat. For two years longer isolated groups continued to resist by maintaining a costly and desperate guerrilla war. It was humiliating for a great empire to find itself defied by two diminutive republics, but even in Britain many liberal thinkers denounced the war as an example of arrogant imperialism. This criticism at home was matched by a wave of anti-British sentiment abroad. With victory the British government sought to make amends. The Boers were promised self-government under British sovereignty, and a sum equal to $15,000,000 was appropriated to rebuild and restock the devastated farms. In 1909 the promise of self-rule was vindicated. The Cape Colony, Natal, the Orange River Colony, and the Transvaal united in a Union of South Africa, with a Senate and a House of Assembly under a Governor-General who represented the British king. The legislature was to meet at Cape Town but the seat of government was fixed at Pretoria.

Of all the British Dominions, the Union of South Africa was burdened with the most complex social and political problems. An ineradicable difference of sentiment, language, and tradition divided the British settlers from the Dutch. There was a further cleavage between rich and poor especially in the mining towns, and there was also an even more important distinction between European and non-European. This last was potentially the gravest problem of all, for the Union of South Africa had a large population of native Africans which outnumbered the European (Dutch and British) ruling caste by four to one. At the close of the Boer War (1902) there were about 1,000,000 settlers of European descent. By 1910 the number had risen to 1,250,000. But the non-European elements had increased from five to almost six millions in the same period, and the introduction of Asiatic laborers, Chinese and Hindus, further endangered the European minority. No attempt was made, therefore, to establish universal suffrage in South Africa. Instead, the franchise was not only limited to citizens of European descent but it was further restricted by wage and

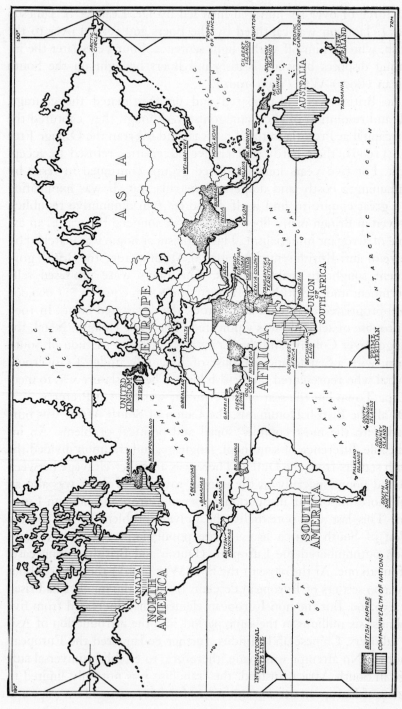

THE BRITISH EMPIRE AFTER WORLD WAR I

BRITISH EMPIRE
COMMONWEALTH OF NATIONS

property qualifications. In this way the wealthier Europeans were assured a controlling voice in the management of political affairs.

The racial problem in Africa suggested on a small scale the racial problems of the British Empire as a whole. The peoples who had submitted to British sovereignty represented all races; only 15 per cent of them were of European descent. The statesmen who shaped policy at London had to maintain naval forces in all the oceans of the world and had to keep in touch with political developments in the remotest regions. But the region which claimed their most rigid attention, the region in which the gravest threat might arise, was Europe itself. The cardinal principle of British policy was to keep the European powers in a self-stabilizing equilibrium so that the Dominions and the distant colonies of the empire might develop in peace.

GERMANY

The course remains the same: full steam ahead!

WILLIAM II

I. RESOURCES: THE PROBLEMS OF ORGANIZATION
AND EXPANSION

UNTIL less than a century ago "the Germanies" were an aggregation of two score large and small states. Germany, as a great power with territorial unity and a centralized government, did not take its place among the nations until the proclamation of the Empire in 1871. Spain, France, and England had achieved political unity under national monarchies four centuries earlier, and this integration had proved a valuable asset to them in their European contests and their fight for empires overseas.

The delay in achieving nationhood affected the character and destiny of the Germans in three important respects. (1) Slowness in fixing territorial frontiers encouraged the intermixture of peoples in the border zones, so that "islands" of German settlers grew up in the Baltic states, in Poland, and in the Ukraine. This migration and dispersion was neither colonization nor conquest but something in between. (2) Lacking national unity and naval resources, the people were too disorganized and too deeply involved in local affairs to join the race for overseas empires. (3) Because Prussia, the most militant and bureaucratic of the German states, took the lead in the work of unification, many Germans before 1871 and almost all of them after that date, were disposed to overvalue the "state" and its role in human affairs. They venerated the state as a power in itself, free from the moral obligations which restrain the individual; and they accepted the idea that the citizen and the group must be subordinate and submissive. These conclusions seemed justifiable because their own experience had shown that too much individualism or "particularism" kept a country impotent. As a consequence they placed undue importance upon unity and discipline.

Once political union was theirs the Germans realized that they had all the resources of a great, a very great, power. Their population was intelligent, frugal, and industrious. It had doubled in a century and by 1914 it reached a total of 67,000,000. They held rich deposits of coal and iron, indispensable for an industrial state, and they could acquire the latest machinery from Britain without waiting generations to develop it. With unification, their businessmen were assured a large central European market and they hastened to expand their factories, equip laboratories, train technologists, and promote the co-ordination of science and manufacture which, within a few decades, made their country the foremost industrial nation of the world. Between 1870 and 1914 the output of its industries increased tenfold and the value of its foreign trade increased 250 per cent.

Partly to weld the state together and partly to encourage business expansion, the government planned an excellent system of internal transport and communication, joining roads, railways, and canals. Harbor facilities were rapidly improved and after 1900 the mercantile and naval tonnage was surpassed only by that of Great Britain. In all parts of the world consumers learned to appreciate the quality of Germany's products; her salesmen even invaded the British Isles, which offered an open market because of the British free-trade policy. The industry of the workers, the skill of the technicians trained in special schools, the resources and natural advantages exploited with foresight and decision by the bankers and businessmen of Berlin, Bremen, Essen, and other centers, made Germany by 1914 the most successful and dynamic of the European states. Between 1880 and 1914 the British share of international trade fell from 23 to 17 per cent, while the German share rose from 9 to 12 per cent. Many Englishmen felt that their relative loss had been Germany's gain. But trade rivalry alone would not have made a war between these powers a growing threat; the United States increased its share of world trade from 10 to 15 per cent in this period without exciting British antagonism. It was not German power alone that excited mistrust but the use the leaders might make of that power; and their purposes seemed to be darkly foreshadowed by their program of armaments.

All the neighbors of Germany watched her rising production, wealth, and energy with envy and alarm. They saw much to admire but more to fear in her spirit and method. Teutonic order and efficiency, the union of science with industry, high standards of education, particularly technological training, the variety of manufactures, the patience and pertinacity of salesmen, the enterprise of German bankers, and the alertness of consular agents in detecting new and promising fields of business — all these set a standard not easy to match. Germany was forging irresistibly ahead, and forging ahead by invading areas and markets which the businessmen of other nations had marked out for themselves. Not only in Europe but in Asia, in Africa, and in South America German trade gains often meant a loss of orders for British, French, Belgian, Dutch, Swiss, Swedish, and American manufacturers. This rivalry in the economic sphere aroused tension and antagonism. The Germans were only one of the competitor nations, but their success, their aggressiveness, the rapid pace they set, and the new methods and techniques they perfected, focused upon them the resentment of less energetic rivals.

For years German chemists led the world in the production of new materials and the discovery of substitutes for old ones. German firms flooded the world with synthetic drugs, fabrics, plastics, and metal alloys which in many cases proved both superior to and cheaper than natural products. One outstanding triumph in the field of industrial chemistry was the development of synthetic dyes; a second was the production of synthetic nitrates. Before the twentieth century over 95 per cent of the world's nitrate supply had come from deposits in Chile, but the Germans perfected a formula for "fixing" the nitrogen which constitutes four-fifths of the atmosphere. By 1914 their chemical plants were producing 12,000 tons of nitrates a year, a valuable addition to the national economy because nitrates are equally indispensable for fertilizers and for explosives. This assured domestic supply, rapidly augmented, helped to carry Germany through the First World War, when imports from Chile were cut off by the British blockade.

Thus German ingenuity helped to solve problems of supply, created new resources, and rendered the industry of the country less dependent upon imports. Moreover, German chemists and engineers tapped new sources of power and production and opened wider fields for exploitation. Although Germans had lagged behind other peoples at the opening of the Oceanic Age when the world was first revealed to Europeans, German chemists and physicists led the way in the modern attack upon matter and laid bare veins of wealth which rivaled the treasures of the Indies.

British Combine

REVIEW OF THE BRITISH GRAND FLEET AT SPITHEAD, 1914

2. DEFENSE: THE PROBLEM OF ENCIRCLEMENT

Had German progress been confined to the arts of peace, opponents might have accepted the competition without alarm. But Germany, in the decades before 1914, became the most powerful and most efficiently militarized state on the Continent. Like the veneration for the state, a hardy respect for military virtues and an acceptance of war as a necessary process in the forging of nations, was widely prevalent. German national pride had been born of the battlefield; the War of Liberation against Napoleon in 1813–1814 had stirred the flame; a war with Denmark (1864) brought the border duchies of Schleswig and Holstein under Prussian control; a war with Austria (1866) settled the issue whether Vienna or Berlin was to be the capital and focal center of the Reich; and a war with France (1870–1871) brought Alsace and Lorraine and a billion dollar indemnity to the victors. As a dramatic touch, the King of Prussia was proclaimed German Emperor in the palace of Louis XIV at Versailles (January 18, 1871), a few days before Paris surrendered to the German army. These associations not only intensified the national spirit, they fused it with militarism and made the army and the state one in German thought. In the long interval of peace from 1871 to 1914 the power of the military caste did not decrease; compulsory military service initiated all youths into the service of the state; industry was developed with a view to war needs as well as profits; roads were built to facilitate the movements of troops and guns as well as goods; and the spirit of military organization and discipline reached into all departments of life. Germany was the Sparta of the modern European world.

Otto von Bismarck, the architect of unification and first chancellor of the new German Reich after 1871, desired a period of peace in which to consolidate the national government he had helped to construct. Until his retirement in 1890 he managed to maintain fairly amicable relations with Austria, Russia, Italy, and Great Britain. By astute and realistic diplomacy he built up an intricate system of alliances which left France isolated and therefore enfeebled. For Bismarck was haunted by a "nightmare of coalitions." He feared that the French would seek revenge for their humiliation in 1870–1871 and his premonition was ultimately vindicated. After he resigned control German diplomacy suffered a long series of reverses. The first setback came when France and Russia concluded a military alliance in 1894. Then France and Britain arrived at an entente or friendly understanding in 1904. Finally France, Russia, and Britain united to form the Triple Entente in 1907.

German statesmen became alarmed as they realized that their country might find itself "encircled" if war developed. To match the armaments of the three entente powers, Germany could rely only upon the aid of Austria-Hungary. Italy was also a nominal ally of Germany and Austria, but this Triple Alliance, though it had been formed in 1882 and renewed at intervals, was unstable. At Berlin the leaders realized that the Italians could not be depended upon for serious military aid, especially in a war against Great Britain. Germany and Austria-Hungary, the Central Powers of Europe, would have to stand or fall together.

The apprehension at Berlin over the mounting threat of war can be read in the successive army bills submitted to the Reichstag. When France and Russia became allies in 1894, the German army was raised from 487,000 to 557,000 men, a move which convinced the French and Russians in turn of the need to strengthen their alliance. When France and Britain established their entente in 1904, the standing army was further increased to 605,000. With each successive crisis in international affairs, from 1908 to 1914, the forces climbed steadily — to 617,000 (1910), 631,000 (1911), 666,000 (1912), and 820,000 (1913). The German high command, which retained control over millions of reservists as well as over the soldiers in service, was an arrogant and independent organization, free from the control of the electors and their representatives in the Reichstag. In theory the high command was subject to the orders of the emperor, but this meant that the real decisions lay with the military cabinet which advised the kaiser on army affairs. In these circles a preponderant influence was exercised by the Junkers, members of the landed nobility and particularly of the aristocracy of East Prussia. The firm monopoly the Junkers retained over the army may be judged by the fact that before 1914 thirty out of thirty-two commanding generals and thirty-seven out of forty-four lieutenant generals were of noble birth. In the lower grades, skill, character, and length of service might assure promotion, but for the highest posts aristocratic lineage was almost essential.

As the diplomatic skies darkened after 1900, the general staff accepted the realities of the international situation and drew up plans for a war on two fronts. Since the country had no strong natural frontiers to serve as defense barriers, it was probable that fighting would prove costly and the battle lines fluid and tenuous. Freedom of movement and the ability to maneuver rapidly would thus prove major advantages. To magnify their striking power and make full strategic use of their inside lines, the Germans completed a network of railways which would enable them to shuttle their forces from the French to the Russian front as needed. They were hopeful that, if war came, they could hold one opponent in check while defeating the other independently and swiftly. They recognized, however, that their most implacable enemy might prove to be *time*, and they prepared to open hostilities with a crushing campaign which would bring speedy victory. For a prolonged war, especially if Germany were blockaded, would ruin trade, deplete resources, and might ultimately reduce the people to defeat through malnutrition and exhaustion.

Despite subsidies and tariffs maintained to encourage and protect agriculture, Germany had ceased to be self-sufficient in the matter of food. As the nation became highly industrialized and the urban population increased, it found itself, like Great Britain, dependent upon imports. By 1914 half the working population was engaged in industry or trade; one-third lived in cities of 20,000 or more; and only one worker in four was left for agriculture. This increasing dependence upon trade was of course one reason why Germany built a navy and sought colonies, but the gamble was a gigantic one because in war her ocean trade, her ships, and her colonies would be hostages of fortune. Her imports, which by 1914 were worth almost $3,000,000,000 annually, were certain to suffer if the sea routes were blockaded. After 1907 it had become increasingly probable that the sea routes *would* be blockaded, for her diplomacy failed to dissolve the accord growing between France, Russia, and Britain. Her overseas investments, the protectorates in Africa, the treaty ports in China, the island bases in the Pacific Ocean (belated acquisitions of the young but lusty German imperialism) would all be severed from the Reich when hostilities commenced. The entente nations could then take over these isolated outposts at leisure. War, for Germany, therefore promised to prove a risky venture, certain to involve heavy fighting in Europe, destruction of trade, loss of colonies, and the likelihood of a long blockade. But these hard probabilities, instead of persuading the government to avoid war, convinced the high command that the war must be made short, sharp, and decisive.

In Europe the area of greatest tension was the Balkan peninsula. A succession of diplomatic crises from 1908 to 1914 brought the central

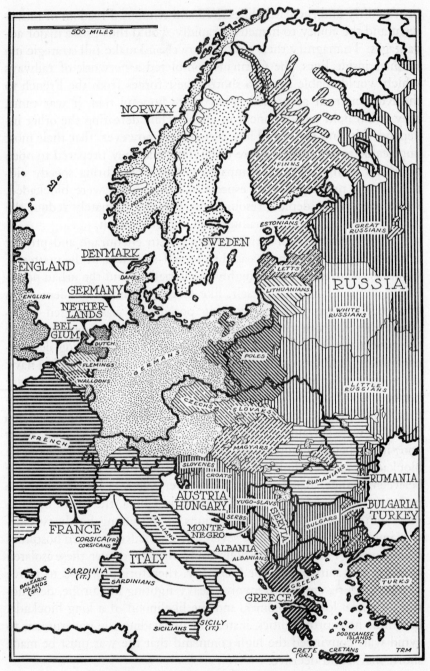

500 MILES

NORWAY

SWEDEN

FINNS

ESTONIANS

GREAT
RUSSIANS

DENMARK

DANES

LETTS

RUSSIA

ENGLAND

ENGLISH

GERMANY

LITHUANIANS

WHITE
RUSSIANS

NETHER-
LANDS

BEL-
GIUM

DUTCH

FLEMINGS

WALLOONS

GERMANS

POLES

CZECHS

SLOVAKS

LITTLE
RUSSIANS

FRENCH

MAGYARS

SLOVENES

CROATS

RUMANIANS

RUMANIA

AUSTRIA
HUNGARY

YUGO-SLAVS

SERBS

SERVIA

BULGARS

BULGARIA
TURKEY

FRANCE

CORSICA(FR.)
CORSICANS

MONTE-
NEGRO

ITALIANS

ALBANIA

ALBANIANS

GREEKS

TURKS

ITALY

SARDINIA
(IT.)

SARDINIANS

BALEARIC
ISLANDS
(SP.)

GREECE

SICILY
(IT.)

SICILIANS

DODECANESE
ISLANDS
(IT.)

CRETE
(GR.)

CRETANS

TRM

NATIONALITIES AND POLITICAL BOUNDARIES IN
MIDDLE EUROPE, 1914

empires into sharp competition with Russia for the control of the lesser Balkan states. German businessmen from the 1880's onward had appreciated the commercial possibilities of the Near East. Great Britain, which enjoyed almost half the Turkish foreign trade, was not at first unduly alarmed by German penetration, but after 1900 a graver note of warning was sounded in London. It was evident that German influence in the Turkish Empire, in Persia (modern Iran), and in the Arabian states was growing rapidly. The Germans had even proceeded so far as to plan a new railway line linking Berlin to Constantinople and running thence to Basra on the Persian Gulf.

The key point in this strategy of expansion was Constantinople. If the Germans obtained the mastery at this "crossroads of empire," it would mean a signal reverse for Britain and a major defeat for Russia. For Constantinople guarded the only exit Russia possessed to the warm seas. A trade depot at Basra, with shipping lines to follow, would bring the Germans to the gates of India and of Turkestan. Russia and Britain, themselves ancient rivals in the Middle East, were moved to adjust their differences and to join forces against the menace. The entente of 1907 set boundaries for the British and Russian spheres of influence in Persia, and Russia recognized the preponderant position of the British in Afghanistan. France, which had maintained trade connections with the Levant since the time of the crusades, was likewise alarmed by the German drive. It was evident that old Europe had become too narrow a field for the expanding forces generated by modern industry and that the Balkan area was the most permeable region and therefore the one most likely to soften under the increasing pressure. This made it also the region in which an open conflict was most likely to develop.

3. SOCIAL JUSTICE: THE PROBLEM OF THE STATE AND THE SOCIALISTS

The new Germany, consolidated in 1871, had a government that was parliamentary in appearance but authoritarian in spirit and practice. The Germans did not have a long history of evolving parliamentary precedents like the British, nor semi-autonomous bodies for local self-government like the English county, parish, and borough, where aspirants for public office could learn the art of politics. Nor had the Germans passed through a century of alternating revolution and reaction, like the French after 1789, whereby various forms of government might be tried out and the virtues or failings of each demonstrated. As a consequence the Germans lacked wide experience in managing their political affairs and were more familiar with the advantages of energetic bureaucratic rule than with the party system, popular assemblies, and the ballot. Since the teaching of history influences the attitude of every people towards different methods of administration, it should be kept in mind that for Central Europeans "election" brought to memory the mode of choosing the Holy Roman Emperors, whose lack of authority and inability to unite their realms had spelled division and war for centuries. The Polish Diet, which "elected" the kings of Poland but granted them no funds or authority to govern, seemed a further example of the weakness of assemblies, an example emphasized by the disintegration and dismemberment of Poland in the eighteenth century. Parliamentary rule had been further discredited for the Germans by the fiasco of 1848–1849, when the Assembly of Frankfort attempted and failed signally to frame a constitutional union for the German states. But what the parliamentarians failed to do with their talk and resolutions and balloting, Prussia, under Bismarck's leadership, achieved. Formed in three wars between 1864 and 1871, the new German Empire bore the stamp of its forging. "Not by speeches and majority votes are the great questions of the day decided," Bismarck proclaimed in a much quoted speech, " — that was the mistake of 1848 and 1849 — but by blood and iron."

The efficiency of the Prussian conscript armies, which brought the Austrians to terms in seven weeks (1866) and the French in six months (1870–1871), seemed a practical vindication of the Prussian system. The extraordinary economic expansion which followed the political unification of 1871 also seemed to offer proof that the bureaucrats in control knew their business. Most Germans were therefore disposed to leave problems of administration to the rulers who had shown themselves expert in these matters. It had long been the practice of the Prussian kings and their ministers to draw army officers from the nobility, and civil servants from the upper *bourgeoisie*. The high standards of loyalty, efficiency, and honesty which characterized most Prussian officials under the monarchy, and the conscientious toil of an army of obedient and industrious clerks, offered a further clue to Prussian influence. In politics, as in most affairs, those who are willing to assume laborious tasks and perform them consistently accrete power by imperceptible degrees. The Prussians (often with the aid of patriotic Germans from other states who joined the Prussian service) led the van in all phases of unification. They fought the French under Napoleon (1806, and 1813–1814); they worked to organize the states in a common customs union (the *Zollverein*) between 1819 and 1844; and they assumed direction and responsibility in the critical years from 1860 to 1870. When Bismarck became chancellor of the new empire, Prussian standards and methods were already admired and imitated throughout the Reich, and the completion of the federalizing process was in a sense a "Prussianization" of Germany. Prussian administrative efficiency and co-ordination, which had linked and energized the scattered domains of the Hohenzollerns and raised Prussia to the rank of a great power in the eighteenth century, inherited in the later nineteenth the task of knitting twenty-five states into a national unit.

The ideal of authoritarian bureaucracy differed from the ideal of responsible government and democratic control which had gained ground in Britain, France, and the United States in the nineteenth century. The new Germany occupied a middle position, geographically and politically. It lay between the western democracies, Britain and France, and the dynastic absolutism of Austria-Hungary and Russia. After 1871 the national government was a compromise between autocratic and popular rule. The Reichstag, a popularly elected chamber with 382 deputies, represented the people, but although the population of the electoral districts shifted, the conservative rural constituencies kept the same number of representatives as urban districts with five or even ten times the number of voters. The states composing the new empire were represented in an upper chamber, the Bundesrat, the members of which were nominated, not elected. As Prussia held seventeen of the fifty-eight votes in the Bundesrat and could control several others, the indissoluble union of states was very largely under Prussian control.

In yet another respect the government remained authoritarian rather than parliamentarian in its functioning. The head of the cabinet, who was known as the chancellor, was nominated by the King of Prussia in his role as German Emperor and was not necessarily acceptable to a majority of the Reichstag. As the chancellor usually named the associate ministers to head the various departments of state, he preserved an almost dictatorial control over the administration. In parliamentary regimes, the essential controls which the representatives of the people exercise over the cabinet lie in their control of money appropriations (which they vote only for those programs which they approve) and in their right to repudiate and overthrow a cabinet at any time by refusing it a vote of confidence. In the new German constitution these controls did not function effectively. The chancellor could and sometimes did ignore the opposition of a majority in the assembly, for he could retain his office as long as the monarch supported him. Freedom to criticize the government, freedom of speech and of the press, which in France was often carried to extremes under the Third Republic, were restrained in Germany. The government maintained a strict supervision over the journals and over all public organizations. An efficient police system preserved order, the highly centralized army instilled a sense of discipline into the young men, and the regimentation which ruled the army and the bureaucracy made itself felt in every field of national activity.

As citizens, the Germans proved themselves docile, law-abiding, and respectful of authority. The rapid rise and bold bid for power of the new empire inspired them with a fervent patriotism which easily became chauvinism. It would seem that these people, modest and unaggressive as individuals, found compensation for their own restraint and frustration by exalting the state. They applauded their leaders when the latter asserted the claims of Germany to a larger influence in international affairs, to "a place in the sun"; and the leaders gratified them by frequent displays of undiplomatic truculence and swordrattling. Such exhibitions of pride and power earned for the kaiser, William II, in particular, a reputation for aggressiveness which made him appear to contemporaries as the "War Lord of Europe." Unfortunately Europe was too small a field for German ambitions. The economic and military aggrandizement of the Reich, sustained by the ardent efforts of industrialists, chemists, engineers, bankers, diplomats, and soldiers, pushed the empire by 1914 into a grandiose policy of *Weltpolitik* or global politics.

One factor in the phenomenal rise of German industrial power, a very significant factor, was the high performance and relatively low wages of the German worker. The need of the state for soldiers, technicians, clerks, and factory hands, as well as farmers, was foreseen and provided for in the school training program. The worker accepted his role and discharged his duties in remarkably faithful fashion. The average income in 1900 was only two-thirds that in Great Britain, although German products were in many respects superior in quality and in workmanship. It was inevitable that in time the workers would grow critical of a system which denied them a richer reward for their labor. The dissemination of socialist doctrines and the rise of a Socialist Party after 1900 gravely alarmed industrial leaders and government heads.

As early as 1880 the alert and realistic Bismarck had foreseen the danger that working class voters might be affected by socialist ideas. He decided to combat the threat by a comprehensive scheme of social insurance which would attach the working classes more firmly to the state. Twenty years before the British government turned to similar measures, he sponsored a Sickness Insurance Law (1883), an Accident Insurance Law (1884), and an Old Age and Invalidity Insurance Law (1889). The funds for the first law were contributed by the workers and the employers; for the second, by the employers; and for the third by workers, employers, and state. These acts, by relieving the worker and his family of the ever-present fear of sickness and swift destitution and by assuring the aged against misery and want, removed much of the insecurity and hardship from their lives and inspired gratitude towards the "paternalistic" state which instituted and supervised this protection.

Bismarck's program of social legislation recognized the truth of the Dutch proverb that to make a man a conservative you must give him something to conserve. The rootless, propertyless urban classes, if they had nothing to lose, would have been more susceptible to the enticements of revolutionaries who promised them a better life under a new order. But the insurance to which they had contributed gave them a stake in the future. Like holders of national bonds, the workers acquired an interest and a motive for defending the existing imperial regime. As the state guaranteed them the benefits of their accumulating policies and promised them a retirement annuity when they were too old to work, they had less reason to become revolutionaries and more reason to hope that the existing government would remain stable.

Bismarck distrusted the populace and saw in the socialists and communists the internal agitators who might destroy the empire which he had consolidated. In 1878 he introduced a law suppressing public meetings, journals, and the collection of funds for socialistic or communistic causes. After 1890, however, when the Iron Chancellor was forced to resign by the new emperor, William II (1888–1918), this law against the socialists was allowed to lapse. William was determined to play a leading part in matters of policy, and the chancellors who followed Bismarck were less independent and masterful men. The earnest but inexpert Leo von Caprivi (1890–1894) was succeeded

by the aged and courtly Prince Chlodwig zu Hohenlohe-Schilling-
fürst (1894–1900). Then came the adroit but somewhat irresolute
Count Bernhard von Bülow (1900–1909) and the conscientious but
colorless Theobald von Bethmann-Hollweg (1909–1917). The kaiser's
erratic moves confused and weakened the policies of his ministers, and
the government met with increasing difficulties and reverses in domestic and foreign affairs. The treatment and reaction of the socialists
affords a striking example of this confusion. Craving popularity and
eager to win the workers, William and his ministers approved a number of concessions between 1890 and 1911. Working hours were limited by law; factory conditions were improved; workers' committees,
formed to negotiate with employers, received recognition; a department of labor was created; accident, sickness, and old age insurance
was broadened and increased; and the entire field of security legislation was embraced in a single act, the Imperial Insurance Code of
1911. Had it been possible to placate the lower classes by paternal legislation, these concessions should have met the situation.

Democracy was on the march, however, and the German people,
seeing the greater political liberty enjoyed by the French, the British,
and the Americans, demanded a larger share in their own government.
The Socialist Party, able to come into the open after 1890, grew rapidly and, as often happens in such cases, became more moderate in its
aims as it increased in numbers. In 1912 it elected 110 members, the
largest single group in the Reichstag. The socialists drew their chief
support from the cities. They were opposed by the militarists because they sought to reduce army appropriations, by the wealthy because they favored inheritance and income taxes, by the landowners
because they wished to lower the tariff on farm produce and import
cheaper food, and by the employer class generally because they demanded better pay for servants, laborers, and factory hands. But although the Social Democrats received over one-third of the votes cast
in the election of 1912 and dominated the Reichstag with the aid of
liberal allies, they could not control the ministers. In 1913 the Reichstag passed a vote of lack of confidence in the government, but the
chancellor, von Bethmann-Hollweg, did not resign, for he regarded
himself as the appointee of the emperor and responsible to him. As a
result crises which in England would have overturned the cabinet and
forced an election passed in Germany with a few heated debates and
resolutions of protest.

For the Social Democrats were not revolutionaries. They hoped to win further advantages for the proletariat and to acquire a larger share in the government, but they had no real desire to shatter it or to plunge Germany into turmoil. Germany in 1914, though shaken by class antagonism, was not seriously divided or weakened. The nation was still too inspired by its emergence to power and its rapid progress to feel profound discontent or to yield to schism. Economic activities were still expanding, foreign trade had doubled in the preceding decade, national pride and prestige had never stood so high. It required the agonies of a four years' war, of a tightening blockade, of hope deferred, malnutrition, and ultimate defeat, to sap the loyalty of the people as a whole towards their kaiser, their political and military leaders, and their system of government. Even after they set up a republic in 1919 amid the chaos of defeat, they did not change their inmost sentiments. It is true that the first president they elected had been a saddler, Friedrich Ebert, but the second was a Field Marshal, Paul von Hindenburg. German political history, so long dominated by the spirit of authoritarianism, suggested the possibility that if socialism triumphed in Germany it might culminate, not in a merger with liberal forces but in the erection of a dictatorship.

FRANCE

*One must be deliberately blind not to realize that the [German]
lust for power, the impact of which makes Europe tremble each
day, has fixed as its policy the extermination of France.*

GEORGES CLEMENCEAU [1]

1. RESOURCES: THE PROBLEM OF POPULATION

"THE fair land of France," as the old chroniclers named it, contains
some of the richest farms, orchards, and vineyards of Europe.
To these gifts Nature has added a moderate climate, moist in the north
and sunny in the south. These advantages help to explain why France
leads in the production of rare wines and why the French are the foremost bread consumers among the nations. With a population not too
densely concentrated (approximately 180 to the square mile) and
large areas that repay cultivation, the French people have remained
largely self-sufficient in the matter of food. In this they have preserved
an advantage lost in the twentieth century by the British, Italians, and
Germans who have become partly dependent upon imported supplies.

The natural richness of the land also helps to explain why relatively
few Frenchmen emigrate, why so many have remained attached to
the soil, and why even city workers, still farmers at heart, so often
keep a small vegetable garden (sometimes no more than a few square
yards in extent) where they can smoke their pipe in the evening while
weeding the lettuce beds. Before 1914 there were still two Frenchmen on the land for one in a factory or shop. The millions of sturdy,
independent farm proprietors formed a powerful stabilizing class, for
as property owners and taxpayers they were disposed to be conservative in politics and conventional in their thinking.

In addition to its agricultural wealth and productivity France
entered the twentieth century with well developed industries. She

[1] Georges Clemenceau, *L'Homme libre*, May 21, 1913.

ranked fourth in the total of her foreign trade in 1900, third in her output of textiles, and third in iron production. Her artisans, long noted for their skill in creating luxury goods, specialized in fine fabrics of cotton, silk, and wool, exquisite laces, perfumes, leather work, glass, porcelain, and jewelry. Since the seventeenth century, when Louis XIV made Versailles the model of elegant life, she had set the fashion for international society. High among the assets of the nation were the profits derived from the tourist trade, for millions of visitors came each year to view the historic châteaux and cathedrals, to shop, to visit the beaches and watering places, and to assist, by their payments for these services, in preserving for France the favorable balance of trade which enabled her to accumulate gold reserves.

A further asset which the French had acquired was the second largest colonial empire in the world. French overseas territories in Africa and Asia ranked next to those of Great Britain in area and population. This extensive list of protectorates and colonies had been acquired in a few generations. Until the nineteenth century the history of French colonial enterprise had been a story of heroic exploration and settlement followed by disheartening reverses and forfeitures. Attempts to found permanent colonies and establish spheres of control in Canada, in Louisiana, in the West Indies, in Egypt, in India, even in Australia, had all been frustrated in the end by superior British sea power. But a new and more progressive chapter in overseas expansion opened for the French in 1830 when they sent a punitive expedition to occupy Algiers. Cautiously but inexorably French imperialism was pushed outward until by 1914 its conquests included 4,000,000 square miles of African and Asian territories, with a colonial population somewhat larger than the 40,000,000 total of France itself. Few, however, aside from soldiers and administrators, left France for the colonies. The French acknowledged their share in the "white man's burden" and undertook their "civilizing mission" among backward peoples. But although they were proud to establish order, build roads and hospitals, garrison and govern their protectorates in other continents, they did not feel impelled to populate the globe as the Spaniards and Portuguese, the British, Italians, Germans, Russians, and Scandinavian peoples were doing. This fact is strikingly demonstrated by the United States census returns for 1940, which show among 11,419,138 foreign-born whites only 102,930 Frenchmen, a figure which places France twentieth among the European states which have contributed to the present population of the United States.

Many thoughtful Frenchmen doubted the value of possessions overseas and opposed the imperial urge which led to such conquests. Their
huge African domains, divided into five administrative divisions —
Morocco, Algeria, Tunisia, French West Africa, and French Equatorial Africa — had been costly to conquer and remained costly to administer. The second great *bloc* of imperial protectorates lay in southeastern Asia, comprising the nominally Chinese provinces of Cochin
China, Cambodia, Tonkin, Annam, and Laos, a combined area larger
than Texas, with a population over 20,000,000. To subdue this empire required many minor military campaigns, expensive to the French
taxpayer in their totality. To hold these distant regions demanded the
presence of armed forces and the maintenance of a powerful navy.

Anti-imperialists stressed these facts. They pointed out that colonial trade did not justify such expansion of territory because it formed
only a small fraction of French external trade. As France had no problems arising from excess home population, and the colonies were in
general unsuited to settlement by Europeans, they would never form
reserves of manpower, and to arm and train the natives as soldiers
might ultimately threaten white supremacy. Thus the French taxpayer, upon whom the burden of defending the empire ultimately fell,
derived no adequate return. The risks implicit in the imperialistic
gamble, and the international rivalries and wars which might develop
from it, provided anti-imperialists with further arguments against the
retention, or at least the extension, of the empire. These risks and rivalries were real and threatening. The Third Republic came close to war
with Italy, with Great Britain, and with Germany in turn, as disputes
over African territories grew sharp; and the value of the claims involved did not warrant the cost and losses of a major war.

Cautious citizens doubted the wisdom of scattering part of their
forces on distant continents when France might have to face at any
moment an attack from across the Rhine or across the Alps. The rising population of Germany threatened in time to become double that
of France; the population of Italy, Russia, and Great Britain was
also increasing. But the population of France remained stationary, and
this alone seemed sufficient reason for keeping Frenchmen at home.
Frenchmen could not ignore this growing numerical weakness; its implications for the future influenced their consideration of all important political issues; and they realized that their own country, with
the smallest population among the great powers, might be reduced in
time to a secondary place in the concert of the nations. For all the

French assets — gold, wheat, machinery, coal, iron, shipping, colonies — could not preserve French potential if manpower failed. Rather, these advantages would become responsibilities because they would excite the envy of more aggressive and prolific peoples. Already by 1914 thousands of Italian, Spanish, Belgian, and other foreign workers crossed into France annually to fill vacancies in field and factory. As the French birth rate, lowest among the European nations, continued to decline, the manpower problem grew more urgent.

2. DEFENSE: THE QUEST FOR ALLIES

The Franco-Prussian War of 1870–1871 made Germany an empire and France a republic. Bismarck was said to favor the republican form of government for France for the same reason he had opposed it in Germany: he conceived democracies and republics were more subject to internal division and proved inept in war because the executive power was divided and dispersed. The fate of France after 1870 seemed to offer some justification for this argument. Royalists and republicans wrestled for control, internal divisions discouraged plans for a war of revenge, and a succession of political scandals discredited the republican regime. The instability of the cabinets made it difficult for the country to pursue a consistent foreign policy or to secure support, for other governments could not readily negotiate or make binding agreements with a ministry which might be out of office before the agreement was complete.

As a result, France for a quarter of a century after 1870 had a diminished prestige and influence in the concert of Europe. This isolation made it impossible for the French to feel secure; and as German industrial and military might continued to grow, the French likewise maintained a conscript army, spent increasing sums on armaments, and pressed their diplomatic campaign for an alliance of states to curb the preponderant power of the Reich. The first successes in this campaign came after Bismarck's retirement, when the system of alliances built up by the great chancellor began to disintegrate. The Three Emperors' League binding Germany, Austria, and Russia had already dissolved (1887), but Bismarck had maintained the Dual Alliance of Germany and Austria-Hungary, the Triple Alliance of Germany, Austria-Hungary, and Italy, and a new Reinsurance Treaty with Russia promising neutrality by the other party if either Germany or Russia were attacked. In 1891 this treaty was allowed to lapse, and three years later Russian military and diplomatic officials agreed to an accord with France. International politics make strange bedfellows; Republican France, most radical of the European regimes, concluded a pact of military support with czarist Russia, most reactionary of the great powers. This accord of 1894, casual and tentative at first, was bound with chains of gold in the years that followed, for the French government authorized loans to Russia for railways, arsenals, guns, and battleships, loans which by 1914 had passed 12,000,000,000 francs. For the German high command this Franco-Russian alliance meant the certainty of a two-front war unless it could be dissolved or hostilities indefinitely averted. It was this pact which first aroused the German fear of encirclement, but the kaiser's advisers long clung to the illusion that they could break it up by a policy which combined bluff, bargaining, and blunt threats.

The French Foreign Office found an agreement with Great Britain more difficult to achieve. Fortunately for their plans, the instability of French cabinet rule was less apparent after 1900, and foreign policy was ably handled for seven years (1898–1905) by a cool-headed and determined minister, Théophile Delcassé. Bismarck, before his death in the same year that Delcassé took office, foresaw the danger of anti-German coalitions which would encircle the Reich. Delcassé, more than any other statesman, was responsible for their creation. His first task had been to smooth over the grave crisis in Anglo-French relations which developed when both powers claimed the Upper Nile region (the Fashoda Affair, 1898). The French were obliged to withdraw; but instead of being angered by this reverse, Delcassé deliberately courted British friendship. The two countries were rivals in the Levant, in Egypt, in Madagascar, and in the Far East, but compromises and concessions so reduced the tension that by 1904 an accord became possible. Unwilling to commit the government to a formal treaty of alliance, which would require parliamentary approval, the British cabinet preferred a friendly understanding, an entente. But, as already explained (see page 23), this entente rendered possible the concentration of the British fleet in the North Sea, promised France and her colonies safety from German naval attack, and adjusted Anglo-French colonial disputes. It also eased the fears of the French that as allies they might have to aid Russia against Britain if Anglo-Russian jealousy brought on a war. Britain and Russia had long been rivals in the Near and Middle East and their relations remained tense and unfriendly.

After 1904 the new balance of power took rapid form. It became the purpose of French diplomacy to draw Britain and Russia together and the purpose was rapidly achieved. The defeat of Russia in the Russo-Japanese War of 1904–1905 was the critical event that speeded the new alignment, for it proved to the British that their fear of Russian strength had been exaggerated and it gave the German-Austrian-Italian combination, the Triple Alliance, a relative preponderance in Europe. Russia, weakened by defeat and rent by revolution, would not be in a condition to wage war effectively for some years. This the French diplomats were swift to appreciate. Under the existing agreements, if Britain as the ally of Japan had gone to war with Russia, France as the ally of Russia would have almost certainly found herself at war with Britain. Such a conflict, weakening to all combatants, would have given the Triple Alliance the mastery of Europe. At Berlin this advantageous turn of events was fully appreciated — too fully, perhaps, for it made Germany truculent. Russia, in grave difficulties, was half persuaded into an alliance with Germany, and the French poured out further loans to hold their wavering ally. To the French, German diplomats hinted broadly that Delcassé and his policy of encirclement had become a threat to peace and he must be dismissed.

Delcassé accordingly resigned (June, 1905) but the German imperialists were not placated. They had watched with jealous eyes the steady increase of French influence in the nominally independent Sultanate of Morocco and they feared that German trade there would suffer if Morocco became a French protectorate. To assuage German protests a conference of the interested powers was convoked (January–March, 1906). The independence and territorial integrity of Morocco were solemnly affirmed, with equal opportunity promised in the Sultanate for the trade of all nations. The French, however, were allowed limited police powers in certain areas, and they continued to expand their influence. As a result the Germans complained that once again they had been thwarted. Since their dreams of colonial expansion required a powerful high seas fleet, they increased their naval program. At the same time they renewed the Triple Alliance ties (June, 1906), and William II sought to weaken France by flattering Nicholas II of Russia and proposing a Russo-German agreement.

The British, alarmed at the German expansion and especially at German naval building, decided that it was time to redress the balance of power. With French diplomats eagerly smoothing negotiations, the British and Russian governments in 1907 established an entente and sought to adjust the disputes which had brought them into opposition in Persia, Afghanistan, and other areas in Asia. The French statesman, Georges Clemenceau, who was premier in these critical years (1906–1909), was delighted to see a Triple Entente (Britain, France, Russia) take shape as a counterweight to the Triple Alliance. The policy which Delcassé had sponsored was succeeding even though he was out of office. Not only had France secured two powerful friends (Britain and Russia) but her potential opponents (Germany, Austria-Hungary, and Italy) as a rival combination had been weakened. By a series of carefully worded conventions, Italy had been placated and promised opportunities to acquire African territory, and Spain had been reconciled. These accords were important, for they made it less likely that Italy would join in a war against France, or that Spain would attempt to close the Strait of Gibraltar to French ships. This gave the French confidence that, if hostilities broke out, their communications with their North African empire would remain open and they could import minerals, extra food, and even Algerian soldiers to defend France.

Yet even with strong allies and the ocean routes safeguarded the French did not feel secure. "For France the danger of invasion is very real," declared Clemenceau in 1908. "We know that on the morrow of the outbreak of war between Germany and England, the German armies will invade France by way of Belgium, and that Germany will seek in France an indemnity for the losses likely to be suffered on the sea at the hands of the English." The French could not count too heavily upon Russian aid, for the confusion, corruption, and inefficiency prevalent in the czar's empire had been revealed in the war with Japan. Nor could the French feel entirely confident of British aid, for France and Britain, despite warm speeches in praise of the entente, were not bound by a formal treaty. As early as 1906 their military representatives had secretly discussed the forces which Britain might land in France if war developed between France and Germany, but without universal military service the British could not promise more than one or two hundred thousand men. The naval understanding between the two governments assured British protection for the French Atlantic and North Sea coasts if the French guarded the Mediterranean. (See page 23.) But even this arrangement, in the absence of a definite treaty, seemed to leave France exposed and possibly defenseless against sea attack.

It was on land, however, that the French expected the war to develop and on land that they knew it would reach a decision. Memories of the invasion of 1870, the siege of Paris, the humiliation of defeat, the loss of Alsace and Lorraine, kept alive in French hearts a conflict of sentiments. Fear of war mingled with and checked the desire for revenge against the Prussians. Few Frenchmen would have maintained that revenge or even the recovery of the lost provinces was worth the certain horrors and losses of a modern armed conflict. Frenchmen, Germans, Russians, Italians, and Englishmen all responded to patriotic appeals when they thought their country was menaced or insulted, but no one save a few intriguers and irresponsible hotheads wanted war. The growing tension, the bulging military budgets, the conscript armies forever expanding, the dreadnoughts and superdreadnoughts, these were all elements in a dark drama, motivated by vast forces beyond any statesman's understanding, any diplomat's control. Distrust bred suspicion, suspicion begot fear, fear became panic. Darkening each diplomatic parley, hovering over every conference table, hung the nightmare vision of the waiting cannon, the gray battleships, the marshaled men, all the inexorable machinery of the nation-in-arms. Everyone realized that this machinery required no more than a word to set it in motion, and once started it could not be arrested. As already explained, the Germans, fearful of encirclement, raised their effectives from 487,000 to 820,000 men in the twenty years before 1914. The sharpest rise came on the eve of the conflict, a rise from 623,000 to 820,000 between 1911 and 1913. The French countered by extending their period of military training to three years and by establishing a reserve of 750,000.

Fear, it has been said, is a poor counselor. The French, because of their sense of insecurity, had worked to build a system of alliances which, opposed to the Triple Alliance, created a precarious equilibrium among the European powers. This balance, the diplomats insisted, was the surest guarantee of peace because each nation would seek to restrain its allies and none would thoughtlessly invoke a war which it stood an even chance of losing. A war, moreover, whether won or lost, was certain to prove burdensome, bloody, and unpredictable. Some militarists even averred with sincerity that the better armed the nations became and the more terrible the weapons science provided, the less risk there was of actual conflict because all sane people would shrink from it and insist upon arbitration. This line of reasoning may have been sound logically but it proved unsound psychologically. The growing threat of hostilities induced a war mentality, a fatalistic sense that something so steadily foreseen and provided for must be inevitable. The balance of power which the diplomats so carefully built up to preserve peace became a mechanism of interlocking parts, so that when the crisis came the powers were dragged one after another into the catastrophe which each had labored to avert and each had prayed it might avoid.

3. SOCIAL JUSTICE: THE PROBLEM OF SOCIALISM AND SYNDICALISM

The Third French Republic was proclaimed on September 4, 1870, after the Second Empire collapsed in defeat and Napoleon III surrendered to the invading Prussians at Sedan. For five months the "Government of National Defense" fought against the armies which had overthrown the empire in five weeks, but the war was already lost; the heroic but belated resistance prolonged it but could not reverse the verdict; and besieged Paris was driven to capitulate in January, 1871. A French National Assembly which met at Bordeaux on February 12 concluded peace two weeks later. The cost for France was the loss of Alsace and most of Lorraine and a billion dollar indemnity.

Like the German Republic of 1919, the Third French Republic was founded in an hour of national humiliation and its first official act was the acceptance of a harsh treaty. Launched in this inauspicious fashion, the new ship of state tacked back and forth uncertainly for several years. Republicans and Royalists, Radicals, Liberals, Clericals and Conservatives, with a dozen minor groups, fused with or fought one another as they strove to form a *bloc* which would give them control. In the outcome the moderate Republicans achieved a leading position with the support of the middle classes. A "Law on the Organization of the Public Powers," passed in January and February, 1875, gave the new regime a constitutional basis. Popular sentiment was still so divided, however, that the critical amendment introducing the word *republic* was carried in the National Assembly by only one vote, 353 to 352. Not until 1879 were the Republicans confident of their supremacy. In that year they won a majority in the Senate as well as in the Chamber of Deputies. Marshal MacMahon, a president with royalist sympathies, who had been installed in 1873, attempted to impose his own choice of ministers upon the chambers, creating a series of crises from 1877 to 1879. Failing in his attempts, he resigned in the latter year before his seven year term was done. As the constitutional laws provided that the presidential office should be filled by a nominee elected by a majority of the deputies and senators voting together, the Republicans replaced him by Jules Grévy, a man who enjoyed their confidence.

The internal history of the Third Republic proved a drama which lacked grandeur. Partly because the journals were free and acrid in their criticism, the political leaders moved in a tarnished setting darkened by party passions and sordid scheming. There were mock-heroic *coups* that failed and unheroic compromises that succeeded, and the parliamentary sessions were punctuated by a series of crises and scandals. To other nations it appeared that the political life of France was not healthy and that ominous undercurrents fed by tides of suspicion and prejudice threatened the stability of the state. Of the many unsettling issues which stirred popular feeling three were serious enough to rock the Republic.

The first of these centered about the handsome and popular general, Georges Boulanger. Named minister of war in 1886, Boulanger achieved extraordinary acclaim by demanding military reforms, more comforts for the army recruits, and a firm, if not defiant, attitude towards Germany. Fifteen years had passed since the humiliation of 1871: the social psychologist might point out, as a parallel, that after a similar period of uneasy adjustments the German Republic of 1919 came under the domination of Adolf Hitler. But Boulanger, despite the hysterical enthusiasm of his followers, was no Hitler. He did not dare to seize power by a *coup d'état*, and after three years *Boulangisme* had been deflated and ceased to be a threat. When the Senate investigated his activities, Boulanger fled from France, his followers repudiated him, and in 1891 he committed suicide.

The second affair which threatened to discredit and possibly wreck the Republic was the Panama scandal. The great engineer and humanitarian, Ferdinand de Lesseps, who had constructed the Suez Canal, headed a company to cut through the Isthmus of Panama. The project proved more difficult and expensive than the promoters anticipated and the company finally went bankrupt in 1889. When indignant investors learned that part of the funds had been used to bribe journalists not to reveal the deficits and that members of the Chamber of Deputies had also accepted loans and favors from the harassed company under conditions which suggested a blend of bribery and extortion, public anger reached a dangerous pitch. Enemies of the Republic seized upon the case as proof that a regime controlled by the middle class and administered by republican politicians would be certain to dissolve in graft and corruption. The Panama scandal forced several politicians from public life and shook the confidence of the electors, but the Republic survived.

The third affair, *the Affair* as it came to be known because it overshadowed the others, was the Dreyfus case. In 1894 a Jewish army officer, Alfred Dreyfus, was sentenced to life imprisonment by a French military court. The charge was treasonable communication with the agents of a foreign power. Convinced that Dreyfus had been arbitrarily condemned, a group of socialists and radical republicans attacked the arrogant army staff which refused to lift the veil of secrecy that obscured the case and denied Dreyfus a new trial. By 1898 society was tragically divided over the bitterly fought issue. The novelist, Émile Zola, publicly accused members of the French high command of shielding the real traitor, a Major Esterhazy. For his audacity, Zola was sentenced to a year's imprisonment, and fled from France, but "truth was on the march" as he had affirmed. In 1899 Dreyfus was brought back from his five years on Devil's Island, tried by a second court martial, and again found guilty, but President Émile Loubet pardoned him and he was finally exonerated by the Supreme Court in 1906. The case against him had been built upon error, forgery, and arbitrary injustice, but the fact which stood out most clearly was the arrogance of the army command, which had persisted in its error as if it were above public criticism and independent of the civil government.

The anti-Dreyfusards, militarists, royalists, and many clericals, were discredited by the outcome of *the Affair*. In 1900 the people showed their revulsion of sentiment by sweeping into office a number of republican and socialist deputies whom they had denounced a few years earlier for daring to doubt Dreyfus's guilt. The left-wing parties, now securely in control, formed a radical coalition pledged to purge the army of royalist influence and to secularize the schools. The reorganization of the army was carried through resolutely and effectively, but in their program of secularization the republicans opened anew the unresolved controversy between church and state.

From its first years the Third Republic had been disturbed by the opposition between clericals and anticlericals. Most ardent republicans favored a complete separation of church and state, and the Primary Education Law of 1882 made no provision for religious instruction in the public schools. Many monarchists were earnest Catholics, and the republican leaders, recalling the conflict between the First French Republic of 1792 and the church, and the historic alliance of the altar and the throne which had persisted for centuries in France, viewed clericalism as a force inimical to the republican regime. After 1890 the clerical question seemed nearer a solution. Church and state had many common aims, especially in the colonies where both labored to extend civilization. In 1891 and 1892 the papal encyclicals *Rerum novarum* and *Inter innumeras*, issued by Leo XIII, instructed French Catholics that it was proper to accept new governments when these became established and were endorsed by the people. The result was a rally of many Catholics to the support of the Republic, while many republicans found much to admire in the wise admonitions the pope offered on social questions and on the strife between capital and labor. Unhappily, these improved relations were again disturbed by the bitterness of the Dreyfus affair.

By 1901 anticlerical sentiment had grown so strong in France that the numerous schools conducted by religious orders were closed by government decree and the orders suppressed (the Associations Law). In 1904 the French ambassador to the Vatican was recalled, and in 1905 the government promulgated a decree separating church and state and terminating the concordat of 1801 which had regulated the appointment and salaries of ecclesiastics. The property of the church was claimed by the state, which allowed private corporations to take over the maintenance of churches. Protestant and Jewish congregations, which had likewise been under state supervision and subsidy since the early nineteenth century, were also disassociated from the state.

The parties of the left, dominant in the Chamber of Deputies since 1900, thus asserted the supremacy of the Republic over the army and the church. To do so, the republicans of the Center had leaned upon the socialist groups, but fear of socialism and of working class movements made the middle classes cautious. The real balance of power rested with the moderate republicans who spoke for the property holders of France. It was not only the great industrialists, bankers, or owners of country estates who kept the government firm in its defense of private property; it was farmers who owned a few acres apiece (a numerous class), the *rentiers* who had purchased government or business bonds and lived on the interest, the small tradesmen and shopkeepers, and the professional groups to whom a diploma and a practice were a form of investment. All these possessed private wealth of one form or another, and they stood together against revolutionary proposals and threats of confiscation. The Third Republic remained in essence a bourgeois republic; it failed to accept real responsibility for the fate of the landless country laborers or the proletarians of the factory towns.

The radical republicans had long chided the moderates for their failure to introduce a frank program of social reform. In earlier, more ardent days, before they achieved power, many republican deputies had advocated an income tax, government ownership of mines, banks, and railways, the abolition of the senate, the substitution of a citizen militia for the professional army. But when the radicals won to power after 1900 they failed signally to attack existing evils. It was the Socialist Party, brilliantly led by Jean Jaurès, which took over their program, heartened the workers, fought the vast outlay for arms and the loans to autocratic Russia, and offered the hand of friendship to German workers. The socialists also directed their attacks against the concentration of wealth in too few hands, against the great industrialists and bankers, and against the bourgeois control of the state. But their demands for a more generous program of benefits for the masses had little effect. No far-reaching measures of social insurance such as Bismarck had sponsored in Germany, no heavy income or inheritance taxes such as Lloyd George wrote into the British budget in 1909, were enacted in France.

It is not surprising, therefore, that French workingmen who sought to better their lot had little faith in the promises of the politicians. Some put their trust in the program of social justice offered by the church, especially after the encyclical of Pope Leo XIII, "On the Condition of Labor," appeared in 1891. Other workers joined cooperative societies or formed labor unions. When sober and moderate leaders failed to exact benefits equal to their hopes, the more radical workers drifted into the ranks of the syndicalists. The *syndicats* were labor organizations which sought to organize all employees in an industry, so that all transportation workers, or all coal miners, might be called out on strike simultaneously. The ultimate ambition of the syndicalist leaders was to unite all the *syndicats* into a *Confédération Générale du Travail*, a general confederation of labor. The executive committee of the C.G.T. could then dictate to the government under threat of a nation-wide strike. Labor appeared at last to be fashioning a weapon with which it could coerce the ruling classes and extort concessions for "the disinherited."

Yet when the weapon was employed it failed to achieve its purpose. Strikes of seamen, miners, electricians, wine-growers, and even government postal employees were attempted between 1906 and 1909, but they were all frustrated by punitive measures or broken up by the action of the police or the army. An attempt by the C.G.T. to call a general strike (1909) ended in failure. The following year a strike of the railway workers was broken by the proclamation of martial law, and engineers and switchmen, who struck as union members, were ordered back to their posts as soldiers.

When loyalty to his union and loyalty to the army conflicted in a Frenchman's mind, he found that patriotism was stronger than class solidarity. The years of military training which all able-bodied male citizens received at an impressionable age conditioned them to obey the call of country and exerted a conservative, disciplinary influence on their characters. As the danger of war increased, it became manifest that class strife within France and strikes which paralyzed industry, weakened the nation and encouraged its opponents. The war mood was a major obstacle to social reform; this fact helps to explain why the socialists advocated international arbitration, a reduction of military service and armaments, the repudiation of imperialistic aims. But the army was the shield of the Republic, and socialist overtures to Germany and criticism of French armaments seemed to ardent French chauvinists to tend toward treason. When war came in 1914 a hotheaded patriot assassinated Jean Jaurès, the socialist deputy and journalist, because he had often pleaded for a more friendly attitude towards the Germans.

At the test of war, the socialist dream that national antagonisms might be softened by an alliance of the working classes of all nations broke down. Nationalism triumphed over class loyalty when the armies marched, and in the German Reichstag and the French Chamber of Deputies members of the socialist groups forgot their earlier resolutions to stand firm in support of a Socialist International. Almost without exception they voted for war and endorsed the war measures of their respective governments.

RUSSIA

The proletariat has no weapon in the struggle for power except organization . . .

NICOLAI LENIN

I. RESOURCES: THE PROBLEMS OF COMMUNICATION AND DEVELOPMENT

THROUGHOUT most of the nineteenth century fear of Russia hung like a vague cloud over the chancelleries of Europe. The vastness of the country with its little-known people and half-guessed resources; the mounting population, estimated to have tripled from some 35,000,000 to 100,000,000 between 1800 and 1900; the enigmatic diplomacy of the czars, now pacifistic, now aggressive — all these factors combined to alarm the Western nations. In 1854–1856 France and Great Britain fought a costly war in the Crimea to check Russian pressure against Turkey, and in 1878 the British were prepared to fight again if necessary, convinced that Russian dreams of expansion threatened Constantinople, Persia, Afghanistan, and even India.

Considered in terms of its population and resources, Russia was potentially the greatest land power of the world. Like the United States, it was a great colonizing power, although its development is not always viewed in that sense because expansion took the form of a spontaneous overflow into vacant, contiguous territories. While Americans pushed their frontier westward, the Russians were moving theirs eastward, settling the plains and penetrating the forests of Siberia, until they established themselves on the shores of the Pacific Ocean. Unlike the United States, however, where roads, railways, post, and telegraph knit all sections together, the Russian realm remained feebly organized, sprawling, and inchoate. Although it expanded until it included one-seventh of the land area of the globe, it was so poorly articulated and so backward in development that its resources were almost untapped, its people uneducated and apathetic, its great potential energies, human and material, unappreciated.

Trade statistics reveal how undeveloped Russia remained as late as 1914, in comparison with the western European nations. The czar's enormous empire imported and exported less than some of the second or third class states. For the last year before World War I her foreign trade totaled about one-half that of the Netherlands, a country with one-twentieth the population and one six-hundredth the area. The nature of the commerce, moreover, indicated the retarded state of the economy. Russia imported coal, chemicals, metalware, machinery, armaments, textiles, and manufactures of all sorts. The exports were primarily agrarian products, cereals, flax, hemp, dairy produce, timber, furs, and leather. These are commodities which agricultural and colonial regions furnish for the industrial states, and the fact that they constituted the greater part of the exports showed that the Muscovite realm was still provincial and almost medieval in its economic life. Indeed, much of the trade was still conducted in village shops, distributed by traveling peddlers, or transacted at annual fairs reminiscent of fifteenth century France or Germany.

This retarded state of the economy was the more surprising because no country was better situated to benefit by the Iron Age. Russia possessed unmeasured reserves of iron ore, coal, oil, minerals, water power, in fact all the prerequisites of a great industrial empire. But capital and initiative were lacking. Most of the financial and technical aid required to develop railroads and factories came from foreign sources, and most of the profit went to foreign investors. Farsighted statesmen, notably Sergei Witte, who served as minister of communications and then of finance after 1892, endeavored to build up transportation and industry until they could become self-supporting and autonomous. But Witte's energetic policies, which opened Russia to the forces of industrialism so rapidly that a rebellious urban proletariat speedily formed, excited opposition from conservative groups and he fell from power in 1905.

The transformation of Germany, the rapid rise of Japan, suggested what the Industrial Revolution might effect in Russia once it gathered momentum. The example of America was even more inspiring, for the forces which had made the United States a great power in the nineteenth century might make Russia a superpower in the twentieth. With vaster plains, more extensive forests, incalculable deposits of minerals, coal, and oil, she awaited enterprising leaders to exploit this wealth. The first requirement was better roads and railroads to link the diverse peoples and provinces and make the empire one great market of continental extent. Power for industries and mechanized agriculture could be developed from coal, oil, and hydroelectric stations. If harnessed, the rivers promised 50,000,000 to 100,000,000 horsepower, more than all the rest of Europe could provide. The possession of such riches was certain to shape the future of the Russian peoples regardless of political developments. The new age of electricity, of mechanized agriculture, trains, trucks, and airplanes, could not fail to benefit Russia perhaps more decisively than any other country, because she was essentially a land empire. "Our greatest enemy," ran an old Russian proverb, "is space." Twentieth century inventions provided the means of rapid overland transportation which could conquer that enemy.

It was not only the natural economic resources which remained undeveloped in 1900. The human resources, the people, were ill-trained and often wastefully employed. Judged by western European or American standards they were deficient in skill and in mechanical equipment, so that they resembled an inefficient labor army which worked hard but produced little. Although Czar Alexander II had abolished serfdom in 1861, most peasants were still the slaves of custom, and those who left the farm or village to seek employment in the rising factory towns were worked overlong in miserable quarters and were poorly paid. A twelve-hour day was considered moderate in nineteenth century Russia; most peasants, servants, and artisans stayed at their tasks thirteen hours or more, and the quality of the work and the health of the worker both suffered. In such a society agitators found ready listeners, so that the growth of trade unions for collective bargaining was rapid once industry created an urban proletariat. After 1900 strikes became frequent and severe, and as they multipled in moments of political crisis they provided a thermometer by which it was easy to gauge the revolutionary fever. In the critical year 1905, for instance, when Russia suffered defeats in the Russo-Japanese War and was shaken by revolutionary tremors, there were five times as many strikes in the czar's empire as in Germany or the United States and ten times as many as in France. In that year nearly 3,000,000 Russian workers left their jobs to protest against long hours, low wages, and political oppression. Employers were forced to yield important concessions to the militant proletariat, but the causes of discontent were as much political as economic.

The Russian labor organizations won consistent gains from 1900 to 1914, improving working conditions so steadily that it seemed possible that reform might continue without revolution. In 1897 strikers vainly demanded a day of eleven and a half hours; fifteen years later they extorted a reduced schedule from one industry after another and a ten-hour day was common. As early as 1903 the government introduced accident insurance, medical aid, and sickness relief, and in 1912 these measures were defined and extended and the employers made legally responsible for the relief payments. Moreover, while hours of labor were decreasing, wage rates increased, rising over 50 per cent between 1900 and 1914; but this benefit was largely offset by the rise in the cost of living, which amounted to 35 per cent for the same period. Nevertheless it was evident that in spite of the inert, divided, and semiautocratic government, Russian trade unions had won important concessions and under a more liberal regime the conditions of the workers would have improved more rapidly. The political incompetence of the czar, Nicholas II, the incompetence of the bureaucracy which the defeats of World War I pitilessly exposed, and the economic hardships caused by war shortages, made the revolution of 1917 inevitable. Yet the revolution did not improve the lot and living standards of the workers as rapidly as their own efforts and the economic progress of 1900–1914 had done, for under the communist regime the unions lost the power to strike and became agencies of the all-powerful state.

The trade unions and other popular movements had also sought to reduce illiteracy among the masses, and hundreds of clubs and libraries were founded after 1900. But enthusiasm was not enough to overcome the lack of adequate funds; the task of educating a great nation called for an energetic government with all the resources of the state behind it. Before mass education, as it was practiced in France, Germany, or the United States, could be applied successfully, there was need for greater standardization of speech, for some of the hundreds of dialects spoken there had no written symbols. The customs, loyalties, tastes, and attitudes of the disparate groups could not easily be welded together. One-third of the czar's subjects were members of minority nationalities, Poles, Finns, Lithuanians, Germans, Jews, Tatars, and others, and these alien elements tended to weaken the national amalgam. The official policy pursued by the Slavophiles in power had long been to Russify these minor groups, but the policy had been applied so stupidly and sometimes so brutally that it had antagonized those it was intended to conciliate and assimilate. What was needed was a central government which could win the free co-operation of all the subject peoples, liberating their energies, preserving their cherished individuality, and substituting cohesion for coercion. It was an ideal not easy to attain and perhaps unattainable.

Yet there could be no question that the Industrial Revolution would introduce new and better aids by which to increase the sense of coherence and homogeneity among the Russian peoples. An industrial economy, which turns out uniform models for wide distribution and depends upon standard equipment and machines with interchangeable parts, imposes uniformity in the daily life of millions. Essential articles, tools, clothing, conveyances, as they become cheap and common and standardized through mass production, grow familiar to an entire population and induce a similarity of tastes and responses. In the same way mass education, with its millions of identical texts, with official instructions multiplied by the rotary press and soon to be supplemented by the effect of the motion picture and the radio, made it possible to integrate the thinking of the 100,000,000 people scattered from Odessa to Archangel and Moscow to Vladivostok.

Thus the stage was already set in 1900 for the coming expansion of the Russian economy, for a synthesis of the energies and the resources of the Russian people. But only an inspired prophet could have predicted in 1900 under what type of regime the impending co-ordination and expansion would take place or have foreseen that the next half-century was to make the great Slav power the scene of the most ambitious collectivist experiment in recorded history.

2. DEFENSE: THE PROBLEMS OF EXPANSION AND EQUIPMENT

To defend the Russian frontiers and to repress outbreaks within the country the czars relied upon a large but widely scattered and somewhat amorphous army. Recruited by conscription, doggedly drilled and disciplined, and toughened by hardships, the Russian soldiers were known for their hardihood and courage. The officers, drawn largely if not exclusively from middle class or aristocratic families, were often inadequately trained. The arms, equipment, food supply, barracks, and hospitals were inferior and sometimes primitive by western European standards.

This backwardness was a serious handicap: Russia possessed the manpower but not the mechanism for waging modern war effectively.

Twentieth century warfare had become industrialized, and the nation which lacked a highly developed industrial system was ill-prepared to supply equipment, transportation, weapons, and ammunition for the millions of men required in modern mass maneuvers. Before 1914 the Russians had to purchase from France, Britain, and even from Germany (their most probable opponent) the rifles, machine guns, cannon, submarines, torpedo boats, and battleships required for defense. The bill for these costly armaments was paid in part by agricultural exports, in part by credits furnished through French bankers. About 1910 the government began a program of construction which aimed to create adequate arsenals, shipyards, foundries, and factories at home. When completed, it was hoped these plants would make Russia largely independent of imports so that her armies could wage a long struggle even if their trade routes with the Western powers were severed. But Russia was far from the desired self-sufficiency when the ordeal of the First World War commenced in 1914.

One of the surest clues to the strategy of the European states can be read in their railway systems. Under the impulse of the new imperialism which developed in the 1880's and 1890's, the railway lines became the spearheads of economic and military drives. Whether the lines projected were to link Berlin to Bagdad or the Cape to Cairo, the thin threads of steel pointed to a horizon dark with war clouds. This proved notably true of the Trans-Siberian Railway which the Russian government completed in 1903. Permission had been obtained to run it across the Chinese province of Manchuria to the Russian port of Vladivostok. This single track line which the Russians hoped to use for the economic penetration of Manchuria placed them in a much stronger position to claim a sphere of control in North China if the Celestial Empire were to be divided among the powers, as then appeared probable.

The only nation able and willing to challenge this plan of expansion was Japan, for the Chinese government was too feeble to resist. To the Japanese, the consolidation of Russian rule in Manchuria and the fortification of Vladivostok threatened to prove a severe check, for Japan also was seeking to expand in the same area. It was imperative for the Japanese to halt the Russians promptly. Once the new railway had brought settlers, and the projects for economic development made Manchurian resources available to them, it would be too late to drive them out. Accordingly, the Japanese concentrated all their naval and military forces for a test, and the conflict opened a year after the Trans-Siberian Railway reached its goal.

The Russians, who had treated Japanese protests with scorn, were caught at a grave disadvantage when their small opponent struck suddenly in February, 1904. Port Arthur, on the Liaotung peninsula, was besieged and finally captured by the Japanese (January, 1905), and the Russian forces, driven back into Manchuria, were defeated in heavy fighting around Mukden (February–March). The Russian Far East naval squadron had been destroyed early in the struggle, permitting the Japanese to reinforce their armies on the mainland at will. The Russian Baltic Fleet, which steamed halfway around the world to render aid, was overwhelmed in the Strait of Tsushima on May 27, 1905. This series of Japanese victories astonished most statesmen of the time, for they had overrated Russian strength and underrated Japanese audacity, organization, and morale. In a treaty negotiated at Portsmouth, New Hampshire, the Russians agreed to surrender their claims to Port Arthur, the Liaotung peninsula, and the southern half of the island of Sakhalin. They also renounced all title to Korea, which the Japanese annexed five years later. Manchuria was restored to Chinese sovereignty.

Had the Russo-Japanese War continued, it is possible that the greater resources of the Russians might have been brought into play, and the Japanese, their finances and reserves overtaxed by the intense effort, might have been reduced to a less advantageous peace. The test had been an unequal one, for the Russians fought at the end of a single track railway five thousand miles long, while the Japanese could bring their full strength, naval, military, and industrial, into action. In the midst of the struggle, moreover, the Russian government was crippled by the outbreak of a revolutionary crisis which is described in the following section. In perspective these factors help the historian to explain the outcome of the war, but their immediate effect was a shift in the balance of power. The Russian Colossus, it appeared, had feet of clay. German diplomats, swift to appreciate the signs of weakness, pressed their demands for colonial territory and commercial concessions upon the French. Partly to placate the kaiser, the French cabinet, as explained earlier, dropped the foreign minister, Delcassé, but at the same time they carried on Delcassé's policies by seeking a closer tie with Britain. The British, on their part, recognizing that Russia was less of a menace than they had supposed, viewed more favorably the French suggestions for a Triple Entente of France, Russia, and Brit-

TRENCH WARFARE IN WORLD WAR I

THE U-9, A GERMAN SUBMARINE RAIDER OF WORLD WAR I

ain. Austria-Hungary, while Russia was still weak and the situation opportune, annexed the late Turkish provinces of Bosnia and Herzegovina (1908). The entente powers, though humiliated at this *coup* which left them without "reciprocal compensation," had little choice but to acquiesce in the expansion of Hapsburg territory. Meanwhile the French, to speed the rearmament of their stricken ally, advanced several billion francs in further loans to the czar's government. The credits helped Nicholas II defy the newly created Duma, which had declined to vote taxes without further guaranties of liberty. Thus the liberal government of the French Republic helped the autocrat of all the Russias to curb liberalism in his empire, demonstrating, as history has often done, that the foreign and the domestic politics of a state operate in separate spheres and sometimes on contradictory principles.

The movement of 1905–1906 came very close to being a definitive revolution. Czardom survived, to endure another decade, but its flaws had been revealed. War made manifest the incompetence of many officials, the unpreparedness of the administrative, diplomatic, military, and naval services, the complacency which had ruled the ministerial councils, and the corruption which marred the system of supply. These revelations brought to a head the discontent latent among the czar's subjects, and resulted in a constitutional experiment after 1906 whereby liberal leaders sought to obtain a share in the government and a chance to reform the social and political structure of the empire. This experiment must now be analyzed.

3. SOCIAL JUSTICE: THE ATTEMPT TO COMPROMISE WITH AUTOCRACY

The western states of Europe, Italy, Spain, France, England, passed through a slow succession of transforming phases between the fifteenth and the twentieth centuries. In eastern Europe the effect of comparable changes was at first delayed and then sharply accelerated. It is not wholly an exaggeration to say that the Russians telescoped five centuries of history into one, meeting concurrently, as it were, movements which the western nations had experienced consecutively. The Renaissance of the sixteenth century, the scientific revolution of the seventeenth, the French Revolution of the eighteenth, and the industrial revolution of the nineteenth all hit Russian society with swift cumulative impact during the span of a man's life. It is not surprising that many Russian intellectuals, sensitive to the currents of their environment, became confused, neurotic, rootless individuals in the later nineteenth century. They were in a very real and painful sense wandering between two worlds.

The contrasts which Western progress created in Russian society were often so startling as to seem incomprehensible. While rural life was still subdued to medieval formulas which fettered villein and landlord alike (serfdom was not legally abolished until 1861), in the factory towns an active proletariat was already perusing communist tracts and organizing labor unions. This fusion or rather juxtaposition of feudal and modern elements was dangerous and explosive, a situation without an exact parallel in any other European state. The land hunger of the peasants, the agitation of the underpaid factory hands, the political aspirations of the small bourgeois class, the grievances of discontented officials, the resentment of oppressed national minorities, and the utopian projects of intellectual radicals combined to generate a revolutionary ferment which by 1905 had become highly dangerous.

The defeats of the Russo-Japanese War crystallized the discontent. It was clear despite the censorship that official folly and blundering had nullified the sacrifices of the common soldiers. Autocracy had demonstrated its defects. Once before, after the Crimean War (1854–1856), military reverses had forced wholesale reforms; and in 1905 liberal critics demanded a radical change. They wanted representative government with a ministry responsible to an elected parliament, on the British or French model. The populace, stirred to action, pressed for reform with mass demonstrations, strikes, and protests. The answer of the government was delivered on "Bloody Sunday" (January 22, 1905) when workers parading to the Winter Palace to lay a petition before the czar were fired upon by the troops. The victims of this unwarranted massacre, seventy dead and over two hundred wounded, became martyrs of the people's cause. When the smoke of those brutal volleys had blown away in the winter air, the Russian masses began to see the czarist regime in a different light. Their sentimental faith in the "Little Father" had been dissipated.

It was not the fault of Nicholas II (1894–1917) that he inherited a revolution. Like his prototype, Louis XVI of France, he was a tragic misfit, well-meaning but irresolute, and stubborn at the wrong moments. He believed, and chose ministers who believed, in the principles of absolutism. By adroit concessions and specious promises he managed to tide over his first crisis and to confuse and divide the revolutionary groups. In a manifesto issued in October, 1905, he declared himself willing to grant guaranties of personal liberty, proposed to call for the election of a Duma (parliament), and promised that in future no legislation would be considered valid without the consent of the Duma. Moderate liberals accepted the program as adequate and became known as Octobrists. The more radical groups, termed the Constitutional Democrats or Cadets, wished to summon a convention which would draw up a formal constitution and fortify it with a Bill of Rights.

This split in the revolutionary forces permitted the czar to modify his pledges. Lack of unity and of first-rate leadership was weakening the forces of reform, and the inertia of centuries turned the wheels of the administration back into their old grooves. The Duma, when it assembled, was dismissed by the czar as too radical in temper. A second one met the same fate. Finally, after restricting the suffrage and exerting official pressure on the electors, the government permitted the assembly of a third Duma in 1907. This legislature proved subservient enough to survive in an anomalous union with an absolute monarchy. The compromise between autocracy and parliamentarism endured until the First World War but foundered in the confusion of the war years.

The revolutionary movement of 1905–1906 had faltered because it lacked organization. The various groups and committees could not agree upon a co-operative program or a common strategy. The Social Democrats, supported chiefly by the urban classes, preached Marxian communism. The Socialist Revolutionaries, more concerned with the condition of the rural population, advocated the break-up of large estates and a redistribution of the land among the peasants. The national minorities, Finns, Poles, Jews, Latvians, Lithuanians, Estonians, hoped to see the revolution lead to self-government or to a federation of semiautonomous republics. These varied aims confused and paralyzed the movement for reform when a common front and a common program were most essential. In the test neither reformers nor revolutionaries were able to make headway against the well-entrenched bureaucracy, the privileged aristocrats, the new industrial magnates who feared a popular regime. The ubiquitous secret police, whose function it was to ferret out all opposition however legitimate, remained loyal to the ruling caste and betrayed liberal plans and objectives while making excuses to arrest the liberal organizers.

The attempt to achieve a compromise with autocracy broke down because Nicholas refused to grant the Dumas the power to attack abuses, and their sessions, though active, were barren of real reform measures. Proposed legislation, intended to improve the status of the workers, create more efficient councils in the provinces, promote education, and encourage economic expansion, largely failed of its purpose. The prestige of the czar declined as his weakness of character became more apparent, and the strange circle of mystics and charlatans who influenced the superstitious czarina increased the impression that the imperial couple were cut off from the advice of able administrators and were subject to the pressure of cabals and favorites. The failure to cope with the forces of discontent within the empire made it clear that a new revolutionary movement might rise at any time.

Two developments in particular contributed to the violence and success of the second revolutionary upheaval which followed, a decade after the first, in 1917. First, the steady increase and more efficient organization of the urban workers made it possible to plan a series of strikes and acts of sabotage which would paralyze the government at the chosen moment. In the second place the outbreak of a new and more exhausting foreign war in 1914 overtaxed Russian resources, exposed more pitilessly than ever the incompetence of the czar and his advisers, and goaded the people to such desperation and misery that revolution became their only hope of relief. The account of the great Russian Revolution of 1917, one of the landmarks of twentieth century history, must wait until a later chapter.

ITALY

Italy's geographical situation is particularly unfavorable.
PROTEST TO THE LEAGUE OF NATIONS, 1927.[1]

1. RESOURCES: THE PROBLEM OF SHORTAGES

IN Roman times Italy had been mistress of the Mediterranean world. In the Renaissance era the flame of Italian genius made the politics, arts, and letters of Italy the models for all Europe. For two thousand years Rome had been a focal point of Western civilization as the city of the Caesars and the city of the popes. Modern Italians are proud to remember that twice their country achieved a primacy among the nations and that it has so long been the home of the classical tradition, sharing with Greece the honor of being the first European center to achieve high culture.

A tradition of leadership is not easy to maintain. Since the fifteenth century Italy had fallen behind the more progressive maritime states of the north. The shift of commercial routes from the Mediterranean to the Atlantic, and the political disunion which persisted in the peninsula, partly account for the decline. Still preserving "the fatal gift of beauty" Italy seemed, in the seventeenth and eighteenth centuries, to enter a long twilight after a golden day. This impression of a land where time had paused, where the sunlight was gentle to the fading palaces and majestic ruins, has doubtless been intensified by the painters. But the economic decay was real enough, for Venice and Genoa lost their banking and trading wealth to Amsterdam and London. Not even the *Risorgimento*, the political and national revival of the nineteenth century which forged Italy into a single kingdom, nor the coming of the Machine Age with its smoking factories and surplus goods, could bring back the economic leadership Italy had once en-

[1] A protest presented to the Preparation Commission for Disarmament, League of Nations, by the Italian government.

joyed. For a shortage of essential commodities denied the Italians their merited importance in the modern world. Coal and iron were lacking, there was no powerful and progressive middle class to promote industrialization, and there was no adequate supply of ready capital in the hands of enterprising men. Nature had denied Italy several of the essentials which made other states great industrial powers.

The people did not lack vitality. Between 1800 and 1914 the population doubled, rising from some 18,000,000 to 36,000,000. Unfortunately this proof of vigor was not an unmixed blessing because the national food supply remained insufficient. The major part of Italy is mountainous terrain, the rainfall is generally inadequate, and although some areas are suited to grape and olive culture there are not sufficient forest regions, grazing lands, or wheat fields. These facts are reflected throughout the countryside in the substitution of stone for wood as building material, in the gray hue of the treeless sections during the dry season, and in the relative scarcity of dairy cattle, the vegetation being in general more suitable for goats. To compensate for a deficiency in cereals, the Italians (who consume almost as much wheat per head as the French) have become dependent upon imported grain; in 1913 they had to purchase 66,000,000 bushels of wheat abroad to supplement the 214,000,000 bushels produced in the country. Foodstuffs, it is important to note, then formed half the annual imports. This involved a serious strain upon the national economy because such imports had to be paid for, and Italy suffered from an adverse trade balance. Even in average years the value of the imports was almost double that of the exports.

Had the Italian cities become highly industrialized, the nation might have paid for imported foodstuffs in manufactures and services. Great Britain, with a population approximately the same and a smaller area, had grown powerful and wealthy through industry while neglecting agriculture. But here again Nature had been niggardly to Italy, for the country lacked coal deposits, and heavy imports of coal, chiefly from British mines, accounted for one-fourth of the annual trade deficit. This shortage of coal and of available iron ore (Italian steel production before 1914 was less than that of the Grand Duchy of Luxembourg) was a critical handicap in the Machine Age. To create armaments, industrial machinery, railways and shipbuilding, steel bridges and skyscrapers, the metallurgical services were definitely inadequate even in peace. Any attempt to embark upon ambitious wars or a program of colonial conquest was certain to reveal these deficiencies and to overstrain the national economy. For Italy, more surely than for any other European power, essays in the new imperialism were extravagant gestures. Colonial ventures could not fail to increase taxation and might founder before the costly initial period had been surmounted and the dividends began to accumulate.

The nineteenth century had been the age of coal and iron. The twentieth, with its diverse discoveries, its multiplicity of new metals and materials and additional sources of power, opened new vistas for Italian enterprise. Oil, like coal, was lacking, but an obvious solution was to dispense with fuels and develop hydroelectric energy. The rivers and cataracts of the peninsula promised an estimated 6,000,000 horsepower, but only one-fourth of this had been developed before the First World War. Silk and silk fabrics, which made up one-fourth of the value of Italian exports, were challenged by the newer synthetic threads developed by the chemists; but if silk culture declined, the textile centers could make the new fabrics. And Italy possessed other assets which might balance competition if wisely employed. Labor was cheap. The high technical skill of many Italian artisans won worldwide respect. The genius which had so long inspired this gifted and beauty-loving people to produce exquisite paintings, statuary, cameos, jewelry, and glassware, also inspired machinists and designers to create articles of striking perfection, from delicate precision instruments on the one hand to expensive automobiles on the other.

The health and living conditions of the people were depressed by the adverse trade and retarded economy. The birth rate was relatively high; but the death rate, especially the infant mortality rate, was also high and remained almost double that of the neighboring state of Switzerland. The average income of Swiss wage earners was nearly three times that of the Italian. The Swiss also benefited from a sounder national economy, lower taxes, and higher standards of education, health, and industry. These comparisons impressed upon thoughtful Italians the possibility that their country might be handicapped by social and political defects as well as by a deficiency of some natural resources. Discouraged by the poverty, low wages, and lack of opportunity in their native provinces, many laborers emigrated to wealthier lands. Some were seasonal migrants, seeking employment in France, Switzerland, or Germany for a part of the year; but several hundred thousand left annually to find permanent homes in the United States or in South America. This exodus inflicted a heavy loss on the nation. There was, however, one compensation. Most of the expatriates sent back remittances to help support their relatives in Italy, and this influx of foreign credit was an important national asset. Foreign currency, especially United States dollars, not only relieved the want of many families with relatives abroad; it also helped redress the trade balance and augment the purchasing power of the *lira*, the Italian monetary unit.

2. DEFENSE: THE PROBLEM OF CHAUVINISM

When the Middle Ages drew to an end in the fourteenth century, the Italian peninsula was divided, like most of Europe, into minute political fragments. Some eighty principalities, duchies, counties, republics, communes, and city-states filled the region from the Po Valley to Sicily. By A.D. 1500, however, these fragments had been fused into a dozen major political units or areas. This rapid progress was acclaimed by Niccolò Machiavelli (1469–1527), who besought the Italians to become a strong and united nation. But the drive towards political unification was arrested and separatism continued until the nineteenth century. The "Kingdom of Italy" created by Napoleon embraced only one-third of the country and collapsed with his overthrow. The achievement of unity had to wait until the labors of Mazzini, Garibaldi, and Cavour were crowned with success in the decade 1860–1870. In 1859 with the aid of Napoleon III and a French army the Austrian garrisons were expelled, and in 1860 the Italian states — Piedmont and Sardinia, Lombardy, Parma, Lucca, Modena, and the Kingdom of Naples, including Sicily — were all linked in a common union. Venetia did not come in until 1866, surrendered by Austria after the Austro-Prussian War, and Rome was not occupied until 1870. The outbreak of war with Prussia in the latter year moved the French government to recall troops it had stationed at Rome to protect the papal patrimony. On September 20, troops of the Italian Kingdom broke through the walls and occupied the city despite the refusal of Pius IX to compromise or accept compensation. The government had attempted to settle the "Roman Question" by force; but for nearly sixty years the papacy declined to recognize the usurping state.

As in the case of the Germans, the completion of national unity stirred the Italians to a high pitch of patriotic exaltation. The entire nation was infected with a passionate pride in its past and a fervent faith in the future, so strong and transforming that it was termed the rebirth or *Risorgimento*. In their enthusiasm the Italians expected to see their new government immediately emulate more prosperous states, acquire a colonial empire, and reclaim segments of the Adriatic littoral which they regarded as "Unredeemed Italy."

The new national government attempted but failed to meet these extravagant expectations. It had assumed the debts of the constituent states, and this fiscal burden, combined with the adverse trade balance, crippled the national finances. The limitation of resources already described, the high rate of illiteracy which demanded a costly campaign of education, the low living standards especially in rural areas, all curtailed revenue. In the face of a perpetual deficit, successive cabinets strove to promote education, stimulate agriculture and so reduce food imports, develop irrigation, erect power plants, improve railways and harbors, and encourage manufacture. But the projects were hindered by lack of funds, by political incompetence and dishonesty, and by costly military and naval armaments.

The twin urge, to seek colonies in Africa and conquests on the Adriatic at the same time, confused foreign policy. In North Africa France was the most serious rival, and the French annexation of Tunis in 1881 inflamed Italian sentiments. This section of Africa lay closest to Italy, across the narrow strait and almost within sight of Sicily. It contained, moreover, the ruins of ancient Carthage, which the Romans had conquered and destroyed after exhausting wars, and the modern Romans were alarmed and angered to see a potential enemy take possession of it. One result of French intervention was to drive Italy into a Triple Alliance with Germany and Austria-Hungary (1882). This secret accord assured Italy of support against France if the two powers clashed in Africa, but it complicated the Italian claims to Trieste and the Trentino, which Austria, now an ally, still held.

From 1876 the parties of the left had a majority in the Italian parliament, and their defiant foreign policy brought discredit and defeat. Francisco Crispi, premier from 1887 to 1891 and again from 1893 to 1896, defied France, pressed Italian claims to Eritrea and Italian Somaliland, and negotiated a treaty (1889) with an Ethiopian ruler, Menelek, which gave Italy an excuse to claim a protectorate over Ethiopia. Despite a desperate financial situation at home, intensified by the scandalous collapse of the Banca Romana (1893), Crispi dispatched an expeditionary force to subjugate Ethiopia (1895). After several reverses the Italian force of 25,000 men was completely defeated at Adowa (March 1, 1896), and the Ethiopians won full recognition of their independence. This check to Italian imperialism caused the fall of the Crispi cabinet, and for several years popular riots, strikes, and general disturbances necessitated frequent appeals to martial law. For the moment, however, African adventures had lost their attraction, and during the first ten years of the new century Italy avoided colonial strife. This policy brought improved relations with France and Britain and a tacit understanding with both these powers that Tripoli might be left free as a sphere for Italian penetration. (See map, p. 15.)

Tripoli was nominally a part of the Turkish Empire. Revived nationalist fervor in Italy moved the premier, Giovanni Giolitti, to dispatch an ultimatum to the Turkish government (September 28, 1911) and follow it by an attack on the coastal towns. A month later Italy proclaimed Tripoli a protectorate, but fighting continued for over a year before the Sultan acknowledged the Italian claims by the Treaty of Lausanne (October 18, 1912). This conflict revealed the weakness of Turkey and so prepared the stage for the Balkan wars of 1912 and 1913. Italy now held a colony, near at hand and fit for settlement although costly to pacify and to administer. Italian patriots were gratified in heart though depleted in pocket. But this Turko-Italian War had wider implications. The German government, which was striving to win the co-operation of the Turks, recognized with annoyance that Italy could upset the aims of the Triple Alliance at will. The French and British could regard Tripoli in Italian hands as a hostage which would help to keep Italy neutral or draw the country to their side. For communications with the new Italian protectorate would prove difficult to preserve against a French and British naval blockade in the Mediterranean.

Italy had never been an enthusiastic member of the Triple Alliance. Although the original pact of 1882 was renewed at intervals, her adherence became increasingly tenuous especially after the British and French entente of 1904. Austrian pressure in the Balkans, and particularly the annexation of Bosnia and Herzegovina in 1908, roused the hostility of Italian nationalists and revived the demands for *Italia irredenta*. Pride in their conscript army and elation over their Tripolitan victories made the Italians a headstrong nation to hold in check. Nor were the politicians of Giolitti's type particularly eager to curb the chauvinist outbursts. To keep in power by appeals to emotion, by compromises, agility, and manipulation, had long been the ruling aim of the cabinet ministers. So, despite the heavy strain which armaments imposed upon the nation, the leaders did little to curb the clamor for a bold foreign policy, although they might have foreseen, had they risen above the expediencies of the moment, that the patriotic passions so constantly excited might lead the country into expensive and unnecessary wars.

When the First World War did break out in 1914, the government failed to stand by Germany and Austria-Hungary and proclaimed its neutrality. For months Italian diplomats bargained with the entente nations and with the Central Powers to discover which side would bid most generously for Italian aid. In 1915, as a consequence of the secret Treaty of London (April 26), Italy joined France, Great Britain, and Russia. The Italians had extorted a high price. Unredeemed Italy was to be wrested from Austria; segments of the Turkish Empire and additional African territory were to be added to the Italian colonial domains. But it remained to be seen whether the economy could stand the strain of a major war, whether the army could secure *Italia irredenta* by force of arms, and whether diplomacy could obtain the promised compensation at the peace table.

3. SOCIAL JUSTICE: THE PROBLEMS OF POVERTY AND POLITICAL INEPTITUDE

For half a century after 1870 the Italian people were governed by a parliamentary regime. The constitution provided for a limited monarchy similar to the British, and a bicameral legislature with a Chamber of Deputies and a Senate resembling that of the Third French Republic. The electorate, limited at first to male citizens of twenty-five or older, who paid forty lire in taxes, was extended in 1881 by reducing the age limit to twenty-one and the tax requirement to nineteen lire. This permitted some 2,000,000 citizens to vote; further extensions of the franchise brought the number to nearly 8,000,000 in 1912. The *forms* of democratic government thus made rapid advances in Italy as in all leading European states during these years. But the people lacked adequate experience in self-government, and democratic formulas failed to function honestly or efficiently. Official pressure, trickery, and bribery were employed on a wide scale. Secret compacts between opposing party leaders, political jobbery and corruption, and maladministration of the finances marred the record of almost all the cabinets and brought the entire constitutional system into discredit.

Much of the legislation passed by successive parliaments remained a dead letter because of bureaucratic inertia, passive opposition, or lack of funds. The northern sections of the kingdom were the more highly industrialized, and the impoverished, agrarian South seemed part of another country if not another century. Even the dialects differed so completely that a Milanese could not readily understand a Neapolitan. Tariffs on manufactures, demanded by northern mill owners to protect them from unlimited foreign competition, raised consumer costs and offended the rural population; import duties on grains, which might keep up the price level for the benefit of the farmers, meant that factory workers must pay more for their bread and cereals. These regional and class interests created conflicts in parliament and provided opportunities for bargains which seldom satisfied even the factions which concluded them.

Constant unrest, acts of violence, and the imposition of military law indicated the unhappy state of the rural districts. Illiteracy, especially in the Neapolitan provinces and in Sicily, remained high and secret societies oppressed and terrorized rich and poor. With such conditions prevalent and a lack of constructive reforms, it is not surprising that emigration, especially from southern Italy, remained a barometer of conditions, rising and falling with the state of the annual crops and the imminence of famine. Among the workers who stayed home, socialist agitators attempted to organize a workers' party, and after 1900 sporadic strikes and radical propaganda increased the tension. Attempts by labor leaders to call a general strike in 1904 led to violence in Turin and other cities, but as this diverted sympathy from the strikers the socialists lost standing in the elections of that year. Demands for the protection of labor, for sickness, old age, and accident insurance, and for limitation of hours and minimum wages failed to move the legislators.

This indifference or inability of the parliament to attack growing problems in the national life undermined public confidence in representative government and turned many against a regime which possessed neither strength nor dignity. Giovanni Giolitti, the most influential political figure in or out of office after 1900, was a skillful contriver and a professed democrat. But his maneuvers were motivated by the need to favor his followers and he lacked a genuine knowledge of the nation's problems and the vision and courage of true statesmanship. The temptation to divert the attention of the people to external objectives, to evade responsibility, and to trick and befuddle opponents, overcame the leaders in office. Italian politics remained a game of wits played by men of few principles for petty and immediate ends.

VII

AUSTRIA–HUNGARY

If there were no Austria it would be necessary to invent one.

FRANTIŠEK PALACKÝ

1. RESOURCES: THE PROBLEMS OF A LANDLOCKED EMPIRE

FOR a thousand years, from the Age of Charlemagne (771–814) to the Era of Napoleon (1799–1814), the most grandiose but least substantial political structure in Europe was the Holy Roman Empire. In theory it was the secular counterpart of the Universal Church, an empire coextensive with Christendom. But this shadowy realm, more theoretical than actual, lost meaning after the close of the Middle Ages, and with the rise of the national states it became little more than a diplomatic fiction. Finally in 1806 the Holy Roman Emperor, Francis II, laid aside his claims and contented himself with the less pretentious title, Francis I, Emperor of Austria.

Had Austria evolved for centuries, as Spain, France, and England did, inside natural frontiers, the population might have attained uniformity of language, a centralized political structure, and national homogeneity. Instead, the island of Germans in Austria and of Magyars in Hungary lived among and were surrounded by minority peoples. The Czechs of Bohemia, the Poles of Galicia, the Slovaks, Croats, Slovenes, Yugoslavs, and Rumanians never coalesced into a compact national state. Austria-Hungary remained primarily a dynastic empire, a composite feudal inheritance. Like the royal realms of the later Middle Ages it took form as an agglomeration of duchies, baronies, free towns, bishoprics, counties, kingdoms, and ecclesiastical estates all in haphazard proximity but all held together by a common allegiance to the House of Hapsburg.

Attempts had been made, notably by Joseph II (1780–1790), to organize the empire into a centralized despotism. Joseph sought to assimilate the minorities, establish uniform laws, and make German the official language, but his measures were blocked by sullen resistance or open rebellion. During the nineteenth century, as national sentiments grew stronger throughout Europe, the dissimilar peoples enclosed within this amorphous empire became more deeply aware of their divergent aspirations. While the Italian states to the south and the German states to the north crystallized into political unions and were welded by the flame of patriotism into nationhood, Austria-Hungary disintegrated slowly but inexorably. The strongest argument for its survival was the fact that no alternative union that might federate the peoples of the Danube Valley appeared practicable. The alternative to Hapsburg rule was apparently the creation of four or five fragmentary states, a solution likely to provoke as many problems as it solved.

The nineteenth century ended Hapsburg claims in Italy, for the achievement of Italian unification between 1859 and 1870 drove Austrian garrisons from Lombardy and Venetia. The loss of these provinces left Austria-Hungary almost completely landlocked. In an age when ocean routes were the most essential highways for trade and transportation this was a severe handicap. Alone among the leading powers, she acquired no colonial spheres of influence. Her foreign trade in 1913, though slightly greater than that of Italy, was less than the total for Belgium. A small segment of the Adriatic shoreline, including the harbor of Trieste, provided one salt-water port of limited facilities, but Trieste lay on an inland sea and was coveted by the Italians. Traffic down the Danube River, of great importance to Austrian merchants, had to pass between Rumania and Bulgaria to reach the Black Sea and thence through the Turkish controlled Straits into the Mediterranean. For Austrian shipping to reach the Atlantic Ocean at Gibraltar or the Indian Ocean via the Suez Canal and Aden, meant a voyage of two to three thousand miles.

Great powers seek outlets, economic and territorial, for their expanding energies. Shut in on the west, north, and east by firmly entrenched and compact states — Italy, Switzerland, Germany, and Russia — Austria-Hungary could expand only to the south, and this meant expansion at the expense of the minor Balkan states. As Russia, likewise landlocked on the south, was also pressing into the Balkans to seek a warm-water port, the danger of a clash between Austria and Russia for control of Constantinople and the Dardanelles increased throughout the nineteenth century. So tense did the political and economic rivalry become in southeast Europe, so complex were the crosscurrents of conspiracy and intrigue in this region, that the Balkans came to be known as the "powder keg" of Europe.

As Russia appeared the greater threat to the general peace in the later nineteenth century, the diplomats of Europe sought to maintain the *status quo* by strengthening Austria. At the Congress of Berlin, summoned in 1878 to check Russian pressure in the Balkan peninsula, the delegates of the remaining great powers assigned to Austria-Hungary the administration of the Turkish provinces of Bosnia and Herzegovina. They thought that these provinces, if attached to the Dual Monarchy, would give the Austrian government control of the Adriatic shoreline from Istria to the Strait of Otranto.

The statesmen at Vienna waited for a favorable moment when they might annex the provinces outright, and the moment came in 1908. In that year a revolution at Constantinople temporarily paralyzed the government of the sultan, Abdul-Hamid II. The "Young Turks" who staged the revolution planned to revive the Ottoman power and to call a parliament. As they intended to include delegates from Bosnia and Herzegovina in order to prove that these provinces were still part of the Turkish Empire, the Austrian government blocked them by a swift *coup*. On October 6, 1908, Vienna announced the formal annexation of Bosnia and Herzegovina to the Austro-Hungarian Empire. Simultaneously, with Austrian approval and encouragement, Bulgaria declared itself independent of all Turkish suzerainty.

The Austrian foreign minister, Alois von Aehrenthal, thought that he had negotiated the *coup* adroitly. Russia could not oppose it because she was still weak from the war of 1904–1905 and could not risk hostilities. Furthermore, the Russian minister, Alexander Izvolski, gave advance consent in return for Aehrenthal's agreement that the Dardanelles might be opened to Russian warships. But this "Buchlau Bargain" (September 16, 1908) broke down because the Russian government repudiated it and Izvolski found it expedient to pretend he had been tricked. The British, moreover, who had extended their entente with France to include Russia, thus creating the Triple Entente (1907), nevertheless opposed opening the Straits to Russian warships. Aehrenthal, however, had foreseen this reaction and maliciously hoped the Buchlau Bargain would stir up trouble in the entente camp by poisoning Anglo-Russian friendship.

In all the capitals there was alarm and in most there was indignation over the Austrian move. At Berlin there was grave anxiety lest Austrian pride and recklessness lead to a war over Balkan issues not worth a battle. But the Germans believed that they must stand firmly behind their ally because they had no other real friend among the great powers and because Austria was laying plans for further expansion that would also benefit Germany. There was talk of an Austrian-controlled railway to run probably from Sarajevo to Saloniki on the Aegean Sea. Such a spearhead of imperialism, by driving a corridor between Serbia and Montenegro, would have greatly strengthened Austrian control in the Balkans and would have blocked the formation of a unified Slav state, a potential development which the Austrian government feared. Furthermore, the railway would have helped to open a better exit for Austrian trade. The Russian foreign minister, Izvolski, admitted that Austria-Hungary needed more outlets to the warm seas, but he fought against any increase in Austrian influence throughout the Balkans. These various aims and compromises suggest how intricate the Balkan situation had become by 1908 and how easily a brusque move there might drag all the powers into open conflict.

Because the crisis of 1908 passed with merely verbal protests Aehrenthal was able to congratulate himself upon his finesse, and the Austrian minister of war, Conrad von Hötzendorf, could boast that the strength of his army and the firmness of the Austro-German alliance had daunted Russia and France. But this easing of the crisis solved nothing: it merely postponed the reckoning. Pressure between Austria and Russia was certain to increase. Both were economically retarded powers; both were feeling the quickening effects of industrial and commercial progress; both needed better trade outlets to the warm seas. The political and diplomatic moves recounted here were but one phase of the growing international pressure, and other factors complicating the situation will be discussed later. One further point should be noted, however. Had Austria-Hungary stood alone in 1908, the entente powers would have found it easy to concede or to block her demands, and Britain and France might even have been ready to meet them by granting outlets on the Adriatic or the Aegean. But Austria in close alliance with Germany was much more formidable, for Austro-German industry and military power, directed into the Balkans and the Near East, might soon prove stronger than Russian, British, or French influence in these regions. The unity of the Austro-German stand demonstrated the solidarity of the Dual Alliance. Had the newly formed Triple Entente been equally firm and united, a general war might have developed. The crisis of 1914 was prefigured in the *coup* of 1908.

For Austria the incorporation of Bosnia and Herzegovina was a questionable gain. It added several million Slavs to the discontented minorities already subject to Emperor Francis Joseph and so increased the nationalist ferment in the empire. This ferment was a serious threat to the government as the following section explains, but it might have been somewhat assuaged if economic prosperity had eased the lives of the populace. But economic progress proved slow, and industry was strangled by the lack of communications and of capital. The Dalmatian coast, which Austria won by moving into Bosnia, contained few harbors or rail connections; and the chief products of the area — wool, timber, fruit, cereals — were largely superfluous to the Austrian economy. The rich Danube basin and the plains of Hungary already satisfied the agrarian needs of the population of the Dual Empire. What Austria required in order to discharge more effectively the role of a great power, was more coal, machinery, iron, arms, and manufactured goods in general. In 1913 the iron production of Austria was only half that of Spain and less than the total output of Sweden or the Grand Duchy of Luxembourg. Hydroelectric power, which might have supplied the deficiency in coal, was largely undeveloped and internal communication inadequate.

The retarded state of industry was a matter of concern to the government, and measures to stimulate trade and manufacture received official support. As part of the program of expansion to the southeast, German and Austrian financiers adopted a project for a railway route to run from Berlin through Vienna, Budapest, Belgrade, Constantinople, and thence across Asia Minor to Bagdad and Basra on the Persian Gulf. This Berlin–Bagdad Railway, which would provide an outlet on the Indian Ocean for the Central European countries, alarmed British shipowners. They feared that mail, freight, and passengers would be diverted to the swifter land route and that economic penetration of the Near East by German traders would curtail British business.

It was true that the construction of such a line under Austro-German auspices was likely to increase the influence which the bankers and industrialists of Berlin were building up in the Near and Middle East. Direct connections from Berlin to Constantinople might also bring Serbia and Turkey into the economic and diplomatic sphere of the Central Powers. If pressed ambitiously, this drive to the east might come to be a threat to British rule in India, for by 1906 the Germans were already seeking concessions for coaling stations and railways in Persia (Iran). The Russian expansionists also viewed this German activity with even greater alarm, for Turkey and the essential Straits, under the shadow of German-Austrian control, would be a serious threat to Russian trade in peace and make a blockade certain in war.

Thus Britain, Russia, and consequently Russia's ally, France, were lined up to oppose the most promising line of expansion open to Austria in the Balkans.

2. DEFENSE: THE PROBLEM OF DISSOLVING FRONTIERS

To the statesmen who directed the destinies of Austria-Hungary the Balkan peninsula was more than a field for economic penetration; it was an area of menacing intrigues. In Belgrade, Bucharest, and Sofia, in Athens and Constantinople, German, Austrian, Russian, French, Italian, and British agents watched events intently and reported every incident to their governments. Representatives of banking, armament, engineering, and shipbuilding firms competed for contracts. In all the Balkan capitals the cabinets balanced offers from the Central Powers against offers from the entente powers, offers of aid in the training and equipment of their armies, offers of loans for the purchase of arms and the construction of strategic railways, roads, and harbors. The aim of each great power, logically enough, was to secure a lien on the smaller states and turn them into pawns in the game of international politics. Britain, France, and Germany, not being in a position to occupy Balkan territory, were in general satisfied to preserve existing frontiers. But for Austria-Hungary and Russia, as already explained, the Balkans were a possible corridor to the outer world. Each sought to extend a protectorate over part or all of the peninsula, and the Balkan countries preserved themselves precariously by playing one power against its opponent, as buffer states must.

To frustrate the dangers implicit in this Balkan ferment and to protect the illogical and dissolving frontiers of the Hapsburg possessions, the Austro-Hungarian government relied upon dynastic and military prestige. Like all other European powers it increased its forces and defense budgets steadily throughout the period of the Armed Peace. From $39,000,000 and 218,000 men in 1875 they climbed to $156,000,-000 and 479,000 men under arms in 1914. Only Russia, Germany, and France possessed larger forces. To Austria, however, the army was an essential element in the preservation of the empire. It filled a dual role: the regiments were at once guardians of the frontiers and garrisons of occupied provinces.

In the Austro-Hungarian Empire before 1914 more than half the subjects were of Slavic descent. These peoples were kept subordinate socially, politically, and economically by the two ruling groups, the Germans of Austria and the Magyars of Hungary. As the Germans

AUSTRIA-HUNGARY, 1914

formed about 25 per cent of the total population and the Magyars about 20 per cent, these two privileged minorities lived in constant apprehension that the more numerous Slavs might come to dominate the empire. For this reason, the annexation of Bosnia and Herzegovina seemed, as noted already, a step of doubtful wisdom. But if left to the nominal suzerainty of the Turks, the peoples of Bosnia and Herzegovina might have united with the Serbs; the Slavs of southern Hungary might have turned in the same direction; and a Pan-Slav state could have taken form under Russian protection. Patriotic societies inspired by such a program were already active in Serbia, and Austrian statesmen felt themselves driven to anticipate and frustrate such ambitions. Without strong support Serbia could not resist Austrian pressure. This had been made clear in 1908 when, Russia being too weak still to risk war, the Serbs unwillingly recognized the Austrian annexation of the provinces and agreed to curb activities directed against the Dual Monarchy. It was an extorted promise and was poorly kept. To the Austrian ruling classes a severe policy seemed simple self-preservation, and Serbian intransigence appeared to justify even military intervention if the plotting continued. But the Austrian difficulties received scant understanding or sympathy in western Europe.

To strengthen its frontiers the Austro-Hungarian government depended upon the ancient adage, *divide et impera*. Local jealousies were sometimes kept alive purposely and minority groups played off against one another with considerable skill. But no political manipulation and no military preparation could make Austria a match for Russia as the trial of strength drew near. The army in 1914 was computed at 479,000 men, but many divisions were too poorly trained and too ill-equipped to be considered first line units, and some were of doubtful loyalty. The Russian armies, though even worse equipped than the Austrian, were formidable because of their vast reserves and the dogged devotion of the peasant soldier. In 1914 the czar's empire was defended by an armed force estimated to exceed 1,500,000 men (more than three times the Austrian standing army), and the Russian war budget of approximately $400,000,000 was three times the Austrian.

This expansion of the Muscovite power was part of an ambitious military and naval program to revive Russian prestige, and it was designed to reach maximum strength about 1917. As the Germany army of 871,000 men in 1914 was almost equalled by the French with 739,000, the German and Austrian chiefs of staff saw the threat of a Franco-Russian offensive as a perpetual challenge. They concerted their plans on the assumption that, if war came, it would be a two-front war, in which the Central Powers would have to face attacks from France and Russia simultaneously. Since Austria and France had no frontier in common, only Germany would face the double attack. The Austrian armies could therefore concentrate their strength on the eastern frontier, but they would have to fight in an area devoid of natural defenses, an area where the battle line might ebb and shift in costly, exhausting fashion. In war as in peace, the Austro-Hungarian empire was to be the victim of "dissolving frontiers."

3. SOCIAL JUSTICE: THE PROBLEMS OF SOCIALISM AND SEPARATISM

Democracy, the second driving force of the nineteenth century, threatened the stability of Austria-Hungary no less gravely than nationalism by setting the weight of numbers against the weight of rank. To broaden the franchise might lead to changes so revolutionary that German and Magyar dominance, and even the dynasty itself, would be swept away. The venerable emperor, Francis Joseph, who had assumed his high office in 1848 at the age of eighteen, strove through a reign of sixty-eight years to hold the national and democratic impulses of his subjects in check. He had learned from Metternich that these twin forces, which became the dominant trends in European politics after the French Revolution, would prove disintegrating influences in the semifeudal society over which he ruled. He was a conservative, educated in the belief that the ideals of benevolent paternalism which his predecessors had exemplified were sound. He had inherited a deep sense of responsibility, lived austerely, applied himself conscientiously to the details of administration, and strove to govern in a spirit of enlightened despotism.

The affection and increasing respect which his subjects felt towards Francis Joseph were perhaps the most genuine bonds holding the empire loyal. Veneration for the dynasty formed among the peoples of Austria-Hungary a sentimental cohesive cult. But it was not so powerful as the mystic Russian veneration for the czar as the Little Father of his people, and it was less compelling than the French national cult of *la patrie*, the German worship of the nation-state, or the social solidarity and sense of imperial destiny which united the British. In the face of disaster no desperate but heroic flame of patriotism would fuse the subjects of Francis Joseph into a nation willing to die rather than accept defeat and dismemberment. Austria-Hungary, it must be repeated, was not a nation in the modern sense, and its fate had already been prefigured before World War I broke it into political fragments.

The political machinery through which Francis Joseph administered his polyglot empire was a cumbrous organization with duplicated parts. In addition to being Emperor of Austria he was King of Hungary, and the Hungarians had their separate constitution, their individual parliament, and their national capital at Budapest. This dual arrangement, which had been established by an *Ausgleich* (Compromise) in 1867, provided that problems of defense, tariff, and foreign policy were to be adjusted by conferences between the twin imperial ministries at Vienna and Budapest. In all other matters of government, however, Austria and Hungary were separate countries although they had a single ruler. This partial decentralization, or federalization, of government had been further extended (1868) by the grant of nominal autonomy to the Croatians of Hungary, and by the establishment of complete autonomy in local affairs for the Poles of Galicia.

The Czechs of Bohemia had received less generous treatment and formed one of the most insubordinate national groups in the empire. They demanded the establishment of Czech schools and insisted that all public officials in Bohemia speak Czech as well as German. When their demands were refused, their deputies in the Austrian parliament obstructed legislation, setting an example for the other discontented minorities to follow. In the stalemate which resulted, the government resorted to an article in the constitution which permitted the enforcement of emergency decrees, i.e., decrees which could be promulgated while the parliament was not in session. The parliament might refuse to vote the annual budget, and did refuse assent several times after 1900, but the government raised the required taxes by authority of special imperial orders. This contest between the authoritarian methods of the monarchy and the protests of the overruled parliament was a further symptom of the divisions weakening the Dual Empire.

Out of this highly complex situation, so full of conflicts and contradictions, three facts stood forth as the twentieth century opened. (1) The intensified ambitions of the nationalist groups could not, apparently, be resolved by any political formula yet tried, whether it looked to the concentration or to the diffusion of the administrative power. (2) The growing influence of the Slavic elements — Czechs, Poles, Slovaks, Ruthenes, Slovenes, Serbs, Croats, and others — made the extension of greater political influence to these peoples almost inevitable; but the dominant ruling groups, the Germans and Magyars, were fearful of extending the franchise and so finding themselves outvoted by superior numbers at the polls. (3) The slow but irresistible growth of modern industry was creating an urban proletariat, and the appearance of a Socialist Party added one more unruly element to the political chaos. As the most influential bankers and industrialists were Germans and the workers were drawn largely from the Slavic groups and classes, the rise of capitalist enterprise and mechanized industry tended to intensify the existing antagonisms dividing the nationalist factions. The less privileged peoples were accumulating a triple grievance: they felt that as peasants and workers they were condemned to social inferiority, that as wage earners they were exploited economically, and that as Slavs they were denied the expression of their national aspirations. United, these varied emotions of discontent made an explosive mixture.

Many proposals were put forward as possible solutions for this administrative puzzle. Perhaps the most promising was a suggestion to transform the empire into a tripartite state, with the Slavs enjoying a semiautonomy similar to that accorded to the Hungarians after 1867. The heir to the imperial throne, the Archduke Francis Ferdinand, was believed to favor this solution. If a decade or two of political peace could be achieved by such a compromise, it was possible a crisis might be averted. The growth of trade, traffic, and manufacture was forging the various sections of the Danubian basin into an economic *bloc,* and the needs of the peoples throughout this area might foster the development of an integrated economic community held together by mutually profitable business interests. But political disintegration came before an economic union could be attained or even seriously attempted. The possibility of such a free-trade federation in the Danube Valley was to revive, however, after World War I.

Whatever program Francis Ferdinand might have encouraged had he succeeded to the throne of Francis Joseph must remain a matter of conjecture, for on June 28, 1914, he was assassinated in Sarajevo by a Bosnian youth. Subsequent investigation revealed that the deed had been planned by a secret society with centers in Serbia and that several Serb army officers and government officials had been aware of the plot. The tension already existing among the Slavic groups in the Balkans and in Austria-Hungary made the assassination the first act in a universal tragedy. The Austrian government reacted with an ultimatum to Serbia, and the shots which killed Francis Ferdinand proved to be the opening volley of World War I.

THE LESSER STATES

The day of small nations has passed away; the day of Empires has come.

JOSEPH CHAMBERLAIN (1904)

I. THE LIMITED AUTONOMY OF SECONDARY STATES

SIX great powers — Britain, Germany, France, Russia, Italy, and Austria-Hungary — dominated Europe in 1900. In a sense it might be said, with some disrespect to the lesser sovereign states, that these six great powers *were* Europe. For over four-fifths of the population, territory, wealth, foreign trade, and armed might of the Continent was vested in them. The secondary powers existed and could exist only as satellites in the orbit of a great power or as buffer states preserved by international agreement.

The "great power" of 1900 possessed, in rough average terms, some 40,000,000 inhabitants and 400,000 square miles of territory. The typical small power had about one-tenth these resources: a population of perhaps 4,000,000 and an area of some 40,000 square miles. Obviously, faced by a superiority of ten to one, a small nation could not resist the encroaching pressure of a neighboring great power unless it enlisted the aid of another to provide a counterpressure. The small countries, in other words, were dependent states. Their governments claimed complete freedom of action and exercised what was nominally "sovereign" power. This diplomatic fiction was carefully preserved, and the rulers of small states seldom avowed openly the considerations which dictated their decisions. For their policies were based (though it was not always expedient to proclaim the fact) upon the primary need for protection. Defense, to the minor power, was less a question of armaments than of alliances. Its diplomatic freedom was commonly restricted, however, to a choice of alliance with one great power (or coalition) or with its competitor. The area on the map, the territorial entity, of a small state was usually determined by agreements reached among the great powers, and further agreements might enlarge, reduce, or obliterate a minor principality.

There were several noteworthy illustrations of this fact. In the later eighteenth century for instance, Poland was expunged from the map between 1772 and 1795, a result of joint partitioning by the Russian, Prussian, and Austrian governments. In the decade 1821–1831 negotiations carried through by the great powers set Greece up as an independent kingdom. In the decade which followed, further accords established Belgium as a sovereign state and dedicated it to perpetual neutrality. The late nineteenth century saw Serbia, Bulgaria, and Rumania gradually freed from the lax suzerainty of the sultan and recognized as sovereign principalities. In these latter cases, the sovereignty of the new states was conditional rather than absolute. The weakened overlordship of the Turks had been supplanted by the less manifest but more masterful pressure of Russian and Austrian militarism, of British naval and mercantile dominance, of German and French loans and economic penetration. The new states were minors in tutelage to the great powers.

This constant dependence upon influences which originated and decisions which were shaped outside their own frontiers was the primary factor to consider when appraising the role of the minor states. However peaceful their policies, however tactful their diplomacy, they found it difficult to avoid entanglement in their neighbors' affairs. When war came they were frequently the first victims, and if they escaped involvement it was a consequence more often than not of the fact that they might be of more service to all the belligerents as neutrals. But even as neutrals their condition was likely to be humiliating if not actually desperate. Napoleon with his laconic logic made the reason for this clearer when he observed that a neutral has two enemies where a belligerent has one.

Most of the diplomatic crises and both the world wars of the twentieth century were precipitated by the ultimatum of a great power to a small state. Wherever an international dispute arose, the anomalous status of some minor country was the most probable point at issue. For the fictions of diplomacy and the facts of power politics were often in flat contradiction. Egypt, for instance, was nominally a part of the Turkish Empire before 1914, but it was under British protection and control. Panama was an independent republic, but an attack on its coast would have aroused the United States to action as swiftly as an invasion of Alaska. By the twentieth century the world had been divided among the great powers into spheres of influence, and political frontiers, especially the frontiers of small states, had lost much of their significance. Maps which showed political boundary lines and nothing more revealed only half, and that the obvious half, of the international picture.

2. SPAIN AND PORTUGAL

For Spain the twentieth century held a tragic ordeal in store. Before the century opened, war with the United States stripped this once dominant colonial power of almost the last outposts of empire remaining to it. Cuba, Puerto Rico, the Philippine Islands, and Guam passed under American protection after a brief and decisive conflict (1898). In European affairs Spain had come to play a minor part, although it possessed a population of 20,000,000 and an area of 196,000 square miles, only slightly less than that of France. But lethargy and bureaucratic inefficiency, economic backwardness, lack of vigor and initiative, widespread poverty in the agrarian sections, illiteracy, and political unrest paralyzed or distracted the energy of the people. In the sixteenth century, the "golden century" of Spain, the shadow of Spanish power had overhung Europe and the enterprise of Spanish colonizers had brought a new world within the orbit of European civilization. Modern Spain, however, failed to maintain this ascendency or to fill the role in world affairs which the traditions, the genius, and the valor of the Spaniards had won for them in the fifteenth and sixteenth centuries.

Economic backwardness and financial insolvency were major factors in retarding the development of Spain. In 1913 her foreign trade was less than that of Sweden or Denmark, amounting in fact to only one-half that of Argentina, once a Spanish colony. Capital was urgently needed to develop mines, factories, and communication systems and to generate hydroelectric power to operate them. Enlightened leadership was likewise needed to reform the schools, to procure credit for new enterprises, to improve public health and sanitation. A far-sighted land policy was needed to raise the living standards of the rural population, to break up the great estates, and to end for the peasantry and sheepherders conditions that verged on peonage. Spain lacked the class which in France had come to form one of the most stable elements in the nation, the millions of independent farmers with a few acres of their own to make them responsible men of property. But it had taken a revolution to transform France from the old regime to the new; and reform in Spain, however instituted, was certain to prove revolutionary in its effects. Whether the needed reforms, agrarian, social, economic, and political, could be carried through without the confusion and suffering of a civil war the century would reveal.

Unlike Spain, Portugal retained into the twentieth century a considerable overseas empire, including the Azores, Madeira, and the Cape Verde Islands; Goa, Damao, and Diu in India; Macao in China; part of Timor in the East Indies; and Angola and Mozambique in Africa. These possessions held a native population greater than the 5,000,000 Portuguese in Europe, and their combined area (1914) was almost one hundred times larger than Portugal itself, a state of only 35,582 square miles. Portugal, like Spain, suffered a severe depletion of manpower in the sixteenth and seventeenth centuries, when Latin America received an estimated 3,000,000 immigrants from the Iberian peninsula. As late as 1750 the Spanish and Portuguese population in the New World was increasing twice as fast as the total for all other European settlements together. Brazil was lost to Portugal in the early decades of the nineteenth century, and the great migration of this century, which carried 50,000,000 Europeans across the Atlantic, further depleted the Spanish and Portuguese home population.

The Portuguese have lacked the naval or military power to defend their far-scattered ports and colonies, retaining them in the past three centuries largely through British aid. If they had passed to a first class power, the Portuguese colonies might have proved a danger to nearby British holdings; so the British were satisfied to leave them in Portuguese control because this helped to assure Portuguese neutrality. The Anglo-Portuguese friendship is of old standing, for it dates from the mid-seventeenth century when the English helped the Portuguese to separate from Spain (1640–1658) and to establish themselves as an independent kingdom once again. In 1703 a closer alliance was negotiated between the two kingdoms, strengthened by a tariff treaty which opened Portugal to British merchandise in return for a reduction of the duty on Portuguese wines entering England. To the British the use of the Portuguese harbors in peace and in war offered important advantages.

Like Spain, modern Portugal has suffered from misgovernment, administrative inefficiency, impoverishment, and illiteracy. In 1910 a revolution dethroned the reigning king, Manoel II, and substituted a republican regime, but reforms promised by the new government were not realized. The Portuguese failed to share in or to benefit greatly from the economic advance which transformed the leading countries of western Europe in the later nineteenth and early twentieth century.

3. THE NETHERLANDS, BELGIUM, SWITZERLAND, AND THE SCANDINAVIAN STATES

The peoples and provinces which now form Belgium and the Dutch Netherlands came very close, historically, to merging into a great power. In the fifteenth century the House of Burgundy controlled most of the area between the crystallizing kingdom of France and the long disunified Germanies, but the attempt of Charles the Bold (1467–1477) to make himself king of this middle and disputed area failed with his death. The Netherlands passed by marriage to the Spanish Hapsburgs and were ruled from Madrid until they revolted against Philip II. The seven northern provinces — Holland, Zeeland, Utrecht, Gelderland, Groningen, Friesland, and Overyssel — proclaimed their independence of Spain in 1581 and became a prosperous sovereign state, but the southern and western provinces submitted to Spain and became the Spanish (and after 1713) the Austrian Netherlands. In 1815 the Congress of Vienna united both sections as the Kingdom of the Netherlands but the Belgians broke away in 1831 and were recognized as a separate kingdom by the powers in 1839.

Had the Kingdom of the United Netherlands remained a unit it might almost have ranked as a great power by the opening of the twentieth century. Although the combined population was still moderately small — about 12,000,000 in 1900 — and the area limited (Netherlands, 12,712 square miles; Belgium, 11,775), the wealth, industry, and colonial possessions of these two states were impressive. Belgo-Dutch foreign trade in the first decade of the century surpassed that of any other European states except Britain and Germany; it exceeded in value the foreign trade of France and of the United States in 1900. The Netherlands overseas empire included a population six times and an area sixty times those of Holland itself. Belgium likewise ruled territories in other continents, chiefly in Africa, with a population double and an area eighty times those of the home state. The density of population in Holland and Belgium, especially in Belgium, was almost the highest in Europe, and the standards of living and per capita wealth were likewise high.

The Netherlands and Belgium, like Portugal, depended upon the open ocean for their trade. A war with Great Britain would invite the destruction of their commerce and the forfeiture of their colonies.

These circumstances help to explain why, when war came to Europe in 1914, Belgium like Portugal was found on the British side, while the Netherlands preserved a precarious neutrality, its trade rigidly regulated by the British blockade.

Switzerland differs from the Netherlands and Belgium in that it has no sea coast and no colonies. Nevertheless the Swiss have succeeded in achieving a remarkable degree of prosperity, based upon their intelligent use of local resources and the expansion of their industries and trade. Circumspect in diplomacy, vigilant in defense, self-respecting and industrious, they entered the twentieth century with a hundred years of peaceful development behind them. The factors which strengthen the bonds of cohesion in most national states are absent in Switzerland, for it does not have the unity of language, uniformity of custom, and centralized administration that distinguish most European countries. Its twenty-two cantons are twenty-two sovereign units, joined voluntarily by a loose federal tie. Slightly more than half the population of about 4,260,000 profess the Protestant faith, slightly less than half are Roman Catholic. There is no single or official language, for a majority of the inhabitants in sixteen cantons speak German; in five French is the accepted tongue; and in one, Italian. Yet despite these disparate influences and local liberties, the Swiss communities maintain a singular firmness and unanimity in preserving their federation. The mountain barriers which divide the cantons from one another also help to preserve Switzerland from attack by its three great neighbors, Germany, France, and Italy. That Geneva was chosen as headquarters by the convention which founded the international Red Cross movement in 1863 and that it became the seat of the League of Nations after 1919, is a tribute to the strict neutrality and broad outlook the Swiss preserve in world affairs.

Denmark, Norway, and Sweden represent another grouping of states which have been closely linked in the past. Had historical trends permitted, the three might today form one unified and powerful state. The crowns of Denmark and Norway were united from 1381 to 1814. Sweden in the seventeenth century almost established a Scandinavian hegemony. But the eighteenth and nineteenth centuries brought political divergence and national autonomy instead of cohesion among these three neighbors. The Norwegian kingdom, detached from Denmark and joined to Sweden in 1814, seceded in 1905. All three, while developing representative institutions and adopting democratic reforms, have remained constitutional monarchies. Sweden, the most highly industrialized, produced 7.4 per cent of the world's iron ore in 1913 and took an early lead in developing the great resources of hydroelectric power. Norway, though likewise favored with abundant waterfalls for such power, remained industrially undeveloped, partly because the energies of the people were engaged on the sea, where the tonnage of their shipping ranked fifth in 1914 among the merchant marines of the world. Sea fishing was also an important occupation and source of gain; the Norwegian taking of cod and herring placed the nation eighth among the world's powers in marketing this commodity before 1914. But Norwegian shipping and fishing suffered heavily during the years of blockade from 1914 to 1918. Denmark, the only one of the three kingdoms which claimed any considerable territory overseas, retained title to Iceland and Greenland and to the Virgin Islands in the West Indies. The last named were sold to the United States in 1917 for $25,000,000, and the protection of Iceland and Greenland rested in reality with the British or the American navy. For Denmark had no navy equal to the task of protecting its empire or its merchant shipping. Its area, 16,575 square miles, makes it much the smallest of the three states. As a flat peninsula and islands, lacking mountains and waterfalls, large forests, or great mineral wealth, it could not match the metallurgical industry of Sweden or the lumber trade of Norway. In compensation, the Danes produce an abundance of farm and dairy commodities which find a market in Germany and England in normal times.

The high level of culture and education maintained in Norway, Denmark, and Sweden has given these nations an influence out of all proportion to their numbers in the literary, artistic, and musical developments of the nineteenth and twentieth centuries. The sculptor, Albert Bertel Thorwaldsen (1770–1844), the literary critic, Georg Brandes (1842–1927), and the writer, Hans Christian Andersen (1805–1875), were Danes. The composer, Edvard Grieg (1843–1907), the dramatist, Henrik Ibsen (1828–1906), and the novelist, Sigrid Undset (1882–   ), were born in Norway; and the dramatist August Strindberg (1849–1912) and the engineer and philanthropist Alfred Nobel (1833–1896) were Swedish.

4. THE BALKAN STATES AND THE TURKISH EMPIRE

In 1453 the Turks ended the Eastern Roman Empire by their capture of Constantinople; in 1683 they were masters of the Balkan peninsula and their armies were encamped before the walls of Vienna. But the

Austrian capital was relieved by a mixed army under John Sobieski, king of Poland, and the Turkish tide began its long retreat. After 1913 only a few square miles around Constantinople remained in Turkish control, and after 1919 the empire of the Crescent, which had once almost ringed the Mediterranean Sea, had shrunk to a republic of some 300,000 square miles with its capital transferred to Ankara.

The slow withdrawal of the Turks from Europe and the disposal to be made of the territories thus liberated created what diplomats called the Near Eastern Question. The area which the Turk had ruled was not a void; the discordant provinces of the Balkan peninsula were inhabited by intractable minorities as hostile towards one another as they were towards their Turkish oppressors. Their uprisings, feuds, and intrigues filled the nineteenth century, creating perpetual crises as the Greeks, Serbs, Bulgars, and Rumanians in turn rose in rebellion and claimed liberty and autonomy. At each crisis the statesmen of Europe worked out a new adjustment but none of their compromises brought tranquillity to the troubled peninsula and its unruly inhabitants. The feuds which throve among the various national groups in this contracted area were rooted in a heritage of immemorial wrongs and were envenomed by conflicting ambitions. Moreover, they were deliberately intensified by intriguers, sometimes agents of the great powers, who sought to play one faction against another for political ends. No segment of Europe reflected more starkly the unstable foundation of European peace in 1914 than the area lying between the Adriatic and the Black Sea.

Four new states had emerged to nationhood in this region during the nineteenth century. The Greeks were the first of the subject peoples successfully to repudiate the Turkish domination and win recognition as an independent kingdom (1829). Enthusiastic liberals throughout Europe and America greeted with admiration the war for freedom waged by these modern Hellenes. The death of the English poet, Lord Byron, while assisting the insurgents, set a seal of romantic approbation on their efforts and their cause. A century ago, when all educated people had been grounded in classical history, the Greek rebels wore the guise of Athenians defying the might of Persia. This literary comparison seriously distorted the facts of the Greek struggle; and it obscured most unjustly the equally heroic contest waged in the same years by others victims of Turkish misrule, notably by the Serbs who had rebelled as early as 1804, by the natives of Moldavia and Wallachia (later Rumania), and by the Bulgars.

Throughout the greater part of the nineteenth century these various insurgent groups conspired and campaigned for freedom. One by one in varying measure they attained it and received the cautious recognition of the great powers in successive treaties and protocols. Moldavia and Wallachia were granted a conditional independence under Russian protection in 1829 and eventually emerged as the Kingdom of Rumania after 1860. The Serbians wrung a promise of autonomy from the sultan in 1830, but they too had to wait until after 1860 before the last Turkish troops were withdrawn. In the 1870's Russian armies helped to liberate the Bulgars, who were granted partial self-government by the powers at the Congress of Berlin in 1878.

The dissensions within the Balkans were a reflection of rivalries without. This fact was amply demonstrated at the Berlin Congress, where the opposing demands of the great powers almost produced an impasse and war was narrowly averted. The representatives of Russia, Austria, and Great Britain were more concerned to frustrate one another and to secure "reciprocal compensation" for any advantage gained by a rival than to harmonize the Balkan feuds or to rectify the injustices which galled these indignant peoples. British and Russian antagonism at Berlin was particularly acute and almost broke up the conference, but a compromise was finally worked out. To maintain a counterpoise to the Russian influence over Rumania and Bulgaria, Austria-Hungary was awarded control of Bosnia and Herzegovina, which remained, however, technically a part of the sultan's empire. Great Britain secured the island of Cyprus, thus strengthening her position in the eastern Mediterranean. The Near Eastern Question, the problem of filling the vacuum created by the retreat of the Turks, was to be solved, it seemed, by the substitution of Russian, Austrian, or British spheres of influence or by the erection of local buffer states under the remote control of these great powers.

At Constantinople the reverses and mutilations of territory inflicted upon the Turkish empire finally produced an indignant protest. A group largely composed of army officers and known as the "Young Turks," forced the abdication of the tyrannical sultan, Abdul-Hamid II (1876–1909). This Turkish Revolution of 1908 replaced one inept regime by another scarcely more effective, but it opened an era of intensified strife in the Near East. In the Balkans, in Turkey itself, and even among the Arabs of the desert, nationalist sentiments were quickened. The Bulgars promptly asserted their complete independence of

Turkish suzerainty. Austria-Hungary, as explained in the preceding chapter, annexed Bosnia and Herzegovina lest the Turks reassert their title or the inhabitants proclaim their independence. It was manifest that the Turkish Empire was falling apart, and the fact encouraged the Italians to press their advantage by occupying the ports of Tripoli in 1911.

The moment seemed opportune to drive the Turks from their last foothold in Europe. In 1912 the Balkan nations momentarily forgot their own rivalries, and Serbia, Montenegro, Greece, and Bulgaria united in a coalition to hasten this result. The allied states, in this First Balkan War, scored a surprising succession of victories, but the great powers kept a careful watch over their satellites to make certain they did not outrun control. At Vienna the persistent fear of a pan-Slav union moved the Austrian diplomats to oppose Serbian aggrandizement. At St. Petersburg there was alarm lest a Serbian, Greek, or Bulgarian army enter Constantinople. The Balkan allies themselves soon fell into dispute over the allocation of the territory liberated, and a Second Balkan War (1913) followed the first. Bulgaria rashly attacked her late confederates, Serbia and Greece, but suffered a swift defeat and forfeited her earlier conquests. Even the Turks resumed the battle against the Bulgars, and Rumania, neutral in the First Balkan War, also opposed the Bulgarian armies. The real clue to this complex struggle, however, lay outside the states actively engaged.

The Balkans were a vital area: no war there could leave the great powers indifferent. The Second Balkan War masked only partly the growing tension between the Triple Alliance (Germany, Austria, Italy) and the Triple Entente (Russia, France, Britain), although none of these powers intervened directly. But the statesmen at Vienna were more determined than ever to limit Serbian gains lest the prestige of an enlarged Serbian (or Yugoslav) state excite envy among the Austrian Slav minorities. To deny Serbia its desired outlet to the Adriatic Sea, Austria and Germany insisted on creating an independent principality of Albania, to be confided to a German prince. It was also suspected that the Austrians encouraged Bulgaria in her treacherous attack upon her late allies. The intent was to humiliate Serbia, and the Bulgarian defeat which nullified this strategy was a reverse for Austria. Russia, on the other hand, was gratified at the success of the Serbs and the enfeeblement of Turkey. The conflict of aims and of alliances was growing more definite, and the most critical center of Near Eastern affairs was the Bosporus. All the divergent strategy could be found, in final analysis, to turn upon the fateful question: Who shall control Constantinople and the Straits?

For five thousand years the Straits had been the scene of strife. Troy, Byzantium, Constantinople, Istanbul, whichever city controlled the passage from the Black Sea to the Mediterranean possessed a rich but perilous heritage. The Turks retained control only because no great power would permit another to seize the key city. But all conspired to influence Turkish politics. By 1914 French armament makers, British mercantile and naval consultants, Austro-German bankers and businessmen, and Russian diplomats and militarists were all converging upon the Turkish capital, bidding for concessions which would give them an advantage. In that highly charged atmosphere, tense with suspicion, a spark could produce an explosion. The explosion came in 1914, but the conflict had been prepared by decades of increasing rivalry.

1914: THE END OF AN ERA

I, the heir of all the ages, in the foremost files of time.

ALFRED TENNYSON

1. THE GREAT CENTURY, 1815–1914

NOT the year 1900, but the year 1914, marked the logical and historical close of the nineteenth century. For one hundred years, from the battle of Waterloo in 1815 to the battle of the Marne in 1914, Europe had been spared any long, lethal, and exhausting wars. There had been revolutionary outbreaks in 1830 and 1848 and the great powers had met in conflict in the Crimean War (1854–1856), the Italian War involving Austria, France, and Sardinia (1859), the Austro-Prussian War (1866), and the Franco-Prussian War (1870–1871). There had also been, especially towards the close of the century, a flurry of minor colonial campaigns. But total wars, spreading throughout the Continent and consuming millions of lives and millions of homes, factories, ships, year after ruinous year — such wars Europe had been spared. The nineteenth century, this century of relative peace, had therefore been a century of hope and optimism, a period of exceptional progress which stands without a parallel in history. It had excelled all others in the development of technology and science, the expansion of production, the increase in material wealth, and the unprecedented rise in European and world population.

The Great Century was also unique in its development of immaterial values, the "priceless intangibles" which give dignity and meaning to life. In all the more advanced countries there was an increasing respect for law and at the same time a more earnest effort to realize "equal justice under law," to provide greater liberties and opportunities for the individual. The citizen gained the right to choose his trade or profession, the opportunity to vote for the legislators who made the laws he must obey, to speak his mind frankly on social and political questions, and to support the group and program which embodied his political aims. He could change his place of abode, seek new employment, or emigrate to new lands if he so desired. In most states a system of public schools was established, and children of talent and ambition, from all ranks, found these schools a selective system which not only trained but discovered and promoted the able and deserving. All these liberties brought the citizen a greater and a gratifying sense of his own worth, stimulated his ambition, quickened his initiative, and enlarged his talents. In a word, these liberties helped to inspire in millions of Europeans and Americans that dynamic drive for self-betterment and for social progress which made the nineteenth century an era of energy, optimism, and achievement unmatched in the annals of recorded history.

In this emancipation of European man France, the United States, and Great Britain played leading roles. The French Revolution of 1789 had proclaimed the "Rights of Man and the Citizen" to Europe in the same year that the First Congress adopted the Bill of Rights which became part of the United States Constitution. But liberty and equality as political ideals cannot be realized without favoring conditions, without institutions that assure social benefits, without citizens trained to respect legal forms above private vengeance, without an adequate standard of living and reasonably stable economic conditions. In these prerequisites Great Britain set an example to the world. The progress of the nineteenth century — the swift mechanization of industry, the magnification of wealth, the improvement in living standards, the extension of European civilization to new lands — all these trends were made possible by the extraordinary economic expansion of the era, and in promoting this expansion Great Britain led the van of progress.

Throughout the nineteenth century Britain remained the dominant naval power of the world. No competing navy or combination of navies seriously challenged that supremacy until after 1900 when the German fleet expanded rapidly. Furthermore, at the close of the Revolutionary and Napoleonic Wars (1792–1815), Britain emerged half a century ahead of all rivals in manufacturing techniques and possessed in addition the reserve capital, the commercial contacts, and the merchant shipping to control world supplies and dominate world markets. This leadership made London the capital of a world economic empire, the first empire in history which may without exaggeration be termed global. The Spaniards, Portuguese, Netherlanders, and French had won posts and dominions in all continents and seas and might assert that the sun never set upon their empires. But the British Empire was global because it included almost one-fourth of the land area of the earth and one-quarter of the human race.

The British maintained their influence through economic rather than naval or military pressure. Aside from a few hundred warships and a few hundred thousand soldiers, Britain lacked armed forces; never before in history, even under the *Pax Romana*, had so many millions of people lived in peace and security, guarded by such limited armaments. For the protection and control of their vast trade empire the British relied chiefly on three favoring factors without which their prosperity would have failed: (1) peace and security on the high seas; (2) cheap and adequate transportation; (3) a stable monetary unit universally acknowledged. These three advantages, essential to profitable trade, the British successfully maintained. Their cruisers policed the seas, prevented acts of war, suppressed piracy, and brought wreckers and mutineers to justice. In this task they were supported as a general rule by other navies. At the same time British navigators and cartographers prepared tide charts and hydrographic surveys for all the oceans. The fact that the prime meridian for calculating longitude and time is a line running through Greenwich, a suburb of London, is a reminder that most nations have adopted the British lead in the arts of navigation and meteorology. The government, the admiralty, and the shipping firms devised regulations for the safe loading and limiting of cargoes (the Plimsoll mark) and the necessary precautions against fire and other marine disasters. Coaling stations, supply depots, and warehouses were established in all parts of the world; and London insurance brokers calculated the risks and helped to reduce the hazards and losses in all forms of mercantile activity. Through these regulations and precautions ocean travel and transport, especially on British ships, was made more safe and predictable with each decade. Such increase in security for life and property encouraged businessmen and investors and furthered the expansion of British influence.

At the same time ocean travel and transport was made as swift and cheap as possible. With the development of the steamship not only luxury articles but goods in bulk could be carried half way round the earth at a cost of a few shillings a ton. In the nineteenth century more than half the international ocean trade of the world was transported in ships of British registry, and the profits from these services made up a considerable part of Britain's "invisible" income. The introduction of the steam engine and the improvement in shipbuilding brought such gains in speed and regularity that ocean voyages, which in 1815 had been a matter of weeks, became by 1914 a matter of days.

The third factor required for stable and profitable trade, a dependable monetary unit, the British also helped to maintain. The pound sterling based upon gold was accepted like British consolidated government bonds as an international standard of value, and other currencies fluctuated in terms of the pound. London, the financial capital of the world, was a power station where switches could be thrown which would send a quickening flow of credit through banking channels to speed a project in distant lands. In this process the newly laid electric cables were of particular value, and the fund of information on world conditions which collected at London made the British capital a clearing house for economic statistics, quotations, and ratings. There the judgments rendered on the evidence at hand might cancel credit facilities, and if the flow of currency were cut off factory wheels might be stilled, store windows darkened, plantations abandoned, and ships marooned, from Lisbon to Lima or Aberdeen to Zanzibar.

This economic supremacy which Britain enjoyed for a century was already declining relatively by 1900. The progressive industrialization of Germany, Belgium, France, and the United States reduced the dependence of Europe and America on the output of British factories. In some cases British bankers themselves loaned the capital which erected industrial plants in other countries. Capital, when free to circulate where it will, seeks the more profitable fields of investment, and the British found it immediately rewarding to subsidize the construction of docks, railways, bridges, shipyards, arsenals, and factories in the Americas, in Russia, in India, and even in Europe. Mines, public utilities, plantations, and finally competitive industries were developed in all the continents on the credit supplied in part from London. At first thought it may appear surprising that the British government did not restrict this extension of aid to alien enterprises which were certain to compete with and curtail the relative advantages which England had accumulated. But the British believed that free trade and a laissez-faire economy were best and that the government should interfere as little as possible in economic activities. They held that "competition is the life of trade" and that "enlightened self-interest" would stimulate each worker and inventor and banker to promote the welfare of society while pursuing his own legitimate advantage. Even after competition grew sharp and threatening, so that German shoes or German cutlery, produced behind the protection of a German tariff wall, invaded the

British home market itself, the British nation persisted in maintaining
a free economy and affirmed until after World War I its disapproval
of protective tariffs.

2. THE LIBERAL STATE

The exceptional prosperity and influence which the British people enjoyed in the nineteenth century gilded their institutions with prestige
and won for their methods of business and administration a world-wide
respect. Responsible parliamentary government and a laissez-faire policy in economic affairs seemed to many observers the clue to British
success, but such an explanation was too limited and too simple: it
would have been almost as just to attribute British laissez-faire ideals
and democratic methods to the acquisition of an empire and the growing economic prosperity. A combination of circumstances, changing
with each century and each decade, had favored the rise of British
power so that by 1840 one-third of the world's international trade was
in British hands. There was, however, no unassailable virtue in British
institutions which could preserve this ascendency against all change.
After 1840, although the total volume of British trade continued to
increase, the total volume of all international trade increased faster.
This meant that the British share declined in relation to the whole, falling to 25 per cent in 1860, to 23 per cent in 1880, to 21 per cent in
1900, and to 17 per cent in 1913.

This relative reduction in British commercial leadership was important, for without the advantages and resources of a paramount economic position Great Britain could not long maintain the naval preponderance or discharge the multifold services which preserved the
empire. It is true that, as world trade increased, a part of this increase
fell to the British self-governing Dominions, so that by 1913 Canada,
Australia, New Zealand, and South Africa together enjoyed a share of
international trade almost one-half as great as that of the United Kingdom. But the Dominions enjoyed fiscal autonomy; they might raise
tariffs against British goods to protect their own developing industries
and might sell their products in foreign markets rather than to British
consumers if this course proved more profitable. Thus Britain's colonies became in a sense competitors. But the most serious rivals which
Great Britain faced in the struggle for international trade were the
United States, which had won a 15 per cent share of world trade by
1913, and the German Empire with 12 per cent. The British people
came to realize that the continued decline of their trade rating was a

serious matter. Business crises, unemployment, shut down mines, closed factories, and idle shipyards foretold increasing difficulties to come, especially as naval and social service costs compelled a steady increase in taxes.

This economic dilemma foreshadowed a condition soon to confront industrial Europe as a whole. The nineteenth century had been an era of business expansion, with new fields of opportunity, new markets for exploitation, new treasures of gold, rare minerals, gems, dyes, plants, woods, rubber, oil, sought out and poured into the world's trade channels year after year. The continents were ransacked for their wealth, often carelessly and wastefully; and backward peoples, uncomprehending and helpless, were persuaded to labor for the white man and to permit the exploitation of their lands, without the power to offer effective resistance. The benefits that came to them through the intrusion of the Europeans were in some cases dubious and in some undesired, but the general result, after pacification, was to bring primitive peoples better government, the white man's medicine, and greater security of life. These improvements, however, were secondary results and not primary motives for the imperialistic conquests. The primary impulse was the quest for profit.

Stimulated by an expanding economy, the leading European nations turned, as Britain had done, to the profits of industry. Germans, French, Belgians, Italians drew upon the supplies of cheap food and raw materials which had become available. The richest commercial fields were exploited first; then, as national appetites grew sharper, vacant areas in every continent were prospected by the agents of one great power or another. Inevitably, the profits of imperialism, so eagerly pursued, brought the leading nations into conflict, and native peoples, growing more alert and better acquainted with European ways, became less submissive. The epidemic of colonial wars at the close of the nineteenth century, already mentioned in our first chapter, were a warning that the world had shrunk rapidly in a few decades. After 1900 it became clear that all further expansion of existing empires or spheres of influence would mean mutual encroachment, rivalry among the powers, and increasing risk of armed conflict.

Newly industrialized nations, like Germany and Japan, which lacked large colonial empires to exploit, were almost certain to challenge the British claim to rule vast areas like Canada, Australia, South Africa, and India, especially as much of this territory was very sparsely settled but rich in resources and crops. British expansion had been achieved, as already noted, with relatively little warfare, and the British Empire was defended by forces remarkably limited and widely dispersed. The British people were not a military nation, had never introduced conscription, and maintained a volunteer army of 100,000 to 200,000 men, the army of a second-rate power. It was not military or even naval prowess which had built up this "Empire on the Seven Seas" but a series of rare opportunities, much expert but unadvertised statesmanship, and broad, humane policies, conceived in a manner at once patient, prudent, and farsighted. At home the same statesmanship had promoted in the United Kingdom a period of increasing material comfort, of broadened liberties, and of remarkable national and social homogeneity. Resolute in defense of their rights, divided in opinion on many points, and highly individualistic, Englishmen nevertheless retained a remarkable talent for cohesive action when a real emergency arose. When vital issues were involved, all lesser disputes were hushed by a spontaneous and unanimous accord as the nation reverted to a monolithic unity, compactness, and strength.

This solidarity of the Anglo-Saxon peoples in the face of danger, joined to a genius for political administration unmatched since Roman times, more nearly explains the greatness of the British than any logical analysis of their national institutions. If a single virtue is to be noted as most significant in their character, it is moderation. They are often greatest for what they forbear to do. Intellectually they recoil before extremes, refusing assent to dogmatic formulas and doctrinaire decisions. The English author and statesman, John Morley, summed up this attitude of mind when he declared, "Perhaps there is no more fatal combination in politics than the deductive method worked by passion." A similar distrust of doctrinaire solutions was voiced by Winston Churchill when he declared, "Sir, we must beware of needless innovation, especially when guided by logic."

Their unwillingness to predict events far in advance and their hesitation to commit themselves to definitive programs or formulas, has earned for the British their well-worn reputation for "muddling through." In war, it has been said, they lose every battle except the last one. But although their tactics, which often appear haphazard, are empirical and pragmatic, the general lines of their policy remain surprisingly strong and consistent. They possess no formal constitution and have no legal check (save the force of precedent and tradition) on the power of the parliament. Their imperial administration is bewildering in its variety and flexibility; they devise solutions, seemingly at random, for a multitude of recurrent problems. But behind a façade of apparent ineptitude and sometimes of salutary neglect, rules and limits do exist, limits imposed by custom and character, which save the British from extreme measures and regrettable excesses.

This British attitude fitted and reflected the conditions of a generous age, a century in which war and fanaticism declined to a remarkably low level. It is important to recognize that British liberalism, like the contemporary liberalism in other countries, was the mood of an era rather than a product of any political formula, program, or set of laws. It represented the fine flowering of individual liberty in an age of economic prosperity, of relative social security, political stability, and religious toleration. Such golden centuries have not been numerous in the annals of mankind.

3. THE "PAX BRITANNICA"

Historians of the future may come to speak of the hundred years which preceded World War I as the century of the *Pax Britannica*. The prestige of liberal government, the theory of free trade, the international gold standard for currency, and the balance of power in Europe were all dependent, in varying degree, upon the maintenance of British sea power and the use which the British made of it.

It is not easy to demonstrate the decisive influence of British naval supremacy because the effect of British policy was so often negative. Only when alternative possibilities are considered, programs which British sea power nullified, does the major fact of nineteenth century history proclaim itself, the fact that it was a century of Anglo-Saxon triumph. If this now seems a preordained development, it did not always appear so. Had Britain failed to recover from the losses of the American War of Independence, had Nelson failed at Trafalgar, had a French invasion or the economic blockade brought England to ruin, world history would have run in very different courses. Without British naval power the French might have kept Louisiana and colonized the Middle West; the Spanish expedition of 1820 might have recovered Mexico; the Monroe Doctrine would scarcely have safeguarded the New World, and European powers might have held most of it, secured the Panama Canal, and divided the Pacific Coast with the Russians. Instead, the peoples of North, Central, and South America were granted a century of development free from serious interference or alien conquest, a fact of first importance for their subsequent history. The political coloring of this New World as well as that of Australia and New Zealand and much of Africa was determined by the pressure of sea power.

No nation in the nineteenth century could hold colonies overseas or dispatch an expedition across the ocean, without in some degree giving hostages to Britain. It has been noted already in earlier chapters that the secondary European states, Portugal, Holland, Belgium, and Denmark, retained their colonial realms with British acquiescence and could not well have defended them against British attack or blockade. Two great land empires were colonized and consolidated in the nineteenth century, one by the Russians, who pushed their settlements northwards to the shores of the Arctic Ocean and eastwards to the Sea of Japan, the second by the United States, which expanded westwards to the Pacific Ocean. These great colonizing movements were an infiltration of empty or thinly populated contiguous territory; they involved no crossing of salt water. The most extensive overseas empire built up in the nineteenth century (aside from British expansion) was the empire which the French conquered in Africa and southeast Asia. This French expansion excited a considerable degree of tension between France and Britain and brought a clash of aims in 1898 (the Fashoda affair) which might have precipitated a war had France been prepared to fight. But such a struggle would have exposed the French overseas protectorates to British attack. Had the Third Republic risked the dispatch of an expeditionary force to defend the territories in West Africa, Madagascar, and Indo-China, where the tricolor had been raised, such a diversion would have weakened the defenses on the Rhine, to the immediate advantage of Germany. This realization cooled the rancors in Paris and the French government withdrew the exploratory force which had offended the British by penetrating the Upper Nile Valley. It is probable that at London, also, the truth that Anglo-French hostility played directly into German hands received due consideration. Looking ahead a decade, British statesmen could already perceive in 1898 that Germany and not France constituted the most serious threat to their imperial power. The overseas empire of the French, like the areas in Africa acquired by the Italians and Germans, might constitute a threat to contiguous British protectorates, but the German high seas fleet at Cuxhaven or Jade Bay constituted a threat to Britain itself.

There were other reasons why French imperialism, although it menaced British colonial expansion in 1898, was likely to prove a diminishing threat. The proclamation of a protectorate and the occupation of territory does not in itself establish an enduring colony. Possession must be reinforced by economic development, by settlement, by capital investments, by a mercantile marine, and above all by adequate naval forces. France at the opening of the twentieth century had a stationary population; all major military reserves were tied down in Europe; the French share of world trade was in relative decline, having fallen from 11 per cent in 1880 to 8 per cent in 1900. In obvious contrast, the German share of international trade had risen from 9 to 12 per cent of the total in the same twenty-year period. The German naval program called for a fleet which outmatched that of France and might come to equal that of Britain. Furthermore, the Germans had also acquired protectorates in Africa, islands in the Pacific, and treaty ports in China, while German manufactures, chemicals, and capital were invading markets which the British had long dominated. These prophetic trends undoubtedly influenced British policy and helped to shape the decisions which brought Britain from a state of diplomatic isolation in 1898 to an entente with France in 1904.

For over three centuries British diplomacy had been dedicated to the maintenance of a balance of power among the nations of Europe. By 1900 the growing German superiority in wealth and armaments persuaded British statesmen that France and Russia might not be able to hold Germany and Austria and Italy in check. The acceleration of German industry, the efficiency of German business methods, the technological progress, and the military and naval program of the Reich threatened the European balance. In population, Germany was already the strongest European state (excluding Russia), and there were Germans outside its frontiers. A British journalist wrote apprehensively in 1906: "Outside the German Empire there are 16,000,000 people of German race in Central Europe, who must gravitate towards Germany. Here are all the elements of a military empire, with 80,000,000 citizens of homogeneous nationality — a stronger empire than Napoleon ever dreamed of." [1]

When, after 1904, Britain united with France, and after 1907 with France and Russia, to form an entente, the action meant that if war came it would be a double war. In Europe, France and Russia would fight Germany and Austria-Hungary. On other continents and on all the oceans British forces would attack German colonies, seize German ships, bases, business assets, and commercial markets. Thus it was the

[1] *Daily Mail* (London), September 16, 1906. In R. J. S. Hoffman, *Great Britain and the German Trade Rivalry, 1875–1914* (Philadelphia: University of Pennsylvania Press, 1933), p. 294.

entry of Great Britain into the alliance against Germany which determined that the war which broke out in 1914 would become a global
war. Without British participation it could have been dismissed more
properly as one more European struggle, for without British involvement it is probable the United States would have remained neutral also.

Between 1914 and 1918 the Germans were to learn, as the French
had learned under Napoleon, that to bid for empire in Europe meant
to forfeit possessions overseas if British sea power remained in command of the oceans. For despite the relative economic decline of British
power, the British navy remained the greatest single influence shaping
world history. By the close of World War I, however, Britain no
longer enjoyed the exceptional supremacy which had made the nineteenth century the century of the *Pax Britannica*. The United States
had developed the wealth, the resources, and the incentive to compete
for naval leadership. This was a momentous fact not only for Britain
but for all the British dominions and colonies and for the remaining
nations of the world. The twentieth century, unlike the nineteenth,
was not to be distinguished by the ascendency of one predominant
naval power. Rather it appeared to promise new patterns of alliance and
conflict, with shifting balance, insecurity, economic confusion, and exhausting wars. An equivalent of the *Pax Britannica* seemed likely to
survive only if the British and United States navies jointly assumed the
task of policing the seas of the world.

4. THE POLICIES THAT PROVOKED A WAR

The history of Europe from 1900 to 1914 was stamped with indelible
irony. For the nations of Europe desired peace, yet they pursued policies which in the end made peace impossible. They perfected machines
with a productive capacity that could raise the standards of living
throughout the world and then used the machines to wage destructive
war. They ignored the international tension caused by their conflicting
policies, and when those policies precipitated an armed conflict they
were taken by surprise and insisted the conflict must be the result of
a secret conspiracy. It is easy to find fault with people who were guilty
of such muddled thinking and mistaken planning, but such belated
criticism is not very profitable. What the historian must seek to do is to
reconstruct the chain of events that resulted in tragedy, and so discover why good intentions produced evil consequences.

Some of the forces which swept Europe into the First World War
have already been noted in describing the problems of the individual

nations. It may be helpful, however, to recapitulate the most important milestones on the road to war, to set them in order and number them and take their bearing. The policies that provoked war, policies never fully grasped in all their multiple effects by those who endorsed them, fall conveniently into four groups: political, economic, military, and diplomatic. The chains of events in each of these fields have cross links — history is an infinitely complex web — but even when the political or the economic or the military events are listed in separate sequence, they suggest how Europe moved towards a general war as if driven by a fatal impulsion which few men read aright.

The basic political development which prepared the stage for a war between the national states was the consolidation of the national state itself. The European states system was in constant evolution from the close of the Middle Ages, but the most recent, most dynamic phase of that development came after the French Revolution. A spirit of intense national patriotism which had the vitality of a secular religion, the conscription of the entire available manpower of the state for military purposes, and the assumption that a national government was a supreme sovereign power which need bow before no superior — these aspects of nationalism did not find full expression until the nineteenth century. As manifested in the ardent campaigns for Italian and German unification, nationalism was considered a noble sentiment, and the sovereign territorial state was accepted as the normal indivisible political unit. Yet a continent crowded with such states spelled anarchy. Thoughtful men pointed out that the claims to unlimited sovereignty asserted by each national government were incompatible with the hopes voiced for continued peace and order among the nations. Individual members of society had learned long since that, if they would live together in harmony, they must forswear their more aggressive impulses and accept and follow common rules of equity in dealing with one another. The national states, which refused to limit their sovereignty and freedom of action, could not fail to come into collision sooner or later, for they did not exist in a vacuum.

With quickened communications shrinking the planet, with commerce growing and populations multiplying, the need for a body of international law to govern the actions of governments towards one another became more urgent each year. Yet the governments steadfastly declined to yield or abate their sovereignty. Each remained the supreme judge of its defense needs, its tariffs and trade and measures of public welfare. Twice between 1899 and 1907 an attempt was made to organize an international body that might serve as a court or government with jurisdiction over international disputes. Delegates from twenty-one states assembled at The Hague in 1899 to discuss the best methods for preserving peace, and their labors resulted in the establishment of a Permanent Court of International Arbitration usually referred to as the Hague Tribunal. This court proved its competence by arbitrating several acrid disputes, notably a controversy between France and Germany over French administration in Morocco (1909) and a conflict between Great Britain and the United States over the Newfoundland fisheries the same year. But even the nations most active in supporting the Hague Tribunal reserved the right to deal with other governments directly and ignore the court if it suited their interests. A second Hague Conference, summoned in 1907, achieved less than the first. The crucial issue had clearly become the steady increase in armaments, which had risen in ten years from $1,000,000,000 to nearly $2,000,000,000 annually, and placed the peace of the world "at the mercy of an accident." But no reduction of military or naval forces could be agreed upon, and the vital question of arms reduction, which had been postponed from 1899 to 1907, was postponed again to a third conference scheduled tentatively for 1915. The conference was never held, for in 1915 the nations were at war.

In the economic field a similar fatality nullified the efforts of the statesmen to reduce the jealousy and tension that estranged the nations, but instead of easing, the tariff contests grew more ruthless. With each decade the economic causes of conflict claimed more attention. The mid-nineteenth century had been the great era of free trade, when world commerce was conceived as a sort of international irrigation system in which the waters, it was hoped, would flow most naturally where they were most needed. But the impulse towards economic nationalism proved too strong. By 1900 only a few nations (Great Britain, the Netherlands, Denmark) adhered to free trade principles; the rest had adopted varying methods of protection and subsidy and had erected and heightened the tariff walls around their own markets. Tariff walls were like dams or gates in the irrigation system of international trade, and like canal gates they could hold back the streams of commerce or divert them into alternate channels. The temptation to impose tariffs was very strong, for import duties offered a government three great advantages. (1) It could "protect" the home market for local manufacturers and farmers by excluding some or all of the foreign steel or wheat or other shipments that might be imported. This pleased local producers and encouraged "national self-sufficiency." (2) The duty paid on shipments, imported despite the tariff, raised government revenues and so saved legislators from imposing more unpopular direct taxes. (3) The loss of markets suffered by foreign traders when they found their goods excluded by a tariff wall might induce them to bargain, and their governments, by reciprocal agreements, could lower their duties in return for similar favors. The higher a nation's tariff, the more generous could it afford to be in its rebates or reductions; whereas a free trade nation, with no tariff to reduce for an equivalent favor, was on an unequal footing and had to offer some other form of concession to secure preferential treatment for its trade.

Tariffs and quotas restricted the flow of trade. Frequently they raised prices artificially in a "protected" country, and sometimes they kept alive uneconomic industries which could operate only when they were protected or subsidized. The ultimate victim was the consumer who paid higher prices, but the general public had little understanding of international economics, whereas the producers, with an interest in "protecting" the national market, could organize pressure groups and help to shape national tariff policy. From about 1880 the spirit of the new imperialism could be detected at work not only in the scramble for markets and territory in Africa or Asia but in the steady rise of tariff walls in Europe and America and in the intensification of tariff wars. Austria, Germany, Russia, France, Italy, Belgium, Spain, and the United States all lifted the tariff rates they had established, and lifted them not once but several times between 1880 and 1914. The average import duties in Europe before World War I ranged from 8 per cent for France to 38 per cent for Russia. Retaliatory tariffs had become an accepted weapon in diplomatic duels, and most nations with colonial empires — France, Italy, and Portugal in particular — were fencing in their overseas possessions in order to secure a major share of their colonial commerce for themselves. Britain, however, still maintained its free trade practices, even when some of the self-governing Dominions imposed duties on British goods.

This tense competition for trade made every open area a field of fierce competition in which leading powers sought to secure a "sphere of influence" and then convert it into a protectorate. Imperialism was economic rather than political in inspiration, trade hunger rather than land hunger, and still more definitely profit hunger. For competition at home had reduced the return that European capitalists could expect on their investments, and they were looking abroad where fantastic profits could often be made in a few years. Inevitably, in the scramble for concessions and the race for profits, British, French, or German merchants, prospectors, and soldiers of fortune, came into conflict and then sought to secure the backing of their governments to support their claims. This contest for the trade or mineral rights or raw products of Morocco or China explains why such countries were centers of diplomatic tension for years. The world was growing too narrow for the great imperial powers, and as each disputed area fell to one claimant or another, the struggle for those remaining grew more grim. Anglo-French rivalry in the Egyptian Sudan almost excited a war in 1898; Franco-German rivalry in Morocco produced three crises between 1905 and 1912; Russo-Japanese rivalry in Manchuria brought on a conflict there in 1904–1905; and Italian demands for Libya were vindicated in the Italo-Turkish War of 1911–1912.

Proof that the political and economic strains which were growing among the nations brought war nearer with each crisis could be read from the armament figures. In every European country the national budgets told the same ominous tale: military and naval expenses doubled between 1880 and 1900, then doubled again between 1900 and 1914; national armies grew until the five continental powers, Russia, Germany, Austria-Hungary, France, and Italy, had 3,000,000 men in their standing armies and millions more in reserve. Each year the rehearsals for war became more convincing, the field maneuvers more realistic. Generals and statesmen, appalled by the grim and inexorable machines they had built up, pondered how to reduce the tension, recognizing that an incident might produce an avalanche. The order for general mobilization, like the signal of a fire alarm, could be issued in any capital at any time, and mobilization meant war. Each nation wanted security, but each was seeking that security by striving to match its offensive force against all anticipated adversaries. The folly of such a policy was gravely summarized by the British foreign minister, Sir Edward Grey. "The increase of armaments," he wrote, "that is intended in each nation to produce consciousness of strength, and a sense of security, does not produce these effects. On the contrary, it produces a consciousness of the strength of other nations and a sense of fear." [1]

Most European people in 1914 took little interest in foreign affairs, and the possibility of a general war seemed like a bad dream that lacked

[1] Lord Grey of Fallodon, *Twenty-Five Years, 1892–1916* (New York: Frederick A. Stokes, 1925), Vol. I, p. 91.

probability or substantiality. People thought of wars as they thought of tropical plagues, as evils which they never expected to see at close quarters though they knew they had been common in barbarous times and still occurred in distant, chaotic countries with poetic names. This mood of complacency and innocence was not altogether surprising, for Europe in 1914 had not known a serious war in almost half a century and had suffered no general international conflict since the fall of Napoleon.

But if the people were ignorant of the danger of war, the diplomats knew better. They had built up, treaty by treaty, the tottering system of alliances which made it almost certain any war would be a universal war. They had watched for over forty years as the powers drew apart and ranged themselves, with delays and hesitations but with a ponderous implacability, in two opposing camps. They had observed the formation of a dual alliance between Germany and Austria-Hungary in 1879, the creation of the "League of the Three Emperors" (Germany, Austria-Hungary, and Russia) in 1881, the accord (kept strictly secret in detail) which joined Germany, Austria-Hungary, and Italy in a Triple Alliance in 1882. Then, as Bismarck's diplomacy passed its zenith, they had watched the slow crumbling of his system of alliances and the cautious construction of a countercombination. The League of the Three Emperors lapsed and was not renewed in 1887; and seven years later France, isolated diplomatically since the defeat of 1870, concluded an agreement with Russia, the core of an alliance that was to balance the Triple Alliance. In 1898 the astute Théophile Delcassé took charge of French foreign policy, narrowly averting a clash with Britain over Egypt as his first service to Anglo-French friendship. (See page 54.) But the diplomatic future was still dark and ambiguous when the twentieth century opened. Britain was still standing aloof from all entanglements or alliances, more distrustful of the Franco-Russian combination than alarmed over the German naval program. In 1902 the British cabinet approved an accord with Japan; the new Oriental power which had arisen so swiftly in the Pacific was to act as a check on Russia in the Far East, with the aid of British credit and material.

Germany, already the strongest industrial and military power in Europe by 1900, had commenced to build a fleet which might in time match that of Britain. This challenge decided the course of British foreign policy: in 1904 Britain and France concluded an entente cordiale, and by 1906 the military staffs of the two powers were discussing what military force Britain could land in France and Belgium to help oppose a possible German attack. The sharp defeat suffered by the Russians in their war with Japan (1904–1905) encouraged the Germans, dismayed the French, and dissipated British apprehensions about Russian strength. The Germans seized the hour of Russian weakness to demand concessions in Morocco from France (1905) and three years later Austria annexed Bosnia and Herzegovina (1908). A stronger entente was needed to hold the Triple Alliance in check, and Britain, France, and Russia concluded a tripartite agreement (1907) which completed the division of the powers into two camps. (See page 55.) Germany, Austria-Hungary, and Italy faced France, Russia, and England in a succession of tests — further crises over Morocco, Crete, Turkey, the Balkan states. Britain concentrated the strongest part of her fleet in the North Sea, facing Germany; Russia made supreme efforts to recover, and expanded her military and naval program with the aid of French loans. All policies seemed to work together towards catastrophe, and the diplomats had no better hope than to slip through each crisis, improvising one solution after another as the days flitted by and the hour approached when no solution could be improvised. The incident that could shatter the armed truce might occur on any envenomed frontier; and the most envenomed area, with the most unruly inhabitants in Europe, lay in the Balkans. At Sarajevo, Bosnia, on June 28, 1914, the Austrian Archduke Francis Ferdinand was assassinated by a Bosnian patriot. The crisis for which no solution could be found had arrived.

PART II

World War I: 1914–1918

THE WAR ON LAND

1914–1918

Modern wars in the life of nations are the same things as examinations in civil life, namely proofs of fitness . . . All politics is economic politics, or war preparedness.

WALTER RATHENAU [1]

1. THE DIPLOMATIC CRISIS OF JULY, 1914

IN June, 1914, the Archduke Francis Ferdinand, nephew and heir apparent to the Emperor Francis Joseph of Austria, visited the provinces of Bosnia and Herzegovina which had been formally annexed to Austria-Hungary six years earlier. (See page 85.) Although many Bosnian subjects were known to be hostile to Austrian rule, no special police precautions were taken to protect the archduke. As he was driving through the streets of Sarajevo, a Bosnian youth, Gavrilo Princip, leaped at the carriage and shot him fatally with a revolver. Had the assassination been the act of a single, self-inspired fanatic, the incident might not have led to an international crisis. But Princip had not acted alone.

Weeks earlier, when the archduke's intended visit to Bosnia became known, the chief of the military intelligence department in the neighboring state of Serbia had learned that Bosnians were planning to kill the distinguished visitor. This official, Colonel Dragutin Dimitri-yevitch, was a leader in a secret Serbian society, the Black Hand, and he and other agents encouraged the plot, provided weapons, and helped Princip and his accomplices to return to Bosnia. Subsequent revelations indicated that several other high officials of the Serbian government, including the prime minister, Nikola Pashitch, also knew something of the plot and failed to halt it, but at the time they dis-

[1] Quoted in Albert T. Lauterbach, *Economics in Uniform* (Princeton, N. J.: Princeton University Press, 1943), p. 64.

avowed all such charges. The Austrian police, who seized Princip and his accomplices after the shooting, learned within a few hours that the youths had received Serbian aid, but the government at Vienna waited three weeks for corroboration before taking action.

Then, on July 23, 1914, Austria-Hungary dispatched to Serbia a note so exigent that it was immediately styled an ultimatum. The Austrian foreign minister, Leopold von Berchtold, had decided upon a stern reckoning with the Serbs; and the minister of war, Conrad von Hötzendorf, was urging immediate mobilization against them. In Berlin Kaiser William II agreed that the Serbs deserved a lesson and he sent assurances of German support. But neither Austrian nor German statesmen anticipated a general war; they thought that if Serbia resisted and Austria had to intervene with armed force, the conflict would be "localized."

The Serbs promptly sought counsel in Paris and St. Petersburg, a recognition that the delicate balance between the Triple Alliance and the Triple Entente was threatened. They were advised that it would be well to behave with circumspection, and they replied to the Austrian note in conciliatory terms within the twenty-four hours von Berchtold had stipulated. They promised to suppress anti-Austrian agitation in journals and schools and to punish Serbian officials convicted of aiding plots against Austrian peace and security. But they explained that to admit Austrian police into Serbia to assist in running down the suspects would violate the Serbian constitution and Serbian sovereignty, and they suggested that this point be settled by other judges. The moderate tone of the Serbians' reply was marred by their simultaneous mobilization for war and an appeal to Russia for aid. The Serb leaders were aware that the president of the French Republic, Raymond Poincaré, and his foreign minister, René Viviani, had visited St. Petersburg from July 20 to July 23 to strengthen the Franco-Russian Alliance. Poincaré was strongly anti-German, though not so outspoken as the Russian foreign minister, Sergei Sazonov, whose hostility towards Austria and Germany was notorious. Von Berchtold was apprehensive that France and Russia might be preparing to stand firm, but this possibility did not persuade him to use greater caution with Serbia. He declared the Serbian response to his note of July 23 to be evasive and unsatisfactory, and on July 28 Austria declared war on the Kingdom of the Serbs.

The rapidity with which the great powers moved towards war seems to prove that the crisis had been of less sudden growth than many observers believed. The Russians commenced to mobilize very quietly as early as July 24 although the full decree was not issued officially until July 30. The British fleet was on summer maneuvers in the North Sea, conveniently ready for action. French mobilization plans moved in concert with those of Russia and ahead of the German preparations. At Berlin the German leaders urged Austria to use greater moderation, but they refused to approve successive British appeals from Sir Edward Grey that the great powers, especially those not directly involved, press a peaceful solution on Austria and Russia. Germany had only one certain ally remaining, the Austro-Hungarian Empire, and dared not desert that ally under threats. On July 29 William II telegraphed an appeal to Nicholas II to halt Russian mobilization. Nicholas postponed the final order until his generals overcame his resistance the following day; then he telegraphed William of his act. After a futile demand, July 31, that Russia demobilize, Germany declared war on August 1. Two days later Germany declared war against France. But these formal gestures were confirmations, not decisions. The decision for war had been taken when the orders for mobilization went out.

Thus an Austrian ultimatum to Serbia brought Russian mobilization against Austria. Honoring the existing treaties which united their policies, Germany supported Austria, and France stood by Russia. Italy held aloof and deserted the Triple Alliance, and Great Britain hesitated to announce her course. The Triple Entente was not a treaty of military alliance. As the crisis grew more threatening and war became more certain, the British cabinet split and the more pacifistic ministers resigned. But the hesitation of the people and the government was resolved after August 3. News that the Germans had demanded free passage for their troops through Belgium and that the Belgian government had refused, made British intervention almost inevitable. Reminding the Germans that the great powers were all pledged to respect Belgian neutrality, the British demanded that the German ultimatum to Belgium be withdrawn at once. When no answer came from Berlin, London announced that a state of war existed between Britain and Germany commencing at midnight, August 4, 1914.

2. THE STRATEGY OF SIEGE

The Germans planned to fight and to win in a swift war; a long struggle was almost certain to turn against them. This fact helps to explain

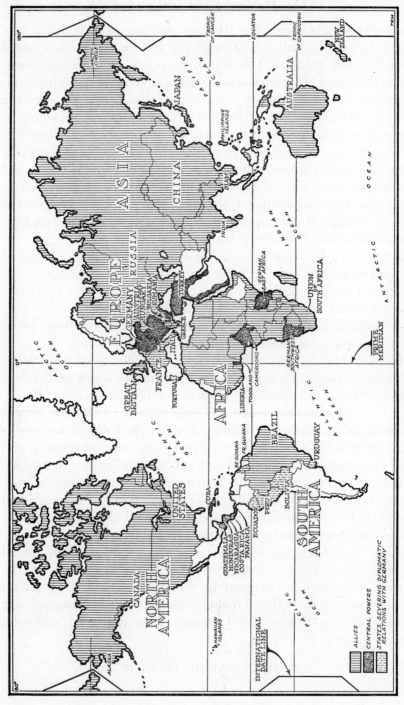

THE CENTRAL POWERS IN WORLD WAR I

ALLIES
CENTRAL POWERS
STATES SEVERING DIPLOMATIC RELATIONS WITH GERMANY

their haste and their ruthlessness. Once the German leaders were convinced that war was certain they forced the issue, hurling ultimatums, opening their drive to the west, invading Belgium and Luxembourg, and pressing into France. That Russia might go to war while France remained neutral was a possibility they dared not count upon. For twenty years they had been preparing for a two-front war, and they would not have dared to send their major forces across the Vistula before they had crushed the enemy across the Rhine. The German general staff knew how steadily entente diplomats had built a circle of enemies around the Central Powers. They assumed that Russia and France would attack together. They prepared their plan of operations on this prefiguration of events, and events then took the expected course because for years it had been the expected course. When in August, 1914, the diplomats lost control of affairs because their deceptions and secret diplomacy had bred distrust and fear in place of understanding and co-operation, they abdicated their responsibilities and the generals took control. But unfortunately the generals, who thus became responsible for the destiny of the European peoples in the hour of crisis, were the prisoners of their own plans.

For the Central Powers the outbreak of war meant that their diplomatic encirclement was transformed into a far more serious military encirclement. Their barricaded frontiers became a menacing ring of battle fronts. In the east they faced Russian armies which stretched from the Baltic Sea to the Rumanian border; in the west the combined French, Belgian, and British forces were soon stretched in unbroken battle line from the North Sea coast to Switzerland; in the south Serbia held off the Austrian attacks valiantly. A glance at the map on the opposite page will show that the encirclement was not complete: there were several breaks in the iron ring. Denmark, the Netherlands, Switzerland, Italy, and Rumania were all neutral in the first stages of the conflict, and the first three remained neutral through the four years of war. To blockade and besiege the Central Powers effectively, it was essential to check the entry and egress of goods, especially war material, through these neutral gates. One certain method of closing the gates was to bring the neutral nations into the war on the entente side. A second was to drive them into the war on the German side and blockade them also. A third was to regulate their trade so strictly that they would have little or no surplus to re-export to the embattled Reich. Thus commercial and military considerations balanced one another. So long as even a small trade with other continents was possible through Dutch and Danish channels, the Germans were prepared to respect the neutrality of the Netherlands and Denmark. Occupation of either country would not have helped break the siege so long as Britain controlled the sea. It was to the southeast, therefore, that the armies of the Central Powers sought and found weak points in the ring that had been forged around them. Their aim was to secure an outlet to further sources of supply while they prepared to knock out their major opponents one at a time.

Such a brief analysis of the "strategy of siege" as it operated in World War I oversimplifies the picture. But it is helpful to stress these elementary principles and to spend some time over a relief map of Europe before taking up the campaigns. A map makes clear almost at once the siege status of the Central Powers and suggests why the position of the peripheral neutrals would be difficult to maintain. Italy, which abandoned the Triple Alliance when war broke out, and affirmed its neutral status, was offered tempting terms from both sides. After months of hesitation the government decided to join the Allied Powers and declared war on Austria in May, 1915. In 1916 Rumania was likewise persuaded to join the Allies, and the battle line in the east was thus extended to the Black Sea. The Central Powers found neutrals which could be induced to join their side. Turkey entered the war in alliance with Austria and Germany in November, 1914, and Bulgaria in October, 1915. This Balkan breach in the iron ring offered a double advantage to the Central Powers. It opened a new gate through which they could obtain wheat, oil, fruit, coffee, tobacco, and other needed commodities, and it closed the route through the Dardanelles to Allied ships. As this was the shortest sea way by which the French and British might have supplied guns, ammunition, and other forms of war material to the Russian armies, the closing of the route was a serious reverse. It crippled Russia and dislocated the plans for a joint offensive from east and west.

In the perspective of history, World War I takes on the outlines of a gigantic siege operation that lasted over four years. One hundred million people dwelling in central Europe resisted the attacks of armies stretched in a vast arc from Belgium to Greece and from the Black Sea to the Baltic. Blockade, attrition, depletion of war materials, of food supplies, of man power, finally broke the spirit and resources of the encircled peoples. After the first two years of conflict the Germans and Austrians found no further allies, whereas their enemies grew in number until thirty-two associated nations were opposed to four. Viewed thus after the event it appears remarkable that the Central Powers held out for four years against such increasing odds. The most remarkable thing, however, is that before losing the war in the fourth year they came remarkably close to winning it on several occasions.

The strategy of the German high command had been decided upon before 1914 and its principles varied little from the plans. Battles are won by achieving a relative superiority of force at the point of attack. As the Germans could concentrate their armies more quickly at any point of the vast perimeter of conflict, they hoped to crush one opponent at a time while holding the others at bay; to strike a blow on the French or Russian front so shattering that the nation thus mangled would sue for a separate peace. This strategy was dictated by the logic of the German position and the factors of modern warfare. The Germans realized that in a prolonged conflict time would work against them because their reserves would ultimately be used up while those of their foes increased. In the years of fighting, Germany, Austria-Hungary, Bulgaria, and Turkey called up 22,850,000 men for military service. In the same period the Allied and Associated Powers marshaled almost twice as many, a total estimated at 42,188,810. The inequality between the two groups of combatants in wealth, food, and industrial resources (especially after the United States entered the war) was even more disproportionate. Coalitions are notoriously inept at coordinating their policies, but it was easy to foresee that, if the Allies held together, reinforced one another, and organized their superior resources effectively, the ultimate defeat of the Central Powers was almost inevitable. The Allies had the world and its supplies to draw upon.

From first to last the campaigns waged by the Germans and Austrians took the form of terrific lunges, first at one point in the encircling battle line and then at another. If sufficient pressure were applied the line could be pushed forward, but it was always stabilized again when the drive had exhausted itself or the enemy applied equal counterpressure. Thus the areas won or lost, when noted on a map, seldom appeared impressive, especially when the territory was measured against the casualties. World War I was predominantly a war of position, a war of costly nibbling and hacking at elaborately fortified entrenchments, and in this respect, also, it resembled a gigantic siege operation.

In planning their drives the Germans possessed two major advantages. First, they held the inside lines, which meant that they could concentrate their strongest forces at the point of attack, using the admirable internal system of German strategic railroads. As their armies advanced into enemy territory, however, this initial advantage diminished, and the difficulty of bringing up fresh troops and supplies became increasingly arduous. This fact partly explains the reduced momentum of Austro-German drives after the first successful stages, and the resulting halt just short of a decisive objective in many cases. The second major advantage which the Germans enjoyed was unity of command. The German general staff, almost entirely independent of civilian control, assumed full direction of the war not only on the German front but in all sectors. In contrast, the Allied armies were widely separated and could not easily concert their movements or reinforce one another. The Russian, British, French, Belgian, and Italian armies were all under independent commands, and the generals directing them were frequently hampered in their actions by the politicians at the head of the several governments and by the criticism permitted in the parliament and the press of the democratic states. These circumstances made it possible for the Germans to hope almost to the last that rivalry and jealousy among the Allied leaders might disrupt their alliance and paralyze their attacks. The hope faded in the final months of the war because unity of command on the vital western front was finally achieved in the spring of 1918. All the Allied forces, French, British, Belgian, and American, were placed under the supreme direction of the French generalissimo, Ferdinand Foch.

These larger issues which dominated World War I must be kept in mind, for they provide the motivation for the campaigns and the explanation of their outcome. In following the course of any war three major factors provide the clue to the strategy, for they pose three problems no commander can ignore in making his calculations. These are the problem of co-ordination and command, the problem of supplies, and the problem of transportation.

3. FROM THE INVASION OF BELGIUM TO THE FALL OF RUMANIA (AUGUST, 1914–DECEMBER, 1916)

The German preparations for an offensive war had been drafted as early as 1893 and were constantly modified until they took form in 1905 as the Schlieffen Plan. Count Alfred von Schlieffen, German chief of staff from 1891 to 1906, was convinced that strategy should aim at the total destruction of the opposing army. He liked to dwell on Hannibal's destruction of a Roman army at Cannae in 216 B.C. as the model battle, or upon Napoleon's victory at Austerlitz in 1805. It seems to

THE WESTERN FRONT, 1914–1918

have escaped the notice of Schlieffen and his followers that although these great commanders won model battles they ultimately lost their wars. Schlieffen's successor, Count Helmuth von Moltke, retained the plan for an offensive war. Assuming that the Russians would require several weeks to mobilize and that Britain, if drawn into the war, could not send more than a few divisions to the Continent, Moltke concentrated nearly 2,000,000 men in the west to strike at France. The French, on their part, had made preparations to invade Lorraine but their offensive never really developed. For after August 3, 1914, German divisions began rolling relentlessly through Belgium, Luxembourg, and northern France, in a vast movement intended to swing five German armies on five concentric arcs, the largest of which would sweep be-

yond Paris before it curved back towards the east. If the plan succeeded the French forces, outflanked and caught like ripe grain inside
the sweep of a scythe, were to be destroyed or captured, and France
eliminated from the war in a few weeks.

The Schlieffen Plan required the German First Army, on the right
wing, to describe the largest arc, and Schlieffen's last instructions had
been to make the right wing strong. But Moltke dispatched his extra
reserves to the Lorraine sector and to the Russian front. By early September the German First Army, after a month of fighting, was still
on schedule and almost within sight of Paris but it was wearied and
weakened. The French, with their Belgian and British allies, had fallen
back without losing contact or morale despite severe pounding, and
they seized the psychological and tactical opportunity for a counterstroke. By September 6 a gap had developed between the German
First and Second Armies. Into this breach the French hurled all their
reserves from Paris, and the German advance was dislocated. After a
week of heavy fighting (first battle of the Marne, September 5–12)
the invaders fell back to the Aisne River where they entrenched themselves. Both adversaries then hurled reserves to right and left in a vain
attempt to outflank the other's lines, and before winter the extended
front had become a fortified system of trenches, barbed wire, and
machine gun nests, stretching from the North Sea near Ostend to the
border of Switzerland. The western front had been "stabilized" and
all the fighting there failed to win a decision in the subsequent four
years of war. The German drive to eliminate France had miscarried.
Despite unprecedented casualties the French fought on, although their
most valuable and productive mining and industrial regions were under
German occupation.

Denied by this narrow margin the decision which they had hoped
for in the west, the Germans sought (and again missed) a definitive
action in the east. Early Russian mobilization, more speedy than had
been anticipated, enabled the czar's forces to break through the screen
of German defenses in East Prussia, and refugees fleeing westward
spread panic among the population of this German province. The situation called for a rapid *riposte*. Under the resolute command of Paul
von Hindenburg and his chief of staff, Erich von Ludendorff, the
Germans transformed the Russian offensive into a debacle at the battle
of Tannenberg (August 25–31). Two-thirds of the invading Russian
divisions were destroyed, and the czar's armies, depleted by the loss of
a million men and an irreplaceable store of guns and munitions, were

thrown onto the defensive. Some Russian victories over the Austrians (who were driven from Galicia and bungled their attempt to invade Serbia) failed to atone for the staggering reverses in the region of the Masurian Lakes. The year 1914 closed with the Central Powers strong and defiant on all fronts.

As concentration was a source of German strength, the Allied governments planned, in 1915, to draw the German armies apart and pin them down in difficult sectors. It was hoped that when the troops of the Central Powers were dispersed their lines would be weakened. This Allied strategy failed to achieve results.

The entry of Turkey into the war in November, 1914, had closed the Dardanelles. To reopen this vital supply route to Russia, Winston Churchill, First Lord of the Admiralty, urged the need for a prompt attack by French and British naval forces in the Mediterranean. Begun hesitantly on February 19, 1915, and delayed by disagreements among various Allied leaders, the assault on the Straits failed and was finally abandoned at the close of 1915. This serious setback shook the prestige of the Allied Powers throughout the Balkans and the Near East.

A Russian spring offensive, which began as planned with the capture of Przemysl on March 22, 1915, met powerful Austro-German counterattacks and recoiled in May. The German commanders, having failed to eliminate France or Russia in the preceding year, now decided to crush the Russian armies in 1915. All through the summer the stubborn Russian divisions were forced back, suffering enormous losses but unbroken in spirit. Man power was their only unlimited asset and they sacrificed it recklessly; but with munitions running low, no adequate factories to replace them, no clear route through which to import arms from Britain, and inadequate transportation in the field, the Russians could not match Germany at industrialized war.

Once again, however, a definitive victory eluded the German generals. The Russian armies fell back but they maintained a fighting front; Russia was temporarily out of action but not out of the war. After occupying part of Lithuania and all of Poland and reaching the Dniester in the south, the Germans halted. Instead of risking a winter campaign on the exposed steppes, they turned upon Serbia. Bulgaria was induced to join them, attacking the Serb armies from the east, while an Austro-German offensive rolled down from the north. In October and November, 1915, the Balkan peninsula was overrun by German, Austrian, and Bulgarian forces, Serbia was crushed, and a direct line of contact established from Berlin to Constantinople. The Allies had failed once again, for although they invaded neutral Greece, the expedition which they had landed at Saloniki on October 5 was too small and too timidly led to aid the Serbs, although it kept Greece more or less unwillingly on the entente side. To critical observers, however, it appeared evident that lack of resolution and lack of adequate forces had crippled the French and British offensives in the Mediterranean during 1915. Even in France and Belgium, where their largest armies were massed, the Allies failed in their attempts to break through the German entrenchments even when the Germans held them with reduced forces.

These military reverses were a heavy blow to the hope of early victory which had misled the Allies at the opening of 1915. The same premature hope that an Allied triumph was near prompted the Italians to declare war on Austria in May, 1915. By the secret Treaty of London (April 26, 1915) they were promised concessions which would make the Adriatic Sea almost an Italian lake, were granted sovereignty over the Dodecanese Islands, and were assured they would receive additional African territory and a share of the Turkish empire if the Allies partitioned it. The financial arrangements included an immediate loan and a portion of the anticipated war indemnity. Although the entry of Italy extended the Austrian battle front from Switzerland to the Adriatic and so welded the ring around the Central Powers more compactly, the Italian armies made little progress against the Austrians and within a year were themselves in need of French and British reinforcements.

If the First World War had been destined to end in victory for the Central Powers, the year 1916 should have brought it. The Russians lacked almost everything essential for a major campaign except valor, and in modern warfare valor is not enough. The Italian and Austrian divisions swayed back and forth on the Isonzo river front, deadlocked in that mountainous terrain. The British did not adopt compulsory military service until January, 1916, and consequently lacked sufficient trained reserves for a mass army. To the German general staff it seemed opportune to revert to their original plan to crush France by a swift, irresistible drive. The French had suffered two years of cruel attrition, holding four-fifths of the western battle line, and the Germans hoped their decimated divisions might collapse under a sufficiently heavy blow.

The first object of the new attack was one of the strongest anchors of the French line, the fortress city of Verdun. At the opening of 1916

General von Falkenhayn pressed men and guns into a few square miles until he achieved a concentration of power which exceeded all precedents. The attacking forces lost heavily for each yard gained, but the French defenders lost more heavily still. Week after week and month after month the unrelenting combat went on, until the French had suffered 350,000 casualties, the Germans 330,000. But the French had sworn "They shall not pass," the key forts of Verdun remained in their hands, and after July 11, 1916, the Germans abandoned their drives and the French retook two miles of ground. By the close of 1916 the lines were much as they had been a year earlier, but neither French nor German military morale quite recovered from this inconclusive mass carnage.

In this same summer of 1916 a second desperate battle was fought out on the Somme. Partly to relieve the pressure on Verdun, partly in the hope of breaking through the German lines and so hastening a decision, 400,000 British and 200,000 French troops were sacrificed in a futile war of attrition, which nowhere penetrated more than seven miles and encountered ever new defenses. With the onset of winter, the deepening mud, shell holes, and quagmires immobilized the attackers, who had depleted their man power, munitions, and morale to a dangerous degree.

One momentary flash lightened the gloom which hung over the Allied nations in that black summer of 1916. On August 27, bribed by extravagant promises and encouraged by the opening of a new Russian offensive, the Rumanian government declared war on Austria. Reprisal was swift and thorough. The Russian drive (the Brusilov Offensive) soon stalled, and the Rumanians, failing to receive support from the Russians or from the Allied expeditionary force at Saloniki, were completely defeated. Their wheat harvest and oil wells passed into the control of the jubilant conquerors. Despite the failure at Verdun the tide of German military success was at the full. The Allies were disheartened. To keep Greece on their side they were driven to bombard and blockade that unhappy country. They had withdrawn from the Dardanelles, lost an army of ten thousand men which invaded Mesopotamia, failed to break the German lines on the Somme, failed to save Rumania, failed to penetrate from Saloniki to the Black Sea and divide Turkey from the Central Powers. This was the moment (December, 1916) chosen by the Germans to propose a peace parley.

Early in 1916 the President of the United States, Woodrow Wilson, had offered to arrange a peace conference whenever British and French statesmen thought the moment opportune. The position of the United States as the most powerful neutral nation made its attitude highly important, and Wilson was in a position to urge a negotiated peace. But the Allied Powers still hoped for a victory and declined to negotiate. When the Germans, on December 12, 1916, proposed peace discussions, they asked Wilson to convey the suggestion to the Allied governments, but they failed to offer any basis for agreement. The Allied statesmen rejected the German overture as "empty and insincere"; and Wilson then followed it with his own proposals (December 18, 1916), suggesting that both sides outline their conception of a reasonable settlement. The Allies demanded the restoration of Belgium, Serbia, and Montenegro, with evacuation of all territory conquered by the Austro-German armies and the release of subject nations under Austro-Hungarian or Turkish rule. At a moment when recent victories had inflated their hopes, the leaders of the Central Powers could not consider such ignominious terms, which only a complete Allied triumph could impose. Peace discussions therefore lapsed and the war continued its destructive course two years longer.

4. THE UNITED STATES ENTERS THE WAR

The outcome of World War I was determined by the fateful decisions taken in 1917, though few people realized their finality at the time. At the opening of 1917 the United States was the only great nation still at peace. The murderous deadlock in Europe had continued for two and a half years without a decision. Russia was on the verge of collapse, France gravely weakened, and Britain enfeebled and frustrated. World War I seemed destined to end in a costly stalemate or a German triumph. This was the moment chosen by the German high command to announce a decision that drew America into the war and reversed the tide of victory. Within two years the impact of American intervention had upset the balance of material power and brought Germany to defeat. It is advisable, therefore, to leave the battle lines of Europe as they stood in January, 1917, and to consider the critical decisions that were taken four thousand miles away in Washington. America, in 1917, was the great unknown factor in the world equation: as soon as American intervention was assured, it became possible to predict the outcome of the war.

Few Europeans or Americans realized that the United States might become a great military power within a year or two; the Germans in particular, with their long military traditions, underrated the fighting spirit and organizing power of the transatlantic democracy. They knew that American factories were already overtaxed to provide guns, shells, and planes for Britain and France, and they did not believe that America could draft, drill, and deliver an army to Europe in time to save the Allied cause from defeat. Led astray by arrogance and miscalculation, the German militarists sealed their doom by their blindness and their bungling diplomacy.

From the opening months of the war, President Woodrow Wilson had directed a sharp correspondence at Berlin in defense of neutral rights. He had also instructed the State Department to protest with vigor against British seizure of neutral cargoes when the British multiplied their lists of contraband and closed the North Sea to neutral shipping. There was a strong mood of isolationism in the United States, especially in the Middle West, as the war progressed, and Wilson's secretary of state, William Jennings Bryan, was frankly pacifistic. Wilson himself strove earnestly to remain impartial, but he found it easier to be patient with British violations of neutral rights than with German violations of the laws of humanity. His most trusted adviser was Colonel Edward M. House, a warm admirer of British foreign secretary Sir Edward Grey. The American ambassador to Britain, Walter Hines Page, was "more British than the British," and American protests were presented at London in a modest and apologetic manner. Wilson had very little respect for professional diplomats in general and conducted many of his most delicate negotiations informally through Colonel House, his "unofficial ambassador."

At the close of 1914 the British declared all food intended for Germany to be contraband of war. The Germans retaliated (February 4, 1915) by declaring the seas around Great Britain a "war zone" which all ships would enter at their peril. The British reply abolished distinctions in contraband and made all shipments presumably destined for enemy countries liable to seizure. This British action was a definite violation of international law concerning blockade and contraband, but it was overshadowed by the more ruthless German acts. On May 1, 1915, an American vessel, the *Gulflight,* was sunk by a submarine without warning. One week later (May 7, 1915) the British ocean liner *Lusitania* was torpedoed off Ireland with a loss of twelve hundred lives, over one hundred being American citizens. The Germans attempted to defend their course on the ground that the *Lusitania* was carrying munitions of war and that British ships often flew American flags to escape attack. The charges were true but American indignation brought the nation so close to a war mood that the German ambassador at Washington, Johann Heinrich von Bernstorff, persuaded his government to heed Wilson's demands. The German government accordingly promised (October, 1915) that submarine commanders would not sink passenger ships without warning unless they resisted or attempted to escape. This course exposed German submarines to much greater risks because armed craft disguised as trading vessels, when halted, could fire upon the U-boat from masked batteries.

The German concessions eased the tension between Washington and Berlin. But Bryan had yielded the State Department to the more aggressive Robert Lansing (June 8, 1915), and it was clear that any further display of German ruthlessness or additional loss of American lives on the seas might bring a break in relations. American attention was distracted in 1916 by the situation in Mexico, when a revolutionary leader, Pancho Villa, invaded New Mexico in March and killed a score of Americans. A punitive force of twelve thousand United States troops entered Mexico to hunt Villa, but pursued him in vain. The incident helped to awaken the American people to a sense of their vulnerability and unpreparedness but they still wanted to avoid intervention in the European struggle. In the election of 1916 Wilson was reelected by a very narrow margin, largely on the slogan, "He kept us out of war." His own sympathy for Britain had been weakened by the British refusal to modify their blockade or accept American mediation to bring peace nearer. At the close of 1916, therefore, Wilson appealed to all the belligerents to indicate their war aims, suggesting that the differences dividing them might not prove as irreconcilable as they appeared. On January 11, 1917, he declared that a compromise settlement would prove the best settlement to the war because only "peace without victory" would endure.

Three months later the United States was at war with Germany. This rapid change had been provoked by a reckless decision of the German high command and hastened by the bungling of German diplomats. On January 31, 1917, Germany announced that unrestricted submarine warfare would commence the following day. The United States immediately severed relations with Germany but the nation was not united on the need for war. Evidence multiplied, however, that German agents were already waging undercover sabotage against American industry. On January 16 the German foreign secretary, Arthur Zimmermann, had proposed secretly that Mexico join Germany and invite Japan to combine for war against the United

States. Mexico was to receive Texas, New Mexico, and Arizona as a reward. When intercepted by the British secret service this Zimmermann Note aroused a storm of indignation in the United States, intensified by the mounting toll of American lives as the submarine campaign grew more desperate. On April 2 Wilson summoned a special session of Congress and called for a declaration of war against the German government. The declaration was passed by a vote of 82 to 6 in the Senate on April 4, and by 373 to 50 in the House of Representatives on April 6.

Field Marshal Paul von Hindenburg, German chief of staff in 1917, later recorded the reasons which led the high command to risk American intervention. "We had a new enemy, economically the most powerful in the world. . . . It was the United States of America, and her advent was perilously near. Would she appear in time to snatch the victor's laurels from our brows? That, and that only, was the decisive question. I believed that I could answer it in the negative." [1] Hindenburg might have pointed out in his own defense that no one, before 1917, had foreseen the decisive impact of the American effort. The French leader, Marshal Joseph Joffre, thought 500,000 men the maximum army the United States would be likely to raise. The largest military detachment which an American officer then in service had commanded before 1917 was twelve thousand men — General John J. Pershing's expeditionary force to Mexico the previous year, which had been made to appear somewhat ridiculous by its failure to capture the elusive Villa. In these circumstances it is not wholly surprising that von Hindenburg, while recognizing American economic resources, failed to allow for the potential military power of the United States.

This rapid mobilization of American might and man power was directed by leaders of exceptional ability. President Wilson had appointed a special Council of National Defense in 1916 (composed of the secretaries of war, navy, interior, commerce, and labor) to study all problems affecting American security. When war was declared much preparatory planning had been done, but the real effort lay ahead. Invoking his war powers, the President created a General Munitions Board, a Railroad War Board, a United Shipping Board, and a Food Administration, to co-ordinate the national economic resources. To provide funds a $4,000,000,000 federal appropriation for defense and a $7,000,000,000 war bond drive were voted, and a Selective Serv-

[1] Thomas G. Frothingham, *The American Reinforcement in the World War* (New York: Doubleday, 1927), p. 10.

ice Act passed by the Congress to raise a national army. The secretary of war, Newton D. Baker, was ably supported by General Tasker H. Bliss as chief of staff; when Bliss left to represent the United States on the Supreme War Council of the Allied and Associated Powers in Europe, he was succeeded by General Peyton C. March. As commander of the American Expeditionary Force the President and his military advisers fixed upon General John J. Pershing, entrusting him with broad powers and supporting him with unwavering confidence. Pershing was responsible for the decisions which made the American Expeditionary Force an independent army from the first, instead of feeding American units as reinforcements into the depleted French and British divisions. The task of conveying the men to Europe was carried through with exceptional speed and security, and the protection furnished by the United States navy proved the competence of the secretary of the navy, Josephus Daniels, and the assistant secretary, Franklin Delano Roosevelt.

In France, General Pershing assumed the titanic task of organizing an expeditionary force which grew to 2,000,000 in a little over a year. Never before had so many men been transported so far or so fast or supplied so lavishly from bases thousands of miles away. The appearance of the fresh, magnificently equipped American troops in the European theater, and the knowledge that another 2,000,000 were in training in America, changed the whole military balance of the war. The miracle of organization which made it possible to transport and maintain such an expeditionary force astonished observers who had imagined it would take many years to make the United States a military nation. But with their characteristic initiative, the leaders applied American business methods and industrial energy to military needs. Under the direction of Colonel Leonard P. Ayers a corps of statisticians with recording and filing devices created the elaborate bureau of records which was the "paper brain" of the War Department. The problem of transporting to the front the tons of food and equipment required for every man in the forces was solved by the Service of Supply in France under General James G. Harbord. No army had ever been better fed or cared for. David Lloyd George, the energetic British prime minister who had organized the munitions supplies for the British Expeditionary Force, confessed his astonishment at the strength and swiftness with which America struck. "Her coming was like an avalanche. . . . Her great army of all ranks gave service that no man would, in 1917, have believed possible."

There is no scale by which it is possible to measure justly the part which American money, supplies, munitions, and men played in the Allied victory. The German collapse in 1918, before Germany had been invaded, was an admission of the overwhelming superiority America still held in reserve but could soon employ. Equally important was the effect of American intervention on the morale of the combatants. It heartened the Allied peoples; it discouraged the Germans and Austrians; and it fell like a judicial verdict upon the ears of all neutrals. The United States, which Lincoln had called the last best hope of earth and which Wilson had made the oracle of democracy, was a symbol of great moral force in the minds and hearts of men. When Wilson, asking the Congress to declare war on Germany, defended his resolution with the statements, "We are but one of the champions of the rights of mankind," and "The world must be made safe for democracy," he passed judgment on Germany and on the German cause. Millions of people outside the boundaries of the United States accepted the verdict.

5. FROM THE HIGH TIDE OF GERMAN SUCCESS TO THE GERMAN SURRENDER (JANUARY, 1917–NOVEMBER, 1918)

The land drives of 1916 had proved indecisive in results and appalling in their mounting carnage. The campaigns of 1917 were equally bloody. On the three hundred mile western front the lethal stalemate continued, although most of the commanders, despite the lessons of Verdun and the Somme, persisted in believing that a "break through" would be possible if sufficient pressure were applied in a narrow section. In April, 1917, the French attacked at St. Quentin and Reims, while the British assailed Arras. The slaughter was so excessive and the gains so negligible that whole French divisions were driven to mutiny. To conceal this critical reaction from the Germans, British forces hastily attacked at Ypres and Cambrai, using tanks for the first time, but their progress was again checked after minimal gains. The armored tank was the most promising weapon yet introduced to break the deadlock of trench warfare, but the British revealed their new device before they had built enough tanks to make the surprise use of them really effective.

Three major developments of the year 1917 overshadowed this introduction of the tank. The first was the German decision to wage unrestricted submarine warfare. This decision was due to the fact that the extremists gained control at German headquarters when the Allied governments refused to consider peace on any terms acceptable to the Central Powers. Within two months this brought about the second major development of 1917, the declaration of war against Germany by the Congress of the United States (April 6). The third development, ultimately to overshadow all others in this eventful year, was the outbreak of the Russian Revolution.

Incompetence in high places, treachery, defeat, lack of food and supplies, war weariness, and revolutionary propaganda had finally broken the patience of the Russian people. Early in March, 1917,[1] the czar's regime foundered in a sea of strikes, while sabotage and mutiny paralyzed the armies. For six months the parliamentary liberals under Alexander Kerensky sought to erect a provisional government and to continue the war against the Central Powers. But the Russian people were weary of a struggle which they identified with the fallen government and with capitalist exploitation. An active and resolute minority of the revolutionists, directed by Nicolai Lenin, hastened the organization of soviets (councils) among workers, soldiers, and peasants, and this ruthless and realistic inner group captured control of the revolutionary movement in November, 1917. Lenin immediately offered the Germans a truce. Russia was out of the war; how completely out, became clear within three months. By the Treaty of Brest-Litovsk (March 3, 1918) the new Soviet regime surrendered Poland, Finland, the Baltic states, and the Ukraine to German domination, and promised to make deliveries of food, raw materials, and indemnity payments to Germany and the German allies.

Victorious in the east, the Germans turned swiftly to the west. There they hoped to win a decision before American aid, in money, materials, and men, could compensate the French, British, and Italians for the loss of Russian assistance. After three years of fighting the Central Powers had achieved that main objective for which they had prepared: the elimination of one of their adversaries and the shattering of the ring around them. In the final outcome, of course, the reinforcements from the United States more than redressed the balance. But before these reinforcements could arrive in strength the Allies had to

---

[1] By the Julian calendar, which was still in use in Russia in 1917, March 11–13, the days which saw czardom overthrown, corresponded to February 26–28. Hence the Russians speak of this as the "February Revolution." Similarly, November 7, 1917, when the Bolsheviki won control, was October 25, Old Style, and this event is therefore the "October Revolution" to the Russians, the "November Revolution" in most European and American accounts.

face a critical interval, during which their exhausted lines were assailed by a foe with superior forces, a foe who could attack at will, choosing the place and the moment. The last great German lunges of 1918 were the most desperate of all; but like the earlier drives they missed the complete success which alone would have justified their cost.

When the paralysis of Russia became apparent in the autumn of 1917, the Germans knew it was safe to withdraw most of their divisions from the eastern front. The men were rested, regrouped, and re-equipped. Then, with no warning, a thunderbolt struck the Italians at Caporetto, on October 24, 1917. Within two weeks the Italian lines had crumbled and the defenders were hurled back almost to the gates of Venice. Over 100,000 Italian soldiers had been killed or disabled, and 250,000 were prisoners. This catastrophic rout gravely weakened the Italian fighting morale. To reinforce the stricken front and keep Italy in the war, the French and British were forced to create a diversion in the north and to spare eleven badly needed divisions to take over part of the Italian lines. This conversion of Italy from an asset to a liability was to make the French and British reluctant, when victory was ultimately won, to concede the Italians all the gains promised them in the secret Treaty of London.

Hope of American aid kept the Allied armies in the field; without such expectation it is doubtful if the French, British, and Italian peoples or their armed forces could have endured the sacrifices exacted after the Russian collapse. The Germans and Austrians, Bulgarians and Turks were likewise weary, sick of the slaughter, and discouraged by the shortage of supplies. More than ever, time had become the essential factor in military calculations. If victory was to be won, the German armies would have to win it in the west, before the United States transported to France the millions of men already in training camps by the opening of 1918.

General Erich von Ludendorff, who had become virtual master of strategy at the German headquarters, promised that one more drive, a *Friedensturm*, would bring the Central Powers peace and victory. The universal spirit of war weariness, which had dissolved Russian resistance, which had weakened the Italian will to fight and depleted French and British morale, affected the German and Austrian people also. But the collapse of Russia buoyed up their confidence. The Treaty of Brest-Litovsk threw open to Germany the resources of the Ukraine and gave the German military leaders a heightened prestige which enabled them to demand the utmost from the exhausted nation. Ludendorff mustered almost 200 divisions, and although losses had cut the average German division to half strength this meant a force of 2,500,-000 men. Against this mass threat the Allies could muster some 167 divisions, or 2,000,000 men, on the French and Belgian front. The Germans, however, had two advantages in addition to superior numbers. They could choose the point of attack, and they possessed a unified command while the Allies were still handicapped by lack of coordination. Hitherto the British, Belgian, French, and Italian staffs had failed to confide in or trust one another fully. Not until March 26, 1918, did the Allied governments and the commanders of the several Allied armies yield to the compulsion of events and set up a unified command on the western front. The French commander-in-chief, the able and cool-headed strategist Ferdinand Foch, was named as generalissimo. His authority, however, was never unquestioned; jealousies continued to divide the armies; and Foch found it necessary to persuade rather than attempt to issue orders to his fellow commanders.

This belated Allied decision to unify the command followed by five days the opening of Ludendorff's spring offensive (March, 1918). The first blow fell upon the British lines at St. Quentin, parted them, and carried the Germans ahead some forty miles through the breach before French reserves, generously poured in, helped to check the Teuton tide. The British lost 250,000 men, one-third as prisoners. But the important railway junction of Arras, goal of the German lunge, remained in Allied hands. Ludendorff had hoped to seize it, separate the French and British armies completely, and roll the British back to the North Sea coast. Two weeks later came a second German lunge which almost cut through to Hazebrouck. The third German drive commenced on May 27, between Soissons and Reims, and carried to within thirty-seven miles of Paris in four days. The invaders had reached the Marne at Château-Thierry and seemed about to realize the decision which had escaped them in 1914.

For the Allies these were desperate days and only the certainty that American help was on the seas nerved them for the ordeal. Reinforcements from the newly formed American Expeditionary Force joined in the defense of Château-Thierry (June 1) and by July the tide of battle had begun to turn. Ludendorff opened a new German thrust around Reims on July 15; in three days it was checked; within a week it had been hurled back. This second battle of the Marne (July 15–August 7) destroyed Ludendorff's confidence. In the east the supplies demanded from Russia could not be delivered because of the chaos in that coun-

try; in the west the great victory drive had broken down. Throughout
the remainder of the summer the Germans were herded relentlessly
backward in a vast and costly rearguard action, as a million fresh American troops swung into action. On September 29, almost in a panic,
Ludendorff urged the German political leaders to open peace negotiations. Bulgaria had collapsed. The resistance of the Turks was disintegrating under Allied attacks and a British-sponsored Arab revolt.
Austria-Hungary, dissolving into minority groups, had ceased to count
as a military empire. The Germans were stunned by the rapidity with
which the high hopes of the spring had turned into the bitterness of
certain defeat. Militarists, soldiers, politicians, and people all suffered
a sudden collapse of morale. Indignation swept in a revolutionary wave
through the cities, the kaiser abdicated, and an interim government
asked for an armistice. This hasty appeal for terms and the German
capitulation in November, 1918, are discussed in Chapter XIII.

XI

THE WAR ON THE SEA

1914–1918

No fair-minded neutral, no matter whether he favors us or not, can doubt our right to defend ourselves against this war of starvation, which is contrary to international law.

THEOBALD VON BETHMANN-HOLLWEG,
GERMAN CHANCELLOR (1916)

1. THE DOUBLE WAR

WORLD WAR I may be more easily understood if it is viewed as a *double* war: a land war fought out primarily in Europe, and a sea war which was global in its range. All major European wars since the seventeenth century have been dual wars in this sense. The War of the Spanish Succession (1702–1713), the Seven Years' War (1756–1763), and the successive coalition wars against France in the era of the Revolution and Napoleon (1793–1814), all saw battles in Europe decide the fate of continents overseas, and decide in favor of the British. A united Europe would have overshadowed and annulled the British hegemony in the colonial world; but a divided Europe, in unstable equilibrium, locked up most of the energies of the nations in a vigilant guarding of frontiers. England fought France because the ambition of Louis XIV and, later, of Napoleon threatened to destroy the balance of power; and all states which sturdily opposed French ascendency were aided by English subsidies and sometimes by English arms. The major task which the British themselves assumed in these protracted struggles was to vanquish the French at sea, to blockade the French coasts, and to capture French commerce and colonies.

In 1914 the British reverted to this historic policy. They joined a coalition of European states against an aggressive and expanding German Reich, a nation of 60,000,000 people which threatened to destroy the balance in Europe. As in former wars, they expected to provide loans and to ship food and arms to their Continental allies, while they themselves conducted the war at sea. Assisted by the French navy, the British set about seizing or blockading all German ships, halting German sea-borne commerce, and occupying German colonies. But they did not anticipate the need to provide any considerable military force. The few divisions they could furnish at the opening of the war were described by the Germans as a "contemptible little army" though they fought valiantly and suffered very heavily in the first retreat to the Marne. Expectation that the war would be over in a few months made it appear unnecessary to train a large force, so that conscription was not introduced into the United Kingdom until January, 1916.

For Germany and Austria the British intervention therefore made little difference at the outset and had the war ended swiftly it would not have mattered profoundly. But the prolongation of the conflict made British naval pressure and increasing military strength a decisive factor. The Central Powers could not eliminate their opponents on the Continent because France, Italy, and to a much lesser degree Russia, were bridgeheads over which the British could continue to pour supplies and men to maintain the opposition. In the closing months of the struggle, when British credit and reserves were near exhaustion, the United States took up the role of provider and base of supplies.

When World War I commenced in August, 1914, the Germans had already lost the diplomatic campaign that preceded hostilities. It is the business of the diplomat, first, to secure the protection and progress of his state without war if possible; second, to enter a war, if war prove unavoidable, with preponderant forces, that is, with a better than even chance of winning; and third, to prove that his country resorted to war under provocation and for good cause, so that it may claim the sympathy of neutrals. The Austrian and German statesmen failed on all these counts and failed again in their estimate of the crisis. They hoped to overcome Serbia in a swift campaign, believing Russia still unready to fight. They were mistaken. They hoped that the British, lacking a large army, would avoid a European war. They were mistaken again. The Austrian attack on Serbia and the German invasion of Belgium marked the Central Powers out as the aggressors and alienated neutral opinion. This was a third failure.

Thus the general ineptitude which had characterized German diplomats for twenty years before 1914 continued to mar their record. Had the Austrians offered the Russians equal compensation in the Balkans, the two powers might have advanced simultaneously towards the warm seas. But with German influence joined to Austrian pressure and directed not only to the Adriatic but to Constantinople, there could be no compromise for Russia but only an abdication of claims which the czars had asserted since the time of Peter the Great two centuries earlier. A further blunder of Berlin diplomacy was the invasion of Belgium. This violation of a small state, the perpetual neutrality of which all the powers were pledged to protect, provided the final impulse which brought Great Britain into the war. Though taken by surprise and reluctant to engage, the British people stood firmly united behind their government in its decision to fight.

In the perspective of history, however, it has become clear that World War I was not the result of a single blunder or a single incident. Nor was it the result of orders issued in the last ten days of July, 1914; those ten days merely set the seal upon the decisions of the previous ten years. Even the British course of action, the most uncertain in appearance, had been all but predetermined. As early as 1902 the British admiralty began to withdraw battleships from the Pacific, in pursuance of an accord reached that year with Japan. From 1904 to 1907 the British and French defined more positively the disposition to be made of their two fleets under the terms of the Entente Cordiale. The naval strategists at London faced a difficult decision: they must guard their home ports and keep open the Mediterranean "life line" at the same time. Since the dawn of civilization the Mediterranean had been a vital area, control of which decided the rise and fall of empires. All the decisive European naval battles (save the destruction of the Spanish Armada in 1588) had been fought in or near the entrance to the Middle Sea. But the British, as already explained, recognized that the developments of the twentieth century were changing this long tradition. In the Russo-Japanese War (1904–1905) the Russian Pacific and Baltic fleets were both largely destroyed in Far Eastern waters by Japanese superiority. This weakening of the Russian fleet, coupled with the construction of the Kiel Canal, promised to give Germany naval preponderance in the Baltic and North Seas. After 1907, therefore, the British fleet was concentrated in the North Sea to face the German threat.

If war developed between France and Germany, the French coasts and colonies would be vulnerable to superior German naval forces unless the British aided France. There was no formal Franco-British treaty of mutual defense. Fortunately, however, as the war clouds darkened over Europe in July, 1914, the British Grand Fleet was due to assemble for summer maneuvers, stripped for service. The British cabinet assured anxious French leaders that the coast would be protected, and it is significant that this assurance was given before the Germans invaded Belgium. When the British foreign secretary, Sir Edward Grey, informed parliament on August 3 that Britain was not bound by treaty and need not enter the war, he addressed an audience which had just learned of the German ultimatum to Belgium. Though two members of the cabinet resigned, the remainder knew, when they committed Great Britain to war on August 4, that the nation was united behind them.

Until the final hour the Germans dared to hope that the British would remain neutral. Yet, had Britain done so, it now seems fairly obvious that France and Russia might have been defeated, leaving Germany in a position to dominate Belgium, the Netherlands, and Denmark, and possibly acquire French colonies. The German High Seas Fleet, with added bases, would then have constituted a more formidable threat, and Britain might have had to fight later with little support from any European country. It was a sense of preservation as well as honor that shaped the British decision. Backed by German industry, technique, wealth, and aggressiveness, the German High Seas Fleet might have achieved parity with the British Grand Fleet in another decade.

In 1914, however, although modern and highly efficient, the German navy was definitely inferior to the British in all major categories. On land, Germany and Austria could fight France and Russia with some prospect of victory. But this was a dual war. On the sea the combined fleets of the Central Powers were clearly outclassed: their combined naval tonnage was about one-third that of their chief opponents, Britain, France, Russia, and Japan. The Japanese, loyal to their treaty with Great Britain (and to their own national interests) declared war on Germany on August 23, 1914, and promptly demonstrated the vulnerability of German overseas possessions by attacking the port of Kiauchow which Germany had occupied on lease from China. By the close of 1914 the Japanese and the British in concert had seized all German-held islands in the Pacific. The naval inferiority of Germany and Austria was increased by losses and by the entry of Italy (1915) and the United States (1917) on the opposing side. In the final years of the struggle the Central Powers were faced by naval odds that had risen to more than five to one. The Allied Powers were supreme on the oceans, and the oceans cover seven-tenths of the globe.

2. CONTROL OF THE SEAS

When the British government announced that a state of war existed between Britain and Germany (August 4, 1914), a veil of official secrecy settled over the oceans like a fog, to hide for the next four years the movements of the fleets. But the British dreadnoughts were at their stations; their main base was Scapa Flow in the Orkney Islands, and their main role was to block any attempt of the German High Seas Fleet to emerge from its home waters. Mines and shore batteries kept the British ships from approaching close to the enemy coasts, and it was not safe for them to penetrate the Baltic Sea. For by widening the Kiel Canal, a project completed in 1914, the Germans made it possible to move their largest warcraft from the Elbe estuary to the Baltic without going around the Danish peninsula. This shorter passage increased the effectiveness of their navy in local waters. Their blockade of the Baltic made it possible for them to import ore and other supplies from Sweden and to prevent Russia from receiving supplies through this most direct and, in peacetime, most important route of Russian sea trade.

Thus the Germans maintained an inner blockade while the British maintained an outer blockade. The map well suggests the problems this involved. The twenty-odd miles of rough water which divided England from France, and the three hundred miles of gray misty waste between Scotland and Norway, were under ceaseless observation. Only an occasional German raider managed to slip through the British patrols. The coming of war caught several German warships in distant oceans and few were able to return. Throughout the closing months of 1914 British, French, and (after August 23) Japanese warships hunted down the isolated German naval units which had been too far dispersed to find a friendly haven.

Two German cruisers, the *Goeben* and the *Breslau*, trapped in the Mediterranean, fled to Turkish waters. Two other cruisers, the *Gneisenau* and the *Scharnhorst*, with some smaller craft, were in the Pacific Ocean and made for home around Cape Horn. After destroying an inferior British force off Chile, these German ships were caught and sunk in the battle of the Falkland Islands on December 8, 1914. Several light German cruisers eluded pursuit for months and some of them inflicted heavy losses upon Allied merchant shipping, but as the war advanced the seas were gradually cleared of these surface raiders. They were like foxes trailed by relentless packs of hounds.

In sporadic forays German cruisers and destroyers darted across the North Sea to scatter shells in British east coast towns, but such ventures had little effect on the progress of the war. Only once did the German High Seas Fleet emerge in strength to clash directly with the British Grand Fleet in a major action. This engagement, fought off Jutland on May 31, 1916, has been adjudged a draw. The Germans inflicted heavier losses on a superior enemy force and then escaped back to port. In marksmanship, maneuvering, and night fighting they outmatched their foes. But the British remained in control of the seas; their slow, constricting blockade was not broken; enforced idleness wore away the valor of the German crews; and when in the final days of the war the fleet was ordered out for a "suicide" battle, the sailors mutinied. Under the terms of the armistice of November, 1918, the greater part of this undamaged navy, over half a million tons of shipping, was surrendered and interned by the British at Scapa Flow. There, six months later, the ships were scuttled by their crews (June 21, 1919). It was an inglorious but defiant end for a fleet which had ranked second among the world's navies.

Control of the seas gave the Allied Powers three marked advantages which increased as the war lengthened. The first of these was the opportunity to draw upon the resources of the world so that almost all the commodities essential for pressing the war were at their command. The vast productive energies and unrivaled industrial equipment of the United States responded to their orders, and munitions from America were soon crossing the Atlantic on a "bridge of boats."

The second advantage which control of the ocean routes gave the Allied nations was the power of blockade. Save with neutral neighbors such as the Netherlands, Switzerland, and Denmark, and with Sweden across the Baltic Sea, German and Austrian foreign trade practically ceased with the outbreak of war. This brought a severe economic loss and a critical shortage of many materials essential for war work, as well as a restriction of food imports. Neutral nations which could no longer trade with the Central Powers naturally offered their accumulating stocks to the Allied governments. The French and British also deprived Germany of some supplies obtainable in Sweden or Switzerland by a practice known as "preclusive purchasing." This consisted in paying higher prices, even extravagant prices, for rare minerals, drugs, and other items, and even if such purchases could not be removed or used by the Allies they might be destroyed to keep them from reaching Germany.

The third advantage which the British in particular derived from Allied naval preponderance was the opportunity to influence neutral nations. Lists of contraband were drawn up and rapidly expanded, so that it speedily became difficult for neutral firms to ship any freight to Europe without British approval. Vessels were searched and their cargoes confiscated if they sought to escape the Allied embargo. The import quotas of neutral states bordering Germany, especially Holland and Denmark, were rigidly checked and limited lest any excess over domestic requirements be re-exported to enemy markets. Business concerns which strove to maintain relations with the Central Powers and defied the blockade might find themselves blacklisted, that is, put in a class which cut them off from all favorable treatment by the countries and corporations friendly to the Allied cause.

This economic pressure naturally drew protests from some neutrals. The United States protested against the right of search exercised by Allied inspectors, and the State Department warned all belligerents that the prohibition of direct or indirect trade with nations still at peace, or even with nations at war, raised unresolved questions of international law. Most neutrals, however, found it expedient to acquiesce in the Allied regulations, to apply for licenses when shipping goods, and to provide the information requested regarding their origin, nature, and intended destination. To secure cargo space for their own commerce and to maintain essential trade relations in a war-torn world, the lesser states co-operated with the Allied agents. For the latter could speed or delay transactions through the multifarious channels of Great Britain's world-wide economic empire. British and Allied spokesmen justified the control they imposed on ocean trade by insisting that they were fighting for the rights of small nations which, like Belgium and Serbia, would be helpless without support against the aggression of Germany and Austria. This argument won increasing assent from a majority of the people in neutral states. The fact that the Allied blockade could be enforced without undue harshness, without violence or loss of life and property, made it much more tolerable than the German submarine campaign. In cases of sharp dispute over cargoes adjudged contraband by the British, the Allied governments sometimes purchased them at prevailing prices or otherwise compensated the producer and shipper. By such tactics, traders who had set out to supply war materials to the Central Powers might find themselves unloading their wares at British docks instead, and that without loss of profit.

3. GERMAN SUBMARINE WARFARE

For Germany and Austria the maintenance of the Allied blockade meant hardship and ultimate exhaustion. This knowledge helps explain their haste to force an early decision on land or to break through the encirclement and open new sources of supply. The advance of the German armies across Belgium and northern France brought valuable mines and industrial plants under German control, but these regions were densely populated and added little to the food supply. The Polish, Serbian, and Rumanian territories occupied by Austro-Russian forces did yield some assets — potato, beet, and cereal crops, wheat, cattle, and oil. But the beleaguered peoples of the Central Powers still lacked certain essentials, fats in particular. The inadequacy of their diet reduced their efficiency, health, and morale. Devitalization of the human machines proved as serious a handicap as the shortage of rubber, copper, mercury, and other materials, lack of which finally stalled the German industries and the German armies.

Early in the war the Germans attempted to retaliate against the blockade, and after a few months their navy undertook to impose a counterblockade. All neutral ships were warned (February 4, 1915) to avoid the waters around the British Isles. As the Germans could not enforce this blockade by stopping and searching ships as the British did, they had decided to resort to a relatively new weapon, the submarine boat. But the *Unterseeboot*, or U-boat, was thin-shelled and vulnerable to gun fire or to ramming, so that it could not safely risk a surface approach. The traditional method of enforcing a sea blockade, which the British respected, was to send an officer on board a halted merchant vessel to study the cargo lists. This was hazardous for submarines because the halted vessel might carry a hidden battery of light guns, or radio news of its plight to a nearby submarine chaser. The Germans therefore announced that all ships which entered a forbidden zone around the British Isles would be sunk by torpedo attack, if necessary without warning.

Such ruthlessness increased the reputation for barbarity which the Germans had already earned by their invasion of Belgium and by the severe reprisals and wanton destruction which they had inflicted in occupied regions. To justify their new policy of submarine warfare they protested that the Allied governments had extended the blockade beyond the limits recognized by international precedent. Furthermore, they insisted that most ships approaching British harbors were armed merchantmen carrying munitions of war, and that these facts made them in effect enemy warships. These arguments, regardless of the truth of the facts alleged, seemed specious to most neutrals. For the civilized world was shocked by the deliberate sinking of defenseless freight and passenger ships in conditions which often left no time for the crew or passengers to save themselves. Even if they managed to launch some lifeboats they might die of starvation and exposure.

The government of the United States, which was already engaged in dispute with the Allied powers over the right of search, promptly took up the rights of neutral shipping so sharply menaced by the German submarine policy. The sinking of the American freighter *Gulflight* and of the British liner *Lusitania* brought a resolute protest from the State Department. After a year of diplomatic pressure, the United States won a promise from the Germans that henceforth passengers and crews would be given adequate warning before merchant ships were sunk. The toll of the U-boats remained nevertheless a serious drain on Allied shipping and a constant threat to naval communication.

Then, at the opening of 1917, the German leaders suddenly abandoned all restraint and announced a policy of unrestricted submarine warfare. They knew that such a retraction of the promises made to the United States and other neutrals the previous year might bring America into the war against them. Apparently four arguments had persuaded them that the risk was worth taking. (1) The Allied blockade was growing tighter and signs of war weariness and malnutrition among their peoples had alarmed the German and Austrian leaders. (2) Despite the military successes against Russia, Rumania, and Serbia, the Central Powers, by January, 1917, had not broken the ring around them nor driven any of their foes (save Rumania) to a dictated peace. (3) The rejection by the Allied governments of the German and Austrian peace overtures of December, 1916, left the rulers of the Central Powers convinced that they had to force a conclusion by victory. (4) The construction of new and improved U-boats, to the number of 120, encouraged the naval experts to predict that unrestricted submarine warfare would destroy 500,000 to 600,000 tons of merchant shipping a month. As this exceeded the highest rate of replacement the Allies could achieve, their ocean transport would be crippled. British industries would languish, the British people would starve, and material aid from the United States could not be effectively transported.

The new campaign had been carefully planned and the forbidden zones now included all the coastline of the Allied countries. The great

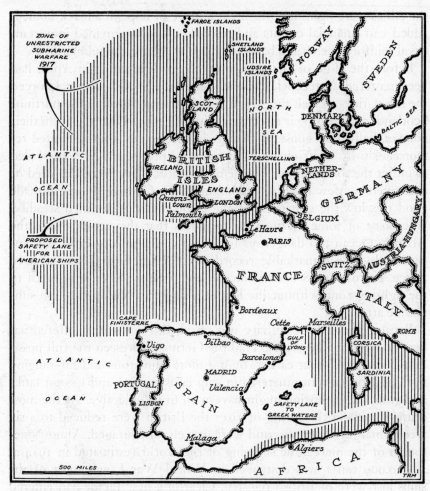

THE SUBMARINE BLOCKADE IN WORLD WAR I

gamble was inaugurated on February 1, 1917; by April the monthly rate of destruction had climbed to 875,000 tons and success seemed assured if it could be maintained. But once again the Germans came close to a triumph only to miss it. The British adopted the convoy system in May, 1917, sending the ships in escorted groups which slowed down the swifter vessels but offered better protection to all. New means of detecting and destroying U-boats were developed, and shipbuilding was speeded up, especially in American shipyards. Most important, however, was the declaration of war by the United States against Germany (April 6, 1917). The intervention of this strong new belligerent not only seemed a moral vindication of the cause for which the Allies were fighting; it brought a surge of hope in a black hour, it added vast financial credits and resources, and it provided important naval reinforcements and bases for the war against the submarines.

Before the close of 1917 this menace, so threatening in April, had been mastered. A steel net, stretched across the English Channel, forced the submarines to seek the Atlantic and to return around the north of Scotland, reducing their effective radius of action. Diverted from their courses, baffled by constant changes in the convoy routes, hunted remorselessly by swift chasers and scouting planes, the U-boats failed to inflict the toll promised by their advocates. Fifty were captured or destroyed in a few months, and although the German shipyards made good this loss the efficiency of the U-boat tactics declined steadily. The boast of some German commanders that they could make the Atlantic Ocean too dangerous for American troops to cross was answered by the remarkable record of the American Expeditionary Force. In 1917–1918 over 2,000,000 combatants were transported to the fighting zone without the loss of a single troopship through submarine attack.

Because the U-boat activity was checked, the threat it offered has been somewhat underrated. Had the Germans foreseen the full possibilities of the U-boat earlier, built a more numerous and far-ranging fleet, and risked more material in ship construction and less on tanks and guns, the campaign might have won to its objective. At the most critical point in the spring of 1917 the British were reduced to a six weeks' margin of supplies and were gravely discouraged. Almost one-fourth of the mercantile shipping of the world (estimated in 1914 at 49,000,000 tons) was destroyed in World War I, and most of the ships lost were of British registry. Clearly, a new factor had entered naval warfare, a factor which offered a challenge to accepted principles of sea power. Had the German submarine blockade proved effective, the Allied powers would have lost control of the sea and with that reversal they would have forfeited the hope of victory.

4. THE INDIRECT ADVANTAGES OF NAVAL ASCENDENCY

From 1914 to 1918 the pressure of sea power shaped the policies of neutral and belligerent nations in a fashion at once compelling and obscure. In its total effect sea power was the most potent instrument used in the war. A few examples will suggest how its omnipresent influence worked for the Allies throughout the four years, directly or indirectly, often making itself felt in unadvertised but fateful ways.

Sea power influenced the Italian course of action strongly. When the Italian leaders kept Italy neutral in August, 1914, and then joined the Entente Powers ten months later, they were moved by a serious respect for French and British naval strength. If they had joined Germany and Austria they would almost certainly have lost their African protectorates, Tripoli, Eritrea, and Italian Somaliland; they would have invited a blockade of their commerce; and they would have exposed their long seacoast, especially the islands of Sicily and Sardinia, to naval attack.

A similar though less calculating prudence may have helped to influence Belgian leaders. Had they yielded in 1914 to German demands they would have abetted the German attack on France. But such a course might have led the British to class Belgium as an enemy state, and the rich Belgian Congo might have been seized as a forfeit. All the European governments with colonial and commercial possessions, especially those of Portugal, Holland, and Denmark, weighed their interests in similar fashion. Their colonies were vulnerable and they were aware of this fact when they suffered the British to search their ships and to curtail their traffic with the Central Powers. They were also aware that British naval ascendency at its firmest was less of a threat to their liberty and livelihood than German military ascendency was likely to prove. Norway was another small neutral which had given hostages to sea power. In 1914 Norway possessed the fifth largest merchant marine in the world, but it lacked a navy to protect this tonnage. Had Norway favored and aided the Central Powers, Allied cruisers could have seized Norwegian ships in all parts of the world, and Norwegian trade would have been cut off or diverted to other routes.

The fate of Greece provided a stern lesson for all neutrals vulnerable to naval attack which dared to offend the Allied governments. The British and French were largely dependent upon Greek ports and bases for a campaign against Turkey or a possible invasion of the Balkan peninsula. The Greek leader, Eleutherios Venizelos, was prepared to bring Greece into the war. The king, Constantine, hesitated, and although a Franco-British expeditionary force landed at Saloniki (October, 1915) the Greek government insisted the country was still neutral. The Allies, after some hesitation, set up a provisional government at Saloniki under Venizelos (1916). An Allied ultimatum to the Greek government at Athens was rejected, and the nation was blockaded and reduced to civil war between the royalist and Venizelist factions. In December, 1916, the British recognized the provisional government of Venizelos. Constantine was forced to resign the following June, and Venizelos declared war against the Central Powers as the Allies desired. Without superior sea power the French and British could not thus have persuaded the Greeks to join them nor established the expeditionary force at Saloniki which held down a large Austro-German army in the Balkans and later hastened the dissolution of the Hapsburg Empire.

The status of some more powerful neutrals, notably Spain and Sweden, was less obviously influenced by sea power, but the influence was operative none the less. The Spanish people enjoyed an unwonted prosperity from 1914 to 1918, selling their mineral ores, wool, and agricultural products to the Allies at inflated prices. They would have sold them with equal readiness to the Germans, but no transportation was available. The naval blockade of the Central Powers thus set the course of Spanish trade and economic co-operation. Sweden, on the other hand, immune from Allied naval attack, without overseas possessions but vulnerable to invasion by the German armies, sustained a role of cautious neutrality. Had it suited either the German or the Russian high command to lengthen the war front, Sweden might have been drawn into belligerency as Greece was. The Swedes strove to divide their exports fairly among the warring powers and to preserve some freedom of action. But the Germans, especially in their period of greatest military ascendency, extorted the major share of Swedish exports, manufactures, chemicals, explosives, and minerals.

Switzerland, ringed by warring powers but most vulnerable to German might, supplied cheese, wine, cereals, timber, manganese, iron, and precision instruments to feed the war economy of the embattled Reich. Had Switzerland possessed a seacoast and colonies, these goods might have gone to Britain. But the best the Allied governments could do with Sweden and Switzerland was to bid for essential products at a higher price, deflecting them in this manner from the German market. The superior financial reserves of the Allied governments and of the United States enabled their agents to outbid the Germans at such "preclusive purchasing."

To concentrate the energies and resources of the British Commonwealth of Nations was a further service made possible through sea power. Manufacturing, mining, shipbuilding, munitions making, and agriculture gained amazingly in all the Dominions under the stimulus of war orders. Expeditionary forces from India, Canada, Australia, New Zealand, and South Africa took an active part in the campaigns, distinguishing themselves in Mesopotamia, Gallipoli, and Flanders. German outposts in the Pacific were seized by Australians and New Zealanders; German South West Africa and German East Africa were invaded by forces from the Union of South Africa. Such imperial co-operation — the manufacture of war supplies, the growing of urgently needed crops, the transportation of armies from the Dominions to the battle areas — all this would have been impossible if the oceans had been closed to the British and open to their foes.

Perhaps the most profound effect of Allied sea power, an effect not easy to measure or to trace, was the direction it gave to the formation of American public opinion. Modern warfare proved expensive beyond all expectancy. Need for more artillery, shells, and ships led the British and French to place unprecedented orders with firms in the United States. The funds to finance these orders were handled by New York bankers, and when the French, and later the British, assets ran out, American financiers arranged credits to cover the cost of further purchases. It is too simple and too mercenary to suggest that the people of the United States joined the Allied and Associated Powers because defeat for France and Britain would have meant loss to American bankers, investors, and industrialists. Many motives mingled and many factors joined to provoke the declaration of war against Germany by the United States on April 6, 1917. But it is undoubtedly true that war trade helped to unite British and American interests.

The people of the United States entered World War I in a crusading spirit. A crusade is a collective enterprise for a moral purpose, and it would be a mistake to underrate the degree to which a common activity with the Allied peoples had affected American views. Co-operation in providing supplies had predisposed millions of citizens in the United States to feel that they had a share in the Allied effort. The submarine warfare which exposed neutrals and combatants to a common peril gave them a common grievance. The close historic connection and the constant communication between Britain and the United States induced a cordial and sympathetic understanding of the British effort, an understanding greatly strengthened by the bonds of a common language. These factors are so important they will be considered elsewhere. Here it should be noted, however, that they were all conditioned by and in a sense contingent upon Anglo-American intercourse, upon shipping, the exchange of cargoes, mails, books, cables, news reports; in other words, upon the lines across the Atlantic Ocean which only sea power could preserve.

XII

THE WAR OF FINANCE, DIPLOMACY,
AND PROPAGANDA

*Without means of payment in dollars — and since November, 1916,
such means of payment had been lacking — the Allies would have
been beaten before the end of 1917. America's entry into the war
saved them.*

ANDRÉ TARDIEU [1]

I. WAR TRADE AND ITS EFFECT UPON NEUTRAL OPINION

MODERN wars are fought on many fronts. The preceding chapter emphasized how inexorably the British battleships, even when lying at anchor and veiled in the mists of Scapa Flow, determined the outcome of distant campaigns. In addition to this naval pressure the Allies commanded other assets, some less tangible but equally pervasive in their effects. Economically and financially the Allies were stronger than the Central Powers. The combined national wealth of Britain, France, Russia, and Italy was double that of Germany and Austria, and after the United States entered the war these economic odds rose to better than four to one. Superior resources gave the British and French governments an advantage from the first in the world markets, for in wartime the prudent businessman prefers to sell for cash. Even victors can go bankrupt, and the producer who sells to the side destined to lose, especially if he sells on credit, is ruined likewise.

Before 1914 it was frequently predicted that a modern war could not last more than a few months because the expense of equipping and maintaining mass armies would soon bankrupt the wealthiest state. The cost, as expected, quickly exceeded all normal estimates but the threat of bankruptcy did not deter the combatant nations. Each year the war expenditures rose, and the ultimate sum directly expended by all the

[1] André Tardieu, *France and America* (Boston: Houghton, Mifflin, 1927), p. 227.

powers engaged has been reckoned at $186,000,000,000. Of this total the Central Powers spent approximately $63,000,000,000 and the Allied and Associated Powers $123,000,000,000. These figures suggest that the Allies spent twice as much as their opponents. They could do so because of the excess wealth and assets which they possessed, but even these resources proved insufficient.

The total British capital invested in foreign countries in 1914 represented about $17,000,000,000. These funds were rapidly converted into available exchange in order that the government at London might pay promptly for ships, services, food, and munitions purchased in all parts of the globe. When the British gold supply and reserves dwindled, loans had to be raised through international banking agencies, especially in the United States. After America joined in the war, the federal government took over from private bankers the problem of providing credits for the Allied Powers and guaranteed payment on their war purchases. By the close of hostilities the advances to the Allied and Associated Powers exceeded $7,000,000,000, a sum equal to five times the public debt of the United States in 1916, the last year of peace. These extensive loans, supplied by the wealthiest nation in the world, re-established the financial credit of the Allied governments, and the flood of munitions and supplies which the credits assured helped to daunt and finally to overwhelm the German armies. At the same time the British, French, and Italians were heartened by the aid of an ally so wealthy and so generous.

Throughout World War I Great Britain strove to maintain "business as usual" in order to pay with manufactured commodities for part of the imports received. Outgoing ships bore cotton goods, cutlery, Scotch whiskey, and anything else Britain could produce and sell, the credits thus amassed being used to purchase raw materials, munitions, and food. The Germans found it almost impossible to maintain their international trade, which before the war had reached $5,000,000,000 and had ranked them second to Great Britain with $7,000,000,000. Unable because of the blockade to sell to any but a few neighboring states, Germany could not build up a fund of foreign exchange by maintaining exports. Like the British they converted their investments abroad into capital, but even when they could purchase necessary goods from distant neutrals they could not readily take delivery of them, for cargoes intended for Germany were contraband of war. Nations which might otherwise have been willing to trade with the Central Powers were discouraged by these difficulties and transferred their commerce to Allied markets instead. With each shipment thus rerouted to London or Cherbourg, whether it was Chilean nitrates, Bolivian tin, Argentine beef, Spanish minerals, or Persian oil, the country producing the cargo became more and more definitely an economic belligerent, an associate in business with the Allied Powers, although it maintained the diplomatic status of a neutral.

In wartime trading a customer's ability to pay promptly and to carry away the goods are primary assets. War conditions create sharp demands but impose vexatious obstacles. Competition for most common commodities becomes keener, the demand for certain essentials grows urgent, prices rise, profits rise, and risks rise also. The possibility of loss through an accident of war, seizure and confiscation, or the purchaser's inability to pay, must all be discounted. Belligerent governments which are in a position to pay cash and assume the responsibility of transportation themselves enjoy an almost insuperable advantage. This advantage the Allied purchasing agents enjoyed, for control of the seas, superior financial resources, and later the financial support of the United States assured them priority. The more completely the Allied and Associated governments came to dominate world trade the more definitely they were in a position to oblige (or disoblige) the neutrals. All nations which fed the Allied war machine tended to become implicated in the Allied effort, and because they helped the Allied cause they were likely to find their sympathy for Allied aims intensified. Association in a common struggle unites men, and this annealing of sentiment, as much perhaps as the profits of war trade, drew neutral peoples into the Allied camp.

2. THE POWER OF PROPAGANDA

The ill success which had marked German diplomacy for two decades before the war opened in 1914 continued throughout the four years of fighting. Only two minor states, Turkey and Bulgaria, aligned themselves with the Central Powers. The Entente Powers, before hostilities ended, were joined by over twenty nations which broke with Germany and participated in the war to greater or lesser degree. It is doubtful if either the Turks or the Bulgarians had much control over the misguided statesmen who committed them to war from motives of fear, greed, or revenge. The Turks had a chronic fear of Russian designs against Constantinople; and as Britain, their erstwhile protector, had joined Russia, they looked to Germany for protection instead. The Bulgars, still smarting from their losses in the Second Balkan War of

1913, co-operated with the Austrians as one means of achieving revenge against the Serbs. There is little evidence that Turks or Bulgars
viewed World War I as a struggle between autocracy and democracy
or between might and right. Their actions were based, or their leaders'
actions were based, on local needs and problems and inspired by national fears, hopes, and prejudices.

The nations which joined the war against the Central Powers were
swayed by many motives. The fact that the Allied Powers won ten
times as many adherents to their cause as the Central Powers attracted
seems proof that to most neutrals the Allied program and methods
made a stronger appeal. Three reasons in particular may be noted to
explain this unequal alignment of belligerents, and two of these reasons
have been listed already. The first was the Allied control of the seas
which exposed all maritime nations to reprisals if they aided the
Central Powers. The second was the fact that economically the neutral states came to depend upon the Allied Powers because world trade
grew into war trade and only a few states, such as Switzerland, were
geographically in a position that permitted economic neutrality. The
third factor was perhaps the most significant of all, but it is difficult to
estimate because it involved intangible values and ethical judgments.
From the day the armies marched, Austria and Germany were stigmatized as the aggressors and were regarded as primarily responsible for
the war. With each year of struggle neutral nations came to view the
conflict more and more starkly as an attack by arrogant autocracies
upon peace-loving democracies. The liberal governments and liberty-
loving peoples of Britain, France, and Italy were pictured as resisting
the leagued tyrants of Central Europe who, with their military advisers
and automaton armies, had plotted to subdue the world. The fact that
czarist Russia and imperial Japan were linked in common effort with
the liberal powers did not seem to affect the force of this argument.

Before 1914 Kaiser William II, by his addiction to martial poses,
military reviews, and bellicose utterances, had identified himself in
many minds as the "War Lord of Europe." When war came, the fact
that Austria attacked Serbia and German armies violated neutral Belgium blackened the reputation of these two powers. The Allied governments had a moral justification for taking up arms: they were fighting for the rights of small nations. Throughout the war, moreover, the
Germans and Austrians fought on conquered territory. They were invaders, and to most people invasion and aggression are synonymous
terms. Their armies came to occupy almost all of Belgium, the rich de-

partments of northeastern France, and a varying area of Russian Poland, Serbia, and Rumania. Repressing a subject population in wartime
is a cruel task at best; it means curfews, patrols, spy hunts, domiciliary
visits, arrests, and the deportation or execution of patriots, underground agents, and saboteurs. It may also involve the arrest of leading
townsmen as hostages, and the wholesale massacre of such innocent
victims or the erasure of entire villages, to avenge a single sniper's bul-
let. With calculated thoroughness, the German forces of occupation
imposed military rule upon the subject populations, and the accounts
of their activities, authenticated and sometimes exaggerated, provided
further evidence to a hostile world of German brutality and barbarism.

In peace conferences before the war an effort had been made to
introduce rules which all nations would accept in order to abate the
savagery of war. At the Hague Conference of 1899 and again in 1907
proposals were introduced to prohibit the use of bacteria or poison gas
in war, to assure humane treatment for the wounded, for prisoners, and
for noncombatants. Civilians and civilian property, whenever possible,
were to be spared. But once war opened, the moderate rules which had
been approved were often ignored. The Germans seized and shot unarmed civilians during their march through Belgium and France; they
fired upon hospitals, burned churches, libraries, and schools, and early
in 1915 loosed poison gas against their foes. Coupled with the admitted
illegality of the submarine campaign, which subjected neutral as well
as enemy merchant ships and their crews to attack without warning,
these examples of German "frightfulness" convinced a majority of
neutrals that the Central Empires were outlaw states which the free
peoples of the world must break and bind for the peace and safety
of mankind. This conviction, fostered by all the devices of publicity
and substantiated by the daily reports of German ruthlessness, mobilized public opinion especially in the United States against the "militarists and warmongers." Public sentiment within the Allied countries was
firm and united from the first. But the neutral nations formed, as it
were, the jury in this international contest of claims and counterclaims.
The fact that neutral opinion turned steadily in favor of the Allied
nations was an asset of incalculable worth, more important perhaps
than superiority in man power, naval strength, or material wealth.

The United States was the only great power still at peace after May,
1915. Apologists for the Allied cause therefore made special efforts to
present their case convincingly before the bar of American opinion.
The British in particular possessed two great advantages in their pub-

licity campaign. In addressing the Americans they were communing with a people who spoke the same language, had studied the same literature, and were in sympathy with British culture and traditions: this was their primary appeal. But a second advantage, of which they made consistent use, was their control of the news channels. In 1914 the British owned one-half the world's submarine cables and had helped to lay much of the remainder. Four hours after the opening of hostilities the German undersea cable lines were cut. Most lines owned by neutrals were subject to British influence, and communication by radio was not yet highly effective for long distances. During four years of war, therefore, the world followed the campaigns through news reports furnished predominantly from Allied sources and edited in London. As ocean going ships carrying mail were likewise subject to inspection, and all communications, books, and journals which the censors judged harmful to the Allied cause might be suppressed or confiscated, the Central Powers were blockaded in a cultural as well as a physical sense.

These limitations made it difficult for the Germans to present their case with the facility and persuasiveness of British and French spokesmen. No one can weigh the effects of such conditions accurately; some German propaganda that did circulate in America was so ineptly presented it did more harm than good to the cause of the Central Powers. The economic expansion and prosperity for farmers and factory workers in America, which resulted in part from Allied war contracts, undoubtedly induced some of them to feel a stronger pro-Ally sentiment. But the most compelling influences which turned the feeling of Americans against Germany were the genuine, not the inflated or spurious, "atrocity" stories, the grim tragedies of the submarine warfare, the malicious destruction practised in American factories to delay supplies for Britain and France, the ineptitude of German diplomats who sought to incite a Mexican attack against the United States, and the intrigues of German consuls and attachés who used their privileged position to inspire strikes, finance spy rings, and plot deeds of sabotage and arson which wrecked American plants and ships and cost American lives. Such activities as these were rightly viewed by most Americans as acts of war committed against a neutral country. Without such preliminaries to excite public indignation, the renewal of the unrestricted submarine campaign on February 1, 1917, might not have brought a declaration of war from Congress two months later. The American people debated for two and a half years before reaching a verdict.

3. THE WAR GUILT THESIS

It has been said that in war truth is the first casualty. Early in the First World War a story circulated through the Allied journals that the kaiser had summoned his military, naval, and political experts to a secret conference at Potsdam in July, 1914, at which the decision was taken to provoke a general war. This story had no factual foundation, but it served as the basis for the "War Guilt Thesis" which thenceforth colored the thinking in Allied countries on the war and the peace. This thesis affirmed that the German and Austrian leaders were guilty of planning war as a deliberate stroke of policy, their motive being an insatiable lust for power. German "militarism" became the standard explanation for the chain of events which led up to hostilities; it was blamed for the competition in armaments, for the series of diplomatic crises, for the failure to negotiate the Austro-Serb dispute when it arose, and for the failure to localize the conflict when it had commenced. Most citizens of the United States, who were in general but meagerly informed on the international rivalries of the Old World, accepted this account readily and came to believe it sincerely.

The size, efficiency, and success of the German armies were cited as further proof that German militarists had prepared and plotted war. Allied lack of success, on the other hand, was attributed to the fact that as peaceful states Britain, France, and Russia had been largely unprepared for the armed conflict. This argument was true in the case of Britain, in the sense that the British lacked a mass army and were driven to introduce military conscription in the midst of the struggle. But militarism and large-scale military preparations for war were not limited to Germany and Austria-Hungary before 1914. The statistics on this question tell a rather confused story, and although statistics do not, of course, provide a complete picture, they offer more or less dispassionate testimony. Statistically, Russia had the largest trained army in the world in 1914, estimated at 1,445,000 men, and the largest armament budget, $520,000,000. France had the highest percentage of men in military service, amounting to 1.87 per cent of the population. Britain had the highest per capita taxation rate for armaments, equivalent to $9.00 a head. It was not wholly true that German increases in armaments had set the pace and forced other nations to follow; the competition seems to have been mutually waged. Between 1910 and 1914 British naval estimates rose from $165,000,000 to $255,000,000, and the French from $65,000,000 to $97,000,000, while the German naval budget increased but slightly, from $110,000,000 to $120,000,000. In the ten years preceding the war Russian military expenditures had increased from $187,500,000 to $399,000,000, the French from $147,000,000 to $218,000,000, and the German from $187,000,000 to $218,000,000. The annual outlay for arms voted by the three entente nations was not only larger than the total for the Triple Alliance but was rising more rapidly. By 1914 Russia, France, and Britain were spending twice as much for arms as Germany, Austria-Hungary, and Italy.

Such figures from the arithmetic of power politics do not prove the thesis of German war guilt and were not stressed by the Allied propagandists. In any case, it is not the possession of military power but the use made of it that marks a nation as aggressive or peaceful. Lust for power, greed for territory and trade, and secret pacts for the spoilation of neighbors were stressed in World War I as characteristics of autocratic regimes dominated by military cliques. It was not publicly admitted by the Allied governments that Britain, France, and Russia had made secret agreements for a future division of territories and spheres of influence after victory might be achieved. These secret treaties in which the Allied Powers, including Italy, defined their claims, remained confidential.[1] The effort of the Allies was represented publicly as a defensive war, waged to protect themselves and the small states of Europe from aggression.

The secret treaties negotiated among the Allied governments suggested that all the warring nations were motivated in part at least by the hope of gain. The fact that the terms of these accords were not openly avowed suggested that the Allied leaders were apprehensive of the effect upon neutral opinion if they made known the rewards they hoped to win through victory. In March, 1915, for instance, France, Russia, and Great Britain reached an understanding that France should recover Alsace-Lorraine and obtain control over the left bank of the Rhine. Russia was to receive German and Austrian Poland and control over Constantinople and the Straits. Britain was to be rewarded with a major share of German colonies and trade. One month later, Italy was persuaded to join the Allies and was promised Trieste, with

---

[1] After the November Revolution in Russia, in 1917, the Russian communist leaders embarrassed the statesmen of the British, French, and Italian foreign offices by revealing some of these treaties. The terms were published in liberal newspapers such as the *Manchester Guardian* and the *New York Evening Post*.

portions of the Tyrol and Dalmatia; and later still plans were laid for partitioning the Turkish Empire among Russia, Britain, France, and Italy. German treaty ports and concessions in China, and island bases in the Pacific Ocean, were pledged to Japan. This arbitrary disposal of the anticipated spoils of victory somewhat disillusioned the people of the United States and liberals in the Allied countries when the treaties came to light. Most of the American people had supposed that Woodrow Wilson spoke for all the Allied and Associated Powers when he affirmed, "We seek no indemnities for ourselves, no material compensation for the sacrifices we shall freely make."

4. THE PEACE PROGRAM

In the ardor of a great collective effort, a war or a revolution, nations idealize their aims. The projects proposed at such times are often half-Utopian, too far above the level of events to be realized, but powerful as stimulants encouraging men to make the sacrifices demanded. It was inevitable amid the suffering and slaughter of the years 1914–1918 that civilized people everywhere should insist that such a tragedy must not recur. The world had been relatively peaceful for generations and the war appeared an extraordinary and unnecessary disaster. There was a widespread insistence that the causes which had contributed to bring on the conflict must be curbed. From the first weeks of the fighting, idealists were shaping programs for a better world-to-be, blueprints for peace which might cure the evils of imperialism, militarism, autocracy, and war.

As these conceptions took clearer form, spokesmen in the Allied and neutral countries listed the major causes of armed conflict and sketched the machinery of arbitration. Everywhere popular hopes were kindled and multitudes were persuaded that this could be made a "war to end war." This faith found its most effective and influential advocate in Woodrow Wilson. As President of the United States he commanded the attention of the world; as head of the greatest neutral nation and, after April, 1917, of the greatest belligerent power, he could speak as one who had judged the issues and would help to shape the peace. His role as an outstanding champion of democracy and of neutral rights made him the logical prophet of the new world society. For in all liberal countries it was accepted as self-evident that the new world order must be founded upon democratic principles and fortified by granting all national groups the right of self-determination.

Wilson had earned a unique prestige as the champion of the rights of mankind. He had dealt patiently but firmly with the threat to neutral rights arising from the Allied blockade and he had defended American lives and property against German ruthlessness by all peaceful means available to him. The lesser neutrals, too weak to challenge British or German infringements of their rights, had learned to look to him to defend their interests also in the turmoil of an embattled world. His success in constraining the Germans to modify their submarine warfare against merchant shipping (1916) added to his reputation abroad and increased his popularity at home. It was ironic that just five months after his re-election in November, 1916, he had to lead the nation into a war which without sacrifice of principle he could no longer avoid.

On January 8, 1918, President Wilson outlined before the Congress of the United States the basic principles and specific readjustments which in his opinion offered the surest foundation for a lasting peace. Summarized in the famous Fourteen Points his program came to be regarded as embodying the terms which the Allied and Associated Powers were fighting to realize. The spirit of idealism and the high regard for the dignity of nations and of individuals which distinguished Wilson's thought made his speeches more effective than cannon in pleading the justice of the Allied cause. The moral advantage, which had lain with the Allied Powers from the opening of the war, made them appear, as the war ended, the "champions of the rights of mankind" in Wilson's words. This lofty and unselfish role they were not able to fill in all respects, and the discrepancy between the ideal aims and the hard realities of international politics produced a schism at the peace table. This conflict, which raged most fiercely about the interpretation of Wilson's Fourteen Points, will be analyzed in the succeeding chapter.

PART III

The Search
for International Stability

THE PROBLEMS OF PEACEMAKING

PARIS, 1919

The atmosphere of Vae victis *is not a good one in which to frame a treaty of lasting peace.*

LORD ROBERT CECIL [1]

I. WAR CASUALTIES AND WAR COSTS

WHEN the order to cease fire halted World War I on November 11, 1918, a stunned humanity prepared to audit the costs of four years' mass destruction. This stocktaking required time. Some estimates are even yet in debate, but the loss of life and the official expenditures have been summarized in round numbers. Eight million dead and twenty million wounded proved that modern war had become systematic mass murder. Through four and a quarter years of fighting, men had died at the rate of six to seven thousand a day. In three particulars the military figures of the First World War surpassed all previous known records: the proportion of the male population called to the colors was higher than in any previous national wars for which computations were available; the absolute total of men mobilized, a total probably in excess of sixty million, was without precedent in history; and the ratio of dead and wounded, in proportion to the total number engaged, had risen sharply. The casualties represented nearly 40 per cent of the combatants, even if it be assumed that some names figured on the casualty lists more than once. With military conscription and the concept of the nation-in-arms the size of modern armies had increased from forces reckoned in the thousands to forces reckoned in the millions. This rapid rise in military strength had been more than matched by a rise in military losses. The figures available suggested that war was growing progressively more deadly as civilization ad-

[1] Lord Robert Cecil, *A Great Experiment* (New York: Oxford University Press, 1941), p. 71.

vanced. In sixteenth century Europe, war killed or wounded perhaps one combatant in twenty. In the eighteenth century the ratio was about one in seven. In the twentieth century it was one in three.

At the close of World War I the casualties of the chief belligerents stood approximately as follows:[1]

	Dead	Wounded
GERMANY	1,808,000	4,247,000
RUSSIA	1,700,000	4,950,000
FRANCE	1,385,000	3,044,000
AUSTRIA-HUNGARY	1,200,000	3,620,000
GREAT BRITAIN	947,000	2,122,000
ITALY	460,000	947,000
TURKEY	325,000	400,000
UNITED STATES	115,000	206,000
	7,940,000	19,536,000

In proportion to population France had endured the heaviest sacrifices. Even the reacquisition of Alsace-Lorraine could not replace numerically the French lives blotted out in the four years' slaughter. For Americans to form an idea of this drain on French man power it is necessary to translate these losses into proportional estimates based upon the population of the United States in 1945. A comparable tragedy for America would mean 5,000,000 servicemen killed and 11,000,000 wounded, a total in excess of all the men in the armed services of the United States in World War II.

France was not the only European nation seriously reduced by the disaster of war. Germany suffered a larger total of war dead, although in proportion to the population of the Reich the percentage was lighter. For Austria-Hungary the burden was almost as great as for Germany. Russian estimates acknowledged a list of slain almost as high as the German total and very probably higher had complete statistics been available. The generation which lived through World War I did not fully comprehend how lethal and devastating armed conflict had become. A comparison of war casualties in Europe since 1100 suggests that between 1900 and 1925 more men died or were wounded on European battlefields than in the preceding eight centuries.[2]

[1] W. L. Langer (editor), *An Encyclopaedia of World History* (Boston: Houghton Mifflin Company, 1940), p. 960.
[2] Pitirim A. Sorokin, *Social and Cultural Dynamics* (New York: American Book Company, 1937), Vol. III, pp. 336–37.

Twentieth century warfare proved more costly in money as well as in lives. Here again historical precedents offered no adequate bases for predictions or reparations. In twenty years of warfare against the French, from 1793 to 1814, the British national debt increased eight-fold. But in the four years from 1914 to 1918 British indebtedness, domestic and foreign, rose from $3,000,000,000 to $35,000,000,000. These figures suggest that war had grown ten times as costly in the course of a century, but as population, production, and living costs had all risen in the same period comparisons are not easily resolved. For all the belligerents of World War I the official direct expense has been calculated at $186,000,000,000. The indirect cost was almost as great. The loss in property cannot be easily measured. The labor and energy diverted to nonproductive or actively destructive ends deprived humanity of all the durable goods which might have been created with the same effort. For projects uncompleted, as for lives cut short, there is no gauge to measure losses. Everywhere, plans for social welfare, programs of health and education, were arrested by the war effort, and a heritage of debt burdened victors and vanquished. War finance and war debts dislocated the machinery of international exchange and condemned the world to years of economic stress and confusion.

After a century of relative order and remarkable progress Europe had entered an era of violence, destruction, fear, and organized hatred. To restore order, confidence, economic stability, and peace demanded statesmanship of a high quality. The task of peacemaking called for realism, a sane estimate of the causes of the strife, an honest acceptance of the motives which moved nations, a clear judgment on the wisdom of the remedies proposed. Unhappily, few of the leaders and fewer still of the citizens in the victor states possessed these rare gifts of heart and mind. The spirit of revenge disguised as self-righteousness and greed masquerading as justice marred the peace settlement in advance.

At least five major misconceptions distorted the program which idealists had drawn up to settle the war-ravaged world. These misconceptions, some ingenuous, some deliberately fostered, all false in part, colored and confused the debates. They must be examined thoughtfully because their cumulative effect was often definitive and sometimes disastrous.

2. MISCONCEPTIONS AND MISCALCULATIONS

The primary misconception which dominated the thought of many millions of people in 1919 was the belief that a few wicked men in high places had planned the war. This was the "conspiracy theory" of war causation, which we have discussed in the preceding chapter. It assumed that certain statesmen, diplomats, and militarists, in collusion with a handful of financiers and industrialists, had plotted the great tragedy. In the course of the fighting, the persistent and effective propaganda of the Allied publicists fastened the dire responsibility for the catastrophe upon the kaiser, the German and Austrian military leaders, and German industrial magnates. Arrogant, irresponsible, and avid for power, these men, it was widely believed, had plunged the world into war to further their own selfish interests.

Such a judgment inevitably raised the question: how could a few malign men come to hold such arbitrary power over the fate of millions? To this question, also, the peoples of the democratic countries believed that they knew the answer, and this was their second misconception. They insisted that the fault lay in the fact that Germany and Austria-Hungary, as conservative monarchies, were subject to autocratic rule. Lacking true democratic traditions and institutions, the peoples of central Europe had been unable to control the army staff and the imperial advisers who shaped the policy of the state. Their governments had been undemocratic and therefore irresponsible. War had come when the autocrats and militarists who planned it considered the moment ripe for the execution of their satanic plans of conquest. In other words, wars were caused by autocrats and militarists who prepared them through secret pacts and understandings.

Against premeditated violence the peace-loving nations, which meant to people in the Allied countries the democratic nations in particular, had of necessity taken some protective measures. But their expenditure for armaments before 1914 proved insufficient. It had required years of effort in the midst of war for them to arm, equip, and train the forces needed to assure victory. The faith that democratic governments always desired peace led to the third major misconception, that if there were no irresponsible autocrats in the world there might be no wars. Woodrow Wilson summarized this deep faith in the common man and in popular government when he issued his ringing declaration that the world must be made "safe for democracy."

Wilson, like millions of his admirers, was deeply and fervently convinced that the world was about to enter a new, more generous, more peaceful, and more democratic era. "The day of conquest and aggrandizement," he proclaimed, "is gone by. So is also the day of secret covenants entered into in the interests of particular governments and likely at some unlooked-for moment to disturb the peace of the world." This was the fourth major misconception. The victors in the First World War were themselves bound by secret commitments which they hesitated to avow, and the peace treaties which terminated the war were drawn up in secret. Conquest and aggrandizement, like militarism, are relative terms. To the defeated nations and to some neutral peoples the democracies appeared militaristic because they had won the war, and their annexation of German colonies by force of arms appeared indistinguishable from conquest and aggrandizement. The world had changed less than the idealists liked to believe.

To safeguard peace in the future and make World War I truly a "war to end war" numerous proposals were offered for the creation of a league of democratic states, the citizens of which would form their governments by self-determination and live at peace with their neighbors, adjusting any disputes by frank and open methods. It was hoped that hatred of war would prove strong enough to persuade all nations, or a controlling majority, to modify their pretensions to absolute sovereignty to the extent of promising to submit all international controversies to a world court and to abide by its decisions. This faith that a world league of states and a world court could preserve peace was the fifth misconception or miscalculation prevalent in 1919.

Idealistic programs can be dangerous when they excite hopes which cannot be realized, for a mood of popular exaltation is certain in such a case to be followed by a sense of disillusionment and betrayal. When the misconceptions of 1919 are summarized, it becomes easy to understand why the war was certain to be followed by disappointment and cynicism. But to understand and interpret a period the student must recognize the faiths which inspired the people living in it. At the height of the war effort millions of people did accept the assertion that a few evil and ambitious leaders had plotted the war; they believed that such misuse of power could occur only in an autocratic regime; they were assured that a democratic nation was a peace-loving nation, that once secret diplomacy and militarism were curbed, war would be curbed also, and that a League of Nations would preserve peace on earth. In the exaltation of a great common struggle, millions of Americans, Englishmen, Frenchmen, and Italians, as well as citizens of the lesser Allied and neutral nations, caught an apocalyptic vision of a world remade. The war, hateful and costly though it proved to be, inspired something like the ardor and expectation of a crusade. The noble intention to build a better world steeled the Allied nations to hold on until victory was certain. The endorsement of their effort and their ideal by the people of the United States was a verdict and a vindication. The encouragement which American aid brought to their faltering morale was as important as the reinforcements which the United States forwarded to second their military efforts.

The subject peoples of Austria-Hungary and even the German socialists and liberals were influenced by the proposals for a fairer world order. They came to hope that if they repudiated the governments which had led them into war they might be welcomed into the society of free nations and be permitted to assist in organizing the League of Nations. By 1918 the faith had become general that a covenant might be drawn up which would assure peace and justice among nations. It was a doctrinaire faith, overwritten with phrases and formulas, a too generous and too credulous belief that political instruments and institutions in and by themselves could remold humanity. But it was, while the mood endured, a living faith. It brought a surge of hope to the European peoples who were stunned and stricken by the war, starved for food, submerged in political chaos by the collapse of the Russian, Austrian, and German imperial regimes. Democratic government and the principle of self-determination appeared a panacea for all their problems, and they had been encouraged to believe that in repudiating their wartime leaders they would escape the penalties of defeat. This miscalculation, which deceived millions in central Europe with a false hope, added to the postwar bitterness, but the Allied spokesmen had intended no deceit. The new, struggling, democratic regimes which appeared in central Europe after 1918 were aided and encouraged by the victor powers. The United States in particular offered generous financial and material aid. The real tragedy lay in the fact that no change in government, no new political tenets or formulas, could resolve the problems of Europe. Economic pressures, class conflicts, national ambitions had been intensified by the war and could not be assuaged.

3. THE VICTORS' PEACE

"The policies of reality and of idealism are at grips," a French journal announced at the opening of January, 1919. Two weeks later the Peace Conference met for its first plenary session. Woodrow Wilson had come to Paris in person as leading delegate for the United States. Knowing the ideals which had stirred the masses in all the belligerent countries, ideals to which he had given such eloquent expression, he

was determined to see the hopes of humanity enshrined in a just settlement. Pitted against him as exponent of the "policies of reality" was
the seventy-nine year old French statesman, Georges Clemenceau, who
had helped to defend Paris against the Prussians in 1870 and had lived
to become president of the French council of ministers in the critical
days of 1917 and 1918. Shrewd, cynical, and disillusioned, Clemenceau
sought but one main guarantee from the peace: security for France
against a future German attack. The third member of the Big Three
was the mercurial Welshman, David Lloyd George, like Clemenceau
the wartime premier of his country, who had steered Britain through
what he later described as a "blood-stained stagger to victory." The
British people re-elected him in December, 1918, and sent him to Paris
to defend their interests, to "hang the kaiser," and to make Germany
pay for the war. Thus Lloyd George came to the Conference with a
definite mandate and the assurance that he had popular support at
home. Clemenceau likewise knew that the French Chamber of Deputies stood behind him, for they voted confidence in his leadership by
398 to 93 on December 29. In contrast, Wilson could no longer feel
assured that the United States Congress would support him, for the
election of November, 1918, had given the Republican Party and
Wilson's opponents control of the Senate and the House of Representatives.

Wilson, Lloyd George, and Clemenceau, with the advice of specialists in all fields with whom they could consult, were the architects of
the Treaty of Versailles. The Italian prime minister, Vittorio Ema-
nuele Orlando, took but a minor part in the discussions, and the Japanese delegates almost none at all. The remainder of the Allied and
Associated Powers shared in the discussions only when their interests
were directly involved; their delegates met with the Big Three on rare
occasions and then by invitation. Much of the preliminary work was
done and some of the sections of the treaty drafted by the fifty-eight
committees and commissions of experts, but all sections were subject
to revision by Wilson, Lloyd George, and Clemenceau.

These three statesmen who framed the Peace of Versailles have been
severely criticized for its deficiencies. The criticism is legitimate in that
they accepted the responsibility of making peace. It may be that they
were too exclusive in their attitude; war concentrates authority and it
is not easy to pass at once to the more leisurely dispersion of power
that is usual in peacetime. It is only just to these leaders to realize the
sense of urgency that drove them on and the limitations and difficulties

under which they worked. No three human beings, however thoughtfully they labored, could have solved the complex and multiple issues
that were referred to the Big Three day after day. They themselves
did not realize how final many of the rapidly phrased decisions would
prove to be. They thought their work was provisory and assumed that
a peace congress would follow the peace conference and review the
preparatory draft. A further point to note in their defense is that they
were not free agents. Each was bound to interpret and as far as possible
to execute the will expressed by a majority in their respective legislatures. They also knew the exalted hopes and expectations which had
stirred the masses and they knew these hopes could not be fully realized. But they dared not disavow either the idealistic aims of the hu-
manitarians or the more selfish program of the nationalists among their
fellow-countrymen lest a revolt of the electorate deprive them of their
mandate.

At every step contrary considerations made a decision difficult.
Overgenerous terms to the defeated nations were certain to rouse criticism from the people in the victorious countries. Overhard terms might
drive the Germans, Austrians, and Hungarians into an alliance with
Soviet Russia. All the statesmen in Paris were harassed by petitioners
and critics, misled by rumors and misrepresentations, exhausted by debates, pressed for time. Inevitably the Big Three compromised, con-
doned, countermanded, and sometimes conceded terms which they
intended to review but forgot as new and more pressing problems
arose. After three or four months the need to end the uncertainty by
proclaiming some sort of settlement, however hasty, to the waiting
world, forced them to conclude their draft, and some of the sections
were thrown together almost as swiftly as a newspaper going to press.
Recommendations from the committees were rushed to the printer.
The Covenant of the League of Nations, composed by Wilson and his
colleagues on the League Commission, was added to the treaty as an
introductory section. Then, before delegates of the minor Allied and
Associated Powers had seen the treaty, the government of the recently
formed German Republic was invited to send delegates to Paris to learn
the terms on which they might have peace.

The haste, the compromises, the provisory nature of the Versailles
treaty, constituted a major weakness in later years when it was under
attack. There can be little question that the proceedings were summary, many of the decisions curt and arbitrary, and the mode of ratification dictatorial. When, on May 6, 1919, the delegates of the Allied

and Associated Powers were called to a plenary session to endorse the terms offered Germany, many of them had seen only a short summary of the 80,000 word document. Only six plenary sessions of the Peace Conference were called between January and June, 1919, and the proceedings at each were formal and almost void of discussion. Despite the wartime denunciations of the evils of secret diplomacy, the condition of the world did not permit open sessions at which all the tangled questions might have been argued. All sovereign states were (theoretically) equal in their rights and privileges. But the realities of the situation overrode theories. With Germany defeated and disarmed, Austria-Hungary dissolved, Russia in revolution and chaos, Italy enfeebled, and Japan remote from European affairs, there were only three powers which remained dominant. The peace was shaped by the representatives of France, Britain, and the United States because these three powers were in a position to do so, and no others were in a position to oppose them.

4. IDEALS AND REALITIES

The settlements imposed upon the defeated states — Germany, Austria, Hungary, Turkey, and Bulgaria — pleased few critics and were destined to provoke years of controversy. This was unavoidable because they were the result of compromises and were shaped in a period of stress, confusion, and bitterness. Many people came to believe that it was the defects in the treaties of 1919–1920 which sowed the seeds for a second world war twenty years later. It would, of course, be more just to say that the treaties were imperfect because they were a compromise between the ideal world society desired by dreamers and the practical, often selfish, demands of over fifty independent sovereign states. As Woodrow Wilson's Fourteen Points summarized most effectively the hopes of the idealists, the fate of the Fourteen Points indicates most clearly the defeat of Wilson's policies.

The first point, "Open covenants, openly arrived at," was disregarded by most of the committees which drew up the peace terms. The deliberations of the Big Three, the labor of the special commissions, and the compromises arranged among the delegates were all pursued in an atmosphere of reticence if not of complete secrecy. It is difficult, however, to see how the diplomats could have proceeded in any other manner without defeating their own intentions. Diplomacy and war both deal with the disputes arising among nations. The maneuvers of the diplomats, like the campaigns of the generals, often depend for their success upon the concealment of objectives, upon actions concerted secretly in advance, upon surprise moves and strategic withdrawals.

The second of the Fourteen Points, "Freedom of the Seas," was set aside before the conference met, largely out of deference to British objections. Point three, the removal of economic barriers, remained an unfulfilled hope, for the treaties created new states in Europe and tariff frontiers were extended instead of being reduced. The fourth point, adequate guarantees of disarmament, was enforced upon the vanquished nations but not carried out by the victors. The German army was reduced to 100,000 men and was deprived of heavy artillery and military aircraft. A belt extending thirty miles beyond the Rhine was demilitarized. The German navy was reduced to six warships with other units in proportion. Equally strict measures of disarmament were drawn up for Austria, Hungary, Bulgaria, and Turkey. These provisions, severe and specific as they were, failed in the outcome to lower European military expenditures or to prevent a renewal of the armament race some years later. The reasons for this failure are discussed in a subsequent chapter.

The fifth point, an impartial adjustment of colonial claims, was defined, before the conference met, as applying only to claims created by the war. Even in this limited sense it was largely overriden and the colonial areas available for distribution were divided among the victors. The sixth point proposed that all Russian territory be evacuated and the Russian people assured that they would be permitted to pursue their political aims without interference. Instead, the Allied governments continued for three years to intervene by force in Russian affairs and to support various anticommunist leaders who harassed the Soviet regime by their insurrections.

Point seven, the evacuation of Belgium by the German forces, was carried out promptly, as well as point eight, the restoration of Alsace and Lorraine to France. Point nine, the readjustment of Italian frontiers "along clearly recognizable lines of nationality," gave rise to a sharp dispute between Wilson and the Italian delegates, Orlando and Sonnino. Before the armistice of November 11, 1918, Wilson had conceded tacitly that Italy had a claim to the Trentino and possibly to Albania. This was in accord with the secret Treaty of London of April, 1915, which had acknowledged the Italian claims to *Italia irredenta*. When it became apparent, however, that the Italians wished to annex areas which would bring half a million Austrians and Yugoslavs under their rule, Wilson appealed to the Italian people over the heads of their leaders. But the nation, strongly nationalistic, rebuffed Wilson's appeal for a fair demarcation and the government at Rome strongly resented the implication that it did not represent the true voice of the people.

Point ten, autonomous development for the peoples of the Austro-Hungarian Empire, meant the dismemberment of that archaic structure. It proved difficult, however, to draw new frontiers which would satisfy the minorities. In the settlement worked out the Slavic peoples were in general accorded the advantage at the expense of the Germans and Magyars. Point eleven, which promised self-determination for the Rumanians, Serbians, and Montenegrins, was achieved in a general and somewhat overgenerous fashion by doubling the size of Rumania and creating a new state, Yugoslavia, to include Serbia, Montenegro, and most of the former provinces of Bosnia and Herzegovina.

Point twelve had proposed a secure sovereignty for the Turkish section of the Ottoman Empire, with self-determination for the subject peoples in the sultan's dominions. This point could be realized only in part, for it contradicted plans which the Allied governments had devised for establishing spheres of influence for themselves in the Arabian peninsula. As a result, the states newly recognized in this area — Lebanon, Syria, Palestine, Transjordania, Iraq, and Saudi Arabia — were regarded as semiprotectorates or mandates, with the French guarding Lebanon and Syria and Great Britain supervising the defense and maintenance of order in the remaining areas.

It should be observed that the Russian Revolution and the separate peace which the Bolshevik leaders concluded with Germany at Brest-Litovsk in March, 1918, canceled the promises made to the czar's government. Russia did not receive control of the Straits nor possession of Constantinople. The defection of Russia likewise made possible a more radical solution of the Polish question. Polish territory held by Germany, Austria-Hungary, and Russia was reunited to form a reborn Polish Republic (point thirteen). This settlement, though easily effected in 1919 when Germany and Russia were weak, was likely to prove precarious when these two powers regained their intrinsic weight in the international system of Europe. The expanded Polish state was sustained by French military ascendency; if French power declined, Polish security was certain to decline with it.

To Wilson and his supporters point fourteen was the most important of all. It proposed the establishment of a League of Nations organized for the preservation of world peace. As chairman of the commission on this league, Wilson helped to draft the covenant and he was eager to see the new experiment launched and its covenant made a fundamental section of all the peace treaties. For he believed the league would prove a court of appeal and a rectifying instrument whereby any errors or injustices implicit in the hastily drawn treaties might later be amended. This hope proved somewhat too sanguine. The league, erected by the victors and enshrined in the "victors' peace," served to maintain the imbalance of that peace rather than to resolve international tensions.

Within a few years it became apparent that the doctrinaire spirit of the League covenant made it an unrealistic document. The views which Wilson and his admirers upheld were couched in admirable phrases but they too often proved inapplicable when pressed down on the obdurate facts. Suggestions for settlements on "clearly recognizable lines of nationality" had a simple and persuasive logic as principles. But the ethnographic patterns of southeastern Europe were hopelessly confused, and no clearly recognizable lines of nationality could be found in many disputed areas. When applied, the formulas of the idealist lost much of their magic.

These formulas, moreover, had a further limitation: they were conceived too exclusively in political terms and they ignored economic realities. Thus, to offer the peoples of the Danube Valley political independence turned the late Hapsburg empire into a patchwork of small states. This created new political frontiers, with attendant tolls and tariff barriers that restricted the flow of trade in an area where communication was already difficult and inadequate. An economic federation of the Danubian states might have solved national grievances better than the attempts to discriminate between the various peoples and to assure each self-determination.

Finally, the principles upon which the League of Nations and the peace treaties were nominally founded were weakened by the fact that they were honored when it suited the makers of the peace to honor them but ignored when it did not. To right an ancient wrong by resurrecting Poland was idealistic but it was dubious statesmanship. Germany and Russia, unrepresented at the Paris Conference, could not be expected to endorse its decrees willingly nor to respect them when a revision of the treaty became possible. Self-determination, however, required that the Poles be granted a large, independent, but vulnerable homeland. Yet the Irish, who had been in rebellion during the war and demanded home rule as vehemently as the Poles, were not permitted to present their case to the conference; and the Egyptian government, which likewise demanded independence, asked for it in vain. There were no clear principles which would resolve all cases, and the attempt to discover and apply such principles exposed the treaty-makers to the charge that, when it suited them, they betrayed the ideals for which the war had been fought.

THE POLITICAL SETTLEMENTS
1919—1920

*Why deceive ourselves? We are making no peace here in Paris.
What is there to make it of? We've really only seen five out of
another thirty years' war. It looks sometimes as if we were drift-
ing into another dark age.*

TASKER H. BLISS

1. THE DISARMAMENT OF GERMANY

PERHAPS no diplomatic congress in European history has been
more promptly and severely assailed than the Paris Peace Conference of 1919. For this harsh criticism neither the policy makers nor
the public were logically to blame: it was an inescapable reaction to
the high expectations and inflated ideals of the war effort. The widespread desire to see a more stable, just, and harmonious world order was
not deep enough to dissolve the rivalries dividing the victors or to repair
the shattered states of Europe. The vanquished nations, permitted no
part in the discussions, and allowed to write no line into the final documents except their signatures, stigmatized the treaty as a *Diktat*, an
imposed decree. It meant little to the Germans that their own generals had dictated still harsher terms to the bewildered Russians a year
earlier. They saw themselves as the victims of a great betrayal and a
great injustice.

Thus the victors found the treaties a disappointment, and the vanquished found them "a mutilation of the fatherland" inspired by "pathological hatred." The terms decreed for Germany as "chief culprit"
were made as specific and severe as if the victors had been dealing with
the Kaiser and his advisers instead of a new government with new
leaders. By the famous "War Guilt Clause" (Article 231) of the Versailles treaty, the delegates of the new Weimar Republic were asked

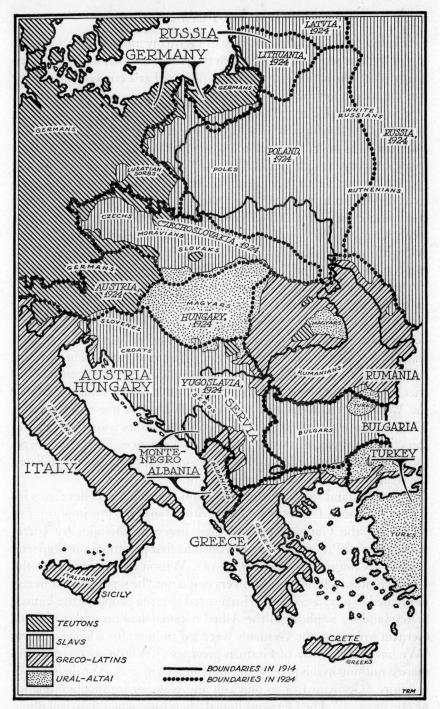

RUSSIA

GERMANY

GERMANS

LATVIA,
1924

LITHUANIA,
1924

GERMANS

WHITE
RUSSIANS

RUSSIA,
1924

POLAND,
1924

POLES

RUTHENIANS

LUSATIAN
SORBS

CZECHS

CZECHOSLOVAKIA, 1924

MORAVIANS

SLOVAKS

GERMANS

AUSTRIA
1924

MAGYARS

MAGYARS

HUNGARY,
1924

SLOVENES

CROATS

RUMANIANS

RUMANIA

AUSTRIA
HUNGARY

YUGOSLAVIA,
1924

SERBS

TURKS

ITALIANS

SERVIA

BULGARS

BULGARIA

MONTE-
NEGRO

ALBANIA

ALBANIANS

TURKEY

ITALY

GREEKS

GREECE

ITALIANS

SICILY

TURKS

CRETE

GREEKS

	TEUTONS
	SLAVS
	GRECO-LATINS
	URAL-ALTAI

BOUNDARIES IN 1914

•••••• BOUNDARIES IN 1924

TRM

NATIONALITIES AND POLITICAL BOUNDARIES IN MIDDLE EUROPE, 1924

to acknowledge "the responsibility of Germany and her allies for causing all the loss and damage to which the Allied and Associated governments and their nationals have been subjected as a consequence of the
war imposed upon them by the aggression of Germany and her allies."

It was inevitable that the inclusion of such a clause in the treaty
would leave a lasting resentment in German hearts. For the Germans
and their allies never accepted the war guilt thesis as justified. The conspiracy theory, which ascribed the war of 1914 to a plot deliberately
formed by the Kaiser and his associates, could not be readily demonstrated. Within a few years after the war ended, historians in many
countries, even in the Allied countries, were distributing the blame
among many leaders in all the capitals of Europe. Thoughtful enquir-
ers, with more and more documents at hand, ceased asking, "Who
caused the war?" and began to ask the more impersonal question,
"What caused the war?" When thus expanded, the question of war
guilt involved numerous factors and reached back many years, so that
it became difficult not to assign some share of the blame to each of the
belligerents. This "revisionist" judgment on the war guilt question
made the penalties imposed upon the defeated nations seem less just,
and within a decade after 1919 many people in the democratic countries, especially in Great Britain and the United States, came to feel that
the Versailles treaty should have embodied a less one-sided verdict.
This change in the mood and opinion of the victors was important because it gave them, as it were, an uneasy conscience. They were therefore confused and divided when, in the 1930's, the Germans repudiated
the treaty provisions and began to rearm.

To understand the German conviction that the Versailles terms involved a breach of faith and a hypocritical betrayal, it is important to
recall that the Germans opened their peace negotiations by corre-
sponding with President Wilson. When he first presented the Fourteen
Points to Congress (January 8, 1918), Wilson had insisted that the
United States and the Allied Powers could not "be separated in interest
or divided in purpose." As he also insisted that the people of the United
States (and by implication the Allied nations) had no wish to impair
German greatness, the Germans were led to hope for a lenient peace.
"We have no jealousy of German greatness," Wilson reiterated, "and
there is nothing in this programme that impairs it. . . . We do not wish
to injure [Germany] or to block in any way her legitimate influence
or power. . . ." The Germans hoped, therefore, when they laid down
their arms, to obtain an assurance in advance that the peace would be

based upon Wilson's Fourteen Points. The British, French, and Italian governments accepted this understanding but they left a loophole by adding that the engagements were "subject to qualifications." They specified, moreover, that they could not accept point two, which guaranteed freedom of the seas, nor promise in advance to ask no indemnities.

Before the armistice was signed on November 11, 1918, the Germans had staged a rebellion, repudiated the Kaiser (who fled to the Netherlands), and overthrown the militarists. They hoped this change of regime would win them a place of equality at the peace table among the democracies, for they replaced the imperial government with a democratic assembly and established the "Weimar Republic" to signalize their conversion. By the terms of the armistice they surrendered their battleships, airplanes, and heavy guns and withdrew their troops from the bridgeheads of the Rhine. Having thus thrown themselves upon the generosity of the victors, they hoped to win a settlement drafted in a spirit of democratic good will at a conference in which their delegates would debate on terms of equality. It was, of course, a proof of political naïveté for them to entertain such hopes. Promises made before a victory, electoral or military, are seldom fulfilled to the letter.

Instead of participating in the settlement of an easy peace the Germans were presented with a treaty which, as they saw it, stripped, shamed, and pilloried them. A proud nation does not willingly accept nor long endure a sentence of shame, and the accumulating pressure of deep national resentment in Germany was a predictable result. The map on page 189 indicates how full of controversy the boundaries of the new German Reich were likely to prove. To assure Poland an outlet to the sea, East Prussia was separated from the remainder of Germany by a "corridor" which extended to the city of Danzig on the Baltic. Danzig itself was made a Free City under the protection of the League of Nations. The problem of passports, tariffs, and customs for passengers and goods crossing or traversing the corridor was certain to excite controversy. A further source of friction was the fact that the boundary lines dividing Poland from the Reich were drawn in a manner to favor the Poles, and some disputed areas where the plebiscites indicated a German majority were assigned to Poland. As the population of the towns was often predominantly German and that of the surrounding countryside predominantly Polish, it is obvious no simple line of division could have been drawn. An exchange of minority elements offered the only certain means of placing all citizens who considered themselves Poles on one side of a line and all who called themselves German on the other. This solution was not widely invoked in 1919, and even if it had been it could not have anticipated all ethnic confusion. Patriotism is an exceedingly complex emotion, in eastern Europe especially so, and there were inhabitants in the disputed areas who were ashamed to avow themselves Germans in the midst of defeat after 1918 but proud to do so when Hitler was dictating to Europe in 1939.

The boundaries drawn for the new state of Czechoslovakia were decided in part by the need to give the Czechs a defensible frontier against Germany. To assure this, the line was fixed at the horseshoe curve through the Bohemian Forest and the Erz and Sudetes Mountains. This meant, as the map suggests, that the western end of the long and narrow state of Czechoslovakia was thrust into the Reich with Germans half-circling it from Silesia to Austria. It also meant that some three million Germans, former subjects of Austria-Hungary, were included as a fretful minority in the Czechoslovak Republic, a minority which proved a Trojan horse and was destined twenty years later to bring about the downfall of the republic. Point ten, of the Fourteen Points, had promised the peoples of Austria-Hungary the freest opportunity of autonomous development. But, as in the case of Poland, no line could be drawn which would separate the various peoples unequivocally and leave no dissatisfied remnants on one or both sides of the new frontiers.

The return to French control of the "lost provinces" of Alsace and Lorraine, which had been annexed to the new German Empire after the defeat of France in 1870–1871, was regarded as the righting of a wrong and was accepted by the Germans without undue resentment. But the assignment of the districts of Eupen and Malmédy to Belgium, and the return of the northern third of Schleswig to Denmark, after a popular vote of the inhabitants, stung German pride. In general, however, these redrawn borders on the west and north of the Reich left no open wounds, and the German government in 1925 voluntarily acknowledged and guaranteed the frontiers fixed by the Versailles treaty between Germany and Belgium and Germany and France. This guarantee was never extended to the frontiers of Germany in the east, however. There the status of all political boundaries had been provisory and unstable for centuries, and the settlement of 1919 was almost certain to be challenged as soon as Germany or Russia, or both together, was strong enough to refashion it.

One mutilation of territory which the Germans would have found most difficult to endure, they were spared. At the peace table the French demanded the cession of the left bank of the Rhine so that a Rhine Republic might be formed to serve as a buffer state between Germany and France. Woodrow Wilson and Lloyd George fought the proposal vigorously; it would, they insisted, create a new irredentist problem more threatening to European harmony than Alsace-Lorraine under German control had proved to be. In the outcome the French were persuaded, most reluctantly, to accept a compromise. The left bank of the Rhine and the bridgeheads on the right bank were to be occupied by Allied forces for fifteen years, and the Saar Valley was to be detached and administered as an independent unit for the same period. The motive for this last provision was economic rather than political. The Saar coal reserves were equal to those of the whole of France, and these mines were to be open to French exploitation during the period of League administration.

French military advisers had urged the creation of a Rhine Republic because they believed such a barrier indispensable if France with 40,-000,000 people was to be safe from Germany with 70,000,000. In 1919 the fear expressed by the French that they would be attacked by a revived Germany appeared excessive to most British and American observers. Henry White, a member of the United States delegation, commented on the French dread of the future. "It is impossible," he wrote from Paris in March, 1919, "to comprehend the extraordinary obsession felt in this country lest Germany within the next few years repeat the actions which she took in 1914." To dispel this "extraordinary obsession" and provide France with a substitute guarantee in place of a neutralized Rhine Republic, the British and American delegates proposed a treaty of mutual aid. Great Britain and the United States were to support France if Germany ever became a threat. Woodrow Wilson approved this accord, but the United States Senate failed to ratify it. The British, on the ground that the American rejection nullified the agreement, likewise let it lapse. The French not unnaturally came to feel that they had surrendered a substantial barrier for a paper promise and had emerged with neither. When the passing years proved the French dread of Germany to be well founded, Frenchmen looked back with increased bitterness to this betrayal, or at least desertion, by their allies.

All the former German colonies, treaty ports, trade concessions in backward countries, foreign investments, merchant ships, undersea cables, and even patents registered in enemy states, which the victor powers had been able to seize during hostilities, were confiscated without return or compensation. A German proposal that the colonies and other property thus obtained should be assessed at a reasonable valuation, and the total credited to Germany as reparations paid, was rejected. The German lease on Kiaochow and economic privileges in Shantung as well as the German title to a number of Pacific islands north of the equator were transferred to Japan. German Pacific islands south of the equator were assigned to Australia, with the exception of German Samoa which went to New Zealand. The Union of South Africa acquired German South West Africa. Great Britain took over German East Africa and divided with France the Cameroon and Togoland territories which the Reich had held in 1914.

In all, Germany ceded 25,000 square miles of territory in Europe, with a population of some 6,000,000; and 1,000,000 square miles overseas, with 12,000,000 inhabitants. But this loss of land and population was only part of the German forfeit. There were also heavy economic penalties which will be listed in the following chapter.

2. THE DISMEMBERMENT OF AUSTRIA-HUNGARY

In drafting terms for the Germans the Allied statesmen had to disarm and discipline a powerful nation. In settling the affairs of Austria-Hungary they were the self-appointed executors of an empire which had ceased to exist. Before 1914, as already explained in Chapter VII, the discontent stirring the national minorities within the Hapsburg Empire threatened to split it apart. The First World War had speeded the process of dissolution, and the Hapsburg dynasty as a unifying influence practically died with the aged Francis Joseph in 1916. His successor, Charles I (1916–1918), inherited a crumbling state. Whole regiments of drafted Slavic troops were deserting to the Russians, and hostility towards the two ruling groups of the empire, the Germans in Austria and the Magyars in Hungary, deepened with defeat and hardship.

As the less unified, less prosperous, and less industrialized of the two Central Powers, Austria-Hungary had followed the German lead throughout the war. But the Austrian forces had suffered even heavier losses than the Germans and the misery mounted steadily. Realizing the exhausted state of his realm, the new emperor determined to act without fully informing his stronger ally, and he opened secret negotiations for peace. The French foreign office responded to the half-official overtures and secured a letter from Charles in which he agreed to use his influence with Germany to support the "just French claims to Alsace-Lorraine." After the negotiations miscarried, the French premier, Clemenceau, published Charles's indiscreet communication, discrediting the emperor with the Germans and with many of his own subjects, who felt he had conceded too much. A lame disavowal of the whole affair, issued from Vienna, convinced no one, and distrust and discouragement grew in the Austrian capital. By 1918 the empire on the Danube was little more than a shell, the defeats of that year shattered it, and in October the empire fell apart after the government had sent out by radio a futile plea for peace. When fighting ceased in November, 1918, there was no longer any central government in Austria-Hungary with which the Allied powers could treat. Partly for this reason, partly because the desire to deal with Germany was more imperative, the Allies waited nearly a year before completing their terms for what remained of Austria and of Hungary.

By these terms the once proud empire of Austria shrank to a third-class state which still bore the name Austria and contained the capital, Vienna. The Treaty of St. Germain, signed in September, 1919, limited the Austrian Germans to this small, landlocked state, 32,000 square miles in area, with a population of 6,500,000, one-third of the people being concentrated in the capital. The Austrians asked permission to unite with Germany, realizing that it would be difficult for their state to exist as a political unit under postwar conditions. But the request was denied. There were, it appeared, strict limits to the principle of self-determination. When the application of this principle promised to augment the population and power of Germany, it was not acceptable to the Allied statesmen who had made it a winning slogan in the war.

Hungary, likewise, became a third-class state, its fate being settled by the Treaty of the Trianon (June, 1920). Three-fourths of the area which had constituted the kingdom of Hungary under the Hapsburgs was assigned to form new states or to enlarge neighbors. On the north, Czechoslovakia was erected as an independent republic. Provinces which the Hapsburgs had ruled since the partition treaties of the eighteenth century were restored to the reconstituted Polish state. The humiliation of Austria proved a boon to Serbia: it was linked to Montenegro, enlarged by the addition of the greater part of Bosnia and Herzegovina and a slice of Bulgaria, and emerged as the kingdom of Yugoslavia. Another fortunate beneficiary of the new apportionment was Rumania which doubled in size, receiving a segment of territory from the late Hungarian realm which matched the area left to the Hungarians themselves. As the Allied powers and the new succession states opposed the restoration of Charles or any other Hapsburg to the throne at Budapest, Hungary remained a kingdom without a king, ruled in the interim by Nicholas Horthy, an admiral without a navy.

With this dissection of Austria-Hungary the Danube Valley lost what political unity it had known while the Hapsburgs ruled. The new frontiers, the deepening of national jealousy, the tariffs, and the constriction of economic life condemned the region to an era of disorder and instability. The new states, patterned according to the ethnical, linguistic, or cultural traditions of the inhabitants, were economic misfits. Their tariff policies and frontier tolls hindered the free exchange of goods. Projects for a Danubian federation to adjust the evils of the situation failed to win acceptance. The low standard of living, especially in the agrarian regions, made agitation easy and politics violent. French influence was paramount in the area immediately after the peace. But the fact that the French did not need the largely agrarian products of the Balkan states and a reviving German economy did, promised to create stresses and strains in the future if Paris pulled one way and Berlin another. For some years, however, the Balkan area remained heaving and uncertain, the final results which would emerge from the shattering of Austria-Hungary still undisclosed. It was as if a planet had exploded in a crowded system; for the time being the fragments continued to group themselves loosely before they were drawn into the field of a larger neighbor. France was too remote to exercise a strong attraction. The ultimate consequence of the dismemberment of Austria-Hungary would not become clear until a revived Germany and a reconstructed Russia clashed and the victor extended a quasi-protectorate over this critical region.

3. POLAND, RUSSIA, AND THE BALTIC STATES

Between 1772 and 1795 Poland disappeared from the map of Europe, partitioned among Austria, Prussia, and Russia. It is of importance to note that the second and third partitioning, in 1792 and 1795, occurred while France was rent by revolution and unable to aid the Poles or to claim reciprocal compensation for the gains made by the Eastern powers. Napoleon I at the height of his career promised the Poles a partial restoration of their fatherland, and Napoleon III encouraged the hopes of Polish patriots. The British likewise, although they did not interfere directly in eastern European affairs, were generally sympathetic

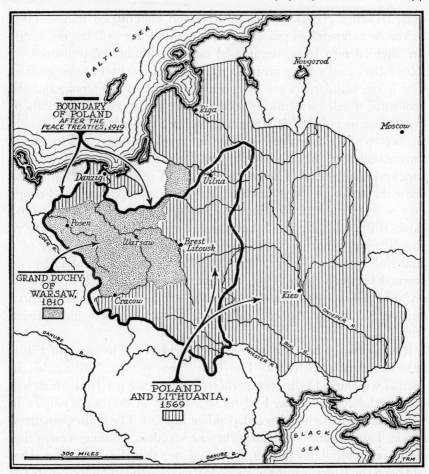

THE FLUID FRONTIERS OF POLAND

towards Polish ambitions. But the three empires, Austria-Hungary, Germany, and Russia, which were co-sharers of the extinct kingdom's territory, had in consequence one point in common in their foreign policies: all were opposed to a revival of Polish nationalism.

In 1918, with Germany defeated, Austria-Hungary shattered, and czarist Russia dissolved in revolution, the restoration of Poland became a possibility, for all effective opposition had for the moment been nullified. It is not surprising, therefore, that Poland reappeared on the map, reconstituted as a state of 140,000 square miles with a population of 30,000,000. By these measurements Poland was a second-class power. But the weaknesses which had undone the ill-fated country in the eighteenth century had not been cured. Poland lacked defensible frontiers, lacked a powerful, progressive, and enlightened middle class, lacked an independent peasantry. The country was still largely agrarian, divided into large, semifeudal estates without the industrial resources to equip a large army or the financial resources to support it. The living standards were low, the people largely illiterate, and the problems of self-government too complex for an electorate without experience in political affairs or democratic procedure. The French, anxious to ally themselves with all the succession states and to pledge a maintenance of the peace settlement, offered the Poles a military alliance and financial aid. The government at Warsaw accepted both and knew that so long as the French army was the most powerful in Europe they were protected. But they were not powerful enough to stand alone. If France failed them they would have to look to Germany or to Russia, and memories of their tragic past brought forebodings of a doubtful future. If Germany and Russia revived, Poland might be crushed between them. The premonitions were justified. Proclaimed on November 8, 1918, the new Poland was to be overwhelmed twenty-one years later by the concerted advance of German and Russian armies.

Russia was the heaviest loser after World War I in terms of European territory transferred. The Rumanians occupied Bessarabia in 1919. Two-thirds of the reconstructed Polish state was land which had been under Russian rule. Finland seceded from the czar's empire in 1917 and was recognized as independent in 1920. The Baltic provinces, Latvia, Estonia, and Lithuania, likewise seceded, winning recognition as sovereign republics (1921). The total area thus detached from what had been the Russian Empire exceeded 300,000 square miles, an area as large as Spain and Italy combined, with a total population of 25,000,-000. These extensive losses were suffered while Russia was exhausted from the war and racked by revolution. It was almost certain that the Russians would favor some revision of these forced concessions as soon as their country recovered unity and vigor. This reassertion of Russian power, when it came, proved as irresistible as the turning of a tide. Within twenty-two years, as subsequent chapters will show, all the lost areas save Finland had been reincorporated into the Russian system and a part of Finland reconquered. (See Chapter XXXIII.)

The succession states, Estonia, Latvia, and Lithuania, during the interval of their independence established regimes based on democratic and republican forms. Estonia, northernmost of the three, is a peninsula lying between the Gulf of Finland and the Gulf of Riga. Its in-

Ewing Galloway

THE GERMAN DELEGATES SIGNING THE TREATY OF VERSAILLES,
AS PAINTED BY SIR WILLIAM ORPEN

BRITISH WARSHIPS IN HONG KONG HARBOR

dependence was recognized by the Soviet government in a treaty of 1920, and the boundaries enclosed an area of 18,353 square miles with a population slightly over one million. Latvia, below Estonia, had a land area almost equal (20,056 squares miles) but a population of nearly two million. It was recognized as independent by the Soviet government in 1920. Lithuania, which likewise obtained recognition of its sovereignty from the Soviet government in 1920, had less success in clarifying its boundaries than its neighbor republics. The Lithuanians claimed an area over 31,000 square miles, with a population of some three million, but the Poles retained nearly one-third of this territory.

In Finland the House of Representatives proclaimed the country an independent sovereign state on December 6, 1917, and a republican constitution was formally adopted on July 17, 1919. Finnish independence was recognized by the Russian revolutionary government on January 9, 1918. The land area of the country (excluding lakes) was 132,589 square miles and the population (1920) 3,364,807.

World War I ended the rule of three famous European dynasties, the Romanovs, the Hohenzollerns, and the Hapsburgs. In the states carved from territories which Nicholas II, William II, and Francis Joseph I had ruled, the favored form of government after 1918 was a republic. Save for Hungary, a kingdom without a king, and the royal houses of Rumania and Yugoslavia (Serbia), the new or reconstructed states of central and eastern Europe formed governments which were democratic and republican in form. But constitutional guarantees do not by themselves make a democracy nor assure representative rule. Strong democratic traditions were lacking. The new statesmen had little or no experience with the complexities of popular government. The electors were untrained in the responsibilities of political initiative. The administrative officials available had nearly all received their training under autocratic monarchies. Fear of a monarchist *coup* or the emergence of a military dictator led the framers of the new constitutions to make the executive office subordinate and secondary. This had the effect of shifting the center of power into the hands of the legislature — or its leaders, since several hundred men cannot well exercise power jointly. The legislators, unused to the checks and balances of a representative system, too often surrendered the power delegated to them by the electors to a cabinet which they could not control, and once in office the ministers tended to assume almost unlimited authority. As all the new constitutions contained clauses which permitted a cabinet to issue "emergency" decrees, and the inexperienced legislators and newly organized law courts were seldom certain how to challenge such decrees, the regimes could very easily be transformed into more or less popular dictatorships. This was especially true in countries where economic ills and deep grievances made the populace responsive to dramatic appeals and drastic measures. Several of the succession states — Poland and Rumania in particular — never really developed representative institutions. The parliaments were a screen behind which a few powerful leaders manipulated the elections, the press, the courts, and the army. But this truth was not readily apparent to the people of the older democracies, to the French, the British, and especially to the Americans. They were, in consequence, unprepared for the rapid revival of dictatorships in Europe, which gained momentum after the economic collapse of 1929.

4. THE END OF THE OTTOMAN EMPIRE

The empire over which the sultans at Constantinople claimed to rule had been shrinking for several centuries before the First World War finally shattered it. All North Africa — Morocco, Algeria, Tunis, Tripoli, and Egypt — had already been detached by 1914 and in Europe the sultan had forfeited all his Balkan provinces except a small area around Constantinople. But so long as the Turkish government controlled the Straits, and claimed the Arabian peninsula with its strategic ports on the Mediterranean, the Red Sea, the Indian Ocean, and the Persian Gulf, Turkey was a power in the Near East despite the backwardness of the people and the corruption and inefficiency of the government.

When Turkey joined Germany in 1914 the broad Arabian lands, one-third the size of the United States in area, were exposed to Allied attack. The British and French encouraged the subject peoples of Asia Minor to revolt against Turkish misrule and supplied bands of insurgent Arabs with arms and money. In secret compacts, Britain, France, Italy, and Russia arranged to partition the sultan's realm among themselves after the war but the withdrawal of Russia and the feebleness of Italy canceled this plan. The defeat of the Turks and the completeness of the Allied victory permitted the peacemakers to divide Asia Minor into half a dozen states under French or British protection. Syria became a French mandate. In Palestine a national home was founded for the Jewish people, with Great Britain as the mandatory power. Transjordania, the Hedjaz, and Iraq were erected into independent Arab states with Britain as protector.

Had Russia remained in the war and shared in the Allied victory, the Russian diplomats might have insisted upon the control of Constantinople and the Straits, which had been promised to them. But Soviet Russia, beset by foes and rent by civil war, was in no position in 1919 to collect on czarist claims and had forsworn imperialist ambitions of conquest for the moment at least. The British were therefore left in a dominant role but they soon discovered that they had assumed heavy and perplexing responsibilities. The Mediterranean was the "life line" of their empire and it was a cardinal maxim of British policy that the Suez Canal and the Red Sea route to India must be safeguarded. But a spirit of independence was stirring the Arab peoples and they were not willing to exchange Turkish sovereignty for British supremacy. In Egypt, Iraq, and Saudi Arabia, movements aiming at complete independence for the native peoples gained rapid headway. In Palestine the attempt to honor the Balfour Declaration of 1917, wherein the British government had promised to establish there a national home for the Jewish people, led to a state of civil war between the local Arab population and the Jewish immigrants. As the British had many millions of Moslem subjects in their empire, they did not wish to antagonize them by dispossessing the Moslems in Palestine. They were therefore driven to restrict the area open to Jews in Palestine and to limit the quota of immigrants. For this they were assailed in turn by ardent Zionists throughout the world.

The sultan at Constantinople accepted the Treaty of Sèvres which dismembered his empire and Turkey became a small state limited to the Anatolian headland. But the defeat and humiliation stirred the nation to revolt, and a powerful reform party headed by an able army officer, Kemal Ataturk, deposed the sultan and set up a republic (1923). The vigorous attempts made to energize and modernize the Turkish people after 1919 will be outlined later. (See Chapter XLV.)

THE ECONOMIC SETTLEMENTS

The time has now come for a heavy reckoning of the accounts.
You have asked for peace. We are prepared to offer you peace.

GEORGES CLEMENCEAU
TO THE GERMAN DELEGATES MAY 7, 1919

1. THE REPARATIONS BILL

IN the midst of the First World War President Wilson affirmed that the democracies, when victory crowned their efforts, would not seek to impose any "punitive damages" upon their defeated foes. David Lloyd George, wartime prime minister of Great Britain, asserted that the British for their part did not favor the infliction of a war indemnity. These unmercenary avowals, however, were wartime statements. The complete collapse of the Central Powers put the unselfishness of the Allied nations to a crucial test, for it left the victors in a position to demand extensive compensations. The British, French, Belgian, and Italian people, many of whom had suffered losses through the air raids and submarine toll or more directly through the wastage of the battlefield, insisted that reparations must be collected. It should be remembered that all the people in the Allied and Associated nations had been studiously indoctrinated with the argument that the Central Powers had plotted the war and waged it with the deliberate intention of destroying their neighbors. In these circumstances reparations appeared logical and just.

The Allied governments therefore sought a formula which would reconcile their earlier assertion that they sought no military indemnities with the later decision that they could and must collect reparations. They solved the contradiction by stipulating at the time of the armistice that the defeated nations must make compensation "for all damage done to the civilian population of the Allies and their property by the aggression of Germany by land, by sea, or from the air." This qualification left them at liberty to assess Germany and her allies an indefinite sum calculated on the value of civilian property destroyed through enemy action during four years of war. In effect it was equivalent to substituting the phrase "reparations for civilian damages" for the phrase "military indemnity."

The Allied peoples believed reparations justified not only as a reasonable compensation for wanton damage but as a warning to any nation which might be disposed to wage aggressive war in the future. It was thought advisable to impress upon the Germans in particular and also upon the Austrians, Hungarians, Bulgarians, and Turks, the fact that nations which allowed their governments to violate humane principles and international obligations would be brought to justice by an international verdict supported by all peace-loving peoples. Such a lesson, it was hoped, would provide a salutary deterrent to any nation which might develop aggressive inclinations later.

In the case of the Germans such reasoning proved faulty. The war had already cost them heavily. If additional penalties and sacrifices could have counteracted all will for militarism and conquest, the terms of the "Carthaginian Peace" should have done so, for these terms were heavy and they were intended to remind the offenders of their misdeeds and to keep reminding them for decades to come. But unfortunately the corrective effect of the penalties miscarried. The Germans considered the penalties undeserved and therefore unjust. The whole nation felt humiliated and embittered. So deeply did they resent the accusation of guilt which they had been forced to acknowledge before the world, that the determination to reverse the verdict of 1918 became a national aspiration. After the first mood of defeat and discouragement ebbed, the German people came slowly but decidedly to the conclusion that their mistake lay not in having waged a war but in having lost it. From that point a number, especially of younger Germans, went on to the conclusion that the way to reverse the ignominious verdict of Versailles was to wage a second war and win it. This idea was not so much a logical and conscious reaction to events as a psychological and subconscious rebellion. The sense of mortification, the indignation burning in German hearts, prepared the nation for a sudden upsurge of chauvinism. Leaders with the temerity to stimulate and capitalize upon this defiant and recalcitrant mood were certain to appear at the appropriate moment. This reaction might have been forecast in 1919. The French did in fact foresee and fear it, but it did not prevent the Allied governments from deluding themselves that they might collect reparations from a presumably docile Germany until

1980. The generation which had made the war was to pay for it throughout the remainder of the century, unless Germany rebelled.

There seemed good reason to believe in 1919 that the German nation could pay substantial reparations for damage done. How much it could pay, the more cautious economists hesitated to predict. Some optimistic British statisticians estimated the total at $100,000,000,000; some set it even higher. Accordingly, the various commissions appointed to collect claims for civilians' injuries inflated their lists, adding charges for property destroyed by fire, shells, air raids, and ship losses, for mines flooded, bridges blown up, farms gutted, orchards slashed, and cattle slain. The sum quickly rose to astronomical figures. Some items not easy to justify under the head of civilian damages were inserted none the less as pensions for soldiers and their dependents; and the loans contracted by Belgium as well as the military expenditures of the Belgian government from 1914 to 1918 were also included. To complete the reparations bill on these extended lines demanded much listing and itemizing, and the compilation seemed likely to take considerable time. In the interim the Germans and their allies were ordered to commence payments in the form of tangible assets.

Protests that Germany was ruined by war and in no condition to meet heavy charges were weighed by the Allied economists. They found that the German government had expended the equivalent of $40,000,000,000 in waging war and that nearly 2,000,000 Germans had perished as war casualties. The health of the nation had been reduced because war economy and the Allied blockade had caused a shortage of essential foods, especially fats, and a deficiency of many raw materials. Before 1914 the wealth of Germany had been rising rapidly because of the highly efficient industrial development. But the armistice and treaty terms deprived Germany of two-fifths of her coal and nearly two-thirds of her iron ore supply, a serious blow to an industrial nation. The treaty also detached one-tenth of the German factories and confiscated the German colonies, foreign investments, commercial concessions, and all merchant ships over 1600 tons. It was possible, however, for Germany to commence some forms of payment immediately, and the nation was ordered to surrender gold and goods to the value of $5,000,000,000 before May 1, 1921. As an initial payment, 250,000 farm animals — horses, cattle, sheep, swine, and goats — were to be transshipped; some millions of tons of coal; up to half the reserves of drugs and chemicals; building materials of all types; locomotives, coaches, and freight cars; industrial machinery, minerals, fertilizer — the list was long and could be lengthened indefinitely. The Allied claims, it appeared, would be limited only by the capacity and willingness of the defeated nations to produce and turn over the materials demanded.

The total reparations bill had not yet been completed when the treaty was laid before the delegates of the German Republic in Paris on May 7, 1919. The failure to mention a specific sum at this time was possibly a tactical, or at least a psychological, error. It left the Germans apprehensive but still hopeful that they might clear off the burden of reparations quickly, as France had cleared off the billion dollar indemnity imposed by the victorious Prussians in 1871. When, two years after Versailles, the Germans finally learned the national mortgage they had assumed in signing the treaty, they were appalled and indignant at the total. After much preliminary debate, the experts had reached a compromise on the calculation of German wealth, the maximum annual payments which might be expected, the mode of transfer, and the final sum with interest charges. In April, 1921, they announced the total: it had been fixed at $31,500,000,000. This did not represent an exact accounting; many items were so confused, many lists so detailed, that they had resisted analysis; but the members of the Commission finally compromised among suggested totals and announced the sum indicated. A schedule of payments had likewise been prepared, calling for the first billion dollars within twenty-five days. If the Germans failed to pay, the Treaty of Versailles provided for penalties, including possible occupation of territory in addition to that already held for military security, the seizure of state property, the diversion of taxes, customs revenue, and other assets of the Reich, and a charge against public utilities and other property owned by the component states and municipalities. The possibility of further assessments and even further increases in the total was not ruled out, and military pressure by the Allied armies of occupation was to be a reserve weapon that would be applied if the Germans failed to meet their obligations under the treaty. Unforeseen developments had already been covered by a blanket clause of the treaty which declared that "all matters relating to the occupation and not provided for by the present Treaty shall be regulated by subsequent agreements, which Germany hereby undertakes to observe." The delegates of the Weimar Republic who signed at Versailles had no logical authority thus to promise in advance that subsequent governments would observe the terms of agreements which had not yet been devised. It is not altogether surprising that

German youths, reading the Treaty of Versailles in later years, came to think of the Weimar regime as a weak and shameful administration which had mortgaged the rights and liberties of the nation throughout future generations.

2. INTERGOVERNMENTAL DEBTS

To the nations which had suffered from a German invasion, especially to the French, the payment of reparations was simple justice, and they looked upon the settlement with the rigidity of a creditor who has been awarded damages against a criminal and evasive defendant. World War I, which the French believed they had done nothing to cause, cost their government an estimated $26,000,000,000. The devastation wrought in the invaded areas added to this a $20,000,000,000 bill for reconstruction. The Allies, recognizing that the republic had borne an excessive share of the common effort and the common destruction, agreed to allot to France 52 per cent of the expected payments from Germany. By the same arrangement, negotiated in 1920, the British Empire was to receive 22 per cent, Italy 10 per cent, Belgium 8 per cent, and the remaining Allied and Associated powers 8 per cent among them. As the Belgians felt and usually voted with the French on the reparations issue, the two shared a 60 per cent equity in the expected payments and were therefore, quite understandably, the most urgently aroused and the most insistent upon reprisals when the payments were in default.

The problem of international debts was one of the most involved problems intensified by the war. It had two sides: the reparations account with all its bitter implications, and the question of intergovernmental loans covering all the credits advanced to one another by the Allied powers. These two phases of international finance had no direct relation to one another, but despite their separate origins they tended to become opposite sides of the same coin, and a swiftly depreciating coin at that. War in the twentieth century had proved so ruinously expensive that the financial reserves of Russia, France, Italy, and Great Britain had become exhausted in turn and by 1917 the United States was the chief source of credit. After the fighting ceased in 1918 the United States continued to make advances to foreign states, largely to aid the program of postwar reconstruction. By 1924 the total obligations owed to the United States by other governments was over $12,000,000,000. Britain, which owed $4,454,000,000 of this sum, was the leading debtor. But Britain was also a creditor; France alone owed her almost $7,000,000,000. Other countries in turn owed France an even larger total, although most of these debts had become mere figures in a ledger. Like the billions of francs which the French had advanced to the imperial government of Russia before its collapse, these loans were uncollectible and some had been frankly repudiated.

The British government proposed that the situation might be clarified by an all-round cancellation. The British were primarily interested in a return to normal trading relations because their prosperity depended so largely on a healthy international trade and they feared that a debt deadlock might delay the trade revival. But the proposal for cancellation was unacceptable to the United States. This government had no equivalent debts outstanding to match the $12,000,000,000 credits owing, and the loss incurred through wiping out the debts would have fallen too largely upon the American taxpayer.

Consequently all the debtor nations (except Soviet Russia) worked out agreements between 1921 and 1930 for refunding and repaying their debts, agreements which brought some order into the bookkeeping but did not assure the execution of the terms arranged. As the chief creditor nation the United States took the lead, concluding over a dozen funding agreements between 1922 and 1926. It was obvious that regardless of the amounts involved some states were in a better condition to pay than others. The American negotiators made allowance for this fact and sought to adjust the ultimate burden to the debtors' capacity to pay. Interest rates were scaled down and the period for repayment extended to sixty-two years, but the principles, both on wartime loans to Allies and on postwar loans for reconstruction, were maintained and added together. The settlement with Britain involved the largest total, amounting to $4,600,000,000 at 3.3 per cent interest. The French debt came next, being funded at $4,025,000,000, but for France the average interest rate was cut to 1.8 per cent. Italy received an especially low rate of 0.4 per cent on a funded debt of $2,042,000,000. These three accounts comprised 92 per cent of the total of $11,671,400,000 in funded debts owed to the United States by Allied or neutral or ex-enemy countries; but as payments and interest soon fell in arrears, the sum owed or in default grew steadily. The British government, which received the least generous concessions in the refunding, made the most earnest efforts to meet the annual payments and repaid a larger share of its debts than France or Italy. But the problem of repayment was increased by the refusal of the United States to accept payment in goods. American producers were alarmed lest foreign nations, needing United States dollars to pay their debts to the United States treasury, would pour floods of low-priced merchandise into the American market. To prevent such competition, Congress was urged to protect the American standard of living by raising the protective tariffs and the Fordney-McCumber Tariff Act of 1922 established the highest rates hitherto tolerated in American history. Unable to ship in sufficient goods or obtain dollars by other means the debtor countries made part payment in gold and silver, but the limited amount of bullion in the world and the fact that more than half the monetary gold had accumulated in the United States made this method impracticable also.

The stand taken by the United States on debt collection decided the British attitude. When Congress made it clear that the debts must be honored, the British negotiated with their debtors in turn, for Britain was likewise a creditor country with some $10,000,000,000 outstanding. This was more than twice the sum she owed the United States, but nine-tenths of the British advances were never collected. To their debtors the British explained that they would base their scale for refunding on the scale set by the United States and if the United States canceled debts Britain would do the same. This was a shrewd policy because they knew that their debtors would almost certainly default, whereas they themselves took their own debt more seriously. After 1930 a general cessation of payments, or universal default, brought into effect something which resembled the original British plan for all-round cancellation. But by that time Great Britain had paid out nearly $250,000,000 more to the United States than the British treasury had received from German reparations and loan repayments combined.

The British reaction to the American stand was adroit but somewhat embarrassing to the United States. For the British repeated that Britain would assess her debtors in proportion to American demands and would reduce the obligations other Allied nations owed in London as soon as the United States reduced the obligations Britain owed in Washington. In effect, this threw the onus of exacting payment upon the American people, and Uncle Sam began to appear in the hostile sections of the European journals as Uncle Shylock. But the United States government still declined to cancel the debts outright, although the foreign loans were refunded at a lower rate of interest and the period for repayment extended. The debtor nations, moreover, found a further argument to justify or attempt to justify a delay in their repayments. It was almost inevitable that, as Germany fell behind on the scheduled reparations transfers, the French and British would insist they could not pay the United States until the Germans paid them. The Germans were thus disposed to see the United States as the ultimate beneficiary and therefore as the ultimate assessor forcing indemnities from them. Despite the idealism and generosity of the American war effort, the vanquished as well as the victor nations, envious of the extraordinary American prosperity of the 1920's, came to see the United States as an opulent power too greedy to forgive battle-racked and impoverished peoples their unequal burden of debt. For the American people the debt controversy was a long lesson in disillusionment which increased their inclination after 1919 to avoid any new entanglement in European quarrels.

3. GERMANY IN DEFAULT

The hardening stand of the United States incited the British, French, Belgians, and Italians to adopt a harsher attitude towards Germany. In April, 1921, the Reparations Commission announced that the total which the Germans must pay over the years would be at least $31,500,-000,000. The immediate effect of this drastic assessment was a depreciation of German currency, a fall in revenue, and a partial default on the preliminary reparations payments already due. In 1922 the Mark (the German monetary unit) continued to decline on the international exchange, and Germany again failed to furnish the stipulated payments in cash, coal, materials, and labor. On January 9, 1923, the Reparations Commission formally announced that Germany was again in default. French and Belgian troops thereupon marched into the Ruhr Valley, the most highly industrialized section of Germany, to enforce the methods of direct action or "sanctions" which the Treaty had prescribed to cover such an eventuality.

Disarmed and demilitarized, the Germans could not fight back actively but they resisted by a passive strike. Business halted in the occupied areas; the mood of noncooperation stiffened throughout all Germany; in the months of enervating deadlock which followed, credit collapsed in a bottomless sea of inflation and the Mark depreciated until it became valueless. All Europe felt the dislocation, the economic life of the Continent was threatened with chaos, and even the French franc lost 25 per cent of its value. Pressure had not solved the problem. At the close of 1923, therefore, the Reparations Commission appointed committees to consider a new program. Accepted in 1924 and known as the "Dawes Plan" because of the active participation of the American delegate, Charles Gates Dawes, in devising it, the new plan offered a way out of the impasse. The German currency was to be stabilized, German industry was to be revitalized (with the aid of a $200,000,000 foreign loan), and the reparations payments were to be reduced temporarily to $250,000,000 a year. Under this schedule the Germans paid nearly two billion dollars in the next five years, and the French and Belgian forces were withdrawn from the Ruhr Valley.

Under the Dawes Plan German industry and economic life made a surprising recovery, aided by the fact that American loans were available to finance the recovery and speed the wheels of production. In 1928 a further modification was introduced, named for another American, Owen D. Young. The total which Germany still owed on reparations was scaled down to the sum of $28,800,000,000, and payments on it were calculated to run for fifty-nine years. With the ratification of this pact the last Allied forces of occupation were withdrawn from the Rhineland (1930), and the German government continued payments to the extent of $685,916,000. Within two years, however, the whole issue had passed into history, for the great depression so dislocated world economy and international finance that on June 21, 1931, President Herbert Hoover proposed a moratorium on international debts. A year later, at Lausanne, representatives of the Allied powers finally accepted the truth that the reparations claims against Germany would never be realized. They proposed a drastic scaling down in the schedule of payments, so drastic that it would have amounted to a practical cancellation of reparations and war debts alike. But once again the United States declined to admit any legal connection between the two types of indebtedness. Germany, however, made no more payments on account of reparations, and after 1931 the British, French, Italian, and other governments made only token payments or none at all on their funded obligations. Finland was the only exception and continued to pay the United States the annual sum agreed upon when it accepted financial aid after separating from Russia in 1917.

Thus reparations and intergovernmental debts, which had been carried as a sort of elastic, marginal item, impressive but unreal, in the budgets of the powers, were written off as bad debts. The records indicated that the Germans had paid $6,200,000,000 on reparations up to September 1, 1924, and an additional $2,600,000,000 between this date and June 30, 1931, a grand total of $8,800,000,000. This did not represent a really crushing burden for a great power; after 1933 the German government found it possible to spend much larger appropriations for military and naval rearmament. But because of the passions aroused the whole question remained clouded and confused. Even the actual amounts paid were variously estimated as debtor or creditor restated them in terms of shifting currencies and set arbitrary values on the payments in kind and in services.

The major problem in the whole tangle, a problem never very clear to the average citizen in New York or London, was not whether Germany could or even would pay, but how she was to pay. It was quite possible to set aside a portion of the annual budget, especially as a demilitarized Germany had no armament expenses, and a part of the national revenue from the state railways or from tariff dues or internal taxes might have been transferred to the account of reparations. But to transfer such amounts out of Germany to the receiving nations was another matter: for this purpose it was necessary to establish credits abroad. Germany could not pay in gold, for her gold reserves were exhausted. The British and French did not wish to accept German manufactures as payment because this glutted markets which they preferred to supply themselves. Payment in kind instead of in coin often proved no blessing to the receiver; while the Germans, for instance, built ships for Britain to replace the tonnage lost in the war, the British shipyard workers were standing idle and claiming unemployment insurance. When French industries received coal from Germany as partial reparations dues, the British coal mines which had previously helped to supply French needs were shut down. This dilemma continued to embarrass the experts, for Germany could make really substantial payments only in goods and labor or by selling German products in the world markets and then transferring the profits thus gained to the reparations account. Either way, German wares reached consumers who might otherwise have bought French or British products.

The Germans, with their workers active and their factories humming, kept abreast of modern methods, improved their machinery, and co-ordinated their industries. To undersell their opponents they were compelled to become more efficient, and they introduced new processes, new synthetic chemicals, new inventions to speed production. In addition they rationalized the management of their great industries into trusts and combines, grouping interdependent factories under the direction of efficiency experts and co-ordinating production by the creation of supertrusts and international cartels.

The legend that Germany was crushed and crippled after World War I by the extortion of a ruinous tribute is thus seen to have little real truth, and it overlooks the fact that the democratic powers, while striving to collect reparations for a decade, were also helping Germany to recover her place in world economy and to rebuild her industries. This aid, it is true, was not always official or even intentional. It was very largely financial aid, advanced in the form of loans negotiated through the great investment brokers of New York, London, Paris, and other capitals. But the effect was to subsidize a vast expansion of German industry. The first five years of peace (1919–1924), with defeat, political disorder, the occupation of the Ruhr Valley, and the ruinous inflation, brought much suffering to the Germans; but this was not in general the result of military occupation or reparations, it was the consequence of economic exhaustion and the loss of the war. The second five years (1924–1929) offered a more cheerful picture. Foreign funds to the extraordinary amount of $7,800,000,000 flowed into Germany, of which $2,400,000,000 came from American investors. Thus two dollars went into Germany for one that came out as part of the reparations schedule, a fact which makes a fair estimate of the financial situation still more difficult to achieve. For after 1931 Germany not only ceased to pay reparations but defaulted on most of the private loans which had been floated by municipalities, public utilities, industries, and banks. In these transactions American investors were again the heaviest losers.

4. PAYMENT DEFERRED

In the final analysis, therefore, it would appear that the United States government not only failed to collect on the loans made to its Allies during World War I; it advanced, and again failed to collect on, large sums lent to a number of European governments after the war. Furthermore, in addition to an official loan of $200,000,000 advanced to the Reichsbank under the Dawes Plan of 1924, American citizens bought German bonds to the total of $2,400,000,000 after 1924, and most of this sum likewise they never recovered, although it helped to finance the recovery of Germany and prepared the way for rapid German rearmament in the 1930's. This situation appears so illogical and has been so widely criticized by many American commentators that it needs more careful study.

After 1922 the war loans and other intergovernmental debts then outstanding were adjusted by a series of agreements negotiated by the United States with its various debtors. By 1930 subsequent arrangements had scaled down the anticipated payments because few of the debtors had met the schedule of annual payments, and some nations were already in default on agreements which still had half a century to run. Collectively, the intergovernmental debts owed to the United States would have amounted to some $22,000,000,000 by 1933 if accounts had been strictly kept. Actually, unpaid principle and interest piled up in the ledgers, but only about one-tenth of the over-all total, or some $2,250,000,000, was ever repaid. Thus some $20,000,000,000 might still be considered as due the United States when payments ceased. French and British observers could point out, however, that the total of unpaid German reparations was even larger, for they estimated it at $25,000,000,000. It was thus possible to argue that the German failure to pay left the United States the loser. But this was an oversimplification of the issue. The United States was not the only creditor unpaid. Great Britain failed to collect on loans and credits of some $10,000,000,000 which had been advanced to associates during and after the war and were later repudiated. France, in addition to the enormous property losses suffered during four years of campaigning and enemy occupation, had also to write off as uncollectible some $700,000,000 lent to her associates and allies.

Private investors in Britain and France and in all the wealthier centers of Europe also lost on loans advanced to speed German expansion in the 1920's. The Germans urgently needed credit and capital to develop new plants, purchase raw material, and exploit their resources, and they offered attractive terms and high interest rates to float bonds on the international money markets. Many Americans had money to invest in the prosperous decade after 1919, and of the $7,800,000,000 borrowed by the Germans one-third came from the United States. Thus a circular system of exchange grew up, whereby American investors, through international financiers, lent billions of dollars to German enterprises, the German government transferred millions of dollars to the French, British, Italian, and Belgian governments as reparations, and the French, British, Italian, and Belgian governments turned a part, but only a part, of the reparations thus obtained back to the United States government to reduce the interallied debts. Out of all these intricate transactions and the bitter arguments they inspired, one fact emerges quite clearly. By 1933 the total of intergovernmental debts and of reparations demands still outstanding was between fifty and sixty billion dollars. But they had become paper obligations, owed back and forth among the nations, and they would never be repaid. (See pages 264–270.)

THE INTERNATIONAL SETTLEMENT
THE LEAGUE OF NATIONS

I can predict with absolute certainty that within another genera-
tion there will be another world war if the nations of the world
do not concert the method to prevent it.

WOODROW WILSON

I. THE SEARCH FOR INTERNATIONAL ORDER

THE idea that all the states or nations of the world should be united in one empire, a society of states, or an international federation, is almost as old as the earliest records of civilization. From the most ancient eras successful conquerors dreamed of universal dominion, and ambitious lawgivers strove to make one code supreme throughout the world of men. Egyptian, Babylonian, Persian, and Chinese dynasts called themselves lords of the world in their day. The Roman Empire, in the first centuries of the Christian era, brought a remarkable degree of uniformity in legislation, custom, and culture to the Mediterranean world and left behind a powerful tradition of universal sovereignty and the memory of the *Pax Romana* or Roman peace. Then Rome declined, the European section of the once mighty empire was split into barbarian kingdoms, and the Roman provinces in Africa and Asia were conquered in the seventh century by the followers of Mohammed. For a thousand years, from the fifth to the fifteenth century, western Europe or Christendom, though shattered into feudal fragments remained united in spirit by the ties of a common religious faith. But after the fifteenth century the rise of national territorial states, the separation of the Protestant denominations from the Catholic Church, and the dissolution of that shadowy political conception, the Holy Roman Empire, left Europe permanently divided. There was no tribunal to which all princes would turn, no international court with the authority to intervene and arbitrate the recurrent controversies which drove the sovereign states to frequent war.

Projects for the establishment of an international court or league were proposed by many eminent thinkers. In the seventeenth century the Duke of Sully, minister of Henry IV of France, formulated a "Grand Design," and the scholar Émeric Crucé urged that human society was in reality one body and that no part of it could suffer without the whole feeling the affliction. In the eighteenth century the Abbé de Saint Pierre and the philosopher Immanuel Kant drafted projects for perpetual peace. In the nineteenth century a host of writers devised a variety of intelligent plans. But none solved in workable fashion the fundamental problem of state sovereignty *vs.* league authority or explained how a national government could pledge itself to accept the decision of an international court yet remain the supreme and sovereign judge of its own actions.

The penalty of this condition of international anarchy was the succession of general wars which darkened European history every few decades. Each major conflict from the sixteenth century on was followed by a mood of horror and remorse and inspired the creation of diplomatic machinery which was intended to avert by frequent conferences, compromise, and arbitration the outbreak of further disastrous conflicts. These various efforts, endorsed sincerely enough by their framers while the dead still lay unburied on the battlefields, never crystallized into an enduring tribunal, and the plans to summon regular international conferences were always abandoned after a few years. The last ambitious attempt of this kind was undertaken a century before the First World War broke out. When the Napoleonic Wars with their mounting casualties culminated in the defeat of France, the Quadruple Alliance of the victorious powers, Britain, Russia, Austria, and Prussia, was set up as the foundation for a Confederation of Europe. After three years the defeated power, France, was admitted to membership. But Great Britain had already begun to draw away, and the Confederation, which lacked any permanent meeting place, any formal structure, any body of officers or recognized secretariat, ceased to be an instrument of diplomacy and became a convenient idea. In theory there was a "Concert of Europe" throughout the nineteenth century. But the relative tranquillity of the era was primarily due to the balance of power favored by Great Britain and to the release of European tensions through expansion overseas and the opening up of the world, so that the dawn of the twentieth century found a Confederation of Europe no nearer reality than before.

By 1900 the exploitable regions of the earth had been very

largely pre-empted, and national rivalries in Europe were intensified yearly by the rivalries of the imperialist powers in their overlapping colonial spheres. The rise of armament budgets and the growing tension convinced many lovers of peace that there was an urgent need for some sort of co-operative action. In 1899 a peace conference called at the suggestion of Czar Nicholas II of Russia met at The Hague. The delegates drew up a formula for the arbitration of disputes among sovereign states and proposed that a permanent court of international justice be established to hear appeals and render decisions. In 1907 a second Hague Peace Conference was convened. But no real progress was achieved in the crucial issue, the limitation of armaments, and the states would not agree in advance to submit their quarrels to the Permanent Court and promise to abide by its decisions. Despite some well-meant gestures and minor concessions, despite the earnest efforts of the peace societies and other public groups which favored disarmament, the Hague Conferences had no real influence upon the foreign or domestic policies of the great powers. The crisis of 1914 found Europe without any peace machinery adequate to avert or even to delay the appeal to arms.

Four years of anguish and eight million war dead brought the nations once more to the conviction that a permanent international body to preserve peace was essential if civilization was to be preserved. Pondering the waste and tragedy of war as the campaigns racked Europe, people everywhere persuaded themselves that the tragedy might easily have been averted, that a World Court, with the prestige and the jurisdiction to arbitrate the Austro-Serb quarrel, would have made a general war inexcusable and unnecessary. Leaders stood forth in all the democratic countries to expound this belated truth — Lord Robert Cecil for Great Britain, General Jan Christian Smuts of South Africa for the British Dominions, Léon Bourgeois for France, Woodrow Wilson for the United States. These eloquent proponents for a league to preserve peace secured a large and inspired following in 1917 and 1918, and the faith that a real and honest attempt would be made after the war to organize such a league heartened the Allied nations in their crusade for victory. When the Paris Peace Conference assembled in January, 1919, all four of the above mentioned statesmen were elected to a "Commission on the League." The commission was entrusted with the task of drafting a constitution for the Association of Nations which Woodrow Wilson had listed among his Fourteen Points. The conference decided that the charter of the League should be embodied in the peace treaties as the cornerstone of a new world order.

2. THE STRUCTURE OF THE LEAGUE OF NATIONS

The form proposed for the League of Nations made it a sort of super-state with machinery capable of discharging the three normal functions of a government: executive, legislative, and judicial. The paramount purpose was to promote peace and security among the nations. At the plenary session of the Peace Conference, which met on January 25, 1919, a resolution was adopted declaring that:

> It is essential to the maintenance of the world settlement, which the Associated Nations are now met to establish, that a League of Nations be created to promote international co-operation, to insure the fulfillment of accepted international obligations, and to provide safeguards against war.

The chief organs of the League were to be two legislative chambers, to be known as the Assembly and the Council. All member states were accorded one vote in the Assembly, great powers and small nations ranking alike in this respect, but each might be represented by one to three delegates. The Council, as first planned, was to consist of nine members. Five of these were to be permanent members and would represent the five great powers, the United States, Great Britain, France, Italy, and Japan. The four nonpermanent members were to be chosen by the Assembly. Later the number of the nonpermanent members was raised to six and finally to nine. The Assembly and the Council were declared competent to debate any question which concerned world peace.

The judicial functions of the League were to be entrusted to a Permanent Court of International Justice, a World Court. This body was organized with eleven (later fifteen) judges, elected for a nine-year term by the Assembly and the Council. Ratified in 1921, the Court was duly installed in 1922, taking its seat not at Geneva where the other League organs and commissions assembled but at The Hague. It was provided that any national governments involved in a dispute might appeal their case to the Court by mutual accord, and it was hoped that many states would bind themselves in advance to ask such arbitration before resorting to war and would promise to accept the decision resulting from such "compulsory arbitration."

The executive powers of the League were the powers most likely to infringe upon the authority of the sovereign states. They were left weak and nebulous. There was no prince or president, no cabinet under the direction of a chairman or prime minister as in parliamentary regimes, no executive committee with a clear mandate or definite delegated powers. A permanent secretariat or bureaucracy headed by a Secretary General who also acted as secretary for the Council and the Assembly meetings preserved the records and provided a rather tenuous line of continuity between sessions. Responsibility in specific fields was delegated to committees on economic affairs, labor, mandates, and minorities. The investigations and recommendations of these committees were supposed to furnish information upon which the Assembly and the Council might take action, but it was easier to compile a body of data on a critical question than to secure any positive result when the chambers met. The Council as the smaller body with the weightier prestige showed the more determined front, but the Assembly, where the smaller nations most in need of protection could unite their protests, gained more confidence as the years passed. But both chambers were inhibited by the knowledge that their enthusiasm or indignation, their debates and their resolutions would prove echoes in a desert of silence unless a majority of the national governments translated them into positive policies.

For the League remained primarily a consultative body; it could recommend a course of action to the member states but it possessed no real coercive powers to enforce respect for its decisions. If, despite League protests, a war came and nations took up arms in violation of their pledges and in defiance of League admonishment, the Council might invite member states to apply an economic boycott against an aggressor. The Council might even recommend armed reprisal against the offender. But the appropriate measures of restraint, economic or military, could be applied only by the governments of individual states. The League itself possessed no weapons, no armed force, and a French proposal to place an international police corps at its disposal was voted down. The weight of a League decision was dependent upon its prestige, upon the strength of public opinion in enlightened nations, and when public opinion was ill-informed, confused, or divided (as is commonly the case when international crises arise) the League lacked the authority to intervene with force and effect. Even if a strongly worded vote of censure condemning a belligerent state were passed by the Assembly and the Council, no means existed for bringing pressure against the troublemaker except through a joint boycott imposed by other members. In theory, this mode of concerted action had appeared promising, but when attempts were made to apply it no effective, co-ordinated boycott could be achieved. The solid front desired could never be established because nonmembers were generally uncooperative, some member states were evasive, and some were in open or secret sympathy with the aggressor. Nevertheless even when the League appeared to fail most impotently, it left a residual judgment in the minds of sober men everywhere, a judgment which identified and condemned those nations which showed aggressive impulses.

3. LIMITATIONS, ABSTENTIONS, AND DESERTIONS

It is easy, after a quarter of a century, to point out the defects that weakened the League of Nations. It was cumbrous in organization, slow and formal in deliberation, unprepared (because seldom in session) to cope with a sudden crisis, unprovided with instruments to check aggression when aggression commenced. The financial resources of this august body were severely restricted, and its annual budget of some $7,000,000 was less than that of leading American universities. Yet all these limitations, which might have been repaired in time, did not cripple the League in fundamental fashion. The real defect of the League as a confederation of sovereign states was the fact that it never was a truly international, independent, world-embracing organization. It never achieved the prestige and standing of a supranational parliament, it never won the active support of all the leading world states, it never attained the neutral and universal character which its founders envisaged for it.

The first and heaviest blow it suffered was dealt by the nation which had seemed its warmest friend. When Woodrow Wilson asked the United States Senate to approve the Treaty of Versailles, which included the League Covenant, the Senate rejected both. His faith in the people still firm, Wilson carried his appeal to the nation, but the election of 1920 sustained his opponents, and the Congress finally voted for a separate peace with Germany in 1921. This repudiation by the American people, who had led the crusade to "make the world safe for democracy" and then abandoned the one organ which seemed a guarantee of peace and justice, crippled the League permanently. Responsibility for this unhappy outcome to ardent hopes was shared by Wilson, his opponents, and the sovereign people of the United States.

Wilson's noble idealism made him a great popular leader but his

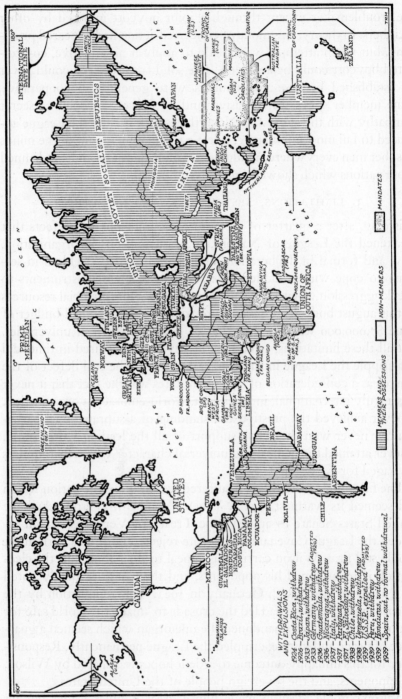

THE LEAGUE OF NATIONS

WITHDRAWALS
AND EXPULSIONS

1924 — Costa Rica, withdrew
1926 — Brazil, withdrew
1933 — Japan, withdrew
1933 — Germany, withdrew (Aug.1926)
1936 — Guatemala, withdrew
1936 — Nicaragua, withdrew
1937 — Italy, withdrew
1937 — Paraguay, withdrew
1937 — El Salvador, withdrew
1938 — Chile, withdrew
1938 — Venezuela, withdrew
1939 — U.S.S.R., expelled (Aug.1935)
1939 — Peru, withdrew
1939 — Honduras, withdrew
1939 — Spain, out, no formal withdrawal

MEMBERS AND
THEIR POSSESSIONS

NON-MEMBERS

MANDATES

unwillingness to compromise proved an insurmountable liability in the final political maneuvering. By the end of his career he had become estranged from almost all his old associates, even from Colonel House. His faith that the people would support him often encouraged him to defy the counsel of political advisers. When he sailed for Paris in December, 1918, the Republicans had just won control of the Senate and the House of Representatives, but he failed to include any of their outstanding statesmen in the American peace commission. The ovations accorded him in London, Paris, and Rome obscured his waning popularity at home, and few heeded the grim warning uttered by the former president, Theodore Roosevelt, "Our Allies and our enemies and Mr. Wilson himself should all understand that Mr. Wilson has no authority to speak for the American people at this time." Had Wilson remained in Washington and permitted his secretary of state, Robert Lansing, to negotiate the peace, he might have felt less personal loss of prestige when the accords were criticized. But he was determined to conduct the negotiations himself and to present his critics in America with a treaty and a league covenant indissolubly linked in one document. He did not believe that the Senate would dare to affront popular hopes by rejecting his work.

He was mistaken. When he presented the Treaty of Versailles to the Senate in July, 1919, with the Covenant of the League of Nations as a preamble, the Senate opposition, led by Henry Cabot Lodge of Massachusetts, recommended several changes or reservations. Wilson commenced a speaking tour in September to win the nation to his views, but he was exhausted by his long efforts and he suffered a paralytic stroke in Colorado which shattered his health. Nevertheless he clung rigidly to his determination that the Treaty and the League Covenant must be ratified without revision. When the draft with reservations came before the Senate in November he instructed his supporters to vote against it. As a result, the necessary two-thirds majority could not be marshaled to ratify the Treaty in amended or unamended form. A last attempt to pass it, with reservations, was made on March 19, 1920, but twenty-three Democrats, obedient to Wilson's behest, joined with die-hard Republicans to vote it down. Had they approved, the amended treaty might have passed by seventy-two votes out of eighty-four senators balloting. To legalize the end of hostilities in some fashion a joint resolution was then passed by both Houses, declaring that the war with Germany was at an end: from his sickbed President Wilson vetoed it. The deadlock was not resolved until Wilson's Republican successor at the White House, Warren G. Harding, signed a resolution ending the state of war between the United States and Germany on July 21, 1921. Separate treaties with Germany, Austria, and Hungary were then negotiated by the State Department and approved by the Senate.

What were the "reservations" which Wilson believed so serious that they would have nullified the Covenant of the League? They concerned four points in particular, and it seems doubtful that their inclusion could have weakened the Covenant so fatally as American exclusion weakened the League. The Senate Committee on Foreign Affairs offered four amendments. They recommended that the United States should not bind itself unequivocally to "preserve as against external aggression the territorial integrity and political independence of all members of the League" (Article 10). They insisted that the United States should define more specifically the provision governing withdrawal from the League (Article 1). They stipulated that the United States could not surrender its right to decide what disputes came within the sphere of the League and what issues the American courts were competent to adjudicate. Finally, the United States, they held, could not accept the competence of the League to investigate or to rule upon questions which involved the application of the Monroe Doctrine.

The Monroe Doctrine was the cornerstone of American foreign policy. When it was announced under President James Monroe in 1823 it was intended as a reply to contemporary threats — to the claims leveled by the Russians at the West Coast from Alaska to California, and to projects of the Spanish and Portuguese monarchs to reassert their control over the peoples of Latin America. But in the course of a century the Doctrine had come to stand in American thought as a "No Trespassing" sign warning all foreign powers against an attempt to acquire territory in the New World, to fortify bases, to intervene, or even to ally themseves with an American republic. Any such interference, it was thought, might threaten the balance of power in the Americas and might compel the United States as the guardian of the New World to establish a powerful army and to construct naval and military fortifications on a costly scale. By maintaining the Monroe Doctrine inviolate the United States had kept the Atlantic and Pacific Oceans between itself and any powerful aggressor.

The importance which Americans attached to the Doctrine was recognized by President Wilson and his associates when they drafted the pertinent clauses in the League Covenant. Article 21 read:

Nothing in this Covenant shall be deemed to affect the validity of international engagements, such as treaties of arbitration or regional understandings like the Monroe Doctrine, for securing the maintenance of peace.

Even this carefully worded assurance did not remove the fear which many Americans felt that membership in the League would involve the nation in foreign disputes, the "entangling alliances" against which Washington had warned the young republic in its early years.

The policy of isolationism had failed in 1917, the United States had gone to war, and 115,000 American soldiers had died. Inevitably, in the mood of disillusionment which followed the great idealism of 1917 and 1918, it seemed as if the noble crusade had failed. Revelation of the secret treaties which had been concluded by the British, French, Russian, and Italian governments for the division of conquered territory made Wilson's lofty arguments for "open covenants openly arrived at" seem naïve and impracticable. Europe, it appeared to many Americans, was rapidly reverting to the evils of secret diplomacy, power politics, and imperialism. This change in sentiment, this mood of disillusionment, this bitter conclusion that the quarrels of the European nations were endless and insoluble and that the United States ought to stay out of them, swayed American opinion very powerfully in 1920. It helps to explain why the Senate repudiated the League of Nations, for many senators, headed by William E. Borah of Idaho and Hiram Johnson of California, feared that if the American republics joined the League they would constantly be drawn into foreign disputes and crises. They also resented the thought that the League Council, sitting in Geneva, Switzerland, might seek to interfere in New World affairs which were, or had been hitherto, the concern of the Pan-American Union.

Thus, from the outset, the United States was absent from the circle of the League, gravely impairing its usefulness. But there were other gaps almost as distressing. In the early years two other great powers, Germany and Russia, were also absent. An association of nations which included no more than four of the seven great powers could be called a "world league" in name only. It is true that the number of great powers within the League was increased to five in 1926 when Germany received a permanent seat on the Council, and this event marked the high tide of League achievement. Yet even in the act of providing a place for the German delegate the League betrayed its intrinsic disunity. Even at this, its most hopeful hour, a dispute on status and a broken pledge provided forewarnings of the decline that soon sapped its usefulness.

The decision to admit Germany to the League was the culmination of a momentary mood usually described as "the Spirit of Locarno." By 1925 Raymond Poincaré and the more adamant Nationalists were out of favor in France; the Conservative Party, usually the more defiant in its foreign policy, had suffered a reverse in England; while the adroit Gustav Stresemann had persuaded the bourgeois and the socialist groups in Germany to support a conciliatory foreign policy. At Locarno, Switzerland, in 1925 Germany, France, and Belgium mutually guaranteed their existing frontiers and agreed to arbitrate future disputes. The accord also provided that Germany might apply for membership in the League. But the move to add one more permanent member to the Council stirred up jealousy and dispute; Poland, Spain, and Brazil all insisted that they merited a permanent Council seat also. The solution adopted was to expand the permanent seats to five and allow the Assembly to elect nine nonpermanent members. When this decision was announced, Spain and Brazil withdrew, Brazil permanently. This was the first of the inauspicious events which marred the optimistic spirit of the hour.

The second flaw in the accord which admitted Germany to League membership was a broken pledge, and that defect was to be magnified until it provided Germany with an excuse for resigning in 1933. When the Germans signed the Versailles treaty in 1919, they had been assured in writing by the chairman of the conference, Georges Clemenceau, that German disarmament was to be the first step in a general reduction and limitation of armaments. By 1926 the Allied commission appointed to supervise German disarmament reported that the process had been carried out in almost all particulars, but no serious attempt was made by the victor powers to fulfill the remainder of the agreement in the years that followed. The Germans argued that this failure proved the bad faith of the French and British governments and invalidated their arguments that it was German militarism which had caused World War I. In 1933 Germany quit the League abruptly.

Thereafter the dissolution of the League proceeded swiftly. The Japanese, offended when their invasion of Manchuria was voted an act of aggression, resigned in March, 1933. The Italians, whose invasion and conquest of Ethiopia moved the League to impose sanctions, defied the worst the League could do and then resigned in 1937. These secessions would have left Great Britain and France the only great powers still in attendance had not Soviet Russia been admitted in 1934. Russian distrust of the Western democracies slowly declined after 1926, and Maxim Litvinov, who became commissar (or minister) for foreign affairs in 1930, brought Russia into the League shortly after the exit of Germany. Thus within fifteen years of its formation the League of Nations, which had never been a truly universal association, shrank to a truncated alliance dominated by Great Britain, France, and Russia.

Public opinion still respected the high ideals upon which the League was founded, and delegates at the sessions did not cease to warn against the increase of armaments and to deplore the growth of aggression and the disregard of treaties. But horror of war is a relative passion; it was strong among the lesser nations which were predestined victims of aggression, and weak among the ambitious nations conscious of power and eager for expansion. Cynics pointed out with some truth that the states which remained within the League were either second and third class countries which could not afford to wage a war or satiated powers which had ample areas in which to expand. The three great powers left in the League after 1937 were not moved wholly by moral considerations in denouncing war. All of them for one reason or another preferred to see a balance of power in Europe and the world, and they made the League an instrument by which violent change might be discredited, denouncing from its forum those restless and hungry nations which threatened world equilibrium or coveted their neighbors' lands. Britain, France, and the Soviet Union could afford to support a policy which "froze" existing frontiers and prohibited further conquest, for they were, as their critics pointed out, "satiated" powers. Taken together, the three empires comprised almost half the land area of the earth.

The fact that the three "have not" powers, Japan, Germany, and Italy, all gave offense to the more peaceful members, were all charged with aggressive and militaristic actions, and all resigned in resentment, suggests a grave defect in the League as an instrument of peace. The German, Italian, and Japanese imperialists insisted that their nations, too, were entitled to large colonial empires, to "living space" or *Lebensraum* as the German expansionists termed it. The idealists who supported the League believed that it might become a mechanism for assuring peaceful change in the world, for lowering obstructive tariffs, opening up neglected areas, and assuring all nations a fair share in world trade and raw materials. But world trade fell sharply after the depression of 1929 and each nation sought selfishly to safeguard its own share. This sharper economic nationalism which drove the powers towards a policy of self-sufficiency, added to the bitterness of the "have not" states. It is important to understand how the dissatisfied imperialists in Berlin, Rome, or Tokyo viewed the League in order to understand why it failed to hold their support. To the Germans it never outgrew its early association with the Versailles pact, it never achieved a truly independent or international status in their eyes. The Italians likewise, who felt that they had been cheated in the peace settlement of 1919, never regarded it with enthusiasm. In all parts of the world there were many people with similar views, people to whom the League never appeared the detached, impartial tribunal they might have trusted but merely a complicated piece of diplomatic machinery constructed by the statesmen who framed the Versailles treaty and controlled by them as a device for protecting their conquests. This was not a just estimate of the League; it was not even a logical estimate, but it was an estimate widely advertised by its foes.

There was a further limitation in the League platform which counted against it among the non-European peoples of the world. The Japanese proposed in 1919 that the League protocol should recognize the equality of races, but their suggestion was rejected by the drafting commission. This decision emphasized the Europocentric bias of the League and its most prominent supporters and relegated two-thirds of the world's population to a position of implied inferiority. The peoples of Africa and Asia, especially those living in territories administered by European powers, such as the Egyptians, Hindus, or Indonesians, were not confident that the League would listen to their complaints with impartiality, if indeed it listened to them at all.

Within Europe those nations disposed from the first to distrust the League as an instrument of the victor powers found some reasons to justify their misgivings. They noted that it was reluctant to criticize any action of its leading members. It hesitated to criticize the French, who insisted upon maintaining the most powerful army in Europe although the Central Powers were disarmed and helpless. It failed to curb Poland (a satellite of France) when the Poles detached Memel from Lithuania in 1920 or when they seized additional territory from Russia in 1921. It failed to enforce arbitration upon the Italians when they shelled Corfu in 1923 and exacted an indemnity from the Greeks in retaliation for a border incident. When it was a matter of enforcing the Versailles terms against the vanquished, however, the League was accused of too much zeal by some critics. Austria, reduced to a third-rate power by the treaty, would normally have merged in a political or at least an economic alliance with Germany. But this choice was forbidden lest Germany grow too strong. The unsound economic condition of the new Austria made a common customs union with Germany a reasonable plan, but neither appeals to the principle of self-determination nor the economic chaos in Austria persuaded the French to permit the *Anschluss* or union proposed. Recourse to the League was vain: as late as 1931 the Court of International Justice declared such a merger contrary to the Treaty of Versailles, a ruling which affronted German patriots.

In the critical tests of the 1930's the League failed each time it sought to check the aggressive moves of a great power. It failed to arrest the Japanese invasion of Manchuria and northern China which commenced in 1931. It failed to halt the Italian invasion and annexation of Ethiopia in 1935 although the Ethiopian government, like the Chinese, appealed repeatedly to Geneva for protection and arbitration. It failed during the desperate Spanish civil war of 1936–1939 to prevent the Germans and Italians from sending thousands of technicians, airmen, and whole divisions of infantry to aid the insurgents, while the Russians supported the Republican government. It failed to prevent German infiltration and occupation of Danzig, although the Free City was under its direct protection. Finally it failed to avert the German attack upon Poland which opened World War II in 1939.

Yet the blame for these failures does not properly belong to the League as an organ. The members of the Council, the delegates to the Assembly, the personnel of the secretariat strove earnestly, despite weakened authority and waning prestige, to uphold its rules and maintain its functions. The fault lay with the statesmen of the leading states, with the public in the advanced nations, who lost faith in the League as an organization. To flout the League became a popular gesture with German, Japanese, and Italian politicians who wished to arouse nationalist enthusiasm by appealing to the chauvinist emotions of their constituents. The League itself did not cease to function: it simply failed to affect the course of events. When the Japanese pushed into Manchuria, the Council adopted a judicious report on the Far Eastern situation and condemned the Japanese government on the charge of military aggression. But the rebuke did not halt the Japanese. When the Italians invaded Ethiopia, the League members agreed to invoke an economic blockade of Italy to restrain the Fascist plan of conquest.

Italy is particularly vulnerable to blockade; the withholding of oil alone might have stalled the Italian drives. But the economic sanctions were too lightly enforced to prove effective. These tests, and these successive proofs that the League could judge a situation, could bring in a verdict, but could not enforce it or persuade an effective majority of the national states to enforce it, were milestones on the road to the Second World War.

As an experiment in collective security the League of Nations failed, but the list of its failures is not the most important part of the record. It was not a wholly abortive experiment. Its successes, and it had many minor successes, have been too readily forgotten. Even its missteps and frustrations had their value, for errors provide a warning. The League sessions helped to set a precedent and a pattern for international co-operation which future generations may recognize more clearly and rate more highly than contemporary observers have done. Its failures are now a part of history but its successes hold the clue to a better international order.

4. SOME ACHIEVEMENTS OF THE LEAGUE

League arbitration was not always vain. In a score of disputes between secondary states the committees at Geneva found a workable solution. In several cases action by the League not only averted hostilities, it even halted open warfare after the fighting had commenced. The tale of such successes makes more encouraging reading than the list of antagonisms unhealed and ruptures which could not be averted.

In 1921–1922 a dispute between Sweden and Finland, both of which claimed possession of the Aaland Islands, was submitted to the League for decision. The verdict, which granted the islanders autonomy under Finnish sovereignty, moderated the controversy. In 1925 border clashes almost brought on a war between Greece and Bulgaria, but arbitration under League auspices assured a peaceful settlement. In 1932 an incipient war between Peru and Colombia was resolved peaceably through League mediation. Several controversial claims arising from the Versailles settlement, confided to the League for adjustment, were likewise arbitrated with success. Under League supervision a plebiscite was held in Upper Silesia in 1921 to resolve the border separating Germany and Poland. A majority of the inhabitants wished the territory in dispute to remain within the German Reich. The League Council recommended a partition of the region which awarded Poland a somewhat more generous share than the vote seemed to justify but which did settle a most acrid dispute without violence and laid down a line of demarcation in a troubled area. A second difficult assignment for which the League should receive honor was its fifteen-year supervision of the Saar Valley. In accordance with the provisions of the Versailles treaty the League conducted a plebiscite in 1935. The results indicated that 90 per cent of the inhabitants desired the reincorporation of the territory in Germany, and the League thereupon approved the reunion of this important mining and industrial area in the Reich. These five cases are examples of patient negotiation and responsible statemanship. They might be duplicated many times over from the records in the League files. The publicity and clamor which accompanied many appeals to the League were often an embarrassment; some of the most effective work accomplished by the League diplomats was successful because it did not reach the headlines of the newspapers. Every sane settlement of an international dispute is likely to be a compromise, and governments sometimes find it easier to withdraw extreme claims if the spotlight has been turned elsewhere. Public excitement, especially when deliberately fanned by governments as part of their offensive, can create an atmosphere so tense and stormy that a calm analysis of the questions at issue becomes impossible.

Some of the soundest and most constructive tasks attempted by League commissions seldom attracted popular attention. Financial aid to the insolvent Austrian republic, advice and assistance to several eastern European nations in combating typhus, improvement in the status of natives in backward regions and obscure protectorates — these and other services were undramatic and passed with little general notice. Yet the existence of a Commission on Mandates with responsibility for scrutinizing conditions in Uganda or Sumatra marked an important change in the attitude of the European states towards the treatment of submerged peoples and the exploitation of colonial areas. The League did not possess a police force which could intervene to prevent injustice, but it could appeal to the enlightened opinion of civilized people in the advanced countries. In Europe and America intelligent and humane citizens read the League reports and besought their governments to introduce corrective measures to benefit forgotten peoples caught in the net of the rival imperialisms.

Perhaps the greatest ultimate benefits conferred by the League will result from its studies on human welfare. Year after year its investigators compiled carefully tested and remarkably objective statistics on the effects of famine, of deficiency diseases, of epidemics, of vaccines and preventive medicine, of vice, slavery, the drug traffic, labor conditions, and many other social problems affecting the welfare of mankind. Many of the evils uncovered were of such a nature that they could be curbed only through international co-operation. Though the League possessed very limited funds its agents performed invaluable services in collecting information and co-ordinating the findings of national and international charitable organizations, in quickening the consciences of civilized peoples, and in making available the facts and figures upon which campaigns for a better and healthier world could be based. For the first indispensable step to all social reform is the compilation of fair and accurate data on the conditions to be remedied. The League of Nations Year Book and other reference works which published trustworthy figures on tax rates, living standards, incomes, vital statistics, literacy, armament budgets, and a hundred equally significant facts, provided an arsenal of useful information. Legislators, reformers, journalists, and lecturers could draw upon the international guides when preparing campaigns or criticizing abuses.

The promotion of intellectual co-operation among the thinkers and artists of all nations was a further aim of the League sponsors. To link culture to culture and class to class through the exchange of scholars, lecturers, scientists, and artists; to hasten the translation of important books; to encourage exchanges in research; and to broaden the channels of international travel and communication were all worthy purposes and all gained strength through League enterprise.

Finally, it is just to note the role played by the International Labor Office, an agency of the League created for the improvement of relations between employers and employees and for the promotion of remedial measures to reduce class tension and class rivalry. Modern society is not only threatened by the devastation of war between nations, it is endangered by the prospect of war within nations, war that could turn one class against another. To find a solution to class antagonisms and so reduce the risk of civil conflicts is a vital function of any organization which aims at assuring peace by collective action. This truth was likewise clear to the idealists who framed the League of Nations.

OIL WELLS AT THE BEAUMONT FIELD, TEXAS

A UNITED STATES AIRCRAFT CARRIER PASSING THROUGH THE PEDRO MIGUEL LOCKS IN THE PANAMA CANAL

Acme

PART IV

The Americas
in the Twentieth Century

THE UNITED STATES
INTERNAL DEVELOPMENT

Send but a song oversea for us
Heart of their hearts who are free . . .
ALGERNON CHARLES SWINBURNE [1]

I. GROWTH

NOWHERE in history is there a story of nation-building so remarkable as the epic of the United States. For a handful of colonists to invade a continent, expand their dominion, and increase their number until in three centuries they formed a united nation of 140,000,000 is an unparalleled achievement. These transplanted Europeans carried overseas the forms of an ancient culture, adapted historic ideals and techniques to the problems of a novel environment, improvised as the need arose new formulas, new tactics, new devices. At times they experimented audaciously. They dared, for example, to adopt a republican form of government, to set up a democratic regime of a type never previously maintained with success in a broad and expanding empire. They not only "brought forth on this continent a new nation," they so governed and developed the nation that it became a leading world power, while its citizens acquired a greater measure of political liberty and material welfare than any other empire of equal size had ever conferred upon so many millions of men.

The "miracle of America," as a French writer described it, filled the people of less fortunate lands with astonishment and envy. By the Americans themselves, however, the bounties of nature and the blessings of security were accepted almost casually. The free citizen of the United States learned to regard as normal a civilization so prodigal in

[1] From the poem, "To Walt Whitman in America."

its production, so unfettered in its creative and mechanical energies, so varied, colorful, and dramatic in its achievements that nothing seemed impossible to American genius. In the years when the first settlers were founding Jamestown and Plymouth, the English Lord Chancellor, Francis Bacon, prophesied that mankind was entering a new age in which science would bring "the enlarging of the bounds of human empire to the effecting of all things possible." In America his prophecy found its most startling measure of fulfillment. From the skyscrapers of Manhattan to the Golden Gate the triumphs of American engineers and scientists suggested the marvels of the *New Atlantis* or a fantasy from a scientific *Arabian Nights' Entertainments*. Modern technology provided for the millions a standard of living which the Caesars might have envied.

All great historical movements tend to take on in retrospect a character of grandeur, of predestination. As Americans of the twentieth century contemplated the growth of their republic they felt increasing admiration for their predecessors and increasing awe for the dangers the nation had survived. Throughout its most vulnerable years a kindly fate had protected and preserved the Union. But with the opening of the twentieth century the era of semi-isolation had passed; the United States had suddenly come of age and inherited a deciding role in world affairs. "This generation of Americans," Franklin Delano Roosevelt reminded the nation in 1936, "has a rendezvous with destiny."

Could a nation so lately fashioned from diverse groups withstand the stress of world competition and world wars? The United States lacked the deep historical roots, the long cultivated loyalties, the tested institutions which gave the European powers their strength and structure. Six generations earlier no one could have predicted with assurance that half of North America would be knit into one republic and dominated by Anglo-Saxon culture. The Spaniards were the first to settle in Florida and California. The French explored the central area from the Great Lakes to New Orleans. The Russians laid claim to Oregon. But thanks to the elasticity of American institutions and the initiative and wisdom of American leaders the earlier colonists of foreign speech and background were incorporated without undue difficulty into the expanding frame of the nation.

This fusion of peoples, who in their European homelands had been foreigners and often foes to one another, was a remarkable reconciliation. Even more remarkable as a test of the New World amalgam was

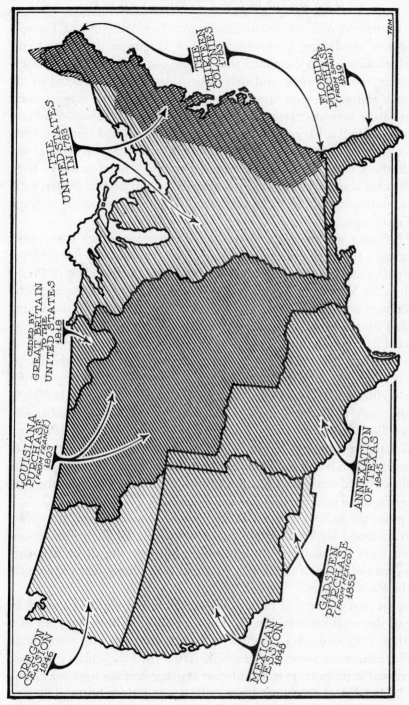

THE EXPANSION OF THE UNITED STATES, 1783–1853

THE THIRTEEN COLONIES 1783

FLORIDA PURCHASE (FROM SPAIN) 1819

THE STATES UNITED IN 1783

CEDED BY GREAT BRITAIN TO THE UNITED STATES 1818

LOUISIANA PURCHASE (FROM FRANCE) 1803

ANNEXATION OF TEXAS 1845

GADSDEN PURCHASE (FROM MEXICO) 1853

OREGON CESSION 1846

MEXICAN CESSION 1848

the absorption of a stream of immigrants from all parts of Europe, people of conflicting nationalities, classes, languages, faiths, and cultural traditions. It is estimated that 50,000,000 emigrants left Europe between 1800 and 1914, and that three-fourths were attracted to the United States. To land-hungry farmers the chance to acquire their own farms was an irresistible lure. To political refugees the New World offered a haven. To the ambitious, the myriad opportunities, the system of free enterprise, the rewards awaiting men with vision made the United States the "Land of Promise." But for native-born Americans above all others the mystery and magnificence of that half-void continent waiting to be conquered formed a perpetual heritage and challenge.

The result was that saga of westward expansion which is the most distinctive theme of American history. The republic was the achievement of pioneers. In the century and a half from the founding of Plymouth to the War of Independence the English colonists conquered the wilderness at a rate of ten square miles a day. After 1783 the young United States, born with a giant's energy and a giant's appetite, expanded its frontiers for the next hundred and fifty years at the rate of fifty square miles a day. Its restless sons were forever on the move, forever heading into uncharted areas, inventing new tactics, testing new techniques, raising a cabin in the clearing or a trading post by the stream, only to abandon them abruptly and move on when other settlers followed on their heels. They learned skills as they needed them, trail making, trapping, hunting, and planting. They built log houses in the woodlands and sod houses on the plains. They followed the ruts of the covered wagons to Oregon and California. They knew the epic of portage and prairie camp and mountain pass. Then at a critical turning point the railway arrived, bringing a revolution in land transport. Ten thousand settlements lost in the immensity of the great central plains were linked by the magic rails, and soon the silver filaments threaded the mazes of the Rocky Mountains to guide a host of pioneers to the Pacific shores.

In the first century of railway construction one-third of the trackage of the world was laid in the United States. Within the span of a lifetime (1830–1900) a network of lines spread out into every state until a saturation point was reached. After 1910 the railway mileage decreased in proportion to population as other vehicles took over some of the burden of transport from railways and river boats. The first automobile show in America was held, appropriately enough, in 1900, as if to signalize that the century of steam had closed and the century of oil and electricity had opened.

Then, in a generation (1890–1910), the frontier passed. Its boisterous influence, which had dominated the rise of American democracy and inspired the virile, self-confident, and often lawless individuality of the range, was curbed by newer forces. With the opening of the twentieth century the United States entered a more disciplined era. Agriculture, which had been the primary source of income hitherto, yielded place to industry and commerce. Urban population overtook and finally surpassed the total of the rural districts. The millions of arriving immigrants, who had poured out onto the farm lands while the richer areas were still unclaimed and unworked, tended after 1900 to settle in the cities, seeking employment in factories, in construction work, in the mining and metallurgical trades. These changes came so swiftly that they created a number of problems which had been unprovided for because few of them had been foreseen.

The crisis caused by this readjustment, the methods adopted to meet this rapid industrialization and urbanization, wove new patterns of American life. After 1900 the citizens of the United States found themselves facing several problems which most European peoples had been coping with for generations. Of these problems the most significant formed the triad already met in earlier chapters: the problem of resources, the problem of defense, and the problem of social justice. Before the twentieth century the favorable conditions in the New World had made these problems much less acute for Americans than they had long proved for Europeans.

2. POPULATION: THE MOVEMENT TO THE CITIES

Within a century and a half, from 1790 to 1940, the population of the United States increased more than thirtyfold, rising from 3,929,214 to 131,669,275. It has been estimated that the world population increased fourfold during the same period, from some 500,000,000 to 2,000,-000,000. This suggests the unusually favorable conditions in the United States where the ratio was eight times the world average. Three forms of increase swelled the American total: the birthrate, the incorporation of settlers already living in territories annexed to the original states, and the influx of immigrants from other lands. Natural increase — that is, children born in the United States — contributed most heavily. French settlers in New Orleans and other points, Spaniards of Florida, Texas, and California, added their national and cultural contribution as

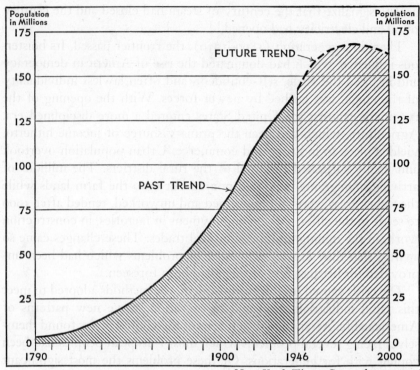

POPULATION OF THE UNITED STATES, 1790–2000

New York Times, September 15, 1946

these and other states were joined to the Union, enriching the national life with their own arts and customs as the Swedes and Dutch of New York and Pennsylvania had done. The names on the land recall Indian and colonial strains, and the surnames of American families suggest the many countries which contributed to the building of the American nation. The Anglo-Saxons, who formed the dominant majority in the Thirteen Colonies, were the most numerous and most successful element, and their influence largely determined the language, laws, and institutions which were to distinguish the new society and the new republic.

The capacity of the United States to attract, absorb, and Americanize immigrants from many lands has been stressed already. This process of achieving a national synthesis was the more remarkable and perhaps the more successful because it was not a compulsory policy or official program. Settlers from overseas adapted themselves to the American climate, landscape, and environment, reacted to their neighbors, accepted and elaborated the laws and customs which the earlier colonists had introduced. Newcomers found the laws and customs in the New World less narrow and repressive than the set pattern of life they had known in Europe. They found that in America society might be said to take shape rather than to be shaped.

Statistics, so far as they are available, indicate that between 1820 and 1943 over 38,000,000 foreigners arrived for permanent residence in the United States. Throughout most of these decades the immigrants from the British Isles outnumbered those from any other European state, but after 1900 the immigration from the northern European countries declined while that from central, southern, and eastern European regions increased. In 1940 about one-fourth, or 34,576,718, of the residents of the forty-eight states had been born in foreign countries or were of foreign or mixed parentage. The distribution of this total according to the leading countries of origin was as follows: [1]

GERMANY	5,236,612
ITALY	4,594,780
CANADA	2,910,159
POLAND	2,905,859
RUSSIA (U.S.S.R.)	2,610,244
EIRE	2,410,951
ENGLAND	1,975,975
SWEDEN	1,301,390
AUSTRIA	1,261,246
MEXICO	1,076,653
OTHER COUNTRIES	8,292,849
	34,576,718

In their first precarious camps and along the expanding frontier American settlers tended to repeat the stages whereby primitive man had once climbed the long ascent to civilization. The first frontiersmen were nomads, fighting or trading with the Indians they encountered and living on the fruits they could gather and the game they could kill. The first exposed settlements were like fortified camps fenced with a stockade. But around every settlement the colonists planted crops; soon they had passed from the hunting to the agricultural life. The arts were born; forges, brick kilns, tanneries, shipyards appeared; and in a few generations trading posts had become cities. The long,

[1] *Statesman's Year Book: 1946* (New York: Macmillan, 1946), p. 499.

unplanned ascent which had cost primitive man more than 300,000 years of effort was scaled in less than 300 years by the colonists. Some Americans like to think of the United States as a self-made nation, but the contrast of those time-sequences rebukes such presumption. At every step in their development the American settlers utilized the knowledge and skill and weapons they had brought with them; at every critical moment they drew upon the support, experience, and technique of their European homelands, upon the most advanced civilization the world had ever known. They did not evolve a civilization; they transplanted one. Despite the severance of political ties they remained a part, culturally, intellectually, and historically, of the European world order, of the Euro-American or Western civilization which is dominant today.

Like Europe in its latest stage, American society has passed recently and rapidly from the agrarian to the urban mode of life. By 1940 manufacturing had become the leading gainful activity. It employed 10,572,842 workers, while the next largest group, those engaged in agriculture, forestry, and fishing, totaled only 8,475,432. This shift from farm and forest to factory, store, and office, provided the most important social and economic change in recent American history, and it is a change which has come about since the grandparents of today were children. In 1870, 53 per cent of the American workers, one out of two, labored on the land. But the towns were calling. The growing demand for helpers in industry, construction trades, commerce, transportation, clerical and professional work turned rural Americans into urbanites. In 1940 nearly 75,000,000 inhabitants lived in cities or in towns of 2500 or more. This trend towards urbanization was not only marked by the movement of people, especially young people, from the country to the town but it was emphasized even more by a migration from the towns to the cities. Large cities grew faster than small ones, and the vaster the metropolis the more powerful its attraction. Between 1910 and 1940 the number of cities of minor size, with populations of 25,000 or less, increased only 15 per cent, although the national census total was rising three times as fast. In the same thirty years the number of cities of major size, with populations ranging from 25,-000 to 1,000,000 or more, increased 80 per cent. To measure this same movement towards the larger cities in another way, it may be noted that the total number of inhabitants in the continental United States in 1940 was about 40,000,000 greater than it had been in 1910. But this increase was unevenly distributed. Approximately one-fifth was registered in towns below 2500 and in unincorporated territory; one-fifth in towns of 2500 to 25,000; and three-fifths, or 24,000,000 of the additional 40,000,000 inhabitants, were in cities over 25,000. The movement to the cities was strong, and it was growing stronger. Two out of three Americans now lived in incorporated towns or cities. One out of three lived in a city of over 25,000 people.

This change meant that a majority of modern Americans would seldom see the open country except when they went on an excursion; the city had become their home and their horizon. How this would affect their right to life, liberty, and the pursuit of happiness no one could easily foretell. Millions of other Americans had survived the dislocation, the reorientation which followed their transplantation from the Old World to the New, and they had made the readjustment with courage and success. Now a new form of migration and reorientation, a sort of pioneering in reverse, was imposing itself upon their descendants. For the rapid shift from country to city, though accepted casually, was a revolution of unpredictable scope. Any rapid change in a people's way of life, no matter how great the advantages it may bring, must disrupt accepted patterns, sever strands of sentiment and tradition, disinherit the generation which nostalgically turns its back upon its own past.

In the earlier pre-urban age, the sights which first grew familiar to an average American child were stars and trees and sunsets. All his life he knew the woods and streams, the kinship of animal life, the processions of the seasons, and the pageantry of nature. The last sound to reach his dying ears might be the lowing of cattle or the crowing of a cock. In contrast, the average American child of today is likely to open his eyes in a city hospital; he sees more neon signs than moonrises; he will learn his letters in crowded schoolrooms and his games behind the wire fences of city playgrounds. Night silences no longer bring the stars nearer, or the distant music of a brook, or the call of a night bird. Those who lie awake in the city know that street lights put the stars to flight and that the most penetrating sounds come from the stream of late unending traffic.

Sentimentalists deplore these changes; sociologists seek to evaluate them. It is true that in the march of progress modern America is leaving behind much that was lovable and picturesque — the little red schoolhouse, the old oaken bucket, the open fireplace, the village blacksmith, hay rides and sleigh rides, the old gray mare, and the old swimming hole. As substitutes, America is acquiring brick schools a

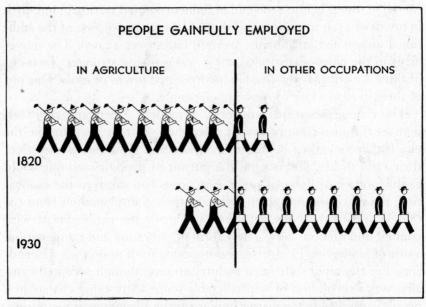

PEOPLE GAINFULLY EMPLOYED

IN AGRICULTURE   IN OTHER OCCUPATIONS

1820

1930

THE SHIFT FROM AGRICULTURE TO OTHER OCCUPATIONS

Each figure represents one-tenth of all workers in the United States at the two dates
indicated.

block in area, hot and cold running water, central heating, train, bus,
and automobile transportation, chain stores, telephones, motion pictures, and radios. Even farming, the most ancient craft, is being transformed by machinery for ploughing, reaping, threshing, milling, milking, cotton picking. The total effect is a wider diffusion of education,
improvements in hygiene and public health, more comfortable standards of living, and an extraordinary reduction in physical toil. Nature
lovers complain that millions of city children are growing up in exile;
they never pick wild strawberries or fish for trout; they identify their
favorite foods by trademarks, and could scarcely tell a field of potatoes from a field of peanuts. It is true that the whole trend towards
urbanization severs man from the soil he trod for countless generations, but the trend is stronger than tradition. Even those who sing
nostalgic songs about the good old days would not readily abandon
electric light for oil lamps if they had to tend the lamps, or prefer
a wood-burning fireplace to a steam radiator if they had to chop
the wood.

When the majority of people in a country change their way of life
they may change their character also, may create new needs and prob-

lems which alter their outlook and their history. Until recent years farm or village life was the normal life for most Americans; today city life is becoming the normal life for their children. A change so momentous perplexes legislators and other planners who attempt to guide the course of public affairs. The earlier centrifugal movement of the population towards the frontier induced a spirit of hardihood and initiative. What effect will the later centripetal movement to the large cities produce on the American character? Will there be a shift in traditional values, a decline of individualism? Will the diversity of talents displayed by the frontiersman yield to functional specialization? What will be the role of government in an urbanized society, and what degree of regimentation will be necessary to regulate the lives of the millions who elect to live in such close proximity?

3. RESOURCES: THE PROBLEM OF CONSERVATION

In the exploitation of natural resources, the production of the necessities and luxuries of life, the people of the United States had forged so far ahead by the twentieth century that this nation led the world in material wealth. In fact it led by such a notable margin that one-half the total manufactured products possessed by mankind were credited to the American people. Although such estimates have little real value or meaning, yet the material prosperity enjoyed in America remains impressive even when it is translated into prosaic terms. One-third of the railway lines of the world, as already mentioned, lie within the United States. One-third to one-half the world's steel and coal are produced here. Two-fifths of the radios, half the telephones, four-fifths of the automobiles of the world are owned by Americans. Twenty-two billion dollars of gold, over four-fifths of the monetary gold in existence, is held by the Treasury Department. In the form of electrical energy, every American citizen has the equivalent of a dozen slaves meeting his needs in a myriad ways so ingenious he accepts their service without appreciating the miracle of it. The average European has only one-fifth as much electric power available to serve him and far fewer contrivances for it to operate.

To supply 140,000,000 consumers and feed the gigantic industries Americans must exploit all the riches of the land and the treasures under it. Their annual consumption of lumber has reached thirteen million square feet; the annual value of metallic products has risen to over $2,000,000,000, of non-metallic products to $5,000,000,000. In the last year before World War II opened in Europe (1939) American manufactures attained a total value of $25,000,000,000. But such figures mean little by themselves. To be appreciated they must be set beside statistics for other nations and the American standard of living contrasted with the welfare of less favored peoples in regions that are not so rich or so well developed.

Not only industry but agriculture has been revolutionized by American energy, ingenuity, and machinery. The continental United States contains regions of rich soil, a varied topography, a rainfall that is adequate and dependable over extensive areas, and climatic zones that range from severe through temperate to semitropical conditions. These natural advantages have enabled the American people to cultivate within their own borders almost all the commodities required for an abundant and variegated diet. The average American commands ten times the food supply of the average Asiatic, and his food is not only more plentiful but infinitely more varied, better balanced, and more palatable. This achievement in food production is the more startling because, in the United States, only one-sixth of the population is engaged in providing food and they have a surplus for export. In most Asiatic regions five-sixths of the people toil on the land to sustain a population which is only one-tenth as well fed.

The cash value of farm income in the United States ranged between $5,000,000,000 and $10,000,000,000 in the 1930's; under the stimulus of war demands it rose to $16,000,000,000 in 1942. Preserved by improved methods of dehydrating, freezing, or canning, this huge surplus produced from American fields, farms, orchards, flocks, herds, and poultry yards provided food for the armed forces and for millions of the needy who faced starvation in war wracked countries. It has been estimated that the state of Kansas alone could produce enough wheat for the people of the United States.

The natural wealth of the New World seemed so inexhaustible that the American people were overreckless in exploiting it. Never in history was a continent plundered so impetuously. By the end of the nineteenth century some of the penalties of waste and wanton destruction were already apparent. In 1871 a Commissioner of Fisheries was appointed to save the coastal fishing grounds from exhaustion. Twenty years later the Department of Agriculture moved to create a national forest reserve, before lumbering, land clearance, and bush fires should destroy the forests beyond recovery. By 1900 the federal government had accepted the grave responsibility of calculating the nation's reserves and resources and measuring them against its future needs. Plans for a national survey, for a national reclamation service, and for the preservation of essential resources in the public domain were pressed by farsighted legislators who recognized the wastefulness of unregulated exploitation.

One prompt result was the passage of stricter Acts designed to safeguard those national forest and mining areas which had not yet been appropriated. Coal, oil, gas, and mineral wealth located in the public domain were subject to federal control, and the Department of the Interior could lease available areas for development under the Mining Act of 1920. Rivers, waterways, dams, irrigation projects, and hydroelectric plants were supervised by a Federal Power Commission. With the swift destruction of the forests the danger of floods had increased. In forested areas a heavy rainfall flows away slowly and part of the water is evaporated by the trees, but in logged-off areas a prolonged rain may wash away the exposed topsoil. Rivulets become gulleys, and rivers swell to floods which spread wide devastation. Nor is this the only danger that may follow unplanned deforestation. In dry seasons the soil which is loose and parched may be carried away by high winds, creating dust storms which destroy crops and livestock over entire states.

The problems of reclaiming marginal lands, replanting forests, controlling floods, irrigating arid valleys, developing electric power were all related to one another. But they reached beyond state lines, and to solve them required expenditures and engineering projects greater than the individual states could undertake. The federal government therefore assumed responsibility and its engineers drafted plans for power and conservation projects on a grandiose scale. The most notable was the Tennessee Valley Authority, organized in 1933. This ambitious undertaking, which required a special Act of Congress, involved the construction of dams to control the whole Tennessee River system. The aim was to improve navigation, assure flood control, and generate electric power. But the project had a further purpose, the development of surplus power and resources that would be available in a national emergency; and this function overshadowed the other activities of the TVA when the United States was drawn into World War II.

Bold ventures in national economic planning, such as the Tennessee Valley Authority and projects undertaken by the Federal Bureau of Reclamation on the Colorado River at Hoover Dam and on the Columbia River at Grand Coulee, though they pay for their cost in rich benefits, are not welcomed unanimously. Many citizens oppose the grant of such extensive powers to the government. They denounce the laws controlling land use and the limitations on mining, lumbering, fishing, and waterway development as "bureaucracy." But Americans have come to recognize that the multiplication of federal commissions and the extension of government control is no momentary or accidental trend. In every industrial country of the world similar measures of "regimentation" have multiplied in the twentieth century. The most notable examples of state planning in the period between the World Wars were Russia, where the Soviet government brought the entire national economy within the scope of successive Five-Year Plans after 1928, and Germany, where after 1933 the social, political, and economic activity of 70,000,000 people were co-ordinated in a vast rearmament program under the National Socialist government. The United States could not easily remain unaffected by the almost universal tendency to bring political, social, and economic forces together to promote national defense; such national planning was the most vigorous expression of twentieth century "statism."

4. THE PROBLEM OF SOCIAL JUSTICE

From colonial times the English settlers in America were distinguished by a hardy self-sufficiency. The royal government in London could not control them strictly and they learned to solve many problems of shelter, supply, transportation, and defense on the spot. Their spirit of local independence made them difficult to govern; they resented any officious interference in their affairs and repudiated new taxes. This attitude continued to distinguish many Americans, especially in frontier regions, after the Thirteen Colonies became the United States. The frontiersmen, like the first settlers, were inclined to trust in themselves and to distrust politicians.

Because exhausting wars, except for the War between the States, were spared Americans until the twentieth century, they could afford the luxury of an unobtrusive government. They could dispense with military conscription and allot to education the funds which less isolated nations dedicated to defense. Largely for this reason their laws were less exigent, their taxes remained lower, their personal liberty was greater, and their freedom flowered in a manner that European countries could not equal. Furthermore, because the resources of the new land seemed more than adequate for the needs of the young nation, there was no good reason to fear an unfavorable trade balance, no need to mortgage the future by asking too much foreign aid, monetary, military, or technical. American sovereignty was more nearly absolute and unhampered than that of any other important nation. This wide independence and relative immunity to foreign interference was important. It provided the living space and the atmosphere in which the democracy of the New World developed.

American democracy could be threatened, however, by internal as well as by external developments. As the nineteenth century advanced a new aristocracy, an aristocracy of money, rose to leadership in the business world and dominated American society. In the era of business expansion which followed the War between the States the conflicting demands of capital and labor, which had already split European classes asunder, became a lively issue in politics. Popular orators argued that the rise of vast personal fortunes, the exercise of monopolies, and the creation of business trusts and corporations would concentrate too much power in the hands of a small ruling group, a plutocracy. Equality of economic opportunity, a foundation stone of American democracy, appeared to be threatened by such concentration of wealth. The question thus arose whether it was not the duty of Congress to prevent by positive legislation undue accumulation of economic power by small private groups.

Hitherto business life in the United States had been left to develop as freely as possible under a system of free contract. Government interference in economic matters was contrary to the laissez-faire spirit of the nineteenth century. The demand for legislation which would assure the laboring classes a fair income and reasonable working conditions and prevent the concentration of economic power in the hands of a few business leaders marked a change in political thinking. This change might be summed up by saying that, for millions of Americans, the eighteenth century maxim, "To govern better, govern less," was being revised to read, "To govern better, govern more." The most important laws passed by Congress after 1900 were adopted as part of a program to promote social justice, preserve the American way of life, and protect the system of free enterprise. The great business trusts, corporations, and monopolies were attacked on the ground that they were becoming a threat to free enterprise. Yet the main difficulty which hindered all attempts to curb the trusts or to dissolve them was the fact that they were themselves a product of the system of free enterprise which Americans valued so highly. It was recognized, furthermore, that without the organizing genius of a few farsighted men, without the accumulation of capital in private hands, and without the unity of management and the standardization required for mass production, the expansion of American business life could hardly have taken place. But it was also recognized that however great the benefits the powerful monopolists had conferred, they had also displayed at times a readiness to pervert politics and corrupt legislators, to discriminate unfairly against their opponents, to exploit the public, and to waste the national resources in their greed for profit.

The first important legislative attempts to limit the power of "big business" were the Interstate Commerce Act (1887) which sought to bring the railways under federal control, and the Sherman Antitrust Act (1890) which declared contracts, combinations, and trusts illegal if they could be shown to be conspiracies in restraint of trade. The enforcement of these Acts depended upon the courts, and as they were called in question by many adverse court decisions the efforts to limit or dissolve the trusts were only partly effective. A supplement to the Sherman Act, known as the Clayton Antitrust Act, was adopted in 1914. It was designed to restrict still more specifically the practice of price discrimination, to forbid exclusive business agreements which violated the principle of free competition, and to hinder the formation of too many interlocking directorates, a device whereby the real control of several corporations might be held by a few key men.

The First World War brought a tightening of government control over business and production. Goods needed for defense and factories making munitions were regulated by government fiat. The War Industries Board, created in 1917, had charge of all war purchases, and a War Finance Commission (1918) advanced the credit from federal funds to recondition factories and subsidize crops. With peace, however, government aid and government control were relaxed. The railroads, which had been unified under federal control in 1917, were restored to private ownership and operation in 1920. In the decade from 1919 to 1929 American business enjoyed a period of extraordinary expansion and prosperity. Prices and wages rose, production multiplied, and the people of the United States, pleased with the increase of material wealth, left the business leaders a large degree of independence. But this tolerance ended abruptly when the inflated market collapsed in 1929. Blaming the bankers, brokers, promoters, and industrialists for the economic crisis, the bank failures and the alarming unemployment, the public demanded angrily why the government had not regulated economic affairs more intelligently and averted the depression.

In the election of 1932 the Republican Party was repudiated by the electorate and the Democrats were swept into power with a large majority. The crisis had fixed the attention of the nation on Washington, and the new president, Franklin Delano Roosevelt, speedily won unusual prestige and popularity. The American faith in laissez-faire ideals and the confidence that businessmen knew best how to assure the prosperity of all had been profoundly shaken. There were widespread and insistent demands for government aid in restoring order and stability. Recognizing this mandate, Roosevelt announced a "New Deal" for the "forgotten man" and a far-reaching program of social reform.

One aim of the New Deal legislation was to bring all business enterprises — banks, corporations, public utilities, transportation systems, investment houses — under stricter federal control. A second aim was to protect the factory and office worker, the farmer, the small storekeeper, the home owner, from the destitution which threatened him as the business depression spread. Relief and rehabilitation for ten million unemployed, federal loans to the banks to safeguard savings, financial aid to farmers threatened with foreclosure, and a civil works program to create jobs were some of the measures adopted by the Democratic Congress which convened in 1933. By 1935 government plans to take permanent care of the indigent and the aged had been embodied in the Social Security Act. With federal contributions, the state governments were to promise $15 a month to aged residents over sixty-five, who were in need; to provide unemployment insurance in the form of payments for a limited period to workers deprived of occupation; and to create a fund which would enable qualified registered workers to retire at sixty-five with a pension of $10 to $15 a month.

These relief measures, federal loans, and contributions to old age and unemployment funds rapidly increased the federal debt. Between 1932 and 1939 it doubled, rising from approximately $20,000,000,000 to $40,000,000,000. New taxes were introduced which struck at corporation profits, increased the income tax and surtax, and placed luxuries and amusements under tribute. These measures suggested that the New Deal leaders considered it expedient not only to curb and regulate "big business" but to redistribute the national income by collecting revenue from the wealthy through surtaxes and other levies and raising the income of the poor by a system of pensions. These changes in policy, so rapidly extended after 1932, indicated a swing towards social and economic control in the United States. The concept of the "weak state" which made its authority felt as little as possible had played its part in American life and been discarded. Federal inspectors, a federal police (the Federal Bureau of Investigation), federal taxes and security regulations were reaching into all parts of the country. Many employers and businessmen complained that they were handicapped by the demand to fill out interminable form sheets, by the visits of government inspectors, by the control exercised over raw materials, by the processing taxes, and by social security rules. They hoped that when the economic crisis which commenced in 1929 had abated, federal control would be relaxed. But a large proportion of small farmers, city workers in mill and office, members of the lower middle class, and the businessman with a small independent firm or store approved of the New Deal. Roosevelt was re-elected in 1936 and in 1940 by imposing majorities, and thus became the first American president to serve a third term. After 1937, however, the increasing danger of war turned the attention of the people to foreign as well as domestic affairs. The measures proposed and the multiplied powers requested by the federal government, in bridging the economic crisis, were prolonged and extended into a broad program of national defense. This organization of economic, military, and naval forces for the protection of the United States can be discussed more logically in connection with foreign affairs.

THE UNITED STATES: FOREIGN AFFAIRS

Be it remembered that unless I had acted exactly as I did act there would now be no Panama Canal. It is folly to assert devotion to an end, and at the same time to condemn the only means by which that end can be attained.

THEODORE ROOSEVELT

1. MANIFEST DESTINY

THE expansion of American economic life in the last decades of the nineteenth century, especially the growth of industry, enabled the United States to overtake Great Britain and Germany and to become the greatest economic power in the world. The American share of international trade did not equal that of Great Britain until 1929. But nine-tenths of American production was absorbed by the home market, where more than a hundred million consumers with the highest living standard in the world constituted a coast to coast market in themselves, a market which could not be barred to American goods by alien tariff walls. The relative self-sufficiency of the United States partially obscured its growing strength, but the European peoples became gradually aware that a giant had arisen across the Atlantic Ocean. Many Americans, however, because they were self-centred and preoccupied with local problems, failed to foresee the important role which their country would soon be called upon to play in world affairs. Only after the surge of frontier expansion and settlement had dwindled did the people of the United States turn their gaze across the oceans. They were surprised to discover that by then they had already acquired commitments in other continents.

Until the twentieth century the United States had suffered little from the wars in Europe, Asia, or Africa. As the dominant power of the New World and guardian of the Americas, it was satisfied to warn all foreign nations not to interfere aggressively in the affairs of the Latin American republics. In 1889 it sought to establish its responsibilities for the defense of this hemisphere more definitely, and formed plans for a permanent league of all the American republics. Since the United States could not fail to exercise preponderance in such an association, the proposal did not thrive. The Argentine Republic in particular was opposed to it, resisting the plans for a common code of international law for the Americas, a co-ordination of Pan-American highways and railways, and the integration of currency and customs rates. But although the move for a genuine Pan-American league failed at this time, it had one positive result. A diplomatic council was established, pledged to meet from time to time for the discussion of common hemisphere problems. With this tentative measure of consolidation the friends of Pan-American solidarity had temporarily to rest content. In fact, for a decade and more inter-American relations deteriorated. The activity of United States forces in the Caribbean, the Spanish-American War of 1898, and the energetic acquisition of the Canal Zone at Panama alienated and alarmed many Latin Americans, who looked with apprehension at the exuberant power of the "Colossus of the North."

A further indication that the United States had taken the road to expansion in the late nineteenth century was the occupation (1893) of the Hawaiian Islands. Two years later the United States government intervened in a dispute between Great Britain and Venezuela and checked British designs against this South American state by insisting upon arbitration. But if the United States was to defend the Latin American republics and extend its protection to islands in the mid Pacific, a strong navy was essential. Ardent patriots and expansionists therefore urged Congress to vote an ambitious program of naval construction to support the more decisive attitude the United States was expected to play in world politics. The outbreak of a revolt in Cuba (1895), which was repressed with great severity by the Spanish authorities there, roused sympathy for the insurgents. In 1898 the unsettled Cuban question led to a war between the United States and Spain. This brief conflict ended the same year in a swift and signal defeat for the Spanish forces. A United States fleet destroyed the Spanish squadron at Manila Bay in the Philippines without the loss of a single American life. A few weeks later a second Spanish squadron was destroyed in Cuban waters. Peace was concluded in August, 1898, Spain ceding to the United States the Philippines, Puerto Rico, and Guam. For the Cubans the war brought independence from Spanish rule, and the United States assumed responsibility for the protection of Cuban liberty by the Platt Amendment (1901) which was incorporated in the Cuban constitution.

The Spanish-American War proclaimed to the world that the United States had become a naval power, with responsibilities which only a great naval power could successfully fulfill. The maintenance of advanced bases in the Pacific, the protection of the Central and South American coasts, and the patrolling of Alaskan waters called for an expanded naval policy. Commitments so far flung could be met only by dividing the American fleet and stationing part in Atlantic, part in Pacific waters. The long voyage around Cape Horn made it difficult to reinforce the reserves in either ocean, and if an emergency arose one section of the fleet might be shattered before the other could arrive to support it. The surest way to strengthen American naval defense was to link the east and west coast bases by a waterway that would accommodate battleships, and this meant the construction of an interoceanic canal across the Isthmus of Panama.

In the 1880's a French company had undertaken to build a Panama Canal, but the venture collapsed in scandal and bankruptcy. The Suez Canal, which linked the Mediterranean to the Red Sea in 1869, had been financed by an international syndicate, but the United States could not remain indifferent if foreign governments built a canal across Panama or Nicaragua. Theodore Roosevelt, who became President of the United States in 1901 when President McKinley was assassinated, personified the new, confident, expansionist mood stirring the American people. He was not a man to delay in a matter of importance nor was he easily daunted by technical, diplomatic, or financial obstacles. When the Republic of Colombia negotiated, and then failed to ratify, an agreement authorizing the United States government to construct a canal at Panama, the project was threatened with indefinite delay. But a convenient revolt broke out in Panama province and Panama seceded from the Republic of Colombia (1903). The State Department at Washington promptly recognized the *de facto* government, which in return immediately ratified the desired canal concession. An accord had already been reached between the United States and Great Britain in 1901, and the property and privileges of the defunct French company were purchased by the United States in 1902. After years of battle against tropical diseases, landslides, labor problems, and technical difficulties, the canal was completed in 1914. The cost was half a billion dollars, but the "big ditch" was an impressive victory for the United States army engineers and ranked as one of the greatest feats of engineering in human history.

2. THE UNITED STATES AND ASIA

When the United States moved firmly into the field of world politics after the Spanish-American War of 1898, most of the great powers were seeking new alignments. Throughout the nineteenth century Great Britain had favored a position of "splendid isolation" but had guarded the balance of power in Europe and the world. The world was shrinking, however, and by 1900 British isolation began to appear less splendid. Alliances were forming which, a few years later, split Europe into two hostile camps and prepared the tragedy of World War I; in 1900 Great Britain stood on the threshold of the new century, hesitating to choose sides.

Germany and Austria-Hungary were knit by a Dual Alliance; France and Russia had formed a military accord in 1894. In 1898 the British made overtures at Berlin, hinting at the benefits of an Anglo-German front against Russia. The front was never formed; but in 1902 the British found another ally who might hold the Russians in check. Forsaking the policy of isolation, the cabinet at London negotiated an alliance with Japan, a move which greatly increased the prestige of the Japanese and encouraged them to press their duel with the Russians for the ultimate control of North China. Few statesmen in 1902 believed that the Japanese would dare to fight the Russians or foresaw that Japan might become an even more formidable threat to the peace of Asia.

The status of China was precarious and unpredictable when the United States began to take an active part in Far Eastern politics. The acquisition of the Philippines in 1898 had carried the Stars and Stripes across the Pacific and linked the destinies of young America with the fate of the ancient Orient. By 1899 this new responsibility was already causing concern to John Hay, the American secretary of state. The decision was taken at Washington to discourage further dismemberment of China by the great powers, and Hay proposed an "open door" policy whereby the powers would promise to admit foreign trade to their spheres of interest in China on the same terms as their own commerce and to respect vested interests which were already there. Some months later Hay sent a second circular note to the powers, urging that the integrity of China should be preserved and trade allowed on equal terms to all without discrimination.

The immediate effect of Hay's overture was not great, for in 1900 Chinese resentment against the "foreign devils" exploded in a futile rebellion known as the Boxer Uprising. The revolt was sternly repressed by an international armed force dispatched jointly by all the interested powers including the United States. Peking was occupied, with considerable looting, and the Chinese forced to assume indemnities of more than $700,000,000 as a penalty for the murder of several hundred Europeans and the destruction of property. The Russians seized the chance to strengthen their hold on Manchuria with several army corps, and the danger that all North China might fall under their domination darkened the outlook for peace.

Russia was not the only aggressive neighbor threatening Chinese sovereignty; in the outcome, China was really saved by the jealousy of the intruders, who blocked one another in their greed for segments of the Celestial Empire. The British, long established at Hong Kong, marked out the valley of the Yangtze Kiang for penetration. The French, masters of Indo-China, were reaching into adjacent Chinese provinces. The Germans secured economic concessions in the province of Shantung. The Japanese, after a brief war with China in 1895, had taken Formosa and demanded "freedom" for Korea, which they hoped to annex. It appeared probable in 1900 that China would soon be parcelled out among the imperialist powers as ruthlessly as Africa had been partitioned in the preceding decades.

These distant rivalries on the other side of the world still seemed remote and uninteresting to most American citizens. But their attention was drawn to the Philippines by the struggle of the insurgent forces there, which resisted for three years after Spain surrendered the islands. To provide bases and coaling stations for the far-ranging United States battleships, now called to the most distant areas of the world's largest ocean, the navy competed with expeditions dispatched by other powers, exploring the numberless groups of Pacific atolls and laying claim to those which might serve for depots, for anchorage, or for coal or cable stations. In some cases, as in the protracted dispute over Samoa, several powers were involved, all interested in strengthening their naval position in the Pacific area.

In 1904 the outbreak of war between Japan and Russia gave a new aspect to the whole Far Eastern question. The Muscovite designs on Manchuria and Port Arthur were halted, for the Japanese naval and military forces defeated the Russians in a series of brilliant and decisive campaigns. Japan moved suddenly into the circle of the great powers,

Russia ceased for the time to appear a serious menace, and statesmen in the leading capitals hastened to gauge the new shift in the balance of power. In 1905 the United States government offered its services as mediator, and the Russo-Japanese War was ended by a treaty signed at Portsmouth, New Hampshire. The terms provided that the Japanese would control Korea (Chosen), receive the southern half of Sakhalin Island, and be granted a lease to the Liaotung peninsula. Manchuria the Russians agreed to restore to Chinese sovereignty. Although this treaty settlement was a triumph for Japan it was greeted there with criticism and rioting. The Japanese had hoped to secure an indemnity and immediate control of Manchuria as a further reward for the sacrifices which had brought victory. The Treaty of Portsmouth appeared to them a proof that European imperialists still hoped to secure the most coveted sections of China for themselves.

The Japanese were the first non-European people to adopt modern scientific and technological methods to solve their national problems, and to apply them with a success that made Japan a great power. The entry of Japan upon the stage of world politics therefore marked the opening of a new act not only in the drama of Far Eastern affairs but in modern history. It signalized the first serious challenge to the supremacy of the white race and the world hegemony of the Europeans. Unrest in Asia, nationalist resistance to British rule in India, the resentments smoldering throughout the Mohammedan world were all stimulated by the Japanese example. For the Japanese had proved that a non-European people could challenge the Europeans at their own imperialistic game and defeat them as Japan had defeated Russia.

Though disappointed in 1905 that they had not won a wider influence in China, the Japanese bided their time. The outbreak of World War I nine years later provided the favorable occasion they desired, for it engaged the great powers in a life and death struggle in the European theater. Nominally an ally of the Entente Powers, Britain, France, and Russia, Japan promptly seized the German leased port of Kiauchow and took over German concessions in Shantung province. Then Tokyo presented in secret an ultimatum of Twenty-one Demands, insisting that the Chinese acknowledge the newly acquired rights in Shantung, extend the Japanese a number of important economic privileges, lease southern Manchuria to Japan for ninety-nine years, and refuse further concessions to other foreign powers. This program, if executed without opposition, would have speedily subordinated all northern China to Japanese control, for with the European nations heavily engaged in their own war the Chinese could look for little help in arms or money from abroad. Nevertheless they held the Japanese off as best they could. Further demands from Tokyo followed in 1916 and 1917. At Washington there was increasing concern over this Japanese penetration on the mainland of Asia, and American statesmen felt that the situation called for a firm stand if China was to be saved. The result was an exchange of notes between the United States and Japan in 1917. The Japanese government agreed to maintain the policy of the "open door" and to respect the political integrity of China. In return, the United States recognized that Japan held "special interests" in China. This none too specific agreement imposed some restraints upon the march of Japanese imperialism but it really decided nothing. The moment was not opportune, however, for the United States to adopt a more resolute course which might have required the dispatch of naval and military forces to the Far East.

For in 1917 the United States had pledged its resources to the European war and could suffer no unnecessary diversion of strength to secondary objectives. Two years later, however, after the collapse of Germany, the Pacific naval squadrons of the United States could be strengthened and a firmer attitude adopted towards Japan. It appeared possible that an unrestricted naval race would develop between the two rivals, with the added risk of a similar competition between the United States and Great Britain. To avert such costly and dangerous rivalry the American government proposed a naval conference which met at Washington in 1922. As a result of the parley a measure of stability was restored in the Far East. Japan returned Kiauchow to China. The territorial integrity and independence of China were reaffirmed in a Nine-Power Treaty, with the United States, Great Britain, France, Italy, Belgium, The Netherlands, Portugal, and Japan as signatories. A ten-year naval holiday was decreed during which no capital ships were to be laid down, and a total capital ship tonnage of 525,000 tons was set for the United States and Britain, with a limit of 325,000 tons for Japan and 175,000 each for France and Italy. This 5:5:3 ratio, as it came to be termed, offended Japanese pride but helped to postpone the intense naval rivalry and building race which had appeared unavoidable.

The relaxation of warlike preparations and the reduction of naval expenditure was welcomed by the American people. A change of mood had come over the nation with the close of the war. Disillusionment at the outcome of foreign ventures, distrust in the terms of the peace settlements, suspicion and cynicism towards the League of Nations, and resentment over the nonpayment of the war debts turned many Americans against new undertakings in distant countries. They argued that if the United States guarded American interests but avoided entangling alliances and wars on other continents, it would be unnecessary to maintain a conscript army or a large and expensive navy. The rewards of imperialism and participation in global responsibilities had ceased to seem attractive. National self-sufficiency appeared the sane and preferable ideal. Reversing the trend of the previous twenty years, the United States after 1918 swung back to a course of cautious isolationism and left the other continents to settle their own quarrels.

This postwar mood remained strong for over a decade and helps to explain why the American people were almost indifferent when the Japanese renewed their penetration of China. In 1931 Japanese forces opened a carefully timed offensive, a military campaign which was in reality an undeclared war. Within a few months they had occupied southern Manchuria and intervened at Shanghai. Conversations were opened between London and Washington on the need for joint Anglo-American action but no action was taken. The League of Nations, of which the United States was not a member, was more resolute in criticizing the Japanese. After investigation it adopted the Lytton Report which condemned the Japanese attacks; but it failed to halt these attacks. Manchuria, proclaimed an autonomous state with the title of Manchukuo, became in actuality a satellite under Japanese rule. To the expansionists at Tokyo, the militarists and industrialists who fostered Japanese imperialism, the hesitancy at Washington and the helplessness of the League were taken as proof that a bold course of action would assure Japanese domination over all East Asia.

Had the United States taken a firmer stand against Japanese expansion in Manchuria and China in 1930 and 1931, the balance of power in the Pacific area might have been altered. The war which came ten years later might have been averted; or, if it had proved inevitable, the American forces would have held stronger positions. But in 1930 the American people were in an isolationist mood. They were absorbed in the domestic crisis resulting from the economic depression, in the spreading unemployment, the falling prices and falling income, and the business failures. They wanted tax reductions and government aid at the same time, a program which could most readily be achieved by reducing "unnecessary" expenses such as battleships. At the same time,

American diplomats wanted to demonstrate American faith in disarmament for the benefit of foreign nations. The result of all these pressures may be read in the concessions made to Japan and to Britain when the Washington Naval Treaty was revised at the London Naval Conference of 1930. The "holiday" on capital ships was extended to 1936, and the ratio on naval tonnage was extended to include several other types of warships besides the giant battleships. Moreover, in balancing up the tonnage for these lesser categories, the British-American-Japanese ratio of 5:5:3 was revised to favor Japan. In small-gun cruisers and destroyers the Japanese were permitted seven-tenths of the parity ratio maintained by Britain and the United States. In submarines Japan and the United States were to be equal.

These real concessions might well have assuaged Japanese pride and canceled Japanese doubts regarding American intentions. For although the naval limitation treaties allowed Britain and America a 10:6 or 10:7 superiority over Japan in absolute tonnage, it must be remembered that the British and American navies were distributed throughout vast reaches of ocean, in the Atlantic and the Pacific, and had almost illimitable reaches of coast line to safeguard. The Japanese navy, entirely concentrated in the Orient, could maintain an almost unassailable supremacy in Far Eastern waters. This supremacy was further assured by the concessions of 1930, which raised Japanese light cruiser strength. But as an additional gesture of reassurance to demonstrate that America had no aggressive intentions, the United States renewed the pledges on Pacific bases which had been incorporated in the Washington Naval Treaty of 1922. These pledges prohibited the construction or expansion of naval bases or fortifications in the Pacific islands. Japan was thus freed from the fear that the United States might strengthen Guam or fortify the Aleutian Islands in a manner to threaten Japanese mastery in Japanese home waters.

The London Naval Treaties proved to the world that the people of the United States, moved by a variety of motives, were prepared to take long strides towards disarmament. In the Atlantic as well as the Pacific American naval strength was cut, for the American heavy cruiser program was reduced while the British won permission to raise their cruiser strength if they deemed it necessary. In the capitals of the world, in London and Paris, in Berlin, Rome, and Tokyo, the American naval limitation, the American hesitation to oppose Japanese moves in China, and the American neutrality laws which followed shortly, all appeared to proclaim the same truth: the United States would defend the Americas but it would not be drawn into the wars of Asia or of Europe. This was, as subsequent history showed, a false assumption. But it was not, in the light of American policies from 1919 to 1939, an implausible assumption. To understand the course which the United States government followed in this twenty-year period, it is important to realize that a majority of the American people throughout these years not only wanted to stay out of foreign wars but believed it was possible to stay out of foreign wars. In their desire to avoid foreign commitments and foreign entanglements they were isolationists. It was only when American involvement in World War II was recognized as unavoidable that the word isolationist became a term of reproach.

3. THE UNITED STATES AND EUROPEAN PEACE

From the first years of their independence the feelings of the American people towards European problems remained contradictory. They wished to remain aloof from the perpetual feuds which rent the Old World, yet with every major conflict from the eighteenth to the twentieth century they found themselves drawn in against their intentions. The Seven Years' War, the Napoleonic Wars, and the First and Second World Wars all cost American lives and endangered American liberties. European wars were contagious; when they lasted more than a year or two it became almost impossible for the United States to escape infection. Nevertheless the desire to stay out, to preserve American isolation, remained the dominant wish of the people and the cardinal aim of their foreign policy. The United States contracted no alliance with any European nation; even in the great collaborative effort of 1917–1918 it was an associated not an allied member of the coalition that defeated the Central Powers. American diplomats worked for peace, advocated a just equilibrium among the states, and frowned upon aggression. But there was a persistent gulf between the aims they approved in principle and the responsibilities they were prepared to undertake. The clause in the League Covenant (Article 10) which bound the members to respect and preserve the territorial integrity and the political independence of all other members, seemed a hazardous commitment. If accepted literally it meant that the United States would have to go to the aid of any foreign nation that was attacked without warrant. The American people preferred to resume their traditional isolation and reject the League of Nations. The decision was in keeping with their preferences and with their past.

It was not prudence alone that kept America outside the League. Even from three thousand miles away the people could see that the Versailles settlement had not solved all issues perfectly and that to guarantee "existing" frontiers might be to perpetuate injustices. Here, indeed, was the hidden worm that sapped the strength of the League from the first. Woodrow Wilson, recognizing that the Versailles treaty contained flaws, had stressed the League as the rectifying instrument which would correct them. But the French and their allies in Europe, who dominated the League sessions when they opened, were adamant against revision: they wanted to hold the gains won in battle and to dedicate the League to the task of "freezing" the existing frontiers. Had the United States been a member, American influence might have held the League closer to its true function as an instrument for adjusting strains and rectifying inequalities. But the United States had withdrawn once more into diplomatic isolation. Although American statesmen visited Geneva to observe League proceedings, the nations assembled there never heard that voice from the New World which had spoken so clearly above the roar of cannon in 1917 and 1918.

Those delegates at Geneva who strove to work out the Wilsonian ideals enjoyed American sympathy but not American aid. The people of the United States read, some with enthusiasm, some with tolerance, some with impatience, and many with indifference, the speeches and the projects for assuring international peace. These moves had three major aims: (1) to fix frontiers and secure each sovereign state against aggression; (2) to reduce armaments; and (3) to promote economic stability and open the world markets and world resources to all people on equitable terms. These were the aims held up in Wilson's Fourteen Points and in the League Covenant.

It is easy to point out, after their efforts for peace miscarried, that the spokesmen for the various powers were seldom frank, impartial, or self-effacing in their demands. Each had a special aim, a national interest to promote. Thus the first problem, the need to fix frontiers and protect all states against aggression, was a problem in which those great powers which were "satiated" and those small powers which were weak had a special interest. France, with the second largest colonial empire in the world but the smallest population of any great power, was quite understandably the leading advocate of immobility after 1918. The French sought and bought allies among the smaller states of Europe, pledging to Poland, Czechoslovakia, Rumania, and Yugoslavia the support of the French army to maintain existing frontiers. These smaller states, which had been created or enlarged by the settlements of 1919–1921, were safe only so long as those settlements were unchallenged, and they consequently supported the French stand. They were, like the French, "antirevisionist" so far as the postwar treaties were concerned, for the revival of German power or the re-creation of the Austro-Hungarian Empire might threaten their existence.

To those nations — Germany, Austria, Hungary, Bulgaria — which had been reduced and penalized by the peace treaties, the protests of the French and their allies that the existing status was satisfactory and that all who sought to undermine it were enemies of peace, seemed hypocritical. These defeated nations and other unsatisfied powers like Italy and Japan were "revisionist" in their diplomacy. They wanted to see some new deals in the game of international politics. This is the basic reason why they could not long support the League of Nations. For the Covenant of the League represented to them the first general postwar attempt to "fix" frontiers and by outlawing war to make the victors safe in their possessions. A durable peace had to be an endurable peace, accepted as such by all participants; otherwise those who felt themselves wronged by it would appeal from a deaf World Court to the decision of the sword. Thus it was clear that no proposal to outlaw war had much chance of success unless the European nations, vanquished as well as victors, could be reasonably assured that the League would act impartially on their claims.

The League never inspired this confidence in the vanquished nations; had the United States joined it, League power and impartiality would have stood higher in the popular estimation. The progress made after 1924 in harmonizing national resentments in Europe was made outside the League sessions rather than within them. Thus a proposal known as the Geneva Protocol (1924), initiated by Ramsay MacDonald as prime minister of Great Britain and by the French premier Edouard Herriot, failed to thrive although it was founded upon the three essential concepts: arbitration, security, and disarmament. But where League proposals failed, regional agreements succeeded. The most important were negotiated at the Locarno Conference held in Switzerland in 1925. Delegates from Britain, France, Italy, Germany, Belgium, Poland, and Czechoslovakia concluded five treaties of arbitration. The most significant was a Rhine Pact, whereby France, Britain, Italy, Germany, and Belgium guaranteed the existing Franco-German and Belgo-German boundary lines. The powers concerned also promised to refer future disputes to arbitration, and Germany exchanged a similar pledge with Poland and Czechoslovakia. Germany thus acknowledged voluntarily the borders drawn by the Versailles treaty-makers in the west; but attempts to secure a similar accord among the states set up in eastern and southern Europe after 1918, to supplement the postwar settlements there by new and voluntary agreements to respect the new frontiers, were unsuccessful. There was no "eastern Locarno."

Nevertheless much had been accomplished to dissipate the fear of war, and the Locarno pledges to avoid an appeal to arms in future disputes were firmly applauded in America. Three years later, in 1928, the United States secretary of state, Frank B. Kellogg, joined with the French foreign minister, Aristide Briand, in drawing up an antiwar pledge which was speedily endorsed by almost fifty nations. The signers of this Briand-Kellogg Peace Pact (or Pact of Paris) renounced war as an instrument of national policy and asserted that they would resolve any future disputes that arose among them by pacific means and that solutions "shall never be sought except by pacific means." Despite its vigorous wording, however, this multilateral treaty for the renunciation of war did little to change the march of events. For even the American State Department which sponsored it did not pretend that the pact was really a renunciation of war: the signatory powers merely renounced wars of aggression. "Every nation," ran the accompanying explanation, "is free at all times and regardless of treaty provisions to defend its territory from attack or invasion and it alone is competent to decide whether circumstances require recourse to war in self-defense." One result of this strange ambiguity was that after 1928 nations preferred to go to war without a declaration and continued to deny in the midst of extensive campaigns that a state of belligerency existed.

Diplomatic protocols that remain too far above the level of events and are couched in high-sounding generalities that lack any specific application, encourage a "flight from reality." It might even be charged that, however noble their intent, they are dangerous to peace because they erect paper screens for those who like to avert their gaze from the brutalities of international strife in other parts of the world and live in artificial isolation. Millions of Americans felt proud and satisfied that their government had sponsored so idealistic a pledge as the Kellogg Pact. They hoped that all the other signatory powers would honor it; but they did not feel obligated to examine it very carefully or to enquire whether it had much relation to the realities of the international situation. Nor did they trouble to ask themselves whether their own policies invariably worked in favor of peace or whether, as the richest and strongest of the industrial powers, the United States always sought to keep open the world markets and the world resources for all peoples on equitable terms.

4. AMERICAN ECONOMIC POLICIES

The role of a detached and self-sufficient power to which the United States reverted after 1919 was conceivable in a political and even in a diplomatic sense, for political and diplomatic ties could be repudiated. But it was impossible for the greatest industrial nation of the world to isolate itself economically. When the First World War ended, the United States called home its armed forces, rejected the general peace settlement which President Wilson had helped to draft, separated itself from its late associates in battle, and made bilateral treaties with its late enemies. America asked no reparations and annexed no share of the conquered territories. But in this proud resumption of its traditional aloofness it did not forget the loans which had been extended to the European nations in their need. The strongest material tie which joined America to Europe after 1919 was financial.

The decision of the United States Congress that the war loans must be honored and not abrogated had a profound effect on European postwar finance. (See pages 206–213.) When Germany defaulted on reparations and the French occupied the Ruhr Valley in reprisal, America took a prompt and effective part in resolving this impasse. A committee of financial experts headed by Charles Gates Dawes devised the Dawes Plan for handling reparations, and their motto, significantly enough, was "Business, not politics." The American nation, which shunned any binding political connection with the European states, readily forged another financial link by providing more than half the $200,000,000 loan required to stabilize German finances. Five years later, when the problem of reparations called for still further readjustment, another American expert, Owen D. Young, headed the committee which formulated a new settlement, the Young Plan.

American interest in questions of international finance was growing more percipient because American commerce with other nations was growing more profitable. Between 1922 and 1929 the national income of the American people rose 40 per cent and their industrial production rose 43 per cent. Their foreign trade also rose, but less swiftly, the increase being only 28 per cent. Imports were turned back by the high tariff rates, which had been raised still higher in the Fordney-McCumber Tariff Act of 1922, and exports were slowed by the fact that foreigners found it difficult to obtain dollar credits with which to pay for them. In exchange for American products the world had only its own products to offer and if these products competed with American output from farm or factory the representatives at Washington were persuaded to add a few bricks to the tariff wall at that point. Between 1914 and 1922 the annual exports from the United States exceeded the imports by over $2,300,000,000, but this unusual surplus of exports was swelled by war shipments to Europe. From 1923 to 1930 the annual excess of exports was about $630,000,000, or approximately $5,000,000,000 for eight years. Much of this surplus built up capital reserves abroad, creating American credits, developing oil properties, plantations, and mines, or opening American branch factories, banks, and agencies. By 1930 the amount of American private capital invested abroad was estimated at $16,000,000,000. This did not include the intergovernmental loans which were almost all in default and represented another pool of (uncollectible) dollar capital exported. These American ventures in the foreign investment field after 1919 did not absorb any dangerous proportion of American private savings, taking about 5 per cent annually. In comparison, the British invested about 30 per cent of their savings abroad annually in the years from 1924 to 1929.

This mounting dollar imperialism of the American people excited the envy of less prosperous nations, but so long as American loans were extended freely there was little complaint. But after the economic crisis of 1929 American capital export declined abruptly and so did American trade. The American dollars sent abroad had helped materially to provide dollar credits to pay for American goods sold abroad. In the disastrous years from 1929 to 1932 the international trade of the world fell two-thirds in value, but American foreign trade fell even faster, for the American share dropped from 29 to 22 per cent of the declining world total within three years. The sum of American exports and imports had reached almost $10,000,000,000 in 1929, but they amounted to less than $3,000,000,000 by 1932.

No one cause and no one country was responsible for the depression of 1929 and the following years, but the policies adopted by several national governments to combat the economic decline almost certainly made it worse. Each nation endeavored to safeguard its own shrinking market with protective walls and a managed currency, and this jealous economic nationalism further impeded the free flow of commerce by increasing tariff obstructions. The United States took the lead in this melancholy competition with the Smoot-Hawley Tariff Act of 1930 which had been drawn up before the depression struck. Britain and other nations followed in 1931. The self-governing Dominions of the British Commonwealth adopted more favorable rates for interempire trade by the Ottawa Agreements of 1932, and Britain, having forsaken free trade at home, likewise abandoned the "open door" policy which had made the colonies a market for the goods of all nations. France, Italy, Spain, Mexico, and many other states also increased their tariffs in retaliation for the Smoot-Hawley tolls. Direct bargaining between governments for specific benefits became more common and world trade was increasingly directed into narrow grooves dug by the multiplication of bilateral agreements. Germany was particularly active in this form of negotiation, and by 1939 four-fifths of the German foreign trade had been canalized. The practical monopoly of many essential commodities enjoyed by leading powers and their superior coercive arguments when negotiating for an exchange, led to extreme hardships for less favored states; and the tightening of the trade restrictions sharply increased the international tension. One writer summarized in a terse prophecy the situation which was growing up: "If goods don't cross frontiers, armies will."

The United States government was widely criticized for its greed in striving to collect the war debts and for "protecting" with a high tariff an industrial system and agricultural resources unmatched anywhere in the world. President Herbert Hoover met the debt situation in 1931 by suggesting a one-year moratorium on all reparation and war debt payments. But both war debts and reparations had ceased by that time to have much meaning; no one seriously expected a resumption of payments after the year was over and no one made an effort to excuse the default. When Franklin D. Roosevelt replaced Hoover as President after the Democratic victory of 1932, however, the United States made a stronger bid to recover its ebbing share of world trade. Abandoning the gold standard, Roosevelt instructed the Treasury to devalue the dollar and to purchase gold in the world market at the equivalent of $35 instead of $20 an ounce. This measure reduced the value of the dollar from 100 to 59 cents but brought a flood of gold from all parts of the world to the United States. To many people it appeared illogical that America should desert the gold standard yet continue to buy and hoard gold, and they were perplexed at a policy which brought $10,000,000,000 worth of surplus gold into the country between 1934 and 1939. But such purchases were, in effect, a new form of capital export. By allowing the producer $35 for every ounce of gold shipped from Australia, South Africa, or other gold-producing countries, the United States Treasury provided foreign credits for the purchase of American goods. Private American capital had ceased to seek foreign markets after 1929, but Treasury payments for the gold imported (and imported at an extravagantly high quotation price) supplied the need of other nations for dollar credits. The excess of American exports over imports, in goods, from 1933 to 1939 was over $3,000,000,000, but in the same period America accepted imports of $10,000,000,000 in gold shipments and paid several billions more than the world price for this imported bullion. In a sense this was equivalent to giving away some $3,000,000,000 or more to balance the trade export surplus.

In defending itself against criticism, the American government could point out that it had not led the way in currency depreciation. The British depreciated the pound sterling by forsaking the gold standard in 1931, and the pound declined one-fourth in value, carrying with it a number of other national currencies which had been tied to the sterling system. These countries with lowered currencies could then sell their goods at a lower price on the world market, and nations which still strove, like the United States, to remain on gold, found their wares too highly priced for most of the world's consumers who had only depreciated currency to offer. The American abandonment of gold at the end of 1933 was followed by a steady recovery in the ailing export trade of the United States, a revival of business and industry, and a rise in the national income.

It is significant that recovery from the Great Depression of 1929–1933 began within the leading states and that trade between states was more severely shattered and required longer to reknit. This was partly due to the fact that, with independent or "unilateral" adjustment of national currencies, the dollar, pound, franc, peseta, and other units of coinage lost contact, and values expressed in one could not readily be translated into another. Fluctuating currencies discourage trade because they increase the uncertainty and the risk of loss, making it difficult for businessmen to preserve agreements or predict market demands. So long as each government continued to change the value of its currency without consultation with other nations, the world monetary situation would remain in a condition not far from anarchy.

In 1933, therefore, an International Monetary and Economic Conference was called at London to discuss currency stabilization. But the American government was persuaded that the chaotic condition of world economy made any plan for a general stabilization of national currencies inopportune and impracticable at this time. The economic ills of the world appeared too serious and too little understood to yield to a "bookkeeper's" solution and each nation was advised to put its own house in order before an attempt was made to re-establish a fixed parity or rigid exchange rate among the money units of the world. From Washington, President Franklin D. Roosevelt warned the Conference that the American people were determined to mend their own fences first.

> The world [he wrote] will not long be lulled by the specious fallacy of achieving a temporary and probably an artificial stability in foreign exchange on the part of a few large countries only. The sound internal economic system of a nation is a greater factor in its well-being than the price of its currency in changing terms of the currencies of other nations.

This sharp rejection of collective stabilization, announced by the greatest economic power of the world, hastened the dissolution of the Conference in July, 1933. With every state striving to save itself, to achieve the greatest possible economic security for the interest of its own people, there was little chance of co-ordinating the world's financial structure. Some countries, however, were better endowed to practice economic self-sufficiency than others, and the United States was the most favorably conditioned of all. For nine-tenths of the economy of the United States was self-contained: America was its own producer, manufacturer, and market. In contrast, Britain and many other states carried on from one-fourth to one-half their business dealings with foreign countries, and for them the disequilibrium of the currency exchange rates introduced an uncontrollable factor into all their business life. To them the powerful but unpredictable moves of the United States in world affairs were frightening and exasperating: like Gulliver, this giant of the Western ocean could capsize a Lilliputian navy by the waves raised up through a careless motion.

THE WAR LOANS AND THEIR REFUNDING [1]
(Figures in millions of dollars)

Country	Amounts of Original Loans			Amounts of Funded Debts	Average Interest Rates over Whole Period
	Pre-Armistice	Post-Armistice	Total		
ARMENIA *	......	12.0	12.0	......	....
AUSTRIA	......	24.0	24.0	24.0	3.3%
BELGIUM	171.8	207.3	379.1	417.8	1.8%
CUBA †	10.0	......	10.0	......	....
CZECHOSLOVAKIA	......	91.9	91.9	185.0	3.3%
ESTONIA	......	14.0	14.0	13.8	3.3%
FINLAND	......	8.3	8.3	9.0	3.3%
FRANCE	1,970.0	1,434.8	3,404.8	4,025.0	1.6%
GREAT BRITAIN	3,696.0	581.0	4,277.0	4,600.0	3.3%
GREECE	......	27.2	27.2	32.5	3.3%
HUNGARY	......	1.7	1.7	2.0	3.3%
ITALY	1,031.0	617.0	1,648.0	2,042.0	0.4%
JUGOSLAVIA	10.6	41.2	51.8	62.9	1.0%
LATVIA	......	5.1	5.1	5.8	3.3%
LIBERIA †	......	......	......	......	....
LITHUANIA	......	5.0	5.0	6.4	3.3%
NICARAGUA *	......	.4	.4	......	....
POLAND	......	159.7	159.7	178.6	3.3%
RUMANIA	......	37.9	37.9	66.6	3.3%
RUSSIA *	187.8	4.8	192.6	......	....
TOTALS	7,077.2	3,273.3	10,350.5	11,671.4	2.1% ‡

* Debts unfunded.   † Debts paid.   ‡ Average for all settlements.

The American people on their part had grown cool towards the problems of the European states, and American patience with the nations which had defaulted on their debts had finally failed. At the monetary conference of 1933 the unsolved problem of war debts was left off the agenda, a tacit admission that the debtor states hoped to forget the whole matter. But creditors have longer memories and in 1934 Roosevelt signed the Debt Default Act passed by the Congress. This Act declared that token payments by the governments which owed the United States funded loans would be held insufficient in future. Borrowers who remained in default were notified by this legislation that they would not be permitted to float loans in the United States until their past obligations had been satisfactorily settled. The warning had no effect. With the exception of Finland the debtor nations remained in default and ceased to remit even a

[1] From Allan Nevins and Louis M. Hacker, *The United States and Its Place in World Affairs, 1918–1943* (Boston: Heath, 1943), p. 174.

token installment. It should be noted, however, that all were not equally indifferent to their obligations. The British had paid almost $2,000,000,000, a sum considerably in excess of their collections from their own debtors. The French paid about $500,000,000. All other governments involved paid together less than the French remittance, so that the United States collected under $3,000,000,000 on debts which, with interest, amounted to over $20,000,000,000 when payments ceased.

5. THE AMERICAN ATTITUDE ON THE ARMAMENT PROBLEM

Even in the midst of the economic depression the European governments found money for arms. This fact helped to increase the impatience many Americans felt for the defaulting debtors who had not yet repaid the money borrowed for the last war. But the question of disarmament, like the question of fixing frontiers and the attainment of economic stability, proved too difficult for the League of Nations and for the diplomats. The most hopeful results were obtained in the first years of peace after 1919. The compulsory demilitarization of the defeated powers, however secured, was at least disarmament. The Washington Naval Conference of 1922 avoided the risk of a naval race between Britain and the United States and fixed a quota for Japan. America, by demobilizing its army divisions and limiting its navy, had set an example in voluntary disarmament.

No comparable agreement for the limitation of military forces was worked out by the European powers. Instead, France and the satellite states aligned with the French, which had inherited the military hegemony of Europe after Germany was disarmed, clung firmly to their advantage. The League of Nations showed no haste to call the promised conference on general arms reduction. Not until 1925 was a "preparatory" commission nominated. It did not hold its first meeting until 1926. Five years passed with an occasional interchange of views and in 1931 the delegates of sixty nations were invited to a Disarmament Conference. The results were almost entirely negative. The French insisted that a sense of security must precede any real move to disarm and argued, with reason, that no adequate system of collective security had yet been established. The American and British delegates strove to reassure the French and to make allowance for their strong distrust of Germany, but no compromise proved acceptable.

When the Conference convened once again in 1933 the prospect had darkened. The Germans, whose recalcitrance was changing to open defiance, now demanded equality of arms with the other powers and the abrogation of the limits placed upon their military forces by the Treaty of Versailles. Adolf Hitler, newly appointed Chancellor of the Reich, declared that he was willing to abandon all German military preparations if the other European powers would disarm, an offer none weighed seriously. The United States offered to reduce its armed forces in proportion as other nations reduced theirs. But all such proposals and counterproposals affected the realities of the situation very little. Land armies are not like battleships; there are no formulas for comparing the strength of a division in the same manner that the speed, thickness of armor, and caliber of guns on a dreadnought may be specified and tested. The quality of training and the morale of an army contain imponderable factors, the degree to which a nation's industries may be counted as war industries is not easy to fix, and the readiness with which youth organizations or air transport lines can prepare specialists for war tasks makes any routine definition of army strength of little value. These complex considerations daunted the commission on disarmament, the more so because the genuine desire to resolve them and to reach an honest formula on arms was too often lacking when the delegates assembled.

In October, 1933, the German government withdrew its delegates from the Conference and announced its impending resignation from the League of Nations. As justification for this move the Germans pointed out that in 1918 the victorious Allies had insisted they had built up their armies to resist German militarism and had implied that they would disband them once Germany was powerless to make war. This promise had not been kept. In 1931 Germany was spending 63 per cent less on armaments than in 1913. But the victor powers had increased their forces while the Germans reduced theirs, the increases in expenditure ranging from a 30 per cent rise for France and Russia since 1913 to an increase of 197 per cent on arms outlay for the United States.[1] The withdrawal of Germany ended the hope of a compromise on armaments. Europe was committed to an uncontrolled militarism, and the League of Nations accepted one more defeat.

Europe had taken the road towards another war, and the American people wanted no part in it. There was a powerful popular agita-

[1] *The Challenge of Disarmament.* Carnegie Endowment for International Peace, April 15, 1932.

tion in 1935 in favor of American neutrality and a strong feeling that intervention in the First World War had been a mistake, that it had been a consequence of clever propaganda by selfish interests. Recalling that the sale of arms to France and Britain and the loss of American lives in the war zone had helped to draw the United States into war in 1917, Congress passed a Neutrality Act in 1935 to avert similar developments if a new war opened. All shipment of war materials to belligerents was placed under embargo, American citizens were warned they could travel on the ships of belligerents only at their own risk, and the President was granted discretionary authority to apply these restrictions.

The neutrality legislation did not preserve the United States from war. From 1935 to 1941 the history of American foreign policy shows a steady involvement in the drama of European conflict. There was, first, a deepening emotional interest in the tragedy. The attitude of most Americans was no longer neutral even in 1937, although the embargo on arms, munitions, and implements of war and the prohibition of loans to belligerents were reaffirmed. A "cash and carry" provision was adopted which largely evaded the earlier decrees. Belligerents were now permitted to purchase what they desired from American sources provided that they paid for all purchases in cash and carried them away in their own ships. As only nations with preponderant sea power could be certain to profit by this provision, the amended measure was likely to favor Britain or France in case of war but not Germany, Italy, or Russia.

The repeated acts of aggression committed by the German National Socialist government after 1937, the inhuman treatment of the Jews, and the reports of brutalities inflicted upon political prisoners in the concentration camps, completed the emotional preparation of the American people for war. Their sympathy was almost wholly on the side of Britain and France when World War II opened in September, 1939. From then until the Japanese attacked Pearl Harbor on December 7, 1941, the attitude of the United States towards the conflict was, in a formal sense, one of neutrality. But in a realistic sense, as the "arsenal of democracy," the United States was aiding Britain and France and its status was that of an ally though not yet a participant in the war.

SECONDARY AMERICAN STATES

Peace is not enough: there must be jobs for all. The only thing the World needs to fear is poverty.

EZEQUIEL PADILLA (1945)
FOREIGN MINISTER OF THE MEXICAN REPUBLIC

I. THE DOMINION OF CANADA

CANADA forms a special link in the international order, for it is a bridge between Great Britain and the United States. Politically it is an autonomous self-governing Dominion in the British Commonwealth of Nations, with a bicameral parliament modeled on that of the mother country and a Governor-General who represents the King-Emperor at London. The Governor-General is little more than a constitutional figurehead, however, and the Canadian parliament would not enjoy greater freedom of action if the office were abolished. For since 1931, when the British parliament enacted the Statute of Westminster, the self-governing Dominions have ranked as sovereign states. This Act provided that no subsequent legislation passed by the British parliament was to extend to any of the Dominions, unless a Dominion requested and consented that this should be the case. A Dominion may even decline to accept a Governor-General, as Eire (the Irish Free State) has done under its constitution of 1937.

As a sovereign nation Canada has negotiated treaties independently of, and even in opposition to, British foreign policy and has voted against British proposals at international conferences. In general, however, Canadian foreign policy has paralleled that of other units of the Commonwealth. Great Britain, in turn, has shown respect for Canadian aims and preferences, as in 1921 when the Anglo-Japanese alliance of 1902 was dissolved, in part out of regard for Canadian and American sentiments. Technically Canada ranks as a kingdom and this distinction has been cited as one reason why the Canadian gov-

ernment does not join the Pan American Union of New World
republics. The real reason is that as a member of the Union Canada
might be drawn more closely within the orbit of the United States
and become involved in contradictory commitments. Had the Dominion been a member of the Pan American Union in 1939, for instance, it could not very well have joined Britain in declaring war on
Germany without separating its policies from the American republics which remained neutral.

In its economic as well as its political relations Canada stands between Britain and the United States. The geographical unity of the
two largest states of North America, Canada and the United States,
would make them economically one if there were no political dividing line. By 1943 American-owned property in Canada and Newfoundland exceeded $4,000,000,000, over one-third the total value
of American-owned property in foreign countries. Canadian commodities and prices react swiftly to quotations on the New York and
Chicago stock market, and Canada differs from all the other British
Dominions in using the dollar instead of the pound as a monetary
unit. But Canadians are vigilant to preserve their economic no less
than their political independence. Their annual exports to the United
States are only slightly greater than those to Britain. Since 1932 a
preferential tariff in favor of Britain and the other British Dominions
has strengthened imperial trade, and approximately half the external
commerce of Canada is now carried on within the empire. Thus in
its economic as well as its political and cultural ties Canada labors to
preserve its role as a bridge between the nations of the English-
speaking world.

If nations were judged by their foreign trade alone, Canada would
rank fifth among the great powers. By the decade 1926–1935 its
foreign trade placed it ahead of Japan, Italy, and Russia. Like the
United States, Canada has advanced with giant strides in the twentieth century, especially in industry. By 1942 automobiles led its exports, surpassing in value even wheat and newsprint. This industrialization has led to the same sharp increase in urban population which
has been already noted in the United States. Over 6,000,000, or approximately one-half the Canadian people, were town dwellers by
1945. But unlike the United States, where the frontier has disappeared, Canada has and must always have a frontier, a belt of vacant
territories between the northernmost settlements and the Polar Sea.
The vast region of Labrador, the shores of Hudson Bay, the North-

west Territories, and the Yukon are comparable to northern Siberia in their climate, vegetation, resources, and remoteness. These areas are not yet fully surveyed and are almost uninhabited, for nine-tenths of the Canadian population is found within a few hundred miles of the United States border. The density of population for the whole of Canada is less than five to the square mile.

The total area of Canada is estimated at 3,694,863 square miles. For a country so vast and so richly endowed by nature the twentieth century must bring rapid developments. As the automobile and the airplane superseded the canoe and the pack horse, and electricity arrived to help in solving the problems of heat, power, and light, large areas of Canada once thought too severe or too inaccessible for colonization were opened to settlers. In developed electric power per head Canada already ranks second among world states, following Norway. In national income per head the country ranks close to the United States and New Zealand, the most favored nations of the world in this respect. The great distances which separate the major Canadian cities, from Montreal to Vancouver, make transportation and communication acute problems. Canadians have built nearly 50,000 miles of railways, more miles per head than any other country can boast. Communication is served by well-developed air mail, radio, telegraph, and telephone systems, with one telephone to eight people as compared with one to six in the United States.

The problem of national defense could easily become serious in a country so large, so wealthy, and so thinly peopled. The British mastery of the seas, almost undisputed throughout the nineteenth century, served as a shield while Canadian settlements spread westward from the Gulf of St. Lawrence to the Pacific Coast. In the twentieth century the growth of American sea power has provided a further naval defense, for an invasion of Canada by any alien power would be resisted by the United States as a threat to the peace of this hemisphere. In addition there is a Royal Canadian Navy established in 1910.

Canada entered the First World War in 1914 and adopted a Compulsory Military Service Act in 1917. In the Second World War, without decreeing compulsory military service for action abroad, Canada nevertheless marshaled almost 1,000,000 men through the various fighting services, the Canadian Army, Canadian Navy, and Canadian Air Force. Since 1945 the question of defense has moved the government to survey more exactly the empty spaces of northern

Canada, a program made possible by sending military expeditions into the Arctic and subarctic regions, with the aid and co-operation of the United States Air Force. The completion of the Alcan Highway to Alaska during World War II has made it possible to establish more military and air bases in the northwest and in Alaska and to explore the resources of this corner of the continent.

Like the United States, Canada grew in a century and a half from a colony to a great nation. The increase has been due to a moderately high birthrate and constant immigration. The total population of the provinces has remained between one-tenth and one-fifteenth that of the United States. In 1800 it was about 400,000; by 1871 it reached 3,689,257; and in 1941 it was estimated at 11,506,655. The tide of immigrants has tended to fluctuate. The number arriving between 1881 and 1890 was 886,000; between 1891 and 1900 it fell to 321,000; but for the decade 1901 to 1910 it rose again to 1,453,000. For the single year 1914 it reached a peak of 367,240. Then the First World War cut it down, and in the last year before the Great Depression it had climbed back only to 167,723 (1929). In the 1930's and early 1940's it fell until it was less than 10,000 a year.

The Canadian government maintains a restrictive immigration policy, accepting for permanent residence only such settlers as it considers the nation can profitably assimilate. In a world in which many countries, especially in the Orient, are overcrowded, this policy is a potential source of controversy and has already created problems within the empire because of the exclusion of applicants from British India. In 1941, of the total Canadian population 5,715,904 were of British origin, 3,483,038 were of French descent, and the remaining 2,232,866 were of various national parentage. But only 1,104,133, or approximately one-tenth of the population in 1941, were foreign born, and of this number 312,473 were from the United States. In exchange for these settlers from the south, one million Canadian-born citizens who emigrated to the United States were living there in 1940. As in the earlier history of the American frontier, newcomers to Canada have moved towards the sparsely settled regions, and the percentage of foreign-born increases from east to west. In Prince Edward Island less than three residents in the hundred are of foreign birth while in British Columbia the percentage is 37.25.

There are two main national groups in Canada, the five to six million people of British descent and the three to four million of French descent. The French Canadians are guaranteed their right to preserve their language, religion, and customs, and have not intermixed with the other elements as most national groups in the United States are disposed to do. Loyal to their ancient French culture, responsive to the influences which stir the Latin as distinct from the Anglo-Saxon peoples, and firmly attached to the Catholic faith, the French-speaking *Canadiens* help to make Canada in yet another sense a *liaison* nation among the peoples of the Western world.

2. MEXICO

Unlike Canada, with its high wage level, modernized power plants, transportation, and industries, Mexico is economically retarded and impoverished. Half the population of 20,000,000 are illiterate; slightly more than half are Indians or are of mixed race. The official language is Spanish but several million Mexican Indians cannot speak it. Two-thirds of the people live by agriculture and only one-fourth are town dwellers. Mexico entered the twentieth century with two pressing problems: the need for land reform and the need to escape the exactions of foreign-owned corporations which were exploiting the resources of the country for the profit of alien investors rather than for the benefit of the Mexicans.

The land question rose out of the hacienda system which had been introduced by the Spanish conquerors three centuries earlier. By the end of the nineteenth century a few families had come to own most of the arable land throughout whole provinces, and a majority of the rural workers were in a state of peonage. Their food was inadequate, their hours of labor excessive, and their homes miserable windowless huts of one or two rooms floored with earth. The rising ferment within the country broke into revolution in 1911. General Don Porfirio Diaz, who had maintained a firm rule since 1876, was overthrown and exiled, and Mexico entered a decade of turmoil.

The revolutionary slogan, "Land and Liberty," was realized slowly in the midst of confusion and civil war. A new constitution, adopted in 1917 and modified in 1929 and 1933, provided for a Chamber of Deputies of 170 members elected for three years and a Senate of fifty-eight members elected for six years. There are two senators from each of the twenty-eight states of the republic and two from the Federal District surrounding Mexico City. The president of the republic is elected by direct popular vote for a term of six years. The political edifice constructed since 1911 is less important than the social and economic changes. Lands confiscated by the government have been allotted to the village assemblies for distribution as family holdings. The rural village is the real administrative unit, and in recognizing this fact the revolution brought about a partial return to the communal society of the Aztecs, known as *ejido*. The new agrarian laws which turned private estates over to the people constituted the essence of the revolution, for some two million families comprising half the Mexican people received individual allotments of land. The rapid increase of the population (a 17 per cent rise between 1930 and 1940) suggests that living conditions have improved. There has also been a vital artistic renaissance, especially in painting, which suggests that the latent energy and talent of these long submerged people may yet astonish more advanced nations.

The second great problem, the question of foreign investments and foreign control of resources, has been resolved in part through confiscation, repudiation, or refunding. The external debt of the republic has been in default since 1914 and amounted to about $235,000,000 in 1940. About 60 per cent of this amount was owed to citizens or corporations under German control. After Mexico declared war on Germany, Italy, and Japan (May, 1942), this three-fifths share of obligations outstanding was repudiated. On one-fifth of the debt, held by investors in the United States, the Mexican government made a settlement accord in December, 1942; but the final fifth, owed to British bondholders, remained in default. British and other foreign investors also held 97 per cent of the mining properties of the republic. As Mexico produces 40 per cent of the world's silver, and silver and gold together constitute one-fourth of the nation's exports, this alien ownership deprived the Mexicans of the management and profit of their most lucrative natural resources.

It was not surprising, therefore, that the government should seek to terminate this era of foreign financial control. In 1937 the main railway lines were declared national property; the railway bonds, half of which were held in London, remained in default. A year later, after negotiations had failed, the Mexican government appropriated the oil properties which had been developed at considerable cost by three foreign companies. An arrangement was concluded between Mexico and the United States in 1942 whereby the American oil properties were valued at $24,000,000 and compensation promised for this amount. Closer and more cordial relations between Washington and Mexico City had become a matter of urgency with the outbreak of World War II, a fact which speeded the settlement of

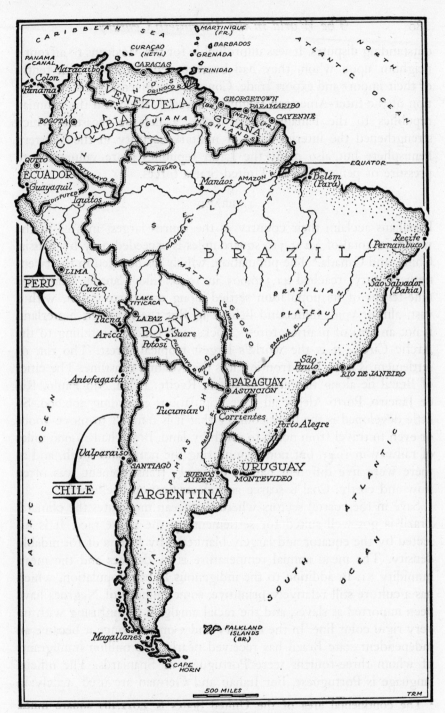

THE SOUTH AMERICAN REPUBLICS

outstanding disputes. It was unprofitable for the Mexicans to affront a neighbor upon whom they had become dependent for nine-tenths of their import and export trade. Consent was given for the construction of the Inter-American Highway across Mexico and the isthmian republics to the Panama Canal Zone, a defense measure which strengthened the interior lines of military security in the Western hemisphere but also made the Latin republics more vulnerable to pressure or penetration by United States forces.

3. BRAZIL

Brazilians acclaim their country as the fourth largest in area in the world; its total of 3,275,510 square miles is exceeded only by Russia, China, and Canada.[1] The population, which has doubled in the twentieth century, reached 41,356,605 in 1940. Like Canada, Brazil has nine-tenths of its population settled along one narrow rim, with a vast, almost void, hinterland behind it. But the Brazilian hinterland is not an area of prairies, forests, rocks, and tundra stretching to the Arctic Circle; it is the world's largest tropical forest. The rim of settlement is not a land frontier; it is the Atlantic coastline. The cities of Brazil lie along this coast — Belém, Recife, Bahia, São Paulo, Rio de Janeiro, Porto Alegre all have populations exceeding 300,000. So little developed is the back country that it is difficult to move goods or even to travel from north to south by land. Brazil had 24,000 miles of railway in 1943, but none connecting the north and south, and as there were five different gauges of track, transshipment was often slow and costly. Coal is scarce and electrification backward.

Save in the coastal sectors where the ocean moderates the climate, Brazil is not well suited for settlement by the white race. It is bisected by the equator and largely blanketed by forests of formidable density. The mean annual temperature is 72 degrees and the mean humidity 81. In addition to the indigenous Indian population, which has a culture still relatively primitive, some millions of Negroes have been imported as slaves, and the racial amalgam is confusing with no very rigid color line. In the century and a quarter since it became an independent state Brazil has received nearly five million immigrants of whom three-fourths were Portuguese or Spaniards. The official language is Portuguese, but Italian and German are used widely in

[1] The continental area of the United States is 3,022,387 square miles. With territories and possessions included the United States controls 3,735,223 square miles and thus exceeds Brazil.

the southern provinces. Successive regimes of a more or less pro-visory nature and frequent constitutional changes have marked Bra-zilian history in the twentieth century.

In Brazil nature is the most intractable adversary, and the oppres-sive climate, prevalence of disease, lack of supplies, of medical aid, of adequate finances, and of trained personnel make progress a tardy but heroic march. The questions of defense, of education, transporta-tion, and exploitation of unmeasured natural resources are being solved slowly in the face of grave obstacles. Like Mexico, Brazil is burdened with a heavy load of external debts, and the cost of servic-ing them is the chief charge on the federal budget: it absorbs a larger share of the taxes than the army and navy and four times the sum al-lotted to health and education. The twenty component states of the republic, and many municipalities, which until recent years enjoyed a large measure of independence, have also borrowed from foreign investors, and a part of these rather dubious loans are in default.

The disabilities which afflict Brazil hold in some degree for all the South and Central American republics. Roads and railways are lack-ing, and the mountains and forests interpose such impassable barriers that internal trade cannot develop easily and communities are isolated. Travel by pack train or river boat is slow, tedious, and sometimes dangerous. No continent has so much to gain from the air age as South America, for the airplane brings mountain plateaus and jungle clearings, once separated by weeks of travel, within a few hours' fly-ing time of one another. Hitherto, trade within and between the more isolated sections of South America has been almost nonexistent. Brazil, for instance, touches every South American republic except Chile and Ecuador, yet two-thirds of its external trade before the Second World War went to the United States and Britain and most of the remainder to European countries.

The lack of a strong domestic market is a serious handicap to the peoples of South America. Their economy is vulnerable because it is dependent upon demands from overseas, and world prices fluctuate uncontrollably. Their exportable commodities, minerals, coffee, rub-ber, tobacco, cocoa, and cotton, may rot in the fields or lie in a store-house in times of surplus. A fall in prices may reduce the plantation owner to bankruptcy and the peon to starvation, for millions of work-ers labor for local landowners or large corporations under condi-tions that are little better than serfdom. It has been estimated that two-thirds of the people of Latin America are physically ill nourished and that one-half suffer from infectious or deficiency diseases. All these disadvantages affect the Brazilians with particular force and no prompt solution is possible, but much may be hoped within the next decades from the reduction of tropical diseases through new drugs and vaccines.

4. THE ARGENTINE REPUBLIC AND THE LESSER STATES

In three respects Argentina offers a direct contrast to Brazil. (1) The hinterland is not impassable tropical forest but open pampas or scrub and steppe land. (2) The climate is not hot and humid but temperate, and most of the country is suitable for settlement by Europeans. (3) The population is almost exclusively of European extraction; there is no Negro element; and there are relatively few Indians or *mestizos*. Since 1900 the population has doubled, reaching 13,516,927 in 1942. Of this number 2,000,000 live in Buenos Aires and Rosario, so that in the inland regions the density falls from thirty to the square mile near the capital to less than two to the square mile in the territories.

Pasture lands comprise two-fifths of the republic, and over them range Argentina's living wealth, the hundred million domesticated animals that form a second population. About one-half the herds are sheep, with 30,000,000 cattle, 7,000,000 horses, and 6,000,000 swine. In Brazilian economy the vital article for export is coffee; in the external trade of the Argentine it is meat, with cereals in the second place. Great Britain has become the leading market for both, and the value of British investments in Argentinian enterprises is estimated at $2,000,000,000.

The Argentine government has often taken the lead in opposing the influence of the United States in South American affairs. There is an influential German group among the predominantly Spanish and Italian population, and in both World Wars the people of Argentina were sympathetic towards Germany. In the Second World War the republic did not sever relations with Germany, Japan, and Italy until the beginning of 1944. A few weeks later a swift *coup* unseated the president, General Pedro Ramirez, who resigned and was replaced by General Edelmiro J. Farrell. The defeat of the Fascist powers in Europe weakened but did not destroy the power of the military group which sought to dominate Argentine politics. In 1946 a new president, Juan Perón, was elected with the support of many workers' votes, but relations between the United States and the Argentine government continued strained.

Argentina carries a heavy public debt, internal and external, which devours one-fourth of the revenue and is partly in default. Uruguay, its small neighbor to the east, matches it in this and in several other characteristics. The sister republic has an external debt which absorbs one-fourth of the state revenue; one-third of the 2,000,000 Uruguayans are concentrated in the capital, Montevideo; and the country is 60 per cent pasture land. Animal products constitute 95 per cent of the exports.

A comparison of the Latin American countries makes it evident that all possess a familiar set of problems, repeated with variations but distressing in their repetition. There is the problem of a mixed population, sometimes half-Indian, largely illiterate, with many of the people in remoter regions unacquainted with Spanish (or, in Brazil, with Portuguese). There is the problem of inadequate transportation, which isolates the republics from one another and shuts provinces and villages in upon themselves. There are the problems of poverty, disease, ignorance, and sloth, and in much of Central and South America the problem of a climate tropical in its heat and humidity. It is significant that the most noteworthy Indian cultures of pre-Columbian times developed on the plateaus of Mexico and the Andes, thousands of feet above the hot and humid lowlands.

There is a second set of problems which might be classed as political. Few Latin American regimes have achieved that stability and continuity which encourages long-term planning and the steady growth of prosperity. This political uncertainty and the frequent civil wars, revolutions, and *coups d'état* which have punctuated Latin American history, have been in part a response to the economic vicissitudes. When conditions which they cannot control and do not understand reduce millions of people to want, they are easily stirred to rebellion especially if they are incited by ambitious and unscrupulous leaders. All the Latin American peoples feel with some reason that they are the victims of foreign exploitation, for all the republics (except Venezuela) have to deal with the problem of a heavy external debt.

This leads to the third set of problems, the economic problems, which beset the people. Much of the profit (in some republics almost all the profit) from the mines, railroads, airlines, telegraph companies, power plants, and other utilities go to foreign investors in the form of dividends. This has created a situation which many resent as economic vassalage. Economic dependence can destroy the political sovereignty of a state. Yet such dependence upon banks and markets outside the country is difficult to avoid if the country has developed a "one commodity" economy. Uruguay, with 95 per cent of its exports limited to animal products, is a striking example of this trend. In Venezuela petroleum formed 95 per cent of the export total in 1941. In Bolivia tin ore has made up 90 per cent of the export value for years. Chile, which once furnished nine-tenths of the world's nitrates, was all but ruined when chemical production and the Great Depression of 1929 broke its monopoly. The vulnerability of a nation with too many of its economic eggs in one basket is self-evident.

The nation which looks to one foreign market for most of its imports is likewise vulnerable. Most Latin American republics purchase at least half their imports from the United States and sell from half to three-fourths of their exports to the same power. This places them at the mercy of American tariff regulations, which might throw their rigid and restricted economy out of adjustment at any time by excluding their chief commodities. This dependence inevitably makes them apprehensive of American displeasure; against it they could do little in retaliation and therefore they could not be sure of any redress. A few figures on foreign trade will suggest how intimate this dependence of a small nation may become. In Costa Rica, Guatemala, and Salvador, for instance, coffee sales provide three-fourths of the value of all exports and hence provide the funds that pay for most imports. As the United States absorbs from 71 to 96 per cent of the exports and provides from 73 to 87 per cent of the imports, North American businessmen are able to influence profoundly the welfare and prosperity of these smaller neighbors. The case is even more conclusive for Honduras, Nicaragua, and Panama, for over 95 per cent of their exports go to the United States and over 75 per cent of their imports are purchased here. These conditions were in part an outgrowth of World War II which cut off trade with Europe, but they indicate a situation which most Latin Americans have to recognize and accept. In economic, financial, and military affairs the United States has established a regional supremacy over the Western hemisphere.

5. HEMISPHERE SOLIDARITY

At the opening of the twentieth century the Latin American republics were at once dependent upon and resentful of the might of the United

States. They accepted the protection and the security assured by the Monroe Doctrine but they were easily inflamed when North American businessmen interfered in their local affairs or United States marines landed on their shores. The State Department at Washington tended to interpret the Monroe Doctrine in ever more succinct and formidable terms, claiming for the United States the privilege of intervening at any time if an American country were threatened by a foreign power. In 1895 President Grover Cleveland asserted this prerogative and championed the Republic of Venezuela against Great Britain in a sharp boundary dispute which had remained unsettled for nearly a century. When the British resisted arbitration, the relations between Washington and London became seriously strained (1895–1896). But the British government, preoccupied with the approaching war in South Africa, did not wish to seek trouble and conceded the "special interest" claimed by the United States in New World affairs. A commission of arbitration divided the disputed territory between Venezuela and British Guiana in 1899, and relations between Britain and the United States rapidly improved.

Relations between the United States and several Latin American republics, on the other hand, became more strained. Four years after the Venezuela controversy was closed, the province of Panama suddenly seceded from the Republic of Colombia. The prompt recognition of this *coup* by the United States, which had helped to inspire and to defend it, seemed proof to many Latin Americans that the "Colossus of the North" threatened their liberties. Theodore Roosevelt justified the intervention on the ground that a canal across the isthmus was essential to world trade and American naval defense, and he insisted that only the United States had the wealth and the will to complete the project. But Colombia was affronted, and the peoples of Central America noted with mounting resentment the readiness with which United States forces interfered in the internal affairs of the Caribbean countries. The liberation of Cuba from Spanish rule (1898) left that island under American "protection" and such protection meant, apparently, that United States forces might be landed whenever disorders occurred. One such intervention came in 1905, and in the same year United States officials assumed charge over the finances of the Dominican Republic. There, likewise, troops followed in 1916. This was the year that United States soldiers marched into Mexico in pursuit of the bandit leader, Pancho Villa; other detachments landed in Haiti; and a second occupation of Cuba followed. In 1926 it was the turn of Nicaragua, where American marines battled the popular liberal leader, Augusto Sandino.

After 1933 this policy of armed intervention was abandoned by the United States and a "Good Neighbor" policy substituted. At the Seventh Pan-American Conference, which met at Montevideo (1933) the United States secretary of state, Cordell Hull, stressed the need for mutual confidence and collaboration among all the American republics. In 1936 at Buenos Aires Pan-American solidarity was further strengthened by an agreement calling for common consultation among all the people of the Americas for their joint defense. Two years later, at Lima, the succeeding conference asserted the absolute sovereignty of all the American states. Thus in less than ten years the new policy sponsored by President Franklin D. Roosevelt and Secretary Hull altered the spirit and the practice of the United States in its relations with its sister republics of the Western hemisphere.

The twenty-one Latin American republics and the Dominion of Canada are all to some degree satellites in an economic sense of the United States. In a world divided by trade rivalries and frequently torn apart by disastrous wars, the Western hemisphere has been fortunate in the twentieth century, for no exhausting and destructive war has leveled its cities or decimated its peoples. This protection is a result of British and American naval strength. As the British have no ambition to disturb the equilibrium of North and South America, and the United States would resist any attempt by another great power to intervene by force, the peace and tranquillity of the hemisphere is guaranteed. Civil wars and revolutions within the American republics are another matter; but as war and violence in any form are a danger, all the American states strive through diplomatic pressure to promote stable government in disturbed areas. The Pan American Union, following the lead of the United States, analyzes the causes of tension or discontent in any part of the continent and advises the local government that conflict and bloodshed or cruel and dictatorial methods of administration are a threat to the peace and welfare of the Union. In this respect, the Pan American Union is like a League of Nations or United Nations Organization operating in one-half of the world. The leadership of the United States in American affairs is recognized by other powers as a "regional understanding" or "regional arrangement."

The peace and equilibrium of the New World may be threatened by economic penetration as well as by active aggression. Before the outbreak of World War II in 1939 the economic advisers at the State

Department in Washington were disturbed at the rapidity with which German, Italian, and Japanese firms were capturing much Latin American trade. The attempt to curb Italian aggression by imposing economic "sanctions" or restrictions during the Ethiopian crisis, the endeavor to deter the Japanese from further penetration of China, and the unofficial boycott of German goods as a protest against Nazi policies, all brought economics to the forefront in the 1930's as an important weapon of coercion. The whole world was dividing into economic areas or blocs — the vast territories of the Union of Soviet Socialist Republics were one economic region with trade under state control; the British Empire was drawing its units into a closer economic organization; the Germans were extending exclusive agreements with the nearby European states to weld an economic empire into a European hegemony; and the Japanese were planning a "New Order" to bring all East Asia under their influence. As the totalitarian states grew more aggressive and more exclusive, the United States took the lead in advising closer co-operation among the American peoples so that, if war came, the Americas would be independent in a political, military, and economic sense.

This growing need for hemisphere solidarity and hemisphere defense was recognized before war came to Europe. At the Eighth International Conference of American States, which met at Lima, Peru, in 1938, the Pan-American republics adopted the Declaration of Lima whereby they agreed to resist jointly any threat of foreign intervention. The following year, when war broke out in Europe, the delegates of the twenty-one American republics met promptly at Panama to proclaim their neutrality and their determination to preserve it. In 1940 they assembled again, this time at Havana, and further concerted their efforts to assure joint action in defense of American territories if they should be threatened.

These conferences and projects for joint action forecast the emergence of a regional league of nations in the Western hemisphere, defended by the United States navy and fortified by numerous air and naval bases extending throughout the Americas and far into the Atlantic and Pacific Oceans. The part these bases were to play in World War II is discussed in a later chapter. To the peoples of America the development of regional solidarity, with all existing frontiers jointly guaranteed, with a balanced inter-American economic order self-regulating and largely self-sufficient, and defense forces adequate to repel invasion, promised a degree of security unknown to the rest of the world. While Europe, Asia, Africa, and even Australia were stricken by war, the Western hemisphere escaped direct attack or devastation. The relative immunity was no mere accident of fortune. The people of the Americas had found statesmen with the skill and vision to make themselves the architects of security.

PART V

The Union
of Soviet Socialist Republics
and the Border States

THE RUSSIAN REVOLUTION: 1917—1928
THE PROVISORY PERIOD

Communism is Soviet government plus electrification of the whole country.

NICOLAI LENIN

1. THE MARCH AND NOVEMBER REVOLUTIONS, 1917

IN an earlier chapter Russia was described as a waking giant but a giant still unable at the opening of the twentieth century to make full use of its strength or even to organize its resources. The great Slav state was still half-medieval in its social structure and half-despotic in its political and police administration. It was a despotism tempered by inertia, however, for most of the officials were corrupt, inefficient, and ignorant. The lack of roads, schools, and factories unfitted Russia for competition with more advanced states. The defeats suffered by the czar's armies and fleets in the Japanese War of 1904–1905 brought a revolutionary crisis and exposed some of the faults in the government, the economy, and the army. But when the First World War broke out in 1914 the Russian divisions were still only half-equipped to march against the better drilled, better staffed, and better armed forces of the Germans. Had a swift victory brought prestige to the arrogant czarist government the success might have preserved it; military defeat and the strain of a long deadlock were a bid for revolution.

In the decades before 1914 the French bondholders lent their Russian ally over 12,000,000,000 francs, for the French knew that they would need Russian assistance in a war against Germany. Later the French complained because these loans were not repaid. But if the Russians failed to repay in gold they could, and did, insist that they had honored the debt with blood. For nearly three years they kept over half the military forces of the Central Powers engaged on the eastern front; and the Russian dead, estimated at 1,700,000, with nearly

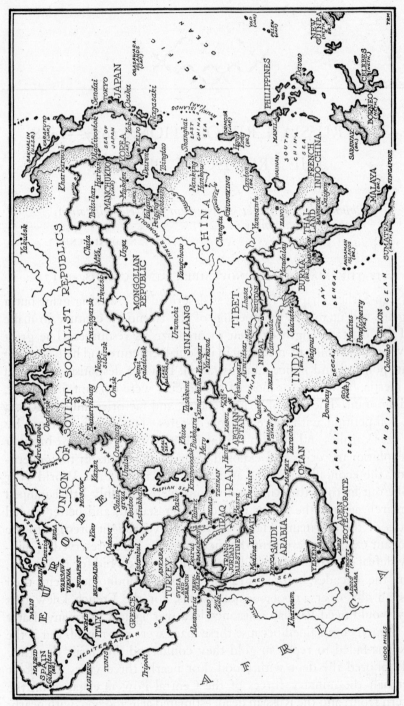

ASIA, 1935

5,000,000 wounded and 2,500,000 prisoners, proved the magnitude of their war effort. Without this eastern war to divide their strength, the Germans could have launched such a powerful and sustained drive in the west that the French Republic must almost certainly have collapsed in 1914, much as twenty-six years later it collapsed before the full strength of the German armies.

For the Russians the cost of holding a battle line from the Baltic to Rumania through thirty-two racking months was a tragic expenditure of man power, as the figures above indicate. Man power was the one asset the government could draw upon recklessly, for the population in 1914 was 125,000,000. But weapons, uniforms, war material of all descriptions were lacking and as Russia could neither manufacture nor import adequate supplies the struggle grew more and more unequal. It is reported that some Russian companies actually marched into battle armed with sticks instead of rifles. By 1917 war-weariness, disgust at the blunders of incompetent officials, rumors of graft, favoritism, and even treachery in high places sapped the morale of the people and of the army. The awaited hour had struck and czardom was bankrupt.

The ministers of the inept czar, Nicholas II, had concealed from him the almost universal exhaustion and discontent of the people. But the war-weariness of the troops at the front had been advertised by the increasing rate of desertions, and in March, 1917, the czar left for the battle lines to inspire the fighting forces. While he was absent a strike was proclaimed in Petrograd (March 8) and crowds paraded through the streets demanding peace, bread, and the end of autocratic government. The revolution of 1905 had commenced with similar demonstrations evoked by the hardships and reverses of the Russo-Japanese War, but in 1905 the populace had been intimidated by displays of force and the demonstrators had been dispersed by the volleys of the imperial troops.

The insurrections of March, 1917, had a different ending. When the hesitant ministry ordered the Petrograd garrison to restore order, the soldiers refused to fire upon the crowds, and some of the regiments fraternized with the striking workmen. At his army headquarters in Mogilev, Nicholas was informed of the disturbances and debated whether to appoint liberal ministers and promise concessions or to repress the agitation by a greater show of force. On March 11, influenced by the advice of his wife, the Czarina Alexandra, he decided to take a firm stand and approved a decree dissolving the Duma. At the same time he dispatched additional forces to Petrograd to restore order. But the situation was now out of his hands. He lacked sufficient loyal troops to enforce his will; and the Duma, instead of dissolving, elected a temporary committee to exercise authority in the crisis. The "vacuum of power" that resulted as the czar's authority declined had to be filled somehow, and the liberal leaders of the Duma feared that if they did not take charge the rebellious soldiers and striking workers would seize control. Already the socialists had organized councils (or soviets) of soldiers' and workmen's delegates to represent the people, and on March 12 some of the socialist leaders formed a general soviet and invited each factory and regiment to send a spokesman to it. While the Duma committee were hesitating, the soviet appealed directly to the army and the people. Thousands of soldiers revolted, deposed or murdered the officers who tried to restrain them, and joined the popular movement.

From its first week, therefore, the March Revolution revealed a division of leadership and of aims between the Duma committee and the socialists. At the outset neither group felt strong enough to wrest power from the other; so the Petrograd soviet (despite the advice of its more radical leaders) endorsed the provisional Duma ministry on March 14. It was a poor bargain for the socialists, for they received only two posts and the ministry was predominantly middle class in sentiment and membership. The liaison officer between the socialists and the Duma was Alexander Kerensky, who held the portfolio of minister of justice. Because of his influence this stopgap government established on March 14 came to be known as the Kerensky regime. It was destined to survive for only seven months.

Apprised of the trend of events in Petrograd, Nicholas attempted to return, but his train was stalled by striking railway workers. The army which he had launched against his rebellious capital dissolved, and most of the soldiers went over to the revolution. Too late he acknowledged the need to compromise and offered liberal reforms which might have saved his throne if they had been advanced a week earlier. But by March 15 the people had tested their strength and taken final measure of the czar's irresolution. They demanded his abdication and refused to accept his brother Michael or his son Alexis in his stead. So on March 15, from his temporary residence at Pskov, the last Czar of All the Russias laid down his crown. His final decree was an order which legalized the provisional government and appointed a liberal nobleman, Prince Lvov, to head the Duma ministry.

The leaders of this provisory government were bourgeois parliamentarians with too little conception of the depth and fury of the revolutionary current. They announced that the new regime would honor the treaties and loans contracted by the government of the deposed czar and that it would continue the war against the Central Powers in concert with the other Allied nations. These proclamations did not please the war-weary Russian masses. But in these early weeks of the revolution a mystic exaltation was sweeping Russia and the people were so full of hope they did not instantly protest. They accepted in good faith the pledges given by the new government. Political prisoners were released; freedom to strike, freedom of speech, and freedom of the press were guaranteed; and a national assembly to be elected by universal suffrage was promised. With these assurances the people felt confident they could carry through their program without difficulty.

But the bourgeois groups which dominated the Duma and the provisional government had no real wish to carry through a genuine revolutionary program. They wanted to guarantee private property, to assure middle-class rule, and to continue the war. To placate the populace, Kerensky persuaded his fellow ministers to promise a few socialistic measures, such as distribution of the land of the czarist nobles among the landless peasant families and the socialization of industry. But these promises were not put into effect except where lawless peasants seized lands for themselves or soviets of factory hands or shopworkers took control of their employer's firm. Neglecting the critical internal state of Russia, the Kerensky cabinet responded to the appeals of the British and French and sought to continue the war. But even Kerensky was unable to galvanize the armies for a new offensive. When the new foreign minister, Paul Miliukov, assured London and Paris (May 1) that Russia would remain in the war until the common victory, the Petrograd socialists denounced such "imperialism." There were angry demonstrations, and Miliukov was forced to resign. The socialists believed that peace was possible for the asking if all belligerents agreed to renounce annexations and indemnities; and as the French and British governments hesitated to do this, the socialists declared that Russia was released from any obligation to continue the war.

A wave of protest now rose against further participation in an imperialist war among bourgeois states. The socialist radicals, or communists, appealed to the workers of Russia and to all the belligerent nations, to unite, to fraternize, and to demand an end to the war. The proletarians, they proclaimed, were dying in the trenches or toiling in the fields and factories, while prices soared above wages and their families starved. The only beneficiaries of the war, ran this communist argument, were the capitalist profiteers in all countries who were "merchants of death" and parasites of patriotism. These appeals to mass prejudice and emotionalism failed to excite a response in France, Britain, America, or Germany, but the Russians, whose sacrifices had been so largely in vain, were susceptible to such propaganda.

The Kerensky regime failed to placate or to keep pace with the mood of the people. On the other hand, the group of more radical revolutionaries who had set up the soviet of workers' and soldiers' delegates in Petrograd on March 12, did catch the drift of popular emotions and extended its influence. Its leaders thus steadily usurped the real power and left the provisional government undermined and weakened. Soviets or committees were organized in factories, towns, garrisons, even among the regiments at the front, and all of them looked for directions to the original or Supreme Soviet at Petrograd. The Germans, happy to see Russia dissolving in chaos, speeded the process of revolutionary fermentation. Agitators who had been exiled from Russia by the police during the czarist regime were now seeking to return to their homeland, and the Germans aided them. In April, 1917, a delegation arrived from Switzerland, of which the most important member was Nicolai Lenin. With his arrival in Petrograd the swing to the left was accelerated.

Lenin's slogan was "All power to the soviets" and he insisted upon a breach with the provisional government. The new communist regime, he said, would rule without the participation of the *bourgeoisie.* Starvation, war-weariness, and land hunger had at last stirred even the patient Russian peasants to action, and as the Kerensky regime failed to move speedily enough, the leading socialist group, the Bolsheviki, endorsed the program of "Land, Peace, Bread," which Lenin advocated. The phrase had a growing, finally an irresistible, appeal. In July, 1917, the soviets made their first attempt to seize power; it failed, and for the moment Lenin and other leaders were in danger. But by November their organization was powerful enough to sweep Kerensky aside. A congress of delegates from all the soviets met and entrusted the direction of their program to a Council of Commissars, headed by Lenin, with Leon Trotsky as minister for foreign affairs. The new Council assumed command on November 7, 1917, supported by the Red Guard, a sort of communist militia, and by a secret police organization which hunted down opposition leaders and silenced rival groups. Thus the Russian Revolution, a vast, surging mood of indignation which had united the overdriven, inarticulate masses, was harnessed by a small group of determined men who had studied the dynamics of popular movements and were prompt and ruthless in seizing control.

The Kerensky government, obedient to the democratic and parliamentary traditions of western Europe, had called for the election of a popular assembly. But when the elected representatives attempted to meet in January, 1918, it was already too late. They were dispersed by the troops of the triumphant Bolsheviki; leaders of the moderate parties were arrested; and all branches of the state, provincial, and even municipal governments were purged of suspects and dissidents. The new soviet leaders announced that the goal of the revolution was a collectivist society. They promised immediate nationalization of the land, control of industry by the workers for the state, and the repudiation of debts contracted by the czar's government. The road down which the new regime so arbitrarily headed was certain to prove a difficult one, for there were forces which would resist the confiscation of land and wealth, and the late allies of Russia — France, Britain, Italy — and associated powers like the United States, would resent the "breach of faith" in deserting the war. The repudiation of foreign debts and attempts to stir the workers in other countries to revolt put a further strain upon Russian relations with the capitalist states.

The upheaval which in less than a year dethroned Nicholas II and elevated Lenin to power was one of the great formative events of the twentieth century. It is easy to picture the Bolshevist *coup* as a simple act of force and terrorism. But it was not force or terrorism which made Lenin an object of mystical veneration to millions of Russians. In all great social crusades people feel themselves united in a supreme assault upon the evils of injustice and oppression. They idealize and revere the leaders who, by heading the movement, expose themselves to the deadliest blows of its enemies. The mood of urgency and exaltation is never quite real or credible to those who do not share it. It is customary to speak of "revolutionary madness" or of psychopathic excesses. The actors in the drama seem to the foreign eye like mad puppets engaged in a bizarre dance to unheard music. But the people who make revolutions are not puppets. They are sensitive to the criticism their violence excites and they exaggerate it; they feel themselves isolated in a world of foes and they grow more desperate

and more defiant. In the great French Revolution the republican leaders declared war against *all* kings; the Russian communists assumed
that *all* capitalist countries were united in a league to destroy the
Soviet Union.

The leaders of such a movement know that the mood of the people is part of the *mystique* of the movement. Successful leaders must
gauge the mood, must speak the ideological language of the hour, but
they must not be confused by it. For the long-term principles of statecraft still hold, and however violently the ship of state is beaten about
by storms the ultimate goals of national policy must not be forgotten.
No modern revolution can long run counter to the trend of national
aggrandizement; rather, under disguised forms, the revolution is likely
to prove a prelude to a war of aggrandizement and conquest. But the
first step is the consolidation of the revolution at home, the transition
from a provisory and therefore precarious regime to a permanent government. To steer a revolution, especially in its first, most turbulent
and unpredictable phases, demands unique qualities in a leader: idealism, realism, and ruthless will. Nicolai Lenin displayed these qualities
from his advent to power at the close of 1917 until his death in 1924.
His successor, Joseph Stalin, showed less interest in ideological issues
but possessed greater skill in political organization and an equally
ruthless will.

2. THE STRUGGLE TO SURVIVE

The first and most urgent problem facing Lenin and his associates was
to conclude peace with the Germans. For Russia the war was lost.
Mass mutinies and the collapse of the transport system, mass strikes
and the failure of the half-developed war industries, had brought the
country to a defenseless state. Negotiations with the Central Powers
were opened in November, 1917, immediately after the Bolsheviki
seized control. The Congress of Soviets, which represented the councils of workers, peasants, and soldiers that had formed themselves during the summer of 1917, proposed that *all* the warring nations make
peace, on the bases of no annexations and no indemnities. But France
and Britain ignored the proposal, and the German militarists were jubilant because they had split their enemies and could now dictate a separate settlement with Russia.

As a result, German confidence overreached itself and the terms
which the kaiser's government offered the Russians were extremely
harsh. After a futile effort to hold out for some modification the Soviet
government yielded. Lenin's realism saved him from Kerensky's illu-

sion that Russia could continue fighting. Accepting the crushing German ultimatum, the soviets made peace at Brest-Litovsk on March 3, 1918. Russia surrendered Finland, Poland, the Baltic provinces, and the Ukraine to German control, and assumed a heavy indemnity. With peace, the Bolshevik faction was able to gain a firmer control of the internal situation. "White" armies of antirevolutionaries which had organized in various provinces to fight the "Red" brigades of the communists were checked; and the program of social reform began to make progress. Reversing the move which Peter the Great had made two centuries earlier, the communist leaders shifted the capital from Petrograd to Moscow, which is deep in the heart of Russia and reasonably secure from invading armies. Thence a flood of decrees went forth, declaring that all banks, industries, mines, railroads, and landed estates would be nationalized. No compensation was offered to former owners in this wholesale confiscation, and the victims, the landowners, capitalists, czarist officials, and army officers who might have opposed the sweeping program, appeared to be temporarily stunned.

Then the opposition forces began to rally, encouraged by the promise of aid from the British, French, and American governments, and the "heroic" period of the revolution began. The Allies had forwarded guns, ammunition, and other supplies to the czar's government before its collapse and they insisted that these shipments must not fall to the Bolsheviki. Expeditionary forces invaded Russia on the fringes of that vast country, landing where they could from Archangel to Vladivostok and Murmansk to Sevastopol. The White armies, encouraged and in some cases armed by the Allied commanders, attempted to overturn the precarious Bolshevik dictatorship. Threatened on all sides, the government was galvanized into ruthless activity. Supplies were requisitioned to feed and arm the Red Guard; desertion and treachery were checked by murderous reprisals. Among the most illustrious victims of the purge were Nicholas II and his entire family, who were shot (July 16, 1918) on the order of the local commissar when a White army neared their place of imprisonment at Ekaterinburg.

Yet even in this dark hour, when the revolution seemed on the point of collapsing in blood and infamy, the masses remained loyal to the leaders in Moscow and relatively few volunteers from the poorer classes rallied to the White generals or supported the Allied expeditionary troops. The Red army, drilled and organized by the energetic commissar for war, Leon Trotsky, fought with a devotion which contrasted with and discredited the bigotry and blindness of many White officers. After two years of savage and often confused struggle in many areas the Allied forces were all withdrawn, the White armies defeated or expelled, and the Soviet government remained master of Russia. But the intense effort, the sacrifices and reprisals, the pride and panic of that "heroic" period when all the world powers appeared in league against the revolution, left a permanent stamp upon that generation in Russia. Distrust of all capitalist nations remained almost a mania, and the people of the Soviet Union withdrew into themselves. They were convinced that until communism triumphed throughout the world they would be an outcast nation and that they must be perpetually on guard against the malice, the treachery, and the aggression of the other powers.

For this reaction the French and British governments were partly to blame. After defeating Germany in 1918 they were naturally in no mood to placate the Bolsheviki who had withdrawn Russia from the war at a critical period, had betrayed the Allied secret agreements to the world, and had repudiated the Russian state debts. On the other hand, the Russian leaders sponsored in 1919 the foundation of the Third International at Moscow, and this body sent agents into the capitalist countries to encourage revolts among the working classes.

Fear that communist doctrines might really excite revolutionary movements troubled the statesmen at Paris, London, and Washington for a decade and more after 1918, increasing the tense and reciprocal antagonism which divided Russia from the western democracies. The French, in particular, who possessed the strongest army in Europe after the Germans capitulated, believed it necessary to guard eastern Europe from communist influence. When the Poles in 1920 attempted to wrest the Ukraine, the "granary of Russia," from the control of the Soviet government, their seizure of Kiev stimulated the Red army to a counterdrive which almost reached Warsaw. French reinforcements came to the aid of the Poles and changed the tide of battle, compelling the invaders to accept a frontier settlement which left 3,000,000 Russians under Polish rule (Treaty of Riga, 1921). This reverse at the hands of the Poles and French, and the Polish ambition to win the Ukraine, further convinced the Russians that they could trust none but their own leaders and must defend themselves by their own efforts.

3. THE SOVIET SYSTEM OF GOVERNMENT

The political structure which the communist leaders erected amid the chaos of war, treachery, famine, and massacre proved dictatorial enough to discipline a racing revolution but elastic enough to allow for expansion and progress. To explain the aims of the revolution to millions of men of all sorts and conditions was a prodigious task in itself, yet unless the millions scattered from the Vistula to Vladivostok and from the Arctic Circle to the borders of Iran, Afghanistan, and Mongolia could be infused with faith in the Soviet regime the revolution could not succeed. The Communist Party recognized the need to reach and stimulate the masses. They formulated their program in terms which would win the alert, modern-minded journalists and technicians who spoke for the city proletariat, and then they rephrased it for the slower comprehension and tribal mentality of herdsmen in central Asia. They had to develop a system which would meet the myriad administrative needs of a society so diversified that it was an international world in itself. The Soviet peoples were split into many cultural strata, into regional units and groups, into tribes and societies which differed in speech, religion, education, manners, and methods of livelihood. A political system strong yet adaptable enough to unite such diverse nations had to be deftly devised and endowed with remarkable virtues. The fact that such a system was forged in the midst of the revolutionary ferment makes it worthy of careful analysis.

The first principle of the Russian Revolution, the ideal of a classless society, was based upon the teaching of Karl Marx. Half a century earlier Marx had prophesied that the capitalist system bore within itself the seeds of its own decay and that a revolution must inevitably ripen which would see the "expropriators" expropriated and the proletarians freed from their chains. But Marx expected this denouement to develop first in one of the more highly industrialized countries of Europe where the urban population was numerous and well organized. Russia was still very largely agrarian in 1917, and in identifying the Russian Revolution with the predicted Communist revolution, Lenin and other leaders who had imbibed Marxian dialectics invoked a theoretical foundation to slip under a confusing but actual situation. In grappling with immediate problems they had at times to depart from the dictates of Marxian method, but in public they usually found it an asset to pretend they could reconcile their course, verbally at least, with the master's teaching. Even revolutionaries have their texts and traditions, and the need to safeguard the "orthodox" ideology against the "heretics" who seek to divert the revolution from its true course makes the struggles for control among the leaders particularly bitter.

To hasten the advent of the classless society in which there would be neither expropriators nor expropriated, the Bolsheviks adopted a program of collectivism. As already noted, private estates, corporations, transport and utility services, mines and factories were "nationalized." Since the propertied classes in Russia had never been large, for there was no powerful and numerous middle class as in western Europe, it proved relatively easy to dispossess and "liquidate" the wealthy. When the Soviet government had to feed and equip the Red army in the civil war, it invoked this same principle of collectivism and seized grain, cattle, tools, clothing, and whatever else was required. It was soon discovered, however, that such "war communism" had serious defects: it was possible to confiscate goods, but capital resources were speedily eaten up and little creative activity survived to replace them. In some provinces the confiscation of grain drove the peasants to rebellion. There was a sharp fall in production as factories were taken over by the workers' soviets, for the new managers were often unskilled in the arts of the ousted employers and the men became unruly and troublesome. By 1920, after three years of revolution, the economic situation had become desperate. Leading industries had shriveled to ruin, famine was making a solitude of stricken rural areas, and in others the farmers were killing off their livestock rather than surrender it under the system of forced requisitions.

The commissars at Moscow were aware of the conditions and sentiments of the masses. The All-Russian Congress of Soviets, which had held its sessions since the first year of the revolution, left a Central Executive Committee of experts in permanent session, and advices from local and provincial soviets kept the communist chiefs informed on the trends in all sections of the union. The function of the congress and the committee, however, was mainly to advise; the executive power and the real authority was exercised by the ministry, the "Council of People's Commissars." Here all the key posts were held by strictly chosen members of the Communist Party, and the party members formed the élite of the bureaucracy and the officer personnel of the army. The party, though it numbered at first only a few hundred thousand members, was the brain and nerve system of the regime. Through its able and vigilant agents on local soviets, it could study ills before they excited disturbances, and the energy and devotion of its acolytes made it an efficient instrument of control. Members, in whatever office or rank they were ordered to serve, were expected to display a standard of zeal and obedience which would inspire all comrades to similar effort in the hope that they, too, might win the honor of election to the party.

It is important to recognize the dual nature of the Russian revolutionary government. The first constitution, adopted by the Fifth All-Russian Congress of Soviets on July 10, 1918, recognized the ascending system of committees or soviets, from the local body in each village to the All-Union Congress at Moscow. Delegates were to be chosen by open ballot. But within the elaborate pyramid the party served as a more or less secret organization which had no legal or constitutional foundation. No other political party was permitted to form, so that the regime was a one-party system. Members of the party were very carefully selected after a period of probation as candidates and the total enrollment during the first ten years of the revolution remained less than 2 per cent of the population. All important posts in the government were held by party members, and government policies were regularly shaped and even overruled by directives from the party committees.

The Russian masses, so newly liberated from the stupidity, inertia, and corruption of the czarist despotism, remained in general docile and dutiful under the direction of the more efficient communist bureaucracy. Collectivism, in agriculture at least, was not unfamiliar to them, for it resembled the organization of the *mir*, the ancient Russian village community. As in medieval Europe, the families which composed a village had long been accustomed to share the land, the labor, and the produce, living very largely as an economic unit dependent upon their local yield. The new masters, however, were not thinking in terms of the needs of a single village; they planned to co-ordinate the energy of all the villages in a vast communal effort. On a scale never before attempted and with consequences still unmeasured and unpredictable, they drafted a program under which the production, consumption, exchange of commodities, income, and working hours of the Russian and allied peoples were to be planned years in advance. Striking out along an unknown road, these despotic innovators abandoned at a stroke the tradition of private property, free enterprise, and the profit motive, and embarked upon the attempt to construct a workers' commonwealth.

4. THE NEW ECONOMIC PLAN

By 1921 the Soviet regime was consolidated and gave promise of surviving. Internal resistance had been crushed, and the other great powers, though still hostile to communism as a creed, had abandoned their attempts to check the revolution by armed intervention or maritime blockade.

The first years of the revolution were an era of constant danger, of sacrifices, suffering, and civil war. They were followed, after 1921, by a more stable and constructive period, but much of the work attempted amid the chaotic conditions persisting in postwar Russia was still provisory and experimental. Lenin had come to realize that to build a collectivist state it was not enough to confiscate and distribute the existing wealth and land. New wealth had to be created and distributed so that Russia could match the Western democracies with a living standard, literacy ratio, and agricultural and industrial output equal to that of the more advanced nations. Above all, Russia must maintain the Red army at a high state of efficiency and develop industrial machinery and the power to drive it, so that the army would be equipped for battle, a battle that would very probably be waged without allies or foreign aid.

The conventional incentive to productive effort, the motive of personal profit, had been outlawed, in theory at least. The individual was to be subordinate to the needs of society. The independent farmer, the business executive, the shopowner, the banker, lawyer, engineer, journalist, artist, all the members of the intelligentsia, as well as the *bourgeoisie* and the ancient nobility, had been destroyed or intimidated by the purges and persecutions. Now it was discovered that many of these key men of the professional classes were indispensable and that some consideration must be paid to them even if their sympathy for the new order was not very deep or sincere. To start the wheels of industry rolling again and train the masses in new techniques, Lenin decided (1921) to revert in part to the methods of private ownership. This "step backward" was termed the New Economic Plan, and those with the energy and courage to accept the chance to re-enter business and perhaps accumulate wealth once again, were known as nepmen.

The re-establishment of a stable currency based on the gold ruble also helped to encourage a renewal of business enterprise. Although external trade remained a state monopoly, the farmers were permitted to sell their grain in the market and small business owners managed their enterprises on an individual basis. Foreign experts were invited to Russia to give instruction in the latest technical improvements. They helped the nepmen to open mines, recondition factories, repair railways and bridges, prospect for oil, coal, minerals, timber, fur, and hydroelectric resources for the generation and distribution of power. The whole vast realm, one-sixth of the land area of the earth, was to be surveyed, and reports on the natural resources of all sections, even the remote Arctic, submitted to the Supreme Economic Council.

The New Economic Plan, though it involved some compromise with capitalist methods and permitted limited private enterprise, was not meant by the leaders as an abandonment of their ideals. They still planned to establish a collectivist society. The nepmen were encouraged to teach their skills and share their knowledge; they were even allowed to amass some private wealth; and prosperous and ambitious peasants (kulaks) were enabled to expand their holdings, hire helpers, and become masters of their own estates. But a day of reckoning awaited them. Once they had served as guides and teachers, once the revolution had reached the point where it could dispense with them, they were to be collectivized or liquidated. When Soviet agriculture and industry were organized they would come entirely under state control, from the largest combine to the smallest farm.

Reversion to the original collectivist program came after 1928. Economists had gathered and checked the essential figures on resources and production, scientists and engineers had been trained for their tasks, schedules had been prepared, and the members of the Communist Party had been instructed and disciplined. With the opening of the new phase foreign experts were superseded by Russians trained to fulfill their functions, foreign imports were matched by Russian products, foreign models of trucks and tractors were assembled by Russian mechanics. The kulaks were persuaded, taxed, or harried into merging their own estates with the collective farms. Private enterprises which employed more than ten workers were stigmatized as "capitalist" and the drive towards state ownership and control of all industry was resumed with vigor. The first "heroic" phase of the Russian Revolution ended about 1921; the second experimental and provisory phase closed about 1927. After that date the revolution entered its third phase, the planned society.

THE RUSSIAN REVOLUTION: 1928—1939
THE PLANNED SOCIETY

In the Soviet Union there is a basis only for the Communist Party.
JOSEPH STALIN (NOVEMBER 26, 1936)

1. THE PRAGMATIC APPROACH

THE hundred years from 1815 to 1914, from the end of the Napoleonic wars to the opening of World War I, were a century increasingly dominated by the ideals of bourgeois democracy. First in Britain and France, and then through most of Europe, constitutional government, middle-class rule, and laissez-faire economy became the prevailing pattern of society. As the nineteenth century was unmarred by any long or destructive wars, and the general standard of living and of health in most European countries rose remarkably, the rule of the middle class was not seriously challenged. The criticism of the landed nobility died away as they were dispossessed or were themselves merged with the triumphant middle class; the criticism of the "proletariat" had not yet swelled to a threatening chorus. But the First World War, with its blunders, suffering, economic dislocation, and widespread ruin brought to a head the growing discontent with the system of bourgeois democracy and unregulated capitalist economy. Bourgeois society was condemned by radical reformers as "plutocracy" and blamed for the major evils of the new era.

One of the most serious charges hurled by critics against the bourgeois state and the system of private property was the accusation that unregulated capitalism leads to economic chaos. Under the liberal regime, individual businessmen enjoyed a wide liberty of action, for the government interfered as little as possible with the economic activities of the citizens while they engaged on their own initiative in free business enterprise. It was assumed that each citizen, pursuing his own enlightened self-interest, would benefit himself, his neighbors, and his country through his enthusiasm and industry.

This sanguine view the socialists and communists attacked, insisting that by its guarantee to protect private property, free competition, and the pursuit of personal profit, the government in reality favored the expropriating class, the capitalists and employers of labor. Instead of assuring a fair field and no favors, said these critics, the existing laws in capitalist society protected the wealthy, whereas it was the proletarians — the wage earners and consumers — who most needed protection against expropriation and discrimination. Thus the capitalist system was blamed for the existence of poverty and the maldistribution of wealth, evils which had of course existed long before the system developed.

But this was not the only fault for which capitalism was held responsible. A profit economy, the critics further insisted, if allowed free play, induced cycles of overexpansion, inflation, financial crisis, contraction of credit, business depression, unemployment, and destitution. Recovery of some measure of prosperity inevitably led to unregulated expansion in a mad pursuit of excessive profits, and the cycle repeated itself. The long history of business depressions lent this theory some weight, for the causes of the periodic economic crises were not easy to analyze.

Karl Marx and Friedrich Engels had pointed out this defect of the capitalist system in their *Manifesto of the Communist Party* issued in 1848.

> For many a decade past the history of industry and commerce is but the history of the revolt of modern productive forces against modern conditions of production, against the property relations that are the conditions for the existence of the *bourgeoisie* and its rule. It is enough to mention the commercial crises that by their periodical return put on its trial, each time more threateningly, the existence of the entire bourgeois society. . . And how does the *bourgeoisie* get over these crises? On the one hand by enforced destruction of a mass of productive forces; on the other, by the conquest of new markets and by the more thorough exploitation of old ones. That is to say, by paving the way for more extensive and more destructive crises, and by diminishing the means whereby crises are prevented. . . . But not only has the *bourgeoisie* forged the weapons that bring death to itself; it has also called into existence the men who are to wield those weapons — the modern working class — the proletarians.

·These Marxian doctrines comforted the proletarians in their struggle for power because there was a poetic justice in the thought of the *bourgeoisie* digging its own grave while the expropriated classes, the proletariat, were predestined to become the expropriators. After the triumph of the proletariat had been consolidated, there would no longer be a capitalist class controlling the machines of production as if they were so much personal property. Or so loyal Marxists professed to believe.

The economic activities of a society, the communists argued, are too vital to be left in private hands. The solution they proposed was a form of collectivism which would make the state supreme in all fields of economic life. Such doctrines were too radical to win speedy acceptance in western Europe or the United States where a powerful, numerous, and well entrenched middle class was satisfied with existing institutions. In Russia, however, no influential middle class with political experience had yet developed. The government had functioned for centuries as a military despotism, and the tradition of a ruthless and arbitrary master at Moscow who exercised absolute control over the lives and possessions of his subjects was almost unquestioned. When czardom fell, the Bolsheviki took over and repaired the machinery of despotism. Because they were more energetic and much better informed than the czar's officials, their fiats had more effect than an imperial ukase; and revolutionary enthusiasm induced the people to accept privation and applaud the decrees from Moscow even when they did not fully comprehend the need or purpose which inspired them.

In theory, the resources and productive capacity of the Union of Soviet Socialist Republics were to be developed by the state for the benefit of the people. The Council of Commissars were stewards with a mandate to improve the living conditions of the masses. It seemed in no way strange to most Russians that the communist leaders should place military needs ahead of material comfort because the czars had always done so. Better food and clothing and housing for the people had to wait while the Red army was equipped, munitions factories built, and strategic roads and railways completed. The plan concerted for the economic organization of the U.S.S.R. was less a peace plan than a war plan. Railway, river, and canal traffic, bridges, roads, hydroelectric dams and power lines, coal, oil, timber, cereals, farm animals, and factory hands — everything was to move or grow or work on a schedule.

The Supreme Economic Council drew up a master sheet by which they proposed to regulate this series of combined operations over a five-year period. Their program, the first Five-Year Plan, went into official effect in October, 1928. The health, education, and recreation, the forms and hours of labor, the factory and farm production, the clothing and the food consumption of over 150,000,000 people were reduced to blueprints. Some of the tabulation was a fiction and more was wishful thinking, but the whole enterprise had a basis in reality and represented a gigantic concentration of effort conceived almost like a military campaign. As the battle proceeded, gains were to be recorded on graphs and charts just as in a laboratory experiment, and details of the operation were to be checked, regulated, and compensated, from month to month and year to year, in the greatest controlled social experiment in history.

The administrative machinery to direct this ambitious scheme had likewise been carefully sketched in advance. All aspects of the social, cultural, and economic life of the Soviet peoples had been studied, as a terrain is studied by intelligence officers before a military campaign. The labor and supplies required for all phases of the various construction projects, the tons of steel, the cubic yards of concrete, the barges, railway engines, trucks, and turnip seeds were all calculated and assigned. Technical schools enrolled students to provide the needed quota of artisans, draftsmen, engineers, metallurgists, agronomists, and surveyors. Special awards and decorations were held out to encourage crews and work units to exceed their assignment, and alert foremen who suggested improvements in method were advanced like officers who distinguished themselves on the field of action. The general aims and rate of progress in all departments of the Five-Year Plan were advertised in posters, journals, and motion pictures, with frequent adjurations to those groups which lagged behind to overcome their handicap.

The introduction of the First Five-Year Plan in 1928 was an indication that the Russian revolution was hardening into its more permanent form. Over a century earlier Napoleon Bonaparte had closed the first decade of the French Revolution with the curt announcement, "The romance of the revolution is over; we must begin its history." In a similar spirit, the men who held control of the Russian revolution at the end of ten years gave it a definitive cast after 1928. The realists had come into power, and the administrative form, the historic pattern of the new society, could now be discerned. This change in mood brought a change in personnel. Leon Trotsky, fiery and eloquent doctrinaire, was expelled from the Communist Party, and several of the Old Guard of the Bolsheviki shared his fate. A sober and realistic Georgian, Joseph Stalin, proved himself the strong man of the inner circle and quietly but inexorably usurped the leading role which Lenin had filled before his death in 1924.

2. THE FIVE-YEAR PLANS IN OPERATION

For the first ten years after 1917 the Soviet leaders were so busy organizing their power, repelling foreign armies that supported the White generals, and putting down internal revolts, that they could not press their economic plans consistently. Between 1917 and 1922 eight-ninths of the Soviet Union was dominated at one moment or another by antisoviet armies, and the disorder and plundering reduced Russian industrial output to one-seventh the level of 1913 and agriculture to one-half.

When the heroic stage had passed and some degree of order and stabilization returned, it became clear that the Russian Revolution was to differ from previous revolutions in European history. In Russia the economic projects of the revolutionists were more significant than the political innovations or the military conquests. By 1928 the economic program began to take definite form and thenceforth the Soviet regime was judged at home and abroad by the success of the "Five-Year Plans" for industrial and agricultural expansion.

A general program for concerting and expanding economic production under the direction of a State Planning Commission (*Gosplan*) was debated as early as 1926. The result was a master plan, put into operation October 1, 1928, which outlined a production schedule for the ensuing five years and was consequently known as the Five-Year Plan. In 1932 the government spokesmen announced that this First Five-Year Plan had been completed in four and a half years and would be followed immediately by a Second Five-Year Plan (1933–1937). This in turn was succeeded by a Third Five-Year Plan (1938–1942) which was still uncompleted when the German armies invaded Russia in June, 1941. But the *Gosplan* had already envisaged (1941) a fifteen-year project of economic expansion, and after World War II ended in 1945 a Fourth Five-Year Plan was launched early in 1946. The rapid economic development of the Soviet Union under the stimulus of these all-embracing programs of national regimentation, national production, and national distribution, must now be analyzed. But a word of caution is necessary when weighing the results. Almost the only figures available on the progress of the plans are official Soviet statistics, and governments seldom belittle the achievements upon which they depend to justify their exactions and their arbitrary use of authority.

To help finance the First Five-Year Plan the Soviet leaders counted upon raising surplus wheat for export, and a drive was instituted to enlarge the acreage under cultivation, to increase the yield per acre, and to simplify labor by the rapid introduction of agricultural machinery. As part of this plan the farm lands were to be combined into large collective units, and the *kolkhoz*, or collective farm community, was held up as the ideal pattern for rural organization. State farms, known as *Sovhoz*, were also introduced. Government experts indicated in advance the crops which were to be sown, and they planned months ahead how they would utilize the surplus. This change in agricultural methods was carried through in spite of resistance and suffering. Some results of it will be analyzed in a later section of this chapter.

In tapping natural resources the communist engineers opened a treasure house, for the Soviet Union is probably the most richly endowed country on earth. Soviet surveyors and scientists calculated that Russia possessed one-fifth of the world's coal deposits, one-fourth of the timber lands, one-half the reserves of oil and of iron ore, and a plentiful share of the various minerals which modern refining methods have made important. In the five years following 1927 Russian gold production doubled, then doubled again in the following five years. Almost all the rare elements and natural salts for which industry has created a sudden demand in recent years can be found within the varied zones of Russia's continental expanses.

On an undertaking so vast as the First Five-Year Plan it was easier to fix a minimum increase at a given percentage than to realize it in actual production. The general averages over several years probably afford a truer picture of what was accomplished than specific figures for separate departments. In agriculture, the authors of the plan called for an increase in crops of over 50 per cent; in industry, an increase in output exceeding 100 per cent. The expenditure for this rapid expansion was calculated at $32,500,000,000, a sum not far from the total which Germany failed to raise in payment of the Reparations Bill.

The First Five-Year Plan succeeded best in the sphere of mechanization and organization. It fell short in the sphere of human standards and human responses, a result which suggested that machines can be improved and their operation co-ordinated more readily than human workers can be changed. It proved simpler to build new factories, powerhouses, railways, locomotives, tractors, and harvesters than to train men to operate them at maximum efficiency. The plan envisaged a reduction of one-third in the costs of production, and a doubling of the output of each worker through machine aids and increased manual skill. These goals were not attained. Furthermore, the living standards of the masses were not raised nearly so rapidly as millions had hoped they would be. For many of the people, living was harder in 1932 than it had been in 1927. The production of consumers' goods lagged behind that of the heavy industries, a Russian equivalent of the German motto: guns before butter.

Food, clothing, housing accommodations, and even amusements were all rationed. Workers who won promotion or served in essential industries gained higher rating and additional food calories, an incentive which helped to spur the ambitious. Night schools and factory instruction, free lectures and reading rooms, made it possible for apprentices to improve their knowledge and skill. All classes were infected by the passion for machinery. Novices were taught to handle tools with reverent care, and the technicians trusted with the operation of delicate machines were warned that they assumed a high responsibility. If, despite instruction and advice, a workman failed to exercise adequate care, he was intimidated by the threat of severe penalties. Engine drivers, switchmen, train dispatchers, electricians, ironworkers — all were warned that carelessness might cost lives, their own lives, if they were convicted of criminal negligence. A schedule of penalties was introduced, not only to punish willful opposition to orders or deliberate sabotage but for errors of neglect or mistakes in judgment.

In this respect, Russian economy under the Five-Year Plans was run with the tempo usually associated with a war economy. There was the same sense of a race against time, of a persistent emergency; and the psychological tension which accompanies a war effort keyed the workers to better than ordinary standards of endurance and devotion. The severity of the penalties imposed for any failure of duty was likewise suggestive of a war atmosphere, when much is at stake and the individual must be sacrificed for the greater security of society. All revolutionary governments are born of an emergency and tend to perpetuate the mood of emergency in order to preserve their extraordinary powers.

In December, 1932, the First Five-Year Plan was officially terminated nine months ahead of schedule. The Second Five-Year Plan, carefully conceived, was immediately set in operation, to govern Soviet economy until December, 1937. The same ambitious attempt at co-ordination of all activities under state direction was retained. The estimated expenditures doubled, from about $32,500,000,000 to some $66,000,000,000. Higher increases and more grandiose goals were set in all fields of production. The preamble to the second plan focused attention upon the need to improve quality as well as quantity and declared that more of the comforts of life would be made available to the masses. The progress of the plan was revealed from time to time through the release of official statistics (no other statistics being available), and the figures cited indicated that the second plan was functioning more smoothly than the first. But the growing tension in Europe after 1936 led all governments to hasten their military programs and direct much of their industrial energy towards greater armament production. The later figures on the Second Five-Year Plan, and on the Third Five-Year Plan which followed it, are therefore of less interest for they do not reveal the true state of Russian war preparations. How thorough these were, not even the Germans gauged correctly although they were nearest to Russia and had most to fear from Russian military expansion.

The effect of the three drives for greater production was more notable in industry than in agriculture. In 1913 industry accounted for only 42 per cent of the Russian total and agriculture for 58 per cent. By 1930 industry was ahead with 53 per cent. By 1938, at the close of the Second Five-Year Plan, the industrial output had reached 77.4 per cent of the expanded national total. This emphasis upon industry, and especially heavy industry, was intentional. The Soviet planners believed that Russia would be unequal to a war with a great industrialized power unless the Red army could be supported by factories capable of producing unlimited war material. The wisdom of this view was to be demonstrated after 1941. The Russian ordeal in World War II, however, and the plans for the further expansion of Russian economy through the Fourth Five-Year Plan of 1946–1950, will be discussed in a later chapter.

3. INTERNAL OPPOSITION AND REPRESSION

In forcing through the drastic changes demanded by the Five-Year Plans the Soviet officials found the industrial workers more manageable than the farmers. Peasants are notoriously obstinate and conservative, and regimenting agricultural labor proved more difficult than regulating factory routines. This partly explains why farm output under the Soviet experiment increased less rapidly than industrial output, which soon outstripped it and held the lead.

The central idea behind the Five-Year Plans was the belief that the application of power-driven machinery would reduce human toil and raise the living standards of the people so swiftly that they would willingly accept the strict regimentation imposed on them. For machine production imposes regimentation; it can operate profitably only when conditions can be standardized for mass production. Factory work is more uniform than farm work, and the production of steel or automobiles or electric light bulbs by mechanical means is thus easier to regulate than the raising of potatoes or pigs. Nevertheless, the Soviet planners believed that agricultural routines could be standardized profitably and that farm tasks could be lightened by collectivist methods. They counted upon the benefits of the new methods to overcome the farmers' conservatism and to persuade farm families to abandon their individual plots and join the collective farms. The independent farmer could not well afford to purchase and operate a power-driven tractor to cultivate a few acres; but the state farms, with thousands of acres under cultivation, were ideally suited to mechanization. The introduction of trucks and tractors was in itself a startling proof of the new age that was coming, and wrought a transformation in the ways of peasant life. In 1916, 99 per cent of the drawing and hauling was still done by draft animals or humans; but by 1939, 66 per cent of this labor had been taken over by the machines.

Such changes not only eased the drudgery of farm work and raised production but they released millions of farm laborers for other vocations or for army service. Yet the changes were not always popular despite the benefits they brought. The drive for collective farms was swift and apparently successful; by 1934 three-fourths of the farm families had been incorporated into the community farms which accounted for 90 per cent of the crop acreage. Yet the peasant's obdurate preference for a piece of land to call his own was still so strong that in 1936 Stalin permitted a modification of the collectivist policy in agriculture. Each family was permitted to retain half an acre for vegetables, poultry, and a few animals. At heart most Russian peasants were still land-hungry.

Behind this concession and behind the march towards collectivism there was a harvest of grim tragedy which is still hidden and can never be known in full. The Soviet officials and the Communist Party carried through the Five-Year Plans against widespread opposition which was crushed with relentless severity by mass arrests, deportations, and executions. What the revolutionary experiment cost in human misery and human lives only the statisticians in the Kremlin could gauge and they kept the figures secret. Neutral observers estimated that under the first three plans, between 1928 and 1941, probably 10,000,000 and possibly 25,000,000 Russians died from famine, forced labor, imprisonment, or execution. This darker side of the picture must be filled in to balance the admitted economic gains which the Five-Year Plans inspired and directed.

It is important to remember that those Russians who were opposed to the policies of the State Planning Commission had no legitimate means of moderating or opposing the policies because under the Soviet system no legal opposition party could exist. No rival political group or groups, temporarily out of office, acted as a check on the government, criticizing its directives and appealing to the voters with an alternate program and an invitation to choose new deputies and new candidates for office. The inner council of the Communist Party debated all important policies before these policies were discussed in the Union Central Executive Committee or approved by the Union Congress of Soviets. Party directives had decisive significance and once the "party line" had been established all loyal officials were expected to accept it implicitly. This unity of effort and of direction was deemed essential to the success of the revolution. The communists never forgot Lenin's warning that most revolutions fail because they do not defend themselves resolutely enough.

Thus opponents of the Soviet administration could not openly declare their opposition. Resistance, in consequence, took two forms. Unorganized popular antagonism revealed itself through sullen inertia, a deliberate slowing down of production, secret sabotage of machinery, fires of incendiary origin, and slaughter of livestock. Official opposition expressed itself in cabals and conspiracies throughout the hierarchy of officeholders and even spread to the staff of the Red army. To understand the shocking purges of the 1930's, the starvation of masses of peasants, and the transportation of millions of suspects to prison camps in Siberia, it is essential to realize that there was much passive opposition and some active plotting against the government and that the secret police were tireless in collecting evidence against any officials who were hostile or even lukewarm in their support of the party line. Suspects were relentlessly eliminated to assure "the safety of the state."

When the earliest Five-Year Plan was introduced in 1928 the first type of opposition (passive resistance) very nearly wrecked it. Millions of peasants with private farms were angered by the order to surrender their grain to the government at a fixed price and to merge their private holdings in the communal units. These more prosperous independent farmers, the kulaks, who thus dared to resent the official economic program, were warned they would be treated as enemies of the revolution. Their resentment grew; rather than raise grain and livestock for official confiscation they slaughtered their livestock and reduced their crops. Between 1928 and 1933 almost half the cattle and hogs in Russia disappeared. Of horses only 15,000,000 survived of an estimated 30,000,000; for sheep and goats the figure in 1933 was a bare 50,000,000, perhaps one-third of the total Russian herds of five years earlier.

This deliberate destruction of food brought misery to the peasants and semistarvation to the towns. Hunger reduced efficiency and the Five-Year Plan was seriously endangered. So Stalin ordered a pause on the "collectivization" of farms in 1930, and forty-eight members of the Commissariat of Agriculture were shot for "oppressing the peasants with thievish exactions."

The resistance of the kulaks was not forgotten, however, nor forgiven. Peasants who still showed themselves noncooperative were arrested and sentenced to prison-camp labor in Siberia. Even those denounced for "insufficient enthusiasm" might be penalized. By 1932 the kulak class had been so despoiled and persecuted that these once prosperous farmers were in a desperate condition. Renewed famine swept the Ukraine; and as the government persisted in collecting the quota of grain prescribed for the region, the famine spread. It is possible that 5,000,000 people (the number may never be known) died of starvation or were herded to prison camps in the terrible winter of 1932–1933 alone. This grim and relentless lesson was a warning to all Russians that there could be no future for those who obstinately defied orders from the Kremlin.

Meanwhile the resistance to the Five-Year Plan and the policies of the Soviet leaders was growing stronger within the party itself. This was a more serious challenge than peasant indignation, for discontented groups inside the bureaucratic ranks might convert the councils to their views. Two groups of critics took shadowy form: the

"Right Deviationists" as they were described, who believed that Stalin had betrayed the revolution by pushing collectivism and industrialization too fast; and the "Left Deviationists" or Trotskyites, who held that Russia could not long survive unless the other nations of the world were converted to communist ideals.

All the critics and malcontents (including Trotsky, who was living in exile in Mexico) insisted that they were seeking to preserve the revolution and to carry through the program Lenin had planned in accord with the teaching of Karl Marx. Foreign observers were puzzled and found that the intrigues, charges, and countercharges in this ideological warfare among the communists made little sense. The one obvious fact which did appear certain was that internal conspiracies and revolts threatened the Soviet regime. In 1934 the assassination of Sergei Kirov, a member of the Presidium and a close aide of Stalin, resulted in more than a hundred executions as the secret police rounded up suspected plotters. A special law was passed (December, 1934) to punish terrorists and traitors and to spur the Department of State Protection (the newly organized police bureau of the Commissariat of Home Affairs) to more ruthless activity.

This hunt for traitors within Russia could be blamed in part upon the threatening international situation. Germany under Hitler was openly rearming, and Japan had resumed an aggressive policy of expansion in China. When Germany, Italy, and Japan united in the Anti-Comintern Pact (1936) the persistent Russian fear of a "capitalist conspiracy against the Soviet Union" flamed up anew. The heads of the state skillfully utilized this dread of a foreign attack to destroy their opponents. All who deviated by a hair's breadth from the party line now came under suspicion. The list of crimes against the state was already vague and terrible enough, but it was lengthened to include ideological offenses. To expound a theory of law which cast doubt on the authority of the Soviets; to interpret history in a manner which weakened the loyalty of soviet citizens; even to praise "bourgeois" books in preference to sound "proletarian" literature might bring a citizen to the attention of the police. Any act or attitude which might impair the strength and stability of the Soviet Union was treasonable, and the most desperate crime of all was to correspond with or abet the agents of foreign governments working to destroy the revolution. With inexorable logic, the public prosecutor argued that the vast majority of Russians were devoted to their government and its leaders. It therefore followed that the few irreconcilable foes of the regime could not hope to organize a strong conspiracy or overthrow the government without foreign aid. Consequently it might be assumed that all secret enemies of the government had leagued themselves with those foreign powers which were plotting to defeat the Soviet armies in a major war.

The result of this panic was a series of "treason trials" from 1934 to 1938 which shocked and astonished civilized nations. Men high in the Soviet hierarchy, Nikolai Bukharin, Aleksei Rykov, Lev Kamenev, and Grigori Zinoviev were tried and executed. To allay suspicion that the charges were fictitious or that the "confessions" attributed to the accused might be fabrications, the Department of State Protection reverted to public trials. Foreign journalists were invited to hear the prisoners doom themselves by public confessions so extravagant that they were attributed to drugs or torture. In January, 1937, sixteen more leaders were shot.

But the most startling trial of that year and the culmination of the "purges" involved several high ranking officers of the Red army. Charges brought against Marshal Mikhail Tukhachevski and seven other Soviet officers involved communication with German and Japanese agents and the betrayal to the Germans of the defense plans of Czechoslovakia, an ally of Russia. The accused were tried by a military court and executed in June, 1937. To the world this seemed a proof of Russian instability. If the victims were guilty, the discontent in the Soviet governing bodies was obviously grave; if the victims were innocent, the purge advertised the desperate fear of Stalin and his associates who felt their control slipping. But the facts seem to suggest another interpretation. Purges were the grim but accepted technique for purifying and energizing party leadership. One-fifth of the party members were expelled in these arduous years; some were later rehabilitated, some kept in prison, some executed. To consider the purges a proof of internal confusion and inefficiency is to misunderstand them in part; and to attribute them to the blind panic of a dictatorial clique, which had no better answer for its critics than a firing squad, is to misread them almost entirely.

Russian leaders were persuaded after 1930 that the rising tariffs and tightening trade barriers adopted by all the capitalistic states would bring the world to another great war. They considered it essential for the Soviet Union to mature its industries and perfect its defenses. The danger of fifth column activities was demonstrated to all by the fate of Spain, Austria, and Czechoslovakia; and the certainty that German agents had sought contacts with rebel factions and dissatisfied army officers in Russia made a scrutiny and purge of traitors opportune. If many innocent victims were also shot on shadowy evidence, this ruthlessness taught all ranks to be more circumspect and dutiful. The detection of possible traitors became especially important after 1935 because the active Soviet army was expanded within two years from 940,000 to 1,300,000. Recruits were drawn, moreover, from classes hitherto suspect and disqualified, from ex-kulak families, and even from Cossack groups. In the ordeal by battle which was approaching, any fifth column elements, any enemy sympathizers or agents in key posts, might ruin the defense and bring overwhelming disaster, and it was therefore of first importance to assure the loyalty of the new army.

A revolution is a struggle between two centuries, two societies, two ways of life, and it produces a perpetual state of "war nerves." Such struggles are never easy or bloodless, and when they are mismanaged, vacillating, or deadlocked, they are particularly tragic because the sacrifice is futile. Revolutionary Russia could not be judged by normal standards. If a smooth compromise, a harmonious transition from the old regime to the new, had been possible, there would have been no revolution. Once started, the movement could be justified only by its success: it had to go forward towards its glorified goals or collapse in obloquy. An ardent leader of the French Revolution, perceiving this truth, confessed that "Nothing so nearly resembles virtue as a great crime." The Soviet leaders knew that they could have no appeal against failure, and they were determined their revolution should not collapse merely because, in Lenin's phrase, "it failed to defend itself."

4. EDUCATION IN THE SOVIET UNION

The impulse to attribute all modern progress in Russia to the revolution and to portray the period before 1917 as an era of almost unrelieved tyranny, misery, and ignorance, has often falsified the communist accounts of Russian history. One example of this is the pretense that the Russian people passed from a state of almost complete illiteracy to complete literacy in less than twenty years after 1917. In actuality, a campaign to reduce illiteracy among the masses, a campaign already in operation before 1900, had made considerable progress before the Bolsheviki put the driving force of the revolutionary government behind it. When the revolution occurred in 1917, one-third of the populace in some provinces and as many as one-half in others had acquired the rudiments of reading and writing. This advance, however, had been largely the result of local initiative, for the inertia of the czarist administration allowed education to languish and without state aid there can be no adequate state school system. Nevertheless it is not unjust to say that with the fall of czardom a new era in education opened in Russia. Especially after the November Revolution the Bolshevik leaders urged on a nation-wide campaign which was to combine practical education with the universal propagation of communist ideals. The men who shaped the Russian Revolution had studied history and pondered the factors in social change. They were aware that to forge a new society it is not sufficient to revise the laws, alter the social patterns, reform the living and working habits of a people. It is also necessary to change their habits of thought.

In their drive to liberate the citizens of the Soviet Union from inherited ideas, the communists turned their attacks against the Russian Orthodox Church. They confiscated church property, expelled the clergy, and dissolved the religious orders. Later, after the first fury of the revolution had subsided, private religious instruction and the holding of religious services were again tolerated. But the attitude of the communists toward religion remained hostile and the exclusive emphasis laid upon a secular outlook and secular aims in the communist youth organizations encouraged a skeptical attitude, to say the least, among the young in matters of religious faith. For the adult population a program of counterpropaganda, designed to weaken faith in religious doctrines, was instituted with official approval. Legal registration replaced the ceremonies of baptism, marriage, and burial services once a monopoly of the clergy, and all records were transferred to the civil authorities. Civil divorce became as easy as civil marriage. No aspect of the communist program excited more vigorous denunciation in other countries than the attack on organized religion, and it was predicted that the new attitude towards marriage and divorce would destroy the sanctity of family life and encourage unlimited license.

Partly as a substitute for religious services, the officials in charge of education and culture organized public concerts, displays, and exhibitions. The articles printed in the newspapers and in books, the offerings of the theaters, motion picture houses, and radio stations were all edited by official censors who decided what the public "needed." Painting, sculpture, and music were likewise expected to reflect proletarian trends. Art galleries and museums for the public were opened in every large community, and education and recreation were fostered by official encouragement and pressure. The consequences proved rewarding, and millions of Russians were brought into contact with literature, art, music, the drama, and the ballet, which might otherwise have remained undiscovered realms to them.

Soviet education had its deficiencies and limitations, however. It did not encourage speculations that ran counter to orthodox Marxian teaching, and criticism of the Communist Party or of the Soviet leadership was severely rebuked. The dominant purpose of the educational campaign was to indoctrinate, to propagandize. Every school, library, factory, collective farm, and homestead was decorated with pictures of Lenin and Stalin. People who could not read were made familiar with the symbols and drilled in the slogans of communism. The virtues of the Soviet form of government, the progress of the Five-Year Plans, the genius of the leadership which had ensured the triumph of the revolution were all emphasized interminably by posters, lectures, motion pictures, books, and newspapers. What percentage of the population used the 70,000 libraries, visited the 28,000 motion picture theaters, and read the 9000 newspapers printed in 70 different languages it is not easy to guess. But it is certain that a majority of the people had encountered the banners hung across the streets of the towns, the health caravans which visited rural fairs to demonstrate lessons in household hygiene, the admonitions in print, in pictographs, and even in public monuments, which urged the onlooker to consider the importance of labor, the evils of drunkenness, the advantages of the communist way of life, and other facts of social significance.

The Soviet system of state education was dominated throughout by a spirit of uncompromising realism. The most expensive and the most rapidly expanding schools were those which trained the architects of the new society, the doctors, laboratory workers, scientists, and engineers who had to staff the clinics, serve the industries, and fill the professional ranks. At a time when millions lacked food the government still found enough foreign exchange to purchase hundreds of academic, scientific, and technological journals from other countries so that its students and inventors might keep abreast of the latest progress throughout the world. Candidates for the academies of military science were picked with special care, and those with the requisite talent were drafted into the bureau of aeronautics, or cartography, or mechanized warfare. The commissars who charted the

322 . The World in the Twentieth Century

Five-Year Plans and outlined an educational curriculum to keep pace with them knew that warfare would become, to a rapidly increasing degree, mechanized. To equip the millions of soldiers who compose a modern army there must be millions of competent workers on the assembly lines. Only an industrialized society can wage a long and successful war in the twentieth century. And only a country with great natural resources and with technicians to explore and exploit those resources can build up an effective industry. It was this conviction that made Soviet education, like the whole social and economic and military program, so relentlessly practical in its aims.

5. POLITICAL AND CULTURAL ASSIMILATION

The largest ethnical group in the Union of Soviet Socialist Republics are the Russians, who constitute three-fourths of the total population. But the Union also includes European and Asiatic peoples from more than sixty nationalities and all levels of culture. Among the minorities of the northwest are the Lapps, a Mongoloid people who number perhaps 30,000. There is a Finnish minority in the Finno-Karelian area; and the Estonians, Latvians, and Lithuanians of the Baltic littoral form distinct nationalist groups each with its own dialect and traditions. White Russians (a subsidiary branch of the main Russian stock) inhabit the flat and marshy tracts which lie between northern Poland and Russia, and below the White Russians live the Ukrainians, with millions of Poles and the descendants of German settlers intermixed. The Moldavians occupy a sliver of territory, between Russia and Rumania, which touches the Black Sea coast below Odessa. Between the Black and Caspian Seas the Soviet frontier extends below the Caucasus Mountains, to include the Georgians, Armenians, and Azerbaijans. Culturally, this transcaucasian region is more Asiatic than European, and farther east still, in Soviet Central Asia, the population becomes definitely Oriental. The Turkmen, Uzbek, Tadzhik, Kirghiz, and Kazakh peoples seem almost wholly alien to Western eyes; the Tadzhiks, like the Azerbaijans, are Moslems, and the Uzbek women have only recently laid aside their veils. Last to be noted in this brief listing of Soviet minority nations are the Yakuts of Siberia, a type not unlike the American Indian, but a progressive people who are rapidly assimilating European culture and standards. This survey has swept around the western, southern, and eastern boundaries of the Soviet Union. On the north the frontiers meet no neighboring nations for they merge into the icefields of the polar regions.

By 1936 the Soviet Union included eleven Soviet Socialist Republics.[1] They were very unequal in size and population, much the most
important being the Russian Soviet Federal Socialist Republic (or
R.S.F.S.R.). This unit comprised over nine-tenths of the area of the
Union, included two-thirds of the total population, and produced
two-thirds of the agricultural and industrial output. (See map, p. 292.)
Second in area and population was the Ukrainian Soviet Socialist Republic with a population of 30,000,000; and third the Bielorussian
(or White Russian) Soviet Socialist Republic with about 6,000,000
people. The legislative body for the Union as a whole was the Supreme Council, a bicameral parliament or congress, consisting of a
Council of the Union and a Council of Nationalities, the members of
which were elected for four years. The executive authority was vested
in a cabinet of ministers, responsible to the Supreme Council, and
known as the Council of the People's Commissars. A constitution vali-
dating this machinery of government was adopted in 1936 and approved by the Supreme Council. It recognized, at least on paper, the
right of any constituent republic to withdraw from the Union. An
amendment in 1944 permitted each of the constituent republics to
have its own commissariat for defense and for foreign affairs. Thus
in international negotiations the Union of Soviet Socialist Republics
might claim to speak as one or as several states, although the real direction of foreign policy rested with the Council of People's Commissars.
When Russia joined the United Nations Organization in 1945 separate
votes were accorded the R.S.F.S.R., Bielorussia, and the Ukraine.

Political organization was less important in the growth of the Soviet Union than the economic and cultural ties which linked the
border regions to European Russia, which was the real core of the Soviet realm and of Soviet strength. Each national group was led to discover for itself the advantages of co-operation with other members

[1] These eleven republics were the Russian Soviet Federal Socialist Republic, the Ukrainian S.S.R., the Bielorussian (or White Russian) S.S.R.,
the Azerbaijan S.S.R., the Georgian S.S.R., the Armenian S.S.R., the
Turkmen S.S.R., the Uzbek S.S.R., the Tadzhik S.S.R., the Kazakh S.S.R.,
and the Kirghiz S.S.R. In 1940 Estonia, Latvia, and Lithuania were admitted as three additional republics, and territory ceded by Finland
and by Rumania was organized as the Karelo-Finnish and the Moldavian
S.S.R. respectively. This brought the total to sixteen, but the administrative structure of the U.S.S.R. as a whole is complex and the status
of many districts and the degree of self-government they retain is not
easy to define.

of the Union. The Soviet officials even fostered the cultural aspirations of the individual peoples, although with more than sixty national groups and dialects to deal with this might seem to invite chaos. Local and isolated peoples learned in varying degrees the improvements that come with books and radios, roads and railways, and with a more systematic development of natural resources. Reciprocal trade arrangements promised to provide raw materials for the Soviet industries and to bring distant tribesmen scientific remedies for the scourges which attacked their children and their herds. Retarded tribesmen were taught to construct more comfortable homes and to sow more productive crops. Within a few years hitherto isolated peoples not only learned of civilization but the more progressive began to operate trucks and tractors, attend motion pictures, buy radios, and build community schools. As the literate minority among them increased, they planned to publish their own newspapers and form their own libraries. These improvements in communication and transport knit them more surely to European Russia and to Moscow, the hub of the Soviet system and civilization, and this trend was encouraged by the Soviet authorities and the Communist Party.

The older generation and the more conservative groups among the less advanced peoples of the hinterland have sometimes shown themselves indifferent and even hostile to civilizing influences. But the young are more imitative and seek to learn about and to master the new techniques. Children learn Russian as well as their local dialect in the schools, they listen to Russian radio programs, and they learn the art of leadership by serving on local committees and joining in activities sponsored by the Soviet officials. The czarist policy of compulsory "Russification" had aroused deep hostility among the minority peoples, but the leaders of the new regime have been more adroit in promoting assimilation. Stalin, himself a Georgian by birth, was aware of the sentiment a smaller nation might feel for its local loyalties and especially its language, and he insisted that the differences of dialect, of dress, and of custom must be respected.

The communist leaders proved their knowledge of social psychology when they inspired these peoples to organize their own republics and enter the Union seemingly on their own initiative and application. In the jungle of international relations it is difficult for a weaker nation to trust a stronger or to separate the ideas of power and malignity. Although leaving to the affiliated republics of central Asia the appearance of autonomy and the illusion of individuality and equal status, the leaders at Moscow knew that in reality they were absorbing them but they were careful to disguise this fact. A superior and more aggressive culture transforms and assimilates less advanced groups which come into close contact with it. Already the more dominant Russian culture is tending to establish uniformity of speech, manners, dress, and ideology among the lesser non-Russian peoples. As Russian is the only language in which all groups can converse, the ablest and best educated students even in remote and alien districts learn to master it, for only those who speak and write Russian are eligible for higher education. The teachers, technicians, journalists, and members of the ruling bureaucracy speak Russian among themselves even though they may address local populations in the dialect of the district. For the children throughout the Soviet Union, as elsewhere, learning is a passionate imitation of the speech and methods of those they most admire. The prestige of Soviet officials, technicians, teachers, and organizers makes them a pattern for the rising generation. This, too, the leaders at Moscow took into their reckoning as they developed the program of the planned society.

XXII

BORDER STATES OF THE SOVIET UNION

It may seem strange that we, who are in favor of the fusion of national cultures in the future into one common culture (both in form and content), with a single common language, are at the same time in favor of the blossoming of the national cultures at the present time, in the period of the dictatorship of the proletariat.

JOSEPH STALIN

1. THE FEAR OF SOVIET RUSSIA

THE communist experiment in Russia which commenced in 1917 was watched with much apprehension by foreign observers in western Europe and the United States. Fear of Soviet Russia was aroused in part because there was considerable social unrest in Europe during the postwar years and the Bolshevik leaders announced that they intended to exploit it. Agents from Moscow attempted to stir the proletariat in other countries to revolt, and with advice and subsidies aided radical groups to make war on capitalism and to demand the abolition of private property. In March, 1919, the Russian communists issued an invitation to communist parties throughout the world to join in forming a Communist International. A First International had been founded in 1864 in an attempt to unite the working classes throughout the world. A Second International, organized later, disintegrated during the First World War of 1914–1918. The new organization, sponsored from Moscow, was therefore termed the "Third International" or "Communist International," and it sought to combine all the workers of all nations in a common program.

It was the professed aim of the Russian communists to create a world communist society. But such an ideal of international affiliation ran counter to the strong national loyalties which divided the nations of the Western world into jealous and disparate territorial states. All Frenchmen were bound by a common loyalty to their fatherland; all Englishmen forgot their private disputes when they believed that the British Isles were in peril. The national state was monolithic and the

A SCENE IN BUENOS AIRES, ARGENTINA

Sovfoto

THE DNIEPER DAM BEFORE ITS DESTRUCTION BY THE GERMANS IN WORLD WAR II

national society was built, as it were, vertically. Communism sought to align class against class and set them in a horizontal opposition. This antinational tenet of the communist program was its greatest weakness, for nationalism is the most powerful political force in the modern state. Although communist groups were organized in almost every country they were never more than a minority, and the accusation that their leaders "took orders from Moscow" damaged their cause and alienated the masses from their standard. In truth, the communist program for a world revolution was never more than a vague project in the minds of a few idealists. As the Russian revolutionary government became more firmly grounded and the danger of foreign attack declined in the years after 1921, the Soviet leaders dissociated their regime from the Third International. Ultimately, during the Second World War, they announced that the International had been disbanded.

Suspicion of Russia and fear of the communist program were fed by the fantastic and unverifiable reports which came out of that secretive land. Numerous refugees who escaped from Red Russia to western Europe and the United States brought gruesome accounts of the perils and sufferings they had survived. The hatred felt by most of these White Russians for the Red regime helped to prejudice their hosts and to build up tension and hostility between Soviet Russia and the neighboring states. As portrayed by the refugees the "dictatorship of the proletariat" was an inhuman tyranny, bringing wholesale arrests, mass executions, and the deportation of hordes of state prisoners to Siberia. It was true that the czarist secret police, the dreaded "Third Section" organized a century earlier under Nicholas I, had been abolished after 1917. But in its place appeared an Extraordinary Commission for the Repression of Counterrevolution, Sabotage, and Speculation (the *Cheka*), which proved more efficient and more ruthless than the Third Section had been. Conspiracies were suspected at all levels, and frequent purges decimated even the highest political and military circles of the hierarchy. Although the *Cheka* was abolished in 1922, it was replaced by the Unified State Political Administration (abbreviated to OGPU), and this in turn became (1934) the Commissariat for Internal Affairs. But the summary arrests, trials, deportations, and executions continued, and some of the most disturbing and (to the outside world) incomprehensible purges involved leading Soviet political and military officials.

To its enemies, therefore, Russian communism appeared an unrelieved tyranny. Yet even while they attacked the Russian experiment and condemned its cruelties, neighbor governments watched Bolshevik policy closely and learned from it. They might close their frontiers to Russian propaganda but they recognized the daring and constructive thought which inspired the social engineering of the planners. For the problems which the latter attacked so courageously were problems which also confronted the nations of eastern Europe and the peoples of a great part of Asia, problems for which they, like the Russians, had to find a solution.

2. THE BARRIER STATES OF EASTERN EUROPE

The most urgent social and economic issue in eastern Europe, from the Baltic to the Balkans, was the agrarian problem, the question of land ownership and exploitation. Much of the best land was still held by landlords who enjoyed an almost feudal status of privilege and prestige, and the fields were worked by envious peasants who yearned for a farm of their own. Before the revolution of 1917 dethroned the landed aristocracy of Russia, active agrarian parties had formed in the neighbor states from Finland to Bulgaria to demand a more equitable distribution of the land among the workers of the soil. After World War I ended in 1918, most of the governments of central and eastern Europe adopted agrarian laws that hastened the break-up of large family estates and increased the number of independent farmer-owners. Fear and prudence were powerful motivating forces in carrying out these reform movements, for the example of Soviet Russia, where all large estates were nationalized without compensation to the former aristocracy, provided a stern warning of what might happen if the hour of reckoning were too long deferred.

Thus the effect of the Russian Revolution was felt even in countries in which the government was officially hostile to communism. The land reforms carried through in Latvia, Estonia, and Lithuania after 1919 were inspired by the general trend. The ruling class in these Baltic countries was largely of German descent, and after the defeat of Germany in 1918 popular disturbances dispossessed and drove out many of the landlords. This expulsion provided an excuse for seizing many of the larger estates and dividing them into small farms of ten to fifty acres. As three-fourths of the people in Latvia, Estonia, and Lithuania lived on the land, the resulting changes in ownership and control, though less violent and dramatic than the Russian program, really constituted a social and economic revolution.

In Finland, which is a large and level land of lakes and forests with one-third of its area beyond the Arctic Circle, less than one-seventh of the countryside is cultivated. Yet it was still primarily an agrarian country in 1918, with two families out of three supporting themselves by agriculture. After the Finns asserted their independence of Russia in 1917, they increased the number of small farms and so created a larger class of independent farmers. By 1940 there were over 100,000 farms of eight to twenty-five acres in Finland, and only a few hundred large farms of 250 acres or more remained undivided.

In Poland, where almost two-thirds of the people likewise lived by farming, the division of the land proceeded more slowly although the same trend was observable. Poland, as reconstructed in 1919, was larger than Finland, claiming approximately 150,000 square miles of territory to 135,000 for Finland. But the population, estimated at 26,473,000 in 1919, was more than eight times that of Finland, which was calculated at 3,081,000. In 1925 the Polish government adopted an agrarian law which provided that some 5,000,000 acres of land would be distributed to peasant farmers. If carried through, this program might have established farms of ten acres as an average and furnished land for half a million families. But the tense political situation made reform difficult. The Poles constituted only 70 per cent of the population, and the minorities — Germans, Ukrainians, Jews, and lesser groups — were not easy to placate and formed a constant political threat. The government, though nominally democratic, was in reality a veiled dictatorship which preserved an unyielding rigidity and a dictatorial tone as a means of concealing its insecurity. By 1926 Poland had become a military and authoritarian state, with Marshal Josef Pilsudski exercising a controlling power behind a screen of parliamentary forms. On Pilsudski's death in 1935 he was succeeded by Edward Smigly-Rydz, who as head of the army maintained the authoritarian regime. It should be noted in extenuation of the leaders that throughout the period between World War I and World War II Poland was a threatened state, with Germany and Russia pressing on its frontiers. The government of a threatened state must keep a firm hold over the nation, build up a strong army, and discourage internal disputes. Insecure governments are seldom tolerant. They fear democratic movements because the formation of political parties, with their campaigns and elections, advertises the rifts within the state and seems an invitation to its enemies to split the nation and crush it piece by piece.

In Czechoslovakia the problem of land reform was attacked with more courage than in Poland. By a drastic agrarian policy the republican government of this newly created state transferred over half the arable land, especially the estates formerly held by German owners, to peasant proprietors. These measures had the desired effect of reducing discontent and discouraging radical demands among the traditionally conservative peasantry. But Czechoslovakia, like Poland, was threatened by the growing power of its neighbors, Russia and Germany, and weakened internally by the agitation of minority groups. The 3,000,-000 Germans of the Sudeten area were a particular problem, for their sympathy lay with their fellow Germans in the Reich. Thus the pressure of political and national feuds and the problem of defense retarded the program and the application of social and economic reforms.

In the states of southeastern Europe agrarian reform was also an urgent issue but the programs followed a more ragged pattern. The Hungarians, in their truncated state of 35,875 square miles with a population of 7,870,000, turned from the bitterness of defeat in 1918 to a brief experiment in communist dictatorship in 1919. Then the conservative forces prevailed in this "kingdom without a king" and the Hapsburg dynasty might have been invited to rule at Budapest if the victorious Allies had permitted such a restoration. Though the dominant role of the ancient Magyar nobility was weakened by the dismemberment of the empire, Hungary still remained a half-feudal, half-archaic country. A land reform Act was adopted in 1920 but it was not widely enforced, and ten years later one-third of the arable land still remained in the possession of a few hundred families. Democratic demands for a secret ballot, popular elections, responsible government, and trial by jury were disregarded by the authoritarian regime. The one real goal that stirred all the Magyars (who composed nine-tenths of the population) was the determination to reverse the terms imposed upon their country by the Treaty of Trianon in 1920.

Rumania and Bulgaria, after World War I, were likewise rent by factional disputes and failed to win political stability. Rumania was swollen by the annexation of what had been Hungarian and Russian territory, while Bulgaria, which had aided the Central Powers, was constricted and embittered by defeat. In both kingdoms peasant parties, eager for land reform, clashed with the propertied groups, the landlords, manufacturers, merchants, and middle class citizens. Those who owned property declared that it was inviolable; those without property agitated for reform and were stigmatized as communists. In the neighbor state of Yugoslavia similar problems and similar feuds provoked political clashes, but Yugoslavia had additional cause for strife in the sectional rivalry and national hostility of the Croats, Serbs, and lesser minority elements. In the kingdom of Greece, poverty, political confusion, and the desire to play a role in Mediterranean politics beyond the scope of Greek resources, made that country too a scene of frequent political disorders. Greece, Yugoslavia, and Bulgaria had the further antagonisms which arise from border incidents and unwilling minorities, for the frontiers which separated the three countries had never been adjusted to the satisfaction of any one of them.

Thus Balkan politics, after the First World War as before it, were complicated by *coups d'état*, assassinations, and foreign intrigues. Britain, France, Italy, Russia, and a reviving Germany all meddled in Balkan affairs as their interests met and clashed in this critical area. But as the Soviet government became stronger Russian influence increased inexorably, although it was often indirect and obscure. As noted above, fear of communism frightened the wealthy and aristocratic classes into many limited concessions, but it also frightened them into clinging more rigidly to political power. The distribution of small farms among the peasant families, on the principle that they would become conservatives if they had something to conserve, was a shrewd policy. But as more peasants became independent farmers and property owners they became a political force and demanded a share in the government of the countries which had so long been ruled by an hereditary aristocracy. Outside of Russia there was no bloody revolution on a grand scale with a complete repudiation of the old order and a frank program of collectivism which renounced the profit motive and the guaranties that protected private property. But wherever the unsolved land question provided a grievance, the peasants and workers of eastern Europe remained half-responsive to Russian influence. This fact was to prepare them to welcome the Soviet soldiers as liberators in the closing campaigns of World War II.

It is important to note that eastern Europe, between 1918 and 1939, was not only a potential battleground of rival powers, of France and Russia or Germany and Russia. It was a battleground on which rival ideologies were competing for the allegiance of the half-comprehending people. Communist doctrines and Soviet policies were a solvent influence; they threatened the social and economic as well as the political foundations upon which the European nations had erected their governments, and they threatened the institutions, particularly the institution of private property, upon which the dominant classes in Europe based their strength and through which they exercised their mastery. The belief of the Soviet leaders at Moscow that all the European governments were leagued against Russia after 1917 was true in the sense that almost all the European governments were opposed to the spread of communism. While France remained the dominant military power on the Continent, the smaller states which bordered the Soviet Union on the west knew that they had a protector. It was an article of French foreign policy in the decade 1920–1930 to preserve a *cordon sanitaire* in eastern Europe that would quarantine Russia and exclude communist influence from Europe. Poland, Czechoslovakia, and Rumania were united in an alliance under French auspices and thus formed a barrier by which the westward spread of the dangerous Marxian ideas infecting Russia might be checked. It was, of course, a second and no less serious duty of these French satellite states to check the revival of German power and German militarism. When, in the decade 1930–1940, German militarism revived despite all checks, the eastern European states went over to the German side voluntarily or else were forced into the German system. In yielding to German demands, the statesmen of Poland, Hungary, and Rumania were swayed by their greater fear of Soviet intentions. The same fear influenced the statesmen at Paris and London as late as 1938, when they sacrificed Czechoslovakia to Germany in the confused belief that it was as important to curb Russia as it was to check Germany.

3. TURKEY, IRAQ, AND IRAN

When the victorious Allies, Britain and France, imposed terms upon Turkey after World War I, they left the sultan, Mohammed VI, a greatly reduced empire of less than 300,000 square miles, including Constantinople and its environs in Europe and the Anatolian headland in Asia Minor. In area the Turkish state was still an impressive block on the map for it was larger than any European country west of Russia. But with its backward population of 13,000,000 and its undeveloped resources and almost primitive economy Turkey after 1918 was a minor power.

Yet there was a latent energy in this truncated state and defeat released it, hurling the Turks out of their ancient and unprogressive channels and hurrying them into far-reaching reforms. Alone among the vanquished nations of World War I, the Turkish people dared to reject the settlement drafted for them (Treaty of Sèvres, 1920) and demand better terms. Though British forces occupied Constantinople and Mohammed VI was compelled to accept the treaty, a Nationalist Assembly which met at Angora (Ankara) repudiated the sultan and organized a movement of national resistance. To chasten these defiant Nationalists, the British encouraged a Greek army to land at Smyrna, but the resulting Greco-Turk War (1921–1922) ended in a disastrous rout for the Greeks. All the leading powers — Great Britain, France, Italy, and Russia — were more willing to let the Turks remain independent than to see Turkey fall under the control of a rival, and this international jealousy enabled the National Assembly at Ankara finally to secure a better settlement. By the Treaty of Lausanne (1923) Turkey renounced all claims to North African lands and to the Arabian peninsula, but in return the Assembly won full recognition of Turkish sovereignty over its remaining provinces. Furthermore, capitulations which had exempted foreigners from the rule of Turkish law, conventions which had permitted foreign powers to intervene to protect Christian minorities, and the reparations claims arising from the First World War were all canceled. The Treaty of Lausanne was a signal triumph for the renascent Turkish state and the first notable defeat for the peace plans outlined by the victors in 1919.

While thus defending Turkish interests abroad, the National Assembly carried through a revolutionary program of reconstruction at home. Between 1920 and 1924 the caliphate was abolished, the sultan, Mohammed VI, deprived of his civil and religious powers and compelled to abdicate, and the energetic organizer, Kemal Ataturk, elected President of the Turkish Republic. By a Fundamental Law (1921) and subsequent constitutional changes Turkish institutions were completely remodeled. All former titles and privileges, civil, military, or religious, were abolished. All adult citizens received the vote, and the elected assembly, representing the people, entrusted full executive authority to the president and his council of commissioners. In carrying out these reforms the Turks were imitating many of the precedents set in Soviet Russia but they did not stress the similarities. Like the Russians they erected a one-party government with strongly centralized control. Like the Russians they provided for elective councils or committees in each province, district, and commune. To speed agriculture and industry the government planning commission introduced a Five-Year Plan in 1934. New codes, based upon Swiss, German, and Italian models, were drawn up to simplify judicial procedure; the metric system of weights and measures was instituted; and the Latin alphabet and Arabic numerals adopted. Mohammedanism remained the religion of the great majority of the people but it was no longer the state religion, and the Moslem religious leaders lost much of their former influence over the schools and the law courts.

In foreign affairs the new regime set a course of careful neutrality. Control of Constantinople and the Straits is an international responsibility. It is a matter of importance to all the nations in the Danube Valley, and to Soviet Russia likewise, that free communication with the Mediterranean should be preserved. In 1925 the Soviet Union and the Turkish Republic concluded a ten-year accord promising neutrality and co-operation, and this pact was later extended to 1945. A further agreement (1941) between Russia and Turkey promised that either party would remain neutral if the other were attacked. The Bosporus and the Dardanelles, demilitarized by the Treaty of Lausanne (1923), were refortified by the Turks under a new convention approved by the powers in 1936. Of all the great powers, Russia would be the most vitally concerned by any shift in Turkish policy. The Russian need for an unobstructed outlet to the warm seas makes Turkey a predestined sphere of Soviet pressure. The same pressure is felt by the neighboring states of Iraq, Iran, and Afghanistan, and this fact helped to unite the four in a common defense pact in 1937.

Iraq, which is dotted with the ruins of Sumerian and Babylonian cities five thousand years old, was erected as an independent kingdom under British mandate after World War I. In 1932 the mandate was terminated and Iraq joined the League of Nations as a sovereign state. As constituted, it formed a country of 116,600 square miles, with a population (1935) of 3,560,435. British advisers assist the monarch and his councillors and help with the organization of the army and the police force. Although Iraq has no common boundary with the Soviet Union its position between Turkey and Iran and its control of the twin rivers, the Tigris and the Euphrates, make it strategically one of the "border states" which block the Russian outlet to the sea.

Iran (Persia) has an area of some 628,000 square miles and a population variously estimated at 10,000,000 to 18,000,000. It is ruled by a cabinet responsible to the National Assembly, and like Turkey it is feeling the impact of Western customs and techniques. Recent legislation has reduced the influence of the Mohammedan priesthood, substituting secular control over the schools and the courts and promulgating a judicial code based upon Swiss and French precedents.

Iranian mineral resources, supposedly rich, remain undeveloped; but oil wells, among the most productive in the Near and Middle East, make Iran a center of competing business interests, British, American, and Russian.

The mountainous country of Afghanistan, with an area of 250,000 square miles and a population of about 12,000,000, is important as a buffer state between Russia and the Indian states. The government is nominally a constitutional monarchy under a Shah, the people are Moslem, and the chief activities are agriculture and sheep raising. Mineral resources are little developed and industry limited but expanding.

4. RUSSIAN EXPANSION IN ASIA

To understand the successes won by the Soviet Union in Asia and the manner in which the Russian communists have secured a working alliance with numerous Asiatic peoples, it is helpful to recall the expansion of Russian influence under the czarist regime. The penetration and settlement of northeastern Asia is one of the great colonizing movements of modern history. Since the sixteenth century Russian explorers, traders, soldiers, and settlers have been pressing eastward, decade after decade, until they arrived on the shores of the Pacific Ocean. Even this did not halt them, for they crossed Bering Strait in the eighteenth century and established settlements in Alaska, with trading posts as far south as California. In 1867 Russian America, as Alaska was called, was sold to the United States, but this withdrawal from America did not mean that the Russians were withdrawing from eastern Asia also. Six years earlier the government of Czar Alexander II founded Vladivostok, "Conqueror of the East," on the Sea of Japan, and the Island of Sakhalin guarding the northern exit to that Sea was annexed in 1875. To link Vladivostok with Irkutsk, Omsk, and ultimately with Moscow, the Trans-Siberian Railway was commenced in 1891 and completed in 1903.

By this eastward expansion the Russians established their claim to a territory that was continental in extent. No other great power was in a position to oppose them or to penetrate into the almost void hinterland of northern Asia. Unlike North and South America, Africa, Australia, and southern Asia, the vast territories of Siberia cannot be reached by maritime routes and can be entered only under exceptional conditions. The Arctic coast of Asia and the Arctic Ocean into which the Siberian rivers empty is sealed with ice most of the year. Northern Asia could thus be explored and settled only as the Russians settled it, by patient expeditions which pressed on through the level forests, the marshes and the tundra, planting towns along the way and wringing a living from the soil of that bleak magnificent land and from the pelts of its furred population.

For three centuries the Russians moved almost unopposed down a corridor of virgin territory, following in general the more temperate routes between the 50th and the 60th parallels of North Latitude. The region was similar in climate, topography, and vegetation to the Canadian provinces from Ontario to the Rocky Mountains. To the north of that four-thousand-mile corridor which they explored lay a vast Arctic region, as in Canada. This was a natural treasure house, an uninhabited empire of coniferous forests, lakes, and tundra. To the south of the Russian line of march lay the little known and politically feeble provinces of Turkestan, Mongolia, and Manchuria. These central Asian areas were populated, though by no means densely populated, by various Kirghiz and Mongolian peoples. But none of them had set up a strong political state or erected military obstacles firm enough to check the eastward march of the Russian colonists. In this the Russians were historically fortunate. Never in the annals of migration, not even by the English colonists in North America, was a continental empire so easily acquired.

By the twentieth century Siberia had become the colonial area of Russian imperialism, a worthy substitute for the overseas empires built up by the maritime powers. But it required the vision of the Soviet planners to recognize that this empire might really become a populous, self-supporting, and healthy dominion of the north by the use of modern methods of transportation, communication, heating, herding, and harvesting. By 1940 this eastern section of the Union of Soviet Socialist Republics, lying between the northern frontiers of China and the Arctic Sea, had a population of 12,000,000, a population larger than that of Canada and growing more rapidly. Several of the cities, such as Novosibirsk, Irkutsk, and Omsk, claimed a quarter of a million inhabitants each. Northern Asia was thus firmly linked to the Soviet Union and garrisoned by a loyal population. At the same time central Asia was coming under the influence of Soviet policies and the outer provinces of Turkestan and China were drawn into the Soviet sphere. The reasons for this successful enlargement of the Soviet Union call for some explanation.

One of the most widely felt and most significant movements which stirred the world population after 1918 was the resentment nursed by millions of subject people against the domination and exploitation of the Europeans. In Africa, in Asia Minor, in Iran, Afghanistan, and India, throughout China, Indo-China, and the East Indies, the stir of native peoples awakening to a sense of indignation at the exactions of European imperialism became an ominous challenge. It was evident to all thoughtful observers that the twentieth century would prove a critical period in the drama of the European hegemony. For the first time in five hundred years the Europeans were to see non-European nations take the offensive against them with a prospect of success.

Alone of European governments, the Russian communist leaders viewed this discontent without alarm. They knew that it could be counted upon to embarrass the major powers, deflect their attention, and disperse their forces to distant spheres of unrest. Furthermore the resentment against imperialism was in a sense an attack upon the capitalistic system and upon the "expropriating classes" as the communists like to style them. In the Asian countries which bordered upon Russia any resentment against other European powers might create a situation which favored Soviet expansion, for the Russians, likewise on hostile terms with European governments, could pose as friends and defenders of the Asiatic peoples against the rapacity of the imperialist powers. This condition of affairs helps in part to explain why Russian influence penetrated eastern and southern Asia with some success after World War I.

The Soviet system of government possessed other and greater advantages in its contacts with neighboring peoples, however. It was elastic enough to permit of indefinite expansion, and it could add new member states to the Union as easily as the United States bestowed statehood on segments of the western territories as these became settled and organized. Secondly, the Soviet system was flexible enough to permit all types of republics, large or small, with populations dense or sparse, civilized or backward, to enter the Union. Thirdly, the communist leaders were prudent enough to avoid any threat of forced Russification of alien peoples, for they knew how deeply this policy had offended minority groups during the czar's regime. All co-operative nations were accepted as sovereign, equal, and free, and no distinction was made between Europeans and Asiatics. Stalin, who was himself a Georgian, well understood the sentiments of the national minorities and helped to shape Soviet policy in dealing with them. The officials from Moscow who prepared the various Eastern nations for admission to the U.S.S.R. acted in general with patience and tact.

The Soviet Union did not impose an alien administration in new provinces, it sought the co-operation of the local councils, tribal assemblies, or other representative agencies which already enjoyed the respect of the local inhabitants. Each region, as it joined the Union of Soviet Socialist Republics, was granted representation on the Soviet Council of Nationalities, and elected its delegates to the Union Congress of Soviets. Variable, adjustable, and elastic, this ingenious method of attracting and incorporating new peoples and provinces within the Soviet Union must be accounted one of the most remarkable triumphs of Soviet statecraft.

PART VI

The Asiatic and Pacific World

INDIA AND THE EAST INDIES

An Indonesian who does not believe in magic is no Indonesian.
A. D. A. DE KAT ANGELINO

I. THE EMPIRE OF INDIA

ALTHOUGH most Europeans and Americans have heard much of India and the "Indian Problem" for years, it is very difficult for them to achieve any clear conception of the country. They are led to wonder why India remains in an undefined state of crisis and to ask why Dominion status, which has worked well in other British states, has not satisfied the Indian peoples. In recent years, since the Indian Nationalists began demanding complete independence, many critics have denounced the British government for failing to grant it. As India holds some 400,000,000 people, almost one-fifth of the human race, the problem of India and of British methods of rule in India is one of great significance. It is one phase of the demand raised by subject peoples everywhere for liberation from the rule of Europeans. Whatever measures the British adopt in their attempt to solve it will have repercussions in all colonial areas, all mandates and protectorates of the great powers, and on all oppressed and exploited peoples.

During World War I the unrest in India gathered strength but there was little violence. This was partly due to the influence of Mohandas K. Gandhi, an ascetic Hindu lawyer known to his followers as the Mahatma or saintly one. After the war ended in 1918, however, Gandhi urged the need for prompt concessions to Indian demands. The British government had promised (1917) that institutions leading to complete self-government would be introduced progressively, but they delayed any positive action. In 1919 a tragic incident at Amritsar, the "Amritsar Massacre," in which a British commander ordered his troops to fire upon an unarmed gathering of Hindus, killing nearly four hundred, aroused deep indignation. The British sought

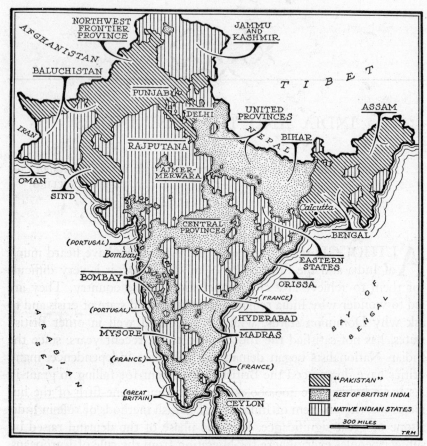

INDIA ON THE EVE OF INDEPENDENCE, 1947

to modify the increasing opposition by passing, later in 1919, the Government of India Act. This set up a dual system of administration (the Dyarchy), whereby the British Governor-General was to divide his power with an Indian Legislature. Provincial legislative councils were likewise to advise the provincial governors, and Indians were to be admitted to the higher as well as the lower ranks of the civil service. Led by Gandhi, the Indian National Congress rejected this compromise as inadequate (1920) and Gandhi preached a campaign of civil disobedience. Despite his pleas to his followers to limit the movement to nonresistance, there was widespread disorder. Gandhi was arrested in March, 1922, and sentenced to six years' imprisonment.

A deepening sense of grievance and a growing spirit of solidarity made the Nationalist movement increasingly powerful. Hindus made their own salt from sea water to avoid the government revenue tax, boycotted the liquor stores to evade the tax on spirits, and even refused to pay the assessments on land. In the cities the industrial workers, a radical element, were organizing and might in time provide a serious revolutionary threat. All classes suffered from the world-wide economic depression which began in 1929. The Indian National Congress now demanded full Dominion status, and when this was not definitely promised, the Congress declared itself in favor of complete independence. Recognizing the need to yield, the British government called a Round Table Conference in 1931 and again in 1932, inviting Indian leaders to assist. The suggestions made were embodied in a new Government of India Act passed in 1935 and put into operation in 1937. One motive for this concession had been the disastrous fall in revenue resulting from the campaign of civil disobedience and the economic depression.

The new experiment provided for the formation of a federation of Governor's Provinces, Chief Commissioner's Provinces, and such Indian states still under local rulers as might join. Government was to be vested in a Governor-General (representing the King-Emperor in London), a Council of State, and a Legislative Assembly. Some members of the Council and the Assembly were to be elected, some appointed. A Council of Ministers, or cabinet, responsible to the legislature, was to assist the Governor-General, and the legislature received power (subject to certain restrictions) to make laws for all persons within British India, all British subjects in other parts of India, and all Indian subjects of the King-Emperor in any part of the world.

In its form and wording this Act seemed to make India, or at least the British-ruled provinces of India, a self-governing Dominion. But this was a superficial and European reading of a situation too complex to be well understood even in India itself. There were four major conditions peculiar to the country which made the attainment of a true national status and real political autonomy a distant and difficult goal. The obstacles to national unity and immediate self-government for India may be conveniently summarized under these four heads.

The first obstacle was lack of social homogeneity. India is not one country or one nation, it is a subcontinent. Its 400,000,000 people range from the highly civilized to the totally primitive and reveal a diversity of racial strains from Aryan to Negroid. There are seven recognized language groups or categories; these are further divided into at least twenty-four subdivisions, and the subdivisions include scores of local dialects. Although some degree of literacy is now claimed for one Indian out of eight, less than one in one hundred have a knowledge of English. Religious differences further segregate the population into rival groups of Hindus, Muslims, Sikhs, Parsees, Buddhists, and Christians, not to name the multitudinous minor sects. Religion is a vital concern in India; rioting between rival sects, especially between Hindus and Mohammedans, is a frequent cause of disorder. The Mohammedans, or Muslims, who form almost one-fourth of the total population, insist that if India becomes independent they must be granted their own self-governing area to be known as Pakistan. Among the Hindus the persistence of strict caste rules, which separate the classes so rigidly that intermarriage or even communication between some of them is forbidden, creates a perplexing barrier to democracy or social unity. It is clear that the peoples of India do not possess, and can scarcely hope to achieve in the near future, that racial, linguistic, and cultural unity which distinguishes the strong, self-governing nation-states of the European world.

The second great obstacle to union and autonomy is the administrative disjunction. To plan, as many Indian Nationalists do, to impose swift political centralization on a society rent by social and religious cleavages, is unrealistic. It is, in fact, a European conception transported by doctrinaire minds to an Oriental setting. India has never possessed an efficient centralized administrative system that could be perpetuated or could serve as a future pattern, and to create a workable one swiftly would tax the greatest lawgiver. Although the British maintained order, peace, and protection in the peninsula for over a century, they brought little symmetry or uniformity to the administration as a whole. Two types of states emerged: those which made up British India and were subject to British rule, and the Indian States, or semiautonomous provinces, the rulers of which were sovereigns "allied" to Great Britain by treaty. British India, the more important section, covered a little more than half the area of the peninsula, but it was the more prosperous portion and included three-fourths of the population. It comprised seventeen provinces, some with local legislatures but most of them split into divisions run by commissioners. These divisions were further subdivided into districts under a local British official who was magistrate, tax collector, and deputy commissioner. The districts were the real units of administration. Thus British India was politically atomized. All real authority rested with a handful of trained and competent British officials, who had wide discretionary powers. The prestige which the British won as alien conquerors, a sort of supercaste, gave them a rare advantage in their supervision of Indian affairs. It is doubtful if the Indian peoples will yield the same respect and obedience to officials of their own choosing. A sudden transition to self-government and the withdrawal of the British ruling hierarchy might open the way to chaos unless it were carried through with caution and dexterity.

A third obstacle to unity and independence is lack of education. The vast majority of the Indian peoples have never been trained to exercise or even to understand the principles of British law or the responsibilities of self-government. Nine-tenths of the population, over 350,000,000 people, live under rural and many under extremely primitive and isolated conditions. Divided by caste, blood, religion, language, and occupation, as well as by political differences, the Indians have much to master in the field of social integration and co-operation. They have been conditioned by centuries of habit to evade, to endure, or to flatter their conquerors, but the masses have never learned to resist, to criticize, or to participate in their own government. They could not soon acquire initiative and experience or adapt themselves in a few years to Western ideals of individualism and democracy.

A fourth obstacle that hinders political consolidation is the attitude of most of the independent princes. These rulers are despots, many of them enlightened despots and some quasiconstitutional despots, but despots none the less by force of immemorial tradition. They are reluctant to associate or combine their hereditary despotisms with the parliamentary regimes which the British provinces slowly developed. Without including the Indian States no unification of all India is possible. Up to 1939 fifty of these States had rejected the invitation to adhere to the federation proposed in the Government of India Act of 1935. Until at least half of them joined the federation, the Act could not become operative. Thus, in a sense, the network of conservative native states, the rulers of which were in general loyal to Britain, were forts of resistance stretched across India. No revolutionary wave could sweep the peninsula from end to end until these "blockhouses" are reduced or amalgamated. It would require decades of political consolidation and a profound social and intellectual revolution to transform India into a united commonwealth.

British financial and manufacturing interests suffered after the Indian legislature won the right to lay import duties upon British goods. But British businessmen had £1,000,000,000 invested in India, and were reluctant to withdraw from the largest foreign market any one nation ever controlled. Regardless of political ties, these economic connections continued to exercise a powerful influence over Anglo-Indian relations. Most of the public utilities, power stations, railways, posts, telephone and telegraph and radio stations, banks, shipyards, and ordnance works functioned under British control or state management. Aircraft manufacture, automobile assembly plants, farm machinery, chemicals, metallurgy, and machine-tool industries were partly nationalized. But so long as the capital essential to such developments, the shipping, the control of raw materials, and the professional personnel remained at the disposal of the British or of Indian industrialists loyal to British rule, the tie with Great Britain remained strong. Even with the political ties dissolved, it seemed probable that Anglo-Indian collaboration on other planes would prove useful and profitable to both peoples.

A divided India would be vulnerable in a world of competing imperialisms: it would almost certainly fall under the domination of some other great power if definitely separated from the British Empire. The Hindus, who comprise two-thirds of the population, might favor an alliance with China if that were practicable. The Muslims, or Mohammedans, a minority of about one-fourth, but an aggressive and influential minority, are more strongly attracted to British rule. Many intellectuals, especially those of the more radical persuasion, look to Russia. These divergent attractions provide one more element of discord and schism rending India apart.

Despite these hazards and unsolved problems the Indian leaders renewed their demands for complete political independence when World War II ended in 1945. The British Labor government, headed by Clement R. Attlee, decided that the time had come for a decision. Early in 1947 the decision was announced from London: the British would withdraw from India within six months, turning over the full responsibilities of self-rule to whatever government or governments the Indians chose to establish. In August, 1947, the transfer of authority was completed. India was divided into two major segments, the Dominion of India (Hindu) and Pakistan (to include areas with a Mohammedan majority). Riots, disorders, and massacres marked the opening of this new chapter in the long history of India. The new Indian governments acknowledged their respect for their late masters by inviting hundreds of British officials to serve under the new regimes.

2. THE BRITISH LEGACY TO INDIA

Thus the British vindicated their oft-repeated promise that their role in India was a tutelary one — that the Indians, like the Canadians, Australians, and South Africans, had been trained for autonomy under British guidance and protection. In the final half-century of British rule, before 1947, India had made exceptional progress. Improvements in agriculture, irrigation, transportation, manufacture, and public hygiene brought a rapid rise in the population, which increased from 283,872,359 in 1901 to 388,997,955 in 1941. In resigning their stewardship the British could take pride in their record of achievements.

The power which the trained British official exercised in India has been described as "bewildered omnipotence." He has also been compared to Mark Twain's Connecticut Yankee at King Arthur's court. Rudyard Kipling in a famous poem bade the British "take up the white man's burden" and serve their captives' need. Idealistic young officials saw themselves as heralds from the future who could bring twentieth-century civilization to millions of Asian peoples living in poverty, ignorance, and superstition. To lead a retarded people from the dark ages to the light of civilization appealed to the missionary impulse which most Europeans share.

In striving to modernize India, the British assumed a task in some ways comparable to that of the national monarchs in Europe at the close of the Middle Ages. The sections made subject to British law corresponded to the disparate segments of a royal domain. The Indian States, ruled by local rajahs and maharajahs, were like baronies of semi-independent vassals whose fiefs had not yet been assimilated. Like the national monarchs the British extended their control through four invaluable instruments of government: they commanded the armed forces of India, the "King's Army"; they established and maintained a standard currency, the "King's coinage"; they developed and administered the main systems of transportation, the "King's highway"; they controlled foreign policy — no Indian state was permitted to form treaties with its neighbors or with any foreign power save through British mediation.

To placate the Indian princes for their lost prerogatives the British left them almost autonomous rights within their own hereditary domains. Some of these rulers agreed to make an annual contribution for the common defense of India and for other services but some did not. The British (again like the early national monarchs) raised a revenue from various monopolies and won the support and contributions of the small but energetic business class. The townsmen compose less than 10 per cent of the population, and they need legal protection in a land of arbitrary despots, uncertain taxes and tariffs, and feudal restrictions. Craftsmen, tradesmen, shopkeepers, moneylenders, professional men of all vocations, who had property or positions or privileges to safeguard, came to rely upon the British law to protect their vulnerable assets. Property needs protection, and men of wealth buy that protection, as they buy any other commodity, where they can obtain it most cheaply and efficiently. Medieval European merchants demonstrated this when they voted subsidies to the king and urged him to extend the royal courts. In the archaic society of India, British supervision of justice created a hierarchy of courts with final appeal to the Privy Council in England. It has been charged that this system brought justice in the sense of legality for existing customs rather than justice in the sense of equity as it is understood in democratic countries. Naturally, those classes which benefit from traditional customs desire to see these customs sanctioned and upheld. The magistrates who presided in the law courts of India, whether they were British or Indian born, understood that their duty was to apply the law. If some of the statutes worked injustice it was the function of the legislator, not of the judge, to reform them.

Many Indian Nationalists affirm that British rule meant a progressive impoverishment for their country despite the real advantages of peace and order that it brought. They insist that India in the seventeenth century was the leading agricultural country of Asia and the industrial workshop of the world and that British conquest and policies in the eighteenth and nineteenth centuries reduced Indian prosperity. Complete independence, they believe, with taxes and tariffs adjusted to benefit India instead of Great Britain, will restore the economic leadership the Indian Empire has lost. The Nationalists also argue that the peasants were even worse off under British rule than in the seventeenth century. The usurers, who hold millions of them in a thralldom of debt which may accumulate through generations, have been fortified in their prerogatives by the decisions of the courts; they are less moneylenders than landlords, and the interest which they exact is "justified" as rent. It is not surprising that the landlord class, the independent peasants who are fortunate enough to own their own farms, the townsmen of middle class status, and the princes in their glittering courts, valued British protection. They feared that a weakening of the British control might bring an agrarian revolution or a communistic upheaval with confiscation of private property.

The Indian quest for unity is still confused and retarded by the complex schisms, vertical and horizontal, which split society. The states of the princes are half-autonomous territorial units, feudal bastions which have still to be reduced. In addition to this vertical segmentation there are weakening horizontal rifts and strata that will not fuse. The caste system, the timeless customs which relegate certain functions and forms of labor to specified groups and classes, make economic, social, and political equality an almost meaningless concept. Despite the introduction of modern machinery and transportation, social evolution cannot be unduly hastened. To suppose that India might traverse in three or four decades the long stages of development which in Europe required three or four centuries, is to misread the tenacity of the Asiatic of the hotter and more humid South. The Indian peoples have defended their preferences and clung to their ways of life for thousands of years despite successive conquests by more energetic Northern invaders. It is possible to impose Western educational methods, jurisprudence, military drill, and factory routine upon acquiescent millions. But tradition is strong. Their training in the new tasks remains mechanical, their thinking wears the gloss of modernity, but the varnish is superficial. The Indian who absorbed a Western education was not better fitted thereby for a happy life within his natural milieu. On the contrary, he often became Europeanized and was isolated from his kindred. British schooling made many Indian intellectuals of the twentieth century cultural exiles, wanderers between the Eastern and the Western worlds. This also was part of the British heritage to India.

3. BURMA, BRITISH MALAYA, FRENCH INDO-CHINA, AND SIAM

Burma is a country of 261,610 square miles (approximately the size of Texas), with a population of some 15,000,000. From 1826 until 1937 Burma and India were joined by the British for administrative purposes. With the application of the new Government of India Act in 1937 Burma became a Crown Colony with a separate constitution. In 1942, after the fall of Singapore, the Japanese invaders "liberated" Burma and declared it an independent state. A Japanese-sponsored regime promptly declared war against Great Britain and the United States, and Burma became the scene of considerable jungle fighting. With the defeat of Japan in 1945 British supremacy was reasserted.

Burma is less densely populated than India but the people possess greater homogeneity. Three-fifths of them are Burmans; the remainder are classed as Indians, Karens, Shans, and other minorities. Buddhism is the dominant, almost the exclusive, religious faith, claiming seven-eighths of the people, but society is not subdivided into rigid castes as in India. Thus Burma, with one widely used language, one prevailing religion, and a fairly homogeneous populace, might be transformed into a unified nation-state more readily than the Indian Empire with its many languages, faiths, castes, and component states. The British administrators, after extending their influence through war and diplomacy as in India, brought the ancient kingdom of Burma and the adjacent Shan states under the rule of a governor and district commissioners. The result was a consolidation of the existing class structure which perpetuated the status of the various groups. Although there is a legislature for British Burma, with two chambers, a small number of European officials form the core of the administration. There is a small middle class of merchants and property owners largely made up of Chinese and Indians, and the native Burmans form the large submerged class of peasants, laborers, and servants. Primary education is in the care of the Buddhist monks who maintain a school in each village, and higher education is fostered by a university and government schools.

British Malaya (the Straits Settlements, Federated and Unfederated Malay States, and some scattered islands) comprise altogether some 55,000 square miles of territory in southeastern Asia, with a population approaching 6,000,000. The Straits Settlements are so named because Singapore guards the most important strait on the sea route between India and China; it is, in fact, one of the half dozen vital "bottlenecks" in the oceanic trade of the world. Before its capture by the Japanese in 1942, this colony was administered by a British Governor who was also High Commissioner for the Malay States and for Brunei in Borneo and British Agent for North Borneo and Sarawak.

French Indo-China before 1939 consisted of the colony of Cochin-China, with four protectorates, Annam, Cambodia, Tonkin, and Laos. This territory had been conquered and organized by the French in less than a century. The total population (1940) was about 25,000,000 and the total area was estimated at 281,174 square miles. Thus in southeastern Asia the French had come to control a region one-fourth larger than France itself, with a population two-thirds as numerous. In 1941 French Indo-China fell under the armed "protection" of the

Japanese, who occupied the chief ports and military bases until the close of the war.

Siam is the only independent native state remaining as a sovereign autonomous principality in southeast Asia. The name of the state was changed to Thailand by decree in 1939, but the traditional name was restored in 1946. The area of Siam is about 200,000 square miles and the population exceeds 15,000,000. After 1932 the government was changed from an absolute to a constitutional monarchy with an elected parliament. In 1941 the French government of Indo-China, acting under Japanese pressure, ceded a section of 21,000 square miles to Siam. The government accepted the enlargement with gratitude and formed an alliance with Japan, a move which involved it in war with Great Britain and the United States. In 1943 the Japanese announced that Siam was to be rewarded further with 75,000 square miles of territory taken from Burma and British Malaya, together with 3,000,000 inhabitants. In reality, the Japanese were bidding for more active aid from the regime, which was secretly in communication with the Anglo-American headquarters. Active underground forces, hostile to the Japanese despite a nominal alliance, aided the democracies and rescued British and American flyers who were forced down in this area.

As an Asiatic state enjoying political autonomy, Siam offers a contrast by which to measure the benefits or ills of the European-ruled colonies which border it. It has survived the march of rival imperialisms in Asia largely because neither the French nor the British would allow the other to annex it. But although it is still autonomous in theory, it is strongly influenced by conditions in the neighboring states of Burma, Indo-China, and Malaya, and its economy and welfare are contingent upon its trade relations with the great powers. Its industry, commerce, mining, lumbering, and even small trade is predominantly under the direction of foreigners. Seven-eighths of the population live by agriculture, lumbering, or other labor on the land, as in similar Asiatic countries. It is worth note, however, that the living conditions and the average wages of laborers are in general higher than in Burma or Indo-China.

4. THE NETHERLANDS INDIES

In the seventeenth century the Netherlanders were the most daring navigators and colonizers in the world, and a rich portion of the maritime empire they then acquired has remained in their control. With their talent for seafaring, trade, and administration, they have made their colonies productive and have drawn extraordinary dividends from them. Their island empire in the East Indies, 735,267 square miles in extent, with a population of 70,000,000, is a living testimony to their shrewdness, tenacity, and business acumen. For although this empire on the eve of World War II had only one-third the area of India and included only one-sixth the population of the British Asian empire, the import and export trade was equal in value to half that of India (1938). Furthermore the surplus value of Indonesian exports over imports for that year was reckoned at $100,000,000, while the surplus value of exports from British India over imports was only $50,000,000.

The chief products of the Netherlands Indies are rubber, petroleum, vegetable oils, tin, sugar, and tea. These six items had come by 1939 to comprise 90 per cent of the exports. The islands proved well suited to a productive economy for the soil is fertile and the rainfall adequate, so that the population can sustain itself without difficulty. Valuable natural resources, especially mineral and oil reserves, awaited modern modes of exploitation to yield enormous profits. The labor supply was provided by the tractable and industrious native population.

The twentieth century brought unrest and demands for more independence even from this carefully guarded society, and the Netherlanders, like the British in India, have been reluctant to bestow self-government. The discontent of the Indonesians is partly economic, for the Netherlanders long sought to supply all the manufactured goods required by the colonial peoples from factories in the home country, and until recent years they discouraged the construction of industrial plants in the islands. This subordination of their economic life has been resented by Indonesian patriots as discrimination, and they have compared the wages and standards of living in the Netherlands with their own. In the islands a monthly wage of $10 is considered reasonable by the employers.

It is not easy for the peoples of the Netherlands East Indies to combine for any collective action. They inhabit islands which stretch for nearly three thousand miles along the equator, the most important being Sumatra, Java, Celebes, most of Borneo, and half of Timor and New Guinea. Since 1916 the Netherlands government has granted the people a share in the administration with an advisory council to represent their interests. But the National Indonesian Party, which first asked Dominion status and finally complete independence, has grown rapidly and after 1945 it opened a war for independence because reforms were withheld. If self-government is attained, it will not be easy for the peoples to achieve unity. The ocean and high mountains separate the provinces and divide the islands. Some regions are almost unexplored and the inhabitants are extremely primitive. There is no simple solution for the language problem, for although Dutch is the official speech, Portuguese is spoken by a minority; Malay, a common dialect throughout the East Indies, is a general medium; and 85 per cent of the natives converse in Javanese or in local idioms.

Like the British and French in their Asian empires, the Netherlanders have failed to introduce a system of schooling well adapted to the culture, the interests, and the mentality of the peoples they rule. Concern for the peace, health, and prosperity of their protectorates has been the dominating mood of the European administrators; they have sought to preserve social conditions rather than reform them. Netherlands officials in general conceived it to be their duty to ratify the position held by an alien (predominantly Chinese) business class in Indonesia; to protect the monopoly of the plantation-owning, trading, and industrial (European) group; and to leave the Indonesian majority to the status of cultivators, artisans, and servants. Such a system of social organization, it has been pointed out, is not really a political government at all. It is economic in function and discriminatory in fact. The administrators control the colony as if it were primarily a factory organized for production rather than a society existing for the development and happiness of the individuals composing it.

When the Japanese occupied Indo-China (1941) and took Singapore (1942), the Netherlands East Indies were exposed to invasion. The Dutch naval and military forces in alliance with British and American detachments attempted in vain to protect the islands. By the close of 1942 the main islands, with the exception of southern New Guinea, were under Japanese control, and the native peoples were informed that they had been "liberated." The resources, especially of oil, rubber, and tin, which the Japanese thus acquired, were extremely valuable to them in the prosecution of the war. After the Japanese defeat in 1945 the Netherlands officials returned and sought with British aid to re-establish their control. (See Chapter XLVI.)

CHINA, JAPAN,
AND THE NEW ORDER IN ASIA

*To most Americans the vast and teeming lands of the Orient
are still* terrae incognitae.

New York Times, EDITORIAL (MAY 12, 1945)

I. CHINA: THE LAND AND THE PEOPLE

THE American student who wishes to gain some general idea of
East Asia might note some comparisons between China and the
United States. Both lie in approximately the same latitudes. Both have
a neighbor to the north, a neighbor with sparsely settled provinces
stretching towards the Arctic; and both have tropical areas, peninsulas
and islands, to the south, for Indo-China and Indonesia may be roughly
likened to Mexico, Central America, and the islands of the Caribbean
Sea. Both the United States and China face the rising sun with a long,
bulging, eastern coastline with numerous ports, and in both the population is heavily concentrated in this northeast section, with sparsely
populated, semiarid regions commencing between one and two thousand miles inland. Still farther inland both have high mountain ranges
to the west and south. But there the comparisons end with two abrupt
differences. For China has a small but powerful neighbor — Japan —
a few hundred miles from what, in America, would be the New England coast. And China has no Far West, no second coastline beyond
the mountains, with growing ports, timbered ranges, rich fruitlands,
fisheries, factories, and shipyards like those which stretch from Oregon to California. Throughout their long history the Chinese have
lived with the knowledge that they had a desert behind them, thinly
peopled by barbarian tribes against whom early emperors constructed
the Great Wall. In front of them lay the widest of the world's oceans,
which, so far as the Chinese knew, had no other shore. Thus Chinese

civilization developed according to its own intrinsic patterns, flourishing on the fertile stretch between two deserts, the desert of the hinterland and the desert of the sea.

Today China commands attention as the oldest continuous civilization in the world and the largest nation-state in point of population. An official estimate of the various provinces in 1936 gave the total of people living in China as 422,707,868. If outlying areas, historically part of the empire, such as Manchuria, Mongolia, and Tibet are added, the total would be 457,835,475. The rate of increase is such that the population had already approached 500,000,000 by 1945. This great bloc of mankind, about one-fourth of the human race, is entrenched on a fertile coastal plain which has been patiently cultivated for thousands of years. Chinese civilization, the Chinese character, and the Chinese way of life have proved remarkably stable and durable. The Chinese possessed their own pictographic and ideographic records 3500 years ago and had developed an advanced culture before 1000 B.C. The character of the people commands respect because of their realism, moderation, cheerfulness, and resiliency. Their economy, predominantly agricultural, has always shaped their family loyalties, their social life, and their concepts of property and of propriety. Most of the arable land is divided into small farms each owned and managed by a single family which pays an annual land tax. Upon this broad base of peasant communities rests a small class of townsmen, a smaller administrative group of soldiers, civil servants, and government officials, and a cultured class of philosophers, writers, and artists. Their subtle poetry and philosophy, exquisite masterpieces of painting, sculpture, metal work, and ceramics, and their delicate and arresting architecture have earned for the Chinese an honored place among the most highly gifted peoples of history. In religion they are tolerant and philosophical. All Chinese revere their ancestors, and most of them practice all three of the leading religions of China, Confucianism, Buddhism, and Taoism.

To this ancient and self-sufficient people the twentieth century brought invasions, revolutions, disorder, and suffering. The loosely ruled, amorphous, dynastic empire, which had endured for so many centuries, was not fitted to resist the encroaching pressures of modern imperialism: it had survived or absorbed its invaders hitherto because of its relative isolation and its great recuperative strength. Until the nineteenth century no great power seriously threatened it from the sea, and the hinterland was protected by the Great Wall, the deserts, and the mountains. That China, with a population no better armed or more militant than the pacifistic Hindus, remained so long immune to European conquest invites some interesting comparisons. North and South America, Africa, and Australia had all been subordinated to the hegemony of the Europeans before the end of the nineteenth century. Maritime Asia, from India to Indo-China, Malaysia, and the islands of the East Indies had likewise succumbed. But the relative unity, isolation, and inaccessibility of China protected it until the later nineteenth and the twentieth century. Then the British pressed into Tibet, the Russians into Manchuria, all the powers demanded treaty ports, and the Japanese, adopting European arms and tactics, opened a campaign for the complete domination of the realm.

It is easier to understand the needs and the problems of modern China when it is realized that the real China lies between the Yellow Sea and French Indo-China. This fertile region, especially the lower valleys of the Hwang Ho and the Yangtze Kiang, contains almost the entire Chinese population. Behind this densely settled lowland area lie the mountains and eternal snows of Tibet and the deserts of Mongolia. These hinterland provinces, equal in area to China proper, are almost empty of inhabitants, for there the population averages less than two to the square mile. In other words, of the 450,000,000 or more Chinese in the republic, less than one in a hundred live in these remote regions of deserts, mountains, and steppes. (See maps, pages 292, 369 and 372.)

A second fact worth remembering about the Chinese people is their profound preoccupation with land cultivation. So intensive and ingenious are their farming, horticulture, and irrigation, that they have been called a nation of gardeners. Over 400,000,000 work on the land. Their diet is 92 per cent cereals and 97 per cent vegetarian. Their habits and loyalties, their arts and crafts, their mental outlook and philosophy are all rooted in the local landscape. Their lack of aggressiveness, their moderation and conservatism, have been attributed to the influence of the land and their dedication to agrarian pursuits. The results are not wholly beneficial. Disease and famine are perpetual threats, four-fifths of the Chinese are illiterate, and almost all suffer from dietary deficiencies.

2. CHINA IN REVOLUTION

By the twentieth century the intrusion of Western influences could no longer be resisted, and the Chinese faced the dilemma of modernizing their institutions and fighting for their freedom or of falling under the domination of the foreigners. An attempt to expel all "foreign devils" (the "Boxer Uprising" of 1900) brought swift retaliation. The affronted powers sent an international expeditionary force which seized the capital, Peking, and imposed a heavy indemnity upon the empire. Indo-China had already fallen under French control, Burma was ruled by the British, Formosa and Korea (Chosen) were claimed by the Japanese, and Manchuria was occupied by the Russians. The Yangtze Valley and Tibet seemed destined to pass under British control also, the French were pressing north from Tonkin, and the Germans claimed concessions in Shantung. The future of China in the opening years of the twentieth century seemed already almost settled, and the powers which had partitioned Africa into protectorates after 1870 seemed determined to join with Japan and Russia in a similar partition of the empire.

In 1911 a revolution shook the Chinese from their lethargy. The boy emperor of the Manchu dynasty, Pu-yi, was dethroned, and China was proclaimed a republic. Several years of disorder followed with disintegration, brigandage, and confusing civil strife. But slowly and laboriously, under the admired though not always very practical statesmanship of Sun Yat-sen, the republic was organized and strengthened. Russian agents were invited to assist the revolutionists, but shortly before he died in 1925 Sun Yat-sen turned against Marxian socialism and rejected it. Possibly a split between the Nationalist Party (the Kuomintang) and the Chinese communists was unavoidable, but the successor of Sun Yat-sen, the more practical and energetic Chiang Kai-shek, forced the issue. Insisting that the communists planned to destroy the Kuomintang, he attacked them successfully and captured Nanking (1926). The communists had been promised help from Russia by Leon Trotsky, but Trotsky's influence was waning before that of Joseph Stalin and Stalin opposed Russian intervention in the Chinese civil war.

After 1926 Chiang Kai-shek emerged as the strong man of China. He had studied at the Tokyo Military College and had visited Soviet Russia. At first he was impressed by the organizing skill of the Soviet agents, but later he came to suspect that they were working for Russia and not for the welfare of the Chinese. Chiang's campaigns against the Chinese communists and their Russian advisers finally drove them from Kwangsi province, and they made a remarkable march (1933) of a thousand miles to Yenan where they re-established their control. They wished to fight the Japanese and in 1937 after a dramatic *coup* in which they captured Chiang and then released him, they gained recognition from the Nationalist government. The Chinese Red army became the Eighth Route Army of the Chinese Republic, and Nationalists and communists were united against the foreign (Japanese) invaders.

These years from 1912 to 1937 were a quarter century of slow but steady recognition that China was a sovereign state. At the Washington Conference (1922) nine powers pledged the independence, territorial integrity, and autonomy of China. In 1924 the government of Soviet Russia renounced all claims to extraterritorial rights and special concessions in China and proposed that the remaining payments due Russia on the Boxer indemnity should be used for education. In 1908 the United States had likewise renounced any further indemnity payments from the Boxer indemnity and established the China Foundation for the Promotion of Education and Culture. But the Western powers did not immediately imitate Russia in giving up the extraterritorial privileges they had extorted. These were special agreements which exempted their citizens in certain areas of China from the jurisdiction of Chinese courts or the penalties of Chinese law. Other conventions of a similar nature permitted European governments to intervene in local Chinese affairs and regulated the import duties which the Chinese might levy against foreign goods.

The threat of military invasion, especially by the Japanese, made it urgent for the Chinese Republic to arm itself and to develop its resources of man power, minerals, industry, and electric power. Only by becoming militarized could China hope to survive in a militant world. After 1924, with the aid of foreign officers, Chiang Kai-shek directed the training of Chinese cadets at a national military academy, and recruits were enrolled and taught the methods of modern warfare. But the program moved slowly, and when the Japanese invaded and occupied Manchuria in 1931–1932, the Chinese armies were not yet ready to meet them with any chance of success. Manchuria was rapidly transformed into the puppet state of Manchukuo, and the Japanese placed the exiled Manchu emperor, Henry Pu-yi, at its head. The failure of the League of Nations or any of the great powers to oppose Japan and halt Japanese aggression proved to the Chinese that they must defend themselves by their own might. With this realization they made a sincere attempt to achieve unity and cohesion. The government pressed through a financial reform (1932), increased the period of military training (1935), approved new railroads, motor roads, and

A PLANTATION SCENE IN JAVA, NETHERLANDS EAST INDIES

air bases, and speeded the purchase of machinery and arms and the equipment of industrial plants. All these moves were jealously watched by the Japanese, who knew that the Chinese Nationalist Party, the Kuomintang, was preparing for the fated conflict with Japan.

The possibility that the almost inexhaustible man power of China might be rapidly converted to industrial or military use raised the question whether China might not within a generation take rank as a first class power. Japan, with much smaller resources of men and territory, had already developed amazingly. But there were certain deficiencies in the Chinese economy and limitations in the Chinese temperament which made prediction hazardous. Coal and iron ore, so essential to the machine age, existed in China but were not abundant or easy to extract. Petroleum, the alternative fuel, which is indispensable for the internal combustion engine, the Chinese lacked entirely. There was adequate hydroelectric energy in reserve, possibly 20,000,000 horsepower, but almost none of it had been harnessed. To develop it would require a large investment for dams, generators, and transmission lines, and the government and the national economy could not well support the cost. Plastics from vegetable sources, and the use of the lighter metals such as aluminum and magnesium, seemed to hold most promise for industrial expansion. There could be no question that the mechanization of industry would increase the local output very greatly, for in 1939 one Chinese worker produced only one-fortieth as much as one American worker equipped with power-driven tools. In agriculture, the wider use of machinery might do little to increase the yield per acre beyond what the skill of the Chinese farmer was already able to extract. But mechanization of agriculture could release millions of land workers for employment at the mechanical trades without reducing the total harvest, and this would permit an expansion of Chinese industry.

Nevertheless there remained certain psychological obstacles to mass production, similar to the resistances which have developed wherever machines have replaced handworkers. The Chinese craftsman is also an artist. He does not adapt himself readily to monotonous piecework, and he can be remarkably stubborn in clinging to his traditional methods. The farm families might not take happily to life in an urban milieu, with its mechanized rhythms, narrowed horizon, and monotonous tasks. A strict routine, even inflexible conventions, the Chinese can understand. But mechanical standardization of labor, goods,

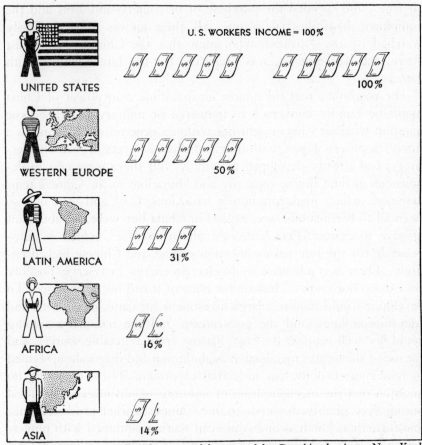

UNITED STATES

U. S. WORKERS INCOME = 100%

100%

WESTERN EUROPE

50%

LATIN AMERICA

31%

AFRICA

16%

ASIA

14%

Based on material prepared by Graphics Institute, New York

HOW STANDARDS OF LIVING IN OTHER COUNTRIES COMPARE
WITH THOSE IN THE UNITED STATES

These incomes are based on the United States workers' average income (1939) with allowance for the difference in price levels in the various regions.

wages, and working hours often affront and antagonize them. The individuality and diversity that persist in Chinese agrarian life are part of a precious heritage. Despite the low living standards, the Chinese preserve a serenity, artistry, and pride in their traditional crafts which they would not readily forfeit. They have shown no great eagerness to exchange their ancient mode of living and imitate the life of the proletarians in the factory towns of Europe and America.

There is one further reason why China cannot for the present assay the role of a great power. It does not possess a strong, efficient central government. The traditional foundations for such a government are lacking; throughout Chinese annals the provincial governors and local army generals have always been half independent, and a central administration cannot be created by decree. Without foreign advisers, foreign supplies, and foreign loans, it is most improbable that the Chinese Nationalist regime could have survived to organize and maintain resistance against the Japanese. Politically, industrially, financially, and psychologically the Chinese are still unprepared to assume a leading role in world affairs. For they are still half in tutelage to Europe and America, still half immersed in their timeless, traditional inertia.

3. JAPAN

The sea has shaped the life of the Japanese people no less decisively than the "good earth" influenced the character of the Chinese. "The life blood of Japan," declares an ancient proverb, "is the water of the sea." The Japanese islands are limited in extent, comprising less than 150,000 square miles, an area smaller than California. Much of the land is mountainous and unsuited to agriculture, and the arable regions are only moderately fertile. Consequently the Japanese like the Chinese can spare little land for pasturage. Herds are an expensive luxury to famished farmers, for one acre devoted to cereals will produce six or seven times as much food, in calories, as it would yield if reserved for grazing dairy cattle. By intensive cultivation, which employs half the population, the Japanese supply their national requirements in cereals and fruits. But they differ from the Chinese in that they have at hand a highly important source of food and fertilizer. The Japanese take in one-fifth of the world catch of salt fish although they constitute less than one twenty-fifth of the world population. Fish is a staple of their diet, and the bones and inedible portions provide mineral fertilizer without which the soil might become exhausted. Furthermore, the problem of communication among the thousands of islands which comprise the archipelago urged the boatman to dare the seas. From earliest history Japan was an amphibious nation. Geographically, the islands are an unrivaled base for an ambitious people who dream of expansion and of empire.

Unlike the Chinese, who were reluctant to accept European techniques and machinery, the Japanese deliberately remade their society, adopting Western science and technology and even the form of Western legal, financial, and political institutions. This policy of imitation and adaptation followed the historic visits (1853–1854) of a United States naval expedition under Commodore Matthew Calbraith Perry whereby the Japanese government was persuaded to approve the Treaty of Kanagawa and to open two ports to American trade. Similar treaties with Great Britain, Russia, and the Netherlands followed within three years. A realistic group of Japanese statesmen, recognizing the inevitable, undertook the extraordinary task of remaking a hitherto isolated Oriental state into a modern world power. With the accession of the young and able Emperor Mutsuhito in 1867 the feudal warlords surrendered their power to the Mikado, and the shogun, a sort of prime minister who had been the power behind the throne, resigned. Attempts to seal the ports once more and to expel all foreigners (a policy supported by a powerful section of the people) were abandoned, and Japan began a period of rapid industrialization on the Western plan. The reign of Mutsuhito from 1868 when he established the capital at Tokyo to his death in 1912 is known as the Meiji Period.

The people of Europe were at first skeptical and somewhat amused when they learned how seriously the Japanese were studying Western ways. But the Japanese knew that their existence as an independent nation was at stake. They chose the best models and followed them faithfully: their navy was copied from the British, their army built on Prussian formulas, their constitution combined British and German elements but leaned towards authoritarianism, their schools owed much to American educational plans, their law courts adopted French and German modes of procedure. Specialists in the natural sciences, in architecture and engineering, in mining, manufacturing, shipbuilding, in every field from history to horticulture, were invited to Japan to give instruction, and Japanese students were sent abroad to observe and to learn. While in China seven-eighths of the people remained illiterate, in Japan a system of compulsory education, planned as early as 1872, was expanded until all boys and girls received elementary schooling and the abler students were encouraged to attend high school and college.

The world was first awakened to the astonishing progress made in Japan during the Meiji Period by the outcome of the Russo-Japanese War of 1904–1905. In a sudden attack the Japanese laid siege to Port Arthur, shutting up the Russian Far Eastern fleet, defeated the Russians in a series of military and naval engagements, and then wisely made peace before the strain of war could exhaust the newly developed state. Although patriots believed the gains inadequate, victory brought control of Korea, where economic penetration had already prepared the way, and won half of Sakhalin Island, while Manchuria, evacuated by the Russians and restored to China, became a field for later penetration. The island of Formosa, which the Japanese had secured in a short war with China in 1895, had given them an important base off the coast between Shanghai and Hong Kong; but Korea, which they formally annexed in 1910, gave them a bridgehead on the mainland. Their preparations for the establishment of a New Order in the Orient under Japanese leadership were completed. All they awaited was a favorable moment to expand.

The outbreak of war in Europe in 1914 diverted the attention of the great powers and created a situation favorable to aggression. As an ally of Great Britain by virtue of a treaty negotiated in 1902, the Japanese declared war upon Germany. But their participation was local and selfish; they reduced the German base at Kiaochow and thus acquired a claim to the concessions in the Chinese province of Shantung which the Germans had extorted from China. Throughout the four years of the war Japanese industry throve on war orders and even more on demands from consumers everywhere whose needs the warring nations could no longer supply adequately. In the decade which followed 1913 Japanese foreign trade almost tripled in value. By 1923 Japan possessed the third largest merchant marine in the world and the third most powerful navy. Such swift triumphant progress might have persuaded even a cautious people that they had an imperial destiny, and the Japanese, intensely proud and patriotic, grew immoderately ambitious. They could not arrest the acceleration of their industrial revolution. Their rapidly expanding economy drove their bankers and industrialists to endorse a program of military expansion to safeguard their markets. Behind the economic drive was the pressure of population, for the nation doubled between 1870 and 1939, to reach 70,000,-000. The island kingdom was narrow and crowded, and the addition of a million citizens a year made the capture of foreign markets and raw materials appear the only solution. Thus the consequences of uncontrolled and dynamic industrialization drove the Japanese down the dangerous and unpredictable road of unbridled imperialism. More fully than any European nation, even Great Britain, the Japanese staked their fate upon the chances of an indefinite expansion of trade.

That trade, however, was dangerously vulnerable. For although the Japanese businessmen sought markets as far afield as Africa and South

America, nine-tenths of their total foreign investment was concentrated in China. A nation which has placed almost all its economic eggs in one basket faces grave risks and must take precautions to safeguard its investments. Any foreign power which increased its influence in China and extorted counterconcessions was a threat to Japanese trade there. But the growing strength of Chinese nationalism was an even greater threat. To hold the favored position which they had gained during the First World War, the Japanese believed they were compelled to press for the complete domination of East Asia. The alternative appeared to be an economic collapse and the twilight of their empire. These facts must be appreciated for they help to explain the defiant manner in which the Japanese faced the condemnation of the League of Nations and the risk they took of exciting Britain, Russia, or the United States to a war for the protection of China. Before 1914 the Japanese had already envisaged a Japanese "Monroe Doctrine" which would proclaim all East Asia their peculiar sphere of influence. The purposeful realization of this plan suggests why they thought it advisable to increase their armaments 400 per cent between 1914 and 1924 and why they deliberately provoked incidents which would appear to justify military intervention in China before the Chinese Nationalist government could organize the republic and build up an effective army for its defense.

Manchuria was for the Japanese the nearest and most attractive segment of China and the province they first sought to win after annexing Korea. It lay beyond the Great Wall to the northeast; it held rich natural resources; and it was not yet densely populated although the Chinese were migrating to it at the rate of a million a year. Once a large Chinese population became entrenched there, conquest would become more difficult, and the Japanese felt the inexorable pressure of time urging them to wrest a decision quickly while fortune favored them. Russia after the close of World War I was involved in the problems of a tremendous revolution. China, after emerging from the revolution which began in 1911, was slowly establishing a modern army, a centralized government, and a system of communications through which to concert and mobilize the vast potential strength of the republic. Manchuria was a rich prize, the loss of which might permanently cripple China as an independent power, for one-half the timber and 40 per cent of the coal and iron reserves on which the Chinese must depend for their industrial development were located there. If the Japanese could get possession first and organize these important resources, they would deal China a heavy blow while enriching themselves. Thus Manchuria was the bridge of destiny over which the Japanese might march to the conquest of East Asia, but it was a bridge which would not forever remain open. They believed by 1930 that they must seize it at once or risk forfeiting it forever.

4. THE "CHINA INCIDENT"

From 1931 to 1941 Japan waged undeclared war in China, and it was a real war although there were partial truces and no declaration of hostilities was issued. It was an ironic commentary on the Briand-Kellogg Pact of 1928 that the nations which had renounced war as an instrument of national policy now waged it without a declaration. Thus the fiction was preserved that a state of war did not exist. The Japanese invasion of China, even when it expanded into a large-scale operation involving hundreds of thousands of soldiers, remained officially the "China Incident."

In September, 1931, on a minor pretext and without adequate justification, the Japanese army opened a drive for the possession of Manchuria. The first step was achieved when they took over the railways and planted garrisons throughout the province. The nominal excuse was the need to suppress bandits; the real reason was the need to get a strong hold on Manchuria so that they could defend it against the Russians or the Chinese Nationalists. This pattern of conquest was a familiar one. It had been employed at one time or another by all the leading European powers, and the Japanese generals and diplomats had learned the lesson thoroughly. The campaign was treated in dispatches as being of minor importance and the whole process of conquest was sedulously minimized.

Indeed, when the Chinese brought the situation to the attention of the Council of the League of Nations, the Japanese went so far as to propose the appointment of a commission to make an investigation. In December, 1931, the League set up the commission, with the British Earl of Lytton as chairman. The members proceeded to visit China, Japan, and Manchuria, where they spent several months.

In the meantime the threatened loss of territory and prestige sobered the disputatious Chinese leaders, and they hastened to compound the rivalry between the communists and the Kuomintang. The Chinese people, too, united in a patriotic attempt to close ranks and offer resistance. Their capacity for armed opposition was of course still limited but they could and did strike at Japanese trade. They resorted to a general boycott, which inflicted such severe losses on the Japanese that the latter in retaliation landed marines at Shanghai at the mouth of the Yangtze Kiang (January, 1932). The resistance offered by the local army was firm and courageous, so firm in fact that the Japanese withdrew (May, 1932) after the Chinese had agreed to end the boycott. The attack on Shanghai was a round without a decision.

By March, however, the Japanese penetration of Manchuria had proceeded so far that certain minorities in the province declared its independence and set up a puppet regime at Hsinking under Henry Pu-yi, the former boy-emperor of China who had been deposed in 1912. The new state was named Manchukuo.

On October 2, 1932, the report of the Lytton Commission was submitted to the League of Nations. The report blamed the Japanese for aggressive actions but recognized that they had paramount economic interests in the area. As a solution it was proposed that the government of China retain political sovereignty in the province while the Japanese exercised economic control and supervision. But the Japanese were not satisfied. They resented the rebuke implicit in the report and in March, 1933, withdrew from the League.

The Chinese government, convinced that the League would do nothing more positive to help it, concluded a temporary truce and Manchuria became a protectorate of Japan. The practical consequence was the addition of 500,000 square miles to the Japanese empire, an area almost as large as California, Oregon, and Texas together, with a population of 40,000,000. The Japanese appetite for further conquests was not dulled by this rich prize.

Nevertheless it was evident that a spirit of defiance was deepening in China and that Japanese tactics had intensified it. Even the six million Chinese settled in other parts of the world were sending contributions to buy airplanes, machine guns, and field hospitals. The Japanese agents decided to alternate force with flattery, and they attempted to focus Chinese resentment upon the imperialist powers of Europe. "British capitalists," declared a Japanese publicist, "are ghosts who absorb our blood and sweat." If the Asiatic peoples would accept Japanese leadership, the proclamation added, the exploitation so long practiced by the Western powers could be ended and the Japanese would organize "Asia for the Asiatics." Some Chinese believed in the sincerity of the slogan; others shrewdly suspected that it really meant not Asia for the Asiatics but Asia for the Japanese. The whole Far Eastern world had become an area of conflict where the competing currents of world politics formed confused patterns. China was influenced by European and American ideals of democracy, by Russian communist dogmas translated to fit Chinese conditions, by the militarism of the Japanese, by the impact of modern scientific methodology and machine tools. The Chinese people, who had narrowly escaped subjugation by the rapacious Europeans, were no more friendly to the idea of subjugation by the Japanese. The pretense that Japan had sent troops into China to help the Chinese set their house in order lost all plausibility when those troops clashed in actual warfare with Chinese divisions.

5. THE SINO-JAPANESE WAR [1]

The ambiguous situation in Manchuria and northern China was deliberately maintained by the Japanese because it gave them all the advantages of peace and of war at the same time. The United States announced unequivocally in 1931 (the Stimson Doctrine) that it would not recognize any change of political status that was brought about by force, and the State Department steadily refused recognition to the newly established empire of Manchukuo. But the Japanese went ahead defiantly, confiscating or converting all foreign investments in their new domain, thus assuring their own economic preponderance in the area. The Russians, who next to the Chinese were most seriously threatened by the large forces of Japanese troops in Manchukuo, soon came to accept the realities of the situation. Unprepared and unwilling to fight a war in the Far East, the Soviet government sold its rights in the Chinese Eastern Railway (1935) which traversed Manchuria and so ended one acute source of tension between Russia and Japan.

The conquest of Manchuria was a flagrant repudiation of the pledges Japan had made as a member of the League of Nations. It was a betrayal of China which as a member of the League had appealed for arbitration and protection. It was a violation of the Briand-Kellogg Peace Pact whereby all signatories renounced war as an instrument of national policy. It was a clear defiance of the Nine Power Treaty of 1922 which had asserted the independence and territorial integrity of China, a treaty to which Japan had likewise given formal assent. Throughout the world the bold success of the Japanese and the

[1] For a further discussion of this topic, see pages 440–443.

futility of the Chinese protests announced the bitter truth that apparently might was right and collective security an illusion in which no weak nation could safely trust.

For the Japanese militarists, success brought confirmation of their faith that audacity paid dividends. Having tested the limits of Russian, American, British, and Chinese patience, and found none of these nations eager to offer real opposition, they opened a new phase of conquest in 1937. Still without a declaration of war, they moved large forces into China, seized railways, highways, and key cities, and blockaded the ports from the sea. Once again the increased threat and aggression coerced the Chinese factions into a measure of unity and the Chinese communist army co-operated with the National government in fighting the invaders. But the Japanese pressed on strongly, seized Nanking (December, 1937), and were in possession of the chief cities and the richest provinces of the country by the close of 1938. Nevertheless the Chinese armies continued to fight when and where they could, encouraged by the stubborn hostility of the people towards Japan, by the contributions from Chinese abroad, and by the tenacious will of General Chiang Kai-shek, who continued to direct the resistance from the new capital at Chungking.

The Japanese aims were not difficult to read, for their policy and methods had not changed. They planned to organize China under a puppet regime similar to that established in Manchukuo, and they began by an attempt to detach the whole northern section of China from allegiance to the Chungking government. They hoped to win the populace by announcing the cancellation of privileges to all foreigners and the termination of the concessions, control of treaty ports and customs, extraterritoriality, and other humiliating conventions which the European powers had extorted in earlier years. But the Japanese, not the Chinese, were to be the real beneficiaries of the change, and for Japan the prize was well worth the winning. Over 400,000,000 Chinese might ultimately be included within the bounds of the Japanese "Co-Prosperity Sphere," and the riches of Malaya, Thailand (Siam), Burma, French Indo-China, the East Indies, and even India might in time fall within the Japanese orbit. The militarists at Tokyo counted upon the outbreak of a war in Europe to engage the attention and exhaust the strength of the Russian, British, French, and United States forces. How sound their calculations proved may be judged by the timing of their strategy. In 1939 they were ready to

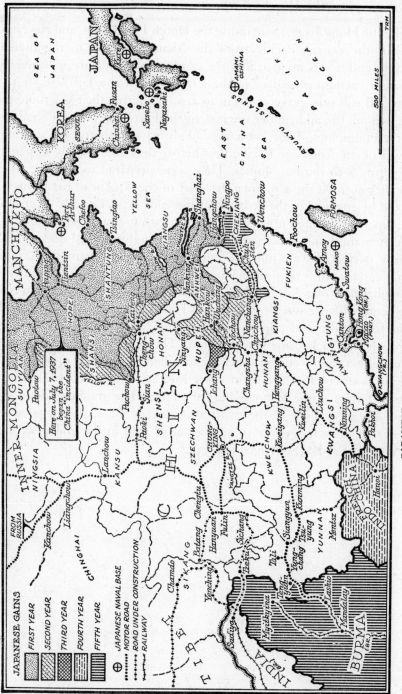

JAPANESE GAINS IN CHINA, 1937–1942

strike for Hong Kong, Singapore, the Dutch East Indies, and the control of the eastern Pacific from the Aleutian Islands to the Indian Ocean; and it was in 1939 that the expected war in Europe began to create a vacuum of power in the Far East. But the Japanese strategists had still one grave problem to resolve: across their sea route to the rich oil, tin, and rubber reserves of the East Indies lay the shadow of the Philippines. They knew they might have to shatter the striking power of the American Pacific fleet before they could safely dispatch large forces to the East Indies. They were prepared to take the risk, but they wanted the assurance that part of the American naval forces would be engaged in the Atlantic at the same time. For this diversion the Japanese counted upon their alliance with Germany and Italy.

When the hour struck, the plans so daringly devised and so patiently perfected were put into rapid and ruthless execution. Within two years (1939–1941) all the important coastal cities of China from Shanghai to Hong Kong were occupied. China lay in a vise between the centers of pressure at Peking and Hanoi. French Indo-China and Siam fell rapidly under Japanese domination, and the invasion of India through Burma became a temptation. The war had become global; but the fact that events in other theaters had created the opportunity meant as surely that events in other theaters would decide the success or failure of the Japanese bid for empire. The grandiose development and grim finale of the effort after 1941 is therefore relegated to a later chapter. It is easier to understand if read in the global setting of World War II. (See pages 529–539.)

XXV

AUSTRALIA, NEW ZEALAND, AND THE PACIFIC ISLANDS

The United States, the British Empire, and Japan agree that the status quo *at the time of the signing of the present Treaty, with regard to fortifications and naval bases, shall be maintained in their respective territories and possessions specified. . .*

ARTICLE XIX. A TREATY . . . LIMITING
NAVAL ARMAMENT. WASHINGTON, 1922.

I. THE COMMONWEALTH OF AUSTRALIA

THE human race is very unevenly distributed over the land areas of the earth. Population maps show a surprising density of settlement in some regions — the Ganges Valley, the Hwang Ho, northwestern Europe — with equally surprising empty regions not far away. It is understandable that the polar and subpolar sections should be almost entirely void of occupants. But it is not easy to discern from political maps why Central Asia, Arabia, North Africa, and Central Australia support less than one inhabitant to the square mile. The main clue may be found, however, by turning to other types of map and comparing the distribution of population with the distribution of rainfall. All the areas mentioned above as empty or almost empty of life, are regions of constant drought, regions so arid that little vegetation can thrive there. Without vegetable life and water there can be little if any animal life, because animals subsist upon vegetation or on other herbivorous animals.

One of the largest arid regions of the earth lies in the heart of Australia. This island continent, almost equal to the United States in area, is one-third desert and another third semidesert. The sections most suitable for habitation lie in the southeast and look towards the Antarctic wastes, so that Australia seems to turn its back upon the great Eurasian and African land masses. This fact helps to explain why it was so long unclaimed and was first colonized, by the British, only at

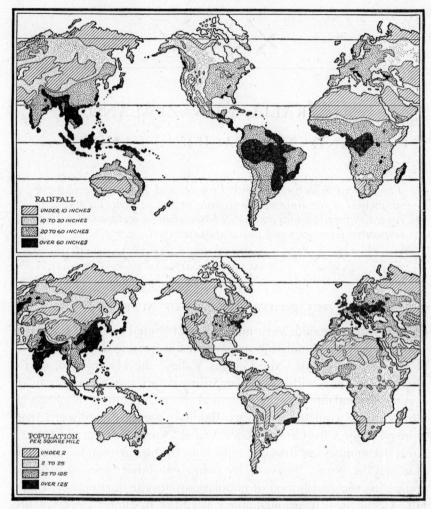

RAINFALL
- UNDER 10 INCHES
- 10 TO 20 INCHES
- 20 TO 60 INCHES
- OVER 60 INCHES

POPULATION
PER SQUARE MILE
- UNDER 2
- 2 TO 25
- 25 TO 125
- OVER 125

WORLD RAINFALL AND POPULATION

the end of the eighteenth century. Within a hundred years it grew into a nation-state and became an important member of the British Commonwealth of Nations. Dominion status was proclaimed in 1901, and by 1942 the population had risen to 7,000,000.

The federal constitution adopted by the Australians bore some resemblance to that of the United States. Although the six component states or territories are unequal in size and population, each elects six senators to the federal Senate. The members of the House of Representatives, also elected by universal suffrage, are distributed according to population. Instead of a president the Commonwealth has a

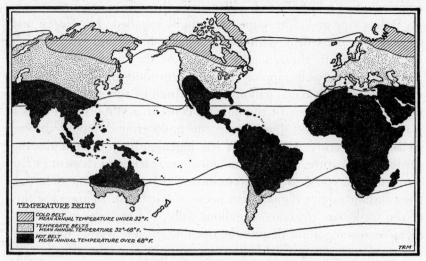

TEMPERATURE BELTS
COLD BELT
MEAN ANNUAL TEMPERATURE UNDER 32°F.
TEMPERATE BELTS
MEAN ANNUAL TEMPERATURE 32°-68°F.
HOT BELT
MEAN ANNUAL TEMPERATURE OVER 68°F.

TRM

WORLD TEMPERATURE BELTS

Governor-General appointed by the British crown. The real executive authority is exercised by the prime minister and his cabinet.

In operation the constitution tended to increase the power of the federal government steadily despite resistance by some of the states, which more than once threatened to secede. Defense, foreign policy, tariffs, internal communication, currency, and pensions were all confided to the federal departments. As tariff control and income and inheritance taxes provided the main sources of revenue, and federal courts secured jurisdiction over labor disputes, the federal power grew inexorably. The problems of defense in the First and Second World Wars hastened this trend to centralization.

The natural advantages provided by open grazing grounds and a moderate climate early encouraged sheep raising in Australia. By 1940 the Commonwealth led the world, with an estimated 116,000,000 head of sheep, ranking ahead of the Soviet Union with 110,000,000, and the United States with 50,000,000. In cattle raising, Australia had moved to fourth place by 1940, claiming a total of 13,000,000. It was surpassed by the three leading cattle countries of the world, the United States, the Soviet Union, and Argentina, in that order.

One-half the total acreage of the country is reserved for pastoral uses, the grasses, bushes, and shrubs supporting the vast grazing flocks and herds. But the rainfall is so undependable that the problem of providing sufficient water remains an acute one, which engineers have attempted to solve by drilling artesian wells. Water holes are soon

emptied when rain fails, and wells remain the only sure source of supply unless long and costly pipe lines can be installed. The largest artesian basin in the world, with twelve smaller basins and artesian reservoirs, lie beneath the semiarid sections of the hinterland. By 1939
there were 9000 wells tapping these underground springs, some of the
wells yielding 2,000,000 gallons daily. Much of this artesian water is
unsatisfactory because of the mineral content, and most of it runs to
waste. None the less, by tapping the underground supply through
wells conveniently spaced, man has ingeniously outwitted the nig-
gardliness of nature. The solution, however, carries an element of risk.
Artesian reservoirs, though constantly fed by underground seepage
from distant rainier regions, can become exhausted. In 1909 the flow
of the wells was 563,000,000 gallons daily, but by 1939 it had fallen
to 340,000,000 gallons despite the opening of new wells. Stabilization
and government control of the water supply were therefore needed
to conserve this natural resource and prevent undue waste and ultimate exhaustion.

Until the twentieth century the prosperity of Australia rested
chiefly upon its capacity to supply raw materials and food to more
highly industrialized states. But in recent decades the Commonwealth
has developed its own industrial machinery with great rapidity.
Though an adequate water supply for hydroelectric power is lacking
and Australia has only about one-fifteenth the potential reserves of
Africa in this respect, there are fortunately rather large deposits of
coal. The rise of industry has been so rapid that by 1941 the net value
of manufactured goods exceeded the total value of products from
the pastoral, dairying, agricultural, mining, forestry, and fishing activities combined. This comparison is interesting as a revelation of the
vital role which manufacture plays in the economy of the modern state.

With a population almost exclusively Anglo-Saxon and a high
standard of living, of wages, and of health, Australia is an outstanding
example of a democratic commonwealth. Maternity, child endowment, and widow's pension payments, provided by the federal government, encourage larger families. A rigid immigration policy, which
practically excludes natives of Africa and Asia, has aroused jealousies
and antagonisms of which the Australians are fully aware. To keep
such a vast country for themselves in a land-hungry world is a formidable problem unless they can expand their population rapidly. It
has not, however, restrained the government from claiming a mandate
over extensive Pacific islands and pressing a title to a segment of the

Antarctic continent as large as Australia itself (1936). The Australians realize that if the protection of the British navy were withdrawn their homeland would be vulnerable to attack by any superior naval power. As early as 1908 they planned to establish a Royal Australian Navy, and they introduced military conscription in 1909.

In the First and Second World Wars the commonwealth ranged itself promptly beside the British people in a joint defense, and Australian forces served with distinction in many fields of the global conflict. The entry of Japan into World War II in 1941 exposed Australia to attack, and its safety was seriously threatened. How it survived, with British and American aid, is related in Chapter XXXVIII.

2. THE DOMINION OF NEW ZEALAND

The Dominion of New Zealand consists of two large and several small islands with a total area of 103,723 square miles. This is slightly larger than Great Britain or almost exactly equal to the state of Colorado. Discovered by the Dutch in 1642 and named for a province of the United Netherlands, New Zealand became a British colony in 1840. A century of development under British protection has made it a proud and progressive commonwealth in a remote corner of the vast Pacific.

The history of Australia and New Zealand suggests some interesting parallels and a few divergencies. The discovery of gold in Australia in 1851 brought half a million newcomers there and added half a billion dollars' worth of gold to world reserves. New Zealand likewise had its gold rush, for the decade 1860–1870 opened with the discovery of deposits at Otago and within ten years a quarter of a million settlers poured into the south island. The Australian aborigines, few, scattered, and primitive, offered little opposition to the incoming Europeans, but in New Zealand the native Maoris were not so easily dispossessed. They were Polynesians of fine physique and high intelligence, and they fought two wars (1843–1848 and 1860–1870) before they yielded. Under the New Zealand constitution they won the rights of residents and voters. They form a group of between 90,000 and 100,000, with four elected members to speak for them in the House of Representatives.

Unlike Australia, New Zealand has no arid regions. No point in the islands is more than eighty miles from the ocean, with the result that every section enjoys adequate rainfall and a temperate climate. The landscape is varied and magnificent. Snow peaks, plateaus, pleasant

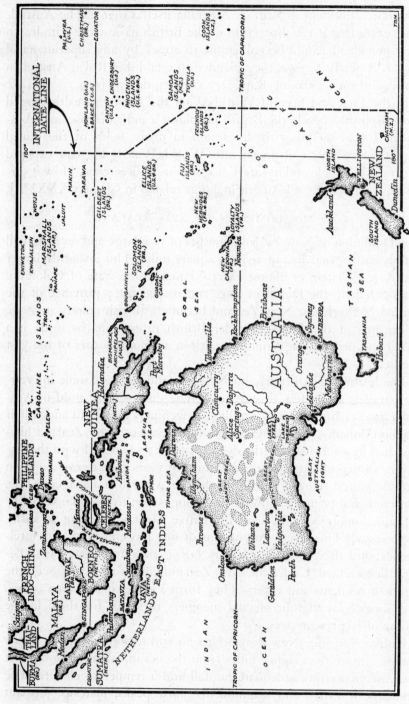

OCEANIA

valleys, rivers, lakes, waterfalls, hot springs, and volcanoes provide an ever-changing scenery. The vegetation is diversified and abundant and most of the land is suitable for farming or grazing. By 1944 the islands supported over 4,000,000 cattle and 33,000,000 sheep. Meat freezing and preserving was the leading industry, with the processing of dairy products second. New Zealand is one of the most richly endowed and healthiest countries in the world. This is reflected by the rapid increase in the population, which reached 1,653,757 in 1944, and in the birth rate of 19.70 per 1000 and death rate of 10.04 (1943). The infant mortality rate is the lowest in the world.

These remarkable social advantages are not wholly the results of climate and geography. Like the early English colonists in America, the New Zealanders left behind many of the obsolete class distinctions, outworn customs, and inherited prejudices which have often constricted the development of European peoples. They not only developed a free society in this remote island realm but they proved to be pioneers in more than one sense and introduced daring democratic innovations. Responsible government was established in 1856. Manhood suffrage followed in 1889; woman suffrage, in 1893. Pioneering also in social and labor legislation, the parliament established industrial conciliation boards and courts of arbitration, with authority to supervise wages, hours of labor, and working conditions. Trade unions increased rapidly, a Federation of Labor was formed in 1907, and a separate Labor Party in 1909. Even more advanced was the progress of social insurance, which commenced with the adoption of old age pensions in 1898. Insurance laws to protect workers against unemployment, sickness, and accidents have followed. Government annuities, benefits, and pensions have been instituted to care for widows, orphans, invalids, and maternity cases, and to help families with a limited income. A Social Security Act passed in 1938 to consolidate some of these services provided that the worker's contribution should consist of a registration fee and a charge on salaries, wages, and other income.

Like Australia, New Zealand has supported Great Britain in the two World Wars and was threatened by Japanese aggression after 1941. By 1944 New Zealand had sent 110,000 men to fight in the various combat zones. Their casualties were the heaviest, in proportion to population, of any nation in the British Commonwealth. The Royal New Zealand Navy, established in 1913, and the Royal New Zealand Air Force are organized to co-operate in the general strategy of empire defense, and in time of war the navy is at the disposal of the British government. In World War II some of the New Zealand ships also operated under the direction of United States naval commanders.

3. THE COMMONWEALTH OF THE PHILIPPINES

When the United States formally acquired the Philippine Islands from Spain in 1899, it took over the responsibility of defending a commonwealth of more than seven thousand islands with a total area slightly larger than New Zealand and about equal to that of Arizona. Most of these islands are dots in the ocean. Less than five hundred have an area of more than one square mile, and only ten or eleven are important. The total population has increased rapidly under American protection, reaching 17,000,000 by 1941, the great majority being native born. Between four and five million speak English, another half million Spanish, and the remainder the various local patois. In 1937 Tagalog, a Malayan dialect, was declared to be the official language but during the transitional period before independence was achieved the teaching of English was compulsory in the free, secular, co-educational schools. About one-half the Filipinos over ten years of age are literate, and four-fifths are followers of the Roman Catholic religion.

When the Filipino people revolted against Spanish rule in 1896 their leader, Emilio Aguinaldo, accepted American aid. But he wished complete independence for the islands, and after the defeat of the Spaniards he opposed American occupation from 1899 until his capture in 1901. The following year the United States Congress established a bicameral legislature for the commonwealth but retained the power to veto its acts. The removal of tariff restrictions and quota limits on trade with the United States provided a market for sugar, tobacco, and other island crops. A desire for complete independence remained strong among the people, although commissions of investigation sent out by the United States government reported that they were not yet equal to the problems of self-rule or the burdens of self-defense.

After 1929, however, the American attitude and sentiment towards Philippine independence underwent a change. American economic penetration of the islands had made less progress than had been anticipated, the free entrance of island crops, notably sugar and tobacco, competed with the produce of American farmers, and the cost of defending possessions in Asian waters added greatly to the naval budget. A plan to set up a transitional regime, leading to independence after twelve years, passed the United States Congress in 1934. Under the provisions of this Tydings-McDuffie Act the Filipinos adopted their own constitution in 1935, choosing Manuel Quezon as their first president. A Popular Party continued to agitate for immediate independence, but Quezon's Nationalist Party held its leadership. The United States continued to supervise defense, foreign relations, finance, and justice, with the understanding that the period of tutelage would terminate in 1946 with full autonomy for the Filipinos. This program was temporarily interrupted by the events of World War II and the Japanese conquest of the islands. Their liberation by United States forces after 1944 and the rapid restoration of local self-government set the stage once more for the promised autonomy. The Act of 1934, however, though it promised the Filipinos their independence as "a separate and self-governing nation," provided that the United States might maintain naval reservations and fueling stations in the islands after granting them independence in 1946.

In contrast to the Philippines, the islands of the Hawaiian archipelago with nearly half a million inhabitants have been drawing tighter their political bonds with the United States. Formally annexed in 1898 and granted the privileges enjoyed by American states through an Act of Congress in 1924, the Territory of Hawaii has at present one delegate in the Congress. There is increasing agitation for full statehood. The important strategic role which Pearl Harbor has come to play in American Pacific defense plans and the fact that one-third of the population is Japanese or of Japanese descent, made the question of bestowing statehood upon this important Territory a complicated one that was not easy to resolve.

4. THE PACIFIC ISLANDS

All the land areas of the earth, if united, would about fill the 55,000,-000 square miles of the Pacific Ocean. This watery hemisphere, with its minute and multitudinous islands, became an ocean of destiny in the twentieth century. The problems of defense and expansion which induced the government of the United States to acquire the Aleutian Islands, Hawaii, and the Philippines before 1900, likewise persuaded alert statesmen in Australia and New Zealand to urge wider British annexation of islands still unclaimed, while French, German, and Japanese imperialists were also raising flags on unconsidered atolls and pressing claims to lonely archipelagoes.

Sovereignty is often difficult to maintain on scattered groups of islets; and as continuous occupation is impossible on most of the South Pacific reefs and atolls because few of them will adequately support even a small population, it has become the custom in the twentieth century to allot the different powers fields of ocean lying between

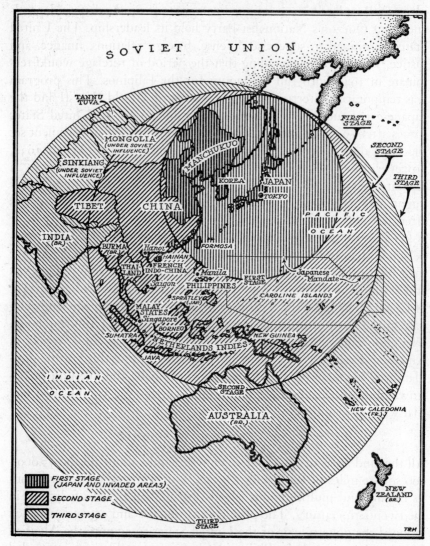

THE JAPANESE DREAM OF EMPIRE

specified degrees of latitude and longitude. Thus, almost without their
knowledge, isolated island peoples who had seldom seen Europeans
except for visiting whalers or missionaries have found themselves
swept into the sphere of influence of a government located on the
other side of the world. The process of demarcation and annexation
was hastened by the events of World War I. By 1919 few islands in
the vast expanse remained unappropriated.

In Oceania, half of New Guinea, with New Britain and New Ireland, became an Australian mandate after World War I. Samoa was mandated to New Zealand. The Fiji, Tonga, Solomon, and Gilbert Islands went to Great Britain with other scattered possessions. In general the equator formed the northern limit of the British area of supervision. North of the equator lay the Japanese mandates, which embraced the Caroline Islands, Yap, the Marianas, and the Marshall Islands. Only a study of the map can make evident how intermeshed the Japanese and American lines of communication became with the extension of Japanese influence. The American stepping stones from Hawaii to the Philippines, especially Midway, Wake, and Guam, lay directly across the Japanese routes of advance. It is not difficult to understand why the people of Australia and New Zealand came to respect American naval strength as their first line of defense against a possible southward thrust by Japan or why, when war did come, they accorded all the facilities at their disposal to the American forces. (See maps, pages 380 and 497.)

The Japanese likewise recognized the probability of American opposition, but they pressed on their plans of expansion with unrelenting patience and precision. Seldom if ever in history has so widely flung an empire been acquired as that built up in half a century by the Japanese. From the annexation of Formosa in 1895 to the seizure of the Philippines and the Netherlands Indies in 1942, they conquered nearly 3,000,000 square miles of territory on the Asian mainland or the islands. Much of this conquered empire was exceptionally rich in natural resources, and the total population numbered nearly 400,000,000, or about one-fifth of the world total. Against this drive of the conquerors from the Land of the Rising Sun the few million Europeans in the areas invaded — the Dutch, Portuguese, Spaniards, British, and Americans — could not maintain themselves. European supremacy in this extended quarter of the globe could be reasserted only after the Anglo-American forces regained sea and air superiority. The rapid advance and retreat of the Japanese hegemony in the twentieth century suggested that most Asiatic and Pacific peoples, unlike the warlike and obdurate Europeans, were unprepared to resist a powerful conquerer. The conditions which had permitted the maritime powers of the West to penetrate the waters of the East with their superior squadrons in the sixteenth century still held. The lands of the East were still at the disposal of the strong invader.

PART VII

Experiments in Government

THE BRITISH EMPIRE–COMMONWEALTH

*Sir, we must beware of needless innovation, especially when
guided by logic.*

WINSTON CHURCHILL

I. THE LOOSENING OF POLITICAL TIES

WHEN World War I ended in 1918 the outstanding victor appeared to be Great Britain. In Asia Minor, the dismemberment of the Ottoman Empire left Palestine, Transjordania, the Kingdom of the Hedjaz, and Iraq to be transformed into British mandates. In Africa, what had been German East Africa, together with a large share of Togoland and the Cameroons, became British mandates also, while German Southwest Africa passed to the Union of South Africa. In the Pacific, German New Guinea and some smaller islands went to Australia, and German Samoan possessions to New Zealand. As a further result of the war the German navy was eliminated and German ocean commerce crippled, leaving the British position at sea relatively stronger. The greater share of the 20,000 miles of undersea cables surrendered by the Germans passed into British control, so that London in 1919 was still the chief center of world communications.

On closer inspection, however, it was evident that these British gains were offset by serious debits. It was true that the territories nominally included in the empire had expanded until they exceeded 13,000,000 square miles, one-fourth of the land area of the earth. But the political ties which held the British Empire together seemed to be dissolving. The Indian Nationalists had increased their demand for independence. In Egypt, which had been proclaimed a British protectorate in 1914 after thirty years of British occupation, a clamorous group of Nationalists were likewise demanding sovereign rights, and Egypt became an independent kingdom in 1922. British forces, however, continued to occupy the hinterland, the Anglo-Egyptian Sudan, and to protect the Suez Canal. In Palestine a bitter feud between the Jewish immigrants and the Moslem population made the problem of maintaining order a difficult and thankless one for the British forces. In the Arab state of Iraq, where a constitutional regime was established by 1924, the people declared themselves ready for self-government, and in 1932 Iraq entered the League of Nations as a sovereign state. It seemed as if the British were schooling their subject peoples to secede, or at least urging them to achieve self-rule and sovereignty.

Another problem in self-government nearer home, the most ancient and envenomed problem in British imperial relations, also found a partial solution after 1919. This was the Irish Question. For centuries the attempts of the British to dominate Ireland had bred revolts and reprisals. True to their conviction that England's extremity was Ireland's opportunity, a group of Irish Nationalists staged an unsuccessful rebellion in 1916 when British fortunes were at their lowest in World War I. Though the revolt was crushed, it left the country in a condition approaching civil war, and after 1919 the Sinn Fein Party was strong enough to insist upon home rule. The Irish Free State became a self-governing Dominion in the British Commonwealth (1922). Northern Ireland (Ulster) was not included. The people of Ulster established their own parliament (1921) but continued to send thirteen members to the historic British parliament at Westminster. The constitution of the new Dominion declared Ireland (Eire) a "sovereign, independent, democratic state." No Governor-General was accepted as representative of the British crown; a president, elected by direct vote of the people, appointed the prime minister, who was known as head of the government. Although the Irish Free State was still associated for some purposes with the British Commonwealth of Nations, the Free State government appointed its own diplomatic representatives to foreign capitals and did not feel itself bound to follow the British lead in foreign policy. In 1939, for example, it did not join the other units of the Commonwealth in the war with Germany.

The emergence of the self-governing Dominions as equal and independent partners in the British Commonwealth marked a new and startling experiment in statecraft. It was, however, a logical step in keeping with a century or more of British practice. The Dominion of Canada had been federated and had acquired a national parliament in 1867; the Commonwealth of Australia had achieved federal unity in 1901; New Zealand became a Dominion in 1907; and the Union of South Africa was formally proclaimed in 1910. The political relationship that linked these self-governing Dominions to Great Britain and to one another thus became a matter for legal speculation because there was no exact precedent which covered it. When the Irish Free State was established in 1922, the independent attitude of the Irish made this question of Dominion status an issue requiring definition. In South Africa, as in Ireland, a powerful political group urged complete political independence of Britain; and in Canada, Australia, and New Zealand there were national-minded citizens who criticized the ambiguous imperial bond.

The question of Dominion status was therefore clarified at a conference which assembled in London in 1926. The rise of the empire had been so largely a spontaneous and unplanned growth that the British and Dominion premiers who debated the issue were themselves uncertain how best to define the numerous and complicated ties which held the imperial structure together. But they agreed on one common conviction. The chief strength of the empire lay in the voluntary and reciprocal attraction of its members, and no attempt to link it more firmly or explicitly by legal formulas or coercive measures would make it stronger. Rather, they thought, a further dissolution of political bonds was in order, and they offered a new definition to describe the political status of Great Britain and the self-governing Dominions. "They are autonomous communities within the British Empire, equal in status, in no way subordinate one to another in any aspect of their domestic or external affairs, though united by a common allegiance to the Crown and fully associated as members of the British Commonwealth of Nations." The logical corollary of this declaration followed five years later (1931) when the British parliament passed the Statute of Westminster. The most important article declared that "no Act of Parliament of the United Kingdom passed after the commencement of this Act shall extend, or be deemed to extend, to a Dominion . . . unless . . . the Dominion has requested, and consented to, the enactment thereof."

2. THE BRITISH ECONOMIC DILEMMA

The British people found it difficult, after 1918, to restore their pre-war prosperity. Disrupted trade, declining industries, ruined markets, increased foreign (especially American) competition, and heavy taxation made the economic future dark. A return of international stability and the revival of world trade promised Britain the surest hope for economic recovery, for British power rested upon the income drawn from commerce and manufacture. If British commerce declined, British influence among the nations would decline with it. Great Britain, as a geographic unit, was the least self-sufficient of the world powers, and the British economic dilemma could be summed up in three words: export or die.

World War I imposed a staggering burden on the British budget. The public debt, which stood at about £650,000,000 in 1913, rose so rapidly during the war and postwar years that by 1933 it had increased tenfold to £6,613,000,000. The taxpayer carried an excessive share in the cost of imperial defense, for the navy policed the oceans, protected the empire, and safeguarded many small nations which would otherwise have been vulnerable to attack. Defense, however, was only one item in an expanding budget. The social services — especially sickness, accident, old age, and unemployment insurance — which had been introduced during the Liberal reform era of 1906–1914, required an increasing share of the national revenue when postwar depression grew severe in 1921. A "dole" of twenty shillings a week to unemployed men and eighteen shillings to women forced a rise in the tax rate when the total of registered unemployed passed one million.

Successive cabinets strove without success to solve the grim problem. In 1922 the wartime prime minister, David Lloyd George, was succeeded by a Conservative, Andrew Bonar Law, who resigned the premiership in 1923 to another Conservative, Stanley Baldwin. A general election at the close of that year brought in the first Labor Cabinet, under Ramsay MacDonald; but before the close of 1924 it was swept out in another general election which opened five years of Conservative rule under the second Baldwin ministry.

In 1926 the mounting discontent of the miners and transport workers and the persistence of unemployment induced a general strike which severely dislocated business for a week. The following year the Conservatives responded by declaring all strikes and lockouts would be held illegal if they endangered the public welfare and the national safety. The financial situation, already strained, became desperate with the world depression which commenced in 1929, and by 1931 it was evident that drastic changes must be made to balance the budget. National and imperial defense expenditures, a dole for 2,000,000 unemployed, relief for the coal mining companies, subsidies for the merchant marine, and carrying charges on public and intergovernmental debts had overtaxed the exchequer. The Labor cabinet, recalled to power in 1929, was in a quandary. It was essential to increase the revenue and to cut expenditures. But the Liberal supporters of the government, with their laissez-faire ideals, refused to sanction a tariff on imports; the Laborites fought any reduction in the government aid for the poorer classes; and the imposition of higher taxes on the wealthy and the business interests threatened to discourage and depress empire trade.

This painful economic crisis split the second Labor ministry of 1929–31. But instead of resigning, MacDonald remained to head a National Coalition government with Conservative, Liberal, and Labor members. This coalition cabinet promptly abandoned the gold standard, with the result that the pound sterling fell from $4.86 to $3.50 in terms of dollar exchange. The government likewise forsook the venerable tradition of free trade (1932) and passed a tariff on imports, while launching a campaign to "Buy British" and negotiating agreements with the Dominions to maintain "imperial preference" in their trading policies. A slow business recovery and the achievement of a balanced budget appeared to justify the course adopted. MacDonald continued to head the cabinet until 1935, but he and those who served with him were expelled from the Labor Party and the cabinet was in reality dominated by the Conservatives or Tories. The abandonment of free trade and laissez-faire principles had left the Liberal Party an impotent minority, and the desertion of MacDonald had split and dismayed the Labor group. General elections in 1931 and 1933, however, gave the coalition government the assurance that the nation was satisfied with its firmer policies.

It was highly significant that the British preserved their parliamentary system intact and made only moderate adjustments to meet the economic confusion and international challenge which shattered many other governments in the years 1919–1939. Even the unexpected abdication of Edward VIII, who succeeded his father George V in 1936 and resigned the same year, failed to disrupt the sober routine of parliamentary rule. This vitality and resilience, in a government which to many foreigners appeared cumbrous and old-fashioned, was not easily to be explained. British administrative methods often impressed the British themselves as time-consuming and unsystematic. British politicians "muddled through" from one dubious compromise to another, and each succeeding generation agreed that things were in a bad way. Yet the British people had surmounted crisis after crisis while neighbor states were plunged into defeat or dislocated by revolution. Hostile critics ascribed the prosperity and prestige of Great Britain to an unexampled series of fortunate accidents. Admirers preferred to credit the growth of the empire and the expansion of British influence to the virtues of British character and the moderation of British methods. Whatever the explanation might be, the British empire at the close of the nineteenth century had become "the world's most successful experiment in international organization." It remained to be seen if the talent the British had developed for muddling through would enable them to meet the challenges of the dynamic twentieth century.

3. BRITISH POLITICAL GENIUS

In their long political development the British had shown a decided preference for evolution rather than revolution. Especially after the civil war and rebellions of the seventeenth century they avoided violent domestic strife. In the nineteenth century responsible government and democracy advanced by constitutional steps, and instead of the sporadic revolutions and new regimes which punctuated French history after 1789 the British adopted a series of legislative measures. The reform bills of 1832, 1867, 1884–1885, and the Parliament Act of 1911 transformed an oligarchy into a working democracy. The progressive steps were taken cautiously and followed no fixed plan or ideological formula. This same reluctance to put too much trust in logic or to constrict the growth of society by insisting upon an excessive uniformity marked British democratic reforms in the twentieth century. The electors showed themselves more responsive to arguments based upon appeals to custom or to practical experience than to arguments supported by axioms and syllogisms.

In 1918, as the war to make the world "safe for democracy" was ending, the British parliament adopted a bill to establish universal manhood suffrage throughout the United Kingdom. The bill also decreed one election day for the entire kingdom and all but ended the practice of plural voting which had permitted certain electors to vote in more than one constituency. But the most significant provision in this Reform Bill of 1918 was the extension of the franchise to every woman over thirty if she or her husband was qualified to vote in local elections. The question of woman suffrage had excited a lively controversy before 1914. During the four years of World War I women had proved their ability to take over much of the men's work in office, industry, and agriculture, and this made it appear more anomalous than ever to deny them legal equality in a democratic country. In 1919 an Act of Parliament decreed that women should enjoy legal equality with men, and should not be disqualified because of their sex from holding public office or entering any profession. Full equality in the exercise of the franchise was not established until 1928 when the Representation of the People Act declared that all electors, men or women, must be twenty-one years of age or older, and must have complied with certain residence qualifications in order to vote.

Equality before the law did not bring genuine equality of opportunity to the women of Great Britain. More powerful than any Act of parliament was the constricting effect of custom, which still disposed people in all ranks to resist a change of status or privilege. In the schools, the professions, and the business world, women were still handicapped by the traditional assumption that men were the superior sex. This almost unanimous opinion, as prevalent among the women as among the men, delayed the emancipation of women. They lacked the fuller measure of freedom and self-confidence attained by their sisters in the Scandinavian countries, in the self-governing Dominions, and in the United States. The fact that there were almost two million more women than men in the United Kingdom (1931) reduced the prospects of marriage for a sizable feminine minority and made the conventional argument that a woman's place was in the home a somewhat ironical platitude for the surplus homemakers.

British conservatism, which provided the chief clue to an understanding of the British character, puzzled foreign observers. They noted in most English people what appeared to be an irrational preference for the traditional method, a preference which often blinded them to suggested improvements or newer techniques. The retention of pounds, shillings, and pence, and the refusal to adopt the decimal system of accounting was an example of this attitude. The preservation of outmoded rituals at the royal receptions, the procedure in the older colleges, the law courts, and the sessions of parliament, reflected still more strongly the British respect for historic precedent. The accumulated body of customs inherited from the past seemed a safe guide to the nation, and glittering generalities were distrusted. This cautious attitude had been eloquently defined and defended by the great parliamentary orator, Edmund Burke, at the end of the eighteenth century. "All your sophisters," he protested, "cannot produce anything better adapted to preserve a rational and manly freedom than the course that we have pursued, who have chosen our nature rather than our speculations, our breasts rather than our inventions, for the great conservatories and magazines of our rights and privileges."

The most paradoxical feature of British conservatism was the fact that this custom-ridden people, who "muddled through" their difficulties and remained so lacking in system that they possessed no written constitution, had nevertheless established a remarkable degree of law and order over one-fourth of the world. This nation so rigid and archaic in its respect for ancient rituals had developed the most popular, most flexible, and most variegated methods of responsible government in political annals. This cautious people so slow to change had preserved the stability of their state in an age of conflict that shattered most contemporary governments. As a system of international cooperation the British Empire-Commonwealth had no parallel. Never before in history had half a billion people of diverse creeds and races been governed and protected by such a small handful of soldiers and administrators as the personnel of the British imperial services. As administrators the British remained most noteworthy for their restraint, and no rulers in history had been less corrupted by power. If the test of political genius was the ability to promote peace and security, to protect individuals and minorities from persecution, to enforce respect for law and for human rights without recourse to cruel and unusual punishments or unnecessary bloodshed, then the British might claim to be the most successful administrators the world had known.

THE FRENCH REPUBLIC

1919—1939

The heart of the French bourgeois is on the left but his pocket book is on the right.

ANDRÉ SIEGFRIED

1. VICTORY WITHOUT SECURITY

THE French people emerged from World War I to face what their aged but indomitable premier, Georges Clemenceau, termed "the grandeur and misery of victory." They had won back the provinces of Alsace and Lorraine, lost to Germany in the Franco-Prussian War of 1870–1871, but they had paid a terrible price. The total population of France in 1914 had been 39,800,000. The total population in 1919, with Alsace and Lorraine re-annexed, was only 38,700,000. A declining birth rate, civilian casualties, and 1,385,000 war dead, had crippled France in its most vulnerable asset, its population. Official efforts to raise the birth rate by suggesting a government bonus for each child failed to check the decline, and the added charge was a burden for a nation already paying pensions to a million mutilated soldiers. The irony of such contrasting policies was summed up in a cartoon showing a tearful Cupid pleading before the French Chamber of Deputies: "I have only my little bow and arrows. Now, if you would give me some machine guns!"

A people haunted by insecurity, military and economic, may well hesitate to raise large families. The decline of the franc discouraged the French almost as much as the decline of the birth rate, and the threat of national insolvency dominated all political discussions. War damage and the cost of reconstruction added twenty billion francs to the national budget, and (as in Britain) the public debt rose tenfold in the twenty years after 1914. The failure to collect all the calculated reparations from Germany, the burden of armaments, and the interest

charges on the government bonds led to the equivalent of national
bankruptcy in 1926. The franc had depreciated to two cents, and the
country seemed headed for the catastrophic type of inflation which
had wrecked German credit three years earlier. In this crisis, Raymond Poincaré formed a National Union Ministry, introduced severe
economies, and "saved the franc." In 1928 it was stabilized at 3.92
cents, but as the prewar rate had been 19.3 cents, this meant in substance an official repudiation of four-fifths of the existing paper debts
of the government and the people. The carrying charges on the national debt and the payment of national bonds as they fell due could
now be settled with depreciated currency. The *rentier* class, which
lived chiefly on the income derived from financial investments, suffered severely by this proceeding but the national credit was re-
established, a sinking fund created to redeem the standing debt, and
the sanctity of private property and private fortunes reaffirmed.

The bitter controversies which flamed up in the Senate and the
Chamber of Deputies over these various financial measures concealed
a deep rift in the national life. The feud between capital and labor,
between bourgeois and socialist, or, in its broadest and simplest expression, between the rich and the poor, threatened to destroy the
Third Republic. As noted in the preceding chapter, the British people were divided by the same class antagonisms after 1918, but the
Laborites and the Tories managed to supplement or modify each
other's policies on strikes, poor relief, armaments, tariff, and taxation.
There were, in Britain, no violent swings from left to right and back
again and no serious disorders. In France, however, the two-party
system had never established itself as a tradition; cabinets were supported by blocs or coalitions of many small parliamentary groups
which united for divergent reasons and for an indefinite time. The
fall of a cabinet was not usually followed, as in England, by a general
election because the Chamber of Deputies served normally for a four-
year term. In practice, the system led to a constant and often unpredictable ebb and shift in party alignments and to frequent cabinet
crises. French ministries formed, broke up, reformed, or were replaced, with a rapidity that bewildered those who sought to divine
government policy. Between 1870 and 1939 the French set up eighty-
eight ministries, four times as many as the British formed during the
same seventy-year period.

Behind the perpetual shifts and crises in France two major social
groups could usually be detected in an unremitting struggle for con-

trol. All property owners, from the great industrialists and bankers to the family group living on a few bonds or a small farm, were united by one common interest: they had a stake in the capitalist system and that stake was legally safeguarded by the institution of private property. On the other hand, all those citizens whose chief asset was their labor or their technical knowledge held a different stake and were likely to ask legislation which would protect *their* main interest, namely, the right to work and receive fair wages and protection. For them the socialist orators demanded higher wages, better working conditions, social insurance, taxes on the unearned incomes and surplus profits of bondholders and capitalists, and government control of public utilities and armament works.

It is a mistake, of course, to think that every Frenchman could be classified as a property owner or as a wage earner. Many were both. It would be a mistake, too, if all wage earners were pictured as voting for socialist deputies and all property owners for moderate republicans. Nevertheless, the general divergence of view which separated the right from the left in the Chamber of Deputies corresponded to a divergence in the economic status of the French classes. It was a divergence which affected every public question: finances, taxation, tariffs, subsidies, social services, labor policy, national defense, and foreign affairs. As one group and then another succeeded in forming a cabinet, domestic and foreign policy vacillated and the lack of any strong or consistent program hastened the decline in French prestige. Within the country the electors lost patience with the perpetual wrangling, the patchwork compromises, and the postponed decisions. Charges of incompetence and graft were flung back and forth in parliament and repeated in the press, and in the confusion of successive crises the people began to despair of their government. This confusion in political aims and ideals prepared the way for the tragic collapse of morale which overtook the nation with the German invasion of 1940.

2. POLITICAL FEUDS AND FACTIONS

The center of gravity in the Chamber of Deputies after 1900 lay a little left of center, and the weightiest group in the successive coalitions of ruling parties was usually that of the moderate republicans. The middle class backed the *bloc national* which led France to victory in World War I, they insisted upon a stern peace for Germany, and they were frightened by the specter of communism which had risen in Russia. On the right of the center groups stood the small party of royalists, spokesmen of a tradition older than the Revolution and austere critics of the Republic; on the left were the socialist and communist groups which opposed or collaborated with the ruling bloc according to the issue of the moment. After 1920 the deepening quarrel between the bourgeois republicans and the socialists made such collaboration difficult. In that year the French Socialist Party voted to unite with the Third International or Comintern, set up at Moscow to foster a world league of communist groups. Thereupon the General Confederation of Labor, a group of French labor unions or *syndicats*, was ordered to dissolve by a court decree, for conservative Frenchmen feared that it might become a tool of Moscow and the spearhead of a proletarian revolution. The political battle between the moderates and the socialists had grown sharper.

For three years the right center kept control of the government. It renewed diplomatic relations with the Vatican and granted the Catholic Church the right to occupy its former property which had been nationalized in 1905. But the failure to extract the promised indemnities from Germany discredited the cabinet of Raymond Poincaré, and in 1924 the *Cartel des Gauches,* a bloc of leftist deputies, elected a cabinet under Edouard Herriot. This leftist government promptly displayed its friendliness towards Russia by recognizing the Soviet regime diplomatically and sought to withdraw the French representative recently appointed to the Vatican. Then the pressing financial problems and the continued decline of the franc brought Poincaré back to the premier's post in 1926. Neither the socialists nor the republicans had a ready solution for the deficit. Socialist enactments, which extended workingmen's compensation benefits to agricultural laborers (1922) and provided employees with insurance against sickness, old age, and other disabilities (1930), added to the tax rate without really placating the laboring classes. A political scandal in 1933 (the Stavisky case) which involved leading politicians in questionable financial deals, so angered the populace that France was threatened by violence and civil disorder. But once again a center coalition cabinet took charge, representing all parties except the royalists, socialists, and communists (1934). Tranquillity was restored but not public confidence. A majority of the people were becoming critical of all parties and scornful of the politicians, an ominous sign in a democracy.

The leftists, as the partisans of radical reforms, attracted many malcontents in this time of general grievance. Socialists and communists united to form a Popular Front (1935) and the following year a Popular Front ministry was installed under Léon Blum. But misfortune pursued the socialists from the hour they assumed office. Strikes in vital industries, rising costs, the hostility of the wealthy, and the decline of the franc hindered their plans for reforms at home while their foreign policy led France into a series of humiliations. The Italians conquered Ethiopia, the Germans refortified the Rhineland, and the Belgians discontinued their military convention with France which had been signed in 1920 to impose a barrier on possible German attacks along the French northeastern frontier. The southern frontier was likewise jeopardized after 1936, for German and Italian aid to the Spanish Nationalists under the insurgent leader, Francisco Franco, made it probable that a pro-Fascist government in Spain would ally itself with the Axis powers. The need to strengthen the Franco-Belgian border, the Franco-Italian frontier, and the Pyrenees, had grown acute, and Blum tried to float government loans and to obtain a grant of authority to control the currency. But a socialist bloc like the Popular Front was not trusted by the wealthier classes, and the Senate, where the powerful financial groups were well entrenched, frustrated Blum's reforms, refusing him the powers he asked to stabilize the franc. In 1937 he resigned, then tried again for a few weeks in 1938 to form a socialist cabinet, and was again defeated. An ominous hint of the tension and bitterness which tinctured the political rift was the discovery (1937) of a conspiracy to overthrow the Republic by an armed *coup* and set up a Fascist or at least an authoritarian dictatorship.

The schism within French political life weakened foreign policy and the smaller states turned towards Berlin instead of Paris. In 1934 King Alexander of Yugoslavia while visiting France on a diplomatic mission was assassinated along with the French foreign minister, Louis Barthou. Attempts to placate Italy by concessions in Africa failed. An alliance with Soviet Russia, hastily signed as a reply to Hitler's announcement that Germany was rearming (1935), frightened the conservatives and remained without force. Anglo-French friendship was strained, and the disorganization of the armament and aircraft industries, which was increased by frequent strikes and by socialist plans for nationalization, further weakened French power at a critical time. The German and Italian governments were united, ruthless, and aggressive; the French cabinets were unsure of their power, inept, and on the defensive. The Maginot Line, the elaborate system of connected fortifications covering the Franco-German frontier, had be

come a symbol of the French people's attitude of mind. They insisted
that it was impregnable. But the Line could not defend the Franco-
Belgian front: it was necessary to extend it. Nor could the Line protect the Italian border: it was necessary to supplement it. (See map,
page 471.) Furthermore, all this emphasis on defense and fortification
warned the allies of France — Poland, Czechoslovakia, Rumania, Yugoslavia, Turkey, Belgium — that France could not rush armies to their
aid as Napoleon I and Napoleon III had done for their lesser confederates. By 1938 the government could not speak with vigor and assurance either in France or in Europe. It was denied the backing of a
confident majority at home such as the British electors gave their nationalist government in these difficult years; it veered from left to
right in its domestic management; and its attempts to follow a resolute
foreign course miscarried or became a feeble echo of British pro-
nouncements.

3. FRENCH DEMOCRACY IN CRISIS

The decline of French prestige after 1933 was matched by the phenomenal rise of Germany. As Frenchmen contrasted the confusion
and the indecision in France with the seeming confidence and strength
of the Nazi regime, many of them grew critical of the democratic
constitution which was supposed to safeguard the revolutionary ideals
of Liberty, Equality, and Fraternity. The fault, however, did not lie
in any inherent defect crippling the machinery of the Third Republic; that parliamentary regime, with all its annoying extravagances
and frictions, had carried France through the exacting test of World
War I. The real difficulty was that by 1938 France was facing two
severe crises at the same time, and whatever remedy the government
adopted for one was almost certain to aggravate the other. The recovery of Germany under Hitler and the formation of the German-
Italian alliance destroyed the European balance. Only a Franco-
Russian military pact could restore equilibrium, but the moderate and
conservative parties in France would not support such an alliance.
Many millions of Frenchmen considered Stalin a greater threat than
Hitler and approved of the suppression of the socialists and the forceful control of labor inaugurated by the Fascists. To some Frenchmen,
as their passions mounted, all communists seemed traitors, saboteurs,
and agents of Moscow, and this extreme view found expression in the
slogan, "Rather Hitler than Léon Blum."

Yet if France could not unite in a genuine military alliance with Russia, how was German aggression to be curbed? The obvious answer appeared to be: by concessions; and in this policy the British cabinet concurred. As a result, the Germans were able to force through their demands at the Munich Conference (1938) and to dismember Czechoslovakia with the acquiescence of the French premier, Edouard Daladier, and the British prime minister, Neville Chamberlain. The Munich Conference, to which Russian delegates were not invited, nullified the anemic Franco-Russian accord of 1935 and demonstrated that France would not stand by her eastern European allies. The governments of Poland, Rumania, and Yugoslavia read the lesson and realized that they might receive as little help in the face of a German attack as the Czechs had received.

The severe diplomatic reverse suffered at Munich should have convinced all Frenchmen that the time had come to stand together, forget faction, and formulate a consistent national policy. The most obvious effect of Munich on French domestic politics, however, was to shatter the Popular Front. The socialist deputies refused to vote on the Munich agreement, and the communists voted against this deal which left Czechoslovakia to Hitler's mercy. Daladier was therefore compelled to turn to the right for support, but the price of that support was the revocation of recent concessions made to French labor by Blum and his colleagues. The government announced that the promise of a forty-hour week could not be kept, a move justified, perhaps, by the need to build up armaments more swiftly, but a move which embittered the laboring classes. The General Confederation of Labor called a series of strikes, and while Europe drifted towards war the French continued to weaken their financial, productive, and military efforts by a strike deadlock and frequent disorders.

The blame for this sacrifice of national efficiency was laid upon the left. Turning still more definitely against the socialists, Daladier asked the Chamber of Deputies for semidictatorial powers. Labor leaders were arrested, strikers threatened with military penalties, while the leading armament makers were encouraged by government orders and the assurances of a fair profit. The fierce partisan attacks against the government, which, under the French rules on freedom of speech and the press, often assumed a vitriolic and defamatory character, were curbed by what amounted to a partial government censorship. These steps freed the ministers from the constant need to defend themselves against attack and to cajole fractious deputies; but it was clear that

France was adopting some of the methods of the totalitarian regimes in order to strengthen the nation against such regimes, an ironic and tragic illustration of the corrupting influence of tyranny. Frenchmen who revered the traditions of liberty which dated from the Revolution of 1789 were troubled by these newer trends. The cabinet of Edouard Daladier, by the spring of 1939, had been granted power to rule by decree with no fixed limit on the use made of this extraordinary authority. The firmer control thus given the French ministers was matched by a firmer attitude among the people and a deepening consciousness of national solidarity. In foreign affairs, the Daladier cabinet negotiated with Britain and with Russia for a united front against the Axis and offered guarantees to Poland, Rumania, and Greece that their independence would be protected. France was not yet herself again — a terrible six-year ordeal lay ahead — but Frenchmen were re-examining the foundations of their national faith.

THE FASCIST EXPERIMENT IN ITALY

For Fascism the State is an absolute before which individuals and groups are relative.

BENITO MUSSOLINI

I. THE PARALYSIS OF PARLIAMENTARY GOVERNMENT

THE system of responsible parliamentary government evolved by the English nation through slow centuries of growth and adopted more spasmodically by the French in the century after 1789, had become by 1919 the distinctive form of administration in all democratic states. The triumph of the democratic nations in World War I was hailed as a vindication of popular rule. Democracy had come to imply a representative system of government under which the electors chose their own lawmakers. The precise forms of the franchise and the functioning of the representative machinery might differ considerably. But the origin and limits of political authority had been defined. The people was the sovereign; the elected congress, parliament, or legislature (of one or two chambers) exercised a delegated power; and the cabinet or council of ministers which directed the departments of government was responsible at all times to the majority in the popular chamber and therefore to the sovereign people. The president or monarch who symbolized the executive power was likewise understood to embody the will of the nation.

This system was designed to remain in equilibrium because it operated through a balance of powers. As developed in England parliamentary democracy was in principle most immediately responsible to the people because a cabinet was obligated to resign at any time if it failed to obtain a vote of confidence from the House of Commons, and the resignation of a cabinet was the signal for a general election. Thus the electors might be consulted at frequent intervals or whenever there was reason to doubt whether the ministers in office had the confidence of the majority. Under this form, true parliamentary government could never be despotic or dictatorial, for a cabinet which promulgated unpopular or tyrannous decrees would be overthrown. Throughout World War I much emphasis was laid by Allied propagandists on the argument that the German and Austrian governments had made war against the will of their people or at least without consulting them. Had the despotically ruled peoples been free to express their will, it was argued, there would probably have been no conflict. The Allied nations were thus fighting for the principle of democracy in order to bring oppressed peoples self-rule and self-determination through popular plebiscites. The essential qualification of a good government, the world was warned, depended upon popular representation. Governments derived their just powers from the consent of the governed.

A people endowed with habits of self-restraint and trained in the art and technique of parliamentary rule, could make the system work remarkably well. But in a country where factional strife was too bitter and the populace tended to divide uncompromisingly on many issues, a feud-ridden parliament might reflect all too faithfully the disunity of the nation. If the level of political morality were low, the prevalence of corruption at the polls and the venality of the deputies might destroy faith in the patriotism and capacity of a parliament. Though the forms of democratic rule remained, the promise of equal justice under law might be vitiated and the political group in power might retain its control through a vast, half-acknowledged conspiracy rather than through enlightened and independent plebiscites. The responsibility of self-government was apparently too severe for some peoples who had not come of age politically. Methods of corruption which created sinecures and softened the application of the laws might be favored by a majority, and the whole government might grow corrupt if that was the kind of government which the majority wanted.

All these defects of a corrupt democracy were prevalent in Italy by the close of World War I, and it was in Italy that disillusionment with the parliamentary system produced the first serious reaction. In 1922 the Italian people accepted the advent of a dictator, Benito Mussolini. Mussolini declared that the function of a government was not to mirror the multiple factions and clashing aims of a divided nation; the function of a government was to govern. The Italians, he warned, were weak because they lacked discipline and divided because they lacked leadership. It was their moral and historic duty to become strong, industrious, and self-sufficient, worthy inheritors of the imperial destiny of the Romans.

Benito Mussolini (1883–1945) was the son of a blacksmith who gained an education by his own efforts and first won attention as the editor of a socialist journal, *Avanti.* During World War I he forsook the Socialist Party and became strongly nationalistic, urging Italian participation in the conflict. Wounded in active service, he re-entered politics. His political acumen had convinced him that nationalism and socialism were the two most powerful trends of the age but that in conflict nationalism would prove stronger than socialism. He therefore planned to unite the elements in each which had the greatest popular appeal, and when he helped to organize a new political party after the war ended, he meditated calling it by some name that would suggest "nationalism" and "socialism" in conjunction. But as the older Socialist Party had repudiated him, he let his followers take the title *Fascisti* instead. Their aggressive bands, or *fasci di combattimento,* opened a violent campaign against socialist and communist groups, broke up their meetings, assaulted their leaders, and wrecked their headquarters. Pretending that the postwar labor strikes and discontent in Italy were leading the nation to communism, the Fascisti posed as saviors of society. The government and the police, they insisted, were too weak and timid to grapple with this communist threat. In the outcome, Mussolini's Black Shirts emerged from the confused struggle with increased strength and prestige. Scores were killed in the daily street fighting which broke out in almost every town, but the Fascists apparently had more courage and fewer scruples than their opponents and struck back more murderously. Their party, with headquarters at Milan, soon dominated northern Italy. By 1921 they had elected thirty-five deputies to the Italian parliament and in 1922, by a "March on Rome," they induced King Victor Emmanuel III to name Mussolini premier.

2. THE FASCIST POLITICAL SYSTEM

This seizure of power was not openly illegal. The Chamber of Deputies supported Mussolini's cabinet by a vote of 306 to 116 and a majority of the people appeared to welcome the Fascist "revolution" as a promise of firmer government and a stricter political morality. They hoped to see a strong, resolute leader bring prosperity to the country by an energetic and frankly nationalist policy, and Mussolini encouraged these hopes by dogmatic slogans such as "Political power creates wealth." It was comforting to the disappointed Italian masses to be assured that they were worthy of greatness, that they had earned greatness, and that their greatness had been betrayed only through weak leadership. Mussolini poured contempt upon the politicians who had taken the people into a war for which they were unprepared and a peace in which they were outwitted. In reality the Italian gains after World War I had not been negligible: Trentino, the south Tyrol, Gorizia, Trieste, Istria, Fiume, and the Dodecanese Islands. But the war costs were excessive for a poor nation, and the failure to acquire more African or Ottoman territory irked Italian pride. Under Fascist discipline, they were assured, their true greatness would be resurrected and the Mediterranean would be "our sea" as in Roman times. This program of expansion intensified the chauvinism of the people. They did not pause to ask how Italy, with severely limited resources, could carry the burden of such an imperial role. For over twenty years they were to follow blindly the exhortations of the new Caesar until his headstrong ambition drove the nation into a new world conflict which brought upon it the miseries of defeat, invasion, and civil war.

A significant and sinister defect of Fascism from its first years was its glorification of force and the brutal persecution to which the Black Shirt militia and security police subjected their opponents. By kidnapping, beating, dosing with castor oil, and sometimes by murder, the Fascists established a reputation for gangsterism which they never outlived. The most infamous example of their methods of intimidation occurred in 1924. Although they secured two-thirds of the popular vote in the elections of that year, victory did not make them generous towards the liberal and socialist minority groups. The opposition, however, was not yet wholly intimidated, and a socialist deputy, Giacomo Matteotti, denounced the Fascists with vigor, insisting that he could produce evidence which would convict some of the leaders of venality and violence. A few days after making these charges, Matteotti was kidnapped and murdered by Fascist partisans. This act of terrorism produced, as Mussolini admitted, "a profound moral oscillation" and led the opposition groups to withdraw from the parliament in protest. But the Fascists clung to power and survived the storm although it was common knowledge that high officials in the regime had approved the measures to silence Matteotti.

Mussolini frequently proclaimed his contempt for parliamentarism and for what he stigmatized as "plutodemocracy," but he hesitated to destroy entirely the organs of representative government. Instead, he brought them under his control or so weakened them that they lacked force enough to oppose "the Party." He left Victor Emmanuel on the throne although he would have preferred a republican state, and he took for himself the position of head of the government. The Senate, the members of which were appointed, was gradually packed with prominent citizens who favored his leadership. The Chamber of Deputies was rendered obedient by a new election law (1923) which reduced the numerous small parties and assured one-party dominance by decreeing that the party which led in the elections (provided it secured at least one-fourth of the ballots cast) would be allotted two-thirds of the seats in the chamber. With its official influence, ruthless methods, and strong organization the Fascist Party could hardly fail to win under such an arrangement. The parliament became a debating society which listened to eulogies of Mussolini and voted its appreciation, but it ceased to exercise any real influence over the ministers. The principle of cabinet responsibility and legislative representation had been nullified.

Mussolini was not satisfied when he had paralyzed parliamentary initiative and rendered the deputies of the nation impotent. He also destroyed what vigor and independence the council of ministers might have retained by assuming eight of the fifteen portfolios himself and he treated the ministers who served under him as secretaries of administrative departments rather than as executive officers. The real policy-making organ of the regime was a new creation, a Grand Council of some thirty members, but it was a body responsible in no direct manner to the king or to the people. The leading Fascist dignitaries who sat on the Grand Council might be considered the actual governing organ of the state, with Mussolini as chairman of the board. The state had become a dictatorship in fact and spirit even though the shells of parliamentary government, the cabinet, the Senate, and the Chamber of Deputies, continued to exist. These too, however, were further modified after 1928.

The rights and liberties of the citizen, which liberal laws and democratic government had been specially devised to protect, withered as the Fascist sun rose high. Freedom of speech became a mockery when an unguarded word might bring a visit from Fascist *squadristi*. Freedom of the press was revoked on the ground that the official censors knew best what news the people should hear. Workers lost the right to strike or to bargain collectively and businessmen found their transactions regulated by government ordinances and by tariff, currency, and priority rules. The economic problems which beset the people were not solved by Fascist methods, but this was not for lack of official interest. Though Mussolini denounced the communists for their heresy in stressing economic pressures as the dominant forces in society, he himself gave a major part of his time to the economic dilemma which faced the Italians. He had declared that political power would create wealth. He had been granted the power. And he had to meet the challenge of a paucity of resources.

3. THE FASCIST ECONOMIC PROGRAM

The most original contribution which the Fascists made to statecraft was the concept of the "Corporative State." Arguing that it was a violation of the integral unity of a nation to divide the country into electoral areas and that electing deputies to represent such districts intensified the spirit of localism in politics, Mussolini asserted that the true units of a modern nation ought to be not *regional* but *functional*. By this he meant that all the citizens who were dependent upon the same general field of activity — upon manufacture, for instance, or agriculture, or transportation — had more essential interests in common than all the families which dwelt in the same province or constituency. The Fascists therefore encouraged the formation of thirteen syndicates, corporate bodies established to regulate and to represent all branches of national activity from agriculture to the arts and learned professions. In 1929 these syndicates were instructed to submit eight hundred names to the Fascist Grand Council. This list, supplemented by two hundred names from other sources, was then reduced by the Council to four hundred, and these carefully selected members became the deputies designate for the next parliament. Those Italians who enjoyed the franchise were permitted to exercise it in a plebiscite, to approve or reject the prescribed list of four hundred names. Very few voters had the temerity to cast a negative ballot.

Although the new syndicates were nominally independent units, in practice they provided the machinery through which the head of the government planned to control production, prices, and working conditions. All labor unions had been dissolved, laborers had lost the right to strike, and many critics saw in Fascism merely the dictatorship of big business. But it was more than that, and the bankers and industrialists of Italy, who had applauded Mussolini's denunciation of communism, found that they as well as the workers had acquired a master. Industry and agriculture were regimented. Stern orders went forth from Il Duce's offices in the Palazzo Venezia at Rome to speed production, and the output of electric power, automobiles, steamships, silk, wheat, and other indices of economic activity rose rapidly. New roads, improved communications, impressive buildings, and grandiose public parades and party spectacles advertised the program to revive the nation's prosperity and prestige. A loan of $100,000,000 from New York bankers helped to stabilize the currency but the national credit remained precarious. The heavy outlay for armaments oppressed the taxpayers, and the rising population kept the problem of an adequate food supply acute. To increase the crops and encourage larger families at the same time the government offered rewards to farmers and to the parents of five or more children, a resort to state aid which did not relieve the taxpayers.

When the years of relative prosperity from 1922 to 1929 were followed by the world depression in the latter year, the Fascist boast that a corporative state could solve the crises which ruined millions in a democratic society was put to the test. The Italian treasury poured out credits, supported ailing industries, tightened the controls over the syndicates, subsidized programs of public works. By 1934 the syndicates had been reshaped into nine main departments of economic activity with over a thousand subsidiary guilds, combines, and labor units. At the head stood a National Council of Corporations of some eight hundred members which by 1936 supplanted the now powerless popular assembly, the Chamber of Deputies. Thus, under the stress of economic pressure and a world crisis, the relics of parliamentary government were further transformed and the corporative organization of society extended. But the results of this transition had still to be tested. The Italian people had little chance to judge the efficiency of the new system because public criticism was restricted, accurate information was so scarce that even government officials were unaware of the true strength of army divisions or the number of aircraft fit for active service, and the populace had to rest content with outbursts of oratory, vehement and vague, and official communiqués from the government press. Foreign observers were disposed to agree that Mussolini had infused new energy into the administration but they regarded his reorganization of the government as primarily a series of changes to consolidate his control. They questioned whether the new machinery or the new men had improved the position of Italy as a great power or solved the economic deficiencies which made imperialism an extravagance for Italy and a major war a desperate gamble.

Like earlier leaders, however, Mussolini found it expedient to divert the attention of the people to imperial objectives. The high cost of overseas conquests, which imposed a heavy burden upon rich and highly industrialized nations like the British, was ruinous for the Italians. But Mussolini insisted that will counted more than wealth and that Fascists must learn to live dangerously. His intervention with large military forces in Ethiopia, Spain, and Albania, ventures which are summarized elsewhere, cost Italy thousands of lives and billions of lire but brought no adequate advantage or economic return. Intervention in World War II (1940) on the side of the Germans, a course to which Mussolini committed the nation against the recommendations of his sanest advisers, brought Italy to defeat and dishonor and the dictator himself to death before an Italian firing squad in 1945. (See page 522.)

4. THE PAPACY

For almost sixty years, from 1870 to 1929, the official relations between the Italian government and the Vatican were interrupted. When forces of the newly unified Italian kingdom drove back the Papal Guard and breached the walls of Rome in 1870, Pope Pius IX withdrew to the Vatican. The occupation of the Papal States and the Eternal City deprived the papacy of its revenue from this patrimony and the pope was no longer free to exercise his responsibilities as head of an Italian principality. He declined, however, to condone the usurpation by accepting the compensation offered by the Italian government. The breach of relations between the papacy and the state continued when Leo XIII was elected in 1878, and dutiful Italian Catholics hesitated to accept office or even to vote for the usurping regime. Succeeding popes, Pius X (1903–1914), Benedict XV (1914–1922), and Pius XI (1922–1939) began their pontificates with the same consistent stand. In 1919, however, Benedict XV affirmed that Catholics might participate in Italian political life and a Catholic Party was formed and rapidly grew influential.

When the Fascists came into power in 1922 their arbitrary acts brought them into frequent conflict with the church. But there was a real desire on both sides to find a solution to the long disagreement, and in 1929 the Fascist state and the papacy reached an accord which was embodied in the Lateran treaty. A small area of about 109 acres in the heart of Rome was declared a sovereign state under the temporal authority of the pope. As compensation for the territory and revenue which had been taken by the Italian kingdom in 1860–1870, the Papacy accepted an indemnity of 1,750,000,000 lire, to be paid partly in bonds and partly in cash. This treaty was supplemented by a concordat to define the position of the church in the Italian state, but despite the care with which the stipulations were drawn all causes of friction were not ended. The educational policies of the government, the militaristic stand which it frequently assumed, and the theories of state supremacy advocated by many Fascist spokesmen drew repeated rebukes from the Vatican.

As head of a church which counted over 300,000,000 followers throughout the world, the pope was mindful of the conflicts that disturbed not only Italian society but peoples in all lands. The communications issued from the Vatican proved how carefully the social, political, economic, and spiritual ills which threatened the peace of the world had been analyzed there. The papal encyclicals and addresses discussed the errors of the time and the rivalries between classes and between nations as well as questions affecting the education of the young, public health and morals, and the condition of the laboring classes. In the encyclical *Rerum novarum* (1891) Leo XIII had enquired so understandingly into the causes of "the misery and wretchedness pressing so unjustly on the majority of the working class" that he was revered as "the workingman's pope." But he warned also that the relative rights of capital and labor were interdependent and difficult to separate or to define and he besought the workers to be on guard against agitators who exhorted them to violence. For neither violent revolt nor peaceful reform could accomplish permanent good unless it was inspired by sound principles. "If then a remedy is desired, let it be sought for in a restoration of sound doctrine, from which alone the preservation of order, and, as a consequence, the defense of true liberty can confidently be expected."

THE NATIONAL SOCIALIST REGIME
IN GERMANY

*The great masses of the people will more easily fall victim to a
great lie than a small one.*

ADOLF HITLER

I. THE ADVENT OF HITLER

THE German democratic republic, born in defeat in 1918–1919,
endured for fourteen years. It was burdened from the outset
with the stigma of surrender and with the dishonor of acknowledg-
ing German war guilt and signing away German territory. Few Germans became deeply devoted to its inglorious annals or regretted its
demise. In 1933 it was supplanted by the Third Reich, a proud and
forceful regime dominated by the National Socialist Party and by the
party leader (Führer), Adolf Hitler. Hitler boasted that his "New
Order" would last a thousand years but it had a shorter life than the
Weimar republic and it ended with his suicide in 1945. The meteoric
rise, the military triumphs, and the calamitous fall of Hitler's empire
was the most fateful drama of the second quarter of the twentieth
century.

Until 1930 Hitler's name was almost unknown even in Germany.
Born an Austrian citizen in 1889, the son of a customs official, he was
a moody and emotional child with artistic yearnings. In 1914 he vol-
unteered for service in the German army and survived the war as a
corporal. At once ambitious and introspective, he knew the bitterness
and frustration of the "little people" and it was in the beer halls and
lodging houses of Vienna and Munich that he first discovered his extraordinary talent. He had been born with the gift of oratory and he
learned how to rouse his depressed listeners to a pitch of hysterical
enthusiasm by his raucous tirades. Humiliation is the harsh stepmother
of ambition, and all Germany, frustrated and resentful, was a predes-

tined audience for his harangues. The audience, however, required over ten years of preparation before it was in the mood to accept Hitler. His early efforts as a political agitator were mere sound and fury. In 1923 he joined with the autocratic field marshal, Erich von Ludendorff, and others in organizing a futile revolt in Munich which was dubbed the "Beer Hall Putsch" by the contemptuous authorities who crushed it. Hitler was sentenced to five years' imprisonment but was released after less than one. While shut up he strung together his aims and ideas in *Mein Kampf (My Battle)*, a book which became a bible for his followers.

Like Mussolini in Italy, Hitler had divined the powerful appeal which lay in a blend of nationalist and socialist propaganda. He joined and soon became a leading spirit in a small group of agitators who called themselves the National Socialist German Workers Party, better known to history as the National Socialists or Nazis. The most dangerous element in the Nazi propaganda was its savage, insistent appeal to national pride. The Germans yearned more intensely than most of them realized to retrieve their lost prestige and vindicate themselves before the world. They believed that an injustice had been done them; that the legend of German war guilt was a hypocritical formula invented by the democracies to excuse Allied extortions and conquests. In dark hours even peaceful Germans doubted if they would ever receive fair treatment unless they rearmed and demanded it. The abortive Beer Hall Putsch was only one of several half-desperate reactions in 1923 to the arrogance of the French, who had marched into the Ruhr Valley to collect on defaulted reparations. With the Dawes Plan the following year and a slow return of German economic prosperity in the years 1924–1929, the fulminations of Hitler and other demagogues attracted less attention and the Nazi Party barely held together. But the economic depression of 1929 and the cancellation of further American loans produced an immediate effect in Germany. National indignation flamed up strongly, the spreading unemployment and hardship were blamed upon reparations, the ten-year-old Versailles *Diktat* became once more the charter of all German woes, and the National Socialist group in the Reichstag rose from 12 to 107 deputies in the election of 1930.

A wave of patriotic fervor was welding the German people into an embattled nation. The socialists still had 143 seats in the Reichstag, and the communists 77, but the defiant slogans of the Nazis were winning new supporters daily. In the presidential election of 1932 the aged Field Marshal Paul von Hindenburg was re-elected, but Hitler ran second and received over 11,000,000 votes. The Nazis were becoming so powerful and so ruthless that they intimidated the rival parties. They had built up a party organization which disposed of large "contributions" and they had become a state within the state through their troops and district leaders. Like the Italian Fascists they gathered their own uniformed police force and action squads to guard Nazi meetings, to break up counter demonstrations, and to extend the party organization and control. The individual liberty and freedom of speech assured by the Weimar constitution made it difficult for the nerveless government of the republic to check these developments.

Thus Hitler's ascent to power was marked by many incidents of violence, coercion, bloodshed, and buffoonery, some of which must forever remain obscure. By 1933 the Nazis were the most powerful party in the Reichstag, and Hindenburg appointed Hitler chancellor. But the Nazis were not ready to stop short with parliamentary control under the Weimar constitution; they wanted a new regime which would assure the dictatorship of the party and a division of the spoils of victory. Hitler's first act was to decree a new election. The Nazi Storm Troopers attacked opposing parties, broke up their meetings, and wrecked their headquarters and printing presses. A conveniently timed fire which destroyed the Reichstag building was immediately blamed upon the communists. Although the new election (March, 1933) gave the Nazis less than half the votes, they dissolved or absorbed the remaining parties and rushed through a bill granting Hitler dictatorial powers for four years.

A revolutionary government, or crisis regime, is always provisory. This is likely to make the men who head it nervous in the face of opposition and arbitrary in the use of their power. The ruthlessness with which Hitler was prepared to exercise his control was demonstrated to Germany and the world in 1934. In June he crushed an alleged plot against his regime by hundreds of summary executions, the victims being shot down without trial. A month later Hindenburg died and Hitler assumed the supreme executive power. The Weimar constitution of 1919 had ceased to have any meaning. The new government was endorsed by a popular plebiscite announced as 88 per cent favorable. There is no good reason to doubt that a majority of the German people were enthusiastically in favor of Hitler's rule. The quickened national pride, the promise of justice for the "little man," the program of public works, the reduction of unemployment, even the authoritarian spirit of the party and the revival of military uniforms and discipline were apparently welcome to most Germans. A mystical exaltation, a blind faith in the Führer and in the destiny of the race, seduced the people into a trance of irresponsibility in which they joyfully surrendered all vital decisions affecting their destiny to the chiefs of the Nazi hierarchy.

2. THE NAZI REVOLUTION

The triumph of the German National Socialists in 1933 dismayed and astonished people in the democratic countries, for it was a repudiation of popular government, a victory of totalitarian over liberal principles and ideals. The totalitarian ideal has been succinctly summarized as: "Everything for the State; nothing against the State; nothing outside the State." How profoundly this philosophy could transform every department of the national life the revolution in Germany soon demonstrated.

The National Socialist Party was declared to be the only official party; all others were dissolved and the formation of independent political groups was forbidden. As members of the Nazi Party had come to form a majority of the Reichstag and Nazis were assigned to all important posts in the cabinet and the administration, it became clear that in Germany, as in Italy and Russia, one party, a well disciplined minority group, was to rule. This arbitrary centralizing tendency also led Hitler to annul the relics of local independence and particularism which the German states still preserved. The Reichsrat, a body somewhat resembling the United States Senate, to which each of the seventeen component German states sent delegates, was abolished, and administrative officers (*Statthalter*) were appointed to govern each state under orders from Berlin. Thus Germany became a unitary national despotism rather than a federal union.

The personal liberty of the citizens was severely curtailed. Nothing illustrates more sharply the divergence between the liberal democratic state and the totalitarian state than the question of individual rights. Since the seventeenth century the idea had gained increasing acceptance in European society that the power of the government in the national states should be restricted in the interest of individual liberty. The totalitarian thinkers reversed this view and insisted that individual liberty must be restricted in the interest of the state. Under the Nazi regime the deciding principle in law was: What benefits the German nation? People's courts were set up to try all offenses against the nation. The vigilance of the police, the secrecy of the trials, and the severity of the sentences created a reign of terror against which few dared to protest because criticism was so easily represented as hostility to the party and the Leader. Those suspected of antisocial or of anti-Nazi activities might be arrested at any time without warning and transported to a concentration camp, a danger to which all citizens were exposed once the traditional legal safeguards of personal liberty had been abrogated. The civilized world was slow to learn and slower to comprehend the inhuman cruelty and systematic extermination practiced in the work camps, and the details which later became available appeared incredible. Throughout the twelve years of Nazi rule, and especially after the outbreak of World War II in 1939, victims who had incurred the ill will of the officials were worked, tortured, starved, poisoned, gassed, or strangled to death, not by the hundreds or by the thousands but by the millions.

The most tragic victims of this official terrorism were the 600,000 German Jews. Before 1933 the Nazis had made antisemitism an article of their creed but after Hitler came to power the persecution became official. Dismissed from all government services, driven out of business and professional life, deprived of the status of citizens, thousands of Jewish families abandoned their homes and property and fled from Germany. Others, unable to flee, became impoverished, and a large proportion, including young children, were herded to the concentration camps. The motives which inspired the Nazis thus to make antisemitism an official policy were a fusion of prejudice and calculation. They needed scapegoats on whom to lay the blame for anything that went wrong. They needed wealth and property to award to party members, and the Jews were active in German business and professional life. It was unwise to blame the French, the British, or even the Russian government too loudly for the defeat and impotence of Germany after 1918, but the Nazis could vent their fury by vague references to a conspiracy of world Jewry to defame and destroy the German race. Although the Jews of Germany had contributed their share to the military effort of 1914–1918, Hitler popularized the fantasy that the collapse of 1918 had come because Jews and communists spread defeatism, that the German people had not been vanquished in a fair fight but had been "stabbed in the back." Such propaganda inevitably marked the Jews and communists out for reprisals as German nationalism revived.

In fine, the Nazis rose to power as a party of protest. They were antiliberal, anticlerical, anticommunist, antisemite. They denounced the great banks and corporations which ruined the "little man" of business, the profiteers who had grown fat on war contracts and currency fluctuations, the alien immigrants who wished to intermarry and contaminate the strain of the "master race." When the Nazis won control, the full fury of this terrible, irrational, manufactured hate fell most forcibly upon the groups that were most recognizable, defenseless, and profitable to plunder. But Jews were by no means the only victims. If figures were available, they might show that ten people of other faiths died in the concentration camps for each Jew that perished there.

3. CONTROL OF THE NATIONAL ECONOMY

The National Socialists abandoned the liberal theories of laissez-faire economy and free business enterprise, substituting instead an intricate system of economic nationalism. The ideal which was held out to the people was *Autarchie* or economic self-sufficiency. Germans were exhorted to increase production and to renounce or find substitutes for foreign commodities which could not be produced at home. All foreign trade was regulated by export and import licenses. Gold and currency could not be taken out of the country nor foreign currency purchased except through official channels. Within the Reich strict rules for the allotment of steel, coal, electric power, petroleum, and other essentials of industry brought all manufacturing trusts under state supervision. As in Soviet Russia, where a state planning commission was co-ordinating all aspects of economic life, so in Germany a board of economic experts strove to make the nation strong and self-sufficient so that it might survive the strains of peace or war. In 1936 the Nazi economists introduced a Four-Year Plan to regulate all phases of economic life in the interests of *Autarchie*.

Unlike the Russian communists, however, the Nazis did not nationalize the land, organize state farms, or collectivize the major industries. On the contrary, the number of small, privately managed farms was increased, and peasant families were encouraged to settle on them as hereditary occupants. There was much exaltation of the mystic affinity of "blood and soil" and the vital relation between the soul of a people and the land they ploughed. But the practical effect of the Nazi agrarian decrees was to produce specific crops and tie the farmer to his task. By similar methods, the workers in the mines and factories were regimented and lost the privilege of striking or even

of changing their occupation at will. The employer became the
"leader" of the group he employed. His main responsibility was to
fill the quota which the government economists demanded of him. In
the first years of the Nazi Revolution the spur of national enthusiasm
and the stimulus of rearmament brought a swift rise in business activity and production, and Hitler was given credit for a program that
had conquered the depression.

There was some basis for this claim though it is questionable
whether the improvement in output could justly be credited to Hitler
or his preachments. Unemployment declined sharply in Germany
after 1932. A vast program of public works, roads, fortifications, military equipment, and, to a lesser extent, of consumers' goods, created
the appearance of unusual prosperity. But the national debt increased
rapidly, the currency was maintained by rigid "pegging," and the
armament outlay was underwritten by compulsory loans from the
people. These obligatory contributions to Nazi funds and charities,
the rising cost of living, and the state regulation of wages left the average German no better off than before. The employers were assured
a more adequate supply of man power, for no one was permitted to be
idle and no workdays were now lost through strikes or lockouts. Like
the workers, the employers found that they had forfeited their independence, they were heavily taxed, and they could not change their
formulas or expand their plants without official approval. Some of the
great financiers and industrialists, who had helped to finance Hitler's
rise, now found that they had become the prisoners of his success.

The dominant impulse in Hitler's complex character was the will
to power; he had no intention of becoming a tool of the German industrialists, the generals, or the Nazi inner circle. Although he was
prepared to reward the industrial magnates with government orders,
subsidies, and monopolies, he was not genuinely solicitous for the
material welfare or economic prospects of the German people or German business. His romantic and egocentric thoughts turned perpetually to new intrigues, to force and conquest, and to mastery over ever
larger bodies of men for the intoxication which cajoling and coercing
these millions brought him. Despite his talk of a Reich which would
endure for a thousand years his triumphs all had a quality of the the-
atrical, they were intense but insubstantial, they left him under an
added compulsion to surpass himself. These defects of his character
were communicated to the regime. It was more predatory than constructive; it ruined its enemies to enrich its adherents; it was under a

compulsion to expand, to feed on new converts, to transform neighbor states into prostrate provinces. The militant spirit of the National Socialist command did not evaporate when they reached the position of a governing clique in Germany; rather, from their new elevation they looked abroad for new areas and new adversaries.

From their first campaign speeches, the Nazis had protested that Germany was denied adequate "living space." Maps showing the wide areas under the British, French, and Soviet Russian flags, with the relatively minute territory controlled by Germany as a contrast, formed a telling item in the arsenal of propaganda. Hitler made envious references to the minerals of the Urals, the wheatfields of the Ukraine, and the oil wells of the Caucasus. Such greed for possessions and supplies suggest the material advantages which the Nazis anticipated from a war of conquest. The German factories after 1935 were purposely integrated for war production, the people were indoctrinated with the idea that Germany must take by force the areas and supplies to which the nation was entitled, and the army was organized for an aggressive strategy of lightning strokes or *Blitzkrieg*. Hermann Göring, second in command in the hierarchy and supervisor of the heavy industries, declared that the slogan of the German people must be "Guns before butter." The consequences of such preparations and such propaganda were a rapid rise in tension and the multiplication of international crises after 1935. "Germany," declared the British statesman Winston Churchill, "must soon either expand or explode."

4. THE REVIVAL OF MILITARISM

The peace terms imposed by the victorious Allies after 1918 stripped the Reich of defenses and arms, and so long as these terms remained in force the Germans lacked the capacity to launch an aggressive war. The Rhineland, the area nearest the French frontier, was demilitarized; the navy was reduced to a few ships; the army was limited to 100,000 men; the manufacture or maintenance of military aircraft was forbidden. Although some feeble efforts were made to evade these limitations (German pilots trained in engineless gliders and a few bands of military-minded youths drilled in secret) Germany remained a third class power in a military sense until after 1930. The fact that the Nazis were then able, in less than ten years, to make Germany the most powerful armed nation in the world showed their will, energy, and gift for organization. But these virtues would have wrought no miracle by themselves. It was possible for Germany to regain the military hegemony of Europe in a decade because Germany was the leading industrial state of the Continent. The steps in the transformation from a peace to a war footing were surprisingly logical once the plan to rearm had been set in motion. The only grave danger was that neighbor nations most directly threatened might unite for a "preventive war" before rearmament was sufficiently advanced to safeguard the Reich.

The Nazis had already violated the implicit terms of the Versailles treaty before they won power in 1933. Their Storm Troops, organized in military formations with weapons and uniforms, were a private army. In 1932 the wavering government of the Weimar Republic removed its ban against these units, a ban it had never seriously attempted to enforce. By the following year the Brown Shirt forces had expanded into a more or less organized militia of some 3,000,000 men. This army of the party was viewed with disfavor and apprehension by the officers of the small professional army who resisted suggestions that the two forces should be merged. In March, 1935, Hitler announced the reintroduction of compulsory military service, thus making all German youths of military age subject to regular army training.

At the same time (March, 1935) he denounced the Versailles treaty, declaring that the German people would no longer be bound by its humiliating limitations which had been imposed by force. Although the government leaders of Britain, France, and Italy took hurried counsel, none offered effective protest to the defiant action of the German chancellor. Hitler had calculated very astutely the differences of opinion between London and Paris and between Paris and Rome, and he did not fear that the powers would combine for joint action. To placate British alarm and alienate Britain from France, he agreed to a Naval Limitation Treaty (June, 1935) whereby German total naval tonnage was to be held to 35 per cent of that of the British Commonwealth. Eight months later, he made another sudden move in his program of rearmament. On March 7, 1936, he ordered German forces to reoccupy the demilitarized Rhineland. The French, British, and American forces which had kept a watch on the Rhine after World War I had been withdrawn since 1930, and once again Hitler's bold and defiant move to strengthen Germany for war met with no effective opposition.

With the formation of the Rome-Berlin Axis the following October the discomfiture of France was almost complete. If they acted in concert, Germany and Italy could attack the French Republic on two frontiers. Germany was rapidly constructing the most powerful air force in the world; her mechanized divisions were reported to possess unprecedented mobility and firing power; and Europe trembled once more before the threats of a warlord at Berlin. The outbreak of a civil war in Spain at the close of 1936 furnished an opportunity for German airmen and engineers to test out their new weapons by helping the insurgent forces. In 1938 the occupation of Austria was accomplished by German tank detachments which raced to Vienna in an unopposed invasion. The military balance had changed with almost bewildering rapidity and all the neighbors of the Reich were suddenly aware that Germany was armed and arrogant and that no fortifications could make a frontier invulnerable.

Once the Reich was rearmed and refortified, Hitler became more indifferent to foreign opinion. He was ready to risk war, he knew the British and French were desperately anxious to avoid it, and he used this knowledge to drive a ruthless bargain. In 1938, at Munich, he extorted cessions which ruined the Czechoslovakian Republic, ended the threat of the Czech armies, and brought the Czech armament factories and resources within his reach. The union of Italy and Germany in a full political and military alliance (May, 1939) gave Germany an ally for war, although that ally was the weakest of the great powers. More important was the negotiation of a commercial pact and a non-aggression treaty at Moscow which assured Russian neutrality (August 23, 1939). Hitler had now completed his political and military plans, and Germany was ready for a test of strength which, with or without war, might reverse the decision of World War I and make Germany supreme. One week after the conclusion of the Moscow accord World War II opened with the march of German armies into Poland. (See page 464.)

PART VIII

The Failure
of Collective Security

ECONOMIC INSECURITY
AND THE GREAT DEPRESSION, 1929—1933

. . . Mankind is tending more and more to regulate the whole of its social life . . .

KARL MANNHEIM

I. THE SENSE OF INSECURITY

AS noted in earlier chapters, there were serious strains and rifts in European society before 1914. The First World War grew out of these unresolved conflicts but the fighting ended no fundamental problem and intensified national antagonisms. As a result the European peoples gained no lasting sense of security from the peace settlement of 1919. Rather, in comparison with the years before 1914, the postwar era seemed threatening and chaotic, and men began to look back to the relative calm of the preceding century as to a golden yesterday. A mood of pessimism and cynicism, of fatalism and futility, spread through the Western world. The discontent and disillusionment, the fear and insecurity and mounting violence offered a marked contrast to the more orderly methods, the respect for legal forms, contracts, and treaties, which had distinguished the leading nations in the nineteenth century. Even the optimistic faith in progress which had inspired civilized peoples before 1914 had lost its earlier intensity. It is important to seek the causes, some of which have already been foreshadowed, which help to account for this change of temper in modern society.

The first unsettling factor to note was the rapid and irreversible increase in the number of city dwellers, especially the urban proletariat. Within half a century all the industrialized nations found that a city population had grown up within their borders which outmatched, outvoted, and outnumbered the once dominant rural and agricultural classes. In Britain, Germany, Belgium, France, the United States, and to a lesser degree in the remaining European countries, the generation which came of age about 1920 was a generation largely born and bred in the cities, shaped and dominated by city patterns and city ideals. The resulting change in the character of the average twentieth century citizen born after 1900 is not easy to analyze or to describe. Yet there was a change, a real and disturbing change, in the mentality and the expectations of this modern generation. It might, perhaps, be summed up by saying that the young people had more superficial self-confidence but less genuine self-reliance than their predecessors.

This was understandable. The sense of security which makes people feel habitually calm and at ease is based upon emotional rather than intellectual certainties. For millions of people the transition to city life tended to weaken the two most fundamental "frames" within which men had oriented themselves and learned to feel at home: the immemorial framework of the family group and the framework of the native village or community. City families were in general smaller than rural families and were often severed from the older generation. They lived in more transient fashion, in rented and often restricted quarters. They had fewer permanent possessions than rural families but more diverse interests. The individuals who composed a city family depended less on one another and less on their immediate neighbors than had been common in village communities. It has frequently been said that modern city dwellers are "rootless," and the charge is just in the sense that millions of city people feel no personal or intimate ties binding them to their block or precinct or at least no bonds comparable to those which attach a man to the fields he has ploughed for years or the villager to the church spire in the shade of which his ancestors are buried.

Children who grew up in a rural environment shared more intimately in family responsibilities, joined early in the common labors, and learned their capacity and their worth. But city children were often a financial burden throughout school years. As members of large classes and neighborhood groups they were submerged in numbers, and when they found work they were likely to pass their days at a mechanical routine with little chance to feel or express their individuality because, to the industry or corporation which they served, they were impersonal and replaceable automatons. Many large firms, recognizing these defects, sought to promote group activities among their employees, to enlist their loyalty by stressing the mutuality of the business relationship, and to reward their fidelity by the distribution of shares or bonuses. But the impersonality of modern business and industrial methods continued to frustrate the individual. In the city environment it was less easy for a human being to devolop those tendrils which unite him to his world and give him the sense of security which comes to those who are known and needed by their fellows. City adolescents reflected this difficulty in achieving emotional adjustment. They learned to be alert and brisk and knowing in manner but they often remained inwardly unsure. The strain and the dissatisfaction which made modern life a burden for millions led to an alarming increase in nervous and mental ailments.

To these psychological hazards of modern life there was added, especially after 1929, a deepening sense of economic insecurity. In earlier times, the man in business for himself, the farmer, carpenter, storekeeper, or general practitioner, did not worry about dismissal because he was his own employer. A poor crop or a business recession might mean some lean years but not sudden unemployment and imminent privation. The factory or office worker, however, who had nothing but his job, lived in fear that his job might fail. This fear lay behind the various government measures, adopted more and more widely in the twentieth century, which promised the working classes some form of insurance against the risks of sickness, accident, disability, and unemployment. The rise in savings accounts, insurance policies, and government social security funds all reflected the need of the workers to lay up some reserve against disaster.

Unfortunately, savings deposited with the banks or the government were not always safe. Bank failure, inflation, ruinous taxes, revolution, or war might destroy the financial security of a whole class or nation. World War I proved to millions of Europeans, who had been subsisting on fixed incomes or annuities, that currency could depreciate and prices soar. The German people learned the full tragedy of inflation after 1920 when their currency depreciated until it became literally worthless. Millions of families watched their wealth, insurance policies, mortgages, pensions, or investments turn to valueless paper. In France the franc lost four-fifths of its prewar value, falling from twenty cents to four. Finally, even the British pound, monetary unit of the world for a century, fluctuated and fell from the gold standard. The impact of these forfeitures shook the confidence of the disinherited classes. Throughout all the industrialized states many people found their jobs dependent upon vast economic forces they could not comprehend and their savings dependent upon financial fluctuations which they could not control. To the young who faced the world after 1920 the old and stable values which their parents had trusted seemed less sure. This was not their misconception; they were living in a disreputable age in which the honor of nations, the sanctity of contracts, and the equity promised by the law were often and brazenly betrayed. Such conditions breed fear even in nations which are spared them. The impoverished classes of central Europe, the fugitives from Russia who had been dispossessed by the revolution, the French families which had lost their men in the war and their savings in the peace, the British who were fighting to hold their threatened leadership in world trade, all felt the prevalent mood of economic insecurity.

A third factor in the general disquiet was the unhinging of international exchange rates. Here sharp national antagonisms added to the bitterness that is always incited by forfeited investments and repudiated debts. In the economic competition after 1920 few nations admitted themselves at fault but all accused their rivals of cheating. The Germans blamed the Treaty of Versailles and the Reparations Bill for the collapse of their currency. The French blamed the German failure to meet reparations payments in full for the fall of the franc. The British blamed a disordered world exchange for their dislocated trade and proposed a cancellation of war debts all around. When the United States, which would suffer the heaviest loss from such a course, declined the suggestion, all debtor states criticized the American government. In reality, the war debts and reparations quarrel was no more than a superficial issue in a much graver problem. World production, agricultural and industrial, had been speeded up and world population doubled in a century. But no adequate machinery had been developed to assure the industrialized countries an equitable share of raw materials or an equitable approach to world markets, with the result that the rival powers fought with tariffs and cartels and currency rules for the trade of a shrinking planet. Nor had any machinery been devised to assure an equitable distribution of wealth, and the maldistribution of purchasing power created needy and depressed classes and famine stricken peoples.

Before its first quarter had ended, the twentieth century revealed itself as a century of deeper violences and sharper vicissitudes than the nineteenth had been. The difference could not be blamed upon any check in material progress and prosperity. In spite of the loss and destruction of World War I the peoples of Europe in 1925 had higher living standards, greater wealth, and a longer life expectancy than they had ever known. But their mood, their methods of government, their political morality had declined since the halcyon years of the long peace, 1871–1914. This decline was to become much more apparent before the second quarter of the century ran its course.

If material prosperity and the progress of science could have assured a stable society, the United States should have held a secure and tranquil population. America led the world in the parade of inventions, discoveries, and technological achievements wherewith science has enriched the life of man. The years 1900–1940 brought a 73 per cent gain in the American population, multiplied 4000 automobiles into 4,000,000, equipped 23,000,000 homes in the land with electric light, popularized the motion picture and radio, developed the airplane and other mechanical wonders, and raised the standard of living, of leisure, of income, and of education to levels unimagined a few generations earlier.

Such achievements might well have filled the American people with a mood of sturdy self-confidence. They did breed a mood of confidence between 1920 and 1929, but it was not a sturdy mood. All the proof of power, the nimble machines which gave each American the services of a score of energy-slaves, failed to equip the citizens of the United States with the faith to meet an economic reverse with firmness. The stock market collapse of 1929 induced a panic which unsettled the nerves of the nation, and American despondency magnified the wave of depression already traversing the globe. If the American people could not have a resolute confidence in that machine age which had bestowed upon them its richest blessings, what confidence could less fortunate nations be expected to display?

2. THE GREAT DEPRESSION

When world trade declined suddenly after 1929, falling over 60 per cent in a few years, economists sought anxiously to analyze the causes of this depression. It seemed dangerous to proceed until business leaders and statesmen had learned how to avert further dislocations so shattering to international prosperity. When no simple or satisfactory explanation could be found and no expedients, however drastic, seemed to arrest the decline, the general disquietude increased. There was more grimness than humor in the reply offered by one economic expert when he was asked how long a business depression could last. The Roman Empire, he reminded his hearers, sank into a depression which lasted a thousand years. Western civilization was undoubtedly ailing but there was no good reason to imply, even allusively, that the malady was fatal. Its most disturbing manifestation was the sense of insecurity which gnawed at the hearts of people everywhere. In some countries of Europe it was to drive them to remedies more desperate than the disease.

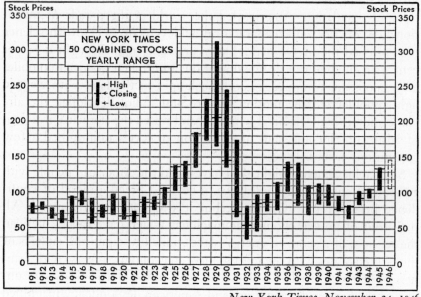

New York Times, November 24, 1946

STOCK QUOTATIONS, 1911–1946

When the first shock of the panic passed and people began to appraise the situation more calmly it became clear that the prosperity of the years before 1929 had been increasingly artificial. Greed for high profits had driven many industrialists to overexpand their plants and investments. Many nations, like the United States, eager to sell their excess manufactures abroad, had attempted at the same time to wall in the home market with tariffs and keep it for themselves. This endeavor to sell more than they bought led the American people to lend prospective purchasers the money wherewith they might buy goods "Made in U.S.A." Without such loans many foreigners could not have obtained the international exchange to pay for their purchases.

Investors with capital accumulating on their hands turned it over to investment brokers who advised them where they might obtain high returns. State governments, municipalities, and corporations which needed credit urgently offered the most tempting rates of interest. One field of rapid expansion was postwar Germany, and under the prevailing system of international credit the Germans by 1929 had borrowed $5,000,000,000 from their neighbors, in part to discharge reparations but also for the construction of new factories, workers' homes, superhighways, and other national improvements. The rapid expansion of business inspired by the necessity of replacing property destroyed in the First World War created a false impression of market demands and consumption in the decade 1919–1929. The sudden acceleration of business and the mounting paper profits of investors made millions greedy, and greed helped them to believe that the prosperity would prove permanent and the expansion of trade and manufacture would persist indefinitely. People did not ask themselves soberly whether the Germans, for example, would be able and willing to pay back their borrowings if their economy suffered a setback nor whether American firms could meet their overextended obligations if supply overtook demand and production slowed down instead of increasing yearly as calculated.

On the stock exchange the quotations on favored stocks doubled and sometimes doubled again. These runaway market quotations gave millions the illusion of wealth but real wealth had not increased at the rate which the climbing stock citations suggested. If all the stockholders and investors had sought to transmute their paper profits into tangible assets they would have found there was neither gold nor goods in existence to exchange for their supposed fortune. When this discrepancy became apparent to a growing number of investors and they began to convert their stocks into more real and substantial forms of wealth, values began to fall because there were more sellers than buyers. When stocks began to fall, investors all over the country tried to unload all at once and the fall became a plunge. Consumers who had thought themselves rich and spent accordingly suddenly ceased to buy. Mounting unemployment from business failures further curtailed the purchasing power of the home market, and production languished while the panic increased. Finally, when American investors no longer poured their money into foreign bonds with high interest rates, foreign firms were no longer able to obtain funds and canceled their orders for American goods. American business of course suffered an additional relapse from these delayed blows. In every country bound up with the economy of the Western world this chain of events was producing business dislocation and depression in varied forms but all increasingly acute.

Normal trade is exchange for mutual advantage. In their zeal for profit too many industrialists and investors had failed to consider sufficiently the one-sidedness of their transactions. While seeking opportunities for foreign expansion they had allowed their most important markets to contract. Thus in all countries agriculture lagged behind the general march towards prosperity and in America it was evident that the farmer's purchasing power was deficient because of his declining share of the national income. City workers, too, even the industrial workers whose efforts helped to produce the wealth of the machine age, found that their wages failed to overtake the rising cost of living. Accordingly the large agrarian and industrial classes, numerically the major market for the nation's mass output, could not absorb an adequate share of the goods their industry brought into existence. Yet even when they could not afford to pay for the commodities which they needed, wage earners were solicited through campaigns of high pressure advertising to buy on credit. This "time payment" program provided a further example of the insecure economy of the "boom" period. When depression struck the country and cut the national income in half, it left millions of puchasers burdened with monthly payments which they had assumed because they expected their incomes to soar instead of to sink.

The "prosperity" of the 1920's therefore concealed an ill-balanced give-and-take, a lopsided distribution of purchasing power. The machinery of production was going ahead full speed and industrial plants expanded. To feed men and machines the output of basic commodities — wheat, sugar, coffee, wool, rubber, tin — was also increasing swiftly. With improved machines and the rationalization of industry more automobiles, textiles, plastics, and electrical devices were produced yearly and produced at a profit. But this profit was not evenly distributed; in some fields the producers had a near-monopoly and held prices up through trusts or cartels. The ultimate effect of such artificial price levels was to deny the consumer manufactured wares he would gladly have bought at a lower cost. Thus many products of industry were too dear for wide mass consumption. But a second trend was also killing the mass market: machines were replacing men. In Europe industrial production continued to rise after 1926 but industrial employment fell. All over the world the workers, especially those who produced basic commodities, found prices rising faster than wages and they lost their purchasing power. Wheat growers, coffee planters, sheep raisers, mine workers, found that the world price for their basic commodity declined the more they produced of it.

By 1928 some commodity stockpiles (tin, for example) were literally a surplus on the market, and when prices collapsed in 1929 the crash was blamed in part upon such overproduction. Producers of basic commodities were urged to "manufacture a shortage" by restricting their output or, if necessary, by burning millions of pounds of coffee or bushels of wheat. Obviously something was out of gear in an economic system which required the use of such wasteful remedies. To speak of a surplus, of overproduction, of excess supplies of wheat or wool in a world where millions were hungry and ill-clothed, was illogical. It seemed apparent that the system of distribution, not the system of production, was at fault.

Many critics explained the depression by blaming it on "the fluctuations of the business cycle." This did not help very much because the business cycle itself was not clearly understood. In earlier centuries "good times" and "bad times" were commonly blamed upon some local development and a business depression attributed to a poor crop, a plague, or a destructive fire. The first "global" depression that may be readily distinguished was that of 1857. This followed the wide business expansion of the early 1850's; it revealed the "cyclical fluctuation" in all its phases — expansion, recession, contraction, and revival. Thereafter economic crises became more world embracing as global economy became more closely knit. The causes and control of depressions and the misery they brought to millions were studied with grave attention. For such crises were the darkest threat (war excepted) which democratic governments and the democratic way of life had to conquer.

The problem of business fluctuations proved so complex that no explanation offered a clear analysis or suggested a sure method of control. Theorists related them to the sun-spot cycle, to an excess of savings, to an excess of production, to greed for profits, to the progress of mechanical invention which substituted machines for men (technological unemployment), and to a myriad other causes. But no theory seemed clear or sufficient. The Great Depression spread panic among the peoples most affected because it implied that the forces shaping modern civilization were beyond man's control or comprehension. The economic cycle which ran from overexpansion to collapse, through reviving production to expansion, overproduction, and collapse again, ought to be harnessed and stabilized by foresight and careful planning. But in countries where free business enterprise was cherished the governments did not have the authority to enforce long-range economic aims. Furthermore, plans which miscarried might make a critical situation worse.

One form of government regulation of business undoubtedly helped to cripple European prosperity: this was selfish and intolerant nationalism. Obstructive tariffs were one sign of this national jealousy. A second was the attempt to monopolize markets through political and military pressure. After 1919, for example, France sought to win the trade of the Balkan states before Germany could recover from World War I. As Germany revived, the French first sought to stabilize economic conditions in Europe by a Pan-European Customs Union in which they might hold their own. The Germans countered with a plan for regional pacts and continued to press their economic drive. This rivalry between France and Germany led the statesmen and militarists to ignore normal trade tides and dam or divert them to national ends. A notable victim of the policy was the Austrian Republic which sought to join Germany in a customs union. French opposition helped to block this projected Austro-German economic accord, and Austrian credit, already precarious, collapsed with the failure of the *Kredit Anstalt*, a leading Austrian bank, in 1931. This clash of purposes illustrates the complexities of the international pattern. National and political antagonism often frustrated those statesmen and economists who had the vision and courage to attempt to cope with the economic confusion. The bank crisis in Vienna increased the panic throughout central Europe; German gold reserves were swiftly depleted; and British efforts to steady the international situation proved unavailing.

On June 20, 1931, President Herbert Hoover proposed a moratorium, a suspension of payments on intergovernmental debts for one year. This proposal included German reparations payments but the Germans were to devote the sums thus withheld to measures of economic recovery. But the world depression had grown too serious and involved for any simple remedy, and Hoover's suggestion likewise failed to arrest the decline. The spread of financial confusion, which diminished the flow of world trade upon which Great Britain depended for prosperity, forced the British government to abandon the gold standard in September, 1931. The pound sterling immediately fell 20 to 30 per cent in value. For the British this result was not entirely a loss, for their debts could now be paid in devaluated pounds and the reduction in wages made British manufactures relatively cheaper and therefore more welcome on the international market. Eighteen months later (April, 1933) the United States likewise abandoned the gold standard, although the major share of the world gold reserve was in this country. Thus the currencies of all the leading nations were unhinged from any fixed value and the unpredictable fluctuations of the dollar, pound, franc, mark, or lira added a further hazard to discourage businessmen from the risks of international commerce. Without fixed policies, respect for contracts, and a stable unit of money with which to reckon costs and prices, traders could not negotiate or bankers calculate the prospects of a project or the worth of securities.

All these factors, which were at once causes and effects, increased the disastrous fall in world commerce after 1929. For that year the total international trade within Europe exceeded $11,000,000,000 (1929 dollar value). Trade between European and non-European countries reached $15,000,000,000. Six years later foreign trade within Europe had shrunk to $4,000,000,000 (1929 dollar value), and European trade with the rest of the world to $5,000,000,000. A fall of two-thirds in the total of all international transactions could not fail to bring ruin or unemployment to millions. The economic prosperity of all the leading nations is very largely dependent upon the profits of manufacture, transportation, banking, and insurance and upon the dividends from money invested in these lucrative activities. But the depression had repercussions which struck at all classes, for with factories idle the output of the mines, the crops from the fields, and the cargoes from distant quarters of the earth all ceased to move.

In countries such as Germany and Italy, where the average income of the workers and their per capita wealth was about half that enjoyed by Englishmen or Frenchmen of equivalent station, the loss and hardship were naturally more pressing. Social unrest impelled all governments to experiment with panaceas which promised to bring temporary relief to a critical situation. The widespread suffering, the mood of bewilderment and anger that stirred the masses, and the demand from the destitute and the unemployed that their leaders find a remedy, must be constantly kept in mind by the student who wishes to understand this clamorous decade 1929–1939. The grandiose national programs, the inflation of the currencies, the mad chauvinism preached by European leaders, were in part dictated by the exigencies of the depression. It was almost inevitable that politicians who could not conquer the economic ills should distract the attention of discontented and angry electors by seeking some minority as a scapegoat for the general misery and by pointing abroad at some foreign rival as the cause of national frustration. It is important to note, too, that in countries which had no long discipline in the methods of democratic self-government, there was a general readiness to look to the government or to a strong and dictatorial leader for a solution to the crisis. In countries where democracy was more firmly rooted and free economic enterprise had flourished more sturdily the individual citizens recognized that recovery must depend very largely upon their own energy and their own constructive efforts.

3. PROGRAMS FOR ECONOMIC RECOVERY

None of the intergovernmental proposals to stimulate the return of prosperity by conferences, proclamations, cancellation or postponement of debt payments, or manipulation of currency rates produced the result desired. In every state, therefore, the leaders turned to measures which might aid in solving their local problems and bring about recuperation in their national economy. The world was too large and complex for legislators to prescribe a program for world recovery, even if they could have agreed upon one; and although the rapidity with which the depression had spread from continent to continent proved that all trading nations were interdependent, they were not co-operative but competitive in their policies. It was therefore of little use to plan measures or promulgate rules for international application, because no real agreement or control or enforcement was possible in a world where each nation-state might adopt a course which weakened its neighbors and nullified any general program for world recovery.

Nations which contained within their political frontiers the raw materials most vital for their economic well-being were fortunate. The United States possessed varied and abundant resources and the population formed a domestic market which could absorb the output of the mills and the crops of the farms. The British Empire-Commonwealth, with colonies and possessions and self-governing Dominions in every clime and continent, could likewise plan to revive its economic life within a framework of "imperial preference." Soviet Russia, where all foreign trade was a monopoly of the state, had its own economic program, its own vast resources, and its own industrial, agrarian, and social needs to satisfy. Such states, especially the United States and Russia, might restore order within their own borders and meet their own needs even if the rest of the world drifted into economic anarchy. But many countries were largely dependent upon one or two products which they must sell in the world market, on coffee or tin or nitrates which they produced in abundance but could not consume themselves. Even leading European states, such as Italy, might be deficient in many resources, coal, oil, and even wheat. For industrialized states, such as Germany and Japan, which had highly developed manufactures to produce and sell, the dislocation of trade and the division of the world into jealously guarded preserves caused increasing difficulty. The ingenuity of their chemists might produce synthetic substitutes for some of the raw materials which they could no longer import. But unless they could achieve complete self-sufficiency (and very few countries could find all the commodities needed within their borders) these states had to export in order to pay for imports, and they could not export to areas which some other power had sealed against them by raising an insurmountable tariff wall.

When their attempts at economic penetration were frustrated, businessmen could hardly fail to remind themselves that the situation might be improved if their government could secure control over the area they desired to exploit. Nations which lacked large colonial empires were easily persuaded that this lack exposed them to undue restrictions and hardships. In Rome, Berlin, and Tokyo the industrialists, the statesmen, and the militarists all recognized that a war of conquest might offer the most obvious solution to their immediate problems. That such a program might prove costly and tragic in its ultimate effects they understood; but they were realists, the pressure of events and the clamor of the people compelled them to offer some positive program, and they craved power. A bold armament campaign might mean increased taxes but it also meant that the government would have large sums of money to spend. Expanded orders for weapons and equipment would assure activity in the heavy industries. By calling additional classes of conscripts for army training, the government could reduce unemployment and provide itself with trained and obedient soldiers who would break a strike or repress internal disorders. Whether a war came or not, military preparedness was the most persuasive argument a dominant party or dictatorial clique could invoke to justify the arbitrary acts, extraordinary expenditures, and illegal usurpation of power practiced by all the totalitarian dictatorships.

It was recognized by thoughtful men everywhere that the "planned recovery" instituted by the German, Japanese, and Italian governments as a means of escaping from the depression was a threat to peace. The existence of a powerful army is in itself a powerful argument for using it. Armament programs, moreover, are always competitive, and even in the less militaristic countries some part of the revenues voted for economic recovery was turned to increased production of arms. As unemployment declined and armaments mounted, it began to seem as if preparation for war was the most certain cure for an economic depression. This grim enigma led one writer to ask the disturbing question: "Is modern industry, then, a sick giant which can rouse itself only to kill?"

THE RESORT TO AGGRESSION:
CHINA, ETHIOPIA, SPAIN, 1933—1936

. . . It is clear that the Disarmament Conference will not fulfill what was its sole object, namely, general disarmament . . .
The German Government is accordingly compelled to leave the Disarmament Conference.

BARON VON NEURATH, GERMAN MINISTER
FOR FOREIGN AFFAIRS (OCTOBER 14, 1933)

1. REARMAMENT

THE preceding chapter described how the leading powers, emerging from the debilitating effects of the world-wide depression, sought individually to mend their national economies. In every state expenditures for national defense played some part in the official plans to revive ailing industries. The years after 1933 brought a universal restoration of militarism, and the armament race was soon more desperate and costly than that which had preceded the outbreak of World War I in 1914. Two motives have been stressed as hastening this fateful development: first, the need to stimulate business and reduce unemployment, if necessary by placing large government orders for weapons and war material; and second, the belief of chauvinists and expansionists that the possession of military, naval, and air power would win advantages and secure spheres of influence for a vigorous nation and enable it to expand.

It will be recalled that the League of Nations was empowered to invite proposals which might lead to a measure of general disarmament. The failure to disarm or to limit armed forces by general agreement after World War I must be attributed to the persistence of international distrust. No nation was willing to reduce its strength in really substantial fashion. The proposals submitted in discussion were always formulated in such a way that they would leave the nation sponsoring them no weaker, relatively, than it had been. This was understandable and logical. The men at the head of a modern state, and especially the naval and military experts whom they consult on questions of national security, have the defense of the state as their highest responsibility. They cannot dutifully approve a step which may expose to increased danger of attack and invasion the nation they are appointed to defend. It is possible, of course, in countries where a cabinet of civilians shapes the national policy that the military and naval advisers may be overruled and the armed forces reduced despite their protest. This is less likely to occur in a country where the general staff dominates the civilian government, a fact which explains why proposals for mutual disarmament made to a government in which the military men are in control have little chance of acceptance.

In war, deception is a primary element of strategy, and in preparing for war concealment is a customary expedient. This applies not only to secret weapons but to the size and nature of the armed forces. All nations fear that their potential enemies may be stronger than they seem and that their acknowledged forces are only a screen for much larger reserves. Armed forces vary in training and quality, and it is easy to deceive a neighbor and to disguise the degree of a nation's military preparation. A sports association or shooting club may train its members in route marches and rifle practice. A flying club, such as young Germans organized for glider experiments, may train war pilots. New automobile highways and railway lines may be constructed to accord with plans secretly approved by the War Department. In industrial plants the possibilities for co-ordinating peace and war production are unlimited. Machines for making tin cans may be set to produce shell cases; bombs and baby carriages may be manufactured with equal ease; standardized alarm clocks are timing mechanisms; lenses and telescopes make range finders; nitrates for fertilizers or for explosives may come from the same chemical plants. The one obvious fact which cannot be disguised or ignored, however, is the industrialization of modern warfare. Without factories to supply them, men cannot fight a major campaign; with adequate factories to supply them, men can be equipped to take the field in a few months.

Thus the military strength of an industrial nation is very difficult to gauge or limit. On the other hand, the regulation of naval armaments can be much more easily achieved, for a battleship takes years to build, it cannot be disguised, and it has no peacetime purpose. Because of these facts and because many experts began to question the value of large battleships in an age of air power, a measure of naval limitation was attained after World War I. The Washington Naval Treaty of 1922 inaugurated a ten-year holiday in the construction of capital ships, and this provision was later extended to 1936. But an attempt made in 1930 to induce the five leading naval powers, Great Britain, the United States, Japan, France, and Italy, to limit their categories of cruisers, destroyers, and submarines brought no general agreement. The French feared to weaken their communications with North Africa, and they refused to accept parity with Italy because they had Atlantic and North Sea ports as well as a Mediterranean coastline to defend. The British, burdened by taxes for the support of the unemployed and weakened by loss of trade, agreed reluctantly to reduce their estimated needs in cruisers and destroyers, and Japan and the United States likewise accepted a limited program of construction. This reduction partly explains why, when war came after 1939, the British were to find themselves desperately short of armed vessels to escort their merchant convoys. The great age of British naval supremacy, when the Royal Navy was equal to any two other fleets in the world, had passed. Yet it is not certain that economic pressure really compelled the reduction in strength which the British accepted, and it is not easy to judge whether this measure of disarmament helped the cause of peace. The candid acknowledgment from London that Britain was limiting her first line of defense left the Japanese more powerful in the Pacific and caused Italy to grow more truculent in the Mediterranean Sea. The Germans likewise speeded up their naval program in defiance of the restrictions laid upon them by the Versailles treaty.

By 1933, however, the Versailles treaty had become almost a dead letter and a new pattern of power was taking shape. The Anglo-French victory in 1918 had made Britain relatively secure at sea and the French army dominant in Europe. Both states therefore sought to limit armaments at that level and preserve a pattern of power which confirmed their leadership. The pattern endured about ten years. When the Germans protested that only the defeated nations had disarmed and demanded that France and her allies reduce their military forces in some equivalent manner, the refusal of the French made them seem arrogant and militaristic. The Germans pressed their advantage, urging that either France must disarm or Germany must be permitted to rearm. A world conference on disarmament, finally summoned by the League of Nations in 1932, accomplished nothing effective. In the midst of the great economic depression the burden of expenditure for defense seemed to most nations more insupportable than ever, but although the conference prolonged its meetings into the following year no agreement resulted. In October, 1933, Adolf Hitler, who had become chancellor of the Third Reich the previous January, recalled the German delegates from the conference. The attempt to limit armaments by international agreement had failed. The world armament bill was already one-third higher than it had been in 1914, and for the next six years it was to rise inexorably until it burst into the crescendo of World War II.

Collective security had failed. For Hitler not only recalled the German delegation from the Disarmament Conference, he announced that Germany was leaving the League of Nations. Two years later he proclaimed openly that Germany had repudiated the Versailles treaty and was prepared to take her place among the world powers on equal terms. In Italy the Fascist Duce, Benito Mussolini, urged his legions to prepare for conquests which would make the modern Italian Empire a worthy successor of the ancient Roman imperium. In Japan the imperialists were planning a "New Order" in Asia. In Europe, Africa, and Asia, the weaker nations, exposed and vulnerable, looked to Geneva for assurance. The League of Nations was to face its final tests and its final humiliations.

2. THE MARCH OF AGGRESSION: CHINA

The argument urged by many pacifists, that armaments did not pay, seemed to be belied by the success of the more aggressive powers, especially after 1931. In the Far East Japan demonstrated to the world that a weaker neighbor might be invaded with impunity and that conquests could be made a source of profit. The motives which inspired the military intervention in Manchuria have been noted already (see p. 364). After September, 1931, Japanese troops moved deeper and deeper into this province, widening the area of conquest, until in 1932 the militarists at Tokyo judged the moment ripe to set up a puppet government and proclaim the "independent" state of Manchukuo. Japanese advisers controlled all important activities of the new regime and Japan established a firm protectorate over the country. From this base the Japanese armies continued their penetration southward, with the evident intention of detaching further Chinese provinces from the rule of the republican government at Nanking.

For the weak and defenseless nations of the world the fate of China provided a grim warning. China was a member of the League and had a clear case. If the sanctity of treaties and the principles of collective security were worth anything, China should have been safe from attack. The Nine Power treaty of 1922, which had been ratified by Japan and eight other nations, guaranteed the territorial integrity and the political independence of the Chinese Republic. In January, 1932, the United States secretary of state notified all signatories of the Nine Power pact that any change of status brought about by armed force and in defiance of existing treaties would not be recognized by the United States. The British government, however, failed to support the American stand promptly and vigorously, and the Japanese were not deterred. The Chinese could offer no strong military opposition but they proclaimed a boycott of Japanese merchandise which caused a fall in imports and a loss to Japanese manufacturers. The Japanese retaliated by a destructive bombardment of Shanghai and landed troops there to occupy the port. On the plea that Japan had "resorted to war" the Chinese government appealed formally to the League of Nations and invited the League Council to review the dispute.

The League dispatched a commission to investigate the causes of the Sino-Japanese clash, but even the presence of officials from Geneva did not halt the desultory fighting in Manchuria and North China. Unfortunately neither the United States nor the Soviet Union was a member of the League, a lack which limited the effectiveness of any policy which the League might adopt. Even Great Britain did not offer strong or consistent support to the Chinese plea for aid. But among many of the minor peoples sentiment ran so strongly in favor of China, and Japanese arrogance was so uncompromising, that the Council adopted the Lytton Report which cautiously criticized the Japanese for their aggressive tactics but recommended a settlement which would have left Japanese influence supreme in the disputed area. The Chinese, losing hope that the League would aid them in any effective manner, made the best they could of a confusing situation and left the Japanese in possession of most of the territory north of the Great Wall. It was evident that the League had suffered one more defeat. The Japanese government dealt it still another by announcing its intention to resign in 1933. In carrying out this decision, the Japanese did not offer to return the Pacific islands which they had received in 1919 under mandate from the League. No one seriously expected that they would do so for all the powers had transformed their mandates into virtual protectorates by that time.

It was still possible for friendly powers to aid China indirectly with loans, supplies, and ammunition if they had the will to do so. But here likewise the almost hopeless inferiority of a weaker state was made clear. With a pretense of scrupulous neutrality, the British government announced that it would not permit British firms to supply arms to either Japan or China, an embargo which embarrassed the Japanese very little because they had the ships to import and the factories to construct implements of war whereas the Chinese were almost wholly dependent upon the arms they could purchase abroad. Lacking large modern industrial plants and deprived of the mines of Manchuria, the Chinese could not hope to equip an army that might match the well trained and well armed Japanese divisions. The Chinese suffered a further handicap in that the Japanese navy could enforce an unofficial blockade of all Chinese ports when it would but the Chinese had no battleships to halt the flow of scrap iron from the United States which helped feed the Japanese armament works. As the peoples of the world observed the unequal struggle waged by the Chinese, their faith in the League as an instrument of international justice fell still lower. The Chinese delegate at Geneva reminded the other League members that China had asked repeatedly for the protection promised it under the Covenant, and concluded with the grave warning that "the absence of any effective action by the League had encouraged those who all along had been proclaiming the belief that might is right." Successful aggression in one part of the world was certain to encourage attempts at aggression elsewhere, and the failure to halt the Japanese in the early stages of their advance into China would persuade them that all China would soon be theirs.

Such was, indeed, the conclusion which the Japanese leaders reached by 1933. Once they were firmly installed in Manchukuo their agents began to expel the personnel, capital, and influence of all European groups and to replace or confiscate foreign investments for the benefit of Japanese business firms. Military conquest and political protection were only stages of consolidation whereby their economic hegemony could be rendered secure. After numerous "incidents" and considerable friction the Russian Soviet government was persuaded to sell its half share in the Chinese Eastern Railway to the new state of Manchukuo, and by 1936 the Japanese had won a position of almost exclusive mastery over an area of North China twice the size of Texas, with a population of 40,000,000. Such rapid penetration and assimilation of new provinces made it seem a fair surmise that they would be able to extend their control over the remainder of the country within a few years and make it the central portion of their "Co-prosperity Sphere," as they liked to style their proposed Asiatic empire.

In execution, however, their plan encountered checks which slowed it down and ultimately reversed it. For ten years after 1931 their armies in China waged successive campaigns until they had subdued ten provinces and brought the four largest cities under their rule. As in Manchuria, they attempted to mask their direction of affairs. After Nanking, the Chinese capital, fell to their armies they established a puppet "Chinese" government. But the legitimate government moved to Chungking and kept up a heroic resistance. With the outbreak of World War II in 1939 the Chinese struggle for survival was merged into the larger global conflict. The history of the Sino-Japanese War after 1939 will therefore be described in a later chapter where it forms part of the Japanese bid for hegemony in the western Pacific, a gigantic gamble which culminated and collapsed between 1941 and 1945. (See pages 529–539.)

3. THE MARCH OF AGGRESSION: ETHIOPIA

It is not easy for the student of history to recapture the lost mood of millions of peace-lovers who saw the steady drift towards a general war after 1933 but were powerless to check it. The fiasco of the Disarmament Conference and the failure to halt Japanese aggression in China excited earnest discussion and the governments of the leading nations were embarrassed by a wave of sharp criticism. There was, however, a deep irony in the international situation which pacifists did not readily appreciate, for the more frankly a people admitted its devotion to peace the more surely an aggressive nation might hope to extort blackmail by the threat of war. In 1934–1935, for instance, a "peace ballot" was circulated in Great Britain as an unofficial test of public opinion. Nearly 12,000,000 citizens voted. Nine out of ten approved of active participation in the League of Nations, favored the reduction of armaments, and endorsed economic pressure against aggressor states. Only seven in ten, however, supported the use of military measures against an aggressor. Although the British cabinet and parliament weighed the results of this ballot thoughtfully, it is not easy to judge how strongly the vote may have influenced British foreign policy. Some critics insisted that it advertised the divided hopes and wishful thinking of the democratic peoples, but in truth their hopes and aims were less divided than they seemed. In a world in which military aggression still occurred, civilized people were seeking to mobilize public opinion against it and to find effective measures short of war that would deter a government from warlike actions. Nevertheless the fact that the British people so clearly wished to avoid war encouraged militarists in Germany, Italy, and Japan to disregard and even to defy British opposition.

The year 1935–1936 brought further reverses to the League which practically ended its prestige and usefulness as an instrument for collective security. The new aggressor and trouble maker was the Italian Fascist government. The Italians had long been dissatisfied with their modest colonial empire and envious of the larger and more profitable dominions ruled by Britain and France. Since the later nineteenth century they had regarded Ethiopia (Abyssinia) as an area of African territory reserved for Italian exploitation, but their attempt to conquer it had met with military defeat in 1896. Ethiopia survived into the twentieth century as an autonomous state under an hereditary monarch and in 1923 was admitted to the League of Nations. As no other region of Africa remained free of European domination the Italian government waited for a favorable opportunity to undertake its conquest. From 1932 onwards it was commonly known that plans for an Ethiopian war had been drawn up by the Italian high command. In 1934 the predictable "border incidents" developed at points where Italian Eritrea and Somaliland joined the Ethiopian frontier. It was evident that Italy was preparing excuses which might serve when the moment came for armed intervention. In January, 1935, the Ethiopian government appealed to the League of Nations. The League was solicited to use its "friendly right" of enquiry to investigate the causes of disagreement which threatened to involve two members, Italy and Ethiopia, in hostilities. The League noted the appeal but postponed action on it.

In March Ethiopia appealed a second time, the delegates citing Article 15 of the League Covenant which prescribed the course to be adopted when peace was directly threatened. Once more the League delayed action. The German government had just announced the reintroduction of military conscription, forbidden them by the Treaty of Versailles, and the European statesmen were preoccupied with this new step towards war. So the months passed and a third and a fourth appeal fell upon deaf ears, while the Italians completed their preparations and opened the fighting with a large-scale invasion of Ethiopia. When thus directly challenged, the League voted that sanctions must be applied to restrain the attack. Only economic sanctions were invoked, however. Oil, the most indispensable article needed by the Italian war machine, was not placed upon the embargo list nor was the Italian line of communications through the Suez Canal severed. Thus, although they suffered some hardship from the restriction of imports, the Italians were able to continue the war. They entered the Ethiopian capital in May, 1935. Thereafter resistance rapidly collapsed. An aggressive military policy had succeeded once again.

4. THE MARCH OF AGGRESSION: SPAIN

The tragedy of China and the assault on Ethiopia befell countries outside the limits of Europe. The Western nations might read about, discuss, and deprecate these events, but most of them, however genuine their concern, considered China and Ethiopia as remote, half-civilized countries where disorder and warfare were perhaps inevitable. But with the year 1936 war came to a European state, war in its most desperate and corrosive form, between people of the same speech and blood. The civil conflict which flamed up in Spain was too close to be ignored and its horrors were magnified by the foreign contingents which joined the opposing armies.

Spanish society had been disordered and Spanish economy moribund before 1914. The First World War brought a measure of prosperity, for the warring powers needed Spanish minerals and raw products; but after 1919 this trade languished. The heavy taxes, the general incompetence of the administration, and the archaic methods of holding and working the land inspired deep discontent. Revolution was averted from year to year by every expedient known to harassed monarchs, but in 1931 a swift upheaval finally unseated Alfonso XIII and replaced the ancient Spanish monarchy by a republic. For five years the new regime strove to extend reforms, distributing the land among the peasants and broadening the basis of education and political liberty. The Spanish people, however, were tragically divided between the old way and the new. Pride, passion, and the hardy individualism characteristic of the Iberian native stock made it difficult to mold society to a disputed pattern. The anticlerical policies proclaimed by the republicans profoundly disturbed millions of believers, for Spain was a country in which the Catholic faith was firmly rooted.

On winning power in 1931 the republicans adopted a new constitution which provided for a unicameral parliament elected by universal suffrage, and a cabinet responsible to the parliament. Decrees proclaiming the separation of church and state, confiscation of church property for national purposes, and secularization of the schools, advertised the anticlerical spirit of the government. Additional measures were voted but not firmly enforced, aiming at the division of large estates among the landless farmers and the nationalization of public utilities.

From the first, however, the republicans were confused and divided by contradictions in their policies and conflicts within their ranks. Some of them were thinking of a revolution similar to the French Revolution of 1789, a series of reforms which would destroy the relics of feudal land tenure, create a class of free tenant farmers, liberate the middle class and encourage business initiative by intelligent legislation, and strip the church and the monastic orders of their wealth and influence. But the Spanish revolt of 1931 was motivated by modern trends as well as by historic traditions. In Barcelona and other industrialized cities a relatively small but well organized body of workers had formed labor unions and studied the writings of Karl Marx. They regarded themselves as brothers-in-arms with the Russian communists, heralds of the latest revolution, which was to establish the classless society in all countries.

The French Revolution had been a bourgeois struggle for power whereas the Russian Revolution was a proletarian struggle for power. Thus eighteenth and twentieth century ideals confused the Spaniards and merged incomprehensively in a pattern of violence. Few foreigners understood the deep issues in dispute. Fewer still were familiar with the fierce regional pride of the Spaniards, many of whom had never renounced their ancient provincial liberties and sense of local independence. Differences of dialect, dress, and custom still disposed millions of the Iberian peoples to think of themselves first as Basques or Catalans and only secondly as Spaniards. Spain was not in the twentieth century a homogeneous nation with one speech, one uniform set of laws, one system of education, such as Britain, France, and Germany had been for generations. In Spain separatism revived at critical moments.

A civil war is always a national tragedy; but when issues are deeply confused and deliberately misrepresented, the tragedy is certain to grow more bitter. Without foreign interference the Spaniards might possibly have worked out a compromise solution and erected a stable government. But a divided country is always a weakened country, and the European powers, already preparing for a general war, were jealous and fearful. Control of Spanish mines, harbors, and airfields was a tempting prize, for Spain would make a useful ally in a European war. The military leaders at Rome and Berlin, who were knitting the Italo-German Pact of Steel (the "Axis" of 1936), appreciated the value of Spain. If they helped to set up a regime there which would be indebted to Germany and Italy for support, they would have won an initial move in the far-reaching strategy of conquest meditated by the Führer and his staff.

Many Spanish republicans, by 1936, while still loyal to the Revolution, were disappointed by the vicissitudes of policy and the divided aims of their leaders. On the other hand, many wealthy landowners and capitalists and many army officers were deeply resentful of the republican program and ready to support a move to restore the monarchy. With German and Italian factories ready to supply guns and planes to these reactionaries it was easy for them to open a sudden attack in July, 1936, which threw the republican regime on the defensive. Assuming the title of Nationalists, the insurgents named General Francisco Franco "Chief of the Spanish State" and pressed a fierce and pitiless attack upon the key centers of republican resistance. Germany and Italy promptly recognized Franco's government; Britain and France sponsored a policy of nonintervention and refused to authorize aid to either side; and Soviet Russia shipped food and arms to the republicans when possible. With a strong Spanish force, some Moorish troops from Morocco, 100,000 Italian soldiers, and German technical advisers and airmen, Franco won the advantage at the cost of bitter and prolonged fighting. When his forces captured Barcelona in January, 1939, Britain and France reluctantly recognized his government, and the fall of Madrid a month later ended the Spanish Republic. The civil war had been waged with a relentlessness and ferocity which appalled civilized peoples. It cost 700,000 lives, caused incalculable property damage, and left millions ruined and hundreds of thousands in exile or in Franco's concentration camps. The national life of the Spanish people was poisoned, and the memory of the countless betrayals, reprisals, and assassinations was a heritage to darken the years.

Once again the pleas of the pacifists and the paper projects of fact-finding commissions had been mocked by the realistic aggressors who were ready for war and not afraid to risk it. The democratic powers had sought to isolate the struggle, but the Anglo-French policy of nonintervention had broken down and the success of Franco and the

Nationalists was celebrated in Rome and Berlin as a victory for the Axis. The well-timed strategy whereby Rome and Berlin alternated their moves, so that the attention of their opponents might be confused and divided, was producing dramatic successes. The Italian dictator, Benito Mussolini, tacitly abandoned Austria to German designs and in return the German government recognized the Italian claim to Ethiopia. By the close of 1936 the Rome-Berlin Axis had come into effective play, and Germany and Japan had likewise concluded an agreement for mutual accord. By 1937 the three militant and authoritarian states, Germany, Italy, and Japan, were linked for the promotion of their varied aims and common advantage.

The only choice left to the democratic powers appeared to be for them to draw together likewise, arm themselves rapidly, and oppose force with force. The world had seen the futility of protests that were not backed up by guns and the willingness to use them. China, Ethiopia, and Spain were proof that aggressive governments which did not fear public criticism or diplomatic rebukes, could and would ignore the protests of irresolute and pacifistic nations. Yet the peaceful peoples still sought to evade this truth, and their leaders, when they proposed appropriations for increased armaments, were defied by complacent legislators immersed in local affairs. Each successive crisis excited a momentary apprehension, a flurry of suggestions, and a stiffening of mind among the democratic nations. Then, as the tension eased, the peoples strove to ignore recent implications and reverted to more optimistic hopes. Throughout the fateful years after 1933 Hitler's cynical assertion that it was difficult to deceive people, but easy to help them deceive themselves, received almost daily confirmation. Faith in the possibility of achieving collective security through honest and patient diplomacy, and hope for the ultimate triumph of right reason, persisted in millions of hearts until the last hours of the peace.

THE FAILURE OF APPEASEMENT: AUSTRIA

ALBANIA, CZECHOSLOVAKIA, 1936–1939

"I believe it is peace for our time."

NEVILLE CHAMBERLAIN, PRIME MINISTER
OF GREAT BRITAIN, SEPTEMBER 30, 1938

I. FORGING THE WEAPONS

AFTER 1935 the armed threat offered by the totalitarian powers
was the dominant force shaping European history. By the end of
that year the German government had reintroduced conscription,
marched troops into the demilitarized Rhineland zone, and announced
that the restrictions on German armed forces imposed by the Versailles *Diktat* were at an end. It was known that the Germans were
creating the most powerful air force in the world and that they had
hundreds of thousands of men at work constructing a defensive line
along the Franco-German frontier. German industry had been co-
ordinated for the production of arms and German economy directed
towards the accumulation of reserves and imports which would enable the nation to survive a naval blockade.

Aware of these warlike preparations, many realistic observers in
Britain and France urged the need for an equally speedy rearmament
by the democratic nations. But the population and the politicians in
power at London and Paris remained divided in mind and aim.
Throughout these years, a French writer protested bitterly, France
had a single aim (security) but a score of cabinets, each of which had
a separate formula for attaining that aim, while Great Britain throughout the same years had a single government but appeared to have a
score of contradictory policies all operative at once. Such comments
merely emphasize the truth that the governments in the democracies
reflected the sad indecision of the people, who were ready to tem-

porize in the hope that with time the critical international situation would improve. Until the close of 1938 it may be said that British and French policies were based upon the calculation that peace might be preserved indefinitely, that it would involve no very heavy sacrifice upon their part, and that the tension in Europe could be eased by concessions which might necessitate the transfer of some small segments of territory and the eclipse of some minor states. The grave defect of this policy was the fact that, if it failed, it would leave the democracies weakened in morale, in prestige, and in allies, and that each concession would magnify the prestige and the bargaining power of their opponents. Thus, as the arrogance and appetite of the aggressive states grew sharper, the timidity and irresolution of the democracies seemed to increase. The futile gestures of appeasement, as it became more obvious that they were futile, filled the French and British electors with anger and they began to upbraid their leaders for a pacifistic attitude which these same electors a few years earlier had enjoined upon their governments as a prescribed course from which they must not deviate. Both leaders and electors blamed the other because both were facing the unpleasant truth that they had been deceived. Hitler's repeated advances, each followed by a solemn pledge that he would make no further territorial demand, finally wakened the Western nations to a rude reality. With a man as erratic and as intoxicated with power as the German chancellor no just and reasonable peace was possible, no engagement durable, no pledge secure. As Hitler's arrogance increased he discarded the pretense of mutual bargaining and summoned statesmen to his presence to hear his decisions. All demands were uttered with an alternative threat. Diplomacy at the German level had become indistinguishable from blackmail.

Why, then, did the democratic nations continue to compromise and bargain with Hitler for nearly seven years after he came into power? There can be no simple answer to such a question: this chapter can attempt no more than a summary of the stages through which peace-loving peoples groped their way until, heartsick and confused still, they found the moral and material strength to cope with the totalitarian powers. The issue between democracy and totalitarianism could not be clearly joined until both ideologies had exhibited themselves in competing action on the twentieth century stage.

The first notable contrast between the two was the treatment accorded to minority groups and critics of the government in democratic and in totalitarian countries. The treatment of minorities reveals whether the laws of a state and the methods of administration assure equal protection of life and property to all citizens. From their first ascent to power the Fascists in Italy and the National Socialists in Germany had violated existing laws, persecuting their political opponents and all minority groups whom they distrusted or whose wealth they coveted, with a brutality which shocked the civilized world.

A second contrast between democratic and totalitarian ideals was clear in their skill in organizing the population and resources of the state for the promotion of national aims. In this test the totalitarian regimes displayed a vigor and efficiency which often produced remarkable results under pressure. Russia under the Five-Year Plans, Italy as a corporative state under the Fascists, and Germany under the state planning introduced by the National Socialists, all proved that the latent energies of a modern nation can be directed and concentrated with remarkable ease by a resolute one-party dictatorship and that such disciplined nations have a greatly increased potentiality for striking sudden and decisive blows. The strength of the totalitarian regimes rested not only upon the material forces they could mobilize, they also rested upon the will to action of a co-ordinated nation. Control of modern methods of communication, of the press, photography, radio, and motion pictures, enabled a dictator to reach every citizen and to polarize the will of the people. The leader became the symbol of this unified national will, the indivisible sovereign nation became articulate when he spoke, and a mystic sense of indestructible strength and irreversible purpose seized upon the masses as they listened to his voice. Never since primitive tribal chiefs harangued their warriors around the council fire, had such instant and intimate accord been fostered between a leader and his followers as the radio established. In the liberal states no equivalent cohesion was achieved by radio because there the people did not listen to only one familiar, authoritative voice but to a thousand differing opinions.

With defiant reiteration totalitarian leaders boasted of their success. The bold moves and confident conquests made by Italy and Germany on the international chess board, their growing military strength, their grandiose public displays and programs of highways, dams, docks, and other engineering projects, all focused attention upon the vigor and assurance of a regimented society. As the citizens in these states heard little save praise for their party, their government, and their leader, it was understandable that they should be impressed and even enthusiastic. Censorship silenced almost all dissenting opinions, but even more effective was the enthusiasm of the masses. Most Russians, Italians, and Germans were honestly and patriotically zealous in their devotion to the state and grateful for its benefits. This likewise was understandable. But it was surprising to find that some critics in democratic countries were converted by such propaganda. In Britain, France, and the United States minority groups began to ask whether liberal forms of government were outmoded, whether democracy was a system too lax and amorphous for twentieth century needs. Advocates of change used the privilege of free speech to extol dictatorships which denied the privilege of free speech. Anti-democrats argued that to permit free business enterprise, unregulated economic competition, and maximum individual liberty was to encourage anarchy. In the time of testing after 1929 the suffering and unemployment of the depression shook the faith of millions. Confusion at home and failure abroad deepened the doubts of those who had begun to wonder whether democratic institutions were strong enough and democratic processes decisive enough to control the forces of the new age.

There was one further source of incertitude which troubled the conscience of many liberal thinkers. Self-critical citizens in Britain and the United States were sensitive to the propaganda of the "have-not" powers. The accusation that the world's colonial spheres were most unequally divided, that the Treaty of Versailles was a vindictive document, that the war guilt clause was a hypocritical and one-sided indictment of Germany, that the extortion of reparations inflicted a galling injustice on the defeated, influenced a wide audience outside Germany. The British and American people were thrown into a half-defensive, half-apologetic mood in which they found it difficult to denounce the Germans with conviction when the National Socialists insisted that Germany must have equality of arms and economic opportunity with other leading powers. Few foreign observers foresaw, in the early days of Nazi power, the lust for revenge and conquest, unabashed and unappeasable, which motivated the National Socialist state. "Justice," one Englishman affirmed sententiously, "is no less justice because it is demanded by a dictator," and the statement suggested the divided mood in which many of his fellow countrymen watched Hitler's rise to power. Thomas Mann, one of the greatest German writers of the age, observed with penetration that until 1938 the Germans held a moral advantage over their opponents because they were united in the conviction that they had wrongs to right, while the democratic peoples were troubled by a misgiving that they were partly in the wrong. Not until after Munich did the democracies feel with equal assurance that their cause was just. Munich made it clear to impartial judges everywhere that no previous mistakes by his opponents and no injustices which the Germans might have endured could excuse Hitler's betrayal of pledges or his willingness to plunge Europe into war to extend his empire.

Though the Munich Conference averted war for the moment it fixed the responsibility for war in advance and fixed it upon the leaders of the German nation. For this dreadful verdict of world opinion, so defiantly earned, a whole generation of Germans was to pay atonement. The march of events in the fateful year 1938 ended the last illusions of peace-loving peoples that the advance of German and Italian conquest could be halted by anything less than armed force. The occupation of Austria, Albania, and part of Czechoslovakia by the Axis provided the final provocations which fired the temper of the French and British people to a fighting mood. These final acts of aggression which preceded the outbreak of war must now be analyzed.

2. THE ANNEXATION OF AUSTRIA

The agony of the civil war in Spain had not yet ended when the Nazi chiefs helped change the destinies of another European state. The troubled and truncated fragment of the defunct Hapsburg empire, the Republic of Austria, was an illogical product of political map-making, for over one-fourth of the 7,000,000 inhabitants were concentrated in the former imperial capital of Vienna. Predominantly German in speech and sentiment, the Austrians requested in 1919 that their provinces might be joined to the German Reich, but such an aggrandizement of Germany aroused fear in France and the *Anschluss* was forbidden. The Italians likewise had approved an independent Austria, for they had no wish to see German boundaries extend to the Brenner Pass. But this Italian opposition was withdrawn after Hitler and Mussolini negotiated the Rome-Berlin accord in 1936. An effective protest by the French was rendered much more difficult after the Germans reoccupied the demilitarized Rhineland zone. By 1938 the stage was set for the *coup* which ended Austrian independence.

The Austrian Republic, as constituted after 1919, was unstable and unsound politically and economically. Despite loans sponsored by the British and French the government at Vienna was unable to avoid a financial collapse in 1931, and the social unrest produced a bloody conflict between socialists and Conservatives in 1934. As in Spain, this civil discord opened the door to foreign intervention. An Austrian group, modeled on and subsidized by the German Nazi Party, agitated for annexation to Germany. An attempted revolt by these Austrian Nazis in 1934 resulted in the assassination of the chancellor, Engelbert Dollfuss, but failed to awaken the expected response among the Austrian people. In the face of failure, Hitler swiftly disavowed this Austrian *Putsch* for power which his agents had secretly encouraged. Four uneasy years later, however, the drama took a different turn.

German nationalism was now on the march. Millions of Germans in neighboring countries — in Austria, Poland, Czechoslovakia, Yugoslavia, and Russia — were taught to agitate for "reunion with the homeland." Maps purporting to show the proportion of Germans throughout Europe, with new boundaries sketched to create a "Great Germany" which would embrace most of central Europe, quickened the pride of German hearts. Eighty million Germans, if politically united and thoroughly armed, would not have to fear for their safety or their future unless they united most of the world against them. Unhappily, the fallacy in their formula for power was that they applied it with such methodical brutality that they ultimately did ally four-fifths of the nations against them.

In the program for expansion which the Nazi strategists openly avowed, Austria was the first important objective. Although the first attempt at seizure failed, further propaganda and more careful preparation made a second operation swift and successful. In March, 1938, on the appointed signal the Austrian National Socialist groups plunged the country into widespread confusion by their demonstrations and threats. The chancellor, Kurt Schuschnigg, was driven to resign. His successor, Arthur Seyss-Inquart, appointed at Hitler's telephoned "invitation," approved the entry of German troops into Austria to maintain order. Within a few weeks the reunion for which the Austrians had asked had been officially proclaimed in Berlin and Vienna. The *Anschluss* was approved almost unanimously by a plebiscite and presented to the world as a *fait accompli*. Such reckless, unilateral changes in the European state system gravely alarmed all the neighbors of Germany, but none dared to offer an effective protest. Clause by clause, Hitler was tearing up the Treaty of Versailles, discarding subsequent accords, and even repudiating pledges which he had himself endorsed.

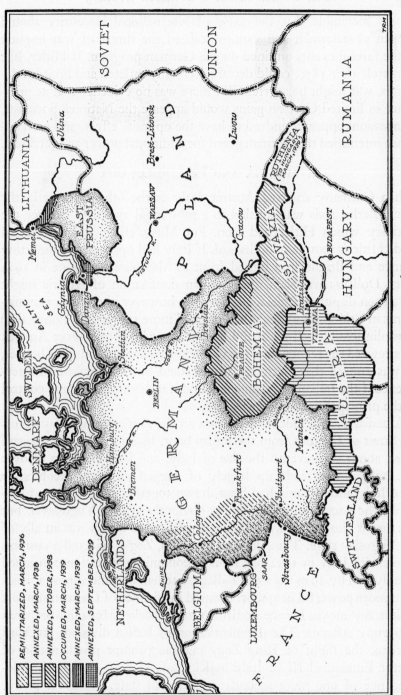

GERMAN MOVES IN EUROPE, 1936–1939

REMILITARIZED, MARCH, 1936
ANNEXED, MARCH, 1938
ANNEXED, OCTOBER, 1938
OCCUPIED, MARCH, 1939
ANNEXED, MARCH, 1939
ANNEXED, SEPTEMBER, 1939

It was inevitable that the sense of international insecurity should deepen as statesmen and nations realized the threat of war implicit in the fateful events outlined on the German program. If Hitler, like Bismarck after 1870, could declare Germany satiated and limit his demands, war might be averted. But there was no evidence that acquiescence in limited German gains would appease the National Socialists. Concessions appeared indeed to have the opposite effect, and each advance intensified the German greed for additional power and territory.

3. ALBANIA AND CZECHOSLOVAKIA

When Germany annexed Austria, Italy as the other partner in the Rome-Berlin Axis was entitled to a substantial award to balance the territory which Hitler had won. For Mussolini's acquiescence had made Hitler's move a good hazard. If Italy had opposed it, supporting France and Britain in a united front as Mussolini had done in 1934 when Dollfuss was slain, the German domination of Austria might have been disputed or delayed. By 1938, however, the Italian commitments in Ethiopia and Spain had claimed more troops and money than Mussolini could well spare and he could not hope to protect Austria. As a reward for recognizing the German advance to the Italian border, he was assured that Germany would stand by Italy against all interference if the Italian government found it necessary to assume control of the principality of Albania.

Albania, a small independent state on the Adriatic coast, lay across the Strait of Otranto from the Italian boot. Its area was 17,374 square miles, about one-seventh the size of Italy, and its population of over one million was made up largely of rugged mountain peoples. In 1926 Italy and Albania had been drawn together by a treaty of alliance. The pact was directed most obviously against Yugoslavia, but this meant also that it was aimed against France which was an ally of the Yugoslav state. The Albanian monarch, Zog I, rejected a customs union with Italy in 1932 but Italian economic penetration continued steadily and by 1939 the small Balkan state had become almost a vassal of its more powerful neighbor. Assured in advance of German support against any moves France or Britain might make, Mussolini prepared to occupy Albania. The disembarkation of Italian divisions on April 7, 1939, the flight of King Zog, and the prompt proclamation of Victor Emmanuel III of Italy as King of Albania, ended the independence of one more secondary European state. No great power made a move to help the Albanians and the resistance which they offered was crushed by the Italian naval, military, and air forces in a few days.

One reason for the indifference shown by the British and French governments over the fate of Albania was the fact that all Europe was watching a greater diplomatic crisis. The hour had struck for Czechoslovakia. When the German legions marched into Austria in 1938 the frontiers of Czechoslovakia were dangerously exposed, for the Germans could now strike the Czech defenses from west and south. Hitler's masterly use of the strategy of the limited objective had become clear: he always gained more than the territory he seized because each gain brought a new objective within his grasp. Precisely as in the case of Austria, he now encouraged the Germans in the Sudetenland to agitate for union with Great Germany. By the autumn of 1938 a Czechoslovakian crisis was ripening much as the Austrian crisis had proceeded six months earlier. But the international tension caused by this new German drive was more serious and the danger of war greater. Britain and France were bound by treaty to help Czechoslovakia defend its independence, and Russia had sound reasons for opposing a German drive eastwards.

At first sight, therefore, Hitler's threats against the Czechoslovak state seemed foolhardy and insensate, for they might impel Britain, France, and Soviet Russia to unite against Germany. France and Russia had been allied since 1935 in a pact which promised mutual support if either were the object of unprovoked aggression. But Hitler knew that the Western democracies were distrustful of Russia and that their ruling classes were hostile towards communism. He counted upon these divisions to paralyze his opponents at the moment when he brought the Sudeten problem to a test and he felt confident that the peace-infatuated ministers at London and Paris would appease him with further territorial concessions rather than resort to war.

The fundamental weakness in the position of the Czechoslovakian government was the fact that 3,000,000 German speaking citizens had been shut within its western frontiers when the borders were drawn in 1919. These "exiles from the Reich" (who had never lived under the German flag in actuality, for they had been subjects of the Austrian Empire before 1918) embarrassed the government at Prague with demands for measures of liberty which amounted to autonomy. To permit them to secede would have delivered the forts guarding the Sudeten hills into German hands. By the summer of 1938 the tension between Czechs and Germans within the republic had grown so acute that civil war seemed imminent. German divisions were waiting for an excuse to justify a march into the Sudetenland, and the French government, believing such a German invasion at hand, ordered a general mobilization to support its pledge of aid to Czechoslovakia.

But Great Britain was less willing than France to enter a war in defense of a minor state in eastern Europe. Possibly the British leaders hoped that Russia would mobilize to oppose a German "drive to the East" or perhaps they foresaw that if the Germans won their way in Czechoslovakia this might bring a Russo-German clash that much nearer. Whatever its motives, the British cabinet was conciliatory in this crisis when conciliation could only mean further concessions to German demands. Three times within two weeks the British prime minister, Neville Chamberlain, hastened to Germany for conferences. At Berchtesgaden on September 15, Hitler insisted that the areas of Czechoslovakia in which Germans predominated must be annexed to the Reich. After deliberation the British and French cabinets advised the Czechs to yield; but by September 22 Hitler had increased his demands to include immediate occupation of the areas claimed and a plebiscite in further portions of the state. Even Chamberlain's patience was strained by these tactics and he returned from a second visit to Hitler (Godesberg, September 22–23) to confer with British and French leaders in London. For five days the crisis mounted, with the Czech army mobilizing and all the great powers preparing for war. Britain and France got ready to support the Czechs in their resistance and Russia, though neglected by the Western powers, affirmed its will to oppose Germany. At Rome the Fascist leaders warned Mussolini that Italy was not equipped to enter a major war as an ally of Germany, but Mussolini stood by his Axis agreement. While President Roosevelt forwarded a message to Hitler urging a conference as the last expedient for averting a general war, Chamberlain and the French premier, Edouard Daladier, pressed Mussolini to use his influence with Hitler to arrange one more meeting. Hitler agreed, arriving at Munich on September 29 with his foreign minister, Joachim von Ribbentrop. Mussolini came with his foreign minister, Galeazzo Ciano, Chamberlain flew to Germany from London, and Daladier hastened from Paris. The Russian government was not invited to participate, a significant omission which strengthened the position of Germany. The Czechs likewise were absent while their fate was settled.

From September 23 to September 29 the peoples of Europe had waited from hour to hour for the sound of the first bombing planes.

News that a last-minute parley had been called at Munich seemed an almost miraculous reprieve, and word that an accord had been signed at midnight was greeted with joy and relief when the confirmation was broadcast on September 30. But peace had been preserved at an ominous price: Russia had been estranged and Czechoslovakia sacrificed. Hitler had won again, for German troops were to march into the disputed areas and take possession within ten days, and claims presented by the Polish and Hungarian governments for Czech territory were likewise to be adjusted. Although the Munich convention provided that an international commission should supervise the occupation and the citizens in disputed areas should indicate their will in a plebiscite, these arrangements were disregarded. The Czechoslovak Republic lost 5,000,000 of its 15,000,000 inhabitants and more than one-fourth of its territory. The fortifications which had guarded the republic against attack in the west passed intact into German hands and the affairs of the shrunken state were left to German supervision.

In a futile attempt to disguise the completeness of their concessions, Chamberlain and Daladier had insisted at Munich that France and Britain would give the reduced Czechoslovak state a formal guarantee against unprovoked aggression and that Germany and Italy should do likewise. These pledges likewise were of no effect. The shattered republic fell apart and the Germans speeded its dismemberment, recognizing Slovakia and Ruthenia as autonomous segments immediately and weakening the helpless government at Prague. In March, 1939, the new president of Czechoslovakia, Emil Hacha, who had succeeded the courageous and statesmanlike Eduard Beneš, came to Berlin and asked Hitler to assume responsibility for the fate of Bohemia and Moravia, while Slovakia and Ruthenia (renamed Carpatho-Ukraine) were likewise assured of German "protection." Within six months a wealthy, well-armed, and independent state had been submerged by the German march of conquest.

The significance of these events, especially in the months which followed the Munich Conference, were clear to the small nations of Europe. Guarantees from Britain and France were no longer effective. Germany had become the dominant power in all central Europe and it was prudent for weak neighbors to come to terms with Hitler before he forced a decision upon them, for his severity increased with delay and his determination remained unshaken by the threat of war. Yet the memory of the holocaust of 1914–1918 was so strong that many Europeans still refused to believe that any responsible statesman would risk another general conflict. Even after Munich, hope revived once more that the nightmare of war had abated. "I believe it is peace for our time," Neville Chamberlain affirmed on his return from that fateful conference, September 30, 1938. Eleven months later the nations plunged into the six-year devastation of World War II.

PART IX

World War II: 1939–1945

FROM THE INVASION OF POLAND
TO THE FALL OF FRANCE

(SEPTEMBER, 1939—JUNE, 1940)

*It has been alleged that, if His Majesty's Government had made
their position more clear in 1914, the great catastrophe would
have been avoided. Whether or not there is any force in that
allegation, His Majesty's Government are resolved that on this
occasion there shall be no such tragic misunderstanding.*

CHAMBERLAIN TO HITLER,
AUGUST 22, 1939

1. THE DIVISION OF POLAND

IN 1934, a year after Hitler came to power, Germany concluded
a ten-year nonaggression pact with the Polish republic. The
pact still had five years to run in the summer of 1939 when German
propagandists opened a war of nerves against the Poles and demanded
that the status of Danzig and the "Corridor" should be revised (see
maps, pages 197 and 455). All Europe was familiar with the tactics
employed by the Nazis when they planned a new stroke of aggression.
There was no doubt that Hitler could seize the Corridor; the only
question was whether the democratic powers would allow him to do
so as a further effort at appeasement or whether they would elect to
fight. The British and French governments warned Hitler firmly that
they would take up arms if he attacked Poland.

Hitler's position had been strengthened the previous May by a
"Pact of Steel" which bound Germany and Italy to engage jointly if
war came. But in August, 1939, Mussolini hesitated, warning Hitler
that recent Italian exertions in Ethiopia, Spain, and Albania had left
Italy without resources for a major war. Hitler and his advisers were
not deterred. They knew that Britain and France had pledged support

to Poland, but these powers had been pledged to aid Czechoslovakia a year earlier and had yielded to avert war. The Germans were confident that threats would succeed again. They were mistaken. Hitler's promise at Munich, that he would respect what remained of Czechoslovakia, a promise he broke within a few months, had left the British and French people without illusions. They would fight for Poland if Poland were attacked.

There remained the question of the Russian reaction, for the destruction of Poland would threaten Russia more directly than Britain or France. Before ordering his armies across the Polish frontier, Hitler sent his adroit foreign minister, Joachim von Ribbentrop, to Moscow to resolve the Russian enigma. There, on August 23, the German and Soviet governments agreed to a mutual nonaggression pact supplemented by commercial treaties. If the democracies went to war and German overseas trade were cut off by a naval blockade, all southern and eastern Europe would still be open to German exploitation. Ribbentrop revealed to the Soviet chiefs the German plan for a swift dismemberment of Poland and agreed that the Russians should occupy the eastern half of these domains.

Deliberately beclouding the last hours of diplomatic talk with fictitious reports and false charges, the Germans attacked Poland on September 1. From London and Paris came grave warnings that the British and French governments would consider themselves at war with Germany unless the invading troops were recalled within twenty-four hours. On September 3 they officially declared war. Britain and France had stood by their pledge, but they were not able to save or even to assist the Poles. German forces estimated at 1,700,000 men opened a concentric attack from East Prussia, Silesia, and Czechoslovakia. They were led by mechanized divisions and supported by overwhelming air superiority. So swift was the advance that the Polish army of 600,000 could not complete its mobilization or concert its plans for resistance and was crushed in two weeks of confused fighting. On September 17 Russian troops swept into Poland from the east, meeting the advancing Germans at Brest-Litovsk two days later. On September 29 the German and Soviet governments divided Poland, the Germans taking some 73,000 square miles with 22,000,000 people under their "protection," and the Russians 77,000 square miles with a population of 13,000,000.

2. RUSSIA WINS DEFENSES TO THE WEST

In the same week that Poland was divided, the Soviet government concluded a treaty with Estonia (September 29) whereby it acquired naval and air bases on Estonian territory. Permission to establish fortified bases in Latvia was secured by a similar pact with the Latvian regime a week later (October 5). A mutual assistance treaty binding Russia and Lithuania followed swiftly (October 10), the Russians ceding Vilna and some contiguous territory but receiving in exchange the right to garrison points of military importance in Lithuania. These moves, which definitely strengthened Russian defenses in eastern Europe and on the Baltic, proclaimed to the world the basic rivalry and distrust which underlay Russo-German relations. In this polite but grim test of power politics above the corpse of the Polish republic, the realism of Stalin had equaled the ruthlessness of Hitler.

Hitler's *Blitzkrieg* or "lightning war" in Poland had cost Germany relatively little in men or material. It had provided a field maneuver under war conditions, giving the commanders an invaluable opportunity to test their new tactics and equipment. For Europe it had provided a terrifying illustration of the striking power of the *Wehrmacht*. But it had involved Germany in a troublesome war with Britain and France and it had antagonized neutral opinion more sharply than before. Hitler was lucid enough to perceive that the main beneficiary of his bold campaign was Russia. The Russians had won more territory than the Germans, had gained control of it without fighting, and had enjoyed a rare chance to observe the German war machine in action. What they learned from the fate of the Polish armies helped them to perfect their own methods of "defense in depth" which were to save Russia when the *Wehrmacht* hurled itself against the Soviet lines two years later.

There was a deep irony about Hitler's position at the close of 1939, an irony which was to haunt him throughout the course of hostilities. He was at war with Britain, a country which he was powerless to invade, and he knew that his advantage over the Russian armies was declining as the Russians hastened their huge program of preparedness. An attack upon France through the Maginot Line was a possibility but it was likely to prove very costly. On the other hand, a Franco-British assault upon the German West Wall appeared even more impracticable. The British and French navies had closed the high seas to German ships but German trade with the Scandinavian countries, Russia, the Balkan States, and Turkey was still open. The Germans could not in the circumstances be blockaded and starved as they were in World War I. The situation had many aspects of a stalemate. Hitler decided, with the Polish question disposed more or less to his satisfaction, to call for a truce with Britain and France. He was even prepared to offer a nonaggression pact and guarantee the security of the British Empire. But his overtures brought no response. Through the winter of 1939–1940 the military stalemate continued and the war correspondents, weary of inactivity, began to write derisively of the "phony war." The implication was unfortunate. There was nothing bloodless or unreal about the war: the adversaries were measuring their strength for a death struggle and when the seven-month overture was ended the main drama commenced.

One campaign there was, however, during this winter prelude which bore on the Russian side the symptoms of a "phony war." This was the Russo-Finnish War, a three months' conflict which opened in November. Unlike the Estonians, Latvians, and Lithuanians, the Finns refused to make concessions which would strengthen Russian defenses on the Karelian isthmus. On November 30, Russian armies attacked Finland in the north, center, and south. For this act of aggression Russia was expelled from the League of Nations (December 14) but the rebuke had no effect. The Finns put up a heroic resistance, especially on the vital Karelian isthmus, and the world watched with amazement the punishing blows which they dealt to the discomfited Russian divisions. But increasing pressure told and when the Russians finally breached the Mannerheim Line the Finns accepted peace. An area of over 16,000 square miles, with a population of nearly half a million, passed to the Union of Soviet Socialist Republics, territory which included the city of Viipuri (Viborg) and a naval base at Hangö.

Though successful in winning their demands, the Russians suffered somewhat in military prestige because of the difficulty they met in overcoming the Finnish forces. But it is possible that they did not on this occasion employ their best troops or material. Hitler had military observers with the Finnish armies, and the Soviet high command had no intention of revealing its latest devices and weapons in a minor engagement. When the Germans met the Russians in 1941 they found that they had underrated a potential enemy, and part of the miscalculation may have arisen from the war in Finland.

3. THE INVASION OF DENMARK AND NORWAY

In the months of waiting during the winter of 1939–1940 the British and German governments threw their production plants into high speed. In all major operations of modern war the problem of supply is a deciding factor, for the planes, tanks, guns, shells, and other equipment are consumed so rapidly that only large reserves can assure replacements in time. All the belligerents sought to place orders in neutral countries. The United States lifted its embargo on the sale of war materials in November, 1939, thus permitting Britain and France to order weapons and carry them overseas in their own ships. This was a significant victory for the democracies. The industrial plants of the United States could almost match the output of all the rest of the world combined, and as the seas were closed to German ships the "cash and carry" rule excluded Germany from the benefits of American production. Cut off from this source of arms, the Germans purchased needed materials from factories in Sweden, Italy, and other nonbelligerent countries.

But even in the adjacent countries of Europe the Germans met with opposition and could not always outbid their enemies. Using their credit reserves, the British and French bargained for supplies which they knew the Germans needed, and in this way diverted the output of Swiss, Spanish, or Swedish mines and factories to their own reserves. If they failed to obtain the exports by offering higher prices, they might apply pressure to the neutral states through the naval blockade. Thus Italy, which was a nonbelligerent, aided Germany by importing and transferring goods from abroad for its Axis partner. In retaliation, the British cut off the sea-borne coal supplies upon which Italian industry largely depended, forcing the Italians to import coal from Germany by the costly haul over the Alps. Belgium, the Netherlands, Switzerland, Denmark, Norway, and Sweden were likewise under pressure. Germany on one side, France and Britain on the other, drove prices up throughout the winter as they bid for the manufactures, dairy products, fish, and any other marketable commodities these secondary states had for sale.

In its ultimate effects this trade war was as important as the military campaigns, but these effects are obscure, undramatic, difficult to trace. To wear an enemy down by reducing his supplies, that is, to establish a partial or complete state of siege, is a principle as old as war. When in September, 1939, the British opened hostilities with Germany,

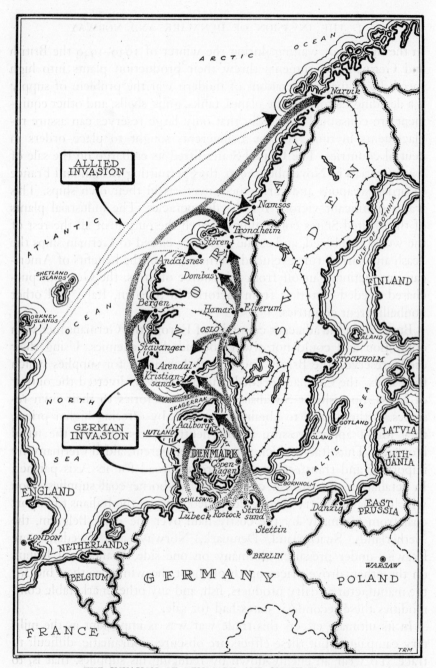

THE INVASION OF DENMARK AND NORWAY, 1940

they immediately halted all German maritime imports and then extended this sea blockade to stop German exports also. The German retort was an attempted blockade of the British Isles by mines and submarine boats. On September 4, one day after the war officially opened, a German U-boat sank the British S.S. *Athenia* without warning, causing a loss of over a hundred lives. Air raids and a new type of "magnetic" mine inflicted heavy destruction on British shipping, forcing the merchant vessels to crowd into the western harbors which were more remote from German airfields. The British navy countered the German moves by multiplying their sea and air patrols, tightening their blockade, scrutinizing all neutral shipping, and sowing mines in German harbors. On February 16, 1940, they seized a German ship in Norwegian coastal waters. Despite protests from the Norwegian government, the British and French announced (April 8) that they had mined Norwegian waters to halt the transit of German vessels which had been eluding the blockade.

The German counterstroke seemed instantaneous but in reality it had been patiently prepared. On April 9, German naval units attacked Norwegian ports, while hundreds of paratroops floated down on the airfields. Oslo, Bergen, Trondheim, Stavanger, and Narvik were occupied in surprise invasions but after their momentary consternation the Norwegians rallied courageously. French and British reinforcements were rushed to aid them and Trondheim, Bergen, and Narvik were temporarily recaptured. But although the invaders suffered some sharp repulses — four cruisers and four troopships were sunk in Oslofiord and several destroyers and troop carriers in Narvik — they maintained almost undisputed mastery of the air. This enabled them to pour in troops at will to any vital point; for the first time in history air power appeared to be the deciding factor in a military campaign.

After two weeks of fighting, the Anglo-French expeditionary forces, which had landed in southern Norway on April 20, were driven out and by June the Norwegian resistance had been broken. The king, Haakon VII, escaped with his ministers to London, where he set up a Norwegian government-in-exile. In Norway a German commissar ordered the establishment of a new regime. All political parties except the *Nasjonal Samling* were dissolved and a puppet government established under a pro-German dictator named Vidkun Quisling. The Norwegian government at London repudiated Quisling as "Minister-President" and after some months he was driven to abolish the constitution and rule as a puppet of the Germans.

A surprise invasion of Denmark, for which there was even less justification, enabled the Germans to occupy that small country without meeting any formal resistance. Though unable to offer active opposition, the Danes refused to co-operate with their conquerors and the five-year occupation which commenced on April 9, 1940, was on the surface a frigid truce that covered a burning resentment and many secret acts of sabotage. Nevertheless the seizure of Denmark, like the conquest of Norway, gave the Germans important advantages. The British people saw one result on their shrinking breakfast menus, for Danish farms had supplied one-third of the bacon, butter, and eggs imported into the United Kingdom. The enemy occupation of Norway, from which the British bought one-third of their fish supply, was a further threat to the national diet, and kippered herrings became scarcer. Occupation of Norway also gave the Germans valuable bases for submarines, surface raiders, and air attacks. The harsh, indented Norwegian coast, which stretches for a thousand miles from the Skagerrak to beyond the Arctic Circle, was an ideal hiding ground for enemy ships seeking to run the blockade. Shrouded by darkness or fog they could slip from fiord to fiord until they escaped into the twilight of the North Atlantic.

4. THE FALL OF FRANCE (MAY–JUNE, 1940)

In war much depends upon maintaining the initiative. The combatant who can time the strokes, choose the battleground, and concentrate superior forces for a surprise attack, enjoys a great advantage tactically and morally. The attacker is the hunter, the conqueror; the attacked are the quarry, the hunted. When a nation suffers a series of reverses and sees its armies driven back repeatedly with heavy loss, its morale may dissolve and a general panic compel it to swift capitulation. The triumphs which the Germans gained in Poland, Denmark, and Norway filled them with reckless confidence, while the French and British armies guarding the western front through the winter stalemate grew more and more discontented. The eight months of "softening up," of waiting, worry, and discouragement, through which the French and British passed between September, 1939, and May, 1940, must be kept in mind for it was a psychological factor of considerable importance.

On May 10, 1940, Hitler struck once again without warning. German divisions were hurled across the frontiers of the neutral Netherlands, Belgium, and Luxembourg. These small countries had little

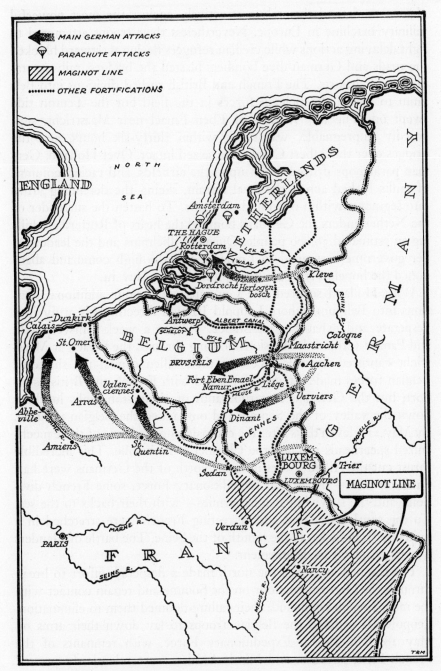

GERMAN INVASION OF THE LOW COUNTRIES AND FRANCE, 1940

chance to defend themselves effectively against the most powerful military machine in Europe. Nevertheless their troops attempted to fight delaying actions while civilian refugees fleeing westward blocked the roads and German dive bombers blasted the bridges, railway stations, and airports. The French and British rushed divisions into Belgium to stiffen the Belgian forces in the field but the Teuton tide swept on. The key fortress of Eben Emael near Maastricht, supposedly impregnable, was taken within thirty-six hours, and the bridges over the Albert Canal were seized intact. Over Holland, German paratroops drifted down upon the airfields, and racing columns of tanks forked across the level terrain, slicing the defending army into segments within one hundred hours. To hasten the surrender of the Netherlanders the Germans bombed the heart of Rotterdam, killing an estimated 30,000 people. Queen Wilhelmina and the leaders of her government escaped to England, and the high command abandoned the hopeless struggle by capitulating on May 14.

With Holland secured, the Germans could pour additional divisions into Belgium, where Leopold III was directing his army in a desperate and exhausting resistance. Within a week Antwerp fell, and Panzer (armored) divisions pouring through the breach at Maastricht captured Brussels. West of their fallen capital the shattered Belgian forces made a temporary stand with French and British support; but the Germans sent thousands of eighty-ton tanks lurching down the valley of the Somme and outflanked the Belgian position. By May 21, eleven days after the campaign opened, one of these mechanized spearheads reached the Channel at Abbeville. This incredible thrust cut the Allied forces in two. North of the Germans were half a million men — the British Expeditionary Force, some French divisions, and the surviving Belgian armies — with their backs to the sea. To the south the dazed and retreating French were stretched in a fluid line from Sedan to the mouth of the Seine. The battle of Flanders was approaching its denouement.

The trapped armies in the north made a desperate effort to break through the German corridor on the Somme and regain contact with the main French command; their failure doomed them to elimination. Leopold III ordered the Belgian troops to lay down their arms on May 28. The British Expeditionary Force, with remnants of the French First, Seventh, and Ninth Armies, were relentlessly pressed back to the shore. Boulogne fell into German hands, then Calais. Only Dunkirk remained as a possible port of escape, and from its shallow beaches daring British craft of every description rescued 335,000 men in the nine days from May 26 to June 3. This "Miracle of Dunkirk" cheered the British people after two months of unbroken disasters. But although most of the men were saved, all their heavy equipment had been lost. Winston Churchill, who had become prime minister in place of Neville Chamberlain on May 10 (the day the Germans struck), rallied the nation with the sober reminder that "Wars are not won by evacuations."

Their swift and conclusive clean-up in the battle of Flanders enabled the Germans to turn their whole armed strength in the west to the battle of France. On June 5 they opened a drive along the Somme. Despite their staggering reverse the French still had courage and confidence, and British reinforcements were shipped to Bordeaux to re-enter the fight. But the Germans' assault seemed irresistible. Within five days they were at the gates of Paris. This was the black hour chosen by the Italian government to strike; for on June 10 Mussolini declared war on France and Britain. On the 14th the Germans were in Paris and the government of the republic escaped to Bordeaux. On the 17th the French premier, Paul Reynaud, his cabinet divided and disheartened, resigned the leadership to the aged Marshal Henri Philippe Pétain. Pétain's first official act was to ask the Germans for an armistice. Despite a magnificent appeal from Churchill offering to fuse the British and French empires in a joint union, despite a stirring broadcast from General Charles de Gaulle urging his countrymen to fight on, the forces of defeatism triumphed and France surrendered. In less than six weeks a nation which a few years earlier had been considered the dominant military power of the world had been conquered and disarmed. The repercussion of the disaster was felt around the world, and in the United States the Atlantic Ocean seemed suddenly to have become a moat and its defense a national necessity.

On June 21, 1940, in the same railway car at Compiègne in which the Germans had signed the armistice terms of November 11, 1918, the French delegates faced Adolf Hitler. The government at Bordeaux now headed by Pétain accepted the terms and the new armistice was signed June 22. A separate settlement with Italy was concluded the following day. For the moment France had ceased to be a great power. Half the country, including Paris, was to be occupied by the Germans, who seized control of the entire seacoast as far as the Spanish border. All naval, military, and air forces of the Third Republic were to be demobilized. The French fleet was to return to French ports, and French war material in the occupied area was to be surrendered.

The British government, promptly declaring that the Pétain regime had betrayed France, severed relations with it (June 23). To keep the warships of their late ally from falling under German control, the British demanded the surrender of those at Oran (July 3). When the French commanders refused, the British sank or captured these ships and seized all French ships in British ports. Thereupon the new government of France broke off relations with London.

The fall of France was not merely a defeat administered to a democracy; it was a defeat for the principle of democracy itself. Since the Revolution of 1789 Paris had been a symbol of liberalism on the continent of Europe. But the rise of totalitarian principles in Italy and Germany had not left the French unstirred. Some politicians and industrialists and many honest and perturbed citizens, appalled by the weakness of the democracies during the era of appeasement, had come to believe that only a one-party government with a strong executive freed from the impediments of parliamentary criticism could save and defend a nation in this iron age. The rise of Hitler had excited envy in France, and the daring though unscrupulous *coups* of the German dictator aroused a desire for similar "strong methods." Some French citizens were still royalists. Other more radical groups looked to Moscow and praised the bold and far-reaching economic plans which had increased Russian industrial and agricultural production. Frenchmen, in other words, were politically confused before World War II opened, delay confused them further, and disaster shattered their weakened faith in the democratic republic. The road to victory had been opened to the Germans by disunion within the French ranks and in a few cases by deliberate treachery.

Defeat brought discredit upon the leading politicians of France, and the parliament itself lost confidence in its capacity to direct the affairs of the humiliated nation. Two weeks after the armistice of June 22 the French Senate and Chamber of Deputies approved a motion to endow the Pétain ministry with the powers of an authoritarian government, making it a quasidictatorship. There was hardly a whisper of opposition; the motion passed the Senate by 395 to 3, and the deputies approved it by 225 to 1. No French government ruling under the shadow of German demands, helpless to defy Hitler, and driven to procrastination and subterfuge in its efforts to ward off heavier exactions, could have played its part with dignity in these dark years.

Pétain inherited an agonizing mandate but he made matters worse by his choice of collaborators. As vice-premier he appointed Pierre Laval, and as the strength of the aged Marshal was failing, the unscrupulous Laval became virtual master of Vichy France, a puppet politician dancing to German demands. A chief of the "collaborationists" who worked with the enemy and were hated for it by sullen French patriots, Laval was driven to assist the Gestapo as it broke up secret resistance groups and dispatched suspects to German prison camps. Like Quisling in Norway, he was to pay with his life after the war ended for this betrayal of his countrymen.

FROM THE FALL OF FRANCE TO THE
GERMAN ATTACK ON RUSSIA

(JUNE, 1940—JUNE, 1941)

Hitler knows he will have to break us in this Island or lose the war.

WINSTON CHURCHILL (JUNE, 1940)

1. THE BATTLE OF BRITAIN: THE AERIAL BLITZ

WHEN the French surrendered in June, 1940, the British were left to face the full might of Germany and Italy. Britain was isolated but she did not stand alone. The Dominions were loyal. The Polish, Free French, Norwegian, and Netherlands governments-in-exile co-operated with as many of their ships, sailors, and reservists as could escape. Anti-Fascists of all nations from all parts of Europe supported the British effort. In the United States and most of Latin America the people were pro-British in sympathy. The speed and success of the German campaigns confronted the Western world with a choice between two systems of government: the more tolerant, decentralized, and apparently haphazard methods of rule which had built up the British Empire, and the ruthless, unpredictable, authoritarian methods of the German Nazis and Italian Fascists. The defeat of Britain would not end the war but enlarge it, for the Germans had shown they could not be appeased by conquests, diplomatic or military. This fact, more powerful than any appeal or propaganda, made Britain appear a bulwark to most neutrals.

Other conquerors in earlier centuries had sought to dominate Europe but the political gyroscope which perpetuated the balance of power among the nation-states always returned to its precarious equilibrium. The British, knowing that submerged forces of opposition would undermine the German domination, made contact with resistance groups that harassed the Nazi troopers by acts of sabotage and terrorism. Even within Germany itself there was a mood of distrust, and secret plots, which grew more serious each year that the war lasted, threatened Hitler's authority. The British were encouraged also by the fact that the German satellite states were hostile to one another and none dared to rely upon German pledges. The leaders in the lesser states could learn little in advance regarding German plans for they were warned that these plans "were locked in the impenetrable bosom of the *Führer*." Mussolini frequently complained, "Hitler always faces me with a *fait accompli*." But the Italian dictator likewise played a double game. One factor which may have encouraged Britain to risk war in September, 1939, was the secret assurance given the minister at Rome that despite the "Pact of Steel" Italy would not fight. Only in June, 1940, when the collapse of France made it appear that the war was over save for the division of the spoils, did Mussolini enter it, a decision which ultimately wrecked his regime and cost him his life.

The cynical diplomacy of the Axis diplomats, the repeated acts of aggression against smaller neighbors, the brutality of the secret police, the persecution of political opponents and minority groups, the horrors that were reported about the extermination camps stirred a revolt of conscience throughout the civilized world. It was a revolt which was to mature through five desperate years while all western Europe cursed Nazi rule.

Historians will speculate why Hitler did not invade England immediately after France fell. The question is a tribute to the power and personality of this erratic genius and it measures him by implication against Napoleon. One hundred and thirty-five years earlier Napoleon had stood at the Channel with an invincible army and gazed at the white cliffs of Dover. But he found Britain "intangible" whereas Hitler possessed not only guns that would reach the nearest ports but also air armadas that could devastate the cities. Had the Germans followed the "heroes of Dunkirk" as they escaped across the Channel, they might have established a bridgehead. But it is extremely doubtful that they could have held it. For German successes were not improvised; their campaigns were long and carefully prepared. Their tanks and dive bombers were trained to fight in co-operation, and they were constructed for land, not for amphibious warfare. So long as the British navy maintained its superiority at sea and the British air force dominated the skies over England a German invasion would have proved a desperate gamble.

On June 18, 1940, exactly a century and a quarter after Napoleon's final defeat at Waterloo, Hitler opened an aerial attack upon Britain. Success had made the Germans oversanguine. They hoped that air bombing would so paralyze manufacture and transportation that the island would succumb without invasion. Through July into August the attacks grew more intense; the world was watching the first air war in history. At first the *Luftwaffe* struck at harbors and shipping. But swarms of British fighter planes, Hurricanes and Spitfires, took such heavy toll of the bombing squadrons that the Germans shifted their attack. They decided that they must wreck the airfields and fire the factories where planes were built, thus crippling the fighter defense. But the new targets were well camouflaged and the plan failed. The defense grew stiffer, accounting for 10 to 15 per cent of the raiders engaged. Once more the Germans shifted tactics, concentrating their September attacks on London in mass raids. They boasted that they would level the heart of the empire with their explosive and incendiary bombs. They came over chiefly at night, flying high to avoid interception and anti-aircraft fire and dropping their cargoes of death at random over the wide metropolis.

By the end of October the air attack began to slow down. The Germans had encountered their first defeat of the war. Defense had cost the British 375 pilots and 800 planes, but 2275 German raiding craft had been destroyed. The *Luftwaffe* was still strong and hundreds of planes still came over nightly to shatter the leading cities, London, Bristol, Plymouth, Southampton, Coventry. But the methods of interception steadily improved, the populace learned to take safer cover, and the fire hazard was reduced. Yet the cost of survival was high. By December 31, 1940, over 20,000 civilians had been killed, and one home out of every five was destroyed or damaged. The assaults, which never wholly ceased, were intensified again in the spring of 1941. The British people suffered the depressing effect of the nightly blackout, the air raid warnings, and the constant tension to the end of the war. The last year of the struggle was to bring still more dreadful forms of flying death, the rocket bombs hurtling from the heavens. But there was no panic, the courage of the populace never faltered, and the government correctly read the popular will to see the war through. When London had been bombed eighty-two out of eighty-five nights running, a motion to consider peace, introduced into parliament in December, 1940, was voted down 341 to 4.

Had the Germans secured even temporary mastery of the air over the Channel and southern ports, they might have planned to pour in a million men by barge and plane. But they could not easily have kept them supplied, and every passing week made the odds against invasion stiffer. British beaches, ports, and highways were mined, fresh divisions trained and armed, troops from the Dominions dispatched to defend the motherland, and production multiplied despite heavy handicaps. To replace part of the war material abandoned in the battle of Flanders the United States Government sold to Britain from its own arsenals several hundred field guns, thousands of machine guns, and nearly a million rifles which had been hoarded since World War I. The later history of the war was to prove that vast amphibious landing operations were entirely possible against well defended beaches. But they called for special types of apparatus, patient preparation, and definite naval and aerial preponderance. The Germans in 1940 possessed none of these advantages in adequate degree. The fall of France had taken them by surprise and they had neither foreseen nor prepared for a military invasion of Britain.

2. THE BATTLE OF THE ATLANTIC

In World War I the greatest, probably the deciding, advantage possessed by the Allied powers was their control of the sea. This mastery was threatened by the German submarine campaign, but by 1918 the convoy system, new detecting devices, and depth bombs had met the U-boat menace successfully. Because the campaign failed and the war was finally won on all fronts, the gravity of Allied shipping losses especially in 1917 passed from the public mind after victory. But British naval experts did not forget. The same prescience which persuaded the air ministry to specialize in fighter planes in sufficient quantity to meet the aerial *Blitz* also moved the navy to develop new antisubmarine weapons. The most effective answer they found was radar, the "electric eye" which could see through fog and darkness. British scientists, collating their discoveries with what they could learn from other countries, pressed on their researches throughout the last years of peace in a desperate race against time.

The territory overrun by the Germans in the first ten months of World War II gave them possession of the entire European coast line

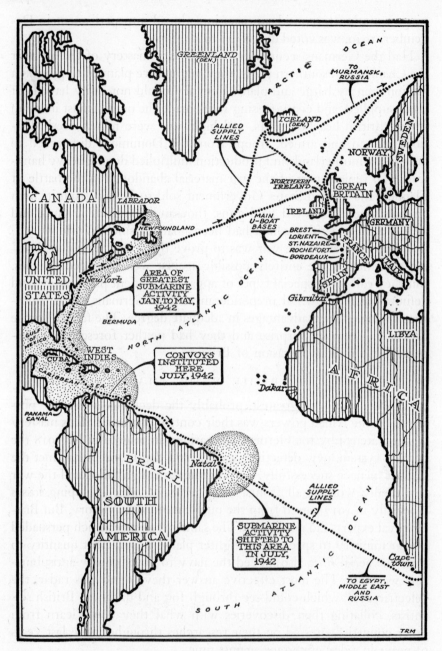

THE BATTLE OF THE ATLANTIC

from Norway to Spain. They had ports and shipyards for their submarines and air bases for bombing raids against British shipping. But they had not built sufficient U-boats and their planes had not been designed for over-ocean scouting. Their attempted blockade of the British Isles was somewhat slow in developing, but with the factories, mines, shipyards, and workers of Europe pressed into service they were confident that they could put Britain out of the war by bombing cities and sinking merchant ships in a crescendo of destruction. With imports failing, factories closed, and the population starving, Britain would yield. But Britain did not yield, and in 1941 what had been largely the air battle of Britain changed and broadened into the shipping battle of the Atlantic.

When supplies from Europe were cut off, the British became almost wholly dependent in the matter of imports upon the food, raw materials, and munitions carried to their ports on the transatlantic convoys. To escape the "wolf packs" of U-boats lying in wait, these convoys had to be guarded by escorts of destroyers, while battle cruisers of the royal navy kept watch to engage the swift German pocket battleships. One enemy cruiser, if it broke through the escort guard to the string of freighters, could wreak fearful havoc in a few minutes. The battle of the Atlantic was won by patient plotting and perpetual vigilance. There were no major naval engagements, few sudden or important victories. One by one the larger units of the German fleet were caught at sea and sunk, or put out of action in port by repeated air raids. The real battle was a gigantic game of hide-and-seek, pursued relentlessly over endless leagues of gray ocean, an ocean sometimes shining and sometimes shrouded but never still and never safe. For such a game fueling bases were indispensable. Planes and scouting ships surveyed the ocean daily, reporting every object they saw moving on, under, or above the water. Although the Irish Free State (Eire) declined to allow the use of its ports, the British (and later the United Nations) gradually acquired adequate bases throughout the North and South Atlantic and from these they were finally able to patrol the convoy routes successfully.

The disruption of commerce and the danger to neutral shipping made all the maritime nations alert to the submarine menace. When German U-boats crossed the Atlantic and appeared in American waters, the United States took the lead in speeding hemisphere defense. American air and naval scouts kept watch offshore and after September, 1940, this patrol service was extended more widely. Fifty over-age but still useful destroyers were traded to Great Britain and in exchange the Americans were granted full facilities at naval and air bases in Newfoundland, Bermuda, the Bahamas, Jamaica, St. Lucia, Trinidad, and British Guiana. As Denmark had succumbed to German occupation, the United States government extended its protection to Greenland (April, 1941) and established bases there. Three months later American troops relieved a British garrison which had been stationed in Iceland to secure it from German raids.

The battle at sea was mounting towards a grim uncertain climax. By 1941 over 7,000,000 tons of British, Allied, and neutral shipping had been lost. The Germans were building U-boats at maximum speed, and the fight to keep the ocean routes clear was the most desperate and unpredictable phase of the struggle for the British. Not only the Empire supply lines but their whole war effort depended upon cargo space. If the battle of the Atlantic had been lost, the war would have been lost.

Not until hostilities were over could the inside story of this Atlantic action be revealed. Hints of the new and ingenious weapons invented by the Germans fell behind the actualities. Mines which exploded if a steel hull passed near them; "acoustical" torpedoes which "heard" a ship's engines and pursued the sound; and radio-controlled flying bombs which could be guided to their target proved the versatility of the German inventors. British and American technicians countered with coils which "demagnetized" steel ships, with towed "noisemakers" that confused the acoustical torpedoes, and with improved detection devices so delicate that their "sonar" sets sometimes picked up the voices of the crew in a lurking submarine. The Germans even resorted to sheathing U-boats with a rubber skin to insulate the sounds. But improved radar came to be even more vital in detection work than sonar sets, for radar sighted the submarines through darkness, fog, or rain. The best answer the Germans found was to equip the U-boats with a ventilation tube or "Schnorckel" which enabled them to use their Diesel engines while submerged. But patience, vigilance, and ingenuity outwitted them. By December, 1943, Grand Admiral Karl Doenitz, head of the German navy, confessed privately that British and American scientists were forging ahead in the technological competition. In an appeal to German engineers, Doenitz declared the Allied forces were winning the sea war not through superior tactics or strategy but through superiority in the field of science and especially in "the modern battle weapon, detection."

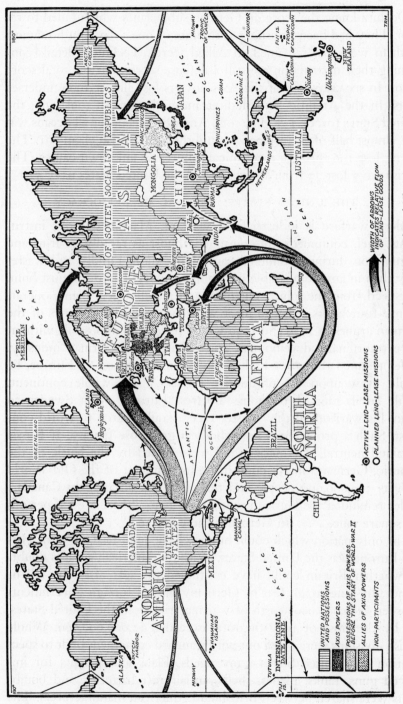

SEA ROUTES AND SUPPLIES UNDER THE LEND-LEASE ACT

Doenitz knew the score on German submarines which failed to return. They had been vanishing at the rate of one a day, but how most of them were lost remained an Allied secret. Technical details concerning their destruction are still a defense secret, but the total score is not. In six years of war the Axis powers lost almost 1000 undersea boats. In the Atlantic and Mediterranean the British took 562; the United States forces, 151. The total American claim for all oceans was 288, almost half of them Japanese, and the total British claim 601. The enemy lost 106 through mechanical failures or unknown causes. The British navy lost 77 from all causes, and the United States navy 52.

3. THE UNITED STATES: ARSENAL OF DEMOCRACY

Modern warfare is industrialized warfare. Machines, tools, instruments, fuel, equipment are consumed almost as rapidly as arms and ammunition during a military campaign — more rapidly and wastefully than in any comparable peacetime activity. Factories must hum, ore speed from the mines, chemical and metallurgical plants operate twenty-four hours a day to meet war demands. The victories of the German armies in 1939 and 1940 would have been impossible without the extraordinary development and efficiency of German industry. Hitler planned that after he had made himself master of Europe, he would draw upon the productive power of the whole continent. While anvils rang throughout "Fortress Europe" from Sweden to Spain, his warriors of the "master race" would march to world conquest. Such a project was not wholly a grandiose fantasy. If Russia remained neutral, if American aid were halted by the battle of the Atlantic, Germany might consolidate its conquest of the Old World with its 500,000,000 people and then leap the oceans. "In Canada," Hitler reminded the German workers in 1940, "there are 2.6 persons per square mile. . . . In Germany there are 360."

The only nation which could outmatch the industrial might of Hitler's Europe was the United States. Without American aid it is doubtful whether Britain could have continued the war after the fall of France. In June, 1940, fear of Germany moved foreign governments to order $800,000,000 worth of war material from the United States; and by the close of 1940 the total exceeded $2,000,000,000. Whole British divisions were fitted out with standard equipment built to specification for United States army needs. Plans and patents for improved guns, tanks, planes, shells, antiaircraft batteries, and bombsights were shared between British and American manufacturers. The

United States had become, as President Roosevelt phrased it in December, 1940, "the great arsenal of democracy."

Unfortunately for the British, however, the financial reserves which they had available for purchases in this country were almost exhausted after a year of struggle. Lacking gold or goods with which to pay, the government at London would have had to cut down its purchases of desperately needed material had the "cash and carry" provision of the earlier neutrality legislation been maintained. But the British plight was solved by the passage of the Lend-Lease Bill, March 11, 1941. Under this new Act, "any country whose defense the President deemed vital to the defense of the United States" became eligible to receive any defense article by sale, transfer, exchange, lease, or loan.

The Lend-Lease Act reassured all embattled or threatened democracies that they might turn to the United States for aid. It also reassured American manufacturers that if they accepted orders from Britain or other states and expanded their plants to meet the demand for war material, they would be reimbursed because the federal government stood behind the transaction. The Act also made it possible for the ships of Great Britain and her allied governments-in-exile to seek repairs in American docks, it provided for the pooling of defense information, and it permitted the immediate transfer to Britain of food and arms for which there was urgent need. By the spring of 1941 the food shortage in England had grown so acute that when the first shipments of cheese, eggs, and evaporated milk sent under Lend-Lease arrived in May, the nation had only a few weeks' reserve rations on hand.

The summer of 1941 marked a turning point in the war for the embattled Britons and the opening of a more encouraging phase of the struggle. They knew thereafter that so long as the Atlantic life line held there would be imports from America to increase their food supply. But the importance of this food from overseas should not obscure the extraordinary campaign won by the British farmer. During 1939, the year that war came, two-thirds of the food consumed in Great Britain was imported. But within the next four years, in a drive to increase home-grown crops, the British more than doubled their domestic food production. By 1943 they were raising 70 per cent and importing only 30 per cent of their own food. This swift achievement, carried through in the midst of a total war, surprised the British themselves. American aid was invaluable to them but even American aid, generous though it was, did not match the increased production of this enterprising people so obdurately intent upon saving themselves.

4. THE BATTLE OF THE BALKANS

In the year which followed the capitulation of France, from June, 1940, to June, 1941, the Axis forces overran the Balkans. Hungary was already a satellite state under German influence. Rumania was "occupied" by October, 1940, to secure for Germany the output of the Ploesti oil fields. Bulgaria joined the Axis powers in a formal alliance on March 1, 1941. But some of the Balkan nations were prepared to fight rather than submit. The Greeks rejected an Italian ultimatum of October 28, 1940, and hurled back Mussolini's troops when they attempted an invasion from Albania. By March, 1941, the Greeks had occupied one-fourth of Albania, and the discomfited Italians were soliciting German aid. It came in the familiar *Blitzkrieg* fashion.

Until the spring of 1941 the Yugoslavs had preserved their freedom of action while the German shadow spread east and south. Yugoslavia was the largest of the Balkan states, with an area of 95,576 square miles, three-fourths that of Italy, and a population of 14,000,000. When German pressure drove their government into accepting a pact of alliance on March 25, the Yugoslav people repudiated the agreement and rallying under their young king, Peter II, they dared the Germans to attack. The result was predictable and mercilessly swift. From Germany, Hungary, Rumania, and Bulgaria the Nazi divisions poured into Yugoslavia and Greece. Belgrade was occupied within a week and the Yugoslav government capitulated after twelve days of resistance (April 17, 1941). To occupy this rough and mountainous land, however, was not to conquer it. Through the remainder of the war hardy bands of Yugoslav patriots harassed the German and Italian forces of occupation.

Greek resistance was broken when Yugoslavia fell. The Greek army which had invaded Albania was cut off when the Germans opened an attack on April 6; it capitulated on April 20. By the 27th the Germans had swept into Athens, and a British expeditionary force of 60,000 men hastily withdrew from the peninsula, losing considerable equipment and several thousand prisoners. By May 20 the Germans held all Greece and were preparing an audacious gamble, an aerial invasion of Crete, which would carry them halfway across the eastern Mediterranean to Egypt. Within ten days Crete fell to the

GERMAN ARMED FORCES LISTENING TO AN ADDRESS BY ADOLF HITLER

THE KRUPP STEEL WORKS AT ESSEN, GERMANY

reckless companies of paratroops and to Nazi reinforcements that defied the British navy and sailed boldly for the island. The surviving British troops and ships, badly mauled by German air power, were withdrawn to Cyprus and Alexandria.

These speedy conquests not only gave the Germans control of the Balkans but made them a serious threat in the Mediterranean, so serious that the British Empire life line to India, via Gibraltar, Suez, and Aden, was rendered useless. By a leap from Crete or by reinforcing the Italian forces in Libya, the Axis might invade Egypt from the west or launch a thrust from the north through Syria and Palestine. Turkey still preserved its precarious neutrality; but in Iraq a pro-Axis leader proclaimed a revolt on May 2. Only a daring march into Bagdad and Mosul by an unsupported British column held the wavering Iraqis neutral. But the situation throughout the Near East was highly critical. The Arab world respects force, and the German legions were weaving for themselves a legend of invincibility. In Syria the representatives of the Vichy French regime were ready to collaborate with Axis troops if they appeared. The danger demanded instant countermeasures. British forces, supported by detachments of Free French, moved against Beirut and Damascus, ending the rule of the Vichy officials in these regions. With control of Syria and Iraq assured, the British were in a better position to overawe Iran where German agents had likewise stirred dissensions. When British and Russian forces entered the country jointly, the Persian government at Tehran agreed to co-operate. These swift and resolute maneuvers in the spring of 1941 erected a line of buffer states across the Near East. Even if the Axis forces seized Constantinople and the Straits, they would still be blocked from the Red Sea or the Persian Gulf (see map, page 637).

5. THE BATTLE OF THE MEDITERRANEAN: ROUND ONE

When the Italian government declared war on France and Britain in June, 1940, Mussolini believed that victory was at hand. France was crushed and it seemed improbable that the British could continue the conflict alone. This hasty miscalculation cost Italy an empire. For the extensive African possessions which the Italians had conquered and sought to colonize in the preceding decades were not easy to defend against an enemy with superior sea power. One strong motive for the German drive towards Egypt in the spring of 1941 was the need to open the Suez Canal to Axis troopships. Only two routes existed by which reinforcements might reach the Italian garrisons in Ethiopia: the water route down the Red Sea and the land route through Egypt.

The British had recognized from the first that of all the Axis conquests Ethiopia and Libya were the most vulnerable because both could be reached only by crossing salt water. On land the Germans had shown themselves irresistible in these opening years of the war but at sea the British still held the advantage. Ethiopia, with the adjacent Italian protectorates of Somaliland and Eritrea, were isolated from the day that Italy entered the war. The Axis victories in Europe brought them no relief. After some initial reverses the British forces began to close in. By the spring of 1941 they were in Mogadiscio and Addis Ababa, and Italian resistance in East Africa was collapsing. It was the first conclusive campaign the British had waged so far in eighteen months darkened by retreats and evacuations, and it was a campaign that succeeded through the pressure of sea power. The lesson was obvious.

The lesson was further emphasized by events in North Africa. In the first months of 1941 the British repelled an Italian force which had advanced from Libya into Egypt. Opening a swift return offensive in December, 1940, imperial troops swept from Mersa Matruh to El Argheila in two months, capturing 114,000 Italian prisoners at a cost of 3000 British casualties. But this brilliant desert campaign was suddenly halted. The German descent on Greece in April, the critical situation in Asia Minor, and the dispatch of German divisions to Libya under the audacious General Erwin Rommel changed the African balance abruptly. On April 3, 1941, the reinforced Axis armies opened a new offensive, seized Bardia, encircled Tobruk, and forced the British back to the Egyptian frontier. The first round of the battle of the Mediterranean had ended in a draw.

Again, as in the previous summer of 1940, the Germans faced the chance for an all-out oversea invasion. This time not Britain but Africa was the goal. Had Hitler thrown his best divisions into Libya, followed them with a major part of the *Luftwaffe,* and possibly risked a drive through Spain to seize Gibraltar, the whole Mediterranean area might have been under his control by the close of 1941. The Italian leaders urged their German allies to the venture. French North Africa would probably have yielded with no more than token resistance. The capture of Malta and Alexandria would have broken British naval power in the inland sea. Hitler and his advisers weighed the project.

A decision, the most momentous decision of the war, faced the Führer. His secret purposes, it is possible, will always remain something of a mystery, but he seems in May, 1941, to have reverted once more to the thought of seducing the British with the offer of a truce.

On May 10, 1941, London was stricken by the worst air attack it had known, 100,000 incendiary bombs raining down upon the blazing city. The same night Rudolf Hess, the Deputy Führer and third ranking chief in the Nazi hierarchy, flew to Scotland on a secret mission. He came to propose peace to the British leaders, but whether he acted on his own initiative or as an accredited agent of Hitler was not made clear. Apparently the British Secret Service had expected his arrival, and it is possible that they learned from conversation with him that Hitler was ready to make peace and even to form an alliance with the British in order to deal with Russia. The British may have warned the Soviet government that Hitler was shifting his divisions to the east for a surprise attack upon the nation with which, less than two years earlier, he had concluded a nonaggression pact.

Tension between Germany and Russia had been growing acute as the Germans drove through the Balkans to the Mediterranean. The Russian foreign minister, Vyacheslav Molotov, visited Berlin to confer with the German foreign minister, Joachim von Ribbentrop, in the spring of 1941, but the price Molotov suggested for a full military alliance with Germany proved too high. The Soviet government felt that it must strengthen its position in face of the augmentation of German power and asked the right to take over Lithuania, Estonia, Latvia, the Karelian isthmus, Bessarabia, and Bukovina, and to extend its influence to the Dardanelles, the Persian Gulf, and the Arabian coast on the east as far as Aden. Apparently Hitler regarded these demands, in the form Molotov outlined, as too great. They would have made Russia a more dangerous adversary without reducing the risk of war. Molotov returned to Moscow after a cold leave-taking.

All spring the German armies had been moving towards the Russian frontier. If war with the Soviet Union was inevitable, the Nazi leaders were not disposed to give the Russians more time; they were persuaded that they could end the threat from the east and then turn to extra-European conquests. But for such imperial campaigns they needed more reserve supplies, and the wheat of the Ukraine, the oil of the Caucasus, the timber and minerals of the Urals were a powerful temptation. Possibly, too, the German specialists in air and mechanized warfare conceived that the Russian steppes in summer offered an ideal terrain for their *Blitzkrieg* strategy. Whatever the motives, Hitler decided to attack Russia. It was one of the most fateful decisions in history.

The Russians were prepared, much better prepared than most foreign observers believed possible. In 1931 Stalin had warned the Soviet peoples of their danger in a world of competing imperialisms. "We are fifty or a hundred years behind the advanced countries. We must make good this distance in ten years. Either we do it or they crush us." In 1941 the ten years were up.

THE WAR BECOMES GLOBAL

(JUNE, 1941—DECEMBER, 1942)

The enemy [Russia] *is already broken and will never rise again.*
ADOLF HITLER (OCTOBER 3, 1941)

1. THE RUSSIAN RETREAT (JUNE–DECEMBER, 1941)

ON June 22, 1941, German armies opened their surprise attack against Russia, sweeping over the frontier on a front of 2000 miles from Finland to Rumania. Auxiliary divisions from Italy and the satellite states gave the German high command an offensive force of 3,000,000 men. To oppose the mighty *Wehrmacht* the Russians had an estimated 2,000,000 men under arms and many millions of trained reservists, but they could not hold back the Teuton tide. Within a week the Germans had reached Grodno, Vilna, and Brest-Litovsk, while the Soviet armies in the north, center, and south continued to fall back with heavy losses. Most foreign observers anticipated a German victory. Reports from American agents abroad were pessimistic, some of them predicting that the Russians would be defeated within three months.

To the British, Hitler's eastern offensive was a reprieve, for so long as the Russians continued to resist strongly the Germans could not attempt an invasion of England. Three weeks after the attack opened, Britain and Russia formed an alliance and the British pledged the Soviet Union all possible aid. In Washington also plans were concerted immediately to dispatch arms to Russia, although there was grave fear that they might arrive too late or fall into enemy hands. Shouldering the burden of decision, prime minister Churchill and President Roosevelt advised rapid shipments, confident that the Russian armies would hold out. In October an agreement was signed in Moscow, promising the Soviet government tanks, planes, guns, gasoline, and other materials from the United States to the value of $1,000,000,000. The British, hard pressed to equip their own forces, nevertheless spared food and weapons. The Russians were demonstrating their determination to fight on to victory. Their farsighted request for machine tools to fit out new munitions factories in the remote Ural region reflected their vision and resolution.

For six months the "bloodiest front" shifted inexorably eastward across the level plains of Russia. This was the real war, an ordeal so savage and exhausting that those participating forgot that there were other fronts. If the military contributions of nations were measured in terms of human sacrifice, the Russian share in the ultimate victory would be twice that of all the other United Nations combined. The Russian battle dead were to mount until they exceeded 3,000,000, or two-thirds of the entire combat losses of the Allies. The total of civilian dead in the war area cannot be ascertained; it may have exceeded the military casualties. For the Germans and their cohorts the eastern front was likewise the real war, for these campaigns probably accounted for two-thirds of the Axis losses in killed, which exceeded 5,000,000 at the end of the war.

The German divisions which marched into Russia in the summer of 1941 were arrogant and strong, for Hitler's legions had never tasted defeat. At first new victories daily added force to their momentum. By the first of July they were in Riga; Smolensk fell to them July 16; after eight weeks of fighting and marching all the Ukraine west of the Dnieper (save Odessa) was in their control. On September 4 they arrived before Leningrad; on the 19th they stormed into Kiev and Poltava. Before the end of October they had taken Bryansk, Vyasma, Odessa, and Kharkov. At the southern extremity of the flaming battle line they were entering the Crimea; in the north they had penetrated the environs of Moscow. The Soviet government shifted to a new capital at Kuibyshev, and Stalin, admitting that the retreat had already cost the defenders 1,500,000 casualties, called upon the Russian people to redouble their efforts.

2. THE RUSSIAN DEFENSE AND THE SECOND GERMAN OFFENSIVE (DECEMBER, 1941–AUGUST, 1942)

The German plan to crush the Soviet armies before winter came broke down before the grim tenacity of the Russian people. With the first snowfall the Russian soldiers, knowing themselves better inured to the cold and more familiar with the terrain, prepared for a counter-

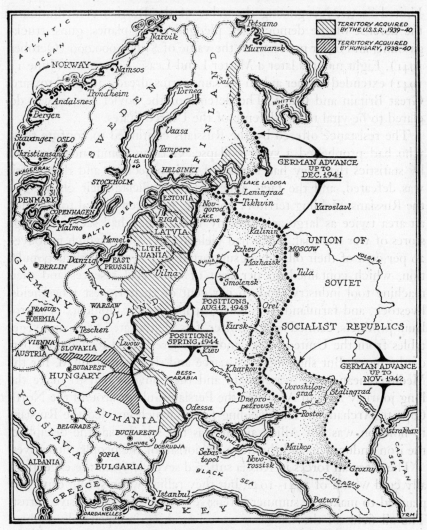

THE GERMAN INVASION OF RUSSIA, 1941-1944

offensive. They recaptured Rostov in the south and relieved the pressure on Moscow in the north. In January, 1942, they retook Mozhaisk, in February Dorogobuzh, in April and May they attacked near Kursk and Kharkov. Encouraged by their recovery from what had seemed irresistible blows, the people settled down for a long war.

From Britain and the United States came an increasing stream of armaments. The British indicated their confidence in Russian faith by transforming the mutual aid pact signed in July, 1941, into a twenty-year treaty of alliance between Britain and the Soviet Union. The

United States, recognizing the value of the Russian contribution to the defense of the democracies, pledged tanks, planes, guns, trucks, gasoline, and other materials to the value of $1,000,000,000 (October, 1941). Eight months later a Master Lend-Lease Agreement (June 11, 1942) extended further aid on the same terms already adopted towards Great Britain and China. The defense of the Soviet Union was declared to be vital to the defense of the United States.

The resistance offered by the Russians continued to confute those who had prophesied a swift collapse. German commanders proved by statistics that they had surpassed their objectives and that Russia was defeated, and the facts appeared to vindicate their claims. For the Russians, yielding territory for time, had been forced to abandon an area twice as large as Germany itself. They had sacrificed huge stores of war material. They had yielded the regions which produced 20 per cent of their oil, which supported 30 per cent of their population, which contained 40 per cent of their coal reserves and their machine tool industry, and 50 per cent of their richest wheatfields, livestock, and farmland. It is true that increasing shipments of petroleum products, canned meats, butter, fats, dehydrated fruits and vegetables from the United States and elsewhere helped to make up part of the losses. But shipping was scarce and shipments limited, for the Mediterranean route was unsafe and the convoys had to make the long journey around Africa to the Persian Gulf or around the North Cape to Archangel. The deciding factor which enabled the Russians to hold on was not Allied aid, it was the self-denial, the discipline, the iron endurance, and the fiery patriotism of the people themselves.

The German forces in Russia suffered severely from the exceptionally cold winter of 1941–1942, but they rallied when spring came and planned to make the summer offensive of 1942 the conclusive thrust. The oil fields of the Caucasus were becoming indispensable to them for they could not elsewhere secure all the gasoline required for their trucks, tanks, and planes. By seizing this supply they could avert a shortage, while the Russian war machine, starved for lack of fuel, would soon be stalled and helpless. Sevastopol, guarding the Crimea, had endured an epic eight-month siege: it was captured by the Germans on July 3. Driving forward along the southern front the invaders reached Voronezh, Millerovo, and Rostov, crossed the Don River, and launched a furious assault against Stalingrad. If they won this key city on the Volga they could cut the last important oil supply route to Russia from the Caspian Sea, for they had already taken

Rostov and Maikop. But Stalingrad held out. Weeks of intense fighting wrecked the city; reinforcements rushed up by both sides devoured each other amid the ruins; shells churned the rubble day after day; but Stalingrad held out. The invaders were making their supreme effort. The *Wehrmacht* struck and struck again with all its collected strength, and it failed to close the Volga. This reverse of 1942 became an Axis disaster at the opening of 1943. Russian pincers closed upon the invading spearhead and 300,000 Axis troops were killed or captured.

3. THE JAPANESE COLLECT AN EMPIRE

The outbreak of war in Europe in 1939 changed the balance of power in the Far East. Within a year the European possessions of the French in Indo-China and of the Dutch in the Netherlands East Indies were left to defend themselves, for the Germans had overrun France and Holland. The British position in Asia had likewise been weakened by the need to recall naval units to hold the sea routes of the Mediterranean and the Atlantic. In the area which lies between China and Australia — in fact throughout the vast segment of the globe which extends from India to Alaska — there was no longer a balance of power but a vacuum of power. Only one strong state remained in that undefended zone, and that state was Japan. The British battleships had been summoned to danger points nearer home than the reaches of the far Pacific. The Russian armies on the borders of Manchukuo desired no clash with the Japanese, for the Soviet generals were waiting for the decision which locked them in battle with the Germans after June, 1941. This was the moment for which the Japanese war lords had waited, the moment when a quarter of the world would be theirs for the taking.

Their war of conquest on the mainland of Asia, euphemistically referred to as the "China Incident,"[1] had brought them control of Manchuria and a dominant position in several provinces of North China. But after ten years of Japanese coercion and cajolery the Chinese Nationalist armies continued to resist and the Chinese people showed little desire to be incorporated into the Co-prosperity Sphere which the Japanese planned to extend over all East Asia. China, moreover, could not supply the indispensable war materials, especially tin, rubber, and oil, which the Japanese required for their industrial and military activities. So they decided that the conquest

[1] See pages 365–370.

of China must be postponed because the conquest of the Dutch East Indies, French Indo-China, and Burma could not wait.

The fall of France misled the Japanese; they concluded that the Axis powers were winning the war and the democracies would be unable to recover sufficiently to hold their empires together. In September, 1940, Japan concluded a military pact with Germany and Italy. The Japanese, however, had no direct interest in the European war; they were thinking of their own advantage, and the accord with Germany and with Italy was rounded out by a nonaggression treaty with Russia on April 13, 1941. This treaty was a "local deal" which suited the Russians because of the impending war in the West and suited the Japanese because it secured their northern flank in China while they moved south. Thus fortune reduced the last serious threat to the Japanese plans for swift expansion. By the summer of 1941 they had occupied bases in French Indo-China (which Vichy France was too feeble to protect), they had contracted a treaty of alliance with Thailand (Siam), and they were demanding the oil and rubber output of the Netherlands East Indies. The British, unwilling to assume over-heavy responsibilities in Asia while they were assailed in Europe, had withdrawn from Shanghai and their North China posts in August, 1940. They still held Hong Kong and their naval base at Singapore, but their ships and garrisons in these areas were not adequate to resist a determined and sustained attack. The Japanese saw a chance for their navy to dominate the eastern Pacific to the Indies and beyond unless the United States joined with Britain in blocking them.

Throughout the summer and autumn of 1941 the United States warned the Japanese cabinet gravely and repeatedly that their program of military expansion might lead to war. After the conference held by President Roosevelt and prime minister Winston Churchill in the North Atlantic (August, 1941) the government at Tokyo received joint warnings from London and Washington. But no compromise could be reached. The Japanese envoys to the United States declared at the end of November that American insistence that Japanese forces be withdrawn from China and Indo-China made further discussion futile.

This diplomatic deadlock was broken on December 7, 1941, by the appearance of Japanese warplanes over Hawaii. A month earlier the United States cabinet had debated whether American forces should strike the first blow but had favored patience and decided to

avoid acts which could be represented as warlike. Thus the Japanese
were able to begin hostilities with a surprise attack and to do appalling
damage in a few hours. Of eighty-eight United States naval craft
located in Pearl Harbor almost all were sunk or damaged. The bombing and fighting planes lined up on nearby airfields were almost entirely destroyed. This sudden stroke, well planned and extraordinarily

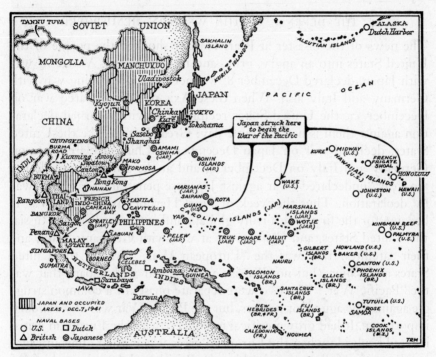

THE JAPANESE OFFENSIVE IN THE PACIFIC, 1941

successful, crippled almost half the United States navy and paralyzed
American striking power in the Pacific. Guam, Midway, and Wake
Island fell under heavy Japanese assaults, and the Philippines, deprived of naval protection and reinforcements, were conquered after
six months of heroic resistance. In the same period other Japanese
forces occupied the Dutch East Indies, captured Singapore and Rangoon, overran Burma, and threatened to invade India. Their naval
raiders seized the Andaman Islands and shelled coastal cities in Ceylon.

Fortune had offered the Japanese an exceptional opportunity but
their skill in exploiting it was impressive and thorough. No nation in
so brief a time had ever acquired an empire so rich, so extensive, and

so densely populated as the area which passed under Japanese control in the six months after Pearl Harbor. By the summer of 1942 it seemed doubtful if anything could halt the Nipponese advance: Australia, New Zealand, even India itself were threatened. But the road to conquest had been cleared for the Japanese by the events in Europe, and events in Europe would decide the outcome of their daring bid for supremacy in East Asia.

4. THE DEFENSE OF THE WESTERN HEMISPHERE

The news of the disaster at Pearl Harbor shocked the people of the United States into an angry, grim, and resolute mood. A state of war with Japan, declared December 8, was accepted as meaning war with Germany and Italy also. When these Axis powers declared war on December 11, the United States reciprocated with a formal declaration against them issued the same day. Great Britain, like the United States, declared war on Japan December 8. China declared war on Germany and Italy on December 9, and at the same time made the ten-year "undeclared" war against Japanese penetration a formal war by declaration. Thus the week of Pearl Harbor saw World War II become for the first time a truly global conflict. Great Britain, Russia, the United States, and China were at war with Germany, Italy, and their satellites: that was the "European War." Britain, the United States and China (but not Russia) were at war with Japan: that was the "Pacific War." The two were separate phases of a common struggle against the aggressor powers, but the Pacific War was of secondary importance. It had grown critical in concert with the European crisis; it would subside when the European crisis was curbed. This interdependence was fully recognized by the British and American chiefs of staff. It was to guide them in their joint preparations and in their war strategy.

As the "arsenal of democracy" the United States had already been a target for Axis saboteurs, but open warfare made the risk of enemy attacks much more serious. The possibility of a blow against the Panama Canal or an invasion of Latin America made hemisphere defense an urgent problem. In 1940 Congress had passed a Selective Service Act, had appropriated $2,500,000,000 for defense, and had authorized the sale of arms to the other American republics under the Pittman Act. The State Department warned all foreign governments that no transfer of territory by one non-American power to another would be recognized if the territory concerned lay in the western hemisphere. The subjugation of Denmark, the Netherlands, and France made it likely that the Germans would attempt to use the colonies of these three countries in the New World for bases, and the United States government was vigilant to prevent such a move. At the Havana Conference of the Pan American Union (July, 1940) the foreign ministers of the twenty-one republics supported the United States in this decision and voted that all should act as "collective trustee" and take over any territory in the New World if there was danger that such territory might be alienated and pass under different sovereignty. The Havana Conference resolved further that all the member republics should make provision for joint defense.

Events were transforming the United States into a strong and militant nation. Plans for a two-ocean navy and the adoption of the Selective Service Act (September, 1940) were proof that the era of isolationism was at an end. The acquisition of naval bases in the Atlantic and Caribbean (September, 1940) and the passage of the Lend-Lease Act (March, 1941) were further milestones on the road to national defense. The Republic of Panama granted the United States the right to establish air defenses outside the Canal Zone, a third set of locks was planned to provide for congestion or accident, and a route was laid out that would link the Canal Zone and the United States by land. This route was to form part of an extensive Pan-American Highway to run from Mexico City through Central America to Santiago, Chile, thence across the Andes to Buenos Aires, and up the Atlantic coast to Rio de Janeiro. An agreement with the Canadian government also provided for the construction of a Pacific highway to Alaska. In 1941 United States forces took up garrison duty in Greenland, Iceland, and Dutch Guiana as a necessary step in securing the western hemisphere from foreign threat.

The outbreak of war between the United States and the Axis powers put Pan-American solidarity to the test. Within six weeks the representatives of the other American republics met at Rio de Janeiro and voted to sever relations with the German, Italian, and Japanese governments. Ecuador granted the United States bases in the Galapagos Islands, and Brazil agreed to a joint defense of the Atlantic sea lanes. An Inter-American Defense Board was established (March, 1942) to co-ordinate the measures for defense adopted by all the American states, and the extension of the Lend-Lease Act the same month proved the readiness of the United States to finance and equip this joint armament project. The defense of each of the American republics had become the concern of all of them.

Defense, however, was not the only Pan-American problem intensified by the war. The disruption of normal trade caused by the blockade of Axis-dominated Europe caused grave inconvenience to most of the Latin American countries. Britain and the United States therefore agreed to purchase food and raw materials and to pay for these supplies with shipments of manufactured goods. As most British and American industries had been diverted to war production, however, Latin American demands could not always be met at once. This meant that credits and advance orders were built up, a process which enabled the people of Central and South America to reduce their debts to Britain and America and so improve their financial prospects for the postwar era. These economic trends united them to the destinies of the Anglo-American bloc, a natural consequence since their trade with the Axis powers was impaired by the blockade.

5. THE BATTLE OF THE MEDITERRANEAN: ROUND TWO (JUNE, 1941–DECEMBER, 1942)

The winter of 1941–1942 was the darkest period of the war for the United Nations. The ships of the United States Pacific fleet which had survived Pearl Harbor were withdrawn to home ports. The British forces in the Far East fared no better: Hong Kong fell to the Japanese December 25, 1941, and the great naval and air base at Singapore capitulated February 15, 1942. Two weeks later the last Allied squadron in the eastern Pacific was eliminated in the battle of the Java Sea (February 27). The British were so weakened by April that the Japanese were in Rangoon and their naval units dared to raid Ceylon.

The astonishing success and rapidity of the Japanese advance into Malaysia, Burma, Java, Sumatra, and Borneo had opened up three possible areas of conquest for their 1942 offensive. They might speed south for a thrust into Australia. They might turn west for a naval and military invasion of India. They might push north from Indo-China and Burma to overwhelm the Chinese Nationalist armies which still defied them from Chungking. The fact that they achieved none of these objectives is an immortal tribute to the vastly outnumbered forces (American, British, Chinese, and Dutch) which still resisted in the Pacific theater of the war. For a year and more it was the impossible task of these ABCD units to guard half the world while the dictates of global strategy called the major reserves of the Allied nations to the other half.

A week after the Pearl Harbor blow, Winston Churchill was in Washington conferring with President Roosevelt. Two courses were open to the American leaders. They might turn the major war effort of the United States against Japan, or they might turn it towards the European theater and make Germany the objective. It is a principle of military strategy that major attention should be directed to the destruction of the enemy's major force. Germany was the heart and core of the Rome-Berlin-Tokyo alliance, the real "axis" of the Axis combination. The objectives open to Japanese attack in 1942 — Australia, China, India — were none of them indispensable to Allied survival. But the German offensive of 1942 (and the initiative still rested with the German high command) might inflict a crippling blow on the Allied nations. The Nazi battalions might plunge across southern Russia to the Caucasus; they might penetrate Asia Minor and Egypt and even link up with Japanese advance columns in India; they might leap to French North Africa and threaten South America from Dakar. If they won supremacy in the Mediterranean they would command North Africa and its supplies, cut the Suez Canal, and halt the flow of arms reaching Russia through Iran. Clearly, Germany was the enemy which could strike the most fateful blows in 1942 and therefore Germany was the foe to watch most closely.

Since Britain and the United States were still on the defensive, their chiefs of staff had to ask themselves where the enemy might paralyze Allied resistance. The most evident answer was: on the sea. Without ships America and Britain would be powerless to strike anywhere and Britain at least would rapidly become powerless to defend herself. This truth was driven home by Winston Churchill when he addressed a secret session of the British parliament in March, 1942. "It is only by shipping," he said, "that the United States or indeed we ourselves can intervene either in the eastern or the western theater." Ships were the key to Allied victory or defeat and there were not enough ships.

One way to relieve this crisis was to reopen the Mediterranean route, for the long convoy trips around Norway and around Africa were dangerous, time-consuming, and uneconomical. But to reopen the Mediterranean seemed impossible in the spring of 1942 because the British forces there could barely hold their own. Malta was subject to daily air raids and even in Alexandria the British battleships were under constant danger of attack. German plans for the summer included the capture of this vital harbor which guarded the adjacent Suez Canal. On May 27 the "Desert Fox," General Erwin Rommel, started a swift drive from Libya. Capturing Tobruk (June 17) the mechanized columns rolled into Egypt until they reached El Alamein, only sixty miles from Alexandria. Meanwhile, a thousand miles to the north the Germans had crashed through the Crimea and were at the gates of the Caucasus. The Arab peoples between the Nile and the Caspian Sea stirred restlessly, loyal to Britain but ready to shift allegiance if British power collapsed. The tide of German success was at the full.

Then, on October 23, 1942, the British Eighth Army leaped forward from El Alamein in a mechanized drive which expelled the Axis forces from Egypt in two weeks. The initiative had slipped from Hitler's hands. For synchronized with this third British offensive from Egypt an Anglo-American expedition commanded by General Dwight D. Eisenhower disembarked in French Morocco and Algeria (November 8). This gigantic amphibious operation, which required 850 ships, resulted in the speedy capture of Casablanca, Oran, and Algiers, and the French garrisons agreed to cease resistance and to co-operate against the Axis forces. The Germans promptly retaliated by moving into unoccupied France and attempted to seize the French warships interned at Toulon, but the ships were scuttled by their crews. Africa was lost to the Axis; but rather than admit it and withdraw, Hitler poured thousands of airborne reinforcements into Tunis and Tripoli. Rommel was ordered to hold to the last those ports nearest to Sicily which, in Allied possession, would provide a springboard for the invasion of Italy. By their promptness in throwing new forces into Africa the Axis powers added to their own ultimate losses but they were successful in their immediate aim: they delayed the Anglo-American entry into Tunis. The battle of the Mediterranean had still a round to go before it became the battle of Italy.

THE TURNING OF THE TIDE

(JANUARY, 1943—JUNE, 1944)

The drive to free the Soviet land has begun.

JOSEPH STALIN (FEBRUARY, 1943)

I. THE BATTLE OF THE MEDITERRANEAN: ROUND THREE

THE destruction of the Axis armies in North Africa was completed between January and May, 1943. From El Alamein the British Eighth Army under General Bernard Montgomery raced a thousand miles westward to Tripoli between October, 1942, and January, 1943. From Morocco Anglo-American forces commanded by General Eisenhower swung eastward in the same months. Both had a common objective: the ports of Bizerte and Tunis through which the Axis nations poured in their reinforcements and from which they must escape if they could escape at all. The problem of supply largely explains why Tunis became the focal center for this last battle on African soil. British and American forces converged by sea through Suez and Gibraltar. German and Italian forces leaped the narrow straits between Sicily and Tunis where the Mediterranean is only a few hundred miles wide. Exposed to attack from east and west, Rommel concentrated his forces, asked Hitler for all possible support, and prepared to hold Tunis to the end. American spearhead detachments, which Eisenhower had hurled towards Tunis as soon as the Allies got ashore on November 8, were checked at the Kasserine Pass. The British on the east were halted in front of Gabès by the Mareth Line. Allied hopes of ending the African campaign by January were dashed. The Americans were unable to take the Kasserine Pass until February 25, 1943. This first great amphibious offensive of the Anglo-American coalition was not a story of unbroken successes; it was an experiment, a rehearsal, which taught the Allied commanders invaluable lessons.

One lesson they already knew: that all supplies and reinforcements which the Axis shipped to Tunisia by sea or by air would pay a toll in transit. Allied submarines and fighting planes cut down Rommel's supplies sharply. Both adversaries were fighting far from their centers of production but sea power won the decision. Though it taxed all the shipping of the United Nations, tanks, planes, guns, gasoline — and men — reached Egypt and Morocco and Algiers, to be rushed to the

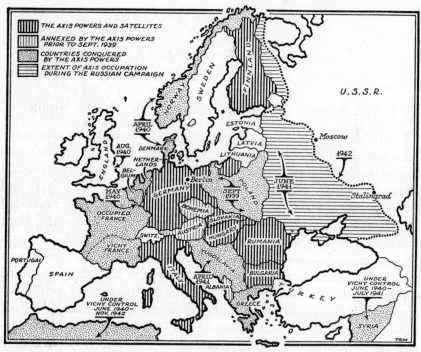

THE AXIS DOMINATION OF EUROPE, 1941–1942

battle line across the cumbered roads of North Africa fouled by the winter rain. The unremitting pressure told so that by April the Allies were crowding the Axis rearguard towards the tip of the Tunisian headland. There the remnants of Rommel's divisions were destroyed or captured in the early days of May. The British entered Tunis on May 7 while the Americans and their French allies captured Bizerte. The last units of the broken Axis army, cut off from escape by the Allied sea and air supremacy, gave themselves up on May 13.

Mussolini had dreamed for twenty years of recreating a "Roman Empire" which would span the Mediterranean. By an irony of history, his last African cohorts capitulated near the site of ancient Carthage, which the Romans had destroyed in 146 B.C. Within three years the Italians had forfeited all their African conquests, possessions ten times the size of Italy with a population of 15,000,000. Their attempts to hold Italian Somaliland, Eritrea, Ethiopia, and Libya had cost the Axis armies an estimated 950,000 military casualties. Of these, 150,000 were taken prisoner in the final week of the Tunisian campaign, May 6–13, 1943.

Undisputed control of North Africa gave the Allies three major advantages. It ended all fear that a German thrust might reach Dakar, where the Atlantic is narrowest and a leap to Brazil most practicable. It reopened to Allied ships the Mediterranean life line to Egypt and the East. It made possible an invasion of Italy and the opening of a battle front within Hitler's "Fortress Europe." Two months after Tunis fell the Allies were in Sicily.

For this second amphibious operation the Anglo-American commanders now had 2500 ships available. Bombing and fighting planes, rolling off the assembly lines in quantity, assured them local command of the air. Wading ashore on July 10, the Allied troops conquered Sicily in a swift campaign of five weeks, at a cost of 22,000 casualties. The Axis losses, eight times as heavy, so daunted the Italian people that on July 25 Mussolini was overthrown in a surprise move and Marshal Pietro Badoglio assumed his place as head of the government. A demand for peace spread through the country, and the Germans, realizing that their ally might capitulate, transformed their divisions in Italy into an army of occupation and seized all strategic centers. Italy sank from the role of an Axis partner to the role of a prostrate state like France, a state that would have to be "liberated." The Italian people themselves appeared to have lost hope and volition.

On September 2, 1943, the British leaped the Strait of Messina to the toe of Italy. A week later a second Allied force, chiefly American units, fought its way ashore at Salerno. Within a month the foot of Italy was cleared and Naples fell on October 1. Then winter weather and strong German resistance halted the advance. A new beachhead was established at Nettuno below Rome (January 2, 1944) but six months of savage fighting, with heavy casualties, ensued before the Eternal City was liberated on June 4. The difficulties of the Italian campaign, and the slow progress against a confident enemy entrenched in terrain unrivaled for defensive fighting, discouraged the Allied

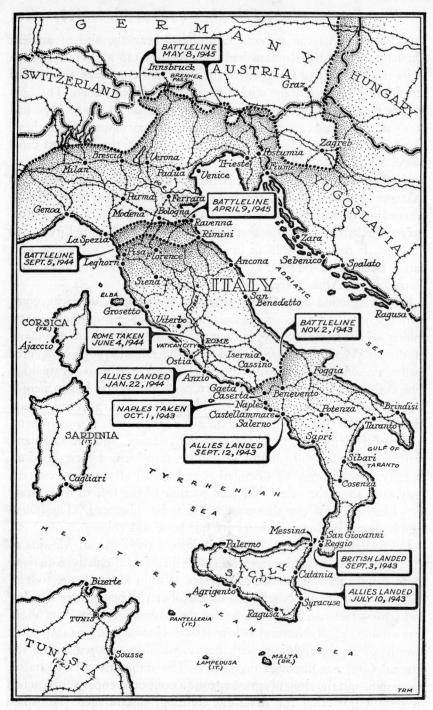

THE FIGHT FOR ITALY, 1943-1945

forces participating. They could not know that their effort was a secondary thrust and that the major operation of 1944 was to be opened in June on the Normandy beaches.

For the Italian people the situation of their country in 1943 and 1944 was confusing and tragic. The government of Marshal Badoglio concluded an armistice with the Allies early in September, 1943. The terms, which were kept secret, provided that the Italians would assist the United Nations, permit Allied military forces to occupy strategic areas, surrender the Italian fleet, and accept temporary Allied control over the national finances, censorship, communication, and transport. Badoglio could not enforce the agreement because his influence did not extend to regions where the Germans still held control. Mussolini, who had been imprisoned after his fall in July, was rescued by his German confederates in September, 1943, and proclaimed a republican regime in northern Italy. Thus two regimes, one dominated by the Germans, one subservient to the Allies, claimed the divided loyalties of the Italian populace. In the long struggle from September, 1943, to May, 1945, Italians served on both sides, but the major fighting to liberate Italy was done by the American, British, French, Polish, Brazilian, and other units which composed the Allied Expeditionary Force. The ruthless and experienced German divisions retreated slowly and stubbornly from one prepared line to the next, and only when Germany itself collapsed did the resistance in Italy cease.

2. THE RESURGENCE OF SOVIET RUSSIA
(JANUARY, 1943–JUNE, 1944)

On the Russian front likewise the Axis armies lost the initiative in 1943. The failure to take Stalingrad by the close of 1942 suggested that their lines were overextended. With the dread winter at hand they should have shortened them, but Hitler forbade a withdrawal. Against the advice of the commanders in the field he gambled on holding the advanced positions won in the summer of 1942, and he lost. For once again the Russians welcomed the winter as their ally, opening a counteroffensive on November 19, 1942. Within ten weeks they closed vast embracing pincers upon twenty-two German divisions besieging Stalingrad, and overwhelmed them. Axis losses exceeded 300,000 and the total mounted as the Russian offensive ground relentlessly forward. In the north, too, a counterdrive relieved Leningrad, which had endured a seventeen-month siege, and brought more thousands of prisoners and tons of war material into Russian possession. February, 1943, was a month of almost daily triumphs and the guns of the Kremlin shook Moscow with their succession of victory salutes. Kursk fell on February 8th, Belgorod the 9th, Rostov the 14th, Kharkov the 16th. By the opening of March, when Rzhev and Vyasma succumbed, the Axis losses in killed or captured were reckoned at 500,000 for the previous ninety days, an average of over 5000 a day.

Then the Germans rallied and fought back desperately. Kharkov was wrested from the Russians once again (March 15) and Belgorod reoccupied a week later. But exhaustion was descending upon both combatants after the winter's incredible work, and the morass of mud that marks the Russian spring chained their feet. For three months (April–July, 1943) there was a breathing spell. The Russians could afford to take it; they were saved. Their winter drive had carried them halfway from the Don to the Dnieper, had recaptured the vital railway hubs at Kursk and Velikiye Luki, and had ended the threat to the Volga-Caspian-Iranian route and the Murmansk-Archangel-Moscow railway.

The strength of the Soviet people grew with every league recovered. Workmen pressed into reconquered towns and began rebuilding before the enemy were out of sight. Peasants returning to their scorched fields buried the dead as they went about their plowing. It was not the spirit of the Soviet soldiers alone that made possible the resurgence of Russia. It was the confidence of almost 200,000,000 people in their cause, in their leaders, and in themselves.

The Germans made plans for large-scale drives to mark their third summer in Russia, but for the first time the Russians had the initiative in summer fighting and they kept it. Orel, Belgorod, and Kharkov were once more in their hands by August; Bryansk and Smolensk fell to them in September. By October, 1943, they had reached the Dnieper; in November they entered Kiev, and in December Zhitomir. The opening months of 1944 concluded the battle of Russia. By May the Soviet troops had liberated the Ukraine, cleared the Crimea, and herded the retreating Axis armies across the borders of Rumania and Poland.

Not even a large-scale map can suggest the magnitude of the Russians' achievement. Within a year they had advanced a thousand miles, from Stalingrad to the Carpathians, transforming the battle of the Caucasus into the battle of the Balkans. But this liberation of the Ukraine had not left other Russian armies marking time. In the center they were at the Polish border, in the north their drives wrested Viipuri from the Finns. It was now the turn of this northern sector to draw the attention of the world, for there in 1944 the battle of Germany was to open. The European struggle was approaching its final phase.

On June 6, 1944, the Allied invasion of Normandy called the Axis forces into action on three major fronts, the Eastern, the Italian, and the Western. The irreparable losses suffered in Russia during three years of exhausting war had left the Germans too weak to hold such extended lines against powerful antagonists. In 1944 it became clear that the Nazi structure was cracking, for the attempt to eliminate Russia had failed and the governments of the Soviet Union, Great Britain, and the United States were bound by a common determination to end the Hitler regime.

The prophets who in 1941 had expected to see Russia defeated after three months were now confronted with a Russia victorious after three years. Four main factors had combined to make this triumph possible. The first was the superb courage and inspired generalship of the Red armies. The second was the energetic development of Russian industry and resources which, despite the mutilation caused by the German occupation, continued to provide the armies with essential munitions and equipment. The third factor was the supplementary material from Britain and America, the thousands of planes, tanks, trucks, the tons of oil, explosives, meat, and concentrated foods. The fourth factor was a negative gain: it was the reduction of German fighting strength by the wrecking of factories, railways, airfields, bridges, and other military targets throughout the Reich, destroyed by raids of British and American bombing planes. The Russians, reasonably enough, emphasized the first two factors because these were the result of their own labor and courage. But the last two factors were also important as contributions to the Russian victories and it is therefore appropriate to pause and consider the role played by Anglo-American production and Anglo-American air power.

3. PRODUCTION AND TRANSPORTATION

When the Soviet Union and the United States entered the general conflict in 1941, World War II became in the literal sense a world war because the population and resources of all the continents were involved. As in World War I the two groups of contestants seemed grossly unequal at first glance. The Axis powers controlled perhaps 3,000,000 square miles of territory and a population of 500,000,000, whereas the United Nations with their empires dominated 40,000,000 square miles and 1,500,000,000 people. For industrial needs — and industry, as already noted, is indispensable in twentieth century warfare — the United Nations possessed more than twice the coal and iron resources and twenty-five times the petroleum output of the totalitarian states.

Clearly, if the United Nations could mobilize their superior resources in men, money, and materials, the Axis empires were doomed. On the other hand, if the Germans, Italians, and Japanese could cut off Russia from Britain and Britain from her empire and from the United States, they might dispose of Russia first, then defeat the British by blockade and starvation, and finally confront the United States. Such was the general aim of Axis global strategy. It grew clearer with the conquest of Norway and France, the isolation of Britain from Europe. It explained the drives for Suez and Singapore, vital "bottle-necks" in main routes of ocean transportation. It motivated the U-boat war on Allied shipping. The effort to seize supplies essential to themselves, while denying them to their opponents, sent the Germans lunging to the Caucasus and the Japanese to the East Indies.

In the First World War it was said that the Allies floated to victory on a sea of oil. In the Second World War the statement was scarcely an exaggeration. Oil provides the most dramatic example of the part a single commodity can play in deciding modern strategy. Mechanized warfare requires thousands upon thousands of jeeps, trucks, tractors, self-propelled guns, tanks, and planes, and these in turn demand oil and gasoline. So consuming was the need for liquid fuel in World War II that one half the cargoes shipped to the American Expeditionary Forces abroad consisted of petroleum or petroleum products. Despite the U-boat war on tankers this stream of oil continued to flow. Had it been interrupted, the armies of the United Nations would have been immobilized, their battle fleets impotent, their planes grounded. There was no real danger of such a paralyzing possibility so long as ocean routes remained open and the ships could sail, for the United Nations monopolized 86 per cent of the world's oil output. The Germans and Italians, on the other hand, found oil production a crucial problem. The Rumanian supply was inadequate; the Caucasian and Persian fields they failed to reach. To supplement their limited reserves they perfected a process for extracting oil from coal, but in the end bombing raids shattered their refineries and extraction plants. To the Italians, who lacked even coal and refining plants, the shortage of oil was crippling, and it kept their ships in port on more than one critical occasion.

The Japanese met the problem of oil requirements more successfully: they seized British Malaya and the Netherlands East Indies which produced about 4 per cent of the world's oil total. Furthermore, the Japanese area of conquest also produced nine-tenths of the world supply of natural rubber, and the loss of this commodity hurt the Allies. The sudden acute shortage which faced the United States, hitherto the world's heaviest rubber consumer, forced the government to develop synthetic rubber as a substitute. By the end of the war the chemists had met the challenge and United States home production of rubber exceeded prewar imports. With similar ingenuity the chemists met the demand for drug substitutes for such specifics as quinine, nine-tenths of which had likewise come from the East Indies. The shortage of tin, half of which had been mined in Malaysia before the war, embarrassed the United Nations to the end of hostilities, but they found alternatives.

The United States was the storehouse and arsenal of the United Nations, and Germany was the industrial core of Axis productive effort. As late as 1942 it was estimated that the Allied countries controlled perhaps 60 per cent of world output of manufactured goods against 40 per cent for the Axis. But the German factories were slowly starved for essential materials; they were bombed with mounting devastation; they were crippled by the lack of skilled man power. As a result the balance of war potential, already adverse, shifted steadily against them. Supplies from Spain, Switzerland, and Sweden, supplies which no Allied naval blockade could intercept, were cut down when the Anglo-American Blockade Committee used its superior financial resources to purchase key products it could not otherwise withhold from the Reich. Prices on some essentials, such as ball bearings, cutting tools, platinum, and tungsten were quoted at ten to one hundred times their peacetime level until the Germans lost purchasing power in this unacknowledged auction.

The problem of transportation, so acute in the first years of the war, was conquered by mass output. So extraordinary was the American achievement in shipbuilding that by 1945 the United States and Britain possessed more merchant shipping (despite losses) than the whole world had claimed in 1939. The construction period for freighters was reduced from thirty weeks to seven, and standardized ships were built in sections and put together like cars on an assembly line.

Almost overnight, shipbuilding became the second largest American industry. Without this bridge of boats the armies could not have moved. Over 26,000,000 tons of construction supplies and equipment were ferried to Britain and nearly 50,000,000 tons of war material to the armies in Europe. The weight of war material per fighting man had increased six-fold since World War I. New machinery, prefabricated barracks, landing ships, bulldozers, and a score of other devices produced by mass methods, made the Service of Supply a producer's nightmare.

In peacetime the United States had formed the largest single and uniform market in the world, and this vast body of consumers had stimulated the rise of organizations equipped to produce a standard product for the millions. This practice in mass production was invaluable in wartime; it enabled the United States to produce $186,000,000,-000 worth of military supplies by doubling its industrial output in five years. The varied weapons and accoutrements required, the enormous rise in output, the experienced personnel demanded, the rehearsals in pilot plants, all created problems which could be met only because American business efficiency had developed machinery for solving them. It is difficult to conceive the meshing and synchronizing of a million minds and a million gears in one co-ordinated enterprise. A modern military campaign is the most awesome example of mass activity the world has ever known and it must function without a hitch or the schedule may be dislocated. When it is remembered that these elaborate undertakings must be planned with secrecy and carried into execution despite every obstacle and destructive measure an alert and ruthless enemy can interpose, the responsibility which the commanders must assume appears insupportable.

4. MASTERY OF THE AIR

The First World War saw air power in its infancy. With the Second World War the air force took its place with the army and the navy as the third department of national defense. Armies and navies could no longer move in safety if they lost command of the skies, and strategy suddenly became a series of problems in three dimensions. A totally new method of outflanking an enemy and of attacking his rear revolutionized the rules of warfare, for paratroops might now be dropped at any point in the enemy's territory and enemy forces might be overwhelmed by "vertical envelopment." Superior naval strength was no longer sufficient to guarantee islands against invasion, warships became dangerously vulnerable to aerial bombs and torpedoes, beleaguered garrisons and marching columns could be attacked or supplied by aerial transport, and civilians living within the widening range of enemy bombing planes were now in the zone of battle.

To outbuild the Axis powers in aircraft and obtain control of the skies over Europe was essential for the defeat of Germany. But the German aircraft plants had a long start and had standardized their designs before the war opened. Their assembly lines were in full operation. In comparison, United States factories were producing only a few hundred combat planes in 1939. As late as 1941, American firms could construct only 2400 planes to meet urgent British needs. But plans for real mass production had been drawn and the results, when they came, literally darkened the skies. By the close of 1942 the United States production rate was 5400 planes a month; six months later it had climbed to 7500 a month, and in 1944 it passed 9000. When the year 1945 opened, American factories had produced 250,000 aircraft in four years and British factories 100,000. Russian plane production had likewise risen phenomenally although exact figures were not available. The United Nations were assured of ultimate dominion in the air. To convey the planes to their field of action in record time and maintain a global air transport service, the Air Transport Command was established with airfields, radio beacons, and weather stations functioning on every continent and ocean.

To Germany this rise in Allied air power brought a terrible retaliation for the ruthless bombing which the *Luftwaffe* had inflicted on Rotterdam and London. German air raids brought death to 60,000 British civilians in the course of the war, but British and American sorties killed 500,000 people in Germany. Against the steel plants and U-boat pens this bombing was only moderately effective. But the synthetic nitrogen plants, munitions works, and especially the airplane factories and oil refineries were crippled by repeated raids. The result was evident by 1944, when the *Luftwaffe* ceased to be a major threat. There were other results, some unintentional but all destructive to the German war effort and the German morale. One-fifth of the dwelling space in German cities was wrecked; 7,500,000 people were made homeless; transportation was seriously deranged. The long ordeal of heavier and heavier raids undoubtedly speeded the material and moral collapse of the German people.

In this long air war the British and American fliers destroyed 55,000 German planes and dropped 2,500,000 tons of bombs over the Reich.

Their own losses in planes exceeded 40,000, and in personnel, 158,000. These casualties were shared about equally between the United States air force and the British air force. The sacrifices were heavy but they won results that were essential to Allied victory and they saved the ground forces months of fighting that would have taken a much higher toll in lives. The destruction of German air supremacy over Europe made the invasion of Europe possible, it prepared the way for the Russian sweep to victory, and it paralyzed the German armies waiting to hurl back the Allies when they invaded Italy and Normandy. The bombing of factories, chemical plants, ammunition depots, railway junctions, and bridges, slowed down German industry and ultimately grounded the *Luftwaffe* and all but immobilized the *Wehrmacht*. With their magnificent railway and highway system severed, and petroleum reserves exhausted or destroyed, the German war machine stalled.

Air superiority also brought the Allies advantages of another sort: it enabled them to anticipate new German weapons and outrace the German scientists. Aerial photographs, checked against reports from secret agents within the Reich, betrayed vital German centers of research and experiment to the British and American intelligence officers. The leading schools for aeronautics and ballistics, the rocket assembly plants and the launching platforms for the robot bombs, the laboratories where German specialists in nuclear physics were working to release atomic energy — all suffered from sudden and shattering raids. Spared the resulting loss of time, material, and personnel, the Germans might have perfected rocket missiles that could reach New York or have won the race to produce the atomic bomb.

XXXVII

THE LIBERATION OF EUROPE

(JUNE, 1944—MAY, 1945)

*Our enormous material superiority gave us an unchallengeable ad-
vantage over our foes . . . More important even than the weapons, however, was the indomitable fighting spirit of the men of
the Allied nations who wielded them.*

GENERAL DWIGHT D. EISENHOWER

I. FROM NORMANDY TO THE RHINE
(JUNE–DECEMBER, 1944)

WITH the spring of 1944 World War II entered its final year.
The slowly consolidated power of the United Nations was
unleashed in a series of offensives of such irresistible momentum that
they overwhelmed Germany by May, 1945, and Japan three months
later.

On D-Day, June 6, 1944, an Allied Expeditionary Force under the
supreme command of General Dwight D. Eisenhower crossed the
English Channel and assailed the Normandy beaches. Throughout
the preceding night paratroops had been dropped behind the coastal
defenses; 600 warships buried German posts and pillboxes under a
barrage of shells; and 10,000 Allied aircraft patrolled the skies. This
naval and air supremacy made it possible for the military forces, transported in 4000 ships, to reach shore and establish beachheads within
a few hours. Deployment proceeded rapidly while the defenders were
still confused and isolated by the naval and aerial bombardment. This
German delay in launching immediate counterattacks has been criticized as a tactical error. For the Allies it proved an important advantage, and their losses were considerably lower than they had expected.
The weakened *Luftwaffe* offered no serious resistance in the air.

Apparently General Erwin Rommel, a master of swift maneuver,
favored fighting the invaders on the beaches with all available German

reserves. But he was overruled by his superior, General Karl von Rundstedt, who hesitated to rush up reserves lest the Normandy attack prove a feint and the major Allied invasion come a few days later in Norway or the Bay of Biscay or in the Mediterranean. The advantage of numbers and initiative had definitely passed to the United Nations. Three-fourths of the German divisions were on the defensive in the east and south and the remainder were insufficient to guard a coastline from Norway to Spain. From Moscow Marshal Stalin sent assurances that the Russian drives would be intensified, to permit no diversion of German strength, and he hailed the Normandy invasion in words which recognized the magnitude of this achievement. "The history of war does not show any such undertaking so broad in conception, so grandiose in scale, and so masterly in execution."

Despite adverse weather the gigantic operation unfolded steadily. All bridges and railroads by which German reinforcements could arrive were blasted from the air or wrecked by the French Forces of the Interior (F.F.I.) which had trained and armed in secret for the hour of liberation. Knowing that all major French ports would be mined and fortified, Allied engineers had improvised two special harbors, constructed in a few days from pontoons, pierheads, causeways, and breakwaters floated across the Channel and moored in place. One harbor was scarcely open before an Atlantic gale destroyed it but the other survived and tanks, guns, supplies, and men were disembarked in unceasing columns. Twenty pipe lines laid under the Channel carried gasoline to the tanks and trucks, and as the battle front advanced the fuel pipes followed it. Within a week of landing the expeditionary forces held a strip of beach sixty miles long, and the capture of Cherbourg on June 27 gave them control of a major port. Through this breach in the "Atlantic Wall" and through other captured ports, over 2,000,000 men, 450,000 vehicles, and 4,000,000 tons of war material were transported to France in the first hundred days after June 6. The Allied command, able to equip British and American troops with effective weapons in almost unlimited quantity, improved their efficiency, speeded their drives, and reduced their battle casualties. The extraordinary effectiveness of the medical services provided maximum advantages for the wounded. Critical cases were treated in the battle zone by auxiliary surgical groups; blood plasma and new drugs reduced the problems of shock and infection; and reparative surgery and improved therapy saved and restored a higher percentage of battle casualties than in any previous war.

In Italy the Allied invading forces had found the people confused and apathetic. In France they found the French Forces of the Interior, valiant resistance groups which had been built up in secret, waiting for the signal to attack. These underground forces aided by harassing the German units; and the realization of the hate they had

THE ANGLO-AMERICAN INVASION OF FRANCE, 1944

inspired among the French populace further demoralized the retreating Nazi troops. By August 23 the Allied armies had crossed the Seine and were approaching Paris, where a spontaneous uprising of the French resistance forces liberated the capital. Brussels celebrated its release from three years of German rule on September 3, and by September 12 American armored columns were across the German frontier. Meanwhile a second amphibious invasion in the south of France (August 15) placed an Allied army ashore on the Mediterranean coast between Marseilles and Nice. There as in the north the liberators found swift support from the resistance groups, the *Maquis*, who assailed the disheartened foe and hunted down French collaborators who had aided Hitler's police.

This speedy liberation of France and Belgium, which cost the Germans 400,000 casualties in four months, raised undue optimism among the peoples of the United Nations. There was, in consequence, a shock of disappointment when the retreating Nazis rallied behind their West Wall in September and halted the Allied advance. A daring attempt to outflank the West Wall defense line by a circling movement through Holland was blocked at Arnhem, where a British airborne division was two-thirds destroyed. It was evident that the Germans would rally and fight fiercely for their homeland and that the "fluid" front of the summer, so favorable to Allied initiative, had hardened.

In preparation for a winter assault on the Rhine, the Allied armies were rested, reinforced, and regrouped. The American First Army and the British Second Army, units of which had recently sliced through northern France and Belgium at thirty miles a day, needed time to recuperate. From the Riviera coast the American Seventh and the French First Army swept up the Rhone Valley to link lines with the American Third Army at Dijon. From the Netherlands to Switzerland the Allies now had six armies, the British Second, then the American Ninth, First, Third, and Seventh, and the French First, hammering at the German frontier. The fall of Antwerp early in November, after a furious resistance by the German garrison, provided an additional and essential port through which the northern armies might be fed.

Defeated in Italy (where Florence fell on August 12), expelled from France, forced back ruthlessly in Russia, the Germans were no longer able to defend their Balkan satellites. A Soviet army swept into Rumania in August; that unstable kingdom promptly reversed alliances and declared war on Germany August 25. Bulgaria capitulated to Russian demands a few weeks later and was granted an armistice. Hungary remained defiant, and fresh Soviet divisions swinging through the Transylvanian Alps and the Iron Gate on the Danube headed for Budapest. The partisan forces of Yugoslavia, which had been battling the German and Italian army of occupation without rest and without reprieve now welcomed the Russians as liberators. In the Baltic region Finland deserted Germany and accepted an armistice on

THE DEVASTATION CAUSED BY A GERMAN ROCKET BOMB, LONDON, 1945

September 3. The Norwegians stirred rebelliously under the German yoke. Wherever possible the Allies aided and armed the partisan groups, but they warned them against premature uprisings. The tragic fate of the Poles proved that Germany could still exact reprisals. Though decimated by five years of starvation and sickness and terrorized by systematic murder, a Polish group in Warsaw rose against the German garrison on August 1. They seized a large part of the city, confident that the Russians, whose advance guards were already in sight, would aid them. But the Russians delayed, and after two months of confused siege the Germans crushed the uprising.

Defeat had dimmed Hitler's prestige, and a widespread plot among his followers, some details of which were known to the Allied intelligence service, was formed to overthrow him. But an attempt by the conspirators to assassinate him and proclaim a new regime (July 20, 1944) miscarried. Several leading German generals and other officials were executed, and the dreaded Heinrich Himmler, head of the security police, became more indispensable to Hitler than ever. The regime which the Germans had acclaimed with delirious plebiscites ten years earlier had become a regime of terror. The fear felt by the multitudes now exceeded the fanatical faith of the few; and the threat of the concentration camp, the Gestapo torture chambers, the noose, and the firing squad hung over Germany, while military defeats darkened like thunderclouds on the horizon.

The rapid fall of German prestige persuaded Hitler to risk his dwindling reserves in a desperate offensive, an attempt to split the Allied armies in Belgium. Field Marshal Karl von Rundstedt opened the drive, with all the advantages of tactical surprise, on December 16. Within a week the unprepared American and British forces in the Luxembourg sector had been hurled back to the Meuse. But General Eisenhower refused to be disconcerted. Rallying divisions on both sides of the "Bulge" to squeeze the German salient, he succeeded in stabilizing the lines before the end of the month. When the year 1945 opened the American, British, and French forces in the west with detachments from the British Dominions, units of Polish and other soldiers from occupied states, and the support of fifty United Nations, were ready for the finale. The assault on Germany was to be fully co-ordinated and relentless. From the Rhine, from the Danube, through Poland, and across East Prussia the invading armies were to press the Reich in a vast combined operation. From the skies the

American air forces and Royal Air Force, with a maximum bomber strength of 14,000 planes protected by 12,000 fighters, would deal the final blow to German transportation and supply.

2. THE BATTLE OF GERMANY (JANUARY–MAY, 1945)

The Russian armies opened the final act of the European war on January 12, 1945. Smashing across Poland they captured Cracow, Tarnow, and Warsaw, and the German line along the Vistula collapsed. Other Russian spearheads were driving to the Baltic shores, liberating Czechoslovakia and splitting East Prussia. From the Vistula the Germans retreated to the Oder, striving to make a stand that would preserve the war industries of Silesia. But the Russian drives gave them no rest. By the end of February the Soviet armies had swept 170 miles from East Prussia to the lower Vistula, and 350 miles from the upper Vistula to the Oder, claiming 800,000 Germans killed and 350,000 captured in a period of forty days. In March the methodical Marshal Gregory Zhukov secured Königsberg on his right and Breslau on his left, freeing his flanks for a final drive on Berlin.

In the west the Allied armies, with over a million men, were likewise poised for the final assault. By February they had driven into Holland and penetrated the Ruhr Valley; by March 5th they were in Trier and Cologne; by the 8th they had crossed the Rhine at Remagen and were piercing the defenses on the eastern bank. Along the north coast British divisions raced for Hamburg and Bremen, while in the center the American Ninth Army seized Essen and then drove towards the Elbe. On April 26 an American advance unit encountered Russian troops at Torgau. Germany had been cut in two.

One week earlier (April 20) the Russian drive from the Oder had reached Berlin. The shattered city, half-leveled by bombing, was shelled and burned anew as the Soviet forces battled the defenders from block to block. Adolf Hitler directed the desperate resistance from the chancellery until April 30, and then killed himself rather than surrender. A provisory government, headed by Admiral Karl Doenitz, opened negotiations with the Allies, and Heinrich Himmler, representing another faction of the defeated government, likewise sought to parley. But the Allied governments knew that the Nationalist Socialist regime was in dissolution and insisted upon unconditional surrender. Many German field commanders were already ordering their men to lay down their arms.

In Italy the British and American armies and the forces of the

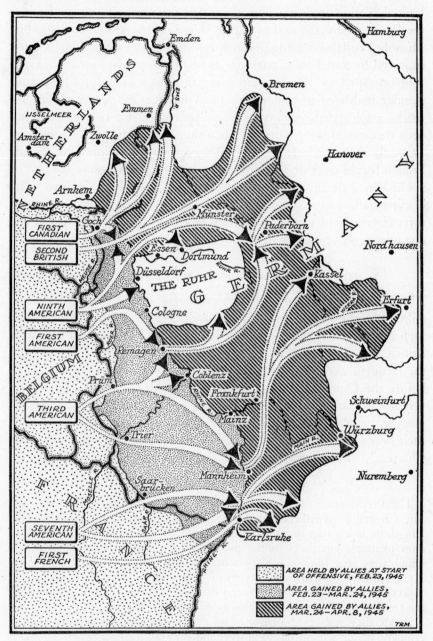

FIRST
CANADIAN

SECOND
BRITISH

NINTH
AMERICAN

FIRST
AMERICAN

THIRD
AMERICAN

SEVENTH
AMERICAN

FIRST
FRENCH

AREA HELD BY ALLIES AT START
OF OFFENSIVE, FEB. 23, 1945

AREA GAINED BY ALLIES,
FEB. 23–MAR. 24, 1945

AREA GAINED BY ALLIES,
MAR. 24–APR. 8, 1945

THE INVASION OF GERMANY FROM THE WEST, 1945

United Nations fighting with them had driven the Germans back to the Po River by the end of April. The German-sustained regime of Mussolini collapsed while Berlin was burning, and the Italian dictator, captured by anti-Fascist partisans as he fled towards Switzerland, was shot on April 28. The million German troops in Italy, whose commander had been in touch with the United States secret service for weeks, capitulated on May 1. Their line of retreat to Germany had been threatened since April 12 when the Russians reached Vienna and pressed on towards Linz and Innsbruck, while United States and French forces were driving from the east towards Munich.

On May 2 Berlin surrendered to the Russians. There the final terms of capitulation were signed on May 8. They provided that all German forces in the field would cease resistance and that fighting would end one minute after midnight.

3. THE CONFERENCES THAT FORGED THE VICTORY

The defeat of Germany was a victory for Allied co-operation: no military coalition in history had delivered such sustained blows with such expert timing and co-ordination. The strategy of United States, British, and Russian commanders had been planned far in advance at the frequent conferences held by the leaders of the Big Three. Even before the United States was attacked, President Franklin D. Roosevelt and prime minister Winston Churchill met off Newfoundland in August, 1941. After discussing common problems they announced their hopes for a better world in a document known as the " Atlantic Charter." [1] Two weeks after Pearl Harbor it was announced that

[1] THE ATLANTIC CHARTER

The President of the United States of America and the Prime Minister, Mr. Churchill, representing His Majesty's Government in the United Kingdom, being met together, deem it right to make known certain common principles in the national policies of their respective countries on which they base their hopes for a better future for the world.

FIRST, their countries seek no aggrandizement, territorial or other;

SECOND, they desire to see no territorial changes that do not accord with the freely expressed wishes of the peoples concerned;

THIRD, they respect the right of all peoples to choose the form of government under which they will live; and they wish to see sovereign rights and self-government restored to those who have been forcibly deprived of them;

FOURTH, they will endeavor, with due respect for their existing obligations, to further the enjoyment by all States, great or small, victor or van-

Churchill was in Washington (December 23, 1941) while the British foreign secretary, Anthony Eden, visited Moscow to consult with premier Stalin. On January 2, 1942, twenty-six nations which had broken with the Axis powers signed a "Declaration of the United Nations" but leadership in the common effort remained with the Big Three — Britain, the United States, and the Soviet Union.

In June, 1942, Churchill visited Washington again and then hastened to Moscow in August. The Russians, fighting desperately against the German drive to the Caucasus, were anxious to know when the British and Americans would relieve some of the pressure by opening a second front in Europe. But Anglo-American strategy had fixed upon the clearance of the Mediterranean as a prior objective. In January, 1943, after the Allied landings in North Africa, Churchill and Roosevelt met at Casablanca in French Morocco. Concerting secret plans for further offensives, they announced to the world that the Axis powers were to be reduced to "unconditional surrender." The following August Churchill and Roosevelt, with a corps of advisers, held further consultations (the Quebec Conference). The most significant meeting of 1943 occurred at Tehran, December 2–7. To most Americans the capital of Persia was a half-unreal city of romantic

---

quished, of access, on equal terms, to the trade and to the raw materials of the world which are needed for their economic prosperity;

FIFTH, they desire to bring about the fullest collaboration between all nations in the economic field with the object of securing, for all, improved labor standards, economic advancement and social security;

SIXTH, after the final destruction of Nazi tyranny, they hope to see established a peace which will afford to all nations the means of dwelling in safety within their own boundaries, and which will afford assurance that all men in all lands may live out their lives in freedom from fear and want;

SEVENTH, such a peace should enable all men to traverse the high seas and oceans without hindrance;

EIGHTH, they believe that all nations of the world, for realistic as well as spiritual reasons, must come to the abandonment of the use of force. Since no future peace can be maintained if land, sea or air armaments continue to be employed by nations which threaten, or may threaten, aggression outside of their frontiers, they believe, pending the establishment of a wider and permanent system of general security, that the disarmament of such nations is essential. They will likewise aid and encourage all other practicable measures which will lighten for peace-loving peoples the crushing burden of armaments.

FRANKLIN D. ROOSEVELT
WINSTON S. CHURCHILL

tales, but the statesmen who met there to doom the Axis were in a grim and realistic mood. With their chiefs of staff, President Roosevelt, prime minister Churchill, and Marshal Stalin reached complete agreement on future operations against Germany. The British and American leaders communicated to Stalin their plans for an invasion of Europe the following spring, and Stalin promised that the Soviet armies would maintain their pressure in the East.

On his journey to the capital of Iran President Roosevelt paused in Cairo for a separate conference with Churchill and the Chinese Generalissimo, Chiang Kai-shek. With the concentration of Allied power in Europe the Pacific war lagged, and it seemed equitable to hearten the Chinese with an assurance that their long struggle against the Japanese was not forgotten. In this global struggle the dictates of strategy made Germany the prior objective, for as Churchill succinctly phrased it, "While the defeat of Japan would not mean the defeat of Germany, the defeat of Germany would infallibly mean the ruin of Japan." In the Pacific as in Europe the tide had turned in 1943, but no attempt was made at this time to predict how long it might take to strip the Japanese of their conquests.

As promised at Tehran, the year 1944 brought an Allied invasion of France, the fall of Paris, Brussels, and Rome, and the sweep of the Anglo-American armies to the Rhine. At the opening of 1945, the "Year of Destiny," Roosevelt visited the Near East a second time. His interview with Churchill and Stalin was held at Yalta, in the newly liberated Crimea. Victory in Europe was already in sight, and at this Crimea Conference (February 4-12, 1945) plans were laid for the joint occupation of Germany and other enemy territory by the armies of the Big Three. Unforeseen problems that might arise with victory were to be settled at a subsequent meeting later in the year; but the Russian government gave assurances at this time that if the Japanese did not yield within three months after the defeat of Germany, the Soviet Union would join Britain and the United States in forcing a decision.

Before the three heads of the victorious powers could meet again, death took Franklin Delano Roosevelt in the hour of victory (April 12, 1945). It was, therefore, President Harry S. Truman who met with Churchill and Stalin at the last war conference of the Big Three. Churchill's magnificent war term was at a close, for the British Labor Party came into power in an election (announced July 26) and Clement R. Attlee headed the new cabinet. But changes in personnel brought no diminution in the Allied effort. At Potsdam, between July 17 and August 2, 1945, the Big Three completed their plans for the occupation of Germany, the demilitarization of the Reich, collection of preliminary reparations, and trial of Nazi war criminals. The further discussions necessary in the preparation of peace treaties were referred to a council of the foreign ministers of the victorious powers.

The Potsdam Conference confirmed and extended the terms which had been imposed upon the Germans after their surrender. The provisional regime of Admiral Karl Doenitz, which had announced Hitler's death to the world on May 1, was dissolved by the Allies, who set up a Control Committee headed by General Dwight D. Eisenhower, Field Marshal Sir Bernard Montgomery, and Marshal Gregory K. Zhukov. Germany was stripped of all annexations made after December 31, 1937, and was divided into four zones under the American, British, French, and Russian forces of occupation. All National Socialist organizations were to be dissolved, Germany disarmed and demilitarized, and industries indispensable for warmaking dismantled. Hope was held out, however, to the peaceful and moderate elements among the German people. They were assured that democratic ideals and efforts at honest and responsible self-government would be respected, and that freedom of speech, press, and religion would be guaranteed in so far as military security and order permitted.

4. WAR COSTS AND BATTLE CASUALTIES

When the fighting in Europe ceased, it became possible to make preliminary estimates of the destruction of property and loss of life. These figures, which could be no more than approximate, were expanded after the capitulation of Japan and demonstrated that World War II was the most costly conflict in history. The expenditures of the belligerent governments for war materials and armaments added up to $1,154,000,000,000. This represented a $317,600,000,000 outlay for the United States, $192,000,000,000 for the Soviet Union, and $120,000,000,000 for Great Britain. The outlay for Germany was calculated at $272,900,000,000, for Italy at $94,000,000,000, and for Japan at $56,000,000,000. The sacrifices made by the Chinese in gold and blood during their prolonged resistance to the Japanese could not be estimated. These official expenditures did not include any allowance for damage to civilian property, which in Great Britain alone exceeded $5,000,000,000. Assuming on good evidence that civilian property in Germany had suffered from ten to fifteen times more heavily, and estimating the loss in other European countries proportionally, the statisticians added a further toll of $230,900,000,000 to the war bill. These figures once more excluded China and were subject to revision, especially in the case of Russia, for property damage in the Soviet Union probably exceeded that in Germany and no bookkeeping could keep up with it.

The number of men killed in action during World War II was set at 10,000,000. More than half these casualties were suffered by the Axis states, Germany leading with 3,250,000 battle dead, and the others in the following order: Japan, 1,500,000; Italy, 200,000; Rumania, 100,000; Hungary, 75,000; Finland, 50,000. Among the United Nations Russia led with an estimated 3,000,000 battle dead, followed by the British Empire with 400,000, the United States with 325,000, France with 167,000, including losses suffered by the Fighting French. For Poland the battle dead were estimated at 125,000; for Yugoslavia in the long guerrilla war, 75,000; Greece, 50,000; Belgium, 7,000; the Netherlands, 6,000; and Norway, 1,000. It should be noted that the last three include only combat deaths during the brief weeks of fighting in 1940. Casualties among the underground forces resisting the Nazis were unobtainable and may have exceeded the total of those who died in uniform.

It is probable that the civilian dead exceeded the total of those killed in battle. Set tentatively at 12,000,000, these nonmilitary casualties raised the total of lives lost in World War II to 22,000,000. The injured were estimated at 34,400,000. Bombing from the air had added a new weapon to the arsenal of war, but the ancient scourges, starvation and disease, took heaviest toll. In China, in Europe, in all parts of the world where people lived in want and squalor and fear, the scarcity of food, lack of drugs and medical care and preventive medicine caused a sharp rise in the rate of disease. It required several years to complete a statistical picture of conditions in the war-ravaged countries and to compute the actual cost in life.

It must be borne in mind that the destruction of files and records, the changes in government, the dispersion and replacement of personnel, disrupted the archival labor upon which population statistics are built. Wherever the tides of war swirled and shifted, millions of people, soldiers and civilians, disappeared. Even on the army lists the number of dead was often exceeded by the number recording as missing. Among civilians the list of displaced or missing persons grew each year. The transfer of millions of workers from one war industry to another, the exodus from bombed cities and conquered provinces, the growth of secret and unidentifiable groups of partisans, the deserters from the armed forces and from labor battalions and factories, the escaped prisoners of war, all helped to create an unparalleled problem of homeless and displaced persons. Only years of patient search can establish the fate of millions who disappeared without trace or record.

No feature of this prolonged mass tragedy so shocked the conscience of the world as the horrors perpetrated in the Axis prison camps. From 1933, when the National Socialists seized power, they had systematically confined thousands of opponents in concentration centers under conditions which became more brutal each year. Rumors of the calculated cruelty, torture, and starvation which the guards inflicted upon the victims in these camps had appalled the civilized peoples of Europe and America before 1939. Hitler's insensate denunciation of the Jews, which excited his followers to a fanatical anti-semitism, drove many of the most brilliant and distinguished artists and scientists of Germany to other lands. Within Germany the persecution of Jews, communists, and any unfortunate minority suspected of opposition to the National Socialist regime, filled the camps.

The outbreak of war intensified the regime of terror. The dreaded security police operated so arbitrarily that no German and no foreigner in the sphere of German influence could feel safe from arrest. For the legal safeguards and the ideals of justice common to all civilized states had been cast aside by the Nazis. Right was defined in 1936 as "what is in the interests of the German people." Prisoners who could be charged with no specific crime might still be condemned if the court considered them punishable "according to the underlying idea of a penal code or according to healthy public sentiment." From all parts of occupied Europe prisoners were dispatched to the concentration camps where millions disappeared without trace. Only after the arrival of the Allied armies of liberation did the world learn the manner of their death. The worst camps had become mass extermination centers, where only the hardiest prisoners, who could endure the starvation, forced labor, beatings, and disease, had a chance of survival. Thousands too weak or sick to work and other thousands deliberately marked for death as Jews or enemy sympathizers were hanged, poisoned, or asphyxiated, sometimes in batches of several hundred a day. After the fighting ceased, committees of investigation from the United States Congress and the British parliament visited Europe to verify the conditions revealed by the Allied military reports and the war dispatches of the newspaper correspondents. The true and terrible price which Europe had paid for submission to Hitler and his regime was now apparent; and the suicide of Hitler, Himmler, Goebbels, and other Nazi leaders did not attenuate the crimes committed under their rule. For the most inexplicable fact in this monstrous story of human degradation was the attitude of the German people. They had acquiesced in conditions which no veil of official secrecy could have wholly hidden from their knowledge. This was their responsibility before the world and before history.

XXXVIII

THE PACIFIC OFFENSIVE

Japan was beaten in the first part of 1945. That was when your submarines and naval aircraft cut off our supplies from the south.
ADMIRAL ZENISHIRO HOSHIMA

I. THE BATTLE FOR BASES

THE rapid conquests made by the Japanese in the six months after their attack on Pearl Harbor (November, 1941–March, 1942) delivered the rubber, oil, tin, quinine, and other products of the East Indies into their hands. Naval units of the United Nations were shattered in the battle of the Java Sea at the end of February, and by March Malaysia, Burma, Java, and Timor had fallen. The threat to Australia, to India, and to China was acute. But in May Allied naval and air power halted Japanese plans against Australia by their victory in the battle of the Coral Sea; in June a Japanese naval force was repelled near Midway Island; and in July the Chinese Nationalist armies defeated a Japanese army in Kiangsi province. Siam (Thailand), the only independent state in southeast Asia, had joined Japan in a treaty of alliance (December 21, 1941), and the Netherlands East Indies had accepted a promise of future independence from their Japanese "liberators." But the Japanese propaganda of "Asia for the Asiatics" failed to excite a revolt in India or to win the co-operation of many Chinese. The "revolt of Asia" against European imperialism, a revolt which the weakened British forces in India could not have controlled, failed to sweep the East as spontaneously as pessimists had prophesied. Perhaps the peoples whom the Japanese were so eager to liberate recognized with Oriental realism that "Asia for the Asiatics" as understood at Tokyo was Asia for the Japanese.

Nevertheless the empire so swiftly collected by the Japanese contained one-quarter of the earth's population. If these 500,000,000 people could have been organized and militarized within a few years they would have become a grave problem to the European world. Yet the Americans and British had no choice but to leave Japan dominant in that wide area for a few years at least. The fall of Singapore closed the direct route between America and the Indian Ocean. Allied ships had to detour south of Australia, and even then they were not safe from enemy raiders from New Britain or the Solomon Islands. These facts partly determined the course of the first American offensive in the Pacific area. On August 7, 1942, United States Marines landed on Guadalcanal. In slow, costly, and courageous fighting, American and Australian forces captured vital bases in New Britain and New Guinea. The threat to Australia and to shipping in the Coral Sea was greatly reduced, especially after November, 1942, when the Japanese lost twenty-eight ships, warcraft and transports, in their attempt to defend Guadalcanal.

No general offensive could be attempted, however, until the American building program gained momentum. Air power in particular was to prove indispensable for the vast Pacific war. On December 7, 1941, the United States possessed only seven first line aircraft carriers. In less than a year combat losses cut the number to three. The emergency was met by rushing new carriers to completion and converting available craft, with such success that two years after Pearl Harbor the total for carriers of all types had risen to fifty. This expansion called for a rapid increase in aircraft, especially fighters. In 1941 new planes built for the navy totalled 3,638; in 1944 the number was 30,070. The cost was enormous, an average of some $4,000,000,000 a year for naval aviation, but the results were decisive because they brought the United States navy to supremacy in the Pacific. In the battles of Midway and the Coral Sea air power proved its value by driving back the Japanese with heavy losses before the battleships could exchange a salvo from their heavy guns.

The value of the battleship had been questioned before the war began and some experts thought these costly vessels too vulnerable in the air age. The lesson of Pearl Harbor and the sinking of the British battleship *Prince of Wales* and the battle cruiser *Repulse* by Japanese dive bombers off Singapore (December, 1941) raised further doubts regarding the worth of capital ships. The United States navy completed only ten battleships and two battle cruisers in the four years from 1941 to 1944 but commissioned six heavy cruisers and twenty-seven light cruisers. The construction of submarines rose sharply, from eleven in 1941 to seventy-seven in 1944. But the most phenomenal development, dictated by the tactics of amphibious warfare, was the program for landing craft. From tiny rafts to 300-foot transports that landed tanks and infantry, the freakish procession grew. Some had shallow bottoms and bows like a drawbridge; some plunged through the waves like a tugboat and climbed the shore like a tank. In 1941 the navy had 123 vessels classed as landing craft. In 1945 the total was 54,206. This wartime expansion affected all categories. The peak of production and the maximum man power was achieved in 1944, for that year saw the size of the fleet almost double within twelve months, while the man power, which totaled 13,149 officers and 206,959 enlisted personnel in 1941, rose to 43,140 officers and 461,376 enlisted personnel in 1944.

The conventional idea of a battle front as a line of demarcation separating distinct areas held by opposing forces lost meaning in World War II. The shadow of Japanese power did not spread like an eclipse across the western Pacific; it would be nearer the fact to picture the Japanese expansion as the rapid spread of a vine. The shipping lines were the long sinuous stalks; ports and islands were holds where the tendrils could seek a grip, strike root if possible, and then spread again. But if the main stalks were cut, the whole vine would wither. This was the conviction which governed Allied strategy.

By 1942 the western Pacific, from Australia to Alaska, had become a series of zones in which American and Japanese forces overlapped and interpenetrated. Both adversaries scattered their submarines along enemy supply lines and raided enemy shipping from the air. Battleships remained in general near their bases where they could be constantly protected by land planes. To take the offensive, therefore, the Americans had to win local air supremacy with carrier-based fighters, rush in landing forces to seize appropriate islands, transform them into airfields, and then repeat the maneuver from these advanced bases. The Japanese held most key islands and the garrisons were prepared to die fighting, a fact which made the first steps in this "island hopping" slow and costly. But as the Americans' strength grew, their offensive strategy became more daring and they speeded their advance by "leap-frog" tactics. Thousands of Japanese were left behind on scattered archipelagoes, to "wither on the vine," as American task forces broke through to seize bases nearer to Japan.

The year 1943, during which the Germans lost the initiative in the European theater, also brought a definite turn of the tide in the Pacific theater. In November American troops assailed the Gilbert Islands and captured them in three days of costly fighting. Two months later (January, 1944) they attacked the Marshall Islands and captured Kwajalein by February 6. Pressing on to strike the important Japanese base at Truk, they reached the Marianas by June. In each case their naval, military, and air force losses were serious but never disastrous, and contrary to custom the defenders suffered heavier casualties than the attackers. By October, 1944, the Americans were ready to risk a daring leap to the Philippines, and General Douglas MacArthur landed on Leyte October 20. A Japanese naval force which attempted to reinforce the 20,000 defenders on Saipan in the Marianas was repelled with considerable losses; a stronger fleet which attempted to halt the landings on Leyte (October 23–27) was vanquished in the second battle of the Philippine Sea. The Japanese lost two battleships, four carriers, six heavy cruisers, three light cruisers, and probably nine destroyers. Avoiding further naval engagements in these waters, they managed none the less to reinforce their troops on Leyte and the fighting was desperate. But the Americans were encouraged by the aid of Filipino guerrilla troops and by the certainty that once they regained the Philippine Islands they could sever the Japanese sea routes to southeast Asia. With American sea and air power cutting their highway of empire, and the newly won bases in the Marianas providing fields for bombing raids on Japan, the economic strength and the striking power of the Japanese would be paralyzed.

A foretaste of the approaching blockade and bombardment came to the Japanese in November, 1944, when land-based Flying Fortresses, operating from Saipan, bombed their home industries. By March, 1945, the American invasion of Iwo Jima had given the United States air forces a base only two hours' flight from the Japanese homeland. American naval forces, fueled at sea and protected by carrier planes, were pressing into the coastal waters of Japan, daring the remnants of the Japanese navy to come out and fight.

2. THE BATTLE OF COMMUNICATIONS AND SUPPLIES

A nation at war may be defeated, as Germany was in 1945, by invading armies which breach the frontiers, storm the capital, and impose peace at the point of the bayonet. This is the logical end of a military campaign: the destruction of the enemy's armed forces and the military occupation of his territory. The war ends because his power to resist has ended, and his "unconditional surrender," symbolized in the signing of a document, marks the moment when hostilities cease. This

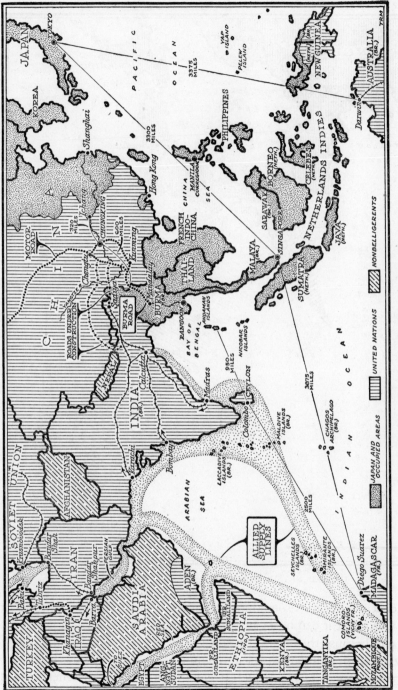

COMMUNICATIONS AND SUPPLY ROUTES IN ASIA

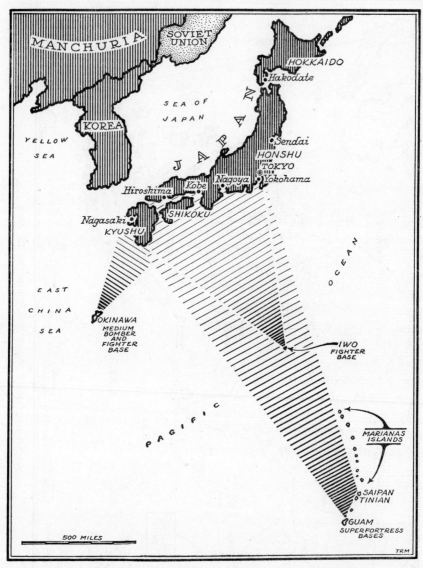

MANCHURIA

SOVIET
UNION

HOKKAIDO

• Hakodate

SEA OF
JAPAN

KOREA

YELLOW
SEA

• Sendai
HONSHU
TOKYO
Nagoya • Yokohama
Hiroshima   Kobe
Nagasaki
KYUSHU   SHIKOKU

EAST

CHINA

SEA

OKINAWA
MEDIUM
BOMBER
AND
FIGHTER
BASE

OCEAN

IWO
FIGHTER
BASE

PACIFIC

MARIANAS
ISLANDS

SAIPAN
TINIAN

GUAM
SUPERFORTRESS
BASES

500 MILES

TRM

UNITED STATES AIR POWER IN THE PACIFIC, 1945

concept of defeat as something definitive is emotionally satisfying to
the victor but it can be a cause of serious confusion. For the war does
not end because the enemy has lost the power to resist. So long as one
citizen remains alive with strength enough to throw a stone the enemy
has some power to resist. Defeat comes not because the enemy loses
the power to resist but because he loses the will to resist. It follows,

therefore, that in war it may be more important to destroy an enemy's will than to destroy his armies. This truth was remarkably illustrated in the defeat of the Japanese, and it demonstrates anew the importance of siege tactics in war. More cities have surrendered to starvation, to the loss of nerve which comes with dwindling reserves and the sense of encircling doom, than were ever conquered by the sword.

Like Great Britain, Japan is an island kingdom, dependent upon the daily arrival and departure of the myriad ships which maintain its economic life. In 1939 the Japanese merchant marine ranked third among the great powers, being exceeded only by that of Great Britain and the United States. The need to import additional supplies for the war effort, to transport equipment for the offensives in China and the Pacific, and to maintain some measure of peacetime trade, over-taxed the marine. The real crisis in shipping, however, was caused by the American aircraft and submarines which inflicted irreparable losses. Despite all efforts to speed shipbuilding, the Japanese found that their available tonnage fell alarmingly after 1942. When they made their bold bid for empire in the western Pacific they had an esti-mated 7,000,000 tons of merchant shipping, but the toll of war was so terrible that by the summer of 1945 scarcely 1,000,000 tons remained afloat. Six out of every seven Japanese tankers, transports, cargo and passenger vessels had been sunk or rendered useless. United States forces had waged a cumulative war of extermination, sinking 134 ves-sels in 1942, 284 in 1943, 492 in 1944. For the seven war months of 1945 the number declined to 132, not for lack of hunters but for lack of quarry. Some of these ships, especially transports, were sunk by gunfire in naval engagements; more were hunted down by aircraft and sunk by bombs or torpedoes. But the majority — almost two-thirds of the craft destroyed — were accounted for by American submarines.

The Japanese navy survived the attrition of war somewhat better than the merchant fleet but it was severely weakened. At the war's end four battleships remained out of twelve, six aircraft carriers out of twenty-five, eleven crusiers out of forty-seven. One-third of the naval vessels sunk were caught by American submarines; others went down under the guns of the fleet or were bombed by naval aircraft. With the establishment of advanced landing fields to supplement the carriers, the air war was speeded relentlessly. By 1945 there was no hiding place left in Japan or the islands where the surviving ships could hide from the daily bombing. Japanese naval power was broken so completely by the close of the war that United States battleships moved into coastal waters to shell factories and dockyards with their heavy guns and then moved away unscathed, meeting no serious opposition.

Several hundred thousand Japanese soldiers had been killed in the losing attempt to hold their Pacific island bases. An indefinite number had been by-passed and remained isolated on their fortified atolls. In Burma their forces suffered several defeats in 1944, losing 50,000 men; and the Burma Road, the only link (aside from air transport) between China and the outside world, was reopened. But the most critical threat to Japanese resistance everywhere came from the severance of sea communications. To import materials from Asia and the East Indies, to feed the industrial workers, to reinforce and supply the divisions battling the Chinese Nationalists, the sea routes had to be kept open. But the sea routes were failing and with the stalk cut the garrisons abroad began to wither on the vine as had been predicted. Japanese military power was still intact but it was losing its power to strike. The question which now concerned the Allied strategists was how strong the army in Japan would prove and how tenaciously it would resist an invasion of the home islands.

3. THE SURRENDER OF JAPAN

Before the collapse of Germany in the spring of 1945, the Combined Chiefs of Staff had completed plans for large-scale amphibious operations against Japan. They estimated that the resources and the fanatical spirit of devotion of the Japanese army, which had made the capture of island bases like Okinawa, Saipan, and Iwo Jima so costly, would enable the cities of the homeland to hold out into 1946 or even longer. It was the boast of the Japanese that their islands had never suffered invasion and that they would resist to the last man. The Allied preparations for a landing were therefore made with great thoroughness and on an impressive scale. Over three thousand ships and a million men were to be available for a double invasion, supported by the naval forces and the thousands of bombers which had brought ruin to the German cities. To those in the secret these dual projects for landing on the Japanese beaches were known by the code names Operation Olympic and Operation Coronet.

The operations never took place. When Germany surrendered, the Japanese were already nearer exhaustion than Allied intelligence officers had surmised. Fuel oil was running low, factories were shattered and burned, machinery worn out or inadequate. In World War II months and even weeks counted in the tense race to perfect and produce improved weapons, and a new model in fighting planes, in torpedoes or rocket bombs, might change the course of a campaign. American and British ingenuity and mass production had outpaced German competition, and the Japanese were less resourceful and inventive than the Germans. In the European theater the Axis troops complained that the Americans fought a "millionaires' war," and the Japanese after their defeat affirmed that they were beaten by machines. Such explanations were in a sense consoling to the vanquished, but they begged an essential question: why were the Allies able to invent and produce and operate more effective machines?

Unused to war and hating the necessity for it, the people of the United States nevertheless pursued the struggle with a spirit of initiative, versatility, and adaptability which conquered incredible obstacles. Unforeseen contingencies that challenged all martial precedents were attacked at top speed and solutions devised which likewise broke all precedents. In almost all fields the technical achievements of the Allied scientists outmatched the best that Axis scientists could invent despite the attention long given in Germany and Italy to war preparation. In the air the Allied bombers surpassed their rivals. In the development of projectiles the "proximity fuse" which exploded a shell by radio contact at the most efficient distance from its target was a product of American engineering genius. The development of radar for reconnaissance and detection was carried to its highest point by Allied technicians. German inventors were working on several terrifying weapons when the war ended, but only the destructive rocket bombs were finished in time to suggest the surprises one more year of war might have brought from the Nazi laboratories. With Germany occupied and the secrets of the German research groups in Allied possession, the Japanese were definitely outclassed. The tenacity, devotion, and self-sacrifice of the soldiers and scientists of Nippon could not cancel this disparity. Japanese technology and industry could not match the precise, plentiful, and lethal weapons turned out by the unbombed factories of America.

It was evident to the members of the Japanese cabinet and to the heads of the army and navy that Japan could not long survive the attacks which the Anglo-American forces would be able to launch after Germany was out of the war. There was the additional probability that the Soviet army might attack on the mainland of Asia, a probability increased by the fact that Russia terminated the Russo-Japanese Nonaggression Pact in April, 1945. But the militarists who had urged the Japanese people to war and assured them that victory was certain found it difficult to acknowledge their mistake. They sought to learn what terms they might expect if Japan surrendered, but they did so indirectly, desiring to preserve their dignity. While they were still hesitating, two swift events at the opening of August, 1945, ended their indecision.

On August 6, 1945, an American superfortress dropped an atomic bomb on Hiroshima, destroying three-fifths of this Japanese city and causing the deaths of 78,150 people. Two days later Russia declared war on Japan and opened a powerful drive upon the Manchurian frontier. The Russian action came exactly three months after the German surrender, fulfilling an understanding reached at the Crimea Conference. The proof that the United States, Great Britain, and Russia were prepared to act in concert to crush Japan made their victory almost inevitable. The British Pacific Fleet, after sailing 25,000 miles in sixty days, had joined in the mounting naval attack; and the Red army, fresh from its victories over the *Wehrmacht,* opened its drive into Manchuria with the familiar and deadly "pincer" strategy which had doomed a million Germans. On August 9 a second atomic bomb was dropped, leveling most of Nagasaki with a heavy toll in lives. Recognizing the appalling cost of further delay, the Japanese cabinet decided to yield on August 10, and the terms presented by the Allied governments were accepted in Tokyo on August 14. The formal ceremony of surrender took place on board the U.S.S. *Missouri* in Tokyo Bay on September 2, after American forces of occupation had already landed in Japan.

The Japanese armies in China, estimated at one million men, yielded to Generalissimo Chiang Kai-shek. Korea was liberated and the inhabitants promised eventual independence. Japanese divisions in Singapore, Burma, and the Netherlands East Indies capitulated to the British commander of the joint Allied forces in Southeast Asia. As in the case of Germany, victory brought release to thousands of prisoners of war who had survived the horrors of Japanese prison camps. Starvation, disease, flogging, and inhuman working conditions had decimated the prison population, and it was estimated that one-fourth of the prisoners in Japanese custody died in captivity. The articles of capitulation provided that the officials responsible for crimes against humanity would be brought to trial.

In Japan the demobilization of the army, dissolution of the general staff, and demilitarization of industry, were speeded by the Allied commander, General Douglas MacArthur. The Mikado, Emperor Hirohito, continued to reign but was stripped of his autocratic powers and voluntarily renounced his traditional claim to divine status. It was evident that the economic dislocation resulting from war damage, loss of ships and markets, and the compression of an excessive population into the mountainous islands of Japan, would make readjustment and rehabilitation in the postwar period extremely difficult. But it was hoped that liberal elements would take control under an amended constitution and bring the people a chance to develop along peaceful lines in a world which desired to impose no undue penalties upon them if they foreswore aggressive intentions.

PART X

The Contemporary World

THE UNITED NATIONS

The mere conquest of our enemies is not enough. We must go on to do all in our power to conquer the doubts and fears, the ignorance and the greed, which made this horror possible . . .

FRANKLIN D. ROOSEVELT (1945)

1. THE UNITED NATIONS ORGANIZE

THE League of Nations, formed in 1919 to promote world order and adjust international disputes, failed to avert the outbreak of a second world war twenty years later. Despite some real successes in arbitration the League had been steadily weakened by defects and discredited by defeats. The gravest limitation, which crippled it from its origin, was the fact that Britain and France were the only permanent members among the great powers and the only important states which took a sustained interest in the meetings. This fact seemed, to hostile minds, sufficient proof that the League was little more than a Franco-British syndicate.

With the outbreak of World War II in 1939 it became apparent to most statesmen in democratic countries that the old League would have to be remodelled or a new one framed after peace was re-established. The need for a mechanism that would reduce the tension among nations had increased. The interdependence of world markets had been advertised to all by the global repercussions of the great depression. The growth of armaments in the 1930's, with the development of new, swift, and terrifying weapons, proved the urgent need for peacemaking machinery. These convictions, intensified by the suffering of the Second World War, evoked a prolific literature and a deep interest in world federation between 1939 and 1945. The nations which had broken with the Axis powers and aligned themselves with the British, American, and Russian governments in the war effort, came by 1943 to represent a majority of the world's population. Their leaders were therefore in a position to endorse plans for a new league,

INTERNATIONAL COURT OF JUSTICE

Fifteen members chosen by the Assembly. They meet in permanent session to decide "judiciable" disputes which arise between nations.

SECURITY COUNCIL

Eleven members — the Big Five permanent, other six elected for two-year terms by Assembly. It investigates international disputes; takes action against aggressors if necessary.

GENERAL ASSEMBLY

Up to five delegates from each of fifty-one member nations, but only one vote for each nation. Its duties are to discuss any questions within the scope of the Charter, and submit recommendations to the Security Council.

ATOMIC ENERGY COMMISSION

Includes eleven members of Security Council plus Canada. Considers all problems relating to atomic energy.

MILITARY STAFF COMMITTEE

Composed of Chiefs of Staff of the Big Five. Under Council, will direct forces against any aggressor nation.

INTERNATIONAL CONTINGENTS OF ARMED FORCES

To be composed of readily available forces, provided by all members for putting down threats to peace.

SECRETARIAT

Secretary General at head; includes research, administrative staffs; reports to Assembly, Security Council.

ECONOMIC AND SOCIAL COUNCIL

Eighteen members elected by Assembly. Coordinates affiliated organizations to remove economic, social roots of war.

TRUSTEESHIP COUNCIL

Includes Big Five and all nations that administer trust territories; others elected by Assembly.

EDUCATIONAL, SCIENTIFIC AND CULTURAL ORGANIZATION

Organized to foster world intellectual cooperation through education, science and culture.

FOOD AND AGRICULTURAL ORGANIZATION

Research and study organization; endeavors to raise world food and nutrition standards.

INTERNATIONAL LABOR ORGANIZATION

Includes labor-management delegates; to raise world employment, welfare standards.

INTERNATIONAL CIVIL AVIATION ORGANIZATION

Deals with the complex economic and legal problems in commercial air transportation.

INTERNATIONAL BANK

Established by the Bretton Woods agreement. Provides loans for reconstruction and development.

INTERNATIONAL MONETARY FUND

Also part of Bretton Woods plan, to be used by members to help stabilize currencies.

WORLD HEALTH ORGANIZATION

Will serve as research organ and as an information center on world medical developments.

INTERNATIONAL REFUGEE ORGANIZATION

Being organized. Successor to UNRRA, will care for refugees; resettle displaced persons.

Graphics Institute for the New York Times

THE STRUCTURE OF THE UNITED NATIONS ORGANIZATION

for which the name "United Nations" was chosen. At successive conferences held in 1943, 1944, and 1945 declarations and resolutions were formulated which could be set forth as a charter for the organization. Of these conferences, the most important were held at Dumbarton Oaks, near Washington, D.C. (August 21–October 7, 1944), at Yalta in the Crimea (February 2–12, 1945), at Mexico City (February 21–March 8, 1945), and at San Francisco (April 25–June 26, 1945).

Composed exclusively of states which had defied the Axis powers, this new international body could not claim to be in the full sense an impartial or all-inclusive world federation. It grew out of the logical and generous desire of the more peaceful nations to discourage aggressors and to promote security and freedom throughout the world. In November, 1943, a United Nations Relief and Rehabilitation Administration was formed by representatives of forty-two nations. Known more briefly as UNRRA, it labored to feed and rehabilitate peoples who had suffered under the Axis yoke. Early in 1944 an organization for educational and cultural reconstruction was proposed; and in July, 1944, a United Nations Monetary and Financial Conference (Bretton Woods Conference) met to plan more stable international currency and exchange rates. These were agencies born under war conditions but they could be made to serve the nations even better when peace returned.

The United Nations became the general world parliament within which all the secondary agencies were expected to work. In October, 1944, delegates of the Big Three — the United States, the British Commonwealth, and the Soviet Union — proposed that the draft charter for the new international body should be submitted for criticism to a conference at which all eligible nations might be represented. The spirit in which the Big Three planned to utilize their impending victory was indicated when their spokesmen, President Roosevelt, prime minister Churchill, and Marshal Joseph Stalin, met at Yalta (February, 1945). While proclaiming their determination to destroy Nazism and Fascism, they announced that the people of liberated Europe would receive the rights of self-government as soon as conditions permitted. The fighting in Germany and Italy had reached its dramatic and terrible finale when the delegates of fifty nations opened their session in San Francisco.[1] In two months (April 25–June 26) they completed a

[1] The nations represented at the San Francisco Conference, which might be considered charter members of the United Nations, were: Argentina, Australia, Belgium, Bolivia, Brazil, the Bielorussian Soviet Socialist Re-

Charter for the United Nations. Ratification by the member governments followed swiftly, the United States Senate adopting it by a vote of 89 to 2. The ratification of Great Britain was deposited on October 20 and that of the Union of Soviet Socialist Republics on October 24. The latter date saw the total ratifications reach 29, the number required to bring the Charter legally into effect. The United Nations thus became an historical reality on October 24, 1945. With this formal appearance of a new world league, the older League of Nations lost meaning. Supplanted and eclipsed, it was dissolved at a final session held at Geneva, April 18, 1946.

It was logical that the Big Three, having borne the chief burden in the defeat of the Axis powers, should assume the lead in creating the United Nations Organization. They had fought and financed the war, and it seemed probable that in a devastated and bankrupt world they would have to finance the program of peace and reconstruction. The main problem at San Francisco, therefore, was to transform the United Nations war machinery into a United Nations peace machinery. The predominant position of the United States, Britain, and Russia was maintained by making them together with France and China permanent members of the Security Council, the executive organ of the new league. There were also to be six nonpermanent members of the Council, and these six would be chosen by the delegates in the Assembly. This second chamber, the Assembly, was to form a sort of international deliberative parliament to which all member states (ultimately, it was hoped, all the states of the world) would send delegates. The third organ of the United Nations was an Economic and Social Council, a body designed to function under the direction of the Assembly and to promote economic stability, friendly intercourse, and general welfare among all peoples. The fourth organ of the United Nations was an International Court of Justice for the adjudication of disputes among national sovereign states.

There was sharp criticism at San Francisco among spokesmen of

---

public, Canada, Chile, China, Colombia, Costa Rica, Cuba, Czechoslovakia, Denmark, the Dominican Republic, Ecuador, Egypt, El Salvador, Ethiopia, France, Greece, Guatemala, Haiti, Honduras, India, Iran, Iraq, the Lebanon Republic, Liberia, Luxembourg, Mexico, the Netherlands, New Zealand, Nicaragua, Norway, Panama, Paraguay, Peru, the Philippine Commonwealth, Saudi Arabia, Turkey, the Ukrainian Soviet Socialist Republic, the Union of South Africa, the Union of Soviet Socialist Republics, the United Kingdom of Great Britain and Northern Ireland, the United States, Uruguay, Venezuela, and Yugoslavia.

"little forty-five" nations, who were dismayed at the powers accorded the "Big Five" (the United States, Great Britain, Russia, France, and China). Article 27 of the Charter provided that important decisions of the Security Council must be approved by seven of its eleven members, including all five of the permanent members. This "unanimity clause" meant in effect that each of the Big Five, if it failed to banish an embarrassing question from the agenda, could at least veto any positive action by the Council after the question had been discussed. The smaller nations saw this as a device to confer immunity on the Big Five while leaving the "little forty-five" subject to action. A further danger foreseen by many critics was that the Big Five would oppose action against a "satellite state" in its own system and that the United Nations would be powerless to investigate conditions in any small state so long as the latter had a "protector" among the Big Five.

The first League of Nations had no authority to employ armed force against an aggressor nation; it could only recommend various forms of diplomatic or economic pressure. As the Security Council of the new league might have to check the rearmament of Germany, Italy, or Japan, or to curb some new aggressor, the nations judged it advisable to place armed forces at the disposal of the Security Council. Article 43 of the Charter provided that, if persuasion failed, members of the United Nations might be called upon by the Security Council to assist in restraining an unruly neighbor even if such action involved war against the recalcitrant state. This Article did not, however, involve any member of the United Nations in blind commitments. The aid, facilities, or military forces which a member state might be asked to provide were to be defined in advance in a special accord made by each national government when it joined the organization. If any state not a member of the Council were asked to provide armed forces, that state would first be invited to send a delegate to participate in the Council debate. Each government would thus be in a position to know, before the call came for armed contingents, the motives which prompted the Council to advise armed intervention. This safeguard protected each country against the possibility that it might be asked to furnish forces to be used against its own interests.

The League of Nations had established a mandate system under which the peoples in retarded areas or protectorates awarded to leading states after World War I remained subject to supervision by the League. The protecting power was supposed to report to the League on the administration and welfare of its charges. Since this system did not always work too well, it was supplanted in the new league by a system of Trusteeships for Dependent Peoples. Territories in which the inhabitants were not yet self-governing, that is, colonies, protectorates, and other regions annexed by a power, were to be honestly and efficiently governed and not exploited for the profit of the conqueror. Members of the United Nations agreed to transmit to the Secretary-General a regular report on the condition of all trusteeships which they administered. The Charter also provided (Article 75) that territories still held under mandates set up after World War I or detached from enemy control as a result of World War II would be placed under the trusteeship system. Some areas held under trusteeship would include bases and other strategic positions, and these the protecting power would hold under direction of the Security Council. It was hoped that this provision would prevent the misuse or illegal fortification of such areas. It was recalled that after World War I the Japanese obtained numerous islands in the Pacific Ocean under mandate, but this did not hinder their plans to turn some of the islands into secret war bases. When Japan resigned from the League in 1933, the League lost all authority over these mandates. The United Nations Council was therefore empowered to exercise more vigilance over strategic areas. But since supervision was entrusted directly to the Security Council and since the Council was dominated by the United States, Britain, and Russia, the risk remained great that each of these powers would veto any positive action if the searchlight of investigation were turned too critically upon its own trusteeships.

The United Nations, as an organization, was a mechanism for easing international tensions and adjusting disputes; it was not a guarantee against the occurrence of such disputes save in the sense that the existence of a law court is a guarantee against crime and violence. Those pessimists who declared that there always had been wars among nations and states and always would be, were reminded that feudal barons once fought one another over a disputed boundary ditch but later learned to submit such property claims to royal arbitrament. Even the rigid code of the duel, which demanded that gentlemen settle disputes "touching their honor" by engaging in personal combat, had been abandoned as respect for law increased. In civilized society, public order and security had been achieved only because the individual citizen agreed to curb his desire for private vengeance and to appeal to the courts for justice, abiding by the judgment rendered. Among nations, however, the code of the duel still reigned; each sovereign people was the judge of its own course and could demand that an opponent yield or settle the issue on "the field of honor." Yet if the will to peace became strong enough among a majority of the world's people, it was a reasonable hope that governments, like private individuals and corporations, would accept the verdict of international courts if those courts spoke for a majority of the human race.

2. THE CONTROL OF ARMAMENTS

The restoration of peace in 1945 brought immediate compulsory disarmament for the defeated powers, Germany, Japan, and their satellite nations. The victorious powers also reduced their war strength but more slowly. A year after the surrender of Japan, the Big Three still had three million soldiers stationed outside their own frontiers. Most of the military divisions garrisoned the conquered countries but some were scattered through "liberated" states also. The largest concentrations of forces were to be found in central Europe. The Russian zone in Germany supported 750,000 Soviet soldiers; and other Soviet detachments, holding strategic points in Finland, Austria, Hungary, Poland, Rumania, Bulgaria, and Yugoslavia, were estimated at almost one million men. In the Far East 200,000 Soviet troops patrolled the Russian zone of Korea, and 75,000 still lingered in Manchuria, executing a protracted withdrawal while stripping the province of machinery and movable wealth.

The British quota of troops still outside the empire limits after a year of pseudopeace was smaller than the Russian total. Moreover, they were much more widely dispersed. About 350,000 occupied the British zone in Germany, with an additional 28,000 stationed in Austria and 45,000 in Italy. Disturbed conditions in Greece kept 50,000 there on the alert, and civil strife in Palestine persisted despite the presence of 110,000 imperial veterans in that distracted land. The number of British soldiers in Iraq, Transjordan, and the Suez Canal zone was not certain but could be estimated at something over 15,000. The conquered Italian empire in Africa, which included Libya, Eritrea, and Italian Somaliland, required another 100,000, part of which were still withdrawing from Egypt. Farther east, in Java and Sumatra, the revolt of the Indonesians throughout the Dutch East Indies, which the Netherlands government could not quell, explained the presence of another 20,000 British soldiers. The total number of British troops still abroad thus approached 750,000. This was less than half the total of Russian soldiers stationed on foreign soil at the close of 1946.

The American armed contingents outside the borders of the United States one year after V-J Day were computed to amount to about 650,000 men. Of these, 300,000, or almost one-half, controlled the American zones in Germany and Austria. Another 25,000 kept order in Italy, especially along the Italo-Yugoslav frontier; 30,000 remained on guard in China, partly to protect American Lend-Lease material; and 50,000 held the American segment of Korea. General Douglas MacArthur's command, which included all the Japanese homeland, required only 140,000; the Philippines and the Pacific Islands accounted for 50,000; and approximately 25,000 held strategic northern bases, anchorages, airfields, and weather stations from Alaska to Greenland. The defense of the Panama Canal and the Caribbean area required a force estimated at 50,000.

When the Assembly of the United Nations took up the delicate issue of disarmament in 1946, it was clear to all that the first step must be a voluntary one: the nations of the world must list their armed forces and reveal how many they had at home and abroad. To obtain such information was extremely difficult. Few secrets are so jealously guarded by modern governments as the strength of their armies and the quality of their weapons. Nevertheless the Assembly voted a resolution (December, 1946) calling upon all national states to announce their armed strength and to permit a full and effective inspection of their war weapons, present and projected. The resolution also recommended that standing armies should be reduced, that atomic weapons should be outlawed, and that control of atomic energy for peaceful purposes should be entrusted to an international body. Having endorsed this resolution "in principle" the Assembly referred it to the Security Council for discussion and implementation.

All governments recognized that the most fateful section of any disarmament treaty would have to define the use of atomic energy in war and peace. On this question the United States, as the only power which had produced and used atomic bombs, could exercise decisive influence and no recommendation was likely to prove workable unless it won the assent of the American government. In January, 1946, the United Nations had appointed an Atomic Energy Commission of twelve, Canada sending a delegate in addition to the eleven member states of the Security Council. In June the United States government notified this Commission that it was prepared to destroy its stock of atomic bombs or to surrender them to an international authority together with all technical secrets of manufacture. There was, however,

LEFT TO RIGHT: WINSTON CHURCHILL, FRANKLIN D. ROOSEVELT, AND JOSEPH STALIN AT THE YALTA CONFERENCE, FEBRUARY, 1945

LEADERS OF THE GERMAN NATIONAL SOCIALIST GOVERNMENT ON TRIAL AT NUREMBERG, 1946

a condition attached to this proposal. Before it surrendered all atomic weapons and renounced the use of the atomic bomb, the United States government insisted that an adequate system for the control of arms, including atomic weapons, must have been agreed upon and put into effective operation throughout the world. Such a system would have to outlaw the manufacture of atomic weapons, maintain an efficient scrutiny over all sources of atomic power, and provide condign punishments for any group or nation which attempted to violate the rules of control.

This American proposal threw the whole issue back upon the United Nations. If the world was to be spared an armament race of exhausting expense and terrifying possibilities, a decision would have to be reached promptly to invest the Security Council or an equivalent body with extraordinary powers. The League of Nations, it was recalled, had possessed the moral authority and legal machinery to identify and proscribe any nation which threatened the peace of the world. But it had not possessed weapons or forces to halt an aggressor. It seemed clear that the United Nations would need an international military police at its command, as recommended in the Charter. Such an international militia could not be organized without the approval and collaboration of the Big Five and more particularly of the Big Three. The test which would decide the real authority of the United Nations therefore lay in the future; the new world league would have to prove itself in action before it could be entrusted with supranational responsibilities.

3. ECONOMIC AND CULTURAL CO-OPERATION

The Charter of the United Nations provided that the health, welfare, and economic progress of the world's millions should be the special concern of an Economic and Social Council elected by the General Assembly. This council or commission of eighteen members began to function in 1946, enlarging its influence through eight subsidiary organizations. To list these secondary agencies and describe their activities will best clarify the ambitious aims and global range of the program for human betterment.

(1) The United Nations Educational, Scientific, and Cultural Organization (UNESCO) was to collect statistics and aid the exchange of useful information. Books, art works, motion picture films, scientific discoveries, new medical treatments, in fact all advances in knowledge which might aid mankind, were to be circulated among the

nations by improvements in communication, in translation, in the exchange of data, of artists, and of teachers.

(2) The specter of world hunger and the problems of increasing world population were confided to the attention of a Food and Agricultural Organization (FAO). This commission of experts drew up plans between 1943 and 1946 for the creation of a world food reserve and compiled valuable information on living conditions, on the average income in all countries, on public health, on nutritional needs and standards, and on the relation between famine and disease. Advance statistics on crops, the movement of trade, and the trend of prices enabled the FAO to predict where famine would strike, and relief could thus be prepared in time to aid countries and classes exposed to extreme need.

(3) Under the League of Nations the International Labor Organization (ILO), created by the peace conference at Paris in 1919, was an autonomous body which co-operated with the League. Its aim and function was the promotion of better working conditions throughout the world. It marshaled statistics, compared living and labor conditions in various countries, sought to clarify relations between employees and employers, and endeavored to encourage reforms by collecting authentic facts and laying them before an enlightened public. This sane and valuable procedure had won wide respect for its recommendations, and it survived the dissolution of the League of Nations and was made a subsidiary of the United Nations.

(4) The rise of air transport to a position of world importance induced the Assembly to approve a special commission to supervise this new activity. Under the Economic and Social Council an International Civil Aviation Organization took form in 1946, its function being to codify rules and simplify the confusion which resulted when millions of passengers and tons of freight swept into the world's airports.

(5) There was a strong demand that something should be done to stabilize business conditions after World War II. The disastrous inflation and collapse which disrupted German, Austrian, and Hungarian economy after 1918 and the great depression after 1929, suggested that economic disorder in one region soon infected neighboring countries and should be remedied before it became acute. In 1944 the delegates of the United Nations organized a World Bank (Bretton Woods Conference). With a capital of $8,000,000,000 and headquarters at Washington, D.C., this bank was authorized to advance loans

to nations which were hindered in their legitimate reconstruction and expansion because of lack of capital.

(6) A further innovation of the Bretton Woods Conference was the creation of an International Monetary Fund. This fund was to act as a regulator and to help prevent the wild fluctuations of national currencies which had dislocated international trade so dangerously in the period between the wars. In 1946 thirty-two nations stabilized their currencies on the basis of the gold dollar. This meant that they agreed not to raise or lower their currency values by more than 10 per cent but they might appeal to the International Monetary Fund for a revision of rates in case of a "fundamental disequilibrium."

(7) Control of communicable diseases, plagues, and plague carriers (rats, lice, mosquitoes, etc.) became an urgent problem during World War II. The rapidity with which millions of men were shifted about the globe exposed them to a variety of new infections, and the increase in air travel brought distant zones and climates into contact. A World Health Organization to study controls and plan the eradication of disease was therefore set up in 1946. Its purpose was to co-ordinate existing agencies and to provide a single commission which would supervise world-wide health conditions.

(8) No problem arising from World War II stirred the conscience of the nations more deeply than the fate of the millions of displaced persons who were rendered homeless by the persecution and devastation of the war years. This problem was first handled by various agencies of the United Nations Relief and Rehabilitation Administration and by military governments which were set up in the occupied countries of Europe. After January 1, 1947, an International Refugee Organization, responsible to the Economic and Security Council, assumed charge of the program for aiding displaced persons.

The United Nations Relief and Rehabilitation Administration came to an end in December, 1946. Organized as an emergency bureau to rush aid to the people of the liberated states and relieve the human misery caused by the war, it spent over $4,000,000,000 in four years and undoubtedly saved thousands and perhaps millions of lives. World War II revealed human nature in its most savage and in its most civilized aspects, but the funds raised by churches and charitable associations to aid the stricken furnished a hopeful contrast to the stark and incredible horrors practiced in the concentration camps. By 1946, however, most European states had recovered sufficiently to care for their own populations. The chief contributors, the United States,

Great Britain, and Canada, which had met the major share of the expense for this venture in international charity, did not feel that it should continue to finance itself through the generosity of a few nations. The United States alone had contributed 68 per cent of the UNRRA costs. World relief was a world problem. How vast a problem it was and how vast a problem it might remain the following section will suggest.

4. HELP FOR THE HOMELESS AND THE HUNGRY

When Germany capitulated in May, 1945, the peoples of Europe had been swept back and forth by the tides of war for over five years. The roads were blocked with thousands of deserting soldiers, escaped prisoners of war, and laborers who had been induced or compelled to serve in the fields and factories which fed the German military machine. Many of these vagrants found their way home unassisted. But within the first year that followed the German surrender more than 12,000,000 refugees in Europe were listed as "displaced persons" by the United Nations Relief and Rehabilitation Administration. The great majority were transported back to the country of their birth, but three very large groups had still to be dealt with at the opening of 1947. One comprised those who for one reason or another did not wish to return to their native land. The second included people of German blood or descent who had been residents of neighboring states in 1939 and were now expelled from Poland, Czechoslovakia, Rumania, and other regions because these liberated nations did not wish to keep a German minority. The third group of exiles were the prisoners of war from the Axis countries. Thousands of Germans were held in England and France, and millions in Russia, to help harvest the crops, build roads, and otherwise make reparation for the damage the German armed forces had visited upon the countries they attacked.

Population displacement on so vast a scale was something new in modern European history. It was not easy to classify many of these migrants or to find a place for them in the postwar world. This was especially true of the political and religious fugitives who had suffered under the various totalitarian regimes. There were 200,000 Spanish republicans who had escaped to France when the Nationalists under Franco overthrew the Spanish Republic (1936–1939). There were 1,200,000 Jews, the most tragic victims of religious and racial persecution and of the systematic decimation practiced in the Fascist controlled areas. Many of these Jews, wishing to forsake Europe, looked

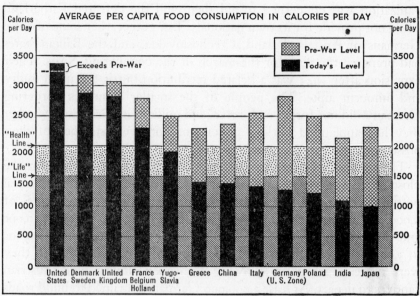

AVERAGE PER CAPITA FOOD CONSUMPTION IN CALORIES PER DAY

Pre-War Level
Today's Level

Exceeds Pre-War

"Health" Line →
"Life" Line →

Calories per Day: 3500, 3000, 2500, 2000, 1500, 1000, 500, 0

United States · Denmark Sweden · United Kingdom · France Belgium Holland · Yugo-Slavia · Greece · China · Italy · Germany (U. S. Zone) · Poland · India · Japan

New York Times, April 28, 1946

WORLD FOOD NEEDS AND FOOD DEFICIENCIES, 1946

abroad to Palestine or to America for a new home. But the quota of immigrants to Palestine was limited by Arab opposition and British policy, and the United States immigration authorities granted visas with increasing reluctance after 1939. Further groups not easy to rehabilitate included political exiles, especially Poles, Yugoslavs, Rumanians, and Russians who refused to return to their native lands, insisting that they would be harshly treated by the communist-dominated postwar governments established there. As UNRRA and later the United Nations Assembly ruled that no refugee was to be repatriated against his will, the British and American military governments in Germany and Austria had to house and feed such exiles indefinitely or find a place for them in some friendly country.

The second group of displaced persons noted above were the Germans who were driven from the "liberated" territories of central and eastern Europe after 1945. Over two million of them were herded out of East Prussia and Silesia as the Poles moved their frontier to the Oder. Millions more left Hungary, Rumania, and Yugoslavia to seek in the mutilated, helpless, and divided Reich the livelihood denied them in the lands bordering the shrunken German state. The fate of these fugitives was especially uncertain because no international organization was concerned to aid them and the defeated Fatherland could not provide for its own nationals. Ten years earlier some of these Germans of Austria, Poland, Czechoslovakia, and the Balkan states had prepared the way for the march of the conquering Nazis. Their expulsion after 1945 was a belated retribution but it fell upon guilty and innocent alike. The people of the smaller countries bordering Germany did not forget or forgive, and millions of Germans, whether they had applauded Hitler's policies or not, were stripped of their possessions and forced to emigrate.

The number of German prisoners of war still in captivity at the close of 1946, a year and a half after the war in Europe ended, was possibly 4,000,000. The United States, which had taken a total of 8,000,000, released them swiftly. The British retained about 150,000 and the French 600,000. But the Russians, who had held 4,000,000 to 5,000,000 when the war closed, released very few, although they were more generous in allowing Rumanian, Italian, and Austrian captives to depart. At least 3,000,000 Germans remained to build roads and railroads in Siberia, to work on farms, run machines, cut timber, and otherwise make reparation through their labor for the destruction wrought by the German armed forces. In Asia about 1,500,000 Japanese prisoners were likewise detained, so that approximately 5,000,000 prisoners of war must be added to the other millions of displaced persons still awaiting repatriation after their years of captivity. Like those other millions, the wounded and disabled, they were the tragic, half-forgotten debris of war's receding tide.

The fate of the world's hungry millions was less dramatic than that of the homeless millions but it was more persistent and more pathetic. When World War II ended, one-fifth of the human race, more than 400,000,000 people, were close to famine and many of them were literally starving. The causes — war damage, economic disorder, unfavorable weather, excessive demands, the unusual waste resulting from war, failure of transport, lack of fertilizers, lack of man power — these causes had cut the world food production to 88 per cent of the 1939 level. European crops were down 20 per cent, North African 50 per cent. South Africa had suffered a drought. The Argentine wheat crop was two-thirds the prewar standard. In India, China, and Burma the rice yield had fallen 25 per cent. Australia and South America were also below normal in their food crops. Only the United States, Canada, and possibly Russia could be counted upon for a surplus in 1946. Had no machinery existed to rush supplies to the most gravely menaced areas, the toll of life that year might have reached an appalling figure. The Combined Food Board which had been set up as an international war agency in 1942, and the United Nations Relief and Rehabilitation Administration, waged a successful campaign against global hunger. Millions starved before the summer harvests of 1946 relieved the acute shortages, but without international co-operation hundreds of millions would have died from lack of food or from the diseases which follow where malnutrition has prepared the way.

In Europe the lands most severely affected were Poland, Austria, Germany, Italy, and Greece. Dietitians had calculated that two thousand calories a day were essential to assure normal health; that fifteen hundred calories per capita was the "life line." Yet in all the countries named above the ratio fell to less than fifteen hundred and many of the people were fortunate to obtain half-rations. When famine prevails over wide areas, relief supplies become a political weapon. The British and Americans accused the Russian military government, and were accused by the Russian authorities in return, of using the promise of food to win starving Europeans to support policies dictated in Washington, London, or Moscow. So suspicious did the Russians become that the British and Americans were using UNRRA shipments to increase their own popularity that UNRRA relief was barred from the Soviet zones.

There was a warning for the world in the famine of 1945–1946 but it was not heeded widely enough. In America the general level of nutrition, despite some specific shortages, was higher than in 1939. Europe, however, had seen the face of famine clearly, and in Asia it had brought tragedy. The Indian famine of 1943 had destroyed a million lives. The famines of 1945 and 1946 were less acute but for two months in 1946 imports of wheat barely sufficed to keep the ailing millions alive. China was more disastrously affected: in 1946 the UNRRA estimates revealed that 40,000,000 people there were dangerously undernourished and 7,000,000 were at starvation point. In Siam, Malaysia, the Dutch East Indies, and French Indo-China, hunger intensified the political unrest, while in Japan and Korea the United States military government strove to relieve the severe distress with imports. After 1946 the specter of mass starvation withdrew from the world's table, but only temporarily. It was evident that several years of unusually good harvests, political tranquillity, and careful planning would be needed to recover the deficits in health and to replenish world reserves. Further droughts, insect plagues, civil wars, or other unfavorable circumstances, would certainly bring hunger back as the most inexorable force dictating human destiny.

THE PEACE TREATIES

1945—1947

The war left two great powers preponderant — the United States of America and Soviet Russia. Great Britain lies midway in geography and way of life.

ERNEST BEVIN, FOREIGN SECRETARY
OF GREAT BRITAIN

I. PROVISORY GOVERNMENTS AND PLEBISCITES

THE death of Adolf Hitler and the collapse of German resistance in the spring of 1945 plunged all central Europe into chaos. Momentarily there was a vacuum of power. The government at Berlin was gone, and because the conquerors refused to recognize any successor to Hitler there could be no continuation of German rule, no transfer of authority. In Vienna, Budapest, Bucharest, and Sofia the situation was the same. Leaders who had collaborated with the Nazis were dead or in hiding, the Russian "liberators" patrolled the streets, and the populace wondered numbly what the future held for them. In that dark hour all the defeated states lacked a government, and the commanders of the invading armies met the situation with the swift pragmatic efficiency of wartime. They set up military governments to administer the American, British, French, and Russian zones of occupation.

No system of administration can be improvised overnight, however. It was inevitable that the new military rulers of the conquered and divided lands should retain some of the local officials, the police agents, clerks, magistrates, postmen, burgomeisters, and other civilian employees of the previous regime. To expel all public functionaries and replace them with Allied troops, or to wait and seek "trustworthy" substitutes, would have invited chaos. The first and most urgent task facing the victors in the hour of triumph was to establish order. Central Europe was an area of shattered cities, bombed bridges, stalled trains, and failing food supplies. To distribute fuel and food, enforce sanitary edicts, quell looting, repair the roads and water mains, and house the homeless were instant responsibilities. Within a few weeks the resolute measures of the military governors began to bring the towns and villages, as units, into a semblance of order.

To restore state governments, to erect a "scaffold" regime that could represent and organize the conquered people in the interim before peace was re-established, was less easy. In all the ex-enemy states provisional regimes were erected in 1945 but none was genuinely autonomous or representative. The temporary premiers or chancellors — Ferruccio Parri and Ivano Bonomi in Italy, Karl Renner in Austria, Peter Groza in Rumania, Kimon Georgiev in Bulgaria, Zoltan Tildy in Hungary — were leaders with limited authority who mediated between their distressed nations and the impatient conquerors. It is the office of an intermediary to serve two masters but in a crisis he must obey the stronger or forfeit his function. Few statesmen can discharge such a role with dignity and fewer still with honor. The leaders who took responsibility in the ex-enemy states in 1945 and 1946 seldom remained in office more than a few months. Their regimes slowly changed to something more representative and more stable as successive plebiscites clarified the political scene.

The most vital decisions affecting Europe after World War II were made not by these leaders but by the European peoples themselves. Within a year a majority of the adult population throughout Europe had gone to the polls to declare their political preferences. The results (not always unchallenged) indicated that more than 90 per cent of the electorate in Russia, Bulgaria, and Yugoslavia registered as communists; in Czechoslovakia the proportion was 30 to 40 per cent; in France and Finland 20 to 30 per cent; in Italy, Belgium, and Hungary 10 to 20 per cent; and in Norway, Sweden, the Netherlands, Austria, Greece, and the United States zone of Germany, less than 10 per cent. These figures suggested that the 400,000,000 inhabitants of Europe west of the Soviet Union hoped to resolve their problems in their own traditional fashions. Europe as a whole was not prepared to embrace Marxian doctrines or establish communist governments.

The elections suggested something more, however. Those countries which did establish communist-controlled regimes, such as Bulgaria and Yugoslavia, were certain to receive firm Russian support at the treaty table. Countries which rejected communism, as Greece and Austria did, would have to look for aid to London and Washington. The terms of the treaties, the amount of reparations, the fixing of disputed boundary lines, would depend upon the great powers, each of which would seek to aid its own favorites. All European states felt the tug of war between the Soviet Union and the western democracies throughout 1945 and 1946 but few were in a position to profit by it. One of the few was France, which secured grain from Russia and a loan from the United States at the same time. But France was one of the Big Four with a vote at the Council of Foreign Ministers.

2. THE COUNCIL OF FOREIGN MINISTERS

Before the Second World War ended in August, 1945, the diplomats of the Big Three — the United States, Great Britain, and Russia — had already laid their plans for making the peace. The purposeful cooperation which Roosevelt, Churchill, and Stalin displayed at their meetings in Tehran (December, 1943) and Yalta (February, 1945) was still evident at the Potsdam Conference which met after the German but before the Japanese surrender (July–August, 1945). The sudden death of Franklin D. Roosevelt the previous April and the replacement of Winston Churchill by the Labor Party prime minister, Clement R. Attlee, in July, changed the heads of two delegations but not the objectives of the three governments. President Harry S. Truman, prime minister Attlee, and Marshal Stalin declared (August 2, 1945) that the foreign ministers of the United States, Great Britain, Russia, France, and China would be given authority "to draw up, with a view to their submission to the United Nations, treaties of peace. . . ."

Thenceforth the inner history of the treaty making was the record of this Council of Foreign Ministers. More specifically, it was the record of what the ministers of the Big Three decided, for the foreign minister of China did not participate in the European settlement and the foreign minister of France was not always invited to the sessions. The Council met nearly two hundred times, in London, in Moscow, in New York, and in Paris and whenever it met the corridors were haunted by journalists and photographers, by delegations from the excluded states, by interpreters and secretaries and international experts, who came to testify armed with briefcases. The Potsdam Declaration had included the ambiguous pronouncement that "whenever the Council is considering a question of direct interest to a state not represented thereon, such state should be invited to send representatives to participate in the discussions and study of that question." But the promise implied in this passage was immediately clouded by the un-equivocal statement that "the Council may adapt its procedure to the particular problem under consideration. In some cases it may hold its own preliminary discussions prior to the participation of other inter-ested states." This warning appeared to imply that the foreign minis-ters of the United States, Great Britain, and Russia might arrange settlements suitable to themselves which the "other interested states" would then have little effective power to revise.

Thus a very grave responsibility rested upon the three foreign min-isters, who became molders of world destiny. Fortunately all three were statesmen of exceptionally broad experience and long training. The American delegate, James Francis Byrnes, was a journalist and jurist who had served fourteen years in the House of Representatives and ten years in the Senate before he was named an associate justice of the Supreme Court in 1941. The following year, at the request of President Roosevelt, he resigned this post to become Director of Eco-nomic Stabilization, and in 1945 President Truman appointed him sec-retary of state at the age of sixty-six. Byrnes was a shrewd, patient, and skillful negotiator and his long political experience in Washing-ton helped him to gauge American public opinion and to keep his policies and commitments within the limits that the United States Sen-ate would ratify.

The British foreign minister, Ernest Bevin, was two years younger than Byrnes. Less suave in manner and less persuasive in debate, he had the determination and truculence of a man who fights hard for the cause he believes in and is not afraid of plain speaking. Bevin was a self-made man; he had worked as a truckdriver, a shop clerk, and a labor union organizer before he was appointed minister of labor in Churchill's coalition war cabinet in 1940. With the triumph of the Labor Party in 1945 this veteran of a hundred labor battles and politi-cal skirmishes became the secretary of state for foreign affairs. As he transferred his attention from internal to external problems his vision broadened and he grasped the global import of British Empire policies. His willingness to support Byrnes in blocking Russian demands and his defense of British "imperialism" annoyed many of his old Labor Party colleagues, who attacked his diplomacy and declared that he had become a Tory imperialist.

The third member of this historic triumvirate was the Russian representative, "the People's Commissar of Foreign Affairs," Vyacheslav Mikhailovich Molotov. A plump, urbane, and smiling man in his middle fifties, Molotov belied his arduous career. For thirty years he had worked at the center of the Russian revolutionary vortex which, like all revolutions, had devoured so many of its own children. He had been an associate of Lenin, a member of the *Politburo* and of the central committee of the Communist Party, president of the Council of People's Commissars, and, after 1939, commissar of foreign affairs. Energetic, affable, and inscrutable, he piqued his opponents by delaying tactics and petty objections and occasionally puzzled them even more by sweeping concessions. Russian distrust of foreign nations and Molotov's own ignorance of English may have inspired some of his unpredictable behavior. The Russians of the revolutionary generation, from commissars to combat troops, never forgot the years when Russia was a nation besieged and they never overcame their distrust of capitalist guile.

The first conference of the Council of Foreign Ministers was held in London from September 11 to October 3, 1945. It was a complete failure. The British and Americans blamed the Russians for the deadlock and were blamed by the Russians in return. Nettled by the criticisms which Byrnes and Bevin offered, Molotov protested indignantly, "You'd think I was on trial!" The Russians were particularly irked by the inclusion of the French representative in the discussions, a move which promised the Western democracies three votes to one for Russia. After three weeks of wrangling, all drafts and formulas were laid aside, and subcommittees were left to work over the problem of reparations and the creation of local governments in the shattered countries of central Europe.

The foreign ministers had agreed to hold their second conference in Moscow, without French or Chinese representation. After conferring for a week they announced (December 24, 1945) that a peace conference of twenty-one nations would be held in Paris the following May. The deadlock had been broken, at least temporarily, and plans for the control of the atomic bomb, for the administration of Japan, Korea, Rumania, and Bulgaria, for the withdrawal of Russian and American forces from China, and for the drafting of treaties for the European states, had all been approved "in principle." This announcement, coming at Christmas time, brought encouragement to a world weary of strife but in reality no definite accord had yet been achieved.

Some common plan was essential, however, unless the Big Three were prepared to face the other eighteen nations invited to meet in Paris in 1946 and face them without a program. To reveal their mutual distrust and deadlocked aims so openly would be to give the secondary powers a ripe opportunity to seize the initiative in the peacemaking. Compromises were therefore in order, and Secretary Byrnes intimated in March that the United States might consider making a loan of one billion dollars to the Soviet Union. Somewhat appeased, Molotov withdrew his objection to the participation of France in the discussions of the Council. The four foreign ministers met in Paris from April 25 to May 16, 1946, with Georges Bidault representing the French Republic. Ernest Bevin vetoed any decision on the German settlement at this time but warned that Great Britain might conclude separate treaties with the other defeated nations if the Council of Foreign Ministers failed to make some progress. The differences between the Western powers and the Soviet Union were sharply accentuated as the ministers clashed on point after point: on the disposition of the Italian colonies, on reparations, on the status of Trieste, on the treatment of the Franco regime in Spain, on the freedom of the elections promised the Rumanians and Bulgarians. But the weeks were passing, and the need to complete draft treaties before the (delayed) conference of the twenty-one nations assembled on July 29 brought the Big Four to an unwilling truce. On July 12 they adjourned after issuing a bland announcement that they were in substantial agreement on all essential issues.

This belated co-operation enabled the Big Four to dominate the Paris Peace Conference of 1946 and reject the demand of the seventeen lesser states for a larger share in shaping the treaties. On July 30 the settlements for Italy, Finland, Hungary, Rumania, and Bulgaria, as drafted by the Council of Foreign Ministers, were laid before the delegates of twenty-one nations.[1] Secretary Byrnes announced that the United States would support the policies approved jointly by the Council (the Big Four) unless these policies "were opposed by a two-thirds vote of the conference as a whole." This meant that unless

---

[1] The twenty-one states participating at the Conference were: Australia, Belgium, Brazil, Canada, China, *Czechoslovakia*, Ethiopia, France, Greece, India, the Netherlands, New Zealand, Norway, *Poland, the Ukraine, the Union of Soviet Socialist Republics*, the Union of South Africa, the United Kingdom, the United States, *White Russia*, and *Yugoslavia*. The six in italics formed the "Slav bloc."

the secondary states could marshal fourteen votes against the treaties as drafted the provisions would probably be enforced. The vanquished nations had no court of appeal. Although representatives from the five defeated states were permitted to appear before the conference and offer their protests, they were given no voice in the deliberations and no vote in the decisions. The treaties might therefore be described as "dictated settlements." They could not be regarded as "negotiated treaties" even though the defeated nations later accepted them, for those nations had not shared in the drafting of the terms which settled their fate. This fact was certain to provide grounds for a revisionist drive in the defeated states in later years.

When the Paris Conference adjourned on October 15, 1946, the five treaties had been approved in outline but the decisions were neither unanimous nor final. The voting repeatedly emphasized the cleavage that divided the east and the west, and the proof that the western nations could line up fifteen votes to override the six Slav states did not appease the latter. This cleavage had been recognized already. The fact that the three Russian Republics (the Union of Soviet Socialist Republics, the Ukrainian Soviet Socialist Republic, and the Bielorussian Soviet Socialist Republic) had the support of the Polish, Czechoslovak, and Yugoslav delegates split Europe into a Soviet and a non-Soviet sphere. While Moscow applauded the loyal stand of its satellites, the United States and Britain demonstrated that steady opposition to their policies might prove unprofitable and that co-operation could bring golden recompense. Thus Czechoslovakia received notice that a credit of $50,000,000 from America was to be "suspended," while Turkey (which had rejected Russian pressure) received a loan for $25,000,000. Austria (which likewise refused to bow to communist policies) was rewarded (October, 1946) with an assurance that America and Britain regarded it as a "liberated" and not as an ex-enemy state. Italy, where the communists likewise failed to win strong support, was fortified with a $50,000,000 loan.

This appeal from both east and west for the co-operation of the smaller states left the essential balance of power unchanged: enlarging the conference to twenty-one nations had merely enlarged the area of discord without resolving the differences. Accordingly the treaties were sent back to the Council of Foreign Ministers, where the drafts had originated. This Council then opened its fourth session of the series in New York on November 4, 1946.

3. THE FIVE TREATIES OF 1946

Unless the Big Four planned to postpone the treaties indefinitely or make peace separately, they had little choice but to approve their imperfect handiwork. The elections of November, 1946, in the United States helped clarify the diplomatic situation, for the vote showed no weakening in the American determination to oppose Russia. The possibility that the new Congress, dominated by the Republicans, might prove more obdurate than the Democratic regime, may have convinced the Russians that it was well to agree with their adversary quickly. Moving with surprising swiftness, the foreign ministers approved the five treaties in December; and the Italians, Hungarians, Rumanians, Bulgarians, and Finns thus knew their fate by the close of the year. The major clauses of each treaty, as they affected the states concerned, will be discussed in subsequent chapters. Here the treaties will be analyzed for their international rather than their specific significance.

(1) The first essential to note about the treaties of 1946 is that they were strictly limited in scope. They dealt (Finland excepted) with countries of south and southeast Europe. Despite the terms, the Italian treaty left the future of Italy indefinite, and the Danubian states could have little real future until Germany was reorganized. The agreements relating to Italy, Hungary, Rumania, and Bulgaria were therefore preliminary formulas, local and provisory. They might be considered as regional arrangements in the great business of global peacemaking.

(2) A second point to weigh was the relative disregard which the Big Four showed not only for the defeated nations but also for the sentiments of the Czechs, Yugoslavs, and Greeks. The Balkan states were "economic colonies" of the more prosperous European powers. They needed British and American and French trade and credit and had little real control over their own economic destiny; yet they resented their dependence on these great industrial states. The Balkans were drawn into one sphere of influence or another as the tide of European mastery ebbed and flowed. In 1919, with Russia in revolution and Germany in defeat, the French dictated Balkan policies. By 1939, German dynamism swept the area into the Teutonic orbit. After 1945, with Germany in eclipse, the Danube Valley lay within the Russian sphere, and a line from Stettin to Trieste marked the western limit of Russian ascendency. The duel waged between Russia and the Western

powers for control of the Balkan area was not primarily a duel for political mastery but for economic monopoly.

(3) This fact becomes more obvious when attention is fixed on a third aspect of the treaties, the importance of the economic clauses. All the enemy nations were held accountable for up to two-thirds of the claims for damages levied against them by the United Nations. Russia claimed $300,000,000 from Finland, $300,000,000 from Rumania, $200,000,000 from Hungary, and $100,000,000 from Italy. The Yugoslavs were awarded $125,000,000 from Italy, $50,000,000 from Hungary, and $25,000,000 from Bulgaria. The Greeks won claims of $105,000,000 from Italy and $45,000,000 from Bulgaria. The Czechs received $50,000,000 in reparations from Hungary, leaving their subsequent claims against Germany to be defined. But reparations formed only part of the economic interests involved. Future trade was also at stake although the Big Four did not openly proclaim their anxiety to monopolize it.

(4) Nevertheless, Balkan commerce and its control formed a fourth point to be considered in judging the treaties. The bitter and prolonged fight waged for the possession of Trieste and for the freedom of the Danube waterway (the two main gates through which seaborne trade from the west might reach the Danube Valley and local produce could be shipped abroad) proved that the Russians, British, French, and Americans all knew the issues involved. If Russia could control these gates, she could also control the economic life of the Balkan region. The decision to make Trieste a free port under the protection of the Security Council of the United Nations and to proclaim the Danube River and the Black Sea an open waterway in which the ships of all nations would have free navigation, were decisions forced through by the Western powers over the stubborn opposition of the Soviet delegates.

To the Western powers freedom of the Danube and the Black Sea was a commercial advantage but for the Russians the concession involved a grave military risk. Russia was not a great naval power. The amphibious invasion of Italy and France in World War II had proved how strongly the British and Americans could strike at any shore their ships could reach. If the Black Sea were open to naval attack, the heart of Russia might be reached through the Crimea and the Black Sea ports. It was fear of such an eventuality that led the Russians to propose to the Turks in 1946 that both governments should unite to fortify the Dardanelles, the straits which connect the Black Sea with the Mediterranean. But the Turks rejected the offer, and the British and Americans applauded them for their refusal. It is essential to see this duel between Russia and the Western powers in its global setting in order to grasp all the issues at stake. The Council of Foreign Ministers was often the scene of a duel to which no one openly alluded, a contest between advocates of two differing systems of economy, of two opposed political philosophies, two ways of life. Implicit also in the discussions was the ancient rivalry between land power and sea power. These contests delayed the peacemaking and postponed to the last the settlement regarding Germany and Japan. The Western allies were concerned chiefly to see that these defeated nations should be restrained from new acts of aggression in the future. But the Russians had a second fear. If Germany and Japan were rendered completely helpless, they might be transformed into possible bases from which more powerful nations could invade the Soviet Union. Americans in particular found it difficult to comprehend such fears for they were slow to realize the implications of American naval preponderance. Had Russia possessed the United States navy after World War II, every mile of the American coastline would have been a vulnerable frontier and the Gulf of St. Lawrence would have been a spear aimed at the vitals of American industry. To the Russians a Black Sea and Danube River open to naval inroads seemed an almost equally perilous breach in the walls of their security.

4. THE RECONSTRUCTION OF GERMANY

Until the segments of the German Reich were reunited and German economy functioned with vigor once more the European states system as a whole could not recover its vitality. The problem which faced the victors of World War II was to rebuild the German economic structure without renewing the menace of German militarism. The problem appeared so complex that the Council of Foreign Ministers left Germany to the last in their discussions, preferring to repair the limbs (the economically dependent states) before they attempted to recombine the four zones of the dismembered Reich and raise it to a responsible place among the powers. The first major decisions on the reconstruction of Germany were not taken until 1947.

The division of Germany into four zones, with separate military governments, separate tariff rates, and separate economies, became so unworkable after a year that the British and Americans agreed to merge their zones and invite the French to unite with them. This move would have left the Reich more or less permanently severed into a Soviet-controlled half and a Western half. The Russians recognized the disadvantages this might bring them and the resentment which Germans in the Russian zone would feel as they saw their fellow-nationals achieving unity. The Russians therefore agreed (December, 1946) to discuss plans for the recombining of the four segments of Germany into one economic whole again.

Fear of German military revival, however, was not dead, and this plan to revive German economic strength was preceded by orders from the Allied Control Council in Berlin to obliterate German military potentials. So sweeping were the new instructions that they prohibited the production or possession by Germans of any type of armament or weapon, and even forbade radar, kites, model airplanes, military maps and ciphers, and experimental research that might have a military application. The few guns and the small stock of ammunition permitted the police were handed out under rigid supervision by the Allied military authorities. This disarmament program, the most stringent in modern history, was inspired by a double motive, the urge to prove to the Germans the distrust the world had conceived for them because of their inhuman use of force, and a desire of the occupying authorities to prove that they had no intention of using German military machinery, arms, or men to make war in the future, perhaps against one another. With the military might of Germany thus completely destroyed the Big Four would be free to ponder the political and economic reconstruction of the Reich.

THE UNITED STATES IN THE ROLE OF
A WORLD POWER

We seek to use our military strength solely to preserve the peace of the world. For we now know that that is the only sure way to make our own freedom secure.
HARRY S. TRUMAN (1945)

1. DEMOBILIZATION AND RECONVERSION

THE people of the United States emerged from the Second World War in a singularly fortunate position. They had suffered no armed invasion like those which devastated France, Italy, and Russia. Their cities had not been blasted to rubble in repeated air raids like the cities of Britain and Japan. Their population had endured no famine or epidemics; their factories had doubled their output within six years; their farmlands were feeding hungry millions in Europe and Asia. The American army was the best equipped and the American navy the most powerful that the world had ever known. The contrast between American prosperity and world poverty had become even more striking than it was before the war. Although the 140,000,000 people in the United States made up only 7 per cent of the global population, they enjoyed over 30 per cent of the world's estimated income and controlled 50 per cent of the world's industrial machinery. Less fortunate nations, enemy or Allied, had watched with awe as the giant republic of the West gathered its resources and struck down its foes. When peace returned they waited with equal apprehension to learn what use the American people would make of their position of world leadership.

The American people themselves did not know the answer. Their first wish, in the exuberance of victory, was to see the millions of service men and women return and to relax the war restrictions on food, travel, consumers' goods, and luxuries. Despite warnings from military and naval experts that too-sudden demobilization might wreck an unsurpassed fighting machine and might leave the nation inadequately protected in a world still full of menace, the personnel of the armed forces was reduced from over twelve to under three million in less than a year. Fears that the release of so many active workers would bring on a wave of unemployment proved groundless. Although the Office of War Mobilization and Reconversion late in 1945 forecast a possible unemployment total of 8,000,000 by the spring of 1946, the Bureau of Labor, when spring came, announced that only 2,310,000 eligible workers were unemployed. By December, 1946, all but 750,000 discharged veterans had found work and were being rapidly absorbed into the business life of the country. A bill signed by President Roosevelt on June 22, 1944, and known as the G. I. Bill of Rights, offered ex-servicemen and women a chance to complete their education or otherwise adjust themselves to civilian life. They might attend school or college with government aid, pursue vocational training, and secure loans and free counsel for building homes or setting themselves up in business. One year after the war ended, readjustment and reconversion had been so smoothly carried out that American production and employment had reached a new peacetime record.

The desire of business leaders to return to the traditional system of free enterprise and free competition led to a swift reduction of the extraordinary powers which the Congress had confided to the executive and to the various government war bureaus. The War Production Board, which had mobilized the economic life of the nation for hostilities, was reformed a few weeks after the Japanese surrender. When it went out of existence on December 15, 1945, it was supplanted by a Civilian Production Administration with severely restricted powers. Although the War Powers Act remained in force, Congress amended the Price Control Act and finally allowed the powers of the Office of Price Administration to lapse. In the hour of victory President Truman urged caution in ending war powers and controls too abruptly. Regulation of commodity prices, wages, and rents had held the cost of living relatively stable throughout the war years, and memories of the excessive price rise and inflation which followed World War I had reconciled the American people to a system of economic regimentation and rationing which was contrary to their experience. To revert to a free competitive economy was not easy. The suspension of the Office of Price Administration in June, 1946, proved too abrupt. Prices soared immediately, and Congress found it advisable to restore partial control for a few months. But by the end of 1946 the attempt to hold the price ceilings had been almost entirely abandoned. This relaxation of price control was hastened by the elections of November, 1946, which gave the Republican Party control of the Senate and the House of Representatives after a fourteen-year period of Democratic rule.

Rising prices and the fear of inflation were the chief economic threats that disturbed the American people in the postwar years. They could still recall the decade of expansion after World War I and the disastrous collapse of 1929. In 1946 war savings and soldiers' pay, added to the swollen national income of the war years, created a situation in which the demand for consumers' goods exceeded the supply. The removal of government controls, which were blamed for the lack of goods, showed the impatience of the buying public, eager for the mechanical marvels which had been promised when industry turned from war to peace production. But the problem was not so simple that the abolition of a few regulations would solve it. No shortage was more acute than housing, which grew into a national scandal as returning veterans by the millions sought in vain for suitable homes. For five years building materials had been diverted to essential factory construction, to dwellings for 400,000 migrant workers summoned to war jobs, and to barracks and offices for military and naval personnel. Old houses had fallen into disrepair and few new ones had been erected. This lack of homes could not be solved quickly, for houses were still largely a product of handworkers and could not be speeded from the assembly line. They had to wait the attention of masons, carpenters, and plasterers, who were unable to cope with the unprecedented demand. Furthermore there was a serious lack of essential building materials. This situation had been foreseen and there was universal criticism at the failure of the government to provide for it.

Thus the people of the United States after 1945 were forcibly reminded that their economy was partly out of joint. They were the richest people in the world. They had amazed other nations by their capacity for organization and production to meet the demands of war. Within six years they had doubled their industrial output, their available electric power, and their national income. They had tripled the amount of money in circulation within their borders and quadrupled their savings, which had soared from thirteen billion to fifty billion dollars. But they could not produce on demand the houses they

needed to shelter millions of families crowded into tenements, room-
ing houses, shacks, and automobile camps. Despite the efforts of the
federal bureaus — the National Housing Agency, the Federal Home
Loan Bank, the Federal Housing Administration, and the Federal
Public Housing Authority — lack of homes remained the chief grievance of the people.

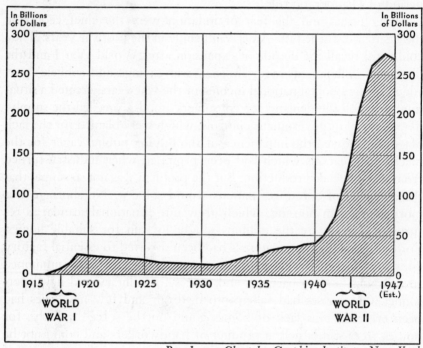

Based on a Chart by Graphics Institute, New York

NATIONAL DEBT OF THE UNITED STATES — BEFORE AND AFTER TWO WORLD WARS

Lack of houses, however, was not the only lack. Clothes, in the
cheaper grades, were almost unobtainable; meat and butter supplies
were limited and erratic; and prices on all commodities were rising
faster than wages. Such conditions excited vociferous protests.

The swift rise in living costs as war controls were lifted resulted in
widespread labor unrest. The first years of peace after 1945 brought
the most threatening strikes in American history, some of them so serious that they almost paralyzed the economic life of the nation. The
New Deal labor legislation of the 1930's had strengthened the power
of the unions and encouraged collective bargaining, so that decisions
handed down under the Wagner Labor Relations Act of 1935 and the

policies shaped by the new National Labor Relations Board, taught the workers the advantages of organization. When all the employees in some basic industry elected to strike, they could disrupt business so profoundly that billions of dollars might be lost in a few weeks. A temporary stoppage of work in the textile industries, the building trades, the automobile factories, or the steel mills meant a rapid spread of unemployment as secondary and dependent industries were affected. But the two fields in which a strike was certain to have the most swift and paralyzing consequences were the railroads and the coal mines. If trains stopped running, cities would starve. If coal mines ceased to produce, the nation's heat and power supplies would vanish. Bituminous coal was the largest single source of energy, accounting for almost half the power used to turn the wheels of industry. Without coal, moreover, three other vital facilities would be crippled, the railroads, the steel mills, and the electric power industry. Despite the construction of enormous hydroelectric dams, in 1945 two-thirds of the electric energy generated in the United States was produced by steam power. These conditions made a coal miners' strike the most ominous labor crisis which could afflict the national economy.

2. ECONOMIC CONFLICTS

While the United States was at war (1941–1945), labor disputes were limited and strikes curbed. Although 12,000,000 to 15,000,000 of the nation's 50,000,000 wage earners were organized in unions by 1945, the union leaders respected the no-strike pledge they had given the government and in general they co-operated with the War Labor Board, the War Manpower Commission, and the War Production Board in maintaining industrial efficiency. The loyalty and sacrifice of the labor army was admirable. The home front suffered its hardships and its casualties as well as the war front, and over 100,000 workers were killed in accidents connected with their occupation during the war years. Living costs rose after 1939, climbing 25 per cent in five years, and wage rates did not always follow. But overtime pay and full employment more than doubled the national income between 1939 and 1945. So long as all workers in essential industries were subject to the directives of the War Manpower Commission, to strike or to forsake a job without authority was a defiance of federal statutes. But the Commission abolished many of these strict controls the day the Japanese surrendered (August 14, 1945), and the labor unions prepared to test their strength.

The first serious postwar strike came in the automobile industry. On October 24, 1945, the employees of the General Motors Corporation, who formed a division of the United Automobile Workers, voted to walk out if their demand for a 30 per cent increase in wages were not granted. General Motors was the largest private employer in the United States, and the strike, which began November 21, 1945, closed eighty plants and withdrew 180,000 workers from productive labor. A settlement increasing pay rates 18.5 cents an hour was reached in January, 1946, but by this time a wave of strikes was sweeping the country. The plans formed by ambitious manufacturers to pour out a flood of consumers' goods before the end of 1946 had to be seriously curtailed. On January 21, 1946, a strike of the steel workers made 750,000 idle. A threatened strike of the International Oil Workers Union was postponed only because the government seized the refineries in question. A closure of the coal mines which caused a severe fuel shortage was settled by the United Mine Workers in May, 1946, only after the government had taken over the mines. The mine operators granted a basic increase of 18.5 cents an hour on the miners' pay, a figure which had come to represent the estimated general rise in living costs.

As strike followed strike, the attitude of the nation and of the Congress grew less sympathetic towards the unions. The sincere though often unsuccessful endeavors of President Truman and of the various federal boards to adjudicate the labor disputes "in the public interest," made the walkouts appear unnecessary and arbitrary when they followed earnest negotiations. It seemed presumptuous for a few thousand organized men to defy government mediation and endanger the national prosperity by disorganizing the work of millions. The public endured grave inconvenience because of the delays in production and delivery service and because of the interruption of telephone, telegraph, and transit facilities. The resulting loss of business built up increasing popular indignation. A test of national sentiment came in the spring of 1946 when 250,000 engineers and trainmen voted to strike, a move which could not fail to disrupt the nation's transport, paralyze business, and endanger the national health by tying up food shipments. As a final step to avoid this national emergency the railroads were taken over by the federal government, but the move did not deter the engineers and trainmen, who ceased work on May 18. Stung by this defiance of the federal authority, President Truman summoned the

Congress on May 25 and asked for emergency powers. By an almost unanimous vote (306 to 13) the legislators authorized the President to curb the wave of strikes by appropriate executive action. No action proved necessary, however, for the trainmen abandoned their strike and returned to work rather than risk penalties for their defiance.

Before the close of 1946 the federal government faced a more critical test when the United Mine Workers struck for the second time within a year. On November 15 their leader, John L. Lewis, notified the secretary of the interior, John A. Krug, that the agreement they had negotiated and signed the previous May would be canceled on November 20. The attorney general thereupon prepared civil and criminal charges against Lewis and the United Mine Workers, and the charges were sustained by a federal court. Lewis was fined $10,000 for contempt because he had refused to heed an injunction to cancel his strike call, and the miners' union was fined $3,500,000 because 400,000 mine workers, at a word from Lewis, had left the pits. The case was appealed to the Supreme Court while throughout the United States coal supplies melted away, lights were dimmed, stock quotations fell, and statisticians calculated that 5,000,000 workers in dependent trades would be idle by December 31. Then, with a sudden change of attitude, Lewis reversed his decision on December 7 and ordered the miners back to work, pending the verdict of the highest court. It was a victory for the government, but it was not a solution. The power of the unions and the role that organized labor would play in American life remained the major issue troubling domestic politics.

The Republican majority which controlled the Congress after November, 1946, considered the Wagner Labor Relations Act of 1935 too favorable to the unions. With the support of Democrats also out of sympathy with New Deal practices, they fashioned a more stringent "book of rules," the Labor-Management Relations Act of 1947. When President Truman vetoed this measure, the House and Senate promptly overrode the veto and the Act went into effect on June 23. The status of 15,000,000 union workers and the terms of 50,000 separate contracts between labor and management were directly affected, but it remained for the courts to rule on the challenged features of the new law. The clauses most likely to arouse labor to battle were those which permitted employers to sue unions for damages, forbade union expenditures for political campaigns, and authorized the federal government to invoke injunctions against strikes which might cripple the national economy. Further sources of controversy were likely to arise from the provisions which outlawed the closed shop, restricted the union shop, and denied bargaining rights to foremen's unions. To administer the new Act the National Labor Relations Board was expanded from three to five members and a general counsel appointed to prosecute unfair labor practices.

3. THE CONCENTRATION OF FEDERAL POWERS

In the United States, as in all leading nations, the years after 1929 brought heavier responsibilities for the national government. Attempts to cope with the great depression, especially the New Deal legislation passed after 1933, led to the creation of many new boards, commissions, and agencies at Washington. The crises of World War II superimposed on these agencies the extraordinary structure of the warborn agencies and bureaus. Even after the second War Powers Act lapsed in 1946 and most of the wartime agencies had been disbanded, the federal government remained a complicated machine, too complicated, many critics insisted, to function efficiently or economically. The era before 1917, when the United States had a negligible public debt, a small army, and a modest body of a few hundred thousand civilian public servants, had passed into history. By 1945 the roster of federal employees exceeded 3,000,000, the armed forces counted 12,000,000 in service, the public debt had reached $260,000,000,000 and the federal government had expanded into a bureaucrat's nightmare. One of the first acts of President Truman, when Congress reassembled in September, 1945, was to ask for authority to reorganize the executive agencies and reduce them to greater efficiency. The move was extended to the legislature also and within a year the Congress had voted to check all lobbyists who came to Washington to press for desired legislation and to scrutinize their expenditures. This measure was intended to free Senators and Representatives from undue pressure by lobbyists and persistent pressure groups. A second and more important clause provided for a simplification of the congressional committee-system. In the course of years the standing committees of Congress had multiplied and overlapped until the Senate had thirty-three and the House of Representatives forty-eight. These were reduced to fifteen and nineteen respectively by the La Follette-Monroney Act (1945). A commission headed by Herbert Hoover was appointed (1947) to suggest improvements in the executive structure.

How vast and embracing the responsibilities of the federal agencies had become was made clear in the "Report on the State of the Union" which President Truman submitted with his budget proposals in January, 1946. His recommendations affecting defense and foreign policy are discussed in subsequent sections of this chapter. His proposals concerning federal powers, labor legislation, and social security proved that the objectives of the New Deal legislation of ten years earlier had been postponed but not abandoned. The government of the United States, the President pointed out, had three main responsibilities to meet: the wise exploitation of the national resources, the advancement of social justice, and the promotion of national defense. Resources were stressed as a primary concern. The President recommended legislation to authorize crop insurance, a permanent housing agency, the stock-piling of strategic materials, control of atomic energy, airport development, and completion of the Great Lakes–St. Lawrence seaway route. A scientific research agency and a program for prepaid medical care were also listed as important aims directly concerned with material expansion, conservation of life, and national security.

The longest sections of the President's report were dedicated to the promotion of social justice. The economic welfare of the American people, the assurance of a fair wage, a reasonable standard of living, health and old age insurance, and greater equality of opportunity, received his particular attention. He urged that the Price Control Act and the war powers of the government be extended beyond June 30, 1946, and that food subsidies be maintained to keep down living costs. To encourage full employment and ease labor disputes he proposed a permanent Fair Employment Practices Act, the establishment of a minimum wage of forty to sixty-five cents an hour, with a later increase to a minimum of seventy or seventy-five cents, and the maintenance of fact-finding boards with increased powers to avert strikes and advise settlements. The United States Employment Service, he suggested, should remain under federal control until 1947 or longer. Unemployment insurance benefits were to be increased, including unemployment allowances for ex-servicemen; and social security benefits were to be allowed to veterans, covering their period of military service.

The emphasis upon research and education under the encouragement of the federal government was a new departure in national politics. On September 6, while the American people were still dazed by the advent of the atomic bomb, President Truman proposed that a central federal research agency be set up on a permanent basis. Subsidized by the national government to the extent of $40,000,000 the first year, this new agency was to co-ordinate existing research activities wherever necessary and to administer funds for future investigations. "The maintenance of our position as a nation," President Truman warned, "will require more emphasis on research expenditure in the future than in the past."

A second field in which federal control, or at least federal aid, seemed destined to increase was public education. In the last year of peace (1940) the expenditure for primary and secondary schools in the United States reached $2,344,049,000. These schools required the services of 875,477 teachers and enrolled 25,433,542 pupils, and an additional 2,611,047 pupils were registered in private or parochial schools. But the cost of education was rising and it was estimated that by 1947 primary, secondary, and higher education would absorb over $3,000,000,000 of state, local, and private funds. To this total the federal government was expected to add $625,000,000. A major share of the federal contribution covered veterans' education; but $90,000,000 was allotted for other needs, for school children's free lunches, for the support of vocational schools, and for the land-grant colleges. Greater financial aid for the schools in the less prosperous states was also indispensable if the students there were to have the educational opportunities they deserved. The expenditure per pupil in the primary and secondary schools varied widely throughout the Union. Figures for the last years of peace showed that school boards in the five most favored states allowed $100 or more annually per pupil for elementary and secondary education, while those in the five least favored states spent less than $35 per pupil. The value of the school property and equipment varied even more unequally, ranging from $526 to $81 per pupil enrolled. Teachers' salaries were likewise depressed in the economically retarded areas, falling as low as one-fifth the rate established in the most favored states.

One method of correcting these inequalities was to allot federal subsidies to cover the deficits in the retarded areas. Few American citizens denied that educational opportunities in a democracy ought to be as nearly equal as possible. But it was not clear that an increase in federal subsidies to the states would provide the best or the only solution. The extraordinary growth of federal authority and the rise in the federal budget was changing the balance of power between local and national government in the United States, and to many thoughtful

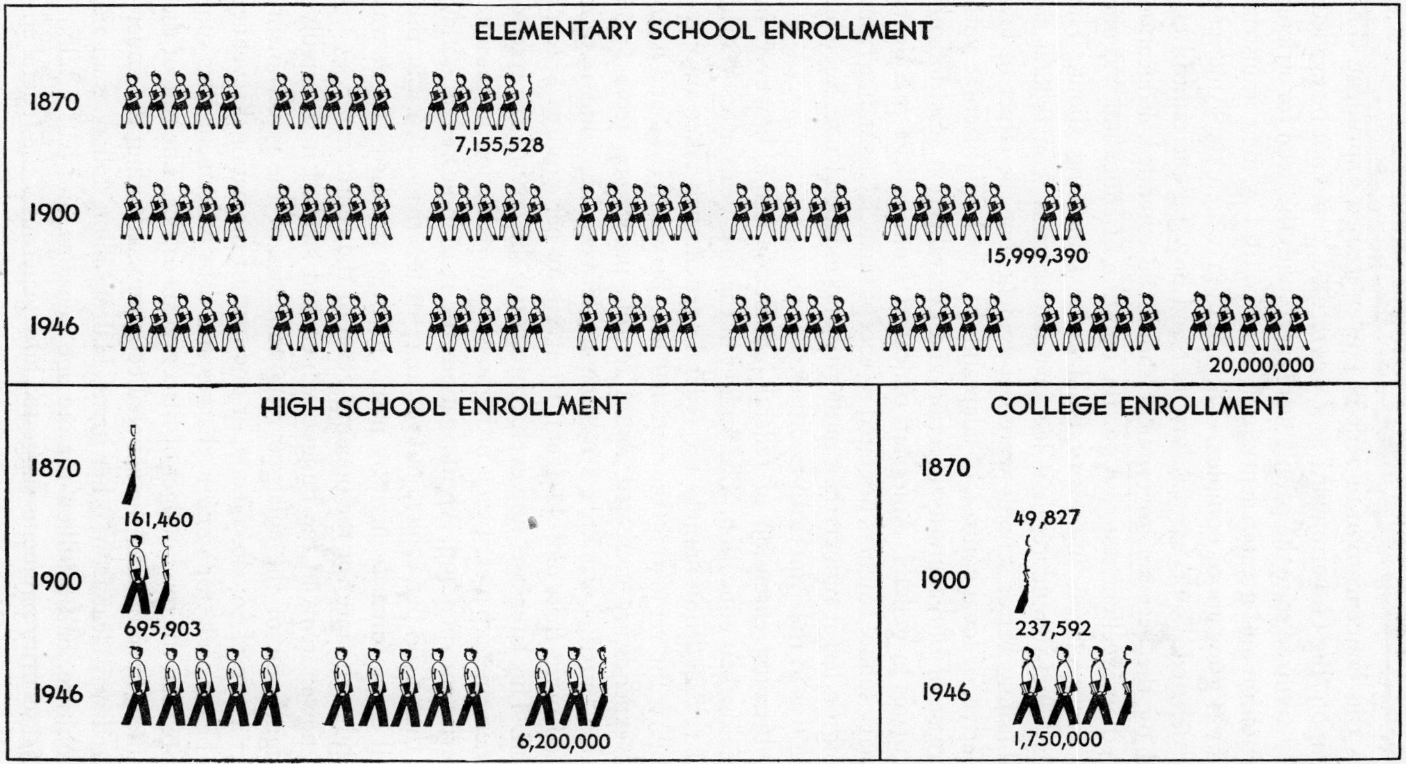

ELEMENTARY SCHOOL ENROLLMENT

1870   7,155,528

1900   15,999,390

1946   20,000,000

HIGH SCHOOL ENROLLMENT

1870   161,460

1900   695,903

1946   6,200,000

COLLEGE ENROLLMENT

1870   49,827

1900   237,592

1946   1,750,000

Based on Chart by Graphics Institute, New York

GROWTH IN AMERICAN STUDENT REGISTRATION, 1870–1946

citizens this concentration of federal power seemed imprudent. The problem of "Big Government," as it was termed, could not be evaded: in every civilized state the people were faced with the need for stricter regimentation and greater centralization of control as their industrial civilization grew more complex. The question which the American people debated, however, was how fast and how far the control exercised by the national government should be extended. Education provided an excellent test case, for the question of education was one which every citizen and every child knew something about. The benefits which would result if less prosperous areas won federal aid in establishing better schools were self-evident; but the effect of loss of initiative, of local control, of adaptability, which might come with an increase of bureaucratic direction and centralization was difficult to calculate. In general, American educators from college presidents to primary school teachers hesitated to accept financial assistance from Washington lest it reduce their authority and independence. Such an attitude was in the American tradition.

The broadest extension of federal jurisdiction came, however, in other fields than education. The budget in the first years after World War II revealed how largely the federal agencies had taken over responsibility for regulating the national life. Between 1915 and 1940 federal expenditure increased almost tenfold per capita, from $7.66 to $70.65. But this was only a beginning. Between 1940 and 1945 it increased more than tenfold again, from $70.65 per head to $719.25 per head. This later rise, however, represented the cost of the war to the American taxpayer; peace brought a rapid reduction in the rate of government spending. Appropriations for 1946 indicated an outlay of less than $500 per capita, and for 1947 of less than $250. But this was still extraordinarily high by past American standards, for it was thirty times the rate for the opening years of the century.

The newer items in the budget, which had swelled it so rapidly, were significant of the enlarged responsibilities of the government. By 1947 a sum of $6,000,000,000, or one-fifth of the national revenue, had to be set aside for interest charges and debt retirement; this sum was more than the total budget of fifteen years earlier. The role of the government in stabilizing the national economy and aiding the underprivileged was clear from other items. Half a billion dollars as an aid to agriculture, half a billion for old age pensions, and half a billion for social security payments suggested how generously the federal administration had assumed the burden of these new experiments. In the years before 1914 half a billion dollars would have covered not merely a secondary item such as pensions for the aged but the entire budget.

By 1947 one outstanding charge had come to dwarf all others, absorbing half the national revenue even in peacetime. This was the appropriation for past wars and for future protection. Pensions and benefits for veterans were calculated at about $5,000,000,000 in the 1947 budget, and the cost of adequate national defense was expected to require at least $10,000,000,000. The United States had entered a new age, an era in which American citizens would have to accustom themselves to military conscription, to the expense of heavy armaments, and to the perpetual fear of attack which had hung over the nations of the Old World for generations. The need for defense in the postwar period, for constant preparedness against airborne invaders or amphibious forces landed along the coasts, was the outstanding factor which added to federal expenditures. How heavy the burden of armaments had become by 1946 few Americans appreciated immediately. All the social services, the public works projects, the aid to farmers, the salaries for 3,000,000 government employees, the subsidies for housing and education, when added together, required a smaller share of the national revenue than the armed services. The wide oceans were no longer an impassable moat for the Americas, as they had been for over a century, and national defense had become the first and most urgent responsibility of the state. This was something new in American annals; it was nothing new to most Europeans who had known the crushing burden of such defense costs all their lives.

4. DEFENSE AND ARMAMENTS

All wars lead to a concentration of military authority. In a democracy the gravest problem of war government is holding the generals and admirals in proper subordination to the civil power, to the legislature freely elected by the nation. In the civil bureaucracy itself, however, some concentration of power is inevitable if a war is to be waged efficiently. The nation cannot be consulted or even informed about important military projects, for secret strategy would not long remain secret if it were debated in popular assemblies. Swift and secret decisions must be made, huge sums of money disbursed without itemized explanations, responsibilities assumed by cabinets and chiefs of staff who shoulder the blame if the operation fails. In all democracies a war is followed by criticism of the generals, by investigations to determine why money was wasted, why lives were sacrificed, why costly enterprises miscarried. This is inevitable. For during hostilities the usual methods of democratic administration are partly curtailed. The representatives of the people, the legislators, are asked to vote confidence in a government and in its policies without being fully informed what those policies are, how much they will cost, and why they are held to be necessary. In Great Britain during World War II the members of parliament were summoned to secret sessions to hear details withheld from the general public and from the press. In the United States the members of the congressional committees on military and naval affairs met with the President, his cabinet officers, the admirals and the generals, to debate war strategy in private conferences. The success of the plans adopted often depended upon the preservation of the most scrupulous secrecy. The key principle of representative government, that all public officials are servants of the people and must be prepared at any time to account for their actions, their movements, their expenditure of government funds, could not be applied in wartime. A veil of secrecy descended, hiding the most important activities of the government from public scrutiny.

All governments maintain a department of military intelligence, receive reports from agents posted in foreign countries, and seek advance information on the weapons, codes, plans, and operations of their foes or potential foes. Espionage and counterespionage play a vital part in war, and because every commander knows that enemy agents are watching tirelessly, the urge to preserve secrecy becomes an obsession. It is inevitable, in such circumstances, that different units and commands must frequently fail to co-ordinate their offensives and may actually obstruct one another because they are not all equally well informed or fail to compare the instructions they have received. Jealousy between the army and the navy or between rival commands may also contribute to dislocation of effort. One Japanese admiral complained, after the surrender of Japan, that he had not only fought the Americans; half the time he was in conflict with the Japanese army as well. If such contradiction in aims could exist in a highly regimented country where unquestioning obedience was a cult, it was inevitable that conflicts of authority would arise in a democracy where the people prized their liberty of action and their right of independent criticism. In general, however, the high degree of co-operation attained by the American services in World War II sur-

Courtesy of Francis B. Morrison

CAPTURED GERMAN OFFICERS ENTERING A UNITED STATES
PRISONER OF WAR CAMP IN FRANCE, 1945

Joint Army Navy Task Force

passed all expectations and contradicted the persistent belief that democracies are too undisciplined to conduct a war successfully.

Unity of command, so highly extolled in war, is never fully achieved. The contrast between military and naval methods, divergence between the civilian and the military points of view, and the rivalry between opposing schools of strategy easily lead to quarrels, deadlocked policies, duplication of records, of research, and of expenditures. One obvious solution for such internal friction and division would be unity of command under a single department of national defense. But overcentralization creates as many problems as it cures. It has often proved self-defeating in the past because no one chief or bureau can readily master and supervise the multitudinous details of a modern defense program. Plans to combine the United States army, navy, and air force into one department of national defense were finally passed by Congress and the new department created in 1947. As Secretary of Defense the President appointed James V. Forrestal. The three coequal branches of the armed forces were united under his able direction, with John Sullivan as Navy Secretary, Kenneth Royall as Army Secretary, and Stuart Symington as Air Secretary. Forrestal viewed war as "the worst possible solution" but he believed that "the capacity to wage war must always be there."

No one knew how profoundly the use of atomic power for war purposes might change the whole conception of national armaments. As the only nation which had perfected the atomic bomb and could experiment with it, the United States enjoyed a temporary advantage but it was an advantage which could easily be lost. The devastating effect of the bomb upon crowded cities had been proved at Hiroshima and Nagasaki; its destructive capacity against ships at sea had still to be tested when World War II ended. In the summer of 1946 the United States navy conducted two experiments at Bikini Atoll in the central Pacific. On July 1, a single bomb, exploded in the air over an anchored naval force, sank five ships, wrecked six, and damaged twenty-five others. Three weeks later a second bomb, exploded under water, proved yet more destructive, sinking ten ships, including a battleship and an aircraft carrier. The conclusions drawn from these experiments were that all naval vessels in future would have to be redesigned in hull and superstructure to minimize the effect of atomic explosions.[1]

---

[1] Until more was known about the effect of atomic explosions on battleships, the vulnerability and value of existing navies could not be easily appraised. The United States emerged from World War II with a total

In peacetime the defense plans of a nation, which are drawn up to meet a hypothetical invasion that may never occur, remain in large measure mere "paper plans" recording the location and function of "paper armies." Few American citizens were aware of the administrative limits or headquarters of the six army areas into which the forty-eight states were divided after World War II. The precautions which the War Department adopted for the protection of Alaska, Hawaii, the Canal Zone, and other exposed segments of the American defense system were likewise little known. But the military experts, pondering the lessons of World War II, decided to raise the strength of American divisions from 15,000 to 18,000 men, to triple the number of their artillery weapons and their fire power, and to transport the complete division, including sixty-ton tanks, by giant air transport planes. The Alcan Highway to Alaska and the Pan-American Highway to the Canal Zone were to be kept open to serve military as well as commercial and tourist needs; and negotiations were pressed with the Canadian military authorities (1946) for joint exploration by Canadian and United States units of the half-uncharted terrain of northern Canada and the Yukon. Airborne and air-supplied armies had become a new factor in military calculations, for they could operate in regions hitherto held to be impenetrable. The Arctic regions thus formed a new, vulnerable, and almost undefended frontier for the Americas. To construct air bases, establish repair shops, reserves of fuel, and living quarters for the maintenance crews in the northern wilderness, became an essential precaution in the air age. The first line of American defense lay between Greenland and Alaska.

Demobilization, or the transition of an army from a wartime to a peacetime status, is an elaborate undertaking, more wasteful in some respects than war itself. A permanent nucleus must be preserved, a

---

of fighting ships almost equal to the combined navies of all other powers. The status of the world navies in 1946 compared as follows:

	United States	Great Britain	Soviet Russia	Italy	France
Battleships	23	14	4	5	4
Heavy Cruisers	26	12	7	1	3
Light Cruisers	41	50	2	9	6
Aircraft Carriers	32	12	0	0	0
Escort Carriers	75	29	0	0	0
Destroyers	353	259	51	11	15
Submarines	206	115	140	21	18
Total	756	491	204	47	46

skeleton army staff, and all the administrative machinery for a phantom army. Each year recruits must be inducted and taught their duties and skills, but they can practice war games only at rehearsals or maneuvers and they match themselves against no substantial enemy. The need to preserve friendly relations with neighboring nations forbids any frontier maneuvers or naval concentrations which might seem like a feint attack or an intimidating gesture. Nevertheless, while preserving a "correct" attitude, all nations which are potential antagonists watch one another warily even in peaceful periods and prepare specific blueprints for invasion and counterinvasion. An increase in the number of army divisions on one side of a frontier is met by the construction of strategic bases or a railway line on the other; the construction of an airfield or submarine pen is matched by an increase in mine layers, a new concentration of antiaircraft batteries, or an enlarged drydock.

The battles of armed infantry are preceded by a battle of birth rates. Man power is an indispensable resource for mass armies, and vital statistics are the indices of approaching victory. A nation with a rapidly rising population can enlarge its armies; a nation with a stationary or a declining population must seek allies or call upon colonial troops if it can command their allegiance. In planning the American armies of the future, strategists have to take into account the change in the birth rate in the United States. In Europe the industrialized states, particularly France, Great Britain, Belgium, Sweden, Czechoslovakia, and Germany, all showed a fall in the birth rate by the middle of the twentieth century. The United States, which had been so rapidly transformed into a predominantly urban and industrial nation after 1850, has revealed the same tendency. The population of 140,000,000 achieved before the close of World War II in 1945, seemed destined to increase slowly to about 160,000,000 by 1970 and then to fall before the close of the century. This decline might place the American people at a serious disadvantage if the man power of China with 450,000,000 people, India with 400,000,000, and the Soviet Union with 200,000,000, could be marshaled and equipped for war. The industrial development of Russia might soon provide arms and equipment for this vast man power of Asia.

These many factors made it extremely difficult for the military advisers of the United States government to forecast defense needs. Their gravest handicap, however, was the fact that in planning the armed defense of the nation they appeared to be planning war because armed defense presupposes war. To millions of Americans it seemed treachery to the dearly won peace to think of the possibility of another war. Congress was therefore under constant pressure to reduce the sums allotted in the budget for the national defense program. The American people turned with relief from the war and its tragedies to plan world reconstruction and world order. How the peace of the world might be preserved was the special problem of the diplomats, but in a larger sense it was also the problem of all peoples and most particularly of all citizens in the leading democratic states.

5. POSTWAR FOREIGN POLICY

A grave decision on foreign policy faced the American people after World War II. Were they prepared to accept the high cost of world leadership or would their traditional preference for isolation and a reduced federal budget persuade them to abandon the world role they had assumed from 1941 to 1945? As they studied the balance sheet of war many Americans felt (as they had felt after 1918) that the European feuds were insoluble, that the United States had done its full share in restoring peace, and that the government had been overhasty in extending aid to other nations which those nations were overhesitant about returning.

In 1919 this mood of postwar disillusionment had led the American people to repudiate the League of Nations and to feel cheated when their debtors defaulted on the war debts. In 1946 the mood of disenchantment was less bitter, the course adopted more realistic and more constructive. Recalling that 90 per cent of the loans advanced to the Allied powers in World War I were never repaid, the government voluntarily renounced the hope of collecting a larger percentage after World War II. By 1946 Lend-Lease credits to other nations had reached $50,000,000,000, a sum five times as large as the war debts owed America in 1919. It seemed self-evident that this enormous sum could never be repaid. The United States promptly wrote off nine-tenths of it in a series of generous agreements with the debtor states.

The leading beneficiary of Lend-Lease was the British Empire, which had received total credits of $31,267,240,530. The extraordinary British exertions in the common struggle had wiped out vast reserves of British capital and the United Kingdom owed $20,000,000,000 to other nations. To repay the credits from America would have bankrupted the British economy. Recognizing this fact, the American government cancelled its claims to all but $650,000,000 for

LEND-LEASE AID EXTENDED BY THE UNITED STATES
TO THIRTY-EIGHT NATIONS; TO JULY 31, 1946 [1]

AMERICAN REPUBLICS		OTHER GOVERNMENTS	
BOLIVIA	$5,633,989.02	BELGIUM	$148,394,457.76
BRAZIL	332,545,226.45	BRITISH EMPIRE,	
CHILE	21,817,478.16	INCLUDING AUSTRALIA,	
COLOMBIA	7,809,732.58	NEW ZEALAND, INDIA,	
COSTA RICA	155,022.73	SOUTH AFRICA	31,267,240,530.63
CUBA	5,739,133.33	CHINA	1,548,794,965.99
DOMINICAN		CZECHOSLOVAKIA	413,398.78
REPUBLIC	1,610,590.38	EGYPT	
ECUADOR	7,063,079.96	(PAID FULLY IN CASH)	1,019,169.14
GUATEMALA	1,819,403.19	ETHIOPIA	5,151,163.25
HAITI	1,449,096.40	FRANCE	
HONDURAS	372,358.11	AND POSSESSIONS	3,207,608,188.75
MEXICO	36,287,010.67	GREECE	75,475,880.30
NICARAGUA	872,841.73	ICELAND	4,795,027.90
PANAMA	83,555.92	IRAN	4,797,092.50
PARAGUAY	1,933,302.00	IRAQ (PAID FULLY IN CASH)	4,144.14
PERU	18,525,771.19	LIBERIA	6,408,240.13
SALVADOR	892,353.28	NETHERLANDS AND	
URUGUAY	7,148,610.13	POSSESSIONS	230,127,717.63
VENEZUELA	4,336,079.35	NORWAY	51,524,124.36
TOTAL	$456,094,634.58	POLAND	16,934,163.60
		U.S.S.R.	11,260,343,603.02
		SAUDI ARABIA	17,417,878.70
		TURKEY	26,640,031.50
		YUGOSLAVIA	32,026,355.58
		Total charge to foreign governments	$48,361,210,768.24

Aid not charged to foreign governments (including
lost shipments, administrative costs, and Lend-Lease
aid diverted to United States forces) $2,578,827,000.00

Total Lend-Lease aid $50,940,037,768.24

Lend-Lease, and made the British a new loan of $3,750,000,000 to
aid their economic recovery. Thus the total British indebtedness to
the United States was set at $4,400,000,000, to be repaid within fifty

[1] *New York Times,* October 19, 1946.

years at 2 per cent interest. Most Americans considered this very favorable treatment and were surprised that spokesmen in the British parliament did not appear to share this view when ratifying the agreement. The attitude of many Englishmen was expressed frankly by one of the leading Liberal weeklies: "It is, of course, aggravating to find that our reward for losing a quarter of our total national wealth in the common cause is to pay tribute for half a century to those who have been enriched by the war."

After Britain, the heaviest borrower under the terms of the Lend-Lease Act was the Soviet Union. Russia received $11,260,343,603 up to July 31, 1946. How this obligation would be settled was not immediately determined: in 1947 the rivalry between the Russians and the Anglo-American forces in Europe, the Near East, and Asia, remained so tense that it seemed wise to leave financial disputes for later negotiation. France came third in the list of Lend-Lease beneficiaries, with a total of $3,207,608,188, and China fourth with $1,548,794,965, debts which could not be repaid soon and which were almost certain to be written off in great measure. These four allies — Britain, Russia, France, and China — had thus received almost 95 per cent of the Lend-Lease aid, the remainder being distributed among thirty-four other Allies as the accompanying table indicates.

Though Lend-Lease shipments might never be repaid in cash or any other tangible form, the American people could still derive great and enduring benefits from this world-wide charity. The distribution of American machinery and factory products made American models and methods known in every continent. Machines, whether for civilian or military purposes, are highly standardized devices. When trucks or planes, pipelines or piston rings, from factories in Connecticut or California, were unloaded at Bombay or Brisbane or Buenos Aires, they advertised the excellence of American machinery. Once in use, moreover, these machines created a market for replacements. Only the factory which built the original model or a factory working with the same specifications could provide the interchangeable parts so essential in repairing modern engines. A fractional difference in the gauge of a cylinder, the bore of a gun, the thread of a screw, prevents this interchange of parts. It is thus an urgent matter for distant purchasers to maintain friendly connections with the country from which they import their farm tractors, their mining equipment, or their arms. For they require additional machines, spare parts, and the standard fuel and lubricants which alone give their trucks, machine tools, or generators high performance.

When governments look abroad for arms and equipment for their soldiers, the question of standard models and standard quality is of paramount importance. As the United States had won an indisputable lead in industry, American models set the standard most widely known after 1945. The Pan-American republics proposed to co-ordinate their armaments with those of their great sister republic of the north, and even the British Ministry of Defense adopted plans to change the measurements and screw-threads of their military equipment to fit the gauges and weapons produced in American factories. (See page 604.) Such co-ordination was not only a tribute to American efficiency in mass production; it was an admission that American aid had played a decisive part in World War II, that it had doomed the Axis nations. The Latin American republics and the nations of the British Commonwealth looked ahead to a future in which they might once again require aid from the nation which had proved itself the arsenal of democracy. Such an alignment of resources, such a co-ordination of weapons between Britain and America had a prophetic significance. It implied that neither the American nor the British government conceived it probable, if the world were again plunged into war, that they would fight otherwise than as allies.

The Americans' attitude towards the United Nations in 1947 differed notably from the suspicion with which they had viewed the League of Nations in 1919. The United States was the most active and most generous member of the United Nations. This leadership made the choice of New York as the capital of the United Nations a fitting gesture. America also assumed a heavy share in the task of financial rehabilitation which faced the postwar world and offered to lead the way on the perilous road towards disarmament. But Secretary of State Byrnes made it clear at the close of 1946 that the United States would not disarm alone, that it would not surrender its weapons until a world authority had been established to supervise global disarmament and keep check on possible aggressors. "The first task which must be undertaken," Byrnes warned, "is the control of atomic energy to assure that it will be used only for human welfare and not for deadly warfare. . . . Our proposals when fully operative would leave the states responsible for the discovery of atomic energy no rights which would not be shared with other members of the United Nations."

On the question of annexations, mandates, and trusteeships, the American attitude had likewise changed in twenty-five years. After World War I the United States lived up to Woodrow Wilson's proud assertion of disinterested idealism. "We desire no conquest, no dominion," he had insisted in 1917. "We seek no indemnities for ourselves, no material compensation for the sacrifices we shall freely make." When peace was concluded at Versailles the United States gained no share of the German colonies, no mandate over liberated segments of the Turkish Empire, no sovereignty over Pacific islands where the German flag had flown in 1914. This failure to secure the customary rewards of victory had cost America dearly, as Byrnes emphasized to a more realistic nation in 1946. For the Pacific atolls which passed under Japanese control after World War I became advance bases for the attacks Japan launched against the Philippines and Hawaii in World War II.

The United States was not prepared to dismantle its defenses, evacuate the Pacific bases captured at high cost, and destroy its unique stock of atomic bombs until the United Nations could guarantee to maintain adequate supervision over all national armaments. Only a world body with power and authority to secure peaceful states against unprovoked aggression could make it safe for those states to lay aside their shields. Until the day of universal disarmament came, the world was destined to remain as it was: a globe divided into spheres of influence in which the great powers ruled by power and prestige and were prepared to defend their rule by force of arms. The 500,000 American troops still abroad more than a year after the fighting had ceased assured the world that the United States would not fail this time to fulfill the global responsibilities which the twentieth century had bequeathed to the American people.

THE BRITISH EMPIRE UNDER
RECONSTRUCTION

*We British have our own commonwealth of nations. These
do not weaken — on the contrary they strengthen — the world
organization.*

WINSTON CHURCHILL (1946)

1. THE BRITISH BALANCE SHEET OF WAR

GREAT BRITAIN fought two great wars against Germany in the
first half of the twentieth century and won both, but the cost in
blood and treasure overstrained British resources. A comparison of
the British losses in World War I and World War II illuminates the
strange odds and vicissitudes of combat. In the four years of World
War I (1914–1918) the toll for the embattled empire was almost one
million dead. In the six years of World War II (1939–1945) its losses,
on the battlefronts and the home front combined, reached about
400,000 dead. The lighter loss of life in the second struggle is surprising because it was the longer and more desperate of the two, an
ordeal in which the people stood fast amid more somber perils than
their ancestors had ever known.

British financial expenditure also appeared at first sight to be somewhat lighter in World War II, but this was a deceptive impression. In
the earlier struggle the public debt multiplied almost tenfold, but in
the six years from 1939 to 1945 it increased only threefold. When
World War II closed the British debt stood at £22,000,000,000 (about
$90,000,000,000 or less than $2000 per capita). The postwar debt
of the United States ($300,000,000,000) was approximately $2050
for each American citizen. Such comparisons can be misleading. A
debt burden of $2000 weighed more heavily on the average Briton
with his smaller income, and Britain had no natural resources equiva-

lent to those of the United States. The chief wealth of the British people lay in their tenacity, skill, and manufacturing techniques. Both America and Britain had learned that the cost of victory comes high, but for the British the cost was so high that it threatened to lower permanently their economy and their standards of living.

This gloomy economic prospect did not daunt the British: they assailed the tasks of reconstruction with energy and vision. During the war, defense needs had overshadowed all others; but as victory neared, the nation turned to audit its resources, prepare a peacetime program, and organize the delayed drive for greater social justice. This shift of attention was already manifest in the general election of July, 1945. The war government headed by Winston Churchill was overthrown, and the Labor Party, which won almost 400 seats in parliament against 240 for all other parties combined, controlled the new cabinet. The Conservatives, with Churchill still at their head, now formed "His Majesty's Loyal Opposition." Thus, even before Japan capitulated in August, 1945, the British people were turning from total war to the equally exacting problems of peace. The triumph of the Labor Party proved that planned production, full employment, adequate health protection, nationalization of basic industries, better housing, better schools, and other social aims were regarded as urgent and overdue. The British electors by a majority of almost 3,000,000 had registered their conviction that Churchill, the dynamic wartime minister, had fulfilled his mission. For the social reforms of peace the Labor Party, headed by the methodical, conscientious, and somewhat colorless Clement R. Attlee, seemed a more suitable agent of the national will. The British respect their statesmen and reward them, but they do not forget that excessive popularity and power confided to one man is a peril to democratic government. This chapter will describe how the British people met the problem of resources, the problem of social justice, and the problem of imperial defense after 1945.

The first step in national bookkeeping was to adjust debits and credits and prepare a peace budget and balance sheet. As in previous wars Great Britain had poured out subsidies to numerous allies, subsidies which totaled over $8,000,000,000 before the war ended. Of this sum, about 60 per cent, or $5,000,000,000, was credited to the United States (charged against American Lend-Lease credits of $30,000,000,000); and 15 per cent or $1,272,000,000 to Russia. Other belligerent states, war governments-in-exile, and neutral nations which received British financial aid, were Poland, France, Greece, Czechoslovakia, Belgium, the Netherlands, Yugoslavia, Norway, and Denmark, and two nonbelligerents, Turkey and Portugal. The Turks received $128,000,000 from London to help them arm against a possible German attack, a heavy outlay for the British but prudent because it kept Turkey secure and neutral.

Few, if any, of the British loans to wartime allies were collectible. Like the American government, the British did not ask or expect a full or prompt settlement. Their chief concern was to see the world return to normal trading, for trade was essential to their survival and it is difficult to trade with insolvent debtors while berating them for nonpayment of old obligations. It seemed better to clear the board of as many old scores as possible, and this generous spirit determined the debt settlement (or more correctly debt cancellation) which the British concluded with the United States. (See pages 586–588.) The British agreed to modify existing empire-preference restrictions in a manner that would promote international commerce and open the world trade lanes more freely to all nations. Finally, they funded their Lend-Lease debts to the United States (reduced to $650,000,000) and they agreed to repay this sum, with 2 per cent interest, over a period of fifty years.[1] By this settlement the two governments hoped to avert the disputes and recriminations over interstate debts which clouded the years after 1918. The United States recognized the excessive and prolonged burden which the British people had carried in the common struggle to crush the Axis powers, and by a generous cancellation of obligations hoped to promote a swifter British recovery.

How swiftly and how completely the British could restore their national prosperity was by no means clear, for their economy had suffered a drastic dislocation. The tripling of their public debt during World War II did not tell the full story of their indebtedness. Part of the war costs had been met by the liquidation of foreign investments. In 1939 British investors held title to an estimated $40,000,000,000 in foreign ventures and this "exported" capital brought them dividends of $1,000,000,000 a year. The government, in contrast, was relatively free from foreign debt and owed the rest of the world the moderate sum of £500,000,000 ($1,800,000,000). But the war inverted this balance. The curtailment of normal commerce, the increased armament burden, the ship losses and property destruction, exhausted credit and transformed Great Britain from the leading lender to the leading bor-

[1] As the British government obtained a new loan of $3,750,000,000 at the same time, the total sum to be repaid was $4,400,000,000. (See page 587.)

rower among the nations. By 1946 international liabilities (omitting Lend-Lease debts to the United States) exceeded £3,500,000,000 ($14,000,000,000). These heavy obligations, which were termed "sterling balances," the British hoped to repay in time but they were in no position to reduce them immediately. They therefore invited the nations, including their own Dominions, which had built up these sterling balances by supplying British war needs, to accept British manufactures in repayment. Portugal and Argentina, for instance, had over £80,000,000 each in sterling credits, but these funds were unavailable or "frozen." If the Portuguese and Argentinians insisted on changing their frozen pounds into dollars, they would weaken British credit and curtail British trade. In their desperate need for imports and exports, the British therefore used the sterling credits as a weapon and offered to unfreeze millions of pounds for the Portuguese, Argentinians, and other nations if they would ship beef, or wine, or sardines, or whatever they produced in surplus, and purchase British wares in exchange. In other words, the nations which had extended credit to Britain could hope for payment more confidently if they did business with Britain, a policy which to American businessmen appeared an unfair form of competition.

2. THE DRIVE FOR MERCANTILE LEADERSHIP

What most Americans did not fully realize was that the British drive to recapture foreign trade was inspired by inexorable needs. They had to "export or die." The United States was a continental market in itself but Great Britain, for a century the "workshop of the world," would be a shop without customers if its overseas trade collapsed. This was the first fact that the British took into account in their postwar bookkeeping. Before 1939 the value of their yearly imports reached almost $5,000,000,000. Half of these essential purchases of food and raw material they paid for with their own exports (chiefly manufactures) which averaged $2,600,000,000 annually. Shipping, banking, insurance, and other services brought in $700,000,000 additional. But this still left the balance of trade adverse by over a billion dollars, and they counted upon the billion a year which came from foreign investments to help rectify the balance. After 1945, with their shipping reduced to 24 per cent of the world total; with $5,000,000,000 of their foreign investments liquidated; with overseas liabilities increased sevenfold from $2,000,000,000 to $14,000,000,000, they faced a serious dilemma. To recover the living standards of prewar days they esti-

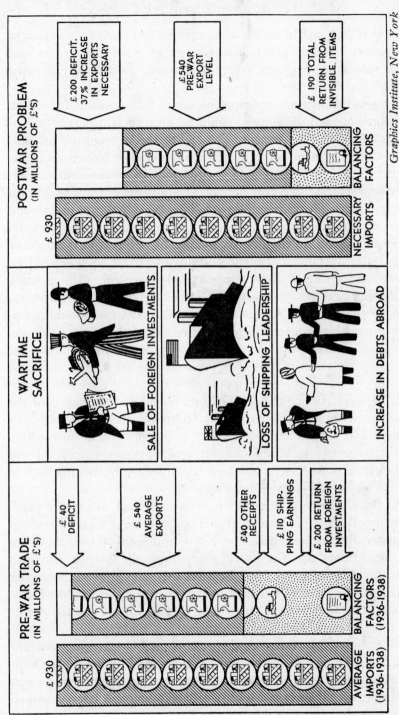

PRE-WAR TRADE
(IN MILLIONS OF £'S)

£ 40 DEFICIT

£ 540 AVERAGE EXPORTS

£40 OTHER RECEIPTS

£ 110 SHIPPING EARNINGS

£ 200 RETURN FROM FOREIGN INVESTMENTS

BALANCING FACTORS (1936-1938)

£ 930

AVERAGE IMPORTS (1936-1938)

WARTIME SACRIFICE

SALE OF FOREIGN INVESTMENTS

LOSS OF SHIPPING LEADERSHIP

INCREASE IN DEBTS ABROAD

POSTWAR PROBLEM
(IN MILLIONS OF £'S)

£ 200 DEFICIT. 37% INCREASE IN EXPORTS NECESSARY

£ 540 PRE-WAR EXPORT LEVEL

£ 190 TOTAL RETURN FROM INVISIBLE ITEMS

BALANCING FACTORS

£ 930

NECESSARY IMPORTS

Graphics Institute, New York

BRITISH TRADE DILEMMA AFTER WORLD WAR II

mated that they would have to raise their export trade by 50 per cent. To improve living standards appreciably they would have to increase export values 100 per cent, which meant they must double the 1938 figures.

Increased export trade was thus the key to British national recovery. Without increased trade there could be little social progress and no guarantee of full employment. The end of the war did not mean an end to the emergency, a fact which the new Labor Government recognized by asking (and obtaining) an extension of its wartime emergency powers for a five-year period. The government was to lead the economic battle for trade and direct all British subjects, as in wartime, in the co-operative effort demanded for survival. The early results were encouraging. In the first six months of peace exports in several fields — steel, metalware, chemicals, tools, electrical equipment, glass, pottery, and artificial silk — climbed well above the 1938 monthly average. But coal, which had formed a staple export for a century, was dropping to a minor place, and exports of cotton goods, which formerly made Manchester world-renowned, had fallen to half the prewar figures. The tragedy of the coal mines was cumulative. They had been ailing for years as the richer veins became exhausted, and many collieries continued in operation only with the aid of government subsidies. In 1946 the mines were all transferred to the state, and the owners received about $750,000,000 indemnification. But state monopoly could not reverse the decline. The rising cost of production made it more and more difficult for coal to compete with oil and hydroelectric power, especially coal mined by antiquated methods in depleted pits and over-extended shafts.

The British postwar trade-drive raised the total of exports to all continents. But the percentage of increase over 1939 levels varied according to the area invaded. For North and South America, where the United States was a powerful competitor, the increase remained slight. For Australia and New Zealand the gains proved more substantial, rising almost 50 per cent over prewar totals. For most European states the increases reached about 70, for Asia 80, and for Africa over 100 per cent. This rapid expansion was not wholly a result of British energy and initiative; there were unique favoring circumstances. With Italy, Germany, and Japan crippled by defeat and military occupation, with most other European states devastated or at least dislocated by war, and with world shipping still largely limited by the war pool and war control, the British enjoyed a great though temporary advantage. They had sufficient ships for all essential imports and exports, their factories had not suffered excessively from German air raids, and they could thus turn their full productive capacity, expanded by war pressures, to filling accumulated orders. For over five years all the nations of the world had been steadily depleted of reserves and resources faster than they could replenish them. The world demand for clothing, fuel, building materials, machinery — and food — was insatiable. It was limited not by capacity to consume but by capacity to pay. Britain was one of the few industrial powers able to profit immediately by meeting these war-sharpened demands.

British trade was dependent upon British shipping. This dependence had increased as British mines became less productive and the minerals and raw materials ferried from other continents filled a larger part in feeding British factories. War losses cut the British share of world tonnage from 30 to 24 per cent between 1939 and 1945, while the registered merchant tonnage of the United States rose from 14 to 51 per cent and that of the Soviet Union from 2 to 3 per cent of the total. One year after peace returned the iron or steel ships of over 1000 tons burden registered for all countries still showed the destructive effects of the submarine warfare. Aside from the rise already noted for Russia and the United States, only the two neutrals, Spain and Sweden, had gained during the war. All other maritime powers had declined in total tonnage, several of them catastrophically. The increase in the world total, from 80,600,000 tons in 1939 to 99,219,900 in 1946, was almost wholly the result of the extraordinary rise in United States shipping. The figures, which do not include army or navy vessels, small boats under 1000 tons, or shipping on inland waterways, suggest the mercantile rank of the nations in 1946. (See next page.)

Although the British Empire, by 1946, had almost regained the same total tonnage in ships as in 1939, the 25 per cent rise in world shipping made the British share relatively less. The shipyards of the British Isles sped new ships down the ways to make good the war depletion and fill waiting orders from abroad. In 1946 Britain led the world in new ship construction, while the United States, unable to operate its 51 per cent of the world's shipping economically, allowed construction to lag, sold its surplus vessels at a loss, or tied them up in port with a skeleton crew. This relative lethargy of the Americans, combined with the ruin which war had brought to the mercantile marine of Germany, Japan, and Italy, offered the British a rare chance to recapture their threatened mercantile supremacy.

MERCANTILE TONNAGE OF THE WORLD

	1939	1946
UNITED STATES	11,681,700	50,389,300
BRITISH EMPIRE	24,053,700	24,009,600
NORWAY	6,931,200	4,477,000
SOVIET RUSSIA	1,597,900	2,626,700
SWEDEN	2,033,100	2,204,000
THE NETHERLANDS	3,424,600	2,035,800
FRANCE	2,998,800	1,612,800
JAPAN	7,145,400	1,432,100
SPAIN	1,051,700	1,253,100
GERMANY	5,177,100	1,160,100
GREECE	2,791,000	1,006,200
DENMARK	1,575,800	952,600
ITALY	3,910,800	691,700
OTHERS	6,227,800	5,368,900
TOTAL	80,600,600	99,219,900

3. THE PROGRAM OF NATIONALIZATION

While waging their war for national survival the British people accepted many strict regulations which in peacetime they would have resisted. Yet when peace came again they did not at once demand the abolition of such controls. Instead, a popular majority accepted the fact that increased social regimentation was a trend of the twentieth century. If the results justified the experiment, they were prepared to yield some of their cherished liberties for the common good. The war hastened a shift towards social control which had been developing since before 1900. This shift towards a socialized, or nationalized, economy, with all essential public facilities subject to state management, was the avowed program of the Labor Party when its leaders took office in 1945.

The British people, however, prefer to make haste slowly and do not welcome rigid plans or ideological programs in politics. The Labor Government moved cautiously along the road to nationalization. For prime minister Attlee and his colleagues knew that of 33,000,000 citizens with a vote, perhaps half had endorsed the Labor candidates, 10,000,000 had favored the opposition groups, and 8,000,000 had not voted at all. With only one-half the electorate behind them, the Labor candidates had no definite mandate to create a socialist state. Nevertheless, during the war years social planners had drawn up projects for improving the schools, guarding the health of the people, and raising the standard of living. When peace came, these plans were dusted off and some of them were carried into effect.

A new Education Act, one of the first reforms, actually went into operation on April 1, 1945, and was thus a measure of the wartime government. Its execution, however, rested with the Labor Cabinet after July, 1945. The Act provided that students in all grades were to have better schooling, better equipment, and better paid teachers. From kindergarten to college public education became one continuous process. Attendance at school was made compulsory for all normal children until they reached fifteen, and part-time instruction was required until they were eighteen. Children who showed exceptional ability were to receive scholarships so that they might complete their secondary school work and attend college. Adults whose education had remained incomplete were invited to renew their studies. The need for more trained technologists, for machinists, electricians, engineers, scientists, and research specialists had been evident in the war crisis. To meet this shortage more technical schools were opened. The Minister of Education also received effective power, hitherto lacking, to direct a national program of public instruction and he was to be aided by two Central Advisory Councils, one for England and one for Wales. All this expansion meant that many new schools were needed, with more teachers and more taxes. The cost of public instruction in 1947 was double that of the prewar years, but the people hoped the outlay would prove a sound national investment. Good schools, they believed, would produce not only more cultured citizens but more useful and more competent citizens. No modern nation could long survive if it failed to find and train specialists for the exacting tasks posed by modern science and statecraft.

Care for the citizen's mind was not enough; it was also essential to care for his body. Many English men and women who sought to serve their country in the war had been rejected as unfit for duty because of poor health or physical defects. To improve the national health the parliament passed a bill (1945) to provide free and unlimited medical care for all through a system of socialized medicine. Many millions of citizens were already protected by some form of health insurance; now all were to be guaranteed medical attention, hospitalization, home nursing, drugs, and appliances as needed, without charge. The Minister of Health had general supervision over the entire program, the

British Medical Association and College of Surgeons were to be invited to collaborate, and the cost was to be defrayed through insurance dues and national taxes.

All public hospitals and clinics were made government property, together with their endowments, and all details of public health came under the direction of local councils to be composed equally of physicians and laymen. The new plan did not abolish the older methods of private medical practice. Patients could still hire a private physician or nurse if they did not wish to avail themselves of state medical aid. Physicians who so desired could continue in private practice; they could also take a part-time share in the public medical services or accept a full-time appointment with a fixed salary at a public health center. It was obvious, however, that the traditional doctor-patient relationship would be modified by this trend towards socialized medicine if it were instituted. British doctors were divided on the merits of the new plan. A majority opposed it, but the spread of new ideas was evident from the large minority which favored it. The rise of a more liberal spirit in medical circles was further reflected in the admission of more women to medical practice. In Great Britain one physician in five was a woman by 1947, whereas in the United States the proportion was only one in twenty.

A third reform which the Labor Government undertook for the national welfare was the improvement of agriculture. Between 1940 and 1945 the farmers almost doubled their crops under the pressure of war needs. When peace came, the government urged them to keep their production high. An Agricultural Research Council, together with medical, scientific, and industrial research agencies, were subsidized from state funds and urged to explore new methods for increasing home resources. The British Isles lacked the vast expanse and the unmeasured natural wealth of the United States and Russia, the oil wells, forests, wheatlands, and hydroelectric power. British copper, lead, and tin mines, once a leading source of world supplies, were nearing exhaustion. More serious still, iron ore was giving out, and the cost of mining coal, as already noted, had risen until many collieries could no longer operate at a profit. These circumstances made it imperative to survey all the empire resources, plan for future needs, and co-ordinate production. The discovery of new diamond mines in Tanganyika and uranium deposits in Canada were no longer viewed as developments to be left to private enterprise; they had become, like all major items connected with economic welfare, a subject for government regulation and supervision. The British, who had "muddled through" so many historic crises, were less certain than formerly that they could always succeed in muddling through. Problems of imperial welfare and imperial defense could not be left to chance in a world in which economic planning had become the fashion.

4. THE DEFENSE OF THE EMPIRE

The British people learned in World War II that their island kingdom, that "precious stone set in a silver sea" was no longer inviolable and that the silver sea no longer served (in Shakespeare's phrase) "as a moat defensive." War planes could cross the Channel in a few minutes; the cities of England were dangerously vulnerable; and the tentacles of British sea power could be severed. Singapore fell in 1942, and although Gibraltar, Malta, and Suez stood off all attacks, the Mediterranean life line of the Empire was closed by Axis raids.

The British Isles had not only become more vulnerable but they had become relatively less important in the British Commonwealth. Though still the undisputed head and center of the Empire, Great Britain was politically one partner among equals. One-third of the English-speaking peoples of the Empire lived in Canada, Australasia, and South Africa by 1945, the reserves of man power and wealth were widely distributed, and the most vital problem in any plan for imperial defense was the problem of communications. Looking ahead, British strategists decided that the unrest in the Arab world, the feuds in Palestine, and the possible expansion of Russian power in the Near East, might close the Mediterranean route in a future war. If this occurred, they would have to send their seaborne supplies around Africa as they had done for a time in World War II. But to protect this southern route and safeguard the South Atlantic and the Indian Ocean they would need air and naval bases along the entire route. These facts were carefully weighed as the British took an inventory of their defense needs in the postwar era.

Sites for suitable African bases were available in Nigeria on the Atlantic coast and in Kenya and Tanganyika on the Indian Ocean. A transcontinental highway, from Lagos in Nigeria to Mombasa in Kenya Colony, would provide an inland route across French Equatorial Africa and the Anglo-Egyptian Sudan, a road that would not only serve for transport but would open up the interior of Africa and form an inner line of defense if necessary. Bisected by the north-south highway system from the Cape of Good Hope to Algiers, these Afri-

can roads would give the British access to and control of the resources
of central Africa, resources which might turn the scale in a future
struggle. They knew that Africa was unbelievably rich in minerals.
Half the world's supply of gold and diamonds was mined there, copper was abundant, and radium and uranium deposits of unknown extent had been located. Though oil and coal were scarce their absence
was not important, for African rivers could produce unequalled reserves of electric power, their potential capacity exceeding that of
North and South America combined.

The decline of French, German, and Italian influence, as a consequence of World War II, left Britain in a position of unquestioned
supremacy throughout the greater part of Africa. Improved medical
knowledge, the automobile, and the airplane, had made the exploration and development of inner Africa relatively safe, rapid, and profitable by the middle of the twentieth century. The economic exploitation of the great natural resources there was inevitable, and as no
serious opposition could be offered by the native peoples and none
was likely to be offered by Russia or the United States, Great Britain
was the logical heir to the Dark Continent. In 1947 the British colonial secretary announced that to speed colonial developments a corporation capitalized at £100,000,000 would be established. The raising of cattle and the growing of wheat, corn, and peanut crops in the
great undeveloped areas of British Africa formed an important part
of the program.

A second line of defense, below the Sahara Desert in tropical Africa,
would offer the British control of an area extremely difficult to attack.
There, if Suez should be shattered and Arabia overrun, the British
might still organize air fleets in the hidden valleys, concentrate reserves, and perhaps manufacture war materials. All wars in which the
British engaged lasted for years because it required years for them to
bring their great but scattered reserves of wealth and resources of
power into effective action. In preparing for the possibility of future
wars British military experts could not neglect the lessons of recent
campaigns. Sea power and control of the sea routes still formed the
essence of British strategy. Singapore and Hong Kong were reoccupied in 1945; the Mediterranean life line was still intact and resolutely
defended. But like Britain itself that route had become more vulnerable in the air age. Although Gibraltar, Malta, and Aden were firmly
held, although the British had two air bases and garrison troops in Iraq,
strong occupation forces in Palestine, a military base in Transjordan,

and 10,000 troops guarding the Suez Canal, they sought safety in dispersion. To be prepared against unfavorable chances, they allowed for the probability that they would have to withdraw all forces from Egypt in deference to Egyptian nationalist sentiments. India, which had supported one-fourth of the imperial forces before 1939, was granted independence in 1947, and the British likewise prepared to

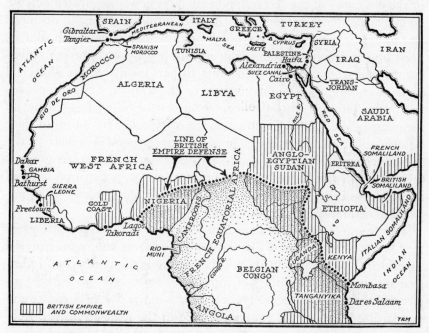

BRITISH DEFENSE LINES IN AFRICA AFTER WORLD WAR II

withdraw from Burma. But the dissolution of political ties did not mean the end of British influence in these areas of Asia. It meant, rather, that the ties would be transformed and the segments of the vast empire would remain bound by a complex mesh of fibers, financial, economic, commercial, legal, and diplomatic.

The Second World War showed how important a unified command and vast supplies of standardized equipment can prove to be in the operations of modern armies. The British accepted these lessons. In 1946 the government introduced a bill to unify the command of the army, navy, and air force under a single ministry of national defense. "The problem which faces us now," declared prime minister Attlee, "is to ensure for the fighting services unity of thought, unity of supreme direction, unity of plan, unity of outlook and, above all, unity of defense doctrine." The separate ministers who headed the army, navy, and air force, together with the ministers for foreign affairs, for finance, for colonies, and for labor and national service, were to meet in council with the prime minister and the new defense minister to decide general questions of policy. When they considered it helpful they could call in other cabinet associates, as the minister of transport or the chairman of the research bureau. This newly organized defense council or defense cabinet was to have authority to make decisions and to act; it was not merely one more advisory commission. But its great power caused no undue concern, for it was a committee of civilian members, responsible at all times to parliament. As an additional bond of empire, the Dominions were to be informed of its discussions and plans through liaison officers who would be exchanged by all members of the British Commonwealth of Nations. By means of their reports and through frequent imperial conferences in which all the self-governing Dominions would participate, the Dominion governments and defense forces were to be kept in close association with all imperial projects. This plan meant, in essence, the creation of an imperial general staff for the entire British Empire.

The Anglo-American victories in World War II were due in great measure to what General Eisenhower called "our enormous material superiority." This was made possible through the unmatched industrial and economic resources of the United States and the British Empire and through the decision reached early in the war to correlate and standardize much of the equipment used in the joint offensives. Recognizing the decisive part which unlimited supplies of standardized munitions and armament might play in the future, the British leaders reached a decision of the highest significance in 1946. They advised changes in British machines and calibers which would bring their patterns and gauges into agreement with American standards. For the British the adoption of American patterns was a concession and in some respects a disadvantage. Such "rationalization" of industrial methods meant that American-made machines and parts could soon compete with British goods in British markets. But the system worked two ways. It also meant that nations which had hitherto bought guns, planes, dynamos, and other equipment for war or peace from American factories, might replenish their supplies from British factories using the same patents and prescriptions. Finally, the co-ordination of arms output by two powers, which together controlled three-fourths of the industrial machinery of the world, meant that these two powers, acting in concert, could grant or withhold the weapons of war to any nation asking for them and unable to supply its own needs.

5. DOMINIONS AND COLONIES

The bonds of empire uniting Great Britain and the Dominions have altered in the twentieth century, as explained in Chapter XXVI, but the economic ties have remained strong. The Irish Free State (Eire), for example, which is a "sovereign independent state" politically, is bound to Great Britain more closely than any other Dominion economically. The Irish pound has the same value as the British pound sterling, and Anglo-Irish trade was so profitable to the Irish during World War II that Britain owed the Free State a sterling balance of almost $1,000,000,000 by 1945. This credit they hoped to pay back by maintaining close economic contacts, a hope based on realities, for one-half the Free State's imports still came from Britain and four-fifths of its exports were sold there.

Next in the order of economic preference came the Union of South Africa. On the eve of World War II the Union exported about two-thirds of its produce to Great Britain and received two-thirds of its imports from the British Isles. New Zealand likewise sent two-thirds of its exports to British markets but purchased only one-third of its imports there. Australia exported almost half and imported one-third. Canada exported only one-third of its products to Britain and bought even less from the motherland.

These estimates varied each year. After 1945 the British drive for overseas trade raised the quota for all the Dominions, but the economic dependence of the various sections of the empire upon British trade was highly illuminating. Where political ties were weakest economic ties were sometimes strongest. Eire and the Union of South Africa, which steer the most independent course (Eire remained neutral in World War II and South Africa very nearly did the same) are the Dominions most dependent upon Britain in their economic life. The British Empire-Commonwealth is thus seen to be an exceptionally complex structure. Its foes have repeatedly predicted its decline or disintegration and then been astonished, in the hour of testing, to find that its multiple economic, financial, judicial, and political bonds could be more durable and persuasive in holding it together than armies, treaties, battleships, or bombing planes.

These circumstances make it extremely difficult to judge the status of the empire in the postwar world when its economy and its political formulas are undergoing revision. In Canada, for example, which is the prototype and the most advanced of the self-governing Dominions, the will to independence led to a new definition or clarification of Anglo-Canadian ties after December 31, 1946. Thenceforth Canadian nationals were to be termed "Canadians" and their passports were to read "Canadian citizen" instead of "British subject." Yet even while asserting this political distinction, the Canadian parliament voted to unite Canada and Britain more closely in their economic affairs by lending Great Britain $1,250,000,000 to speed trade recovery. This sum (larger in proportion to Canada's 12,000,000 people than the United States loan to Britain of $3,750,000,000) was to be spent almost wholly in Canada to purchase supplies needed by Britain. In addition, a four-year wheat agreement was negotiated whereby the Canadians pledged shipments to Britain of 140,000,000 to 160,000,000 bushels annually. Such trade pacts hold the imperial structure intact despite loosened political formulas.

Perhaps the most ambiguous relationship within the frame of the empire is that which unites Great Britain and India. Both political and economic ties between the two have weakened in the twentieth century and Indian will to independence has grown strong and vocal. For Britain the secession of India will mean a considerable dislocation. One-fourth of the British armed forces were customarily stationed (and partly financed) there, and India long provided the most important overseas market for British exports. These facts lost importance after World War I. The Indians provided increasingly for their own needs, and by 1939 they were receiving only about 8 per cent of British exports or approximately the same amount as the Union of South Africa or the Commonwealth of Australia which had only a small fraction of the Indian total in population. During World War II Indian industry expanded under war stimulus, exports to Britain rose rapidly, but imports from Britain declined. Instead of being a debtor, India became a creditor. British investments equivalent to more than $1,000,000,000 were liquidated and paid off, and the Indian people and government accumulated sterling credits of $6,000,000,000. In 1944 the legislature approved a fifteen-year program which aimed to provide the power, chiefly hydroelectric, which would make India a more modern and more industrialized state. The dams which furnished the power would also double the crops through irrigation and nitrate fertilizers, transforming the life of the masses in Bengal, Orissa, Madras, the Deccan, and other provinces. Industrialization promised further aid for raising the standard of living among India's 400,000,000 people. But economic progress was dependent upon political order and stability. The British decision to withdraw from India (1947) left the responsibility of government and the control of their destiny to the Indian peoples. This development is discussed further in Chapter XLVI.

THE UNION
OF SOVIET SOCIALIST REPUBLICS

I do not believe in a real danger of a "new war."

JOSEPH STALIN (1946)

I. RUSSIAN ECONOMIC RECOVERY AND EXPANSION

THE longest and the fiercest campaigns of World War II were fought in Russia. The destruction of life and property, calculated at perhaps 12,000,000 Russian dead and $100,000,000,000 in property damage, was a staggering loss for any nation to survive. In addition the Soviet Union incurred war expenditures of something approaching $200,000,000,000. Only a country with extraordinary resources in man power and materials could have supported this depletion, and to most governments the task of rebuilding the ruined cities would have seemed a sufficiently ambitious postwar program. But the rulers of Russia returned at once to the interrupted projects for social and economic development which had been outlined in the three Five-Year Plans of 1928–1942. In 1946 premier Stalin proposed three more Five-Year Plans which, if duly completed, would prepare the Soviet for "any eventuality" before 1960.

In setting these new goals, Stalin emphasized the progress already made under Soviet leadership. The output of coal, oil, pig iron, and steel, all vital indices of modern industry, increased three to five times between 1913 and 1940. But he warned that an equivalent increase was needed by 1960 if Russia were to be secure and self-sufficient in peace and war. To rouse enthusiasm for the new (Fourth) Five-Year Plan of 1946 production figures were posted in the factories and constantly revised, and the progress achieved since the revolution was advertised to vindicate the leadership of the Communist Party.

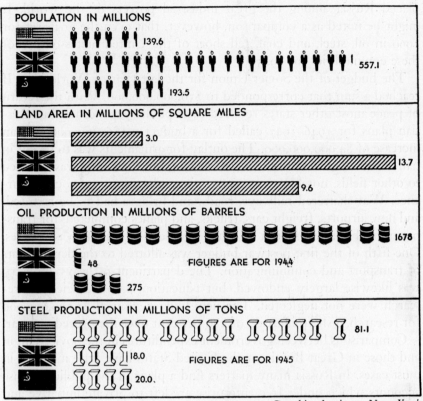

Graphics Institute, New York

THE UNITED STATES, THE BRITISH EMPIRE, AND RUSSIA AFTER
WORLD WAR II: A COMPARISON

RUSSIAN PRODUCTION IN METRIC TONS

	1913	1940	Goal
Coal	29,000,000	166,000,000	500,000,000
Oil	9,000,000	31,000,000	60,000,000
Pig Iron	4,200,000	15,000,000	50,000,000
Steel	4,200,000	18,300,000	60,000,000

At the same time the planners demanded a doubling of available electric power within five years. These advances were impressive, especially as an indication of industrial progress. In 1913 the products of the machine had formed only two-fifths of the total Russian production, but by 1940 they accounted for four-fifths. This expansion placed Russia among the great industrial powers of the world. It might be noted as a comparison, however, that even the goals set for 1960 in oil, steel, and coal, fell short of the United States output of these commodities for 1945.

The budget of the Soviet Union for the last year of World War II reached a sum that corresponded to $56,000,000,000. With the return of peace most other states reduced their public expenditure but Russian plans for 1946–1947 called for a budget of $60,000,000,000, an increase of $4,000,000,000. The outlay for armaments was to be cut in half, as was logical with the war at an end, but the saving was diverted to other fields, notably to transportation, education, and social insurance. War-shattered railways, roads, and bridges had to be restored, and new airports, freight cars, trucks, and planes completed, for transportation has always been an acute problem in Russia's vast wastes. One-fifth of the first postwar budget was allotted to the departments of transport and communication. The department of heavy industry was likewise largely endowed, but education, art, and scientific research were not neglected. The new budget allowed $1,000,000,000 for research, a sharp increase of 240 per cent over the preceding year.

Comparisons between government expenditures in the Soviet Union and those in Great Britain or the United States have little meaning in most cases. In Russia many matters find a place in the public expense accounts which under free enterprise are left to private initiative and private management. This fact helps to explain why Britain and the United States reduced their wartime budgets promptly and restored some activities, temporarily assumed by the war government, to private hands. In Russia the collectivist experiment precluded such disencumberment, and economic life remained a state problem and industrial and agricultural expansion proceeded at state expense.

2. POLITICAL ORGANIZATION AND PRACTICE

When the British people held their general election in 1945, and the American people in 1946, they rejected the party which had carried them through the war. This political change, which put the outs in and the ins out, was a feature of the two-party system common to British and American politics. In the Soviet Union, however, there was no alternative party which could be elected to power in place of the communists. When the voters, 100,000,000 strong, went to the polls in 1946, they re-elected the Communist Party candidates almost unanimously. Joseph Stalin remained chief of the Council of Ministers (premier), chairman of the Ministry of the Armed Forces (general-issimo), and secretary-general of the Central Executive Committee of the Communist Party. Vyacheslav M. Molotov, as a vice-chairman of the Council of Commissars, and Commissar for Foreign Affairs, directed the international policies of the Union. The technical head of the state is the Chairman of the Praesidium of the Supreme Council of the Union. Mikhail Ivanovitch Kalinin, who had filled this somewhat negative role with quiet dignity since 1919, retired in 1946 and was succeeded by the first vice-chairman of the Praesidium, Nikolai Mikhailovitch Shvernik.

After 1945 Stalin was the only outstanding leader of World War II who remained in power. Winston Churchill, the second of the Big Three, who had electrified the British people with his superlative eloquence in their ordeal, was out of office. Franklin Delano Roosevelt, with his vision, his courage, his gaiety and magnetism, had died as the final victory dawned, and was already a legend. The crash of their empires had destroyed the dictators, Mussolini and Hitler, in the spring of the climactic year 1945. But Stalin remained, in peace as in war, the iron man of the Kremlin, imperturbable, inscrutable, and impressive. His prestige and authority were greater than ever; his ascendancy over his associates in the Communist Party seemed absolute; his occasional utterances, concise and unadorned but compelling in their realism, were pondered by an attentive world.

The mystery which had veiled the inner councils of the Soviet regime for thirty years persisted in the postwar period. The plans and purposes of the Political Bureau (Politburo) of the Central Committee of the All-Union Communist Party formed the policies which shaped Russia's destiny, but few outside the nine members of that powerful cabal knew whither those policies tended. Russia was a riddle to foreigners because Russian actions so often seemed to be controlled by invisible strings or by a prearranged complicity that was officially disavowed. In external affairs, for example, the Constituent Republics of the Soviet Union were accorded the privilege of setting up their own Commissariats for Foreign Affairs. Each republic, it was announced, might send out its own envoys, conclude its own treaties with other governments, and even withdraw from the Soviet Union if it so preferred. This move, which went into effect in 1944, permitted the Russians to claim separate representation for four separate republics of the Soviet Union at the Paris Peace Conference in 1946. But in practice the Commissariat for Foreign Affairs for the U.S.S.R. as a whole determined foreign policy, and the delegations of the individual republics played a prearranged and far from independent role in international negotiations. The purported decentralization was thus found to mask an actual increase in Soviet diplomatic strength and bargaining power.

Another aspect of Soviet politics which never ceased to baffle foreign observers was the frequent trials and purges of officials. This "cleansing of the party ranks" seemed to resemble a recurrent use of political proscription rather than a genuine self-rectifying impulse of the people. Apologists pointed out that under a one-party system the party had to diagnose its own failings and accuse its own members if they forsook their duties, for no opposition existed to keep vigilant watch on officeholders. Consequently, Communist Party members were exhorted to supervise one another and to report any evidences of graft, incompetence, or laxity. They were also exhorted to set an example of zeal and to inspire the inert masses with revolutionary ardor. The Communist Party members were a small group numerically. Between 1939 and 1945 they increased from about 2,000,000 to approximately 5,000,000, that is, from 1 per cent to perhaps 3 per cent of the total population.

In 1946 the party was instructed to make a rigorous examination of the records and qualifications of all members, old and new, and to purify the ranks of unworthy personnel. Any officials or groups in military or civilian services which were too powerful or too independent, were demoted, dispersed, or reorganized in weaker units. The brilliant commanders who had led the Russian armies to victory were retired with honor or dispatched to distant posts. Technicians, engineers, and directors of the great productive farms or industrial combines were scrutinized and shifted. Peasants who had profited from "black market" sales were forced to surrender their profits, and groups which had grown overly nationalistic under the patriotic stimulus of the war fever were diluted by population transfers. As part of this policy the autonomous republics of the Crimea and Checchen-Ingush were reduced to the status of provinces, and party leaders in the Ukraine, whose records during the German occupation appeared suspicious, were shot as wartime collaborators. On the collective farms the workers were invited to name any administrators who used their official authority to extort special privileges, and those found guilty of "plundering and pilfering" were severely punished.

Such criticism was not limited to administrators on the collective farms. Factory directors, doctors, inspectors, engineers, bookkeepers, plant foremen, and even machinists who mishandled their tools, came under investigation. Failure to maintain the quota assigned brought swift rebuke, for the Ministry of State Control constantly checked all production figures. Inspectors rated the efficiency of farms and factories. Workers were constantly adjured to cut down waste, to expose falsification, to seek better methods that would speed production, increase output, and inspire the workers to improve their skill. Despite the great effort made to establish better schools, the lack of technicians, of skilled machinists, and of experienced foremen and officials remained the gravest obstacle to industrial progress. This fact partly explains the purges; it was necessary to compel the worker to concentrate his attention, obey instructions, and cherish his tools, and millions who had not been trained to such exacting labor had to be terrified into compliance by extravagantly severe penalties and by dramatic examples chosen from all ranks.

3. SOCIAL PROGRESS

A society in a state of revolution is an embattled society, and the people who make a revolution suffer the same moods as people in a besieged city. They live under conditions of tension which make them fearful and suspicious, and their fears and suspicions often make them cruel. The Russian people were thrown into a state of emergency by the First World War. The emergency increased with the revolution of 1917. The desperate struggle to survive and the civil war which rent the Soviet Union for years allowed no respite or relaxation of the tension. After ten years of provisory progress, with sacrifice and suffering, the Five-Year Plans artificially stimulated the ardor and anxiety of the people. Hitler's invasion and the "Great Patriotic War" of 1941–1945 renewed the sense of urgency and exacted the utmost devotion and fortitude from the masses. For millions of Russians living in 1946 existence as far back as they could remember had been a desperate and unrelenting struggle against famine and disease and the treachery of internal and external foes. This long ordeal must be kept in mind by all who seek to read the Russian mind. The hesitation which the Soviet peoples often feel towards foreigners, the suspicion and secrecy they sometimes show towards one another, the severity they exercise towards traitors or renegades in their midst, are siege symptoms. Equally symptomatic are the pride and enthusiasm they feel for their leaders and for themselves because they have saved themselves, as they believe, solely through their own heroic exertions in a world largely dedicated to destroying them.

A people so beset, or a people who believe themselves to be so beset, judge all activity by the degree to which it serves the common struggle. Everything a citizen does or says or reads or thinks takes on a "social significance." There can be little relaxation, little toleration of idleness or frivolity. Russian newspapers, radio programs, books, and paintings are expected to serve a serious purpose, the "mobilization of the Soviet people for the building of a socialist society and the protection of the Soviet homeland." When Russian artists and writers have neglected this primary social aim they have often been severely criticized, a feature of the purges which has been misunderstood and often ridiculed in other lands. The leading Soviet motion picture producer, Sergei Eisenstein, was attacked on the ground that he advocated the erroneous formula, "art for art's sake." Song writers were denounced for producing songs which gave cheap romantic pleasure. Even the great composer, Dimitri Shostakovitch, was criticized because his *Ninth Symphony* was light, fanciful, and traditional and lacked the "warm ideological conviction" more notable in his compositions celebrating the October Revolution and the battle of Leningrad. Such insistent subordination of art to politics kept much Soviet creative effort at the level of propaganda, and "ideological art" of this nature was seldom admired or imitated outside the Soviet Union.

Even inside the Union the problem of informing and influencing 200,000,000 people in orthodox revolutionary style remained a difficult assignment. There was an unreconcilable diversity about the Soviet peoples which made total assimilation and homogeneity unattainable. Although by 1940 more than 9000 newspapers carried the officially approved press dispatches to all parts of the Union, these newspapers were published in seventy different languages. The 44,000 different books issued that year appeared in 111 languages, and the 2100 journals and magazines in 48. But the most influential newspapers, *Izvestia* which was the official organ of the Supreme Council of the U.S.S.R. and *Pravda* which was the organ of the All-Union Communist Party, were issued in Moscow and all published matter was supervised by the Administration of Literature and Publications which in turn was responsible to the Commissariat of Public Instruction. It was thus possible to guide the public insensibly in the direction planned and to encourage all Russians to master the officially ap-

proved language of Moscow. In this campaign the silent and the talking picture as well as the radio were supremely effective. The 28,000
motion picture theaters of the Soviet Union brought carefully prepared films to the masses, films which glorified the Communist Party
and celebrated the great collectivist experiment in which all Soviet
peoples were participating from Poland to Manchuria and from the
Arctic Ocean to the Indian hills.

One universal organization and instrument for spreading socialist
ideals among the Soviet peoples was the schools to which millions of
adults turned to complete their neglected training. Education was
made obligatory for all boys and girls over the age of seven, and by
1945 there were 32,000,000 pupils in attendance. The young were
honored as the prime asset of the nation and the chief hope of the
future. Their health and education were the first concern of the government, and bonuses were voted to encourage larger families. After
1943 the Commissariat of Public Health paid 400 rubles to the mothers
of three children, with a rise in the bonus level for each additional
child. A mother of ten received 5000 rubles, and 300 monthly for each
child in excess of ten. This official encouragement had a notable effect. By 1945 the birth rate, as officially proclaimed, had risen one-
third above the prewar ratio of forty-four per thousand of population.
This placed the Russian rate nearly three times as high as the birth rate
(twenty per thousand) which prevailed in the United States in 1944.

4. THE DEFENSE OF THE SOVIET UNION

With the collapse of German power in the débâcle of 1945 eastern
Europe from the Baltic to the Balkans passed under Russian domination. Between fifty and a hundred divisions of the Red army remained
to garrison the enemy territory and protect the liberated states. The
Soviet leaders intended to disarm not only Germany but also the
smaller states — Finland, Hungary, Rumania, and Bulgaria — which
the Germans had used as springboards when they launched their attack upon Russia. The Soviet diplomats insisted that these buffer states
must be kept under control or restored to independence under governments satisfactory to the Soviet government. This policy suggested
that the rulers of Russia planned to erect a "rampart of republics" under pro-Soviet regimes in the area from Finland to Yugoslavia and that
they also hoped to extend Russian influence beyond their frontiers in
the Near, Middle, and Far East.

To British and American observers these attempts to exert pressure

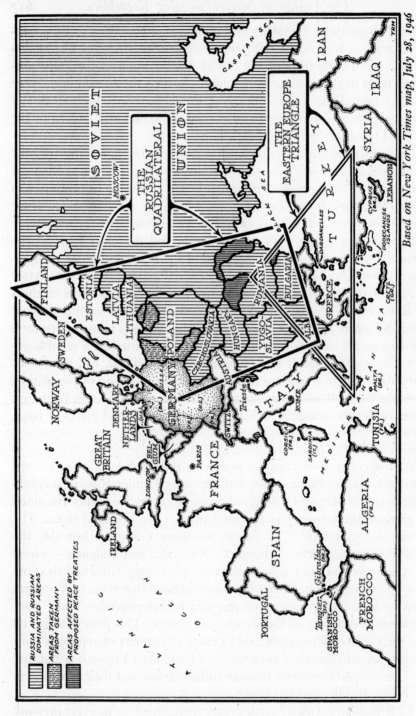

RUSSIAN INFLUENCE IN EUROPE AFTER WORLD WAR II

Based on New York Times map, July 28, 1946

in eastern Europe, in Turkey and Iran, Manchuria and Korea seemed like a threat. That the leaders could be seriously afraid of a possible invasion through these "gates" was not regarded as plausible, for the Western peoples had no wish or intention of attacking Russia. Moreover, World War II left the Red army the most powerful military force in the world, and the rapid expansion of industry made that army almost self-sufficient for equipment and weapons. In the first year of peace the defense budget, though reduced from the wartime level, was still considerably higher than the sum which the United States government planned to expend on its army. The control of the Red army was centralized in 1946 through the creation of a single unified ministry of the armed forces, and all Soviet defense agencies, land, air, and sea, were entrusted to the supreme direction of Generalissimo Stalin. This consolidation assured a closer co-ordination of all units, but the vast area of the country made it necessary to preserve local headquarters also under loyal regional commanders. Each army division scattered from Yugoslavia to Manchuria was supplied by armament factories in its own district when this was possible. Thus the Soviet Union became stronger through a centralization of command but a decentralization of the service of supply. Like an ocean liner which can keep afloat even though several compartments become flooded, the new Russia would be capable of surviving and fighting even though several regions were overrun by the enemy. The air fleet, like the army, was divided into self-sufficing squadrons, one major section defending the western half of the Union and another the eastern half. There was also a third air unit, an Independent Striking Force, which was highly mobile and included its own special ground crews and service of supply. This Independent Force remained under the direct orders of the supreme command.

The navy, although it was the third largest in the world in 1946, was far inferior to the army as an effective force. Its chief strength lay in its defense units; it was not a high seas fleet. Of battleships Russia possessed four, to twenty-three for the United States; in heavy cruisers the ratio was seven to twenty-six; in light cruisers, two to forty-one. The Russians had no aircraft carriers or escort carriers, without which no modern navy dare venture far from the protection of its land-based fighter planes. The destroyer total for Russia was fifty-one, to 353 for the United States, and the submarine total 140 to 206. These ships were distributed, of necessity, at widely separated bases, in the White Sea, the Baltic Sea, the Black Sea, and the Japan Sea. Inland rivers and canals made it possible to transfer all but the largest ships from north to south, but no means existed for moving warships from European waters to Vladivostok save to take them apart and ship them by rail, or sail them through the Suez Canal, across the Indian Ocean, and up the China coast. The Soviet government, like the government of the United States, had to base its defense plans on a two-ocean navy. It could not assemble all its strength in one area swiftly, and its fleet in general was constructed for inland seas rather than for the world's oceans.

5. THE FOREIGN POLICY OF THE U.S.S.R.

The key to Russian foreign policy from the time of Peter the Great (1689–1725) was the urge to find a way to the sea, especially to open "windows to the west" in the Baltic or windows to the south through the Black Sea or the Indian Ocean. This ambition was still strong in 1941, so strong that it wrecked the Russo-German accord negotiated two years earlier. As allies of the German National Socialists the Soviet troops had moved into Estonia, Latvia, and Lithuania and had occupied eastern Poland. They had also annexed Bessarabia and they pressed Hitler for an agreement which would permit Russian control of the Dardanelles and a free hand for Soviet manipulators in Iraq and Iran. Hitler and his foreign minister, Joachim von Ribbentrop, weighed these demands from Moscow in 1940 and 1941. A Russian advance into Anatolia and Iran would cut Germany off from expansion in the Near East, and Hitler, who was planning his drive for Suez and Africa through Greece and possibly through Syria, considered the Soviet price of alliance excessive. Rejecting the benefits of the Russian pact, which had protected Germany from a two-front war, he hurled his hitherto invincible *Wehrmacht* across the Soviet frontier in June, 1941.

The German attack forced a rapid reversal of Soviet strategy and made Russia the ally of Britain and the United States. But long-held Russian policies had not altered: outlets on the seas, especially the warm seas, were still the goal. The British and American leaders, however, were no more eager than Hitler had been to permit Russia to take over the Dardanelles or expand to the Persian Gulf, and they were cool to hints that some of the Italian possessions in Africa would be acceptable to the Soviet Union as "trusteeships." The British were more concerned than the Americans to preserve the *status quo* in the Near East and in the Balkans. They pressed for an invasion of Hitler's "Fortress Europe" through Italy, Greece, or the Danube Valley rather than in the Normandy area. Had British policy prevailed in this question, Europe might have been invaded and Germany overthrown by Anglo-American armies fighting their way up from the south while the Russians drove west to Berlin. Such an offensive might have been longer and would almost certainly have been more costly than the invasion of France. But at the end of the fighting it would have left the Balkan peninsula under Anglo-American rather than Russian occupation.

Limits of shipping precluded two Allied invasions of equal strength in northern and southern Europe simultaneously. While the armies commanded by General Eisenhower drove from Normandy to the Elbe, the Red army swept across the Balkan states almost to the borders of Switzerland. The future areas of occupation in Europe were already discussed when the Big Three leaders met at Yalta in February, 1945. (See page 524.) The war in the Pacific was discussed also, and the Russians agreed that, if Japan held out after Germany was crushed, the Soviet government would not wait more than three months to attack Japan in Manchuria. For this aid, however, the Russians asked a tangible reward, and the terms, which were not revealed until a year later, were embodied in a secret agreement signed by Joseph Stalin, Franklin D. Roosevelt, and Winston Churchill. This agreement promised Russia the southern half of Sakhalin and the Kurile Islands, a lease on the naval base of Port Arthur and free access to and use of the internationalized port of Darien, joint operation with China of the Chinese Eastern Railway and the South Manchurian Railway, and the maintenance of the *status quo* in the Mongolian People's Republic. In return, Russian aid was pledged for the defeat of Japan, and the Soviet government agreed to conclude a pact of friendship and alliance with the Chinese National government headed by Generalissimo Chiang Kai-shek. The task of reconciling the Chinese Nationalists to the loss of Outer Mongolia and to Russian interests in Manchuria, fell to President Roosevelt and to the United States Department of State.

The Yalta accord not only listed the gains to which Russia would be entitled after the defeat of Japan. Stalin, Churchill, and Roosevelt declared specifically that "the heads of the three great powers have agreed that these claims of the Soviet Union shall be unquestionably fulfilled after Japan has been defeated." This clause bound Britain and the United States to respect Russian expansion in the Far East and the dominant role which the Soviet government seemed destined to play there in the period after the close of World War II.

XLIV

THE EUROPEAN STATES AFTER
WORLD WAR II

*I do not think that I could in all conscience serve the nation well
. . . by presiding in impotence over an impotent state.*

CHARLES DE GAULLE (1946)

I. THE FOURTH FRENCH REPUBLIC

FRANCE emerged from the disasters and humiliations of World War II as "The Fourth French Republic." The First Republic had been proclaimed in 1792 in the midst of the great French Revolution. The Second Republic was born of the revolutionary ferment of 1848 and transformed within four years into the Second Empire under Napoleon III. The Third Republic was proclaimed in 1870 after the defeat and capture of Napoleon III by the Prussians, and it came to an end in 1940 when the German armies under Hitler were in Paris once again. The interim regime (1940–1944) of Marshal Henri Philippe Pétain, established at Vichy, collapsed when the Fighting French forces rose to aid the Anglo-American armies of liberation which invaded Normandy in June, 1944. General Charles de Gaulle, leader of the Fighting French and of the French government-in-exile, which had never acknowledged Pétain's Vichy regime, became the hero of liberated France and the temporary head of the newly proclaimed Fourth Republic.

Like all governments erected in the midst of turmoil and revolution, the provisory postwar regime of 1944–1946 was an unstable edifice. De Gaulle himself was a military man, conservative and somewhat authoritarian in temper. The underground forces which had aided in the defeat and expulsion of the Germans were often recruited and led by leftists, sometimes by communist organizers, who had tended to see the struggle against the Germans as a class struggle also and had identified (or confused) the collaborators who had aided the enemy with the "plutocrats." The political uncertainty and political divisions which weakened France under the Third Republic seemed likely to persist and weaken the Fourth Republic also. For several months after their liberation the French people disputed and voted and disputed again in their efforts to find the form of government which would divide them least. Their successive elections showed them to be split into three main political groups very nearly equal in strength. When they chose a National Constituent Assembly in October, 1945, the communists led with 151 seats, the Popular Republican Movement (liberal but anti-Marxist) came second with 150, the socialists won 139, and minor groups combined had 62. The constitution prepared by this Assembly (which was a provisory parliament as well as a constitutional convention) was submitted to the nation for a plebiscite in May, 1946. The French electors rejected it by some 10,000,000 noes against 9,000,000 yeas, the first time a proposed constitution had failed to win approval in a popular vote. In June, therefore, a new election was held to bring the Assembly into closer harmony with the will of the electorate. The results indicated a shift to the right. The Popular Republicans led with 165 seats, the communists fell to second place with 145, and the socialists dropped to 128. This reorganized Assembly then undertook to revise the constitutional draft, and the revised charter was accepted in October by 9,200,467 yeas to 7,790,676 noes, a not very enthusiastic popular majority. French women, newly granted equality before the law and the right to vote, participated in the election.

The first election under the new constitution was held on November 10, 1946. The division of parties in the resulting Legislative Assembly proved that France was still split into three dominant groups, for the communists polled about five and one-half million votes, the Popular Republican Movement slightly over five million, and the socialists three and one-half million. The Popular Republicans had lost prestige through the defection of General de Gaulle, who had retired from leadership early in 1946 as a protest against the factional strife and had denounced the constitution on the ground that it set up an impotent head over an impotent government. Despite his criticism, the new government was formed with the organization of a second chamber known as the Council of the Republic in December and the election of a president of the republic in January, 1947.

The delay in settling political problems, and the great doubt as to how far leftward France might swing if the communists and socialists should combine to dominate the government, checked economic recovery. The nation had suffered heavily during five years of war and occupation, more heavily in lives lost and property damaged than Great Britain. It was estimated that half a million French citizens had lost their lives as a result of military casualties, air raids, the ceaseless strife and reprisals of the underground warfare, and the deportation and death of Frenchmen transferred to German prison camps. The total French population in 1946 was slightly over 39,000,000, a decline of over a million from the figure for 1936. The presence of 1,670,000 foreigners helped to disguise the falling French birth rate, and the Minister of Population not only encouraged this foreign influx but offered to allow the 700,000 German war prisoners to remain permanently if they so wished. The French leaders recognized that economic recovery would be retarded by the acute man power shortage. More than 2,000,000 buildings had been wrecked and 5,000,000 people needed new or improved habitations. France had been an open battlefield not once only but twice in World War II, and the struggle of the underground forces had multiplied the damage. Throughout France there were 7000 miles of ruined roads, 2300 fallen bridges or wrecked railway passes, buried mines to locate and destroy, and 1800 towns and cities to reconstruct.

Like the British and Russian economists, the government advisers drew up a "master plan" to stimulate and co-ordinate production. This French version of the Five-Year Plan called for an increase of 25 per cent by 1950 over the levels of 1939, the year of previous maximum output. Electric power, steel, textiles, machinery, transportation facilities, and farming were all to be expanded. Government commissions set the goals and directed needed improvements in the methods of production. Since the major source of French wealth was still agriculture, plans were made to modernize the farms by introducing 50,000 tractors a year, by distributing dairy machines, and by constructing canning and refrigerating plants to preserve the crops.

The most critical issue, in France as elsewhere in Europe, was the question of collectivization or nationalization of industry. The socialists insisted that the key activities, such as coal mining, electric power production, transportation, steel refining, banking, and communication, must be nationalized at once. They claimed that such action was essential if the government were to integrate economic life, speed recovery, and raise the standards of living of the workers. The defenders of the older order and all those who favored private ownership of property and free business enterprise, declared that the attempts already made by the socialists and the communists to nationalize industry before 1939 had paralyzed production and frustrated rearmament plans, thus contributing to the débâcle of 1940. The solution of this contest, the roots of which reached deep into political, social, and economic life, could not be foretold, but the future power and prestige of France clearly depended upon the ability of the French to create a parliamentary system and a government that would be strong enough to govern.

2. LESSER STATES OF NORTHERN EUROPE

In Belgium after World War II the leading social and political factor was still the ancient rift between the Flemings and the Walloons. The French-speaking Walloons had in general a higher living standard, were better educated, and possessed the more thoroughly industrialized sections of Belgium. From them the socialist and communist parties drew their main support. The liberation of Belgium from German occupation in 1944 was followed by the restoration of the parliament of 1940 but not by the restoration of Leopold II. For although the Catholic and the more conservative groups favored the return of the legitimate king, the liberals, socialists, and communists opposed the move. The first postwar election (1946) showed a solid Fleming vote which helped the Catholic party to win almost half the seats in the senate and the assembly and appeared to forecast the victory of royalism over republicanism. The election also emphasized the rising strength of the Flemish half of the nation. With a higher birth rate, rapidly developing industries, and effective political leadership the Flemings seemed destined to escape from the inferior status hitherto accorded them.

In the first years of the postwar period the Belgians made a swift economic recovery, climbing within two years to 75 per cent of their prewar level of prosperity. Although the coalition government contained left-wing deputies with radical ideas, the policy of the cabinet as a whole was a cautious one. The promise of more prosperous times, stimulated by a proposed customs union with the Netherlands and by profitable development of the resources of the Congo, which contained half the world's known deposits of uranium, kept the working classes fairly content and reduced the communist vote to one-tenth of the total.

In the Netherlands as in Belgium political life after 1945 returned to prewar channels. Queen Wilhelmina, who had spent the war years in exile, resumed her throne. The first election (1946) gave the Catholic Party one-third of the votes as in prewar contests, and a cautious coalition government took office and began to deal conservatively with the major problems. Of these the most immediate and most critical was the revolt of the Indonesians in the Dutch East Indies. The collapse of Dutch power in 1942 and the years of Japanese domination had awakened the peoples of the islands to greater political awareness and they set up their own governments in Java and Sumatra when the Japanese capitulated in 1945. At the moment the Dutch could not quell the disorders and the help of British forces was required until the close of 1946. Peace was restored by promising the Indonesians self-rule within the framework of the Netherlands Empire. (See Chapter XLVI.)

A second problem which perplexed the Dutch was their claim against the Germans for damage caused them in the war. As compensation they asked both money payments and the cession of border territory. The new boundary line they proposed not only rectified the frontier but it gave the Dutch a better defensive line. The 120,000 German inhabitants were offered the privilege of becoming Dutch citizens or moving elsewhere. As further recompense for the $10,000,-000,000 damage claims they pressed against Germany the Dutch suggested that mining concessions in the Reich should be opened to them and they asked guarantees that Germany should be forbidden to raise discriminatory tariffs against their trade. The final settlement had to await the general treaty with Germany which was to be drawn up by the Council of Foreign Ministers.

The Kingdom of Denmark, which was overrun by German armed forces in the spring of 1940, was liberated without any serious disorder or destruction in 1945. Danish overseas colonies in Greenland and Iceland had been garrisoned and protected during the war by British or American forces. In 1944 the people of Iceland dissolved their political ties with Denmark through a referendum and proclaimed themselves an independent republic. The American garrison there was recalled in 1946 but the airfields constructed at American expense remained available for the use of the United States air force.

Norway, conquered by the Germans in 1940 after a brief but brave resistance, likewise escaped from the war with relatively light property damage. The public debt increased fivefold in the war years, but deposits in the savings banks also increased considerably. By 1946 Norway had largely recovered from the blockade. The seven million tons of merchant shipping which had ranked Norway third among the mercantile powers of the world in 1939 had been reduced to four and a half million in 1946, but Norway still ranked third in the list. Trade with Great Britain revived rapidly with peace. The British undertook to provide weapons for the Norwegian armed forces and to place the nation in a stronger state of defense. Although the population of Norway was only 3,000,000 in 1945, one-tenth of the people had emigrated, chiefly to the United States, and many thousands were almost constantly at sea. The skill and courage of Norwegian sailors, whalers, and fishermen made them known throughout the globe.

The Swedish people preserved their neutrality throughout World War II as they had done throughout World War I, but it was no easy task. The threat of a German invasion was imminent at all times and especially acute after Norway was overrun in 1940 and Germany invaded Russia in 1941. When the German hegemony was broken in 1945, it was replaced by a Russian preponderance which alarmed the Swedes almost as much. Sweden has such long and vulnerable frontiers that the limited population of 7,000,000 is insufficient to provide an army which could guard all points securely, despite the excellence of Swedish arsenals and the valor of Swedish soldiers. Adjusting themselves to the realities of the postwar world, the Swedes strove to achieve amicable relations with the Soviet Union. In 1946 the government negotiated a trade agreement with Russia, granting a loan of 1,000,000,000 kroner to promote better economic relations. This sum (equivalent to $278,000,000), which represented about 6 per cent of the Swedish national income, was expected to divert Swedish trade from the Western markets towards Russia. Provision was made for the Russians to repay the loan within fifteen years at 3 per cent interest. In general, the chance to pour goods into the Russian market was welcomed in Sweden, for with Germany bankrupt and disorganized by defeat, the steel products, precision and optical instruments, and electrical equipment in which the Swedes excel might have lacked a ready purchaser. In return Russia offered Sweden scrap iron, manganese, chromium ore, lead, anthracite, and petroleum products.

In their first election of the postwar era (July, 1945) the Swedes re-elected the Social Democratic Party to power. Per Albin Hansson, who had been prime minister almost without a break since 1932, retained his office. His phrase, "Swedish socialism is simply democracy," well suggested the moderate drift towards collectivism and nationalization of major public utilities which has distinguished Swedish politics in the twentieth century.

The defeat suffered by the Finns in their "winter war" with Russia (1939–1940) was described in an earlier chapter. (See page 466.) When the German armies swept into Russia in 1941, the Finns collaborated and temporarily regained their lost areas. But the German reverses after 1943 soon made their position desperate. Soviet troops invaded their country in 1944 and the government agreed to a truce. A treaty was negotiated through British mediation by which Russia received the Port of Petsamo on the Arctic Ocean, the right to build a naval base at Porkkala on the Gulf of Finland, and the demilitarization of the Aaland Islands at the entrance to the Gulf of Bothnia. In addition the Finns were to pay Russia a $300,000,000 indemnity. This placed them under a crushing fiscal burden, for their public debt had increased tenfold in the years of war, from 6,000,000,000 Markkaa in 1939 to over 60,000,000,000 Markkaa in 1945. The military clauses of the treaty limited their army to 34,400 men, their navy to 4500, and their air force to 3000 and 90 planes.

3. GERMANY

For several years after 1945 history seemed to have turned backward in central Europe and there was no longer "a Germany" but "the Germanies" as in the days before Bismarck. Political unity, for the time at least, had died with Hitler and the Reich was a devastated and dismembered area. In the four zones administered by the American, British, Russian, and French armies of occupation four differing methods of treatment were applied to the conquered and confused inhabitants. Despite their divergent policies, however, there were two points upon which all the military governors agreed. They wished to punish those Germans, the "war criminals," who had been particularly cruel and vicious in their days of power and they wanted to collect reparations and indemnities for the losses which the Germans had caused them in the war.

Under the Potsdam Agreement approved by President Harry S. Truman, prime minister Clement R. Attlee, and Joseph Stalin in August, 1945, German affairs were to be supervised by a Control Council of the Big Four until the Council of Foreign Ministers of the same Big Four drew up a treaty of peace. The Control Council was located at Berlin, which was divided into four zones, American, British, Russian, and French, with sentries at all boundaries and police to arrest or turn back those who attempted to cross from one zone to another without authority. Thus the German capital and Germany itself was ostentatiously subdivided and shackled, but the precaution was understandable in view of the terrifying revival of German aggression after World War I.

The public trial of twenty-two leading German war criminals opened at Nuremberg in November, 1945. In October, 1946, twelve were sentenced to death, seven to varying terms of imprisonment, and three were acquitted. The ignominious punishment meted out to these leading soldiers and statesmen of the National Socialist regime marked a new attempt to create an international court to judge crimes against peace, against humanity, and against defenseless minorities. The agreement dated August 8, 1945, whereby the American, British, and Russian governments undertook to try the war criminals was subsequently endorsed by nineteen member states of the United Nations, but the legality of the proceedings troubled many jurists. When other nations learned, however, from the carefully compiled testimony of the court, how vicious and merciless the Nazi leaders had been in the treatment of their victims, very few voices were raised against the judicial verdict or the execution of the condemned. Hermann Göring, Hitler's second in command, took poison; but eleven others, headed by the former foreign minister Joachim von Ribbentrop and by Field Marshal General Wilhelm Keitel, were hanged on October 16, 1946.

The International Military Tribunal at Nuremberg likewise condemned several National Socialist organizations, including the Elite Guard, the Leadership Corps, the Security Service, and the Gestapo (secret police) and denounced their activities as criminal. In all zones of Germany an attempt was made to identify and bring to trial, or at least to remove from office, all German officials who had been active in the National Socialist Party. The task proved arduous and exhausting. In the first year of occupation the United States military government investigated over a million suspected Nazis and convicted nearly 200,000. German courts were entrusted with part of the labor with an invitation to "clean their own house," but they moved so slowly that little progress was made. The people as a whole had no deep sense of responsibility. Although evidence continued to accumulate that between five and ten million people had been starved, beaten, and tortured to death in the concentration camps, a crime without parallel in modern times or in civilized history, the Germans appeared apathetic and made little effort to uncover the agents who had organized and directed this systematic mass murder.

In all four military zones of occupied Germany the reputable citizens were encouraged to organize political groups, study the methods of democratic self-government, and hold elections. The results indicated that the population had no great initiative and was anxious to avoid extremes. In the western zones voters supported the Christian Socialist Party and the Social Democrats, that is, they indicated a preference for sober, co-operative social reforms and frowned on radical innovations, anticlerical measures, and Marxian ideology. In the Russian zone, however, a communist-dominated group fused with the socialists and won a majority of slightly more than 50 per cent of the votes.

The most urgent question that confronted the Big Four in their administration of the occupied Reich was the economic survival of the German people. A year of experiment with four semiautonomous zones produced such confusion and paralysis that the foreign ministers of the United States, Britain, Russia, and France faced the truth that economic re-unification was essential to German recovery. The Germans could not feed themselves as a nation or produce for export unless they could combine their resources and efforts. With German production cut to less than half the 1938 total, all central Europe became a stricken area. Torn between contrary purposes, the urge to level German industries to the ground and the urge to build them up so that they could produce reparations, the victors found their greed stronger than their lust for revenge. They began to emphasize the importance of a sound German economy in a sound European economy. The need to keep Germany disarmed was reiterated, but the possibility of restoring peaceful industries was accepted and approved. By the opening of 1947 the Big Four were ready to endorse measures for greater economic production, and the period of extreme decentralization was at an end. But before the foreign ministers drafted a settlement for Germany they decided to reconstruct the satellite states.

4. EASTERN EUROPE AND THE BALKANS

The smaller states of eastern and southeastern Europe, whatever their fate had been in the war, found themselves all equally helpless in the peace. Some had been temporarily "absorbed" by Germany (Austria); some had been compelled to accept German "protection" (Czechoslovakia); some beaten down by force (Poland, Yugoslavia);

and some bribed or coerced into a German alliance (Hungary, Rumania, Bulgaria). After 1945, however, their lot depended upon their location (inside or outside the Russian sphere) rather than on their wartime allegiances. In areas occupied by the Soviet armies the inhabitants were invited to set up a provisory regime, almost always procommunist. In areas where American, British, or French forces were stationed, local governments were created on a more liberal, parliamentary model. How much real freedom the people exercised in these secondary states it was not easy to guess. But all held elections within two years of the German surrender and all set up more or less representative assemblies to negotiate with the Big Four.

In Austria, with the German influence removed, a political pattern emerged that had changed little in essentials from that of twenty years earlier. About one-fifth of the population belonged to the business, professional, or financially independent groups. The remaining four-fifths were workers or peasants. When the electors (with ex-Nazis disfranchised) chose a government in 1945, they gave the Catholic People's Party 50 per cent of the votes, the Socialist Party 44 per cent, and the communists 6 per cent. Karl Renner, a socialist, was elected President of the Second Austrian Republic, and Leopold Figl, of the Catholic People's Party, formed a cabinet drawn from all parties according to their strength in the elections. The low communist vote ranged Austria with the Western rather than with the Soviet bloc. Britain and the United States rewarded the new regime with loans and removed Austria from the ranks of ex-enemy states by declaring the Austrians a "liberated" people. It did not suit the diplomats of the Western democracies to recall too precisely in 1946 the large majority (officially 99.72 per cent) by which the Austrians had voted for union with Germany in 1938.

In Czechoslovakia the communists proved somewhat stronger than in Austria, casting 2,700,000 out of 7,000,000 ballots in the election of 1946. Although it was estimated that 60,000 victims had been executed by the Germans in Czechoslovakia, the country escaped the major horrors of war and with peace it recovered rapidly. The extreme eastern tip (Ruthenia) was transferred to the Soviet Union (Treaty of Moscow, 1945) but the remainder of Czechoslovakia was reconstituted as an independent state with Dr. Eduard Beneš as president. Lying within the zone of Russian influence the Czechs found it prudent to preserve close and friendly relations with their eastern neighbors and supported Soviet policies in the peacemaking.

Poland after World War II was a swollen state still weak from the wounds of war and the dislocation of resettlement plans and territorial transfers. The Russian advance pushed the frontiers more than a hundred miles westward. The Poles received half of East Prussia, Silesia, and most of Pomerania, and proceeded to expel the German population from the annexed lands. No stable or permanent state seemed likely to evolve from the geographical and ethnological contradictions implicit in the Polish conquests. It was evident that Poland would exist in the future, as in the recent past, through German or Russian "protection" or as a buffer state which both these powers arranged to tolerate or to divide.

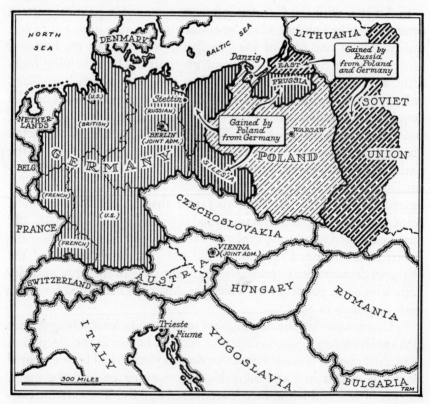

GERMANY AND POLAND, 1945

The Austrians cast their lot with the Western democracies after World War II but the Hungarians were divided between east and west, between communism and capitalism. After World War I they had known a brief attempt at Red rule under a communist leader, Bela Kun, and they had recoiled from the memory for twenty years. But in 1944 Russian communist armies liberated them from German domination, and exiled Hungarian communists hastened home to help organize a new regime at Budapest. In the first postwar election the Communist Party polled 17 per cent of the votes, but the Smallholders Party, a moderate group, came out well ahead and formed a coalition cabinet. Hungarian credit had been ruined by defeat, and the government battled for a year to control a wild inflationary trend. The moderate groups, represented by the Smallholders Party, were out-maneuvered in June, 1947, and a swift *coup* by the leftist minority transformed Hungary into a communist state in close alliance with Soviet Russia. The peace terms drafted by the Council of Foreign Ministers for Hungary set the indemnity to Russia at $200,000,000 with an additional $50,000,000 to Czechoslovakia and Yugoslavia. The military provisions of the treaty limited the Hungarian army to 65,000 men, prohibited a navy, and permitted only ninety aircraft with an Air Force personnel of 5000 or less.

Rumania likewise was reduced to military impotence by the treaty restrictions proposed by the Big Four. An army of 125,000, a navy with a personnel of 5000, and an air force of 150 planes and 8000 officers and men was a minimal allowance for a nation of 17,000,000 people. The Rumanians were ordered to pay $300,000,000 in reparations to the Soviet Union, to which they ceded all Bessarabia and northern Bukovina. They also ceded southern Dobruja on the Black Sea coast to Bulgaria, but these losses were made up in part by the acquisition of Transylvania from Hungary. In their politics the Rumanians swung towards communism after 1945, and the National Democratic Front led by Peter Groza won 348 of the 414 seats in the assembly. This was a triumph for the communists. There were immediate charges that the election had not been free or honest; and the position of the twenty-five year old king, Michael I, was rendered increasingly difficult.

Bulgaria, like Rumania a defeated state, received similar punishment from the Big Four. The Bulgarian army was limited to 55,000 men, the navy to 3500, and the air force to 5200 men and 90 planes. Bulgaria retained the southern Dobruja, as noted above, but was ordered to pay $25,000,000 to Yugoslavia and $45,000,000 to Greece. A referendum banished the young king, Simeon II; and Georgi Dimitrov, head of the Bulgarian Communist Party, became premier in 1946. The communist triumph appeared to be complete, with 90 per cent of the electorate supporting this party.

In Yugoslavia also the communists won 90 per cent of the votes and the regime of Marshal Tito (Josip Broz) was firmly established. The Yugoslavs were fiercely indignant over the Big Four settlement which made Trieste a free port under the protection of the Security Council of the United Nations. Although Great Britain and the United States recognized the Yugoslav government of Marshal Tito (1945), which had driven King Peter II from the throne, relations between Yugoslavia and the Western democracies remained unsatisfactory. The cession of the territory known as Venezia Giulia and some islands in the Adriatic, which Italy transferred to Yugoslavia, failed to satisfy Yugoslav ambitions.

5. ITALY AND THE IBERIAN PENINSULA

The status of Italy in World War II was highly complicated. As an ally of Germany, Italy attacked France, Greece, and Yugoslavia and sent the Germans aid on the Russian front, losing 60,000 men in these Axis ventures. After Mussolini fell from power, Italy became a "co-belligerent" of the United Nations and lost 17,000 men fighting against the Germans. The confusion of this tragic war record, the loss of the empire in Africa, and the uncertainty regarding the terms that would be accorded by the Big Four left the Italian people resentful and disillusioned after 1945. Amid the clash of rival political parties and the trial of Fascist "criminals," the Italians voted to abolish the monarchy, banished King Victor Emmanuel III, and set up a republic (1946). A coalition cabinet under premier Alcide de Gasperi sought to restore peace and restrain the communists who obtained almost one-fifth of the popular vote in national and communal elections.

Italian losses in World War II were, territorially, the heaviest of any belligerent. In Europe there was a slight rectification of the Franco-Italian frontier above Nice which gave Briga and Tenda to France. Venezia Giulia, as noted already, was given to Yugoslavia, and Trieste became a free territory. These areas were small, however, compared to Italian losses overseas. The Dodecanese Islands were restored to Greece, and the Italian African Empire, over 1,200,000 square miles in extent in 1939, was forfeited. Libya, Eritrea, Italian Somaliland, and Ethiopia were not returned despite Italian pleas; and Albania which the Italian forces occupied in 1939, was also lost to them.

In drawing up peace terms for Italy the Big Four showed scant mercy. The naval, military, and air clauses ordered that the army be cut to 250,000 men, the navy to 22,500, and the air force to 25,000.

Several areas in Italy, and Sicily, Sardinia, and other Mediterranean bases were to be demilitarized as well as the frontiers with France and Yugoslavia. Although the British and Americans suggested that Italy be spared the payment of any financial indemnity, Russian claims for $100,000,000, Yugoslav claims for $125,000,000, and Greek claims for $105,000,000 were pressed despite the parlous state of Italian economy. A harsh clause in the treaty (Article 69) provided that the Allied powers might seize property of the Italian state or Italian citizens lying within the territory of such powers if the reparations claims were not met. Italy, on the other hand, had to renounce all claims against the Allies and surrendered all rights in Albania, Ethiopia, and China. These terms in their totality were less severe than the conditions of the armistice under which the Italians surrendered to the United Nations in 1943, for the armistice required total disarmament, occupation of all Italian territory, and full costs for such occupation. Nevertheless, the Italian people were convinced in 1946 as they had been in 1919 that they had been dealt with unjustly. There could be little doubt that as Italy recovered from the trauma of war an ache for vindication and a patriotic urge to revise the treaty of 1946 would burn in Italian hearts.

For the people of Spain and Portugal, who preserved their neutrality successfully, World War II brought economic gains. The Portuguese leaned towards Great Britain, honoring an alliance of the two states which had lasted from the seventeenth century. At the same time, however, the Portuguese maintained commercial and diplomatic relations with Germany, disregarding German protests when the British and Americans used the Azores as an air and naval base in hunting U-boats. The government at Lisbon was authoritarian in spirit and was based upon a republican constitution (*Estado novo*) adopted in 1933. A general election held after the end of the war (1945) confirmed the rule of the National Union Party headed by the premier, Dr. Antonio de Oliveira Salazar. But the curtailment of the war trade boom meant a reduction in profits for the Portuguese, and their living standards, low at the best of times, suffered a decline.

In Spain the government of General Francisco Franco faced a critical and hostile world after Germany and Italy were defeated. Franco had overthrown the Spanish Republic and fought his way to power (1936–1939) with the aid of arms and reinforcements supplied by Mussolini and Hitler. The Russians, who had sought to strengthen the ill-fated Spanish Republican government, demanded in 1945 that

Franco should be forced to abdicate. When demands for his removal were laid before the United Nations Assembly, he liberated some of the thousands of Republican prisoners still in Spanish jails and invited exiled Republicans to return under an amnesty. The Assembly resolved that member states be urged to recall their diplomatic representatives from Madrid, but any active intervention in Spanish affairs was not easy to execute. It seemed best to allow the Spaniards time in which to reconstruct their own government. There was no doubt that millions of them were stirred by grievances against the Franco regime, by memories of the reprisals and brutalities of the civil war, by resentment against the arrogance of the army, and by the pressure of hunger and postwar economic depression. But they were also haunted by memories of the fratricidal strife which Franco's victory had terminated and they were fearful that his overthrow might bring a new struggle between the communist and conservative parties in Spain.

This inclination to let the dead past bury its dead, this craving not merely for a political amnesty but for a political amnesia that would cancel past hates and penalties and the poison of revenge, was common to millions of European people after 1945. The issues, the ideologies, the promises of the war years had all been tarnished. Save for Britain and Russia all the European nations were losers, all had wrongs to forget, and all had political groups which had backed the Axis and feared reprisals. This fact helps to explain the lack of idealism and initiative, the indifference to democracy and authoritarianism as programs, and the willingness to accept almost any political party that seemed to promise a strong majority and a strong government. For the moment imperial conquests had lost their lure, even progress seemed a myth, and most Europeans were glad to cultivate their gardens if they could find any to cultivate.

THE MEDITERRANEAN AREA AND
THE NEAR EAST

The Governments of the United States of America, the Union of Soviet Socialist Republics, and the United Kingdom are at one with the Government of Iran in their desire for the maintenance of the independence, sovereignty, and territorial integrity of Iran.

TEHRAN CONFERENCE (1943)

I. GREECE, TURKEY, AND IRAN

THE lands lying between the Mediterranean Sea and the Indian Ocean seem fated to remain a troubled region in the twentieth century. This fact was already foreshadowed at the opening of the period. German plans to complete a railway line from Berlin to Bagdad had then excited British, French, and Russian business leaders to protest, and the fear that this railway would prove a spearhead for German imperial conquest helped bring on the First World War. Arabia, long regarded as economically sterile, became a focus of world attention when engineers discovered that the Persian Gulf was the center of one of the richest petroleum fields of the globe. A race to win concessions from Iraq, Iran, and the Arabian emirs followed, with the British and French leading. The defeat and dismemberment of Turkey in World War I left Britain and France predominant in the Near East after 1918 and for several years their monopoly was not seriously challenged. But the revival of Russian expansion under Soviet direction made it inevitable that the Russians would resume their historic drive to the south and would seek more influence over the Dardanelles, the Persian Gulf, and possibly the Red Sea coast and North Africa. This Russian pressure became stronger after 1945. Finally, the United States also became a power in Near Eastern affairs after 1945, for American businessmen had secured rich oil concessions in the Persian Gulf area. Thus all the Big Four powers were competitors in this politically backward and economically undeveloped region.

The condition of Greece in the twentieth century made that country a factor of the Near Eastern problem although geographically Greece was part of Europe. Its political status, like that of Turkey, Iran, and Egypt, was a matter of grave international concern because the great power which could use the Greek ports and islands as bases could seal the exits of the Adriatic and the Black Seas. This fact must be kept in mind, for it is the key to the undercover struggle which Britain and Russia waged after 1945 to control the Greek government. The Communist Party in Greece was discredited, British troops remained in the peninsula to repress the communist guerrillas, and an election (1946) indicated a monarchist majority. The king of the Hellenes, George II, returned to Athens, and a royalist government headed by Constantine Tsaldaris as premier restored order with some severity. In 1947 George II died and was succeeded by his brother Paul.

To strengthen the monarchy and make it more popular with the people, Great Britain extended a loan of $50,000,000 and secured for Greece the restoration of the Dodecanese Islands, which had been held by the Italians since 1912. The British were anxious to assure stability under the monarchy because Greece was the only country left in the Balkan peninsula which was not ruled by a communist government after 1945. British investors had a further reason to fear a communist triumph for it might be followed by a repudiation of the public debt, 70 per cent of which was held by foreigners. When Britain found the cost of supporting Greece too heavy, the United States Congress adopted an Act (May, 1947) to extend up to $400,000,000 aid to Greece and Turkey.

The Turkish Republic, like the Greek monarchy, could not stand alone against Russian pressure after World War II. Although the Turks maintained their neutrality successfully during the six years of armed struggle they found the Russian advance into the Balkans in 1945 and 1946 as grave a threat as the German drives of 1940 to 1944. To apply pressure, the Russians interfered with Turkish trade in the Black Sea and the Danubian countries. This trade loss and the burden of keeping large military forces in constant readiness forced the Turks to turn to Britain and the United States for aid, and not in vain. Unofficial hints from Russian sources had informed the Turks that the pressure would cease if Turkey ceded Kars and Ardahan, including an

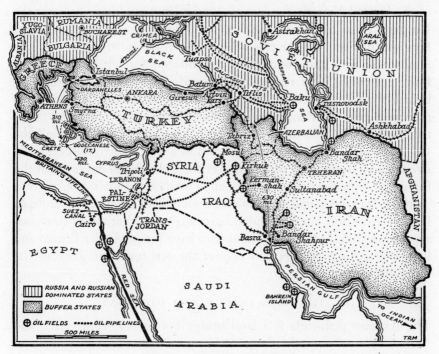

GREECE, TURKEY, AND IRAN

undefined segment of northeast Turkey, and permitted a joint Russo-Turkish fortification of the Dardanelles. But Britain and the United States advised the Turkish government to refuse. Great Britain had already advanced over $100,000,000 to the Turks during the war to strengthen their defenses and promised further credits. The United States granted Turkey a loan (1946) of $25,000,000 for the development of railways and the purchase of machinery. In 1947, the Turks became eligible for further aid from the United States under the Act to provide Assistance for Greece and Turkey. Warned by this stiffening of the Anglo-American attitude, the Russians did not press their demands too heavily but the situation remained delicate.

To the east of Turkey, the pressure of Russian expansion disrupted Iran. Mastery of the oil wells and ports on the Persian Gulf would have been highly profitable to the Soviet planners who were drafting the new Five-Year Plan of 1946. A revolt in the northern province of Azerbaijan provided an excuse for Soviet forces to intervene, or rather to remain, for Iran had been under American, British, and Russian protection during the war. The government appealed to the Assembly of the United Nations, for loss of Azerbaijan would have brought the Russians close to Tehran and severed direct connections between Iran and Turkey. At the end of 1946 the Russians suddenly adopted a more cautious and conciliatory attitude on foreign issues and the Iranian incident was temporarily closed. The "rebel" regime collapsed, the leaders fled to Russia, and the Iranian government forces reoccupied the Azerbaijan region. Thus a wall of resistance was maintained from Albania to the border of Afghanistan to "contain" the weight of Soviet pressure southwards. But a wall or dam is likely to be swept away if any part of it is breached, and it is strongest when the forces on opposing sides are equal. To preserve their sovereignty, Turkey, Iran, Iraq, and Afghanistan concluded an Eastern (Saadbad) Pact in 1937 and later extended it to 1948. In addition to this non-aggression pact, both Turkey and Iran have the pledge of Britain and Russia that these powers will respect the territorial integrity of the two buffer states.

2. THE ARAB LEAGUE AND PALESTINE

The Arabian peninsula is a land bridge between Europe, Asia, and Africa. Famous since the dawn of history for its cities, its trade, and its caravan routes, Arabia and its fringes have cradled a score of empires in the past five thousand years. Its modern history, however, has been less impressive than its past. Only in recent years have the Arab peoples awakened to a realization of their unity of interests and undertaken to explore and exploit the full natural resources of their homeland for themselves. Like other peoples whose development had been delayed, they found that they must learn the new techniques and acquire the machinery which extracts treasure from the earth, for the alternative which faced them was to become the economic vassals of more aggressive nations.

After the dismemberment of the Turkish Empire in 1918 the liberated Arabs began to organize a Pan-Arab League which came into formal existence in 1944. This new federation included seven independent states of the Near East, Egypt, Syria, Lebanon, Iraq, Transjordan, Saudi Arabia, and Yemen. The total area of these states exceeded 1,000,000 square miles and the total population (exact figures are unobtainable) probably reached 35,000,000. It was obvious that if these seven governments could concert their strength and develop their combined resources, they might build a powerful Arab Empire in the Near East.

Among the resources of these lands the natural oil deposits rapidly became the most important asset in the twentieth century. The quadrilateral formed by the Red Sea, the Black Sea, the Caspian Sea, and the Persian Gulf is the second richest oil-producing area of the world. Its annual output of 300,000,000 barrels was increased during World War II and the untapped reserves, placed at more than 10,000,000,000 barrels, make it a prize of first importance. All the great powers competed for concessions and by 1945 the area had been roughly divided into four zones. The Russians monopolized northern Iran. The British held a thousand-mile strip along the north shore of the Persian Gulf and beyond to the environs of Bagdad. United States oil companies obtained options to most of the interior realm of Saudi Arabia. The remaining, peripheral territory — Iraq, Syria, Transjordan, the Red Sea littoral, Aden, and Yemen — were exploited individually or jointly by British, American, French, and Dutch interests. Britain and the United States, however, were the dominant powers, and the oil pipelines which carried the liquid freight from Kirkuk to Tripoli and Haifa, from the Persian wells to Basra and Abadan, and from Saudi Arabia to the Syrian ports, were as vital as railway lines and equally vulnerable. Good relations with the local governments were not always easy to maintain, for the tribesmen were fierce and independent. To win the assistance of King ibn-Saud of Saudi Arabia, the United States advanced his government a loan of $10,000,000 in 1946. By that year American companies in Saudi Arabia were already producing 200,000 barrels a day, one-fourth of which was set aside for the United States navy. The United States army was permitted to maintain an important airport at Dhahran.

The rise of ibn-Saud was closely joined to Arab nationalism in the Near East. Formerly the various tribes and emirates had exhausted their fighting energies in local raids and ancestral feuds, but in 1930 a century-old quarrel between the Arab dynasties of Hejaz and Iraq was settled and in 1932 the kingdoms of Hejaz and Nejd were combined. The outstanding leader in this labor of union and consolidation was the Sultan of Nejd, Abdul-Aziz ibn-Saud, who took the title (1932) of King of Saudi Arabia. In 1938 ibn-Saud granted extensive oil concessions to the Standard Oil Company of California and, while preserving friendly relations with the British, he turned increasingly towards the United States for financial aid, for professional advice in modernizing his realm, and for mechanical equipment. His success in maintaining order, guarding the Mohammedan pilgrims on their visits

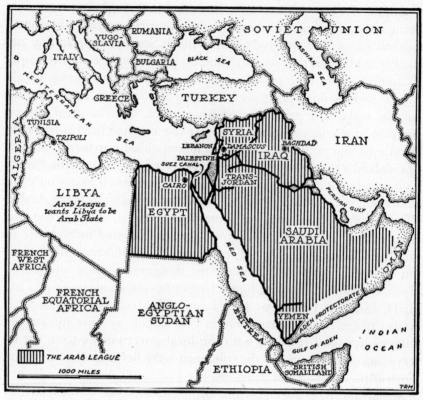

THE ARAB LEAGUE

to Mecca, and curbing his quarrelsome subjects, won high praise. But many Arabs resented the foreigners who drew treasures in oil from beneath the Arabian sands; and the introduction of new ways of life, new machinery, new standards of diet, sanitation, clothing, and housing produced jealousies and armed clashes. The automobile was replacing the camel, straight roads cut across the deserts where the Bedouin once roamed as free as the wind, and the tribesmen wedded to the old ways rebelled against the change.

This rebellion was particularly strong and particularly tragic in Palestine. The "national home for the Jewish people" established there after World War I in accordance with the Balfour Declaration (1917), had grown by 1946 to a state of 10,429 square miles (almost equal to Maryland) with a population approaching two million. The frightful persecution and systematic extermination to which the Jews of Europe were exposed under Axis rule made their desire for a national homeland and place of refuge more urgent than ever. But unhappily the Arab population of Palestine, which numbered over a million in 1946, was not reconciled to the admission of Jewish immigrants. Before 1918 the Arabs had formed almost nine-tenths of the Palestinian population but as the ratio thereafter dropped steadily, the Arabs accused the British of dispossessing them in favor of the incoming Jews. Since Palestine was a British mandate under the League of Nations, the British had to meet criticism from Jews and Arabs alike.

The Balfour Declaration, issued in the year when British and Arab forces liberated Palestine from Turkish rule in the First World War (1917) affirmed that

> His Majesty's Government view with favor the establishment in Palestine of a national home for the Jewish people, and will use their best endeavours to facilitate the achievement of that object, it being clearly understood that nothing shall be done which may prejudice the civil and religious rights of existing non-Jewish communities in Palestine or the rights and political status enjoyed by Jews in any other country.

By 1939, when the influx of Jewish settlers had raised the Jewish population of Palestine from 50,000 to 500,000 (a tenfold increase) in the short space of twenty years, the British government leaders argued that Britain had fulfilled the Declaration. Further entry of Jews was to be firmly restricted by a quota system. This restrictive policy was denounced by the Zionist leaders, who hoped to develop a powerful Jewish state, as a betrayal by the British. But the Arabs were growing alarmed at the rapid expansion of Jewish settlements and declared in their turn that the "civil and religious rights of existing non-Jewish communities in Palestine" had been violated and the Moslem population was in danger of becoming a religious minority in a Jewish state or of abandoning their possessions and emigrating. These conflicting claims made the Palestine question a problem of world concern after 1945.

In Europe and America the sufferings of the Jewish minorities in the countries subjected by the Germans excited profound sympathy for these persecuted peoples. It seemed just that they should have a national homeland. In 1946 President Truman of the United States urged that 100,000 Jewish refugees be admitted to Palestine immediately. The steady objection of the British government to Jewish immigration was little understood; and the repeated acts of terrorism perpetrated by ardent Zionists in Palestine, as protests against the British policy, cost many lives. But the British were looking beyond the moment and beyond the isolated question of Palestine itself. They were aware that the entire Mohammedan world was awakening to sympathy for the Arabs of Palestine, and Great Britain, with 100,000,000 Mohammedans within the empire, could not rashly invite a holy war.

In 1947 the British government announced its intention to withdraw from Palestine and leave to the United Nations the problem of finding and imposing a solution of the Arab-Zionist feud. Projects for the division of Palestine into Jewish and Arab states were accepted with reservations by the Jewish leaders but repudiated by the representatives of the Arab League. A United Nations Special Committee on Palestine heard protests from the Arab Higher Committee for Palestine and the Jewish Agency for Palestine, and the spirit of these protests made it plain that no solution acceptable to both parties could be anticipated. The dilemma facing the United Nations posed a clear test of its authority, for if it adopted the program of its Special Committee, and the Arabs, the Jews, or both, resisted the proposed settlement, the United Nations Security Council would have to enforce the settlement. Failure to do so would advertise its impotence before the world.

3. THE MEDITERRANEAN SHORES

World War II left the status of the entire Mediterranean area in doubt. France was weakened, Italy disarmed. From Spain to Syria and Egypt to Morocco the nations knew that their destiny was likely to be determined by three powers which stood outside the Mediterranean world altogether, by Great Britain, Russia, and the United States of America. As Russia lacked a powerful navy for distant ventures, and the United States had never played a leading part in the affairs of the Old World, the Mediterranean seemed very largely a British sphere after 1945.

The Italian colonial empire in Africa remained in British possession after the fighting ceased and would form a logical trusteeship for that power under the United Nations. Though British forces were withdrawing from Egypt, they remained strongly posted in adjoining areas, in Palestine and Transjordan, at Tobruk and Benghazi in Libya, and at the key points, Aden, Suez, and Gibraltar. These bases appeared to assure continued British supremacy in the Mediterranean. It would not, however, prove an uncontested supremacy. For American naval forces continued to move about the area, and the American army retained the use of airfields at Tripoli, Cairo, Dhahran, and Karachi, indicating that American air fleets would continue to fly the course across North Africa to the Persian Gulf and on to India, China, and the Philippines. The United States merchant marine likewise had invaded the Mediterranean in force, and American ships were assuming a larger share of cargo-carrying on the inland sea. This was important for future relations between the United States and Mediterranean countries.

The French colonial dominions on the Mediterranean shores changed their status during World War II. Inevitably, the German occupation of France and the humiliating role of the Vichy regime of Marshal Pétain weakened the ties of empire, and secession or revolt threatened all parts of the French overseas domain. The fate of French Indo-China is discussed in the following chapter. In Asia Minor the states of Syria and Lebanon, which had been French mandates since 1920, were granted independence by the French National Committee of Liberation (the Free French) in a decree that took effect January 1, 1944. In Algeria the landing of Allied (Anglo-American and Free French) forces in November, 1942, opened a new period of mixed military control. Although Algeria remains a part of the French Empire, the population of about 8,000,000 has agitated for greater independence and self-rule. For northern Algeria the French created three *départements* with the administration on French lines in some communes and limited rights of citizenship in the *communes mixtes* where the natives predominated. The territories of southern Algeria remained a separate colony under military command. The government of Tunis differed from that of Algiers; the Bey (the hereditary ruler) retained his throne when Tunis became a French protectorate after 1881, and the administration was directed from the French Foreign Office.

Morocco, the third French-controlled province of North Africa, is technically an independent sultanate. It is divided into three zones, the French (153,870 square miles), the Spanish (18,009 square miles), and the Tangier (225 square miles). The total population is about 8,000,000, of which 7,000,000 live in the French zone. The native people are predominantly Moslem and largely illiterate; but there are about 300,000 Europeans and 175,000 native Jews. The government is theoretically an absolute monarchy but the real control is exercised by the protecting powers. The Resident-General for the French zone directs an elaborate bureaucratic administration from Rabat. In the Spanish zone a High Commissioner at Tetuan exercises authority in the name of the sultan. The Tangier zone is under the protection of the powers which signed the Convention of Algeciras (1906), and their consuls-general, as a Committee of Control, watch over the local administration.

The emergence of Egypt as an independent kingdom has set a pattern for other North African states. In 1936 an Anglo-Egyptian Treaty of Alliance confirmed the independent status of Egypt which the British had recognized in 1922. All British forces are to be withdrawn from the kingdom but the status of the Anglo-Egyptian Sudan remains in question. The Egyptian government has recognized the special interest of Great Britain in the defense of the Suez Canal, and a force of 10,000 British troops and 400 airmen are to guard the canal zone until the Egyptian army can guarantee adequate defense. A British military mission advises the Egyptian general staff on armaments. The government is parliamentary, with a Chamber of Deputies elected by universal male suffrage and a Senate of 147 members, three-fifths of whom are elected and two-fifths appointed by the king. The monarchy is hereditary, the executive power exercised by a Council of Ministers appointed by the king but responsible to the parliament. Until the Egyptian government brings the law courts up to European standards foreigners are protected by trial in "mixed courts" and are guaranteed against fiscal discrimination.

XLVI

ASIA

The three Foreign Secretaries exchanged views with regard to the situation in China. . . . They affirmed their adherence to the policy of non-interference in the internal affairs of China.

STATEMENT ISSUED BY BYRNES, BEVIN,
AND MOLOTOV AT MOSCOW, DECEMBER 27, 1945

1. INDIA, BURMA, AND MALAYA

FOR the billion inhabitants of South and East Asia, World War II had significant consequences. The most important events of the war and postwar years were first, the temporary defeat of the European forces (British, French, Dutch, Portuguese, and American) and the substitution of Japanese imperialism over a great part of East Asia and the East Indies; second, the collapse of the Japanese Empire and the return of European and American armed forces; and third, the compromises worked out between the European governments and the various Asiatic peoples eager for complete self-rule.

To most Europeans the swiftness and completeness of the Japanese defeat in 1945 obscured the fact that the Japanese conquest of East Asian lands had not always proved unwelcome to the local inhabitants. Where resentment against the Europeans was strong, the Japanese posed as "liberators" and were sometimes accepted as such. With Japan in eclipse after 1945, the Easterners, who must bow to power, found it convenient to disavow their collaboration and accept the return of European hegemony. But the Japanese, who had hitherto defied that hegemony and were now the chief victims of it, were merged by that very denouement in the common destiny of the Asiatics. The broadcast in which Emperor Hirohito of Japan announced the Japanese surrender (August 14, 1945) contained a message to all the peoples of East Asia who had supported the Japanese cause. "We cannot but express the deepest sense of regret," Hirohito concluded, "to our allied Nations of East Asia, who have consistently co-operated with the [Japanese] Empire towards the emancipation of East Asia." As the last free expression of the emperor before he became subordinate to the Supreme Allied Commander and the occupation forces, this broadcast had deeper meaning for the peoples of the East than for the nations of the West.

For the population of India political independence was already in sight before World War II and they made no move to help the Japanese "liberate" Asia. The chief hindrance to the creation of an independent national government for all India was the persistent Hindu-Moslem feud. In 1946 a Central Legislative Assembly was convened, to administer Indian affairs while a Constituent Assembly drafted a constitution. The Constituent Assembly was to consist entirely of Indian jurists (except for the British Governor-General) and was to represent the leading political groups of India according to their strength in the popular elections. All the Indian states were likewise invited to share in the work of constitution making, and if the rulers chose, these states could be included in the proposed Union of All India.

The alternative to an All-India Union was almost certainly a civil war. Rioting and bloodshed spread dangerously in the summer of 1946 and over 5000 people were killed in a few months. Most of the outbreaks sprang from religious hostility. The Mohammedan minority was so distrustful that their leader, Mohammed Ali Jinnah, at first hesitated to accept the five seats on the Governor-General's Council which the Viceroy, Viscount Wavell, offered his party. Progress towards Indian self-government could not be hastened under such conditions, for until the leaders proved that they could assure peace and order and restrain the fanaticism of their followers, the British hesitated to resign their authority. To withdraw before an effective administration was well established and working harmoniously, might plunge 400,000,000 people into a gruesome civil conflict.

By February, 1947, however, the British Labor cabinet was prepared to take this risk. The prime minister, Clement R. Attlee, announced that Great Britain would hand over all power in India to the Indians the following June, and that Rear Admiral Viscount Mountbatten would replace Viscount Wavell as viceroy to complete the transference of authority. When June arrived, the British offered a final plan which left to the Indians themselves the task of deciding whether they would create a united nation or not. Areas in the northwest and northeast, where Mohammedans predominated, might become a separate state with a separate congress (Pakistan); the provinces of British India outside Pakistan might form a second state (Hindustan); and the independent realms of the Indian princes might decide their own future status. With this proposal the British laid down their burden of empire in India and renounced political responsibility for the fate of more than 400,000,000 people. How the new India would organize itself, avoid civil war, and defend its interests in a war-haunted age the future would reveal.

India had suffered no invasion or severe losses in World War II and the opportunity to supply war materials to the United Nations stimulated industry. Far different was the fate of Burma, the scene of two land campaigns, much scattered jungle fighting, and three years of air war. Railways, bridges, and towns were shattered, rice fields ruined, river craft destroyed, cattle slaughtered. The social demoralization which came with war and the Japanese occupation set the Burmese back a generation. Schools closed, banditry increased, trade died. The Burmese had formerly subsisted by exporting timber, rice, and oil, chiefly to India, and the collapse of their foreign commerce during the years of Japanese occupation left them bankrupt. Without foreign capital and equipment Burmese economy could not recover readily. The British government, therefore, outlined a program of political and financial reconstruction.

As a first step in the rehabilitation of Burma the British Governor appointed a small Executive Council and a larger advisory Legislative Council of fifty members (1945). Self-government had been promised the Burmans since 1935 and was to go into effect as soon as a representative Constituent Assembly completed a constitution. One uncertain problem was the disposition of more than thirty Shan states, which had been part of the Burmese kingdom originally but had been administered since 1922 by their own chiefs under British commissioners. As soon as the Burman legislators showed that they could govern the country firmly, pacify the more primitive mountain peoples of the highlands, and restore the shattered economy, Burma was to take its place as a self-governing Dominion within the British Commonwealth. Its economic connection with India remained close, for Indian bankers owned one-third of the rice fields and India absorbed three-fourths of the foreign trade.

The future political status of Malaya was announced by the British in 1945. The nine states of the peninsula together with the settlements of Penang and Malacca were joined to form the constitutional

Union of Malaya. Singapore, the great British naval base which the
Japanese had captured in 1942, remained a separate British colony.
Each state in the new Union retained its existing government with an
advisory council and a British resident to assist the local ruler. But for
the Malayan Union as a whole the British government appointed a
Governor-General and a Commander-in-Chief, and also a Governor
and a Commander-in-Chief for the colony of Singapore.

2. THE EAST INDIES AND INDO-CHINA

When the Japanese resistance collapsed in 1945 the peoples of the
Netherlands East Indies set up independent regimes in Java, Sumatra,
Borneo, and the Celebes, demanding recognition for their newly proclaimed "Indonesian Republic." This movement of revolt, though it
was described as "nationalism," was in reality a mood rather than a
movement, a defiant resentment against the rule of Europeans in the
East. If the uprisings in the Dutch possessions had spread widely and
the Indonesians there had resisted all attempts of the Netherlands
government to re-establish control after the Japanese surrender, the
whole of East Asia might have become involved in the rebellion.
Netherlands forces were insufficient to deal with the outbreaks in
1945 and British troops were called on to protect Europeans and their
property in the islands affected. The Celebes and Dutch Borneo were
easily reconquered but in Java and Sumatra the Indonesians had taken
over the civil and military administration. They held hundreds of
Europeans as hostages and established a "republican cabinet" with Dr.
Soekarno as president and Dr. Sutan Sjahrir as premier.

The possession of arms surrendered by the Japanese gave the Indonesian insurgents a temporary advantage but they could not hope to
hold out long unless they won the assistance of Russia or some other
great power, and this they failed to do. Without shipping or machinery they were unable to restore the oil industry on which the
prosperity of Sumatra largely depended and they could not even
maintain effective communication among the islands of their "republic" which stretch for 3000 miles along the equator. With British mediation, therefore, a compromise was worked out and the
Netherlands forces returned to police the islands at the close of
1946. All British forces, which had reached 92,000 men, were withdrawn.

The compromise which restored an uneasy peace in Indonesia met

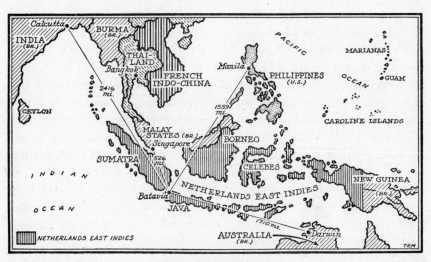

THE EAST INDIES

the demands of the insurgent leaders half-way. The Indonesian Republic was to remain subject to the House of Orange and to acknowledge Queen Wilhelmina as sovereign. It was to comprise Java, Sumatra, and the smaller island of Madura, which together contained almost three-fourths of the population. Recognition of this republic, however, was to be only the first step in a general program to create a United States of Indonesia. Netherlands Borneo and New Guinea, Bali, the Celebes, the Moluccas, and the Lesser Sundas were to be linked in a federal alliance, and an amendment to the Constitution of the Netherlands would then be adopted to permit an alliance of the United States of Indonesia with the Kingdom of the Netherlands. This solution, which prefigured an empire of independent co-equal Dominions united by loyalty to the Crown, seemed a replica of the British Commonwealth of Nations. It was clear, however, that the Netherlands East Indies were a complex society and that many years might be required to adjust relationships between Europeans and Asiatics. The legal and economic rights of European investors and colonists in the East provided one thorny issue. In the Union the problems of defense, foreign affairs, currency, and economic policy were to be debated by joint commissions acting under the authority of the Crown. Until the formal establishment of the Union, Dutch and Indonesian officials were to labor side by side to seek a just and workable compromise on all disputed relations. Civil war or sharp business crises would threaten the prosperity of the islands and harm all parties with benefit to none.

The French in Indo-China, like the Dutch in Indonesia, faced a revolt when they moved back after the Japanese defeat. They sought to overcome the discontent by a show of military force and a few concessions. But the nationalist movement had grown steadily from 1941 to 1945, and the Annamese proclaimed their complete independence as the Viet-Nam Republic. In 1946 an accord was drawn up whereby the French government recognized the Viet-Nam Republic, composed of the provinces of Tonking and Annam, as an autonomous unit in the Federation of Indo-China. But the relationship of the new republic to the areas (Laos, Cambodia, and Cochin-China) which were still under French rule was not clearly defined and fighting broke out again in December, 1946. The issue was not an affair of colonial politics alone; the settlement in Indo-China was certain to be influenced by the rifts in France itself. The French communists favored generous terms for the insurgents in the colonies, while the moderates and rightists urged a firm policy of repression. This divergence between left and right on the question of imperialist rule was common to almost all European countries.

The Kingdom of Thailand (Siam), which had become an ally of Japan during the Second World War, made peace with Britain and India at the opening of 1946. Territory which had been annexed with Japanese aid from the British Malay States and from French Indo-China was restored. Siam was then admitted to the United Nations as an independent state.

3. CHINA

In 1946 the National (Kuomintang) government of the Chinese Republic moved from its wartime capital at Chungking to the permanent capital at Nanking. China had survived eight years and more of war with Japan, the invaders had penetrated thirteen provinces and occupied the four largest cities, but in 1945 all Japanese forces laid down their arms. The National government, headed by Generalissimo Chiang Kai-shek, was strengthened by victory and by the formal recognition of Chinese independence. The special privileges and extraterritorial rights which the powers had extorted from China in earlier years were canceled as recognition that China was now fully autonomous. Between 1942 and 1946 the United States, Great

Britain, Russia, the Netherlands, Belgium, and France concluded treaties which acknowledged the national sovereignty of the Chinese people.

On the day the Japanese capitulation was announced (August 14, 1945) the Chinese government concluded a treaty of friendship and alliance with the Soviet Union. The Soviet government promised that it would not interfere in the internal affairs of China, agreed that Manchuria should be restored to Chinese sovereignty, and offered moral support and material assistance in the rehabilitation of China. In return, China recognized the independence of Outer Mongolia, agreed that the Chinese Eastern and the South Manchurian Railway should be jointly owned and operated by the Chinese and Russian governments, and consented to joint use by both governments of the naval base at Port Arthur.

This Russo-Chinese treaty had been foreshadowed six months earlier in the Yalta Agreement concluded by President Roosevelt, prime minister Churchill, and Marshal Stalin. (See page 619.) Although the terms were not revealed for a year, this accord provided that Russia would enter the war against Japan with the guarantee that after victory Outer Mongolia would retain its independent status, Russian rights surrendered to Japan in 1905 would be restored, the southern half of Sakhalin Island would be returned to Russian sovereignty, the port of Dairen would be internationalized, Port Arthur would be reopened to Russia as a naval base, and the Chinese Eastern and the South Manchurian Railways would be operated jointly by Soviet-Chinese management and Soviet interests in Manchuria would be guaranteed protection under Chinese sovereignty.

The future of China depended very largely on the disposal made of Manchuria. This northern dominion had a population of almost 50,000,000. The Japanese, during their period of occupation after 1931, invested a sum equal to $1,000,000,000 to develop the iron and coal mines, build railroads, improve the soya bean crop, and make Dairen the second largest port of East Asia. Recovery of Manchuria with its industries intact would have compensated China for ten years of exhausting war. But when peace came, the Russian forces were sweeping the Japanese from Manchuria and despite Chinese protests they seized much of the movable property as war booty and destroyed more. Steel production was cut in half in a few months and the output of electrical energy fell 90 per cent. How much of the damage could be blamed upon the Russians and how much was the result of indiscriminate pillage no one could say with certainty, but the total damage was calculated by the American reparations mission at $858,000,000.

Had Generalissimo Chiang Kai-shek been able to march his Nationalist armies into Manchuria promptly, the Russians would have had less excuse for remaining in occupation and inciting or at least permitting so much wanton damage. But Chiang could not act with decision because he was not entirely master in his own domain. The Chinese communists, who had collaborated with Chiang against the Japanese, reclaimed their independence of action once victory had been achieved. In the province of Yenan, in much of Shansi, Shantung, Jehol, Chahar, and all Manchuria north of Hsinking, the communists controlled the civil and military administration. Before they would accept Chiang's authority they insisted upon a more liberal policy, a democratic assembly, and a fair share in the national government.

This split between the Kuomintang and the communists had divided China for twenty years, for although both groups were at one in their opposition to foreign imperialism and aggression, they were divided on questions of internal reform and social betterment. The Kuomintang, like all revolutionary regimes, had become more conservative with the years and had been increasingly dominated by the banking and landowning classes. Since this left the peasants without leadership, the communists prepared a program of agrarian reform which challenged the privileges of the bankers and great landlords. The communists were revolutionaries but not in the sense that the "communist proletarians" in a capitalist society are revolutionaries. China had no organized city proletariat because China had no large-scale industry. On the other hand, the communist teaching that the working class should control the tools of labor made sense to the Chinese farmer when he was assured that communism meant he would have a farm of his own. The Chinese was not interested in urban Marxism or Soviet collectivism but he was interested in land he could till without unendurable rents or taxes.

After 1945 sporadic fighting between the Nationalist armies and the communist armies continued irresolutely as Chiang maneuvered patiently to bring the northern provinces under control without undue cost or bloodshed. The endless pattern of Chinese history seemed about to repeat itself with years of smoldering civil war. But in the twentieth century China was no longer an empire to itself. A war in modern China could spread into a world conflict if the Russians aided the communists actively and the Americans continued to maintain their armed forces in Asia. The Soviet government, with occupation forces in Korea and Manchuria, was suspicious of the United States marines stationed in Shantung and Jehol and watchful of the American moves in Korea and Japan. How much help the Russians were willing to furnish the communists was not certain but the United States frankly aided Chiang Kai-shek with money and materials. Lend-Lease supplies were transferred to the National government and American naval vessels at Tsingtao were organized into the nucleus of a Chinese navy. By 1946 the Chinese had fifty vessels totaling 60,000 tons and were hopeful that the United States would transfer several hundred warcraft to their flag.

4. JAPAN

Before the Japanese surrendered in August, 1945, the victor powers had decided what the future status of Japan should be. The Japanese were to be restricted to their own islands. They would have to demobilize their armed forces, disavow the nationalist agencies that promoted aggression, dismantle their war industries, and dissolve the great trusts and business combines which had fed the military machine. To lead them along the path towards democracy, the British and Americans planned to encourage freedom of speech and press, the broader distribution of income and land-ownership, and the introduction of a constitution that would guarantee all Japanese the benefits of political liberty and personal freedom. In the transitional period while these reforms were in preparation, Japan would be an occupied country with American forces encamped at all important strategic centers and American and Russian troops controlling separate zones in Korea. At Tokyo a four-power Council representing the United States, Britain, Russia, and China, and at Washington a Far Eastern Commission representing the United States, Britain, Russia, France, China, the Netherlands, Canada, Australia, New Zealand, and the Philippine Commonwealth, would decide questions of basic policy. The Supreme Allied Commander in Japan was General Douglas MacArthur and his headquarters at Tokyo was the instrument through which the decisions of the Allied governments were transmitted to the Japanese administration. This plan for the control of the proud but defeated nation which had dominated East Asia a few months earlier worked smoothly and effectively from the day of occupation.

Unlike Germany, where the National Socialist government collapsed and left a void, Japan still had a functioning and highly efficient administration when the Allied forces took over control. The Mikado continued to reign, the Japanese police maintained order, and a majority of the civil servants stayed at their posts. This Allied decision to use the existing government while liberalizing and reforming it by degrees was severely criticized as too mild a method of dealing with Japanese militarism. But the method had the great advantage that it enabled General MacArthur to manage the nation as an organized entity. Japanese society never became the sullen, amorphous, half-paralyzed organism that the German nation remained for some years after Germany was divided into segments by the Allied armies of occupation.

The Japanese officials, from the Emperor down, were polite and acquiescent. They offered no resistance as Japanese army officers were brought to trial before American military courts and condemned for war atrocities and Japanese statesmen were arraigned under the new edicts which made the plotting of aggressive war a crime. The picture of the Mikado was removed from the schools and Hirohito announced in a New Year's broadcast (January 1, 1946) that the divinity attributed to occupants of the imperial throne was a myth. A new constitution was drafted with the aid of legal advisers from MacArthur's headquarters and adopted by the House of Representatives and House of Peers after these bodies had been "purified" by the expulsion of all political leaders closely identified with the program of aggression.

Genuine political evolution can seldom be forced. But the establishment of a free press, the spread of free discussion and criticism, and the enfranchisement of women slowly penetrated among the Japanese people. The crucial test of a new order, however, is the degree of prosperity that it brings, and the liberalized postwar government of Japan faced a dark economic future which weakened its popularity. Despite shipments of 500,000 tons of food from America, the people were close to starvation in the first year of peace. Fuel was scarce, fertilizer was lacking for the farm lands, and external trade was almost extinguished. The silk industry seemed half ruined, three-fourths of the cotton spindles had been destroyed, three-fourths of the merchant shipping was lost, and raw materials were lacking to rebuild the stricken cities or revive the silent factories. Only the farmers preserved a modest but secure standard of living from their scrupulously tilled acres.

The Japanese nation as a whole, with almost 80,000,000 people increasing at the rate of 800,000 a year, could not subsist by farming, however. A lively export trade was as essential to the Japanese as to the British, and the Allied governments therefore faced the problem of helping Japanese industry to recover or leaving the Japanese with an annual deficit caused by the excess of imports over exports. Twentieth-century Japan could not be suddenly thrown back to the self-sufficing, isolated, feudal-agrarian economy of a century earlier. It was an industrialized state with all Asia for a market and a billion possible customers. Electrical equipment, pottery, metalware, toys, and above all, textiles (cotton, rayon, silk, and wool) produced by skilled factory workers at low cost, could restore the trade balance. Armaments were forbidden, chemicals supervised, silk endangered by the growing use of nylon; but despite such handicaps trade could revive. If the economic dilemma facing the Japanese was not solved by a return to exchange trade, they would not have means to purchase oil, ore, fertilizer, raw wool, and raw cotton, and their farms and factories would starve. What was more tragic was that they would lack means to import rice, soya beans, sugar, and other foods for their surplus millions, and the population too would face starvation. This economic dilemma rather than the creation of democratic institutions was the problem which the Allied military advisers had to solve. When people are starving to death it is profitless to hand them a ballot and a pamphlet on the benefits of democracy.

The republic of Korea (85,000 square miles) is slightly larger than the state of Kansas but it differs in almost every other respect. Korea is mountainous, densely populated (25,000,000 inhabitants), and no point in it is more than a hundred miles from the sea. In 1895 the Japanese detached Korea from Chinese sovereignty and annexed it after the Russo-Japanese War of 1904–1905. To the Koreans the defeat of the Japanese in 1945 meant liberation but they soon discovered that they had exchanged one master for two. At the Yalta Conference (1945) the Big Three agreed that Russia would occupy the northern half and the United States the southern half when the Japanese were expelled. A joint Soviet-American military commission discussed a merger of the two zones in 1946 but no accord was reached, and the American military authorities decided to set up a democratic regime in their zone. The Russians, fearful that Korea might one day become a "landing wharf" for an Anglo-American invasion of East Asia, viewed this courting of the Koreans with suspicion and sponsored a communist government for northern Korea. Thus it became the tragic fate of the Koreans, like the Germans, to be divided between two opposed world powers, and the future of Korea, like that of Manchuria and China, became a matter of international politics and the international balance of power.

PART XI

Western Culture
in the Twentieth Century

SCIENCE AND TECHNOLOGY

$$E = mc^2$$

ALBERT EINSTEIN

Science is taking on a new aspect which is neither purely physical nor purely biological. It is becoming the study of organisms.

ALFRED NORTH WHITEHEAD

I. THE REVOLUTION IN PHYSICS

ANY philosophy which teaches that the facts of the universe may be explained by the existence and nature of matter is known as a materialistic philosophy. A civilization in which people devote themselves too exclusively to material interests and values is described as a materialistic civilization. For the people of Europe and America the nineteenth century was an age of materialism. They were deeply impressed by the extraordinary progress of the natural sciences and by the rise in living standards which came with advances in technology and machine production. Materialistic philosophy persisted into the twentieth century but what form it would assume, through what unifying concept it would express itself, was not immediately clear. If the answer were referred to the scientists and engineers, it appeared likely that some term such as "dynamism" or "energism" would serve better than "materialism" to suggest the mood of twentieth-century civilization. Instead of matter, force or energy was proposed as the primal element, the ultimate reality of the cosmos. A brief survey of the more recent developments in physics may help to explain how this shift in emphasis came about. It should be remembered, however, that any brief explanation must of necessity be oversimplified and incomplete.

The early years of the twentieth century saw a great number of scientific discoveries which altered the foundations upon which nineteenth century physics had rested. Not since the speculations of

Copernicus upset the Ptolemaic astronomy four centuries earlier had European man's conception of the physical world suffered such a rude reversal. The fundamentals of physical science in acceptance before 1900 were the Newtonian laws of motion and the twin principles of the conservation of mass and of the conservation of energy. Simply stated, these hypotheses taught that bodies in space, whether they were molecules or galaxies, moved in obedience to invariable formulas which could be expressed mathematically in terms of the mass of the bodies, their velocity, and the distance between them. Matter, the substance of which the universe was presumably composed, was regarded as indestructible and its forms were classified by the chemists who distinguished ninety-two graduated elements, each element having constant, recognizable properties and a fixed atomic weight. Though matter might alter its form, the total mass remained constant, for not one atom could be created or lost. Through similar reasoning it was assumed that energy could be neither created nor annihilated so that, whatever form it might take, the sum remained constant. It was assumed that matter (solid, liquid, or gaseous) formed the normal vehicle by which energy was conveyed and through which it manifested itself, although this conclusion made it very puzzling to explain how the radiant energy of the sun, for example, could traverse the 90,000,000 miles of empty space between the sun and the earth. This difficulty was smoothed away, however, by postulating the existence of an immaterial, omnipresent medium termed the ether, a weightless, frictionless, infinitely elastic medium which could transmit waves of radiant energy at an extraordinary speed. The velocity of light in this ether had been carefully computed and was found to be approximately 186,300 miles per second.

Such were the more general concepts upon which physical science rested at the close of the nineteenth century. But already a series of destructive attacks had begun which endangered or modified all these major hypotheses. Ingenious experiments (1881 and later), which were devised to detect the theoretical ether, all produced negative results; the ether, it appeared, would give no evidence of its existence. In 1895 the discovery of X rays by Wilhelm Konrad Roentgen opened the field of radioactivity with all its startling possibilities. The investigations of Pierre Curie (1859–1906), Marie Curie (1867–1934), Ernest Rutherford (1871–1937), and many other physicists, revealed that certain forms of matter, high in the table of the elements, were disintegrating. The implications of this discovery were revolutionary because they indicated that matter might be transmuted into energy, thus challenging the law of the conservation of matter. In 1901 Max Planck (1858–1947), a German physicist, noted that energy was apparently ejected from the atom in spurts or "packets" and not radiated in a flow of uniform waves. Planck's Quantum Theory led to the conjecture that within the atom many of the accepted principles of physics failed to operate, a disquieting possibility to those scientists who placed their faith in the universal validity of their generalizations. Philosophy, as some observers were happy to proclaim, was having its revenge on physics or at least upon certain dogmatically minded scientists.

Einstein, Rutherford, and others step by step added information and theory to Planck's work. The atom itself had now become the problem child of physics, for it was not possible to conceive, as the Greeks had done, that this ultimate particle of matter was "solid, massy, hard, impenetrable." Instead, it had become a universe in itself with a structure which somewhat resembled a solar system. At its core was a small, heavy nucleus, about which a varying number of electrons revolved like planets or satellites around a sun. This nucleus carried positive charges of electricity, their potential balanced by the negative charges of the ambient electrons. The radiations given off by elements of very high atomic weight, as uranium and radium, were found to consist of alpha particles (the nuclei of helium atoms), beta particles (electrons moving at very high speeds), and gamma rays (radiations similar to X rays, one quantum or particle of which was named a photon). In their behavior and their effects these radiations seemed neither waves of energy nor particles of matter but something between the two. It was clear that the oversimple nineteenth century theories about the nature of matter and energy required revision.

Further evidence that these earlier views were inadequate to account for observed phenomena came from the astronomers. On estimating the mass of some stars the astrophysicists obtained values which indicated a density of more than one ton to the cubic inch, a state of compression inconceivable under prevailing theories. Other stellar measurements suggested that light (which presumably had no mass) was affected by the pull of a gravitational field, a fact which likewise eluded explanation if the rigid distinction between matter and energy were upheld.

Thus the hypothetical ether, the wave theory of radiation, the law of the conservation of matter and the law of the conservation of energy, the nature of the atom, and the principles of causality and of mechanical determinism were all exposed to attack. Concepts cautiously built up and tested through four centuries of physical experimentation were crumbling, and a newer system of physics and a newer mathematics were needed to supplant them. The most important advance in the development of the new mathematics came in 1905 when Albert Einstein offered his special Theory of Relativity. Time and space, he submitted, were not absolute, as Newton had suggested, but were both relative to the observer. In a universe in which nothing could be taken as immovable, all calculations of time and space were variable and would prove valid only for observers who worked under identical conditions. These generalizations on space and time measurements Einstein later extended (1916) to include gravitational phenomena, and in 1929 he published his Unified Field Theory which sought to correlate the mathematical laws governing electromagnetism with the other fields of natural phenomena. Under the impact of the new discoveries and the validation of Einstein's theory of relativity, Newton's concepts of space, time, and gravitation had to be reformulated, for mass had become a variable or relative function in the new equations. It now appeared that the mass of a body depended upon its rate of movement; a body which weighed one ton by conventional standards and scales might, if its velocity were increased until it approached the speed of light, become incalculably heavy. If it reached the speed of light its mass would (theoretically) approach infinity. This speculation suggested that the physicists might have found a new constant to replace the repudiated notions of absolute time and absolute space. This new constant was the velocity of light (approximately 186,300 miles per second) and the speed of light accordingly emerged as the basis of the new physics.

Einstein's principle of relativity offered a clue to several other contradictions which had puzzled physicists and astronomers. But its most important practical application was his assumption, stated as early as 1905, that mass and energy would prove to be equivalent and that proof of this equivalence might be found in the behavior of radioactive elements. Studies in nuclear physics had already indicated, as mentioned above, that under exceptional conditions, or at least in a manner which made detection very difficult, matter might slowly disintegrate and escape in the form of radiations or particles of energy. The most delicate scales could not record this loss of mass in a disintegrating body because the loss was infinitesimal, but the energy which resulted could be calculated because, relative to the mass forfeited, it was almost fantastically great. Einstein computed that the amount of nuclear energy for a given mass could be expressed by the formula $E = mc^2$, using E to represent the energy, m the mass, and c the velocity of light. This innocent-appearing formula concealed an astounding possibility. If valid and workable, it meant that one pound of matter, if it could be transmuted into energy, would be equivalent to all the power produced by all the electric industries of the United States in one month (1939 output). Forty years after Einstein published his paper containing the special theory of relativity, a group of physicists in the United States, drawing on the work done in the laboratories of all the leading nations, put the hypothesis on the equivalence of mass and energy to the test. Its first practical demonstration was the atomic bomb.

Besides these illustrations from the field of physics many others might be cited to suggest how the dual empires of science interpenetrate, the empire of abstract theory and the empire of practical technology. Even to list the fields of scientific investigation and the major discoveries in each would demand disproportionate space here. For science now reaches into every area of modern man's endeavor. Esoteric speculations by a professor of geophysics or seismology regarding the interior of the earth may pay sudden dividends to hard-headed businessmen by affording a clue to oil deposits. Experiments undertaken from curiosity by a laboratory assistant may lead to a process which ruins an ancient industry and lays the foundation of a mightier one. Obscure elements like tungsten or helium, unnoted until recent years, acquire international value almost over night. Formulas for fixing the nitrogen of the air to provide synthetic nitrates or for extracting gasoline from coal products can spell the difference between defeat and victory in war. So rapid and so revolutionary have been the changes wrought by scientific method and scientific thinking that the scientist has become the magician and the *enfant terrible* of modern society. His modest guesses abolish a plague or overturn a school of philosophy; his prescriptions bring life or death, poverty or plenty, to uncomprehending millions; his sibylline equations direct the course of destiny.

2. MACHINERY AND TECHNOLOGY

If a citizen of ancient Rome or Babylon could visit the modern world the feature of Western civilization which would astonish him most would be the wide use of power-driven machinery. Even wind and water mills were little known in ancient times; their possibilities were not generally realized until the later Middle Ages. Steam engines, which wrought a prodigious revolution in manufacture and transportation, have been in use less than two centuries. The internal combustion engine, and electricity with all its myriad uses, have been developed for general public convenience in the last fifty years. Without the application of power for running the machines, the industrial development of the modern age and the marvels of mass production would have been impossible. The average Chinese workman, for example, can produce one-thirtieth or less than the average American workman. The Chinese is as patient and industrious as the American but he lacks power-driven tools. Man's muscular energy, the first form of power he ever used, is still in many countries the form of energy he depends upon even for the heaviest tasks. Yet one pound of coal, efficiently burned in a machine, can liberate more energy than one strong man furnishes in an eight-hour day. The standard of living in every society bears a direct relation to the per capita energy available for productive purposes.

Without the application of power to machinery the locomotive, the steamship, the automobile, and the airplane could not have been developed. It is instructive to note how inventions overlap and help to promote one another. Some early airplanes, for instance, were actually designed for steam-driven engines. But these first ponderous engines were rapidly superseded and within fifty years engineers had designed internal combustion engines so light yet strong that they produced one horsepower for each pound of their own weight. The rocket and jet plane introduced further improvements which rendered gasoline engines obsolete for stratospheric flight at speeds transcending that of sound.

The attainment of high speeds, however, is not the most important development in modern transportation. Such mechanical triumphs as the stratosphere plane, which can carry mail and passengers across the Atlantic in a few hours, are of less economic significance at present than the slower cargo ships, the freight trains, and the motor trucks on the highways. In general transportation, although time is important, cost may be more important still. In the past century or so the minimum time interval for crossing the Atlantic has been reduced from a few weeks to a few days and now to a few hours. For the millions living in Europe and America, however, the really vital reduction in this period was the reduction in freight rates, which declined until it became possible to ship one ton of wheat one mile by land and five miles by water at a cost of one cent. This fall in freight rates constituted the real revolution in transportation. For lower freight costs meant that food surpluses could be inexpensively shipped half way round the world to supply hungry cities. Cheap food is more vital for the survival and happiness of mankind than high-speed passenger service or air mail.

Not only transportation but communication also was revolutionized in the Age of Electricity. The electric telegraph developed by Samuel F. B. Morse (1832) and the laying of submarine cables (1851 and later), linked countries and continents together and made possible the instantaneous transmission of news. The invention of wireless telegraphy by Guglielmo Marconi (1895) extended the possibilities of this lightning-swift transmission and opened the way for the radio, radiotelephone, telephoto and radiophoto, and television.

The first and chief beneficiaries of the electric telegraph were the newspapers, which were soon scouring the world for a digest of the day's events. The printed word remained until the twentieth century the only medium by which an exact and uniform message could be prepared for millions of people at the same time. The invention of printing about 1440 thus tended for nearly five hundred years to favor an influential class of journalists and writers who exercised a virtual monopoly over the most effective channel of public information. The pen came to share with the sword and scepter the perquisites of power, and the press was able to make itself such a strong and independent instrument that the writers were sometimes called the Fourth Estate of society.

The technological advances of the twentieth century challenged this "rule of the graphocracy." The monopoly of type was broken and several newer methods of communication which could convey an identical message to millions at the same moment were brought to completion. The motion picture (1899), the radio (1920), the talking picture (1925), and the development of television, opened a new age in communication. The social effects of the new inventions were far reaching and unpredictable, but it was certain that they would influence public taste in art and music and that they held great possibilities as a means of public education. But their employment also exposed the dangers which lay in their misuse, for they were promptly and unscrupulously utilized by political leaders, in particular by Hitler and Mussolini, with tragic consequences.

The technological advances of the nineteenth and twentieth

centuries multiplied prodigiously the amount of power available for human needs and created ingenious mechanical slaves to perform a hundred daily services. But it has been well said that he who hath a slave hath a master. The use of machines bred habits in modern man which only the machines could satisfy and his dependence upon his mechanical servants increased yearly. This meant, in turn, that he became dependent upon those who kept his machines in repair. When the automobile, telephone, or radio, the electric refrigerator, elevator, or lighting system broke down, a mechanic with special knowledge and skill was required to repair it. This increasing social reliance upon technicians, engineers, and other vocational specialists created a serious problem in highly industrialized countries. The number of specialists available for complex tasks often proved inadequate and the skill required for independent work at the highest technical levels could be acquired by relatively few. Thus a program which would assure the selection and training of sufficient scientists and engineers to operate the machines and man the laboratories, surgeries, drafting rooms, power stations, and radio chains, became a matter of urgency. In time of war the need for experts with special training became still more desperate and governments were driven to conscript the entire adult population and draft those with the requisite intelligence to staff industries and services essential to the national life.

In calculating the role and the social importance of the machine in contemporary society, it is helpful to note that most machines fall into one of two classes. The first group includes all those designed primarily for power production, the engines, small or vast, which serve to amplify the strength of human muscles. The second comprises what may be termed precision instruments. These delicate devices have become incredibly numerous. The thermostat which regulates the temperature of a room, the safety catch which holds an elevator motionless until the door is closed, the electric guard which delays an approaching train until the right switch has locked, are but three simple examples out of many thousand. These instruments have come to perform tasks too delicate for human fingers. They have been endowed with perceptions finer than the human senses. They have been entrusted with duties which would exhaust human patience and the human will.

Most of the more complex mechanical marvels, invented to further production or to promote research, are unappreciated save by the technicians who operate them, but a description of one or two will suggest their complexity and sensitivity. To study objects too small to be seen by the naked eye, modern scientists improved the microscope until they found that the wave length of light set a maximum useful magnification of about 800 diameters. By the use of ultraviolet light, with higher wave frequencies, a magnification of 2000 diameters was achieved. There further observation by optical means appeared to be halted by an insoluble physical problem. So the scientists turned to high speed electrons, guided and focused them to reproduce enlarged images, and succeeded in magnifying infinitesimal objects from 50,000 to 200,000 times. With this electron microscope viruses which cause a number of diseases in plants and animals can be identified and photographed; the search for them, which had been described as "flying blind over unknown territory," now yielded to precise observation, and the chance of finding a remedy for several baffling infections was immeasurably increased.

A second illustration, perhaps more astonishing, of the amplification of human powers by the machine, was provided by the "mechanical brain" or electronic computing machine. These bewildering mechanisms (several types were developed) helped to solve the involved mathematical calculations encountered in physics, astronomy, aerodynamics, and other abstruse sciences. Problems which would require thousands of years to work out if left to a single human computer, were answered in a few hours by these electrical integrators. So complicated were their operations that some machines employed 18,000 vacuum tubes and weighed hundreds of tons.

It is true that instruments as expensive and intricate as this were invented by and for mathematical experts. But millions of ordinary people came to depend upon other selective mechanisms such as the dial telephone exchange, which is almost as extraordinary in its performance. By the middle of the twentieth century civilized man was accepting without surprise and almost without thought his intimate dependence upon the servile steam engine, the sleepless generators, the obedient electrons. Only through an occasional labor strike or a temporary failure of power did he receive a warning of the fate which might overtake his cities if some unforeseen calamity arrested the machines.

3. THE PROLONGATION OF HUMAN LIFE

In a much quoted passage the English philosopher Thomas Hobbes declared that the life of man in a state of nature was "solitary, poore, nasty, brutish, and short." Men founded governments, Hobbes explained, in order that their lives might be more securely guarded and their property protected. A fair test of the efficacy of any government is the average life span of the citizens who share its benefits. Every high civilization has not merely enriched but has prolonged human life, at least for the privileged classes. Measured by this standard modern Western civilization may be considered the highest known to history. A child born in ancient Rome probably had a life expectancy of about twenty-five years; the American child born a century ago might expect to live to forty; the child born today in the United States and other highly favored countries has a life expectancy of over sixty years. This is more than twice the average which still obtains in modern India and China. Of the many factors which help to account for the higher mortality rate in Asiatic countries the most important are lack of medical care and of proper diet. In the Western world science has prolonged human life by curbing disease and by assuring a more abundant food supply.

Until the nineteenth century doctors fought diseases "in the dark"; they could not see or recognize the germs that slew nor could they discover how epidemics were spread. The story of the microbe hunters is a fascinating epic of modern medicine. One by one the deadliest microbes were identified and combated, the great plagues curbed, the death toll cut. Three forms of strategy, three methods of defense were

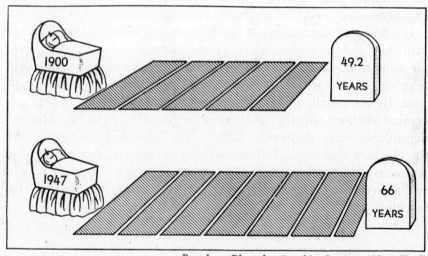

Based on Chart by Graphics Institute, New York

GROWTH IN LIFE EXPECTANCY IN THE UNITED STATES, 1900–1947

developed for this unremitting war. The first method was to check the spread of communicable diseases by more scrupulous quarantine regulations, by asepsis and antisepsis, and by the destruction of recognized plague-carriers such as rats, lice, and mosquitoes. A second means of defense was the development of exact tests which would detect a disease in its primary stages and so permit prompt quarantine and early treatment. A third method was the cultivation of serums and vaccines which would immunize human beings against the attack of specific bacteria. To carry out these more stringent precautions, doctors appealed to the state to make vaccination against such diseases as smallpox compulsory, and invoked laws to govern the inspection of food markets and eating places, the pasteurization of city milk supplies, and decontamination of sewage. Improved hospitals, health clinics for the poor, and more rigid training for doctors and nurses also formed part of the campaign. Public health became an issue in all leading countries, and a declining mortality rate, especially in maternity cases and among children under one year of age, came to be recognized as an index of social, economic, and educational progress.

A new era of surgery opened after 1900 with the utilization of X rays for diagnosis. Further improvements in anaesthetics, in equipment, in knowledge and professional skill, and in the compilation and analysis of case records, made the calculation of chances more precise and permitted operations of a delicacy hitherto unattempted. New treatments were devised, of which the use of radioactive substances in the treatment of cancer was an example. New drugs were synthesized, one of the most important being insulin, injections of which curbed diabetes. A clearer insight into the metabolism of the body was gained by the careful study of the various glands, the functions of which were found to be extremely complex and exceedingly important for health and normal growth.

One important trend in medical science was the resolution taken by physicians to treat the patient as a total personality and so avoid the danger of overspecialization which had sometimes led them to classify him by one label, such as a goitre case or an appendectomy. The need to consider the patient's mental as well as his physical state was emphasized by the fact that, while infectious and organic diseases were yielding to medical science, mental ills appeared to be increasing. By 1945 one-half the hospital beds in the United States were occupied by patients classified as mental cases, and the cost of caring for them laid a heavy burden upon the hospital staffs and upon the taxpayers who supported the state institutions in which a majority of these patients were lodged. This increase was accounted for in part by the fact that more attention was directed to mental ills and that the type symptoms of psychoses were more readily diagnosed. The forms of abnormal psychology and the working of the subconscious mind were revealed by psychoanalysis, a mode of mental therapy developed by Sigmund Freud (1856–1939), a Viennese physician, and his followers. New methods of diagnosis based upon the interpretation of dreams, upon hypnosis and trances, and upon posthypnotic suggestion, promised further advances in mental healing.

As public health became a matter of increasing concern to legislators, laws were introduced to provide for state controlled insurance funds which would protect the workers against the risks of accident or sickness and the misery of a poverty-stricken old age. Free medical examinations, hospitalization, maternity and child care, and free clinical advice were provided by many national governments, these experiments in socialized medicine and state aid being in general a feature of the unemployment Acts and other social security legislation. In addition, many private corporations and industries established clinics and medical services for their employees. The popularity of group insurance policies, which offered indemnities for sickness, accidents, and occupational hazards, was another notable feature in the program of health protection, and the insurance companies contributed to the public educational campaigns for the reduction of accidents and diseases. The endowment of charitable foundations, hospitals, clinics, nursing aid, and counseling services were further evidence of the public and private interest in the drive to save lives.

Modern medical research is a collective enterprise. The once popular concept of the lonely genius isolated on the frontiers of science is largely myth. Most modern scientists work in intimate collaboration, sharing knowledge and exchanging hypotheses. Major discoveries and newer techniques in medicine are tested in research centers which coordinate schools, hospitals, libraries, and laboratories. Many of these are state agencies. Others are supported by private gifts, by chemical firms, drug manufacturers, instrument makers, and other interested groups. The funds devoted to research by business and industry in countries like the United States have come to rival the budgets of university medical schools and public boards of health. All these agencies in combination have contributed to the advance in public health and hygiene in the twentieth century, and it is difficult to apportion the credit among them.

But the field on which medical science has demonstrated its life salvaging techniques most brilliantly is, ironically enough, the battlefield. Statistics on the health of American soldiers for the past half century record some of the more astonishing results of compulsory medical care. In the Spanish American War one United States soldier in seven sickened of typhoid; by World War II typhoid had been almost entirely eliminated. In 1900 nine out of ten victims of tetanus infection died; by 1945 tetanus serums had reduced the incidence of the disease by 90 per cent. In World War I (1917–1918) the mortality rate for cases of meningitis was almost one in two; in World War II it was one in twenty-five. As a consequence of immunization and of the service and safeguards provided by the medical units, the death rate from disease in the American forces in World War II was one-twentieth that of World War I. Care of the wounded was also improved remarkably. American soldiers received more prompt and effective care on the field, and 97 per cent of those injured in action who reached a hospital survived, as compared with 92 per cent in World War I. The use of blood transfusions to overcome the effects of shock and hemorrhage, and the prescription of sulfa drugs, penicillin, and other agents, cut the risk of infection phenomenally. Previously it had been the rule that 75 per cent or more of all compound-fracture cases resulted in bone infections, but for American casualties in World War II this rate was cut to 5 per cent.

4. THE SATISFACTION OF HUMAN NEEDS

The war on disease could not by itself have doubled the world population in less than a century; this triumph of the modern age was also due to the reduction of famine. Food, the most persistent of human needs, was more plentifully produced and more economically distributed in the twentieth century than ever before in history. The reasons for this advance were closely connected with the progress in science and technology, with the mechanization of agriculture and transportation, and with the invention of new techniques for raising and preserving food.

The exploitation of neglected but fertile lands, notably the wheat-growing areas of the United States, Canada, and Russia, and the opening up of the sheep and cattle pastures of America, Australia, and Argentina, greatly augmented the world food supply. The surplus from these thinly peopled regions helped to feed the congested cities of Europe. At the same time the development of better fertilizers, of sturdier breeds of farm animals, of both plant and animal hybrids more resistant to adverse climate and disease, of improved methods of pest control and weed eradication, of more prolific grains and more intelligent irrigation, all worked together to multiply the farmer's yield. The story of the campaigns waged against plant parasites is a saga of modern scientific conquests. Agriculture, which after hunting is the oldest human vocation, did not become a science until recent times but when it did so the studies pursued in agricultural colleges and government experimental stations transformed it in revolutionary fashion within a few generations.

On a short range view the resulting rise in the world food supply was gratifying; on longer study it began to appear ominous. For the increased food yield of the nineteenth century and the early decades of the twentieth came about very largely through the extension of farming activities into hitherto uncultivated areas. By 1940 no new regions of equal richness remained. The invention of farm machinery, which enabled fewer men to work much larger farms, did not in itself greatly increase the yield per acre of such existing farms. The introduction of modern methods and machinery into Asia, for instance, would not improve the yield but would merely release nine-tenths of the peasants from the toil of intensive cultivation. Agricultural science, though it improves the strains, protects the crop, and reduces the man-hours required, can promise no such limitless increase in output as industrial science has created. The production of steel, the generation of electric power, the manufacture of automobiles or radios may be multiplied tenfold or even a hundredfold in a few years, but the crop yield per acre for cultivated land is relatively fixed however the harvest is gathered. Competent estimates indicate that each human being alive today could utilize the products from two and one-half acres of arable land if his various needs were adequately met. The total crop land of the earth has been calculated at four billion acres, or less than two acres per head for the present world population. In large sections of Asia the population sustains itself on an average of one acre of arable land per head, but the living standards are low, the diet deficient, and survival precarious. The earth has no new continents to reveal and its marginal crop lands can be cultivated only in the face of increasing costs and diminishing returns. Excessive cultivation and erosion withdraw millions of acres yearly from productive use.

These estimates suggest that unless the area and yield of the present crop lands can be steadily increased or other sources of food supply uncovered, the search for adequate nutriment may become desperate. If, as present trends indicate, the world population doubles again in less than a century, the arable crop land might average less than one acre per head, with living standards lowered to sustenance level. It is probable that before such a condition is reached, natural curbs on population will begin to operate; in Europe, where population pressure exceeds the domestic food supply and imported food is essential, the birth rate has declined one-third in half a century. But in India, where living standards are much lower and famines are still frequent and severe, the population is increasing over 1 per cent per year. Improvements in sanitation and preventive medicine are the chief explanation, in India and throughout the world, for the reduction of the death rate, but it may be a questionable boon to save people from plague if they are doomed to die later of starvation.

A further threat of famine may result from the fact that several densely populated areas of the world, such as western Europe, have become partly dependent on imported food. If war or accident or hungry millions elsewhere deflected the food cargoes, if technical difficulties crippled the ingenious machines for the canning, freezing, dehydrating, and processing of food, Europe might have to feed itself. Whether it could do so is not clear. But the progress of scientific discovery is unpredictable and its surprises are far from exhausted. The success achieved by the chemists in synthesizing many essential drugs, vitamins, and commercial products encourage the hope that they may also provide a solution to the food problem.

Compared to hunger, the demand for clothing, shelter, and warmth is a secondary human need, and a need which modern technology may be able to meet more certainly. Although world supplies of coal and oil for fuel and energy have shrunk, the resources of "white coal" or hydroelectric power will endure until the rivers run dry. Nuclear or atomic energy, still in the experimental stage as a source of industrial power, offers a substitute as efficient as coal and possibly more economical. In isolated regions without fuel supplies atomic energy might be used to generate electricity. Synthetics and plastics for all purposes, from fine spun fibers to building blocks, provide alternatives to silk, wool, leather, rubber, wood, and other organic products once considered irreplaceable. Man is thus becoming less dependent upon the plant and animal world for everything save food. But the enjoyment of these new products of the technological revolution is denied to all save a minority of the earth's inhabitants by problems of trade, tariff, transport, distribution, and, above all, lack of purchasing power. Modern man has invented the machines to satisfy most of his material needs. The furniture for a new world society, with comfortable standards of living for all, is ready to come off the assembly lines. But man has not yet found the means to pay for that furniture or to share it equitably. The solution to this problem lies in the realm of human nature, and the sciences which deal with man — anthropology, psychology, sociology — are the least exact and the slowest to advance. Because they are sciences of classification rather than sciences of measurement they are slow to yield results comparable to those brilliant mathematical generalizations by which the scientists extended their empire over the physical world.

ARCHITECTURE, ART, AND MUSIC

*The whole art of today, even in its most transitory forms, is
obeying an obscure need of subordination to some collective task
still unknown; and this need suggests to our art — confused and
diverse though it be in appearance — the direction of its lines and
the quality of its tones.*

ELIE FAURE [1]

I. ARCHITECTURE

ALL works of architecture produced under an advanced civilization are of deep interest to the historian. The fabrics employed
for building proclaim the initiative, the techniques, and the means of
transport available to the builders. The form and size of a structure
suggest the aesthetic ideals and the engineering skill of the architects.
The function to which any public building is dedicated tells something of the collective activities and aims of the people for whom it
was erected. When these three tests: fabric, form, and function, are
applied to contemporary architecture, they offer proof that Western
man is living in a daring and dynamic age.

From the dawn of civilization, before 5000 B.C., men planned their
more durable structures of stone or brick. The adoption of iron and
steel for building purposes in the nineteenth century opened possibilities of development so radical that they are still only half recognized.
The skyscraper was one of the first triumphs of the new technique
and it has been celebrated as a typical symbol of the modern age, but
it is not the most appropriate symbol in form or function. Towers,
however built, are not a novelty. Even less so were the modern
churches, theaters, stadiums. The architects introduced steel frames
and ferroconcrete walls, but they used these new materials with little
regard for their possibilities and preferred to continue the imitation of

[1] Elie Faure, *Modern Art*, Introduction, p. xxiii. New York: Harper and
Brothers, 1924.

classical forms and to reproduce tiresome replicas of ancient monuments. The thoughtful visitor, approaching any of the great European or American cities which sprang up so rapidly in the nineteenth century, is dismayed by the lack of any rule of uniformity or ground plan, by the chaos of competing styles, and by the anarchy of the urban skyline. Columns, arches, buttresses, cupolas, even gargoyles and crenelated battlements appear as decorative historical motifs on buildings constructed of iron and concrete for purposes strictly contemporary and utilitarian. Efforts to escape from such sycophantic stylism and to develop an authentic architecture adapted to the needs of modern life finally inspired the movement known as Functionalism. Louis Sullivan and Frank Lloyd Wright in the United States and Otto Wagner in Germany were leaders in this movement, departing from stylistic precedents to project homes, factories, railway terminals, and office buildings conceived in clarity, stripped of ornamental superfluities, economical of space, austerely efficient, and obedient to the mechanical rigors of the age of power.

If the term *architecture* is taken in its broader sense of construction in general, it would include much of the most important engineering work of today. For grandeur of dimension some of the hydroelectric dams of recent years exceed the pyramids in mass. For patterns of formal beauty the steelwork of radio towers and suspension bridges can challenge the arabesques of the East. As engineering achievements, the canals and traffic routes that transect the continents achieve a magnitude inconceivable until modern times. As triumphs of design, strength, and structural integrity the ocean liner, the battleship, and the airplane set a standard not hitherto approached by works of human invention.

All these examples and many others which might be listed belong to the architecture of power. From hydroelectric generators to transcontinental airliners they are functionally related to the harnessing of energy or the movement of mass. Historians of the future, when they assess the architecture of this age, may well find an airport more typical than the Pentagon Building, and the George Washington Bridge more representative than Rockefeller Center. For such critics will be seeking to identify the forms of art and architecture which best exemplify the spirit of twentieth century civilization. The most distinctive characteristic of modern Western society is the dependence men have placed in their machines. It is through machinery that modern men bend natural forces to their will, harnessing unlimited horsepower for easier transportation, for a thousand delicate services, for mass production, and, in war, for mass destruction. The great blast furnaces, elevators, dynamos, and battleships may therefore be chosen by later commentators as the authentic expressions of this age, more truly symbolic than its churches, libraries, or museums, its monuments, its music, or its art.

2. PAINTING

No one prevailing trend or dominant school has given unity to the aesthetic formulas of the twentieth century. The discipline and dignity of the classical rules, the fantasy and fecundity of the romantic spirit, the faithful depiction of nature for which the realists strove, all have contributed something to the vortex of contemporary art. The resulting impression, at close range, is often one of purposeless ferment and confusion. Inevitably, much contemporary art is unresolved; the history of a still living organism can never be completely indicated. To those who watch his efforts the artist in travail appears a distracted spirit, torn by divergent aims and abashed by the plenitude of his material. For the creative spirits of the twentieth century the multiplicity of models, the clamorous competition of new schools, the invention of new instruments of expression and new techniques, impose a task of selection and clarification so immense that it is almost overwhelming.

The entire world of the present and all the civilizations of the past have been laid under tribute to enrich the art of today. African masks and Polynesian idols, ancient Egyptian tombs and Aztec temples, Hindu loomwork and Chinese landscapes have yielded fragmentary inspiration to the artists of the West in their impatient search for new mediums and new forms. In the resultant *mélange* three or four major tendencies may be discerned, but the manner in which these may one day coalesce to produce an art truly expressive of the modern age has not yet become apparent.

In 1900 European painting was still dominated by the modern French masters, of whom the greatest was Paul Cézanne (1839–1906). Cézanne was born in Provence and was a boyhood friend of the great French novelist Émile Zola. The two pledged themselves to creative work and each achieved a position of first importance in his field. But Zola developed early, while Cézanne matured his talents through slow and painful experimentation. He learned the realist technique but soon moved beyond the realists of his day, who were still copying

nature with uninspired fidelity. He came under the influence of
Camille Pissarro (1831–1903) and the impressionists but this too was
only a stage in his artistic growth. His most noteworthy trait was the
emphasis which he laid upon structure, although his independence of
vision sometimes led him into a deliberate distortion of form. It has
been said that Cézanne attempted, out of his own spirit, "to give architecture to the universe," and he thus reaffirmed the primacy of the
artist's own intractable individuality as the most positive force in
painting. For this he has been hailed as the founder of a new movement described variously as postimpressionism and as expressionism.
But the contemporary world was slow to recognize his greatness. An
exhibition of his work in Paris in 1904 brought belated acknowledg-
ments which still fell short of his deserts, and two years later he was
dead at the age of sixty-seven.

Cézanne's contemporary, the Dutch painter Vincent van Gogh,
was even less honored in his short and haunted lifetime. Only his
brother Theo fully believed in his genius, and even Theo's solicitude
could not save him from insanity and suicide at thirty-eight. Van
Gogh was fascinated by sunlight and the emblazonment of massed
color. He defied conventional realist standards even more arbitrarily
than Cézanne, using prodigious splashes of blue and green and yellow
not primarily to reproduce what he saw but to convey to the be-
holder the mood which an object excited in him. This personal or
subjective attitude was characteristic of the postimpressionists. They
fought against conventionalized arrangements, forms, and harmonies,
for it was their obdurate determination to be original despite critics
who ridiculed and a public which ignored them.

Even among themselves, however, the advanced painters were not
often in accord. Paul Gauguin (1848–1903), who abandoned a bank
ledger for the painter's palette in 1881, splashed on his colors in pure
blocks of light, like Van Gogh, and drew inspiration from Oriental
prints and the primitive art of the Pacific islanders. When Gauguin
visited Van Gogh in Provence in 1888 their arguments so tormented
the Dutch painter that he drew a knife on his friend and then in remorse used it to cut off his own ear. Such eccentric behavior on the
part of a few artists persuaded many people that the newer schools in
painting, sculpture, and music were filled with extraordinary characters who were violent and unpredictable if not actually mad. Gauguin
himself added to the legend by fleeing Europe altogether. In 1891 he
moved to Tahiti and later to the Marquesas, where he painted a num-

George E. Kidder Smith, for the Museum of Modern Art, New York

THE MINISTRY OF EDUCATION AND HEALTH, RIO DE JANEIRO, BRAZIL

"RIPPED," BY VASILY KANDINSKY

ber of notable studies of tropical landscapes and brown Maori women, sometimes adding titles in the native dialect as in his *Te Arii Vahine* or suggesting puzzling captions of his own as in his *Spirit of the Dead Watching*.

The postimpressionists and expressionists sometimes carried their eccentric distortions to such extremes that the objects which they represented were incomprehensible to anyone else. Yet this arrogant individualism, by liberating fresh talent and encouraging more experimental techniques, helped twentieth century painters to break with an outmoded naturalism and its frozen formulas. For naturalism, according to its detractors, had degenerated into mere photography, whereas the modernist painters were creative because they probed below the surface with their penetrating vision. What they discerned they then projected upon canvas, not with photographic fidelity but with a masterful selection, using all the tricks of design, dramatization, and symbolism to emphasize what they considered significant.

The search for new material carried some painters far afield. Henri Matisse (1869–   ), a rebel like Cézanne against impressionist clichés, turned like Gauguin to primitive art for inspiration and copied the distorted modeling of Negro and American Indian carvings. The Spaniard, Pablo Picasso (1881–   ), who studied in France, likewise analyzed Negro and Polynesian sculpture in his quest for what he considered essential rhythms. Picasso also helped to inspire a movement known as Cubism, which induced painters to project objects in quaint geometrical guises, the avowed aim being to convey the "essence" of their real structure. Finally, the defiant individualism of some postimpressionists and modernists led them to abandon all attempts to represent objects directly. They sought instead to convey the mood, spirit, or rhythm of a landscape, a machine, or a human being, designing cubes, whorls, intersecting planes, and artful splashes of light and shade, all of which were intended to have significance and to create a mood without representing any identifiable object. This nonobjective art and extreme abstractionism did not capture the public taste but in modified forms it exerted a wide influence upon all the pictorial arts. The preference for skein-like geometric patterns, the employment of distorted forms, the projection of truncated, fragmentary, or incongruous objects into a picture, the achievement of weird and beautiful effects and compelling rhythms, all testified to the power and originality of the modern schools.

One charge frequently made against postimpressionist art was that it remained esoteric and left the masses unaware of, or at least unresponsive to, its message. This charge was refuted in part by the increasing popularity of murals in the decoration of public buildings, especially murals designed to create "atmosphere" by the employment of symbolical or nonobjective art as a medium. Some noteworthy advances were made, especially in Russia and Mexico, in developing mural art for the enjoyment of the people; but as murals are a form of painting which cannot well be lent for foreign exhibition or exported to other lands, this work remained almost unknown outside the Soviet Union and the Mexican Republic. North Americans were slow to appreciate the remarkable renaissance of painting in Mexico, where the genius of Diego Rivera (1886–   ) fused the historical motifs of Mexican Indian art with the symbols of the proletarian revolution and the rhythms of the machine age. His painting in its freedom, symbolism, and power was often compared with that of his great Mexican contemporary, José Clemente Orozco (1883–   ), a modernist of somewhat different inspiration. Orozco's murals in the National Preparatory School in Mexico City and in the House of Tiles helped to make Mexican fresco painting the most vital and suggestive art development in the New World in the interval between the World Wars.

3. SCULPTURE

Sculpture, like painting, has passed through a highly experimental phase since 1900 and has displayed the same obscurity, exaggeration, and expressive distortion. The modern search for new forms, for individuality of treatment, and for the expression of disembodied force (an impulse sometimes described as energism) was already foreshadowed in the works of Auguste Rodin (1840–1917). Rodin could model bronze or marble figures that shone with a grave sweetness or glowed with timeless passion, as he proved with such popular masterpieces as *The Eternal Idol* and *The Kiss*. He could also fix a human personality in a portrait bust or statue, his flambuoyant *Balzac* being perhaps his most arresting triumph in this genre. Despite Rodin's reverence for classical and neoclassical standards, he had felt the romantic movement of the earlier nineteenth century as well as the realism that followed and there were dual impulses in his nature. The inner conflict drove him at times to contrast serenity with ugliness and beauty with decrepitude and death. He could shape emaciated and distorted forms as fraught with agony as medieval wood carvings of martyred saints.

His *Burghers of Calais* became famous; his hunched and brooding figure, *The Thinker*, was attacked and defended with vehemence; and his most grandiose project was a relief study showing hundreds of naked forms descending into hell, a tragic and remorseless holocaust which recalled the *Last Judgment* of Michelangelo.

This search for striking means to convey a dire intensity of mood also inspired many other sculptors, among whom the German Wilhelm Lehmbruck (1881–1919) was worthy of study. His *Kneeling Woman* and *Mother and Child* as well as several sensitive portrait studies and figures showed his addiction to elongated forms and also his spirituality and compassion. His *Youth Mourning* was selected as a memorial for German soldiers killed in World War I. Lehmbruck himself might almost be counted a war casualty, for he killed himself in the mood of general despair which swept the Reich in 1919.

The American-born sculptor, Jacob Epstein (1880–   ), who did his most notable work in Europe after 1905, became a controversial figure with his bronze portrait heads, his experiments in "abstract" sculpture, and his much criticized treatment of religious subjects, including a bronze *Christ* (1920) and a titanic alabaster *Adam* (1939). With him, as a plastic artist of international fame, may be ranked the Yugoslav friend and pupil of Rodin, Ivan Meštrović (1883–   ), who designed the memorial chapel at Belgrade which the Yugoslavs erected to their unknown soldier of World War I. He also treated in a highly individual style a number of subjects drawn from mythology, folklore, and religion and completed portraits in bronze of many famous contemporaries.

The trend towards abstractionism, already noted in painting, affected sculpture also. Some artists made a cult of weird and shapeless studies which provoked and mystified the critics. Since modern sculpture is in some respects an orphan art, the defiant gestures of some sculptors may be in part an attempt to wrest recognition from a negligent public. Statuary is little used by the architects and landscape artists of today, and the unadorned severity of functional architecture offers few niches for busts and fewer pedestals for group compositions.

But as the conventional sculpture of nymphs and cupids that charmed an elder generation passed out of favor, the new age of mass production demanded beauty and elegance in utilitarian objects and mundane patterns. Young artists of the twentieth century, with a talent for designs and mechanisms, helped to add grace and beauty to daily life by perfecting bathroom fixtures and automobile fenders, lighting appliances and electric signs. The modern wielder of brush or chisel could find a thousand new techniques and machine tools to challenge him as he was caught up by the quickening current of the industrial arts.

4. MUSIC

The most powerful influence in nineteenth century music was the romantic movement, which reached its apogee about 1860 in Richard Wagner's *Tristan und Isolde* and *Tannhäuser*. The late nineteenth century is sometimes designated as the postromantic or post-Wagnerian era, during which two elements that had been emphasized by Wagner's arrogant genius continued to influence his successors. The first of these impulses was Wagner's nationalist cult, which made him defend his music as the great art of the future and the most authentic voice of the German soul. The artist, Wagner proclaimed, was impotent unless the nation (*das Volk*) spoke through him. Wagner liked to insist, "Not ye, wise ones, therefore, are the inventors, but the Folk, for need drove the Folk to invention," a glorification of that mystical entity, the Folk or Nation, which was to play such an important part in twentieth-century German thought. The second element in Wagner's art which profoundly influenced subsequent composers was his virtuosity and experimentalism, especially the harmonic chromaticism which he elaborated to express his titanic romantic inspirations. Both these aspects of the master's work were imitated (Wagner would have said pirated and debased) within a few years of his death in 1883.

With Claude Debussy (1862–1918) and his generation the great Wagnerian tradition was divided and distributed and the Wagnerian formulas adapted to modernist moods and aims. Debussy's opera *Pelléas et Mélisande* (1902) was comparable in plot to Wagner's *Tristan und Isolde;* it dealt with the ancient tragedy of a heroine married to one man but in love with another, with death as the inexorable resolution. Despite such comparisons, however, *Pelléas et Mélisande* was hailed by French critics as proof that French music had emancipated itself from the tyranny of Wagner. They pointed out how seductively the tempest and clamor of orchestral brass, which Wagner had marshaled with such overwhelming effect, was subdued by Debussy's art to the more delicate tremor of harps and violins. Music was yielding to the prevalent vogue of impressionism. It became (or attempted) a fusion of all the art forms, for this was an ideal much vaunted around 1900. Debussy was credited with drawing inspiration from the impressionist painters and also from the cadences of Stephen Mallarmé (1842–1898) and Paul Verlaine (1844–1896), French symbolist poets of rare enchantment. Debussyism, warm admirers said, was "a reconciliation of music and poetry, of music and painting." With *L'Après-midi d'un Faune* the reconciliation was broadened to include the art of the dance also, for Waslaw Nijinsky (1890–   ), the greatest dancer of the age, took Paris by storm when he appeared with the Ballet Russe in a choreographic rendition of Debussy's symphonic poem. The Russian Ballet came as a revelation to western Europe and America in the years after 1909, for its language, like that of music itself, was universal.

Yet the bitter and exaggerated feuds, such as that between loyal Wagnerites and enthusiastic admirers of Debussy, advertised the problems which faced the modern composer. He was expected to be nationalist and internationalist at the same time. Music, which should have crossed all political boundaries free of toll, was caught repeatedly in the web of European rivalries. Although it was the most expressive, multilingual, and universal of the arts, it had been swept by the twentieth century into the vortices of nationalist passion, and political rivalries threatened to separate the European peoples into jealous and exclusive culture groups even in their musical preferences.

Like the romantic poets and painters, the romantic composers drew inspiration from national and local themes. This spirit of "folk" loyalty grew more intense throughout the nineteenth century and induced many composers to improvise upon old songs of the countryside and to adapt anonymous ballads and folk dances for modern instrumentation. Other examples of the same impulse were musical compositions infused with local color and sometimes named for a specific locality or remembered scene; like landscape painters the musicians sought to capture the spirit and atmosphere of a beloved mountain lake, vale, forest scene, or island. German, French, and Italian nationalism early found musical expression through schools with a strong and independent tradition. The pressure of Russian expansion and the Pan-Slav spirit may be discerned in the nineteenth-century works of Piotr Ilich Tschaikowsky (1840–1893) and his compeers, and the new Russia of the twentieth century in the strongly Slavic idiosyncrasies of Igor Stravinsky (1882–   ) whose ballet music, commencing with the *Fire Bird* (1910), won international acclaim by its succinct "telegraphic" style.

In secondary European states and among peoples struggling for self-determination music often played a vital part in the national revival. The Bohemian (Czech) aspirations to independence sounded through the symphonic works of Frederick Smetana (1824–1884) and Anton Dvořák (1841–1904). The Polish will to freedom is associated with the polonaises of Frédéric Chopin (1809–1849) and with the concert appearances of Ignace Jan Paderewski (1860–1941). The Scandinavian countries, emerging from the dominant shadow of German culture, produced musicians of national character and international fame in the Norwegian, Edvard Grieg (1843–1907), and the Finn, Jean Sibelius (1865–   ). Themes drawn from folk music also provided inspiration for the Spanish composer, Manuel de Falla (1876–   ), and the Hungarian, Béla Bartòk (1881–1945). British, French, and Italian schools have in general been less responsive to the rich sources of the folklore tradition.

Aside from the influence of nationalism the most vital force in modernist music has been its spirit of experimentalism. New possibilities have opened up with the invention of new instruments and the extraordinary improvement in electrical recording and reproducing mechanisms. These stimuli have made the twentieth century an age of such vigorous improvisation and audacious invention that many critics protest at the chaos and nihilism they discover in the clash of contemporary schools. Music lovers of conventional tastes, who revere the traditional masters, are affronted by what they consider the decadence or anarchism of ultramodernist technique. The experimentalists, who cultivate the possibilities of atonality, polytonality, division of the semitone, and other procedures too recondite for discussion here, insist that only in this way can music remain a living art. History, they point out, is largely a record of cultural forms which grew sterile through obsequious imitation and died within the prison house of their formalized technique.

While it is generally agreed that European music took a new turn toward the close of the nineteenth century, there is as yet no general accord on the probable course of its future development. Like the expressionist painters and sculptors, the composers have sometimes borrowed alien rhythms and untunable scores from Asian, African, and Amerindian peoples. Such borrowing inevitably emphasizes the lack of homogeneity in modern music, but it also proves the receptivity and fecundity of the modernist schools. National loyalties have often tended to confine a musical genius too narrowly, limiting him to forms and sources indigenous to his native land. But a juster sense of the universality of their art has driven a larger number of composers to adopt devices and techniques from all available fields, thus enriching the musical heritage of Western civilization. This crossing of many divergent schools, principles, and techniques exemplifies the experimentalism of the modernist composers. Without such experimentalism the multiple themes, elaborate textures, adventurous rhythm, tonality, instrumentation, and orchestration of many contemporary musical works would have been unthinkable.

Finally, it should be noted that music has won an extraordinary influence and appeal in the twentieth century because of the new mediums of transmission. The phonograph, the radio, and the sound pictures have made all types of composition from operas and symphonies to popular songs available to the public at low cost. What effect this popularization may have on the future of music is not yet clear. A trend towards vulgarization of musical offerings must be anticipated and discounted but the general result should almost certainly be to raise the composer to a more honored rank and more impressive role in the cultural life of the age.

It is difficult to appraise the value of contemporary art. All judgments passed upon artists and art works are certain to be revised and sometimes reversed by later generations. Men and events do not take on their proper proportions until they become part of the historic past. Like a landscape glimpsed from a speeding train the historical present is a pageant of imminent shapes which dissolve almost instantly into a flux of changing relations. Only those objects which reappear in perspective, anchored by distance, achieve an air of proportion and durability. The reviewer who attempts to gauge the stature of his contemporaries should caution his readers that all values are subject to change without notice, that truth, as Leonardo da Vinci insisted, is the daughter of time. It is a sobering thought to recall that in 1800 many critics considered Vulpius, a minor dramatist now almost forgotten, to be a greater genius than Goethe. Quite possibly, according to their standards, they were correct, but Goethe was not writing according to their standards. It is equally probable that the greatest creative spirits of the twentieth century are not widely recognized as such because they are not working within the traditions by which their contemporaries have been taught to measure greatness in the arts.

LITERATURE

To regard all things and principles of things as inconstant modes or fashions has more and more become the tendency of modern thought.

WALTER PATER

1. TWENTIETH CENTURY TRENDS

IN the opening year of the twentieth century the philosopher George Santayana passed a harsh judgment on contemporary literature. The ability to see life steadily and see it whole, he concluded, had been denied to the present age. What moral strength he could discern in contemporary writing seemed at best "a blind and miscellaneous vehemence," and the poetry of the time was "the poetry of barbarism." Fifteen years later the German philosopher, Oswald Spengler, announced even more positively that Western civilization had passed its prime. In the deepening twilight of Western man's decline no creative art on the grand scale could be expected of him, because genuine creative art was inconceivable with the spirit of a culture so far spent. What passed for art in the twentieth century, Spengler wrote, was "impotence and falsehood." Such discouraging verdicts should not be accepted too credulously; every age has its Jeremiahs. But these criticisms do emphasize the truth that twentieth century literature, like twentieth century art, is not rooted in an assured tradition; it is provisory, experimental, and plastic, which means that much of it appears confused, inchoate, and fragmentary.

The modern age is not an age of great poets. Throughout the nineteenth century metrical forms lost ground steadily before the more realistic appeal of prose. No great epic in the tradition of Homer, Virgil, Dante, or Milton was produced to sweep together the thought currents of the age, and although many poetic dramas were written in the nineteenth century few were long remembered. In the twentieth century poetry became the medium for numerous schools of experimenters who hoped to restore it to leadership. Their products, the best of which were short lyrical compositions, sometimes achieved a brief intensity and sometimes an extravagant obscurity. None of the more novel modes of meter, rhyme, or assonance that were adopted or attempted won an assured position or captured the public taste.

The mood of indecision, so pronounced in twentieth-century art, held the poets likewise in a state of suspension. They seemed to be waiting for some synthesis of aesthetic and social values which had failed to manifest itself. Some sanguine critics hailed this hesitation (like the analogous frustration that afflicted many painters, sculptors, and musicians) as "a vigorous, experimental indecision." Others insisted that the poets and writers were numbed by the cultural conflicts and moral nihilism of the age. Their common frustration was brilliantly satirized by Thomas Stearns Eliot (1888–   ) whose volume *Waste Land* (1922) provided a title for a barren poetic era. It became the habit in literary circles to speak of disillusioned American and English writers who competed for attention after World War I as "the lost generation." A comparable mood of disillusioned romanticism had followed the Napoleonic wars a century earlier.

The most fertile literary field and the most profitable to cultivate after 1918 was popular journalism, especially ephemeral articles and stories for the periodicals, tailored to the momentary taste. One vigorous development of the period was a direct response to the progress of inventions, for the talking picture and the radio created a sudden urgent demand for lively dialogue. Radio scripts, written for the ear and not the eye, threw off the clichés of typography and added a mintage of new and lustrous idioms to the language. But "commercial writing," like advertising copy, though it might influence millions, was not considered art. Radio drama and script writing, although its influence grew yearly, remained an experimental literary form too independent and often too extravagant to be rated by conventional formulas.

The public appetite for fiction grew rapidly with shorter working hours and increased leisure. Numerous talented writers in Europe and America brought the short story to a high degree of compression and sophistication, and all types of popular periodicals multiplied to keep pace with the demands of the increasingly literate masses. The market thus expanded was supplied with fiction of varying quality, short sketches, popular biographies, news of the day, and educational articles. Though it reached millions of readers, many of whom read nothing else, this material was almost all too casual and formless to be classed as literature or at least as serious literature.

To merit the attention of the student of history a written work must fit into the framework of its period and throw light upon the major aspirations and dilemmas of a society. In the Western world of the twentieth century the novel and the drama remained the conventional vehicles for prose writers with a message for their time. The leading novelists and dramatists revealed three trends in particular which cut across national and linguistic barriers and proclaimed the intellectual cleavages within contemporary culture. These three trends, which will be discussed in turn, are the disintegration of middle class values, the quest of the individual for an inner real self, and the prestige and influence of science and technology in contemporary art and thought.

2. THE DISINTEGRATION OF BOURGEOIS VALUES

During the nineteenth century the well-to-do bourgeois supplanted the more elegant aristocrat as the social arbiter in matters of taste and fashion. Bourgeois standards of morality and deportment, of financial integrity and civic duty, determined the pattern and ethical framework of European society. The cult of "respectability" that was so dear to the middle class concealed a great deal of hypocrisy, selfishness, and complacency but even the social rebels who deplored such standards and decrees confessed that it was all but futile to fight against them.

In an age when the middle classes dominated society and set the standards, most novelists and dramatists respected the tastes and prejudices of such influential patrons. Nineteenth century authors gauged the public demand shrewdly and set themselves to gratify, entertain, and sometimes to shock that public, for they knew the conventional attitudes, tastes, and reactions that decided the group response. For most of the century the reading public remained remarkably stable and uniform in its preferences, but by 1900 this public had split and new groups with clashing loyalties had engaged in battle. The bourgeois liberal no longer dominated the social scene so securely, for the socialist groups, with their opposing views on property and government, were demanding reading matter that defended their point of view. The "bourgeois synthesis" was disintegrating and was to be succeeded by an era of confused conflict while competing social ideologies divided the European world. No dominant synthesis or dominant social class gave a firm pattern to twentieth-century civilization.

The ideals of the middle classes had never, of course, enjoyed a wholly unquestioned ascendency. Great literature is at once the record, the mirror, and the conscience of a society; and the most powerful novelists of the nineteenth century had frequently castigated bourgeois complacency. Honoré de Balzac (1799–1850), Charles Dickens (1812–1870), William Makepeace Thackeray (1811–1863), and Émile Zola (1840–1902) each in his fashion laid bare the evils of selfishness, snobbery, money worship, and inhumanity which were concealed by the façade of material prosperity and liberal dogmas. Despite such criticism, despite inequities and inequalities, the liberal synthesis held together and bourgeois society resisted change.

It is not easy to fix a date at which it might be said that here the dissolution of the synthesis became a reality. Signs of change appeared with the emergence of socialism as a political force strong enough to challenge control of government. Literature reflected the new moods. In Germany Gerhard Hauptmann's stark drama *The Weavers* (1892) shocked polite audiences by its depiction of the crushing poverty that could persist in an age of progress. Although Hauptmann described his work as "A Drama of the Forties" it was easy to compare his description of poverty among the Silesian miners in his grandfather's time with conditions in any country where industrialism had enslaved large groups of workers. Published two years after the laws against socialism had been dropped in Germany and the Social Democrats were commencing their march towards power, Hauptmann's disturbing masterpiece was a *Tendenzwerk*, a work with a critical application to contemporary trends. It offended Kaiser William II and the official classes but it won international fame for its author. Hauptmann was awarded the Nobel Prize for Literature in 1912.

A second German writer whose labors won him this coveted distinction (1929) was Thomas Mann (1875–   ) whose novels likewise reflected the passing of the bourgeois synthesis. In *Buddenbrooks* (1901) he described life in the trading city of Lübeck, his birthplace, and traced the slow paralysis which overtook a German merchant family as its ideals withered and its vigor waned. Wealth, complacency, and the inability to change destroyed the Buddenbrooks. But the deterioration which Mann diagnosed with an artist's insight was vaster than the tragic decline of a single family; it was the sickness of a whole acquisitive society, of a whole continent. This hint of contagion, of a universal malady, became the dominant mood in *The Magic Mountain* (1924). In this novel Mann laid his plot in a tuberculosis sanitarium. With acute intuition and deep artistry he showed how all the characters were influenced by the awareness of disease so that even those who escaped its physical ravages suffered a psychological distortion of values. *The Magic Mountain* has been interpreted as a parable on the impotence, futility, and illusion which may engulf the most sensitive and percipient members of a decadent social order. Thomas Mann left Germany in 1933 when the National Socialists seized control and in 1940 he became an American citizen.

In England Mann's contemporary John Galsworthy (1867–1933) constructed the realistic annals of a middle class family, the Forsytes. Like the Buddenbrooks, the leading characters of *The Forsyte Saga* revealed the slow disintegration and the deepening uncertainty of a society which was losing its faith, its bearings, and its economic independence. Galsworthy commenced this six volume history with *A Man of Property* (1906) and closed with *Swan Song* (1928). His central character, Soames Forsyte, epitomized the shrewd, calculating, class-conscious bourgeois who has "arrived." Soames with his caution, conservatism, and selfishness was not a lovable character but Galsworthy dissected him, his family, his acquaintances, and a multitude of minor figures with such understanding and compassion that the Forsyte novels became in spirit a sympathetic social history of England from Victoria to George V.

Much more critical than Galsworthy and more pungent in his treatment of the English middle class was the Irish playwright George Bernard Shaw (1856–   ). Shaw frankly avowed himself a socialist when the word still shocked the respectable and timorous, and he turned the full force of his wit against the most cherished bourgeois idols. Shams and pretences, the bland assumptions that sustained the ruling classes in particular, excited his ire and he delighted in deflating the traditions of British superiority, masculine superiority, and middle class superiority. The "Philistines," the pompous, narrow-minded, complacent people who feared all new ideas, were his special target and he fought for the new movements in art, music, drama, and literature against persistent Philistine disapproval. He championed the paintings of James McNeill Whistler after they had been rejected by the Royal Academy. He defended the operas of Richard Wagner in *The Perfect Wagnerite* (1898) when many cultivated people shuddered at them as cacophony. He avowed his admiration and indebtedness to Ibsen in *The Quintessence of Ibsenism* (1891). In his own plays he was as much a critic as a creator and his prefaces were sometimes more lively than the dialogue. His first popular triumph came in 1904 with *John Bull's Other Island,* which he followed with over twenty-five plays in as many years, as well as several novels and a flood of lectures, articles, and reviews. Some of his best known stage plays were *Major Barbara* (1905), *Man and Superman* (1903), *Pygmalion* (1912), and *Saint Joan* (1923), all of which ridiculed masculine pretensions in a way to delight the feminists.

Henrik Ibsen (1828–1906), the Norwegian poet and dramatist, opened many of the campaigns which Shaw was to carry on but Ibsen wrote with a heavier pen. His best known drama was *A Doll's House* (1879), in which he provided the feminists (who were demanding a more equal status for women) with a defiant rallying cry. The heroine of *A Doll's House,* Nora Helmer, left her husband and children because the role of childlike dependency, mental and emotional, which her husband expected her to maintain had become unreal and unendurable. Helmer was baffled by his wife's revolt and reminded her of her "sacred duties": "Before all else, you are a wife and mother." But Nora insisted that she had other duties equally sacred, duties to herself. "Before all else," she replied, "I am a reasonable human being. . . . I must think things over for myself and get to understand them." She walked calmly out of her home and with the closing of a door off-stage the curtain fell. So radical was this ending considered at the time that it had to be reversed when the play was first presented in Germany. Nora turned back at the final moment to beg her husband's forgiveness.

In several compelling dramas — *An Enemy of the People* (1882), *The Pillars of Society* (1877), *Ghosts* (1881), *Hedda Gabler* (1890), *The Master Builder* (1892), and others — Ibsen pursued his incisive exposure of what he considered false and corrupting standards in modern society. He enlisted his audiences on the side of the free soul who struggles to see life with honest eyes and who dares, like Nora, to defy the frustrating dictates of a blind conventionalism. Ibsen recognized the selfishness, arrogance, and incapacity of privileged and entrenched classes, and he felt the sickness that was blighting the promised Utopia of the romantics, for he had begun as a romantic poet himself. But he could only dramatize the social conflict; he could not propose a remedy. His defiant heroes and heroines were all lonely rebels; they were never formed to be the leaders of popular causes. This limitation, which Ibsen shared with most of the "writers of protest" of his day, was important historically. For it was not until artists and writers felt themselves lifted on the crest of a growing "wave of

the future," not until they began to call a new society into existence
to dethrone and supplant the old, that their influence could properly
be called formative. This change was still in the future when Ibsen
wrote; he lived in a Europe still dominated by the "genteel tradition"
and the "Victorian compromise."

In France the literature of the nineteenth century culminated in the
Naturalist school, headed by Émile Zola (1840–1902). Taking the
whole of society for his field, Zola observed and classified it with
the patience of a sociologist, publishing twenty volumes in one series,
Les Rougon-Macquart (1871–1893), as well as many additional novels,
articles, and critical essays. In *Le Ventre de Paris* he laid bare the
lower levels of Parisian society; in *L'Assommoir* he revealed the evils
of the drink traffic and the effects of alcoholism; in *La Terre* he de-
picted French peasant life without illusion or flattery; and in *La
Débâcle* he exposed the incompetence which can exist in a bureaucratic war department. *La Débâcle* appeared in 1892. Six years later
Zola attacked the military hierarchy of the French army command
more directly in his famous manifesto *J'Accuse*, in which he charged
that the Jewish officer, Alfred Dreyfus, had been unjustly condemned
for treason and that members of the highest military circles knew this
but opposed his exoneration. Charged with libel, Zola fled to England
to avoid prison but with the revelation of Dreyfus' innocence he was
vindicated. Returning to France, he died a few years later and his
ashes were transferred to the Panthéon in 1908.

Another French writer who defended Dreyfus was Jacques Anatole Thibault (1844–1924), better known as Anatole France. Witty,
satirical, and iconoclastic, a true spiritual disciple of Voltaire, France
wrote largely for skeptical, sophisticated readers who enjoyed his
urbane ridicule. His mockery was directed at the ideals and the institutions, the manners, the morals, and the follies of men, and he
dissected religion, government, art, and philosophy with polished
irony. In general France's novels were more derisive than constructive in their social criticism and although he was generally regarded
as the foremost French writer of his time his stature has diminished
with the years.

Perhaps the worthiest successor of Zola as an "historian of French
society" was Louis Farrigule, who wrote under the pen name of Jules
Romains. In a series of fourteen interwoven novels (twenty-seven in
the French edition) published between 1906 and 1946 under the title
Men of Good Will, Romains explored and analyzed the world of his

contemporaries. His first book opened at an arbitrary date, October 6, 1908; his last closed on October 7, 1933. Within that quarter century the "men of good will" who dreamed of building a better world saw the greatest civilization the world had known half shattered by war. Romains indicates how inescapably the events and forces of the age touch all characters in a society from convicts to cabinet ministers. So detailed are his descriptions, so numerous his characters, that no reader could recollect them all. This submergence of the individual in the multitude was intentional. The author wished to prove that the principles and forces which mold a society are more significant and more worthy of study than the individuals who compose it. Romains, like Zola, regarded society as a collectivity; he believed that a novelist must do more than dissect personalities or construct a moving plot and paint a milieu. The real artist or writer, he held, will seek to integrate all social activities and functions. This theory or creed came to be termed *unanimism.* A comparable American attempt to survey an entire society may be studied in the experiments of John Dos Passos (1896–   ), particularly *The Forty-second Parallel* (1930) and *Nineteen-Nineteen* (1931).

In the United States the deepening mood of social awareness, criticism, and discontent also helped to produce the heavily written novels of Theodore Dreiser (1871–1946) which contained dour indictments of the milieu and institutions against which Dreiser's characters struggled. His first important work, *Sister Carrie,* appeared in 1900; his most notable, *An American Tragedy,* in 1925. In 1927 he made a visit to Russia with the even better known American novelist, Sinclair Lewis (1885–   ). Lewis was a more gifted writer than Dreiser with a livelier style and he won a much greater popularity. His most telling passages were those in which he satirized the manners, ambitions, and immature emotions of American middle class people and denounced the cultural sterility to which they devoted their leisure. His best known novels were *Main Street* (1920), a savage exposure of the provincialism of the Middle West; *Babbitt* (1922) and *Dodsworth* (1929), portraying American businessmen and business methods; and *Arrowsmith* (1925), celebrating medical research and the war against disease. The impetuous moods, savage, affectionate, idealistic, and vitriolic by turns, in which Lewis wrote, left even his best prose with a surface full of splinters, but his studies of the American character, etched with gall but seldom lacking a touch of incisive truth, won him the Nobel Prize for Literature in 1930. In 1947 he once more reached the best seller lists with *Kingsblood Royal*, a dramatic arraignment of racial intolerance. Lewis' love of controversial issues had inspired him to attack one of the most provocative and explosive issues of the twentieth century, the question of the color line and interracial relations.

3. THE SEARCH FOR THE INNER SELF

The second trend in contemporary literature noted at the opening of this chapter was the search for an inner real self. This search became an absorbing and passionate quest with many twentieth-century writers. New psychological theories propounded by Sigmund Freud (1856–1939) and Alfred Adler (1870–1937), two Viennese psychologists, laid great stress upon the subconscious mind and the part which subconscious impulses play in human thought and conduct. Freud explained with the aid of an elaborate terminology that desires and hungers which adults may not wish to recognize in themselves often find expression in disguised or "sublimated" forms. It was no new thing for students of human nature to delve for hidden motives in human actions but the cult of psychoanalysis won wide popularity. One reason for this was its timeliness; it offered a new justification for the deepening urge towards introspection which was already a mark or, as some preferred to call it, a malady distinguishing the age. Twentieth-century man was narcissistic; he was fascinated by the image which he found reflected in the well of his own consciousness.

The novelists readily gratified this growing penchant for character dissection. Henry James (1843–1916), a brother of the psychologist and philosopher William James (1842–1910), brought the fictional analysis of personality to an extraordinary degree of refinement while studiously respecting the bounds of bourgeois decorum. The situations which James delighted to analyze were social scenes where Americans and Europeans mingled, and his lifetime residence in the Old World slowly alienated him from the New. His art like his characters was overintellectualized and his world and values belonged to the nineteenth rather than the twentieth century. Despite his rich and observant mind he missed or dismissed much that was most vital in the contemporary world and his delicate and muted prose was largely dedicated to describing a society already imprisoned in time.

The French novelist Marcel Proust (1871–1922) likewise lived for yesterday. In an eleven volume sequence published as *Remembrance of Things Past* he reconstructed the milieu of aristocratic Parisian families and recaptured the aura of lost days by an ardent use of memory and imagination. With his leading characters the remembered impression of experiences was often more intense and more emotionally satisfactory than the actuality. Such nostalgic convictions that it is better to have lived than to live is not usually the mark of a robust personality or a vigorous society, and preoccupation with inward thoughts and elusive impulses easily deteriorates into neuroticism. Proust symbolized a trend, especially notable in France, towards what has been termed escapism. The escapist makes art real in order to make life remote. The high percentage of introverted and neurasthenic characters among the *dramatis personae* of twentieth-century literature was a further symptom of the moral nihilism of the age. Too many individuals were spiritually vitiated and rootless and as readers are drawn to books which discuss people like themselves, disillusioned writers found a spent and disillusioned public to share their moods.

With several authors, the most influential being the Irishman James Joyce (1882–1941), the pursuit of the inner real self became a fantastic hunt through a nightmare world. Joyce's masterpiece, entitled *Ulysses,* was published in 1922 and revealed the unusual erudition and verbal inventiveness which enabled him to give a new vitality to the "stream of consciousness" theory of fiction writing. He created bizarre composite words and novel arresting symbols to suggest the uncensored, kaleidoscopic impressions which raced through the mind of his central character. His arbitrary disregard for conventional prose patterns had a strong effect upon younger writers. This Joycean search into the subconscious for the essential core of reality, the core which forms the inmost personal identity of a human being, also fascinated the Italian dramatist, Luigi Pirandello (1867–1936). In a succession of plays and novels he bewildered his audiences with the unresolved riddle of personality. He matched living characters against their more exigent and intense counterparts invented by themselves or by the artist and contrived new variations on the ancient axiom that a thing must be identical with itself. In some of his stories and plays the identity of leading characters and their relationship to one another was intentionally confused beyond resolution. His titles, *Six Characters in Search of an Author* and *Right You Are If You Think So,* emphasized this concern with the conflict between the real and the imagined world.

The paradox of personality and the powerful influence of the new schools of psychology were further illustrated by the dramas of the leading American playwright, Eugene O'Neill (1888–   ). In more than a score of noteworthy dramas O'Neill ranged from comedy to tragedy, from mysticism to naturalism, but his unending theme was human character and his aim was to lay bare the mainsprings of human action. *The Great God Brown* (1925) exposed the pathos and egotism that inflate the heart of an average man and demonstrated with dramatic irony how difficult it is for most people to discard their false masks even with those they love. *Strange Interlude* (1927) sought to present the characters on two levels of consciousness at once: their spoken conversation was interspersed with "asides" for the benefit of the audience in which they thought aloud the curious thread of their private impressions. As a dramatic device this dual method of projecting a character had obvious advantages but it tended to make the play too verbal and to paralyze the action. In *Mourning Becomes Electra* (1931) O'Neill reworked a theme (the tragedy of the House of Atreus) which had been treated by the Greek dramatists Aeschylus, Euripedes, and Sophocles. Transposed to a modern setting, this ancient tale of illicit love and murder proved again how deeply O'Neill was preoccupied with the role of fate, heredity, and passion in shaping human destiny. After a decade of silence he returned with a new play, *The Iceman Cometh* (1946), in which he suggested the function which infirmities and illusions fill in cushioning weak human beings against what would otherwise be the unbearable realities of their existence.

In American fiction during the years that followed World War I the search for the inner self gave significance to the novels of Ernest Hemingway (1898–   ), Thomas Wolfe (1900–1938), and others. From *The Sun Also Rises* (1926) to *For Whom the Bell Tolls* (1940) Hemingway's heroes fought their vagabond destiny with a hardboiled romanticism, searching their souls for the best way to achieve "grace under strain" in a sick and shattered world. Thomas Wolfe lacked Hemingway's sense of compression and structure; he poured out sprawling volumes of intense and sometimes rhythmic and poetic prose. His novels were limited in scope by their autobiographical inspiration but the lyric passion and savage protest of *Look Homeward, Angel* (1929), *Of Time and the River* (1935), *You Can't Go Home Again* (1940), and other works placed Wolfe among the giants of American literature.

In their disillusioned romanticism writers like Hemingway and Wolfe voiced the protest of twentieth-century man against the mechanisms of fate which threaten perpetually to extinguish his personality. The romantic hero may seek escape from his Hamlet complex in action or, as in the novels of Joseph Conrad, in a proud self-denial. Conrad (Teodor Jozef Konrad Korzeniowski, 1857–1924), a Pole by birth, composed some of the greatest sea romances in the English language. His persistent theme was the riddle of the romantic personality and its war with fate. In *Lord Jim* (1900), his favorite among his novels, he created a character who was also a type, an exile cut off from his past, without hope and without faith, yet still wedded inexorably to "a shadowy ideal of conduct." Lord Jim symbolizes, like many another character in contemporary fiction, the dilemma of modern man. His inner real self remains an enigma; he passes away under a cloud, "inscrutable at heart" and "excessively romantic," leaving no one certain what it was he sought. That is his significance, for as Conrad concludes, "We ought to know. He is one of us — "

4. THE INFLUENCE OF SCIENCE

The third trend in contemporary literature, the influence of the natural sciences and of technology, was a deepening force in the thought and writing of the twentieth century. It was not, however, a force that can be readily measured. The artist and the scientist regard the universe from different points of view and utilize experience for opposite purposes. The case of a Goethe or a Leonardo da Vinci proves that artistic and scientific talents may exist in the same individual and be developed to a high degree. But this does not prove that art and science are easy to reconcile. The rules of art are aesthetic principles, and the experiences of the artist are formulated very largely as personal value judgments although he may believe them valid for all mankind. The laws of science, on the other hand, are more objective relationships which the scientist believes he has detected in the natural order and which he states in the most impersonal and unambiguous terms available. The poet is at home with myths; he likes to personify his relationships and may personify inanimate things. Science proceeds by the depersonification of myths. An illustration may help to clarify this distinction. Every national literature contains poems to the nightingale. The value of each consists in its originality, in the unique personal response evoked in the poet by his experience. On the other hand, every encyclopaedia of ornithology contains a scientifically exact description of the nightingale, and the chief virtue of each account lies in its unequivocal agreement in all essentials with other accounts.

Many modern poets, recognizing science as the dominant influence of the age, have attempted to honor it and to celebrate technical advances and inventions. But few have found the subject matter of science acceptable to the muse. The most exacting discipline, the most intricate technique, the most extraordinary implements which man has perfected for pushing back the frontiers of the unknown all operate today in the domain of the natural sciences, and to this domain the poets are generally hostile or indifferent.

To honor the scientist as a modern Ulysses, a man of many inventions who sails beyond the boundaries of the familiar to wrest secrets from stars and atoms, is the obvious theme for an epic of the age. There seems to be no good reason why the lathe, the throttle, or the microscope might not acquire in time an aura of romance like the sword or spinning wheel. In Belgium, the most highly industrialized state in Europe, one poet at least applied himself to the work of immortalizing the triumphs of the factory and the laboratory. Emile Verhaeren (1855–1916) could transform orderly and organized workshops into a setting for his own black and gold moods. He saw prosaic investigations grow big with the imminent discovery of new and monstrous forces, and the microscope amaze with revelations of bizarre, unbidden loveliness. The romance of science as an instrument of man's insatiable lust for knowledge and will to power also inspired the British poet Alfred Noyes (1880–   ) who composed a trilogy, *The Torch Bearers* (1922–1930), to honor the great discoverers in suitable verse.

The most effective and most widely read tributes to the great inventors, engineers, and technologists were written at a less ambitious level and the general public received most of its knowledge of scientific progress through journals or adventure stories. The French novelist, Jules Verne (1828–1905), was the first to make pseudoscientific fiction a genre and utilize the latest investigations of the specialists as a background for fantastic adventures under water (*Twenty Thousand Leagues under the Sea*) or in the blackness of interstellar space (*From the Earth to the Moon*).

It was impossible to honor the works of the great scientists and engineers without applauding the men who conceived them. The adulation which Europe paid Ferdinand de Lesseps (1805–1894), the engineer responsible for the Suez Canal, proved that society was shifting its values. The acclaim reserved for physicists like Marie Curie (1867–1934), bacteriologists like Robert Koch (1843–1910), and mathematicians like Albert Einstein (1879–   ) indicated that scientists might take rank in popular esteem with statesmen, soldiers, artists, and saints as leaders of humanity. The growing pride and interest in science was retroactive and the technological revolution induced a flood of historical studies on all the great investigators of the physical world, from Archimedes and Leonardo da Vinci to James Watt and Michael Faraday.

Of those English writers who caught the spirit and preached the triumphs of the scientific age to the public the most famous was Herbert George Wells (1866–1946). Some of his novels (*The War in the Air* and *In the Days of the Comet*) were social prophecy with a scientific flavor. Others deviated into lectures on the value of scientific training and the need for social planning, for Wells was one of the earliest members of the Fabian Society which sought to re-educate the British people. His most successful books were science adventure stories such as *The Island of Dr. Moreau* and *The Invisible Man* which were really high class "thrillers." Some of the admiration for scientists and technicians which inspired Wells may also be discerned in the American novelist Sinclair Lewis. Scenes laid in the laboratory of the chemist or biologist, the operating room of the surgeon, and even the tower of the astronomer have become popular in modern fiction and drama. The demand for science stories with prophetic forecasts of technological wonders yet to come has stimulated a new school of science fiction since Jules Verne and H. G. Wells set the pattern. But the progress of scientific studies in anthropology and especially in the life of prehistoric man also inspired fresh interest in primitive society. This gave rise to a varied literature in the twentieth century, from Jack London's *The Son of the Wolf* (1900) to Vardis Fisher's *Darkness and the Deep* (1943).

Not all novelists viewed the advance of science as an unmixed blessing for mankind. The pessimism of Thomas Hardy (1840–1928), reflected in his novels from *Desperate Remedies* (1871) to *Jude the Obscure* (1895), was grounded in a mechanistic concept of the universe and its iron laws. Hardy questioned whether the architect of such a world could be more than an automaton, "mighty to build and blend, but impotent to tend" the human castaways marooned in its bleak immensities. Other writers, who escaped what might be termed the philosophical blight of scientific determinism, became victims of a "clinical methodology." A morbid concentration upon pathological symptoms and case histories led them to overburden their pages with ill-mastered medical lore. There was also a group of defiant authors who rebelled against the mechanized routine of living which science seemed to propose for future generations. In the novels of Aldous Huxley (1894–   ) the "brave new world" of science took on the guise of a monstrous and mechanically efficient prison for humanity. Even more disturbing were the fantastic conceptions of the Czech playwright, Karel Čapek (1890–1938), who, in *Rossom's Universal Robots* (1920) and other dramas, suggested the fate which might await human personality in a society reduced to a pattern of undeviating functionalism. The destiny which he forecast for the last human beings was a blind alley, a society as stereotyped as an insect community, in which men had become the slaves of their tireless and inexorable machines.

PHILOSOPHY AND RELIGION

The decline of Western Civilization, at first thought an event limited in time and space like the comparable sunset of the Classical Culture, is a philosophical drama that, in its entirety, comprehends all the major problems of existence.

OSWALD SPENGLER

I. POSITIVISM AND PRAGMATISM

POETS and philosophers sometimes entertain concepts so vast and nebulous that the historian, while hesitating to reject them as untrue, always refers to them with reservations. One such concept is expressed in the lines by Arthur O'Shaughnessy:

> Each age is a dream that is dying
> Or one that is coming to birth.

Few thinkers would deny that each age does have a distinctive mood or time-spirit (*Zeitgeist*) or that each social group has a collective life of its own. The problem is to decide what degree of independent reality should be ascribed to a Time-Spirit, a Group-Being, or to such vital abstractions as The Nation or The State. The members of every human society are united by immaterial ties, by common ideas and affections, habits and hopes, memories and myths. In their totality these shared imponderable affirmations make up the intellectual and emotional heritage of the group, its group-mind or group-soul or group-character. Each generation accepts almost unconsciously and perpetuates almost unthinkingly the loyalties and the legends, the social customs and inherited traits which distinguish their group from rival groups, constraining its members to combine for common aims and react to common threats as if the group were one body.

The philosopher, whose vocation it is to isolate and ponder all generalizations and abstractions, sometimes comes to the conclusion that the complex of ideas accepted by his generation or group is outdated and illogical. When the mythology of a society no longer corresponds to its current needs and knowledge, some thinker proposes an amended synthesis, a more comfortable intellectual framework or "world view," which arranges the discoveries and beliefs of the time in a more acceptable pattern. In the past hundred years the intellectual leaders of Europe and America have attempted several "adventures in synthesis" in the effort to construct an intellectual mansion wherein modern man might feel at home.

During the first half of the nineteenth century philosophy and philosophers enjoyed a high reputation among the European peoples. In the second half of the century, however, philosophy was eclipsed by the dazzling achievements of the scientists and technicians. The scientists seemed to be vindicating their search for laws and their mastery of matter with such a brilliant series of discoveries that leading philosophers were deeply impressed. They hastened to propose a system of philosophy grounded in the system and methods of the physicist and mathematician. Three consequences which resulted from this attempted fusion of philosophy and science are interesting to trace.

The first of these was a powerful movement in philosophy which received the name of positivism. The positivists boasted that they had abandoned abstract "metaphysical" notions in favor of those facts and laws which the scientists were showing to be "positive" or demonstrable. Positivism, as an attitude of mind or mode of enquiry, had many forerunners; it could be traced to the seventeenth century or back to the Greek philosophers, if one chose. But the acknowledged founder of the positivist school in the nineteenth century was the Frenchman Auguste Comte (1798–1857), who used the term *positivism* as the opposite of idealism. Positivism or Comtism, systematized in England by Herbert Spencer (1820–1903), appealed to many who prided themselves upon being practical, hardheaded thinkers and its influence spread strongly after 1850. But positivism was a limited philosophy with serious defects. It postulated a universe that was conceived fundamentally in inorganic terms; even living beings and human societies were analyzed as if their behavior differed in no essential particular from combining crystals or dissolving galaxies. The belief that living forms and inorganic matter were ultimately one and therefore obedient to the same laws, found apparent support two years after Comte's death in the theory of biological evolution proposed by Charles Darwin in *The Origin of Species* (1859). But Darwin's thought, which at first seemed to offer support to the philosophy of positivism, was so revolutionary that it shook off the shackles of physics and diverted the search for truth into the organic world.

Darwin's announcement that biological species could have originated through a process of natural selection was the most important scientific generalization of the century, for it dissolved one of the last certitudes upon which most philosophers had rested their conjectures. From earliest times the observable fact that all the species of the plant and animal world reproduced "after their kind" had been taken as proof that species were fixed and immutable. This immutability, preserved by known species through countless vicissitudes and unnoted generations, seemed proof that organic types had been fixed once and forever. A pattern which could persist even though its mortal replicas perished implied an unchanging reality behind the flux of things, and this persistence vindicated man's faith in eternal verities. But if Darwin were correct, if species, like individuals, were fleeting shadows reflected in the river of time, then notions of design derived from the assumed immutability of species, notions identified by Plato as eternal Ideas or Archetypes, lost much of their philosophic certainty. Thus it seemed probable that the wedding of science and philosophy, which had produced positivism as its first offspring, would produce agnosticism as its second.

One effect of Darwin's theories was to emphasize the struggle for existence and thus to make the will as important as the intellect in the unending battle for survival. This view had already been propounded by the German philosopher Arthur Schopenhauer (1788–1860) in *The World as Will and Idea* (1818). Another effect of Darwin's teaching was to make the concept of adaptability, of internal adjustment to external change on the part of an organism, vitally important and hence to emphasize resource and initiative as virtues favoring survival. One result of these converging currents — of the preference for the positive, the concrete, the workable, and the emphasis upon struggle, will, adaptability, initiative — was a new and popular philosophy which came to be known as pragmatism.

Pragmatism as a system of thought is most often associated with the name of William James (1842–1910). It was fitting that an American philosopher should expound most brilliantly a philosophy which stressed energy, initiative, and improvisation as the virtues of modern man and deprecated blind obedience to any formal pattern. Americans were "pragmatic" by necessity and tradition; the pioneers and frontiersmen had learned to judge ideas and methods by the practical formula, "It's true if it works." With other thinkers of similar mind William James concluded that in a world of ceaseless change and chance even the laws of nature might be but useful approximations and the laws of men but group habits or group responses which had become stereotyped. Under this view, the "truth" of a proposition, a philosophy, a social system, seemed to depend upon how well it served man's need. Immediate human experience became the ultimate test by which men proved things good or bad, right or wrong. There was nothing certain under the sun except struggle and variety, change and chance.

Intelligence, according to the pragmatic view of things, was a faculty developed by the higher animals which helped them to orient themselves and to survive. All matter appeared to be under a compulsion to change and all living organisms obeyed an inner urge to evolve, so that life was forever dynamic and the life force akin to will rather than to reason or logic. Any philosophy which exalted the life force was likely at this point to receive a favorable hearing, and an eloquent exponent of such a philosophy was found in the Frenchman Henri Bergson (1859–1941). Bergson published his *Creative Evolution* in 1906 and proposed the phrase *élan vital* for the vital urge behind the phenomena of evolution. Scornful of metaphysics and formal logic, he insisted that life constantly strove to surpass itself and that it must be studied as a process, not imprisoned in a system. His opinions, expanded and popularized by others, called attention to a critical development in twentieth-century thought, a development sometimes styled the anti-intellectualist revolt or the flight from reason. Before and after World War I a number of critics assailed the primacy long accorded the reason and insisted that will, intuition, and emotion were equally authentic touchstones for discovering reality. This revolt against reason was reflected in politics and in the revolutionary ideologies of the age. It is easy to see that doctrines which declared change to be inevitable, which stressed will and initiative as leading virtues and implied that triumphant force was the final arbiter of things, would appeal to revolutionary groups.

The final ingredient needed to complete a political philosophy of struggle and power was a glorification of the "leadership principle." The superior individual and the superior race must be presented as destined to dominate. For this faith the German philosopher Friedrich Nietzsche (1844–1900) provided a convenient basis with his

doctrine of the superman. Nietzsche's superman was an overcompen-
sation for his own limitations, an exceptional individual imbued with
a "master morality" instead of a "slave morality." Slaves exalt pity
and mercy and charity because their one hope lies in persuading their
masters to accept and practice these virtues. But the true superman,
endowed with an incorruptible "master morality," resists such weakness and operates with the impersonal ruthlessness of a natural force
because he is "beyond good and evil." Nietzsche's arguments were
much more subtle and persuasive than this curt summary suggests but
in sum they provided a rationale for irresponsible arrogance.

It would be a mistake, of course, to suppose that the philosophy of
Nietzsche or of any other academic thinker could set armies in motion. The authoritarian state, which became the supreme power and
the fiat maker for millions of Europeans in the twentieth century,
was not erected by philosophers but by men of action. Philosophy
was merely the mirror in which coming events cast their shadows
before. The right of the superior individual or race to rule the lesser
breeds was implicit in Nietzsche; the vital role of the will was developed by Schopenhauer; the significance of energism and intuition
emerged in Bergson's work; the argument that a cause or a stratagem
might be justified if it succeeded could be read into pragmatist teaching. Totalitarian dictators of the twentieth century found "philosophic irrationalism" already ripe for their purposes and they cari-
catured and pillaged the philosophers' ideas without scruple. Radical
socialists and syndicalists appealing for "direct action" justified it as
energism, and mob demonstrations were displays of voluntarism. Institutions grounded in the older, orderly methods of systematic enquiry and reasoned compromise (the parliaments, the law courts, the
legal safeguards that protected the individual and private property)
were attacked by the dictators as bulwarks of bourgeois privilege.
The real motive for the attack was the firm opposition these liberal
institutions offered to Caesarism, to authoritarianism, to one-party
government. Constitutional checks and balances had to be abolished
as obstacles to the national will before the dictators could exercise un-
trammeled and arbitrary power. But once these slowly erected safeguards of individual freedom had been leveled there was no court of
appeal against the tyranny of the naked act. "Justice," ran a National
Socialist maxim, "is whatever benefits the German people." "Every
force is a moral force," wrote Giovanni Gentile, the philosopher of
Fascism, "for it is always an expression of will." In all political con-

tests under Fascism, the group that won could sit in judgment on the case, and its judgment would be final and irreversible — or so the Fascist deluded himself into believing. This was a doctrine of pure political expediency justified by a philosophy of irrationalism.

2. SOCIOLOGY

Sociology is the science which treats of the nature and development of society; it is therefore the school in which the academic theorist and the practicing politician can best exchange ideas. In every social conflict ideas are weapons; and a new philosophical synthesis, as it wins adherents, prepares the way for a political readjustment. As already noted, when popular leaders appeal to the will, intuition, or emotion of their followers instead of stressing traditional methods and rational considerations, they are likely to excite a maximum of enthusiasm and a minimum of thought. This is one reason why all revolutionists make a point of appealing to the young, for the young are more ardent and less calculating than the old.

The revolt against reason in the twentieth century was in part a revolt against the statistics which supported the *status quo* — against the frozen formulas of the ledgers, the bank rates, the tabulations of trade and population and national wealth and annual earnings, which seemed to condemn certain classes and nations to inferiority. It was also a protest against the legal formulas, the political axioms, the aesthetic creeds which ruling groups had set up to justify the *status quo* and provide a reasoned defense, a rationale, for their way of life. Classes and nations which felt themselves disinherited were easily persuaded that life is more important than formulas, that "the Becoming" is more real than "the Become," that cramped nations with a rising population have a right to more "living space." Through all such arguments, however, there runs an implicit assumption that human society is an organic growth and that a nation with the will to expand and the ability to expand has a right to expand. The philosopher might observe that what this represented, in an abstract sense, was a triumph of biology over physics and that the concept of the universe-as-organism was superseding the concept of the universe-as-machine. In the narrower world of politics, this meant that arguments which emphasized the nation as a cultural organism were becoming more persuasive than theories which treated the state as a mechanical structure.

In the nineteenth century the most influential criticism of society and philosophy of history combined was the contribution of Karl Marx (1818–1883). His great work *Das Kapital,* in three volumes (1867–1895), was completed by Friedrich Engels. Marx fathered the economic interpretation of history. He insisted that the means by which men earned their living and produced material wealth determined their social, political, and intellectual activities and beliefs. When one dominant class (the expropriators) was supplanted by another it meant that a change had taken place in the economic structure of a society. The political revolution which usually accompanied such a change was a secondary phenomenon motivated by the economic forces at work, and Marx held that most historians had been misled hitherto because they did not penetrate behind the political changes. Bourgeois writers were still teaching complacently that the social struggle had ended with the bourgeois conquest of political power, which they identified with democracy or popular rule. But Marx foresaw a further, a proletarian revolution in the making. This proletarian revolution he regarded as historically and logically inevitable, his dialectical materialism ordained it, and he urged the workers of the world to unite in preparation for the day. The dictatorship of the proletariat would come in due time, however, whether the individual worker welcomed or opposed it: that was an aspect of its inevitability.

This Marxian theory of economic determinism, popularized and distorted at times, became the inspiration and the comfort of the militant proletarians. So profoundly had Marx labored as he integrated his ideas that he provided the intellectual leaders of the working classes with a philosophy of revolution and a program of action in one. He himself was too subtle and too independent a thinker to approve most of the simplified "synopses" of his philosophy which became popular. "I am not a Marxist," he protested in his later years. But he had founded a new school of sociology and he left a younger generation of sociologists and socialists to split hairs over the finer points of his doctrine.

It fell to a French engineer and social theorist, Georges Sorel (1847–1922), to formulate the most popular philosophy of direct action or activism for the militant proletariat. Sorel's *Reflections on Violence* (1910) was not his most representative work but it was seized upon by revolutionary syndicalists who planned to conquer power through the organization of labor and the use of the general strike. Sorel was persuaded that the nerveless bourgeois class would shortly be unseated and he suggested that if the proletarian elite failed to seize control when the moment came some more enterprising group would do so. He emphasized energy, will, and decision above pure intellectualism as the indispensable qualities in a leader and he broke with the orthodox Marxian theorists by denying that the triumph of the proletariat was assured through the inexorable processes of dialectical materialism. For Sorèl saw life not as an intelligible historic process but as irrational and chaotic strife; he preached a dynamic activism as the key to social mastery; and he stressed the function of a disciplined and heroic elite group as the instrument with which power could be won and wielded. Such a doctrine could be borrowed and misused by any faction not too squeamish to seek power by strenuous methods, and Mussolini later credited Sorel with helping to provide a theoretic basis for Italian Fascism.

Sorel's contemporary, the Italian sociologist Vilfredo Pareto (1848–1923), who was likewise trained as an engineer, added to the philosophical ferment by seeking to distinguish the "logical" from the "nonlogical" activities of men in society. From his wide reading of history, Pareto concluded that the "rationalizations" or "ideals" which social groups set up were what he termed *derivations*. By derivations he meant façades or fictions that screened the basic, instinctive, and often irrational motives which moved people to act. The astute leader, whose intuition enabled him to see through these deceptions that masked human desires, could harness the direct and primal drives of human nature. This mastery of the nonlogical forces in society, Pareto implied, explained much of the influence achieved by dictators and ruling groups or elites. The amoral leader could juggle conventional symbols, could guide and goad men with slogans they had learned to obey unthinkingly. Such deluded subordinates became efficient tools of the leader's ruthless will. Hitler reduced this phase of Pareto's philosophy to an aphorism when he observed that it is difficult to deceive people but easy to help them to deceive themselves.

Pareto also evolved a cyclical theory of social change, roughly grounded on the idea that after any aggressive social group (the "lions") fought their way to the top, they tended to grow cautious and to conserve their conquests by ruse and rationalization. The "lions" became "foxes." When the foxes so far forsook their courage and clarity of vision that they believed the fables and derivations they had invented to justify their privileges, they were ripe for liquidation by a new group of "lions." As the fate of fallen empires was clarified by modern scholarly research, many other thinkers besides Pareto searched the past for a clue to the inner causes, the sociological laws of human progress. The impassioned antiquarianism which drove some twentieth-century students to turn their back on the astonishing civilization of their own day and sift the dust of forgotten cities had a practical motive. The dynamic rhythms of modern life and the destructive forces which science had let loose made social discipline, social wisdom, and social prognosis imperative. It was hoped that the study of past societies would provide clues and antidotes for dealing with the perils of the present. H. G. Wells put forward the sobering suggestion that modern man was engaged in a race between education and disaster. By repeated autopsies on the remains of dead civilizations the sociologists hoped to discover the causative factors in cultural decline.

Twentieth-century man, having broken up the roads behind him, was troubled by a sense of desolation and singularity which made him nostalgic for the past. "We await, today, the philosopher who will inform us in what language history is written, and how we are to read it," Oswald Spengler wrote in his *Decline of the West* (1918). Spengler believed that he himself had found the key to this language, that he could forecast the future course of Western civilization and could even indicate the general morphology of all cultures. The central concept of his work was his conviction that each culture is an independent growth, that each has its distinctive physiognomy, its unique life cycle, and its characteristic changes from youth to age. No two cultures were identical; in fact the aesthetic, legal, mathematical, and religious symbolism in which one people clothed their aspirations could never be fully comprehended by any other people. But because all cultures (unless damaged or destroyed) completed analogous life cycles, the successive phases in the literature, architecture, social structure, and world view of one culture might be equated with the similar phases in the life history of all other cultures of which man had record. Spengler thus assigned a special sense of his own to the term *contemporary*. For him, Alexander the Great and Napoleon were "contemporaries" because they appeared at the same relative moment in their respective cultures.

The concept of historical parallelisms, the discovery that history repeats itself with variations, was nothing novel. What gave Spengler's thesis distinction was his belief that he would demonstrate why each true culture had a normal life span of about one thousand years, and his confidence that he could distinguish the sequence of changes which must overtake it because those changes were implicit in its organic destiny. In the final phase, when it had hardened into a civilization, a culture might perpetuate itself in spiritless, stereotyped fashion for generations but it could no longer grow because its creative period was ended. Western civilization, Spengler deduced, had now reached this late, rigid, megalopolitan phase. This pessimistic prophecy found an echo in many minds after it was published in 1918, for the First World War seemed an augury of European disintegration.

Spengler's attempt was the most grandiose and poetic but it was not the only contemporary essay in historical synthesis and integration. The new vistas into the past that were opened by the historians and archeologists and the new theories on the nature of man and society formulated by anthropologists, psychologists, and sociologists, challenged bold minds to generalize. In England, Arnold Joseph Toynbee (1889–   ) commenced an erudite and far-ranging *Study of History* notable for its lively imagery and dramatic conception. Toynbee found his central clue to the rise of cultures in the challenge of the natural enviroment and the response each human society made to it. If the challenge were too easy, it might fail to stimulate a vital response which favored growth. If it were too strenuous, it might arrest a promising culture or render it abortive. Even triumphant adaptation had its perils and penalties, for a people who conquered an adverse environment by will and enterprise might remain wedded to a perfected technique when later challenges required a different reaction. It appeared to Toynbee that nonmaterial factors, imponderables such as will, energy, and religious convictions, often proved more conclusive in shaping the destiny of nations than economic pressures or political institutions. The collapse and disintegration of a flourishing culture might come, he suggested, from external pressures which it failed to resist or from an internal conflict between the rational aims of a society and its nonrational impulses. Thus Toynbee's philosophy of history fused several old and new concepts in a provocative but mystifying interpretation of human history, a reassessment which provoked more speculations than it resolved. Unfortunately the outbreak of World War II delayed the completion of the author's compendious project, but the first six volumes of *A Study of History* (1935–1939) were compressed into a helpful one volume presentation by D. C. Somervell (1947).

Ewing Galloway

THE MASTER CONTROL ROOM OF THE NATIONAL BROADCASTING COMPANY IN RADIO CITY, NEW YORK

Courtesy of Paul H. Donaldson

ELECTRONIC CALCULATING MACHINE, HARVARD UNIVERSITY

In the same years the Russo-American sociologist, Pitirim A. Soro-kin (1889–   ), published an elaborate work on *Social and Cultural Dynamics* in four volumes (1937–1941). Sorokin investigated the Graeco-Roman and Western European civilizations, with briefer analyses of Egyptian, Babylonian, Hindu, Arabic, and Chinese cultures, in an effort to probe the secrets of cultural integration and cultural unity. Like Spengler, he concluded that integrated cultures reacted as if they had a life and synergy of their own. A cultural system could adapt itself to resist external changes. It sometimes fell "sick" and recovered in a manner that suggested the reaction of a biological organism. It absorbed or expelled intrusive alien elements. It appeared to develop immunity to repeated external infections. With good fortune, it preserved its functional equilibrium until it had run its course and then it declined and disintegrated in logical fulfillment of its own socioeconomic life and destiny.

In his attempt to explain and to predict social changes Sorokin distinguished three major phases through which a culture might pass. These he termed the Ideational, Idealistic, and Sensate. He concluded that Western civilization exhibited the symptoms of an overripe Sensate culture and that it would shortly decline. But he was more optimistic than Spengler in that he did not rule out the possibility of a revival under the stimulus of some alternate fluctuation of its inner energies.

The influences which brought the "inner energies" of a culture to a climax remained a mystery. What caused the peaks of creative activity which historians discerned, or thought they discerned, in Egypt of the fourteenth, and Greece of the fifth century before Christ, or in Italy of the Renaissance period? This question the American anthropologist, Alfred Louis Kroeber (1876–   ), set himself to investigate in his *Configurations of Culture Growth* (1944). His study shed considerable light on the nature, pattern, and duration of each "cultural efflorescence" which he analyzed, but he refrained from generalizations for which he conceived the time was not yet ripe. Whether all cultures have an ordained life cycle, whether they must age and die, whether it is necessary for them to be cross fertilized with other cultures to preserve their vigor, whether they can be reborn through some self-generated metamorphosis, all these were questions on which, in Kroeber's cautious opinion, no conclusive judgment could yet be formulated.

For the student of contemporary history and contemporary

thought one element of interest in these attempts to "grasp at the hem of destiny" lies in the use of biological or morphological images and comparisons. Spengler and Sorokin in particular drew their analogies from the world of living organisms in preference to the world of mathematics and mechanics. Since the time of Galileo and Newton Western philosophy had been overshadowed by the formulas of physics, and thinkers had in general conceived the universe as a vast machine and society as a pattern or structure. This trend appeared to have reversed itself by the twentieth century, and the newer conception of the universe pictured it as something between a machine and a self-adapting, self-creating, and self-perpetuating organism.

3. EDUCATION

It has become the custom to judge the educational standards of a country today by the literacy or illiteracy of its citizens. For over a century illiteracy has been declining in all the countries of Europe and America. The progress has been most rapid in recent decades. In 1900, for instance, three-fourths of the Russian people were still listed as illiterate but after the revolution of 1917 the percentage of those who could not read or write was reduced sharply within a generation. In the United States one-fourth of the soldiers called for service in World War I were found to be functionally illiterate and remedies were pressed to improve this average. In Europe energetic campaigns for adult education and the introduction of compulsory schooling for all children have had remarkable results so that by 1946 illiteracy had become an exceptional disability in all but the most backward areas. Throughout Africa and much of Asia, however, which hold more than half the human race, the capacity to read and write still remained an uncommon accomplishment. Among the Chinese 70 per cent of the people were counted as illiterate in 1946. For India the rate was computed at 88 per cent; for the East Indies at 95 per cent; and for most of the Near East it was set as high as 98 per cent. The absence of any accurate statistics and any wholly satisfactory standard of examination made it difficult to compute the ratio of illiteracy for the global population as a whole. It seemed probable, however, that after World War II the illiterates still outnumbered the literates by two to one.

The ancient questions, "What shall the young be taught, for what shall the young be taught, and by whom shall the young be taught?" became critical issues in many countries in the twentieth century. For among most civilized nations public education had become a state service, and the public schools, supported by the taxpayers, were expected to train the young to be loyal and useful citizens. In Prussia the right of the state to enforce the education of the young had been proclaimed as early as 1794. In France a national system of public education was decreed during the French Revolution, and school attendance by all French children between the ages of six and thirteen was made compulsory in 1882. In Great Britain compulsory education was introduced in 1876, and full-time education for all children from five to fifteen was decreed in 1945. The first law passed to provide for compulsory school attendance in the United States (Massachusetts, 1852) set an example which was followed by all forty-eight states before 1921. (See graph, page 579.)

The manner in which the national system of education was administered in each country and the degree to which educational policy was subordinated to political control varied greatly from one nation to another. In Great Britain the minister of education did not receive effective power to promote a system of uniform national education until 1945, and in most of the British self-governing Dominions there was no national minister of education and no central agency with power to consolidate the school programs of the provinces or municipalities. In the United States the federal Bureau of Education attached to the Department of the Interior collected and distributed information, but it had no authority to formulate policy and there was no federal machinery through which a national program of education could be synthesized. This decentralization of authority, which left the responsibility for education to local boards, placed the United States in sharp contrast to the authoritarian states. In Soviet Russia the curricula of the schools and the discipline of the young people enrolled in the youth organizations were prescribed by the Soviet commissar of education, and the avowed aim of the schools was to train loyal citizens and indoctrinate them with communist ideals. Under the Fascist government in Italy the school administration was thoroughly revised in order to make it (in the words of the minister of education) "Fascist in its system, method, structure, and style." German education after the National Socialists came into power in 1933 was transformed even more drastically to subordinate it to the policies of the government, and the Reich minister for education declared categorically that "the whole function of all education is to create a Nazi."

In the democratic countries the idea of using the schools to indoctrinate the children with the views of a political party was not popular. The democratic way of life emphasized the dignity and responsibility of the individual, and democratic government was defended as a guarantee that all citizens should enjoy equal justice under law and equality of rights. Among those rights, freedom in seeking information and the privilege of independent judgment ranked high. It was recognized that no legislation could make all men equal in intelligence or endow all children born in the country with equal ability or health or stature. But free schools which all children were required to attend for seven years or longer (unless they received equivalent training otherwise) promised equality of educational opportunity. Free text books, free medical attention, and free meals for school children were further services often established to equalize opportunity.

One form of inequality which could not be solved by these methods, however, was regional inequality. If all local schools were supported by local taxes, the equipment and the teachers' salaries in economically retarded areas would remain below the general level. Recognizing the education of the young to be a responsibility of the whole nation, most governments have sought to improve the quality of public instruction in retarded areas by subsidies from the federal (or national) taxes. A government which turns over part of the national revenue for the support of the public schools, however, is likely to take an increasing interest in the curriculum and standards of those schools.

The educational aims which prevail in a democratic society have been defined as instruction without indoctrination. To devise a balanced curriculum which could ground the students in sound principles and train them to reason for themselves presented no simple problem. A complete absence of any general directives or policies was an invitation to anarchy; but firm direction and strict discipline might be denounced as regimentation. In the United States even the provision requiring public school pupils to salute the flag was fought in the courts as an infringement of individual liberty. Plans to direct students towards the more useful as contrasted with the more admired cultural courses, or to rate them on their capacities and limit their choice of careers, also provoked resentment. One illustration of the laissez-faire philosophy of education may be noted in the attitude of the United States government towards scientific training and research. Only in times of acute crises did the government make any decided effort to draw upon the potential resources of the nation's technical schools and scientific personnel. The National Academy of Sciences was organized by an Act of Congress in the midst of the war between the states (1863). The National Research Council was established by executive order during the First World War (1916). The Office of Scientific Research and Development dated from 1941, the year in which the United States entered World War II. This relative neglect of science as a handmaid of government, except in periods of crisis, meant that research and experiment in America remained almost entirely a private matter without official supervision or subsidy. The burden of scientific investigation was borne by the educational institutes and the industrial organizations. This was in keeping with the liberal traditions of free competitive enterprise.

It was also in keeping with the tradition which regarded the individual as the chief end of the educational process and revered private initiative as something too precious to be endangered by even the shadow of bureaucratic coercion. All educational systems designed for a free society had to compromise between two aims. The child was to be stimulated to develop its richest potentialities. If its talents were exceptional it was offered exceptional inducements to excel, and the end sought was the attainment of a well-adjusted personality and a well-ripened intelligence. Where choices had to be made in school the inclination of the student was given consideration; of several aptitudes it was the skill which he most wished to perfect, not the service which would perhaps make him most useful to society, that he learned. This ideal of fostering individual development was honored in all the democratic countries. In the United States it was emphasized most notably through the progressive movement in education. The theory underlying it was the conviction that the individual is unique, that independence of judgment and·character, the interaction of free, competing personalities, and the energies released when each citizen is permitted to prepare himself for and to seek the work which he prefers, will compensate for the mistakes, the false starts, and the abuse of freedom certain to occur under a system of maximum choice and minimum compulsion.

The second educational aim, with which the first must be harmonized, is the welfare of the society of which the individual forms one unit. In fulfilling this aim the public school functions as a mechanism or organ for the graduation of useful citizens, the needs of the state are kept in view, and the shaping and utilization of human units is adjusted to the general plan of social expansion. These two aims — the individual and the social — are not necessarily antagonistic; all programs of public education must combine them in some workable formula. The political philosophy prevailing in a country, and the wealth, security, and character of the citizens, usually determine whether the preferences of the individual or the needs of the state shall be considered first in education.

Under authoritarian governments the trend towards regimentation in public school programs is much more emphatic than in liberal societies. The Russian Soviet regime as part of its successive Five-Year Plans co-ordinated the technical schools and research institutes with the general program for mobilizing all human resources. The German governments from the foundation of the empire in 1871 to the Third Reich (1933–1945) sought to link education and industry in a productive union and to shape both towards military ends. The same held true for Fascist Italy after 1922. In the twentieth century most plans for social reform, most revolutionary programs, have accepted the raising of living standards as primarily a problem of education and the application of scientific formulas to the satisfaction of human needs. In all the above-mentioned countries government funds were provided to speed the training of the scientific personnel without which it was impossible to carry through the technological advances that were counted upon to transform society.

The perennial flaw in the planned educational system is that efficiency is so often achieved at the expense of initiative. When a school is formalized and overcentralized the teaching process loses flexibility. The spirit of experimentation, innovation, and individual inventiveness seems to flourish more spontaneously under a system of decentralized control. Especially where private schools are free to compete with the state schools, and in both new programs and new teaching experiments are tried out frequently, the inertia and hostility to change which so easily overtakes any entrenched officialdom is more successfully held at bay.

4. RELIGION

It is not possible to classify the peoples of the world into distinct religious groups with exactness, partly because of inadequate information and partly because many millions of individuals might equally well be included in several groups or faiths or in none at all. In 1947 general estimates placed the total number of Christians at almost one-third the world population, or about 600,000,000. Of these more than half, or 315,000,000, were counted as Roman Catholics; 117,000,000 as Orthodox (Eastern) Catholics; and the remainder as Protestants. The Mohammedans of the world were estimated at 220,000,000, and the Jews at 15,000,000. These figures accounted for 800,000,000 or perhaps 900,000,000 in a world population of over 2,000,000,000. Totals for the leading religious groups of Asia are little better than reasoned guesses. The Indian census of 1941 indicated that almost two-thirds or about 255,000,000 of the people were Hindus, and one-third or 95,000,000 were Mohammedans. The Chinese population, according to an official estimate of 1936, included 48,000,000 Mohammedans, and over 400,000,000 people who accepted Confucianism, Buddhism, Taoism, or all three.

In Europe during the twentieth century several sharp conflicts developed between the national governments and the established churches. The concordat between the French government and the Holy See, which had been in force since 1801, was abrogated by the government of the Third French Republic in 1905. The concordat negotiated between the Italian Fascist government and the papacy in 1929 was strained by the arbitrary policies of the Fascist state. The National Socialist government of Germany concluded a concordat with the papacy in 1933 but the interference of German state officials in religious affairs and the spirit which dictated the Nazi program for training the young, provoked a series of rebukes from the Catholic bishops. The German Evangelical (Lutheran) Church likewise resisted Nazi policies when they infringed upon religious liberty and Christian teaching, but without seriously modifying the trend towards dictatorship in Germany. In Spain the republican regime set up after the revolution of 1931 pursued an anticlerical policy, dissolving the religious orders and confiscating the property of the Catholic Church. This policy was reversed and the property restored by the Nationalist government which established itself after the Civil War of 1936–1939.

The most bitter and far-reaching conflict waged between the forces of church and state in the first half of the twentieth century began in Russia in 1917. The communist leaders who secured direction of the revolutionary movement at the close of that year were opposed to the existence of the Russian Orthodox Church. They considered it a bulwark of the discredited czarist regime and they

denounced religion as "the opium of the masses." An official campaign to obliterate the symbols and even the memory of the Orthodox faith brought systematic persecution to the clergy, state confiscation of religious edifices for schools, theaters, museums, and libraries, and the organization of a league of militant atheists to distribute antireligious propaganda and to weaken the hold of the Orthodox Church on the affection of the masses. As the new regime overcame the counterrevolutionary factions, and the Communist Party consolidated its power, the campaign against the church was relaxed. The Soviet constitution of 1936 declared that freedom of religious worship (and of antireligious propaganda) were equally guaranteed to all citizens. Although a majority of the younger generation who had received their education in the secular schools preserved a nonreligious attitude and sometimes an antireligious bias, many of the older Russians after a quarter century of communist rule still clung to their religious faith. By 1940 there were eight thousand churches open, with sixty thousand priests officiating. The Russian Orthodox Church had split, however, into an "Old Church" and a "New Church," both with headquarters at Moscow. There was no longer any danger that organized religion, or any church in Russia, could become a state within a state or could offer a serious threat to the Communist Party or the government. All religious activities were restricted in scope, all funds limited, and all practices of the clergy were subject to supervision by the Council of Peoples' Commissars.
→The rising spirit of irrationalism, the fierce international rivalries, and the fanaticism and brutality which spread in political life after World War I, threatened the moral foundation of Western civilization. To observers with a deep religious sense it seemed clear that these evils were traceable to the materialism, selfishness, and moral nihilism of the period. Believing that a spirit of Christian charity was the indispensable remedy for social ills, religious leaders in Europe and America pleaded for a return to religion and closer co-operation among the congregations of all Christian churches.

This desire to promote cultural and humanitarian ideals found practical expression during World War II, and after it, in campaigns of international, nonsectarian charity on a scale unique in history. Churches, governments, and peoples, as well as international relief organizations like the International Red Cross and the United Nations Relief and Rehabilitation Administration, distributed food, clothing, and medicaments worth billions of dollars to relieve the sickness and famine which spread with war. These practical proofs of the strength of human brotherhood saved millions of lives in the "hungry forties." They also helped to soften wartime hates and to dissipate the spirit of international distrust. Mankind was learning once again that the sanest therapy for fear was mutual service.

For the people of the United States, who contributed more largely to the cause of world charity than any other nation, the help extended was in part a conscience offering. The strong can afford to be generous, and the United States emerged from World War II the strongest, the wealthiest, and technologically the best equipped nation on earth. But in gaining such might it had sacrificed some of the idealism which had impressed the world after its victory in 1918. American citizens were only half aware of their responsibilities as a great power and less than half aware of the fear and suspicion which their armaments had aroused. The United States, which was almost immune to direct attack itself, had dealt its enemies paralyzing blows, blows which had been pushed home without respite and without pity. These things would not be forgotten by a shattered world; and religious leaders, as they called their congregations to give thanks for American victory, called upon them also to acknowledge what that victory cost. "We shall leave behind us after victory," warned one religious journal,[1] "nothing of the acclaim for knight errantry which greeted our participation in World War I and remained as a universal reservoir of good feeling. . . . Our obliteration bombing will rest like a curse upon the fair name of our country for generations. The very stones in the debris of what were once noble cities will cry out against us long after peace has settled down. As men labor to restore their homes and public buildings they will say, 'The Americans did this.' And the story will be told with endless repetition of the women and children, the aged and the sick, who were caught in the flame and crushed in the ruin rained down from American planes. . . . We are not coming out of this war bringing with us our traditional reputation as a noble and disinterested friend of civilization. We are coming out as a Great Power, and any acclaim we shall receive henceforth will be a cool but respectful tribute to our power rather than a spontaneous and hearty expression of trust and affection. This will hold no less for our allies than for our enemies."

[1] *The Christian Century*, May 30, 1945.

AIDS FOR ADDITIONAL STUDY

AND READING LISTS

THE investigation of man's past has been expanded and intensified most remarkably in the last few generations. Students curious to know more concerning history as a discipline, how historians work, and where they find their material, should read *The Gateway to History* by Allan Nevins (Boston: Heath, 1938). Contemporary history, such as this present text discusses, is still largely in the making, still uncrystallized. It is enriched daily by new publications, and as these are often superior to the older treatments the student will wish to know how to discover them swiftly through reference works and bibliographies.

It is encouraging to remember, no matter how elusive a research topic may seem to be, that thousands of experts are constantly at work making data available for the enquirer. To find pertinent material without wasting time is a proof of expert training. *Making Books Work* by Jennie M. Flexner (New York: Simon & Schuster, 1943) and *The Library Key*, 6th ed. revised (New York, Wilson, 1946) provide excellent advice on how to use a library. For a "bibliography of bibliographies" which lists reference works on all subjects consult *A Guide to Reference Books* (6th ed., 1936), compiled by I. G. Mudge, or *Basic Reference Books*, by Louis Shores (1939), both sponsored by the American Library Association. These are professional aids which catalogue all departments of knowledge; but there are special guides prepared for the student of history.

A Guide to Historical Literature, edited by G. M. Dutcher and associates (New York: Macmillan, 1931), is very helpful for works on all fields of history to 1930. L. J. Ragatz has assembled *A Bibliography for the Study of European History, 1815–1939*, with supplements (Ann Arbor: Edwards Bros., 1942), and *The Literature of European Imperialism. A Bibliography* (Washington: Paul Pearlman, 1944). Publications on international developments for the years 1919–1932 are listed in W. L. Langer and H. F. Armstrong, *Foreign Affairs Bibliography* (New York: Harper, 1933) and for 1932–1942 in *Foreign Affairs Bibliography*, compiled by R. G. Woolbert for the Council of Foreign Relations (New York: Harper, 1945). Many useful studies on history in the making appear first in journals or periodicals, and for these a ready aid is the

Readers' Guide to Periodical Literature (New York: Wilson, 1900 to date).

The student seeking facts and dates, especially on very recent history, will find help in such annual publications as *The Statesman's Year-Book*, which furnishes statistics and lists of books covering all the states of the world (New York: Macmillan, 1864 to date); in *The World Almanac* (New York: World Telegram, 1868 to date), which is a mine of tabulated information; and in *Information Please Almanac* (New York: Doubleday, 1947). The *Statistical Abstract* (1878 to date), published by the United States Government, digests and indexes the information collected by government agencies. Other national governments issue similar handbooks. W. L. Langer (ed.), *An Encyclopaedia of World History* (Boston: Houghton, Mifflin, 1940) is invaluable as a compressed, factual summary of developments in all countries and periods. For facts about individuals a first recourse should be the collections such as the *Dictionary of National Biography* (22 vols., 1885–1901, with supplements) for eminent Englishmen, and the *Dictionary of American Biography* (20 vols., 1928–1937) for distinguished Americans. Other nations have similar compilations, and foreign celebrities may also be found in the various encyclopaedias of which the *Encyclopaedia Britannica* and the *Encyclopaedia of the Social Sciences* (15 vols., 1930–1935) are especially helpful for historical matter.

The stage upon which the dramas of history are played quite frequently determines the outcome, but few history students give sufficient heed to geography. A lively introduction to this aspect of history is Roderick Peattie, *Geography in Human Destiny* (New York: Stewart, 1940). Map collections on specific countries and regions are cited in the chapter reading lists which follow hereafter. Four atlases of global range and contemporary relevance are *The University Atlas*, edited by G. Goodal and H. C. Darby (3rd ed., Chicago: Denoyer-Geppert, 1944); *Atlas of Global Geography*, by Erwin Raisz (New York: Harper, 1944); *Look at the World*, edited by R. E. Harrison (New York: Knopf, 1944); and *Global Geography*, by Eugene Staley and associates (New York: Crowell, 1944).

PART I

EUROPE: 1900—1914

Europe Since 1815

ACHORN, ERIK. *European Civilization and Politics Since 1815*
New York: Harcourt, Brace, 1934

BOSSENBROOK, WILLIAM J., and others. *Development of Contemporary Civilization. A History of Western Civilization*, Part II
Boston: Heath, 1940

GILLESPIE, JAMES EDWARD. *Europe in Perspective: 1815 to the Present*
New York: Harcourt, Brace, 1942

HALL, WALTER PHELPS, and DAVIS, WILLIAM STEARNS. *The Course of Europe Since Waterloo*. New York: Appleton-Century, 1941

HAYES, CARLETON J. H. *A Political and Cultural History of Modern Europe.* Vol. II: *A Century of Predominantly Industrial Society Since 1830.* Shorter rev. ed. New York: Macmillan, 1939

SCHAPIRO, J. SALWYN. *Modern and Contemporary European History, 1815–1940.* New ed. Boston: Houghton Mifflin, 1940

Europe Since 1870

ALBJERG, VICTOR L., and ALBJERG, MARGUERITE H. *From Sedan to Stresa: Europe Since 1870.* New York: Van Nostrand, 1937

BENNS, F. LEE. *European History Since 1870*
2nd ed. New York: Crofts, 1941

HALL, WALTER PHELPS. *World Wars and Revolutions: the Course of Europe Since 1900.* New York: Appleton-Century, 1943

SLOSSON, PRESTON WILLIAM. *Europe Since 1870*
Boston: Houghton Mifflin, 1935

SWAIN, JOSEPH W. *Beginning the Twentieth Century: a History of Europe from 1870 to the Present.* New York: Norton, 1938

(Texts of more limited temporal or regional application are listed below with the sections to which they apply.)

Collections of Source Material

Contemporary Civilization Source Book. Part II
New York: Columbia University Press, 1941

COMMAGER, HENRY STEELE. *Documents of American History.* 2 vols. 3rd ed. New York: Crofts, 1942

COOKE, W. H., and STICKNEY, EDITH P. *Readings in European International Relations since* 1879. New York: Harper, 1931

LANGSAM, WALTER C., and EAGAN, JAMES M. *Documents and Readings in the History of Europe since* 1918. New York: Lippincott, 1939

SCOTT, JONATHAN F., and BALTZLY, ALEXANDER. *Readings in European History since* 1814. New York: Crofts, 1930

SPROUT, HAROLD, and SPROUT, MARGARET. *Foundations of National Power: Readings on World Politics and American Security*
Princeton: Princeton University Press, 1946

CHAPTER I: *INTRODUCTION*

ABBOTT, W. C. *The Expansion of Europe: a Social and Political History of the Modern World,* 1415–1815. 2nd rev. ed. New York: Crofts, 1938

BINKLEY, ROBERT C. *Realism and Naturalism,* 1852–1871. The Rise of Modern Europe, Vol. XVI. New York: Harper, 1935

BRUUN, GEOFFREY. *Europe in Evolution,* 1415–1815
Boston: Houghton Mifflin, 1945

CLOUGH, S. B., and COLE, C. W. *Economic History of Europe.* Rev. ed.
Boston: Heath, 1946

CROCE, BENEDETTO. *History of Europe in the Nineteenth Century*
New York: Harcourt, Brace, 1933

DAWSON, CHRISTOPHER. *The Making of Europe*
New York: Sheed and Ward, 1945

DIETZ, F. C. *The Industrial Revolution.* Berkshire Studies in European History. New York: Holt, 1927

FEIS, HERBERT. *Europe, the World's Banker,* 1870–1914
New Haven: Yale University Press, 1930

FISHER, H. A. L. *A History of Europe.* 3 vols.
Boston: Houghton Mifflin, 1935–1936

FUETER, EDUARD. *World History,* 1815–1920
New York: Harcourt, Brace, 1922

HAYES, C. J. H. *A Generation of Materialism,* 1871–1900. The Rise of Modern Europe, Vol. XVII. New York: Harper, 1941

HEATON, HERBERT. *Economic History of Europe*
New York: Harper, 1936

HOBSON, J. A. *Evolution of Modern Capitalism: a Study of Machine Production.* Rev. ed. New York: Scribner's, 1926

—— *Imperialism: A Study.* 3rd ed.
New York: Macmillan, 1938

HOSKINS, H. L. *European Imperialism in Africa.* Berkshire Studies in European History. New York: Holt, 1930

LANGER, W. L. *The Diplomacy of Imperialism,* 1890–1902
New York: Knopf, 1935

MUMFORD, LEWIS. *Technics and Civilization*
New York: Harcourt, Brace, 1934

NUSSBAUM, F. L. *A History of the Economic Institutions of Modern Europe.* New York: Crofts, 1933

RANDALL, J. H., JR. *The Making of the Modern Mind.* Rev. ed.
Boston: Houghton Mifflin, 1940

TOWNSEND, MARY E., and PEAKE, CYRUS H. *European Colonial Expansion since* 1871. New York: Lippincott, 1941

USHER, A. P. *A History of Mechanical Inventions*
New York: McGraw-Hill, 1929

(See also Suggestions for Further Reading, Chapter IX)

CHAPTER II: *GREAT BRITAIN*

BEER, MAX. *A History of British Socialism*
New York: Norton, 1942

Cambridge History of the British Empire
New York: Macmillan, 1929–

CLAPHAM, J. H. *An Economic History of Modern Britain.* 3 vols.
New York: Macmillan, 1931–1938

COLE, G. D. H. *A Short History of the British Working Class Movement,* 1789–1937. 3 vols. in 1. New York: Macmillan, 1938

COLE, G. D. H., and POSTGATE, R. W. *The British Common People,* 1746–1946
New York: Knopf, 1947

DIETZ, F. C. *An Economic History of England*
New York: Holt, 1942

ELTON, LORD. *Imperial Commonwealth*
New York: Reynal and Hitchcock, 1946

ENSOR, R. C. K. *England, 1870–1914*. Oxford History of England
New York: Oxford University Press, 1936

HOFFMAN, R. J. S. *Great Britain and the German Trade Rivalry, 1875–1914*. Philadelphia: University of Pennsylvania Press, 1933

MARDER, A. J. *The Anatomy of British Sea Power: a History of British Naval Policy in the Pre-Dreadnought Era, 1880–1905*
New York: Knopf, 1940

MARRIOTT, SIR J. A. R. *Modern England, 1885–1939: a History of My Own Times*. London: Methuen, 1943

NEVINS, ALLAN, and BREBNER, J. B. *The Making of Modern Britain*
New York: Norton, 1943

ROBINSON, HOWARD. *The Development of the British Empire*. Rev. ed.
Boston: Houghton Mifflin, 1936

STEMBRIDGE, J. H. *An Atlas of the British Commonwealth and Empire*
New York: Oxford University Press, 1944

TREVELYAN, G. M. *British History in the Nineteenth Century and After, 1782–1919*. New York: Longmans, Green, 1938

TROTTER, R. G. *The British Empire-Commonwealth*. Berkshire Studies in European History. New York: Holt, 1932

WILLIAMSON, J. A. *A Short History of British Expansion*. 2nd ed.
New York: Macmillan, 1930

(See also Suggestions for Further Reading, Chapter XXVI)

Chapter III: *GERMANY*

BRANDENBURG, ERICH. *From Bismarck to the World War: a History of German Foreign Policy*. New York: Oxford University Press, 1927

BROOK, W. F. *A Social and Economic History of Germany from William II to Hitler, 1888–1939*. New York: Oxford University Press, 1939

DAWSON, W. H. *The German Empire, 1867–1914, and the Unity Movement*. 2 vols. New York: Macmillan, 1919

FULLER, J. V. *Bismarck's Diplomacy at its Zenith*
Cambridge: Harvard University Press, 1922

HALE, O. J. *Germany and the Diplomatic Revolution: a Study in Diplomacy and the Press*
Philadelphia: University of Pennsylvania Press, 1931

LUTZ, R. H. *The Fall of the German Empire*, 1914–1918. 2 vols.
Stanford: Stanford University Press, 1932

ROBERTSON, C. G. *Bismarck*
New York: Holt, 1919

ROSENBERG, ARTHUR. *The Birth of the German Republic*, 1871–1918
New York: Oxford University Press, 1932

SCHMITT, B. E. *Triple Alliance and Triple Entente*. Berkshire Studies in
European History. New York: Holt, 1934

SHUSTER, GEORGE N., and BERGSTRASSER, ARNOLD. *Germany: a Short History*
New York: Norton, 1944

STEINBERG, S. H. *A Short History of Germany*
New York: Macmillan, 1946

VALENTIN, VEIT. *The German People*. New York: Knopf, 1946

VEBLEN, THORSTEIN. *Imperial Germany and the Industrial Revolution*. New
ed. New York: Macmillan, 1939

    (See also Suggestions for Further Reading, Chapter XXIX)

CHAPTER IV: *FRANCE*

BROGAN, D. W. *France under the Republic: the Development of Modern
France*, 1870–1939. New York: Harper, 1940

BRUUN, GEOFFREY. *Clemenceau*. Makers of Modern Europe
Cambridge: Harvard University Press, 1943

CLAPHAM, J. H. *The Economic Development of France and Germany*,
1815–1914. 4th ed. New York: Macmillan, 1937

GUÉRARD, ALBERT L. *France: a Short History*. New York: Norton, 1946

JACKSON, J. H. *Jean Jaurès, his Life and Work*
New York: Norton, 1944

LANGER, W. L. *The Franco-Russian Alliance*, 1890–1894
Cambridge: Harvard University Press, 1929

MC KAY, D. C. (ed.). *The Dreyfus Case, by the Man, Alfred Dreyfus, and
his Son, Pierre Dreyfus*. New Haven: Yale University Press, 1937

MOON, P. T. *The Labor Problem and the Social Catholic Movement in
France*. New York: Macmillan, 1921

PORTER, C. W. *The Career of Théophile Delcassé*
Philadelphia: University of Pennsylvania Press, 1936

POWER, THOMAS F., JR. *Jules Ferry and the Renaissance of French Imperialism*. New York: Columbia University Press, 1944

PRIESTLEY, H. I. *France Overseas: a Study of Modern Imperialism*
New York: Appleton-Century, 1938

SCHUMAN, F. L. *War and Diplomacy in the French Republic*
New York: McGraw-Hill, 1931

SOLTAU, R. H. *French Parties and Politics, 1871–1921*
New York: Oxford University Press, 1930

STUART, G. H. *French Foreign Policy from Fashoda to Sarajevo*
New York: Century, 1921

(See also Suggestions for Further Reading, Chapter XXVII)

CHAPTER V: *RUSSIA*

FLORINSKY, M. T. *The End of the Russian Empire*
New Haven: Yale University Press, 1931

GOLDER, F. A. (ed.). *Documents of Russian History, 1914–1917*
New York: Appleton-Century, 1927

HENDERSON, DANIEL. *From the Volga to the Yukon: the Russian March to Alaska and California.* New York: Hastings House, 1945

KARPOVICH, MICHAEL. *Imperial Russia, 1801–1917.* Berkshire Studies in European History. New York: Holt, 1932

KERNER, R. J. *The Urge to the Sea: the Course of Russian History*
Berkeley: University of California Press, 1942

MARTIN, JOHN S. *A Picture History of Russia*
New York: Crown Publishers, 1945

MAVOR, JAMES. *An Economic History of Russia.* 2nd ed. rev.
New York: Dutton, 1925

PAVLOVSKY, GEORGE. *Agricultural Russia on the Eve of the Revolution*
London: Routledge, 1930

ROBINSON, G. T. *Rural Russia under the Old Regime*
New York: Longmans, 1932

SKRINE, F. H. *The Expansion of Russia.* 3rd ed.
New York: Macmillan, 1915

VERNADSKY, GEORGE. *Political and Diplomatic History of Russia*
Boston: Little, Brown, 1936

(See also Suggestions for Further Reading, Chapters XX and XXI)

Chapter VI: *ITALY*

CROCE, BENEDETTO. *A History of Italy*, 1871–1915
Oxford: Clarendon Press, 1929

FOERSTER, ROBERT F. *The Italian Emigration of our Times.*
Cambridge: Harvard University Press, 1919

HALPERIN, S. W. *The Separation of Church and State in Italian Thought from Cavour to Mussolini*
Chicago: University of Chicago Press, 1937

HENTZE, MARGOT. *Pre-Fascist Italy: the Rise and Fall of the Parliamentary Regime*. New York: Norton, 1939

MC CLENNAN, GEORGE B. *Modern Italy: a Short History*
Princeton: Princeton University Press, 1933

MARRIOTT, SIR J. A. R. *The Makers of Modern Italy*
New York: Oxford University Press, 1933

SALOMONE, WILLIAM A. *Italian Democracy in the Making: the Political Scene in the Giolittian Era*, 1900–1914
Princeton: Princeton University Press, 1945

SALVATORELLI, LUIGI. *A Concise History of Italy*
New York: Oxford University Press, 1940

SFORZA, CARLO. *Contemporary Italy*. New York: Dutton, 1944

SPRIGGE, CECIL J. *The Development of Modern Italy*
New Haven: Yale University Press, 1944

WALLACE, W. K. *Greater Italy*. New York: Scribner's, 1917

(See also Suggestions for Further Reading, Chapter XXVIII)

Chapter VII: *AUSTRIA–HUNGARY*

FAY, SIDNEY B. *The Origins of the War.* 2 vols. Rev. ed.
New York: Macmillan, 1930

GEWEHR, W. M. *The Rise of Nationalism in the Balkans*, 1800–1930. Berkshire Studies in European History. New York: Holt, 1931

HELMRICH, E. C. *The Diplomacy of the Balkan Wars*, 1912–1913
Cambridge: Harvard University Press, 1938

JASZI, OSCAR. *The Dissolution of the Hapsburg Monarchy*
Chicago: University of Chicago Press, 1929

LENGYEL, EMIL. *The Danube*. New York: Random House, 1939

PRIBRAM, A. F. *Austrian Foreign Policy*, 1908–1918
  London: Allen and Unwin, 1923

REDLICH, JOSEPH. *Austrian War Government*
  New Haven: Yale University Press, 1929

—— *Emperor Francis Joseph of Austria*
  New York: Macmillan, 1929

SCHEVILL, FERDINAND, and GEWEHR, W. M. *History of the Balkan Peninsula*
  New York: Harcourt, Brace, 1933

SCHMITT, B. E. *The Coming of the War.* 2 vols.
  New York: Scribner's, 1930

—— *The Annexation of Bosnia*, 1908–1909
  Cambridge (England): Cambridge University Press, 1937

TAYLOR, A. J. P. *The Hapsburg Monarchy*, 1815–1918
  New York: Macmillan, 1941

CHAPTER VIII: *THE LESSER STATES*

ARNESON, BEN A. *The Democratic Monarchies of Scandinavia.* The Governments of Modern Europe. New York: Van Nostrand, 1939

BARNOUW, ADRIAAN J. *The Making of Modern Holland*
  New York: Norton, 1944

CHILDS, M. W. *Sweden: the Middle Way.* Rev. ed.
  New Haven: Yale University Press, 1939

CLARK, CHARLES U. *United Rumania*
  New York: Dodd Mead, 1932

ELBOGEN, ISMAR. *A Century of Jewish Life*
  Philadelphia: Jewish Publication Society of America, 1944

FORSTER, EDWARD S. *A Short History of Modern Greece*, 1821–1914
  London: Methuen, 1941

GJERSET, KNUT. *A History of the Norwegian People*
  New York: Macmillan, 1927

GORIS, JAN ALBERT (ed.). *Belgium.* United Nations Series.
  Berkeley: University of California Press, 1945

HUME, M. A. S. *Modern Spain*
  London: Allen and Unwin, 1923

IORGA, NICOLAE. *A History of Rumania: Land, People, Civilization*
  London: T. F. Unwin, 1925

MILLER, WILLIAM. *History of the Greek People,* 1821–1921
   New York: Dutton, 1923

—— *The Ottoman Empire and its Successors,* 1801–1927. 4th ed.
   New York: Macmillan, 1936

OECHSLI, WILHELM. *History of Switzerland,* 1499–1914
   Cambridge: Cambridge University Press, 1922

RAPPARD, WILLIAM E. *The Government of Switzerland.* The Governments
   of Modern Europe. New York: Van Nostrand, 1936

RIEMENS, HENRIK. *The Netherlands: Story of a Free People*
   New York: Duell, Sloan and Pearce, 1944

(See also Suggestions for Further Reading, Chapters XIV, XIX, and XXII)

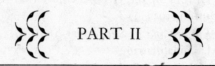

PART II

WORLD WAR I: 1914—1918

Europe and the World Since 1914

BENNS, F. LEE. *Europe Since* 1914. 6th ed.
New York: Crofts, 1946

CHAMBERS, FRANK P., and others. *The Age of Conflict*, 1914–1943
New York: Harcourt, Brace, 1943

HAINES, C. GROVE, and HOFFMAN, ROSS J. S. *The Origins and Background of the Second World War*. New York: Oxford University Press, 1943

LANGSAM, WALTER C. *The World Since* 1914. 5th ed.
New York: Macmillan, 1943

MAY, A. J. *Europe and Two World Wars*
New York: Scribner's, 1947

CHAPTER IX: 1914: *THE END OF AN ERA*

BRINTON, CRANE. *English Political Thought in the Nineteenth Century*
London: Benn, 1933

DICKINSON, G. L. *The International Anarchy*, 1904–1914
New York: Century, 1926

FISCHER, ERIC. *The Passing of the European Age*
Cambridge: Harvard University Press, 1943

HAYES, C. J. H. *The Historical Evolution of Modern Nationalism*
New York: R. R. Smith, 1931

LASKI, HAROLD J. *The Rise of European Liberalism*
New York: Harper, 1936

LATOURETTE, KENNETH S. *The Great Century, A.D.* 1800*–A.D.* 1914. A History of the Expansion of Christianity, Vol. IV
New York: Harper, 1941

MARVIN, F. S. *The Century of Hope: a Sketch of Western Progress from 1815 to the Great War*. New York: Oxford University Press, 1919

POLYANI, KARL. *The Great Transformation*
New York: Farrar and Rinehart, 1944

SONTAG, R. J. *European Diplomatic History*, 1871–1932
New York: Century, 1933

WINSLOW, C. E. A. *The Conquest of Epidemic Disease*
Princeton: Princeton University Press, 1943

CHAPTER X: *THE WAR ON LAND* 1914–1918

CHURCHILL, WINSTON S. *The Unknown War: the Eastern Front*. The World Crisis, Vol. IV. New York: Scribner's, 1931

CRUTTWELL, C. R. M. F. *A History of the Great War*, 1914–1918
New York: Oxford University Press, 1936

EARLE, EDWARD M. (ed.). *Makers of Modern Strategy: Military Thought from Machiavelli to Hitler*
Princeton: Princeton University Press, 1943

FROTHINGHAM, T. G. *A Guide to the Military History of the World War*, 1914–1918. Boston: Little, Brown, 1920

JOHNSON, D. W. *Battlefields of the World War, Western and Southern Fronts: a Study in Military Geography*
New York: Oxford University Press, 1921

LIDDELL HART, B. H. *A History of the World War*, 1914–1918
Boston: Little, Brown, 1934

MC ENTEE, G. L. *Italy's Part in Winning the World War*
Princeton: Princeton University Press, 1934

NEWMAN, JAMES R. *The Tools of War*
New York: Doubleday, Doran, 1942

VAGTS, ALFRED. *The History of Militarism: Romance and Reality of a Profession*. New York: Norton, 1938

CHAPTER XI: *THE WAR ON THE SEA* 1914–1918

BRODIE, BERNARD. *A Guide to Naval Strategy*. Rev. ed.
Princeton: Princeton University Press, 1944

DICKSON, M. R. *The Food Front in World War I*
Washington: American Council on Public Affairs, 1944

FAYLE, C. E. *The War and the Shipping Industry*
New Haven: Yale University Press, 1927

── *A Short History of the World's Shipping Industry*
London: Allen and Unwin, 1933

FROTHINGHAM, T. G. *The Naval History of the World War.* 3 vols.
Cambridge: Harvard University Press, 1924–26

GILSON, R., and PRENDERGAST, M. *The German Submarine War* 1914–1918
London: Constable, 1931

GUICHARD, LOUIS. *The Naval Blockade,* 1914–1918. Ed. and trans. by C. R.
Turner. New York: Appleton-Century, 1930

LEAGUE OF NATIONS. Economic, Financial and Transit Department. *Agricultural Production in Continental Europe during the* 1914–1918 *War and Reconstruction Period*
New York: Columbia University Press, 1944

LUTZ, R. H., and BANE, S. L. *The Blockade of Germany after the Armistice,* 1918–1919. *Selected Documents . . .*
Stanford: Stanford University Press, 1943

MITCHELL, DONALD W. *History of the Modern American Navy from* 1883 *through Pearl Harbor.* New York: Knopf, 1946

PARMALEE, M. F. *Blockade and Sea Power: Blockade,* 1914–1919, *and its Significance for a World State.* New York: Crowell, 1924

CHAPTER XII: *THE WAR OF FINANCE, DIPLOMACY,*

AND PROPAGANDA

BARUCH, BERNARD. *American Industry in the War: a Report on the War Industries Board.* New York: Prentice-Hall, 1941

BOGART, ERNEST L. *Direct and Indirect Costs of the Great World War.*
Carnegie Endowment for Preliminary Economic Studies of the War
New York: Oxford University Press, 1920

BRUNTZ, GEORGE G. *Allied Propaganda and the Collapse of the German Empire in* 1918. Stanford: Stanford University Press, 1938

CHAMBERS, FRANK P. *The War behind the War,* 1914–1918: *a History of the Political and Civilian Fronts.* New York: Harcourt, Brace, 1939

DEARLE, N. B. *An Economic Chronicle of the Great War for Great Britain and Ireland.* New Haven: Yale University Press, 1929

FORSTER, KENT. *The Failures of Peace: the Search for a Negotiated Peace during the First World War*
Washington: American Council on Public Affairs, 1941

GRADY, HENRY F. *British War Finance*, 1914–1919
New York: Columbia University Press, 1927

MAURICE, SIR FREDERICK. *The Armistices of* 1918
New York: Oxford University Press, 1943

PETERSON, H. C. *Propaganda for War: the Campaign against American Neutrality*, 1914–1917. Norman: University of Oklahoma Press, 1939

READ, JAMES M. *Atrocity Propaganda*, 1914–1919
New Haven: Yale University Press, 1941

RUDIN, HARRY R. *Armistice*, 1918
New Haven: Yale University Press, 1944

SEYMOUR, CHARLES. *American Diplomacy during the World War*
Baltimore: Johns Hopkins Press, 1934

VAN DER SLICE, AUSTIN. *International Labor, Diplomacy and Peace*, 1914–1919. Philadelphia: University of Pennsylvania Press, 1941

PART III

The Search for International Stability

Europe and the World Since 1918

JACKSON, JOHN HAMPTON. *A Short History of the World Since* 1918
   Boston: Little, Brown, 1939
SOWARD, FREDERICK H. *Twenty-five Troubled Years:* 1918–1943
   New York: Oxford University Press, 1943

CHAPTER XIII: *THE PROBLEMS OF PEACEMAKING*

PARIS, 1919

BAILEY, THOMAS A. *Woodrow Wilson and the Lost Peace*
   New York: Macmillan, 1944
BIRDSALL, PAUL. *Versailles Twenty Years After*
   New York: Reynal and Hitchcock, 1941
BONSAL, STEPHEN. *Unfinished Business*
   New York: Doubleday, Doran, 1944
— *Suitors and Suppliants: the Little Nations at Versailles*
   New York: Prentice-Hall, 1946
BURLINGAME, ROGER, and STEVENS, AUDEN. *Victory without Peace*
   New York: Harcourt, Brace, 1944
LLOYD GEORGE, DAVID. *Memoirs of the Peace Conference.* 2 vols.
   New Haven: Yale University Press, 1939
MOWAT, R. B. *The History of European Diplomacy,* 1914–1925
   New York: Longmans, Green, 1931
NICOLSON, HAROLD. *Peacemaking* 1919. *Being Reminiscences of the Paris
   Peace Conference.* Boston: Houghton Mifflin, 1933
NOBLE, G. B. *Policies and Opinions at Paris,* 1919. *Wilsonian Diplomacy,
   the Versailles Peace, and French Public Opinion.*
   New York: Macmillan, 1935

SHOTWELL, JAMES T. *At the Paris Peace Conference*
New York: Macmillan, 1937

WHEELER-BENNETT, J. W. *The Forgotten Peace: Brest-Litovsk, March,*
1918. New York: Morrow, 1939

CHAPTER XIV: *THE POLITICAL SETTLEMENTS*

1919–1920

ALBRECHT-CARRIÉ, RENÉ. *Italy at the Paris Peace Conference*
New York: Columbia University Press, 1938

BEER, GEORGE L. *African Questions at the Peace Conference*
New York: Macmillan, 1923

BUELL, RAYMOND L. *Poland: Key to Europe*
New York: Knopf, 1939

CARNEGIE ENDOWMENT FOR INTERNATIONAL PEACE. *The Treaties of Peace,*
1919–1923. 2 vols. New York: 1924

HOGG, ROBERT D. *Yugoslavia*
London: MacDonald, 1944

HOWARD, HARRY N. *The Partition of Turkey: a Diplomatic History* 1913–
1923. Norman: University of Oklahoma Press, 1931

LUCKAU, ALMA M. *The German Delegation at the Paris Peace Conference*
New York: Columbia University Press, 1941

LUTZ, R. H. *The German Revolution,* 1918–1919
Stanford: Stanford University Press, 1922

MITRANY, DAVID. *The Effect of the War in Southeastern Europe*
New Haven: Yale University Press, 1936

ROUCEK, JOSEPH S. *Contemporary Roumania and her Problems: a Study in
Modern Nationalism.* Stanford: Stanford University Press, 1932

SIMONDS, FRANK H. *How Europe Made Peace without America*
Garden City: Doubleday Page, 1927

STEPHENS, W. E. *Revisions of the Treaty of Versailles*
New York: Columbia University Press, 1939

STRAKHOVSKY, LEONID I. *Intervention at Archangel*
Princeton: Princeton University Press, 1944.

THOMSON, S. HARRISON. *Czechoslovakia in European History*
Princeton: Princeton University Press, 1943

CHAPTER XV: *THE ECONOMIC SETTLEMENTS*

BARUCH, BERNARD M. *The Making of the Reparation and Economic Sections of the Treaty.* New York: Harper, 1920

BERGMAN, KARL. *The History of Reparations*
Boston: Houghton Mifflin, 1927

BURNETT, PHILIP M. *Reparations at the Paris Peace Conference from the Standpoint of the American Delegation*
New York: Columbia University Press, 1940

CHURCHILL, WINSTON S. *The Aftermath, 1918–1928.* The World Crisis, Vol. V. New York: Scribner's, 1929

DAWES, CHARLES GATES. *A Journal of Reparations*
New York: Macmillan, 1939

DAY, J. P. *Introduction to World Economic History since the Great War*
New York: Macmillan, 1939

FRASURE, CARL M. *British Policy on War Debts and Reparations*
Philadelphia: Dorrance, 1940

GREBLER, LEO, and WINKLER, WILHELM. *The Cost of the War to Germany and Austria-Hungary.* New Haven: Yale University Press, 1936

LEAGUE OF NATIONS. *International Currency Experience. Lessons of the Inter-War Period.* New York: Columbia University Press, 1944

SIMONDS, F. H. *The A.B.C. of War Debts*
New York: Harper, 1933

CHAPTER XVI: *THE INTERNATIONAL SETTLEMENT:*

THE LEAGUE OF NATIONS

BAILEY, THOMAS A. *Woodrow Wilson and the Great Betrayal*
New York: Macmillan, 1945

CORY, HELEN M. *Compulsory Arbitration of International Disputes*
New York: Columbia University Press, 1932

FLEMING, DENNA F. *The United States and the League of Nations, 1918–1920.* New York: Putnam, 1932

—— *The United States and World Organization*
New York: Columbia University Press, 1938

GREAVES, H. R. G. *The League Committees and World Order*
New York: Oxford University Press, 1931

HOWARD-ELLIS, C. *The Origin, Structure, and Working of the League of Nations*. Boston: Houghton Mifflin, 1928

HUDSON, MANLEY O. *The Permanent Court of International Justice, 1920–1942*. New York: Macmillan, 1942

JONES, S. S. *The Scandinavian States and the League of Nations*
New York: American Scandinavian Foundation, 1939

MILLER, D. H. *The Drafting of the Covenant.* 2 vols.
New York: Putnam, 1928

RAMSHOFEN-WERTHEIMER, EGON F. *The International Secretariat: a Great Experiment in International Administration*
New York: Columbia University Press, 1945

RAPPARD, WILLIAM E. *The Quest for Peace since the World War*
Cambridge: Harvard University Press, 1940

PART IV

The Americas in the Twentieth Century

CREIGHTON, DONALD G. *Dominion of the North: a History of Canada*
Boston: Houghton Mifflin, 1944

HICKS, JOHN D. *A Short History of American Democracy*
Boston: Houghton Mifflin, 1944

HOCKETT, HOMER C., and SCHLESINGER, ARTHUR M. *Land of the Free*
New York: Macmillan, 1944

MORISON, SAMUEL E., and COMMAGER, HENRY STEELE. *The Growth of the American Republic.* 2 vols.
New York: Oxford University Press, 1942

MUNRO, DANA G. *The Latin American Republics: A History*
New York: Appleton-Century, 1942

NICHOLS, JEANNETTE P. *Twentieth Century United States: a History*
New York: Appleton-Century, 1943

PAXSON, FREDERIC L. *Recent History of the United States.* Rev. ed.
Boston: Houghton Mifflin, 1927

SCHLESINGER, ARTHUR M. *Political and Social Growth of the American People: 1865–1940.* New York: Macmillan, 1941

WILLIAMS, M. W. *The People and Politics of Latin America.* Rev. ed.
Boston: Ginn, 1945

WITTKE, CARL. *A History of Canada.* New York: Crofts, 1941

Chapter XVII: *THE UNITED STATES: INTERNAL DEVELOPMENT*

BEARD, CHARLES A., and BEARD, MARY R. *The Rise of American Civilization.*
Rev. and enlarged ed. 2 vols. in 1. New York: Macmillan, 1933

COCHRAN, THOMAS C., and MILLER, WILLIAM. *The Age of Enterprise. A Social History of Industrial America.* New York: Macmillan, 1942

FAULKNER, HAROLD U. *American Economic History*
New York: Harper, 1935

FAULKNER, HAROLD U. *The Quest for Social Justice.* A History of American Life, Vol. XI. New York: Macmillan, 1931

HANSEN, MARCUS L. *The Emigrant in American History*
Cambridge: Harvard University Press, 1940

HOWARD, ROBERT W. *Two Billion Acre Farm: an Informal History of American Agriculture.* New York: Doubleday, Doran, 1945

LORD, CLIFFORD L., and LORD, ELIZABETH E. *Historical Atlas of the United States.* New York: Holt, 1944

MAY, EARL C. *Principio to Wheeling: 1715–1945: a Pageant of Iron and Steel.* New York: Harper, 1945

PARRINGTON, V. L. *Main Currents in American Thought.* 3 vols.
New York: Harcourt, Brace, 1927–1930

PRINGLE, H. F. *Theodore Roosevelt: a Biography*
New York: Harcourt, Brace, 1931

RAUCH, BASIL. *The History of the New Deal*
New York: Creative Age Press, 1944

SCHLESINGER, ARTHUR M. *The Rise of the City,* 1878–1898. A History of American Life, Vol. X. New York: Macmillan, 1933

—— *The New Deal in Action.* New York: Macmillan, 1940

SLOSSON, P. W. *The Great Crusade and After,* 1914–1928. A History of American Life, Vol. XII. New York: Macmillan, 1930

ZEVIN, B. D. (ed.). *Nothing to Fear: the Selected Addresses of Franklin Delano Roosevelt,* 1932–1945
Boston: Houghton Mifflin, 1946

CHAPTER XVIII: *THE UNITED STATES: FOREIGN AFFAIRS*

BAILEY, THOMAS A. *A Diplomatic History of the American People.* 2nd ed.
New York: Crofts, 1942

BARTLETT, RUHL J. (ed.). *The Record of American Diplomacy: Documents and Readings in the History of American Foreign Relations*
New York: Knopf, 1947

BEMIS, SAMUEL F. *A Diplomatic History of the United States.* Rev. ed.
New York: Holt, 1942

BISSON, T. A. *America's Far Eastern Policy.* Institute of Pacific Relations
New York: Macmillan, 1945

DULLES, FOSTER R. *The Road to Teheran: the Story of Russia and America,* 1781–1943. Princeton: Princeton University Press, 1944

DU VAL, MILES P. *Cadiz to Cathay: the Story of the Long Struggle for a Waterway across the American Isthmus*
Stanford: Stanford University Press, 1940

HANSEN, ALVIN H. *America's Role in World Economy*
New York: Norton, 1945

LATOURETTE, KENNETH S. *The United States Moves across the Pacific*
New York: Harper, 1946

MC INNIS, EDGAR W. *The Unguarded Frontier: a History of American-Canadian Relations.* New York: Doubleday, Doran, 1942

NEVINS, ALLAN, and HACKER, LOUIS M. (eds.). *The United States and its Place in World Affairs, 1918–1943.* Boston: Heath, 1943

PEFFER, NATHANIEL. *America's Place in the World*
New York: Viking, 1945

SPYKMAN, NICHOLAS J. *America's Strategy in World Politics*
New York: Harcourt, Brace, 1942

Chapter XIX: *SECONDARY AMERICAN STATES*

BALL, MARGARET. *The Problem of Inter-American Organization*
Stanford: Stanford University Press, 1944

BLANSHARD, PAUL. *Democracy and Empire in the Caribbean*
New York: Macmillan, 1947

CHAPMAN, C. E. *A History of the Cuban Republic: a Study in Hispanic American Politics.* New York: Macmillan, 1927

CLOKIE, H. MC D. *Canadian Government and Politics*
New York: Longmans, Green, 1945

CRAWFORD, W. REX. *A Century of Latin American Thought*
Cambridge: Harvard University Press, 1944

CREIGHTON, DONALD GRANT. *Dominion of the North: a History of Canada*
Boston: Houghton Mifflin, 1944

ELLSWORTH, P. T. *Chile: an Economy in Transition*
New York: Macmillan, 1944

HARRIS, SEYMOUR E. *Economic Problems of Latin America*
New York: McGraw-Hill, 1945

HISS, PHILIP H. *Netherlands America: the Dutch Territories in the West*
New York: Duell, Sloan and Pearce, 1943

MUNRO, DANA G. *The Latin American Republics: a History*
New York: Appleton-Century, 1942

Pan-American Yearbook. New York: Macmillan, 1945–

PARKES, HENRY B. *A History of Mexico*
    Boston: Houghton Mifflin, 1938

RENNIE, YSABEL F. *The Argentine Republic*
    New York: Macmillan, 1945

RIPPY, J. F. *Latin America and World Politics.* 3rd ed.
    New York: Knopf, 1938

SMITH, T. LYNN. *Brazil, People and Institutions*
    Baton Rouge: Louisiana State University Press, 1946

STRODE, HUDSON. *Timeless Mexico*
    New York: Harcourt, Brace, 1944

TANNENBAUM, FRANK. *The Mexican Agrarian Revolution*
    New York: Macmillan, 1929

WHITE, JOHN W. *Argentina: the Life Story of a Nation*
    New York: Viking Press, 1942

WILLIAMS, M. W. *The People and Politics of Latin America.* Rev. ed.
    Boston: Ginn, 1945

WITTKE, CARL. *A History of Canada.* Rev. ed.
    New York: Crofts, 1941

WYTHE, GEORGE. *Industry in Latin America*
    New York: Columbia University Press, 1945

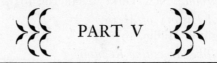

PART V

THE UNION OF SOVIET SOCIALIST REPUBLICS
AND ITS BORDER STATES

CHAPTER XX: *THE RUSSIAN REVOLUTION: THE PROVISORY PERIOD*, 1917–1928

CHAMBERLIN, W. H. *The Russian Revolution*, 1917–1921. 2 vols.
New York: Macmillan, 1935

— *Russia's Iron Age*. Boston: Little, Brown, 1934

COATES, WILLIAM P., and COATES, ZELDA. *Armed Intervention in Russia*
1918–1922. London: Gollancz, 1935

DURANTY, WALTER. *U.S.S.R. The Story of Soviet Russia*
New York: Lippincott, 1944

FLORINSKY, MICHAEL T. *Towards an Understanding of the U.S.S.R.*
New York: Macmillan, 1939

HARPER, SAMUEL N. *The Government of the Soviet Union*
New York: Van Nostrand, 1938

JAMES, C. L. R. *World Revolution*, 1917–1936. *The Rise and Fall of the
Communist International*. New York: Pioneer, 1937

MEIKSINS, GREGORY. *The Baltic Riddle*
New York: Fisher, 1943

NORMANO, J. F. *The Spirit of Russian Economics*
New York: John Day, 1945

SOUVARINE, B. *Stalin: a Critical History of Bolshevism*
New York: Alliance, 1939

STEMBRIDGE, JASPER H. *An Atlas of the U.S.S.R.*
New York: Oxford University Press, 1942

TROTSKY, LEON. *My Life: an Attempt at an Autobiography*
New York: Scribner's, 1930

VERNADSKY, GEORGE. *Lenin: Red Dictator*
New Haven: Yale University Press, 1931

WEBB, SIDNEY, and WEBB, BEATRICE. *Soviet Communism: a New Civilization?* 2 vols. New York: Scribner's, 1938

CHAPTER XXI: *THE RUSSIAN REVOLUTION:*

THE PLANNED SOCIETY, 1928–1939

CRESSEY, GEORGE B. *The Basis of Soviet Strength*
New York: Whittlesey House, 1945

DALLIN, DAVID J. *Soviet Russia's Foreign Policy,* 1939–1942
New Haven: Yale University Press, 1942

HANS, NICHOLAS, and HESSEN, SERGIUS. *Educational Policy in Soviet Russia*
London: P. S. King, 1930

HARPER, SAMUEL N. *Civic Training in Soviet Russia*
Chicago: University of Chicago Press, 1929

HOOVER, C. B. *The Economic Life of Soviet Russia*
New York: Macmillan, 1931

KING, BEATRICE. *Changing Man: The Soviet Education System of the
U.S.S.R.* New York: Viking Press, 1937

LAUTERBACH, RICHARD E. *These Are the Russians*
New York: Harper, 1945

LENGYEL, EMIL. *Siberia.* New York: Random House, 1943

MOORE, HARRIET L. *Soviet Far Eastern Policy,* 1931–1945
Princeton: Princeton University Press, 1946

SCHUMAN, FREDERICK L. *Soviet Policies at Home and Abroad*
New York: Knopf, 1946

SNOW, EDGAR. *The Pattern of Soviet Power*
New York: Random House, 1945

STRONG, ANNA L. *Peoples of the U.S.S.R.* New York: Macmillan, 1944

CHAPTER XXII: *THE BORDER STATES OF THE*

SOVIET UNION

ALLEN, HENRY E. *The Turkish Transformation: a Study in Social and Religious Development.* Chicago: University of Chicago Press, 1935

FOSTER, HENRY A. *The Making of Modern Iraq: a Product of World Forces*
Norman: University of Oklahoma Press, 1935

HAAS, WILLIAM S. *Iran*
New York: Columbia University Press, 1946

HITTI, PHILIP K. *The Arabs: a Short History for Americans*
Princeton: Princeton University Press, 1945

BEN-HORIN, ELIAHU. *The Middle East: Crossroads of History*
New York: Norton, 1943

JACKH, ERNEST. *The Rising Crescent: Turkey*
New York: Farrar and Rinehart, 1944

JACKSON, JOHN H. *Estonia*
New York: Norton, 1941

KERNER, ROBERT J. (ed.). *Czechoslovakia.* United Nations Series.
Berkeley: University of California Press, 1940

NEWMAN, BERNARD. *Balkan Background*
New York: Macmillan, 1944

NORINS, MARTIN R. *Gateway to Asia: Sinkiang, Frontier of the Chinese Far West.* Institute of Pacific Relations. New York: John Day, 1944

PRIBIĆEVIĆ, STOYAN. *World without End: the Saga of Southeastern Europe*
New York: Reynal and Hitchcock, 1939

REDDAWAY, W. F., and others (eds.). *The Cambridge History of Poland*
New York: Macmillan, 1941

SETON-WATSON, HUGH. *Eastern Europe between the Wars, 1918–1941*
New York: Macmillan, 1945

SHOTWELL, JAMES T., and LASERSON, MAX M. *Poland and Russia, 1919–1945*
New York: Columbia University Press, 1945

SHOTWELL, JAMES T. *Turkey at the Straits: a Short History*
New York: Macmillan, 1940

STARK, FREYA. *The Arab Island: the Middle East*
New York: Knopf, 1945

STAVRIANOS, L. S. *Balkan Federation: a History of the Movement towards Balkan Unity in Modern Times.* Northampton: Smith College, 1944

WUORINEN, JOHN H. *Nationalism in Modern Finland*
New York: Columbia University Press, 1931

PART VI

The Asiatic and Pacific World

CLYDE, PAUL H. *A History of the Modern and Contemporary Far East*
New York: Prentice-Hall, 1937

LATOURETTE, KENNETH S. *A Short History of the Far East*
New York: Macmillan, 1946

VINACKE, H. M. *A History of the Far East in Modern Times*. 4th ed.
New York: Crofts, 1941

Chapter XXIII: *INDIA AND THE EAST INDIES*

Cambridge History of India. Vol. VI, *The Indian Empire*, 1858–1918
New York: Macmillan, 1932

COUPLAND, R. *The Indian Problem: Report on the Constitutional Problem
in India.* New York: Oxford University Press, 1944

CRESSEY, G. B. *Asia's Lands and Peoples*. New York: McGraw-Hill, 1944

EMERSON, RUPERT. *Malaysia: a Study in Direct and Indirect Rule*
New York: Macmillan, 1937

FURNIVALL, J. S. *Netherlands India: a Study in Plural Economy*
New York: Macmillan, 1944

GULL, E. M. *British Economic Interests in the Far East*. Royal Institute of
International Affairs. New York: Oxford University Press, 1943

HARTOG, MABEL. *India in Outline*
New York: Macmillan, 1944

HUDSON, G. F., and RAJCHMAN, MARTHE. *An Atlas of Far Eastern Politics*
London: Faber and Faber, 1943

KAT ANGELINO, A. D. A. DE. *Colonial Policy.* 2 vols.
Chicago: University of Chicago Press, 1931

KENNEDY, RAYMOND. *The Ageless Indies*
New York: John Day, 1942

LASKER, BRUNO. *Peoples of Southeast Asia*
New York: Knopf, 1944

MOON, PENDEREL. *Strangers in India*
London: Faber and Faber, 1944

MORAES, F. R., and STIMSON, ROBERT. *Introduction to India*
New York: Oxford University Press, 1943

NEHRU, JAWAHARLAL. *The Discovery of India*
New York: John Day, 1946

PANIKAR, K. M. *India and the Indian Ocean: the Influence of Sea Power on Indian History.* New York: Macmillan, 1945

ROBEQUAIN, CHARLES. *The Economic Development of French Indo-China*
New York: Oxford University Press, 1944

TAYLOR, EDMOND. *Richer by Asia*
Boston: Houghton Mifflin, 1947

VANDENBOSCH, AMRY. *The Dutch East Indies: Its Government, Problems and Politics.* 2nd ed. Berkeley: University of California Press, 1941

VLEKKE, BERNARD H. M. *Nusantara: a History of the East Indian Archipelago.* Cambridge: Harvard University Press, 1943

Chapter XXIV: *CHINA, JAPAN, AND THE NEW ORDER IN ASIA*

ABEND, HALLETT. *Treaty Ports.* New York: Doubleday, Doran, 1944

CARUS, CLAYTON D., and MC NICHOLS, CHARLES L. *Japan: its Resources and Industries.* New York: Harper, 1944

CHANG, CHUNG-FU. *The Anglo-Japanese Alliance*
Baltimore: Johns Hopkins Press, 1931

China Handbook: 1937–1943. Chinese Ministry of Information
New York: Macmillan, 1944

CROW, CARL. *China Takes her Place.* New York: Harper, 1944

DULLES, F. R. *China and America: the Story of their Relations Since* 1784
Princeton: Princeton University Press, 1946

EMBREE, JOHN F. *The Japanese Nation: a Social Survey*
New York: Farrar and Rinehart, 1945

GRAJDANZEV, ANDREW J. *Modern Korea*
New York: John Day, 1944

HUGHES, E. R. *The Invasion of China by the Western World.* Pioneer Histories. London: A. and C. Black, 1937

KERNER, ROBERT J. *Northeastern Asia: a Selected Bibliography in Oriental and European Languages.* 2 vols.
Berkeley: University of California Press, 1939

LATTIMORE, OWEN. *Solution in Asia.* Boston: Little, Brown, 1945

LATTIMORE, OWEN, and LATTIMORE, ELEANOR. *The Making of Modern China.* New York: Norton, 1944

MALLORY, WALTER H. *China: Land of Famine*
New York: American Geographical Society, 1926

OLIVER, ROBERT T. *Korea: Forgotten Nation*
Washington: American Council on Public Affairs, 1944

ROSINGER, LAWRENCE K. *China's Crisis.* New York: Knopf, 1945

ROWE, DAVID N. *China among the Powers*
New York: Harcourt, Brace, 1945

SHIH, KUO-HENG. *China Enters the Machine Age*
Cambridge: Harvard University Press, 1944

STAMP, LAURENCE D. *Asia: an Economic and Regional Geography*
New York: Dutton, 1936

CHAPTER XXV: *AUSTRALIA, NEW ZEALAND, AND*

THE PHILIPPINES

Australia and the Pacific. Australian Institute of International Affairs.
Princeton: Princeton University Press, 1943

CLARK, BLAKE. *Hawaii: The 49th State*
New York: Doubleday, 1947

CONDLIFFE, JOHN B. *New Zealand in the Making.* New ed.
Chicago: University of Chicago Press, 1930

GRATTAN, C. HARTLEY. *Introducing Australia*
New York: John Day, 1942

HAAS, W. H. (ed.). *The American Empire: A Study of the Outlying Territories of the United States*
Chicago: University of Chicago Press, 1940

HAYDEN, JOSEPH R. *The Philippines: a Study in National Development*
New York: Macmillan, 1942

KEESING, FELIX M. *The South Seas in the Modern World.* Institute of Pacific Relations. New York: John Day, 1942

MALCOLM, GEORGE A. *The Commonwealth of the Philippines*
New York: Appleton-Century, 1936

MITCHELL, K. L. *Industrialization of the Western Pacific*. Institute of Pacific Relations. New York: John Day, 1942

NASH, WALTER. *New Zealand, a Democracy that Works*
New York: Duell, Sloan and Pearce, 1943

OSBORN, FAIRFIELD. *The Pacific World*
New York: Norton, 1944

PRICE, WILLARD. *Japan's Islands of Mystery: the Pacific Mandates*
New York: John Day, 1944

REED, STEPHEN W. *The Making of Modern New Guinea, with Special Reference to Culture Contact*
Philadelphia: Institute of Pacific Relations, 1943

REEVES, W. P. *State Experiments in Australia and New Zealand*
New York: Dutton, 1925

TAYLOR, GRIFFITH. *Australia: a Study of Warm Environments and their Effect on British Settlement*. Reprint. New York: Dutton, 1943

⁂ PART VII ⁂

Experiments in Government

BEUKEMA, HERMAN, and others. *Contemporary Foreign Governments*
New York: Rinehart, 1946

RAPPARD, W. E., and others. *Source Book on European Governments*
New York: Van Nostrand, 1939

SHOTWELL, JAMES T., and others. *The Governments of Continental Europe*
New York: Macmillan, 1940

Chapter XXVI: *THE BRITISH EMPIRE–COMMONWEALTH*

BRINTON, CRANE. *The United States and Britain*
Cambridge: Harvard University Press, 1945

BURNHAM, T. H., and HOSKINS, G. O. *Iron and Steel in Britain*
New York: Norton, 1943

DE KIEWIET, C. W. *A History of South Africa, Social and Economic*
New York: Oxford University Press, 1941

HANCOCK, W. K. *Survey of British Commonwealth Affairs.* 2 vols.
New York: Oxford University Press, 1942

HANNA, PAUL L. *British Policy in Palestine*
Washington: American Council of Public Affairs, 1942

HAYDEN, MARY, and MOONAN, G. A. *A Short History of the Irish People*
New York: Longmans, Green, 1939

MAC MANUS, SEUMAS. *The Story of the Irish Race: a Popular History of Ireland.* 4th ed. rev. New York: Devin Adair, 1944

SIEGFRIED, ANDRÉ. *England's Crisis*
New York: Harcourt, Brace, 1931

SIMNETT, W. E. *The British Colonial Empire*
New York: Norton, 1942

VITON, ALBERT. *Great Britain: An Empire in Transition*
New York: John Day, 1940

WALKER, ERIC A. *The British Empire*
New York: Oxford University Press, 1943

WHEARE, K. C. *The Statute of Westminster and Dominion Status*
New York: Oxford University Press, 1938
(See also Suggestions for Further Reading, Chapter II)

CHAPTER XXVII: *THE FRENCH REPUBLIC:* 1919–1939

BAINVILLE, JACQUES. *The French Republic, 1870–1935*
Toronto: Nelson, 1936
BROGAN, D. W. *France under the Republic:* 1870–1939
New York: Harper, 1940
CAMERON, ELIZABETH R. *Prologue to Appeasement: a Study of French Foreign Policy.* Washington: American Council on Public Affairs, 1942
CLOUGH, S. B. *France: A History of National Economics,* 1789–1939
New York: Scribner's, 1939
COT, PIERRE. *Triumph of Treason.* Chicago: Ziff-Davis, 1944
GÉRAUD, ANDRÉ (PERTINAX). *The Gravediggers of France*
New York: Maison Française, 1944
MAILLAND, PIERRE. *France*
New York: Oxford University Press, 1943
PICKLES, DOROTHY M. *France between the Republics:* 1940–1945
London: Contact, 1945
SPENGLER, JOHN JOSEPH. *France Faces Depopulation*
Durham: Duke University Press, 1939
STERN, JACQUES. *The French Colonies, Past and Future*
New York: Didier, 1944
WERTH, ALEXANDER. *The Twilight of France, 1933–1940*
New York: Harper, 1942
(See also Suggestions for Further Reading, Chapter IV)

CHAPTER XXVIII: *THE FASCIST EXPERIMENT IN ITALY*

BOJANO, FILIPPO. *In the Wake of the Goosestep*
Chicago: Ziff-Davis, 1945
BINCHY, DANIEL A. *Church and State in Fascist Italy*
New York: Oxford University Press, 1942

EBERSTEIN, W. *Fascist Italy*
   New York: American Book Company, 1939

FIELD, G. L. *The Syndical and Corporative Institutions of Italian Fascism*
   New York: Columbia University Press, 1938

FINER, HERMAN. *Mussolini's Italy*. New York: Holt, 1935

HUGHES, EMMET J. *The Church and the Liberal Society*
   Princeton: Princeton University Press, 1944

HUGHES, PHILIP. *The Popes' New Order: A Systematic Summary of the Social Encyclicals and Addresses, from Leo XIII to Pius XII*
   New York: Macmillan, 1944

MACARTNEY, MAXWELL H. H., and CREMONA, PAUL. *Italy's Foreign and Colonial Policy*. 1914–1937
   New York: Oxford University Press, 1938

MATHEWS, HERBERT L. *The Fruits of Fascism*
   New York: Harcourt, Brace, 1943

MEGARO, GAUDENS. *Mussolini in the Making*
   Boston: Houghton Mifflin, 1938

NAUGHTON, JAMES W., S.J. *Pius XII on World Problems*
   New York: The America Press, 1943

SCHNEIDER, H. W. *The Fascist Government of Italy*
   New York: Van Nostrand, 1936

STEINER, H. ARTHUR. *Government in Fascist Italy*
   New York: McGraw-Hill, 1938

WELK, W. G. *Fascist Economic Policy: an Analysis of Italy's Economic Experiment*. Cambridge: Harvard University Press, 1938

WRIGHT, JOHN J. *National Patriotism in Papal Teaching*
   Boston: Stratford, 1942

(See also Suggestions for Further Reading, Chapter VI)

CHAPTER XXIX: *THE NATIONAL SOCIALIST REGIME IN GERMANY*

BASCH, ANTONIN. *The Danube Basin and the German Economic Sphere*
   New York: Columbia University Press, 1943

BRECHT, ALBERT. *Prelude to Silence: the End of the German Republic*
   New York: Oxford University Press, 1944

EBERSTEIN, WILLIAM. *The Nazi State*
   New York: Farrar and Rinehart, 1942

FRASER, LINDLEY. *Germany between Two Wars: a Study of Propaganda and War Guilt.* New York: Oxford University Press, 1945

GROSS, FELIKS. *Crossroads of Two Continents*
New York: Columbia University Press, 1945

GUILLEBAUD, CLAUDE W. *The Social Policy of Nazi Germany*
New York: Macmillan, 1941

HALPERIN, S. WILLIAM. *Germany Tried Democracy: a Political History of the Reich from* 1918 *to* 1933. New York: Crowell, 1946

HEIDEN, KONRAD. *History of National Socialism*
New York: Knopf, 1934

—— *Der Fuehrer.* Boston: Houghton Mifflin, 1944

—— *Hitler's Rise to Power.* Boston: Houghton Mifflin, 1943

JORDAN, MAX. *Beyond all Fronts: a Bystander's Notes on this Thirty Years' War.* Milwaukee: Bruce, 1945

KESSLER, COUNT HARRY. *Walter Rathenau*
New York: Harcourt, Brace, 1930

LICHTENBERGER, HENRI. *The Third Reich*
New York: Graystone, 1937

NEUMANN, FRANZ. *Behemoth: the Structure and Practice of National Socialism.* Enlarged ed. New York: Oxford University Press, 1944

OLDEN, RUDOLF. *Stresemann.* New York: Dutton, 1930

PRANGE, GORDON (ed.). *Hitler's Words: Two Decades of National Socialism,* 1923–1943
Washington: American Council on Public Affairs, 1944

ROSENBERG, ARTHUR. *A History of the German Republic*
London: Methuen, 1936

ROSINSKI, HERBERT. *The German Army.* Reprint
Washington: Infantry Journal, 1944

SCHUMAN, F. L. *Germany Since* 1918. Berkshire Studies in European History. New York: Holt, 1937

—— *The Nazi Dictatorship.* New York: Knopf, 1936

WHEELER-BENNETT, J. W. *Wooden Titan (Paul von Hindenburg)*
New York: Macmillan, 1936

PART VIII

THE FAILURE OF COLLECTIVE SECURITY

HODGES, CHARLES. *The Background of International Relations*
New York: John Wiley, 1931

LEE, DWIGHT E. *Ten Years: the World on the Way to War*, 1930–1940
Boston: Houghton Mifflin, 1942

SIMONDS, F. H., and EMENY, BROOKS. *The Great Powers in World Politics.*
3rd ed. New York: American Book Co., 1939

CHAPTER XXX: *ECONOMIC INSECURITY AND THE*
GREAT DEPRESSION

BECKER, CARL L. *Modern Democracy*
New Haven: Yale University Press, 1941

BERGE, WENDELL. *Cartels: Challenge to a Free World*
Washington: Public Affairs Press, 1944

KRANOLD, HERMAN. *The International Distribution of Raw Materials*
New York: Harper, 1939

LASKI, HAROLD. *Reflections on the Revolution of our Time*
New York: Viking, 1943

LEITH, C. K., FURNESS, J. W., and LEWIS, CLEORA. *World Minerals and
World Peace.* Washington: Brookings Institution, 1943

LIPPINCOTT, ISAAC. *The Development of Modern World Trade*
New York: Appleton-Century, 1936

OAKESHOTT, MICHAEL. *Social and Political Doctrines of Contemporary Europe.* New York: Macmillan, 1942

RAJCHMAN, MARTHE. *Europe: An Atlas of Human Geography*
New York: Morrow, 1944

RANDALL, JOHN HERMAN, JR. *Our Changing Civilization: How Science and
Machines Are Reconstructing Modern Life*
New York: Stokes, 1929

ROBBINS, LIONEL C. *The Great Depression*
New York: Macmillan, 1934

SIEGFRIED, ANDRÉ. *Suez and Panama*
New York: Harcourt, Brace, 1940

STALEY, EUGENE. *Raw Materials in Peace and War*
New York: Council on Foreign Relations, 1937

—— *World Economy in Transition: the Conflict between Technology and Politics.* New York: Council on Foreign Relations, 1939

STURMTHAL, ADOLF F. *The Tragedy of European Labor*, 1918–1939
New York: Columbia University Press, 1943

TAYLOR, HENRY C., and TAYLOR, ANNE D. *World Trade in Agricultural Products.* New York: Macmillan, 1943

WASSERMAN, LOUIS. *Modern Political Philosophies and What They Mean*
Philadelphia: Blakiston, 1944

WHITTLESEY, DERWENT. *The Earth and the State: a Study of Political Geography.* New York: Holt, 1939

CHAPTER XXXI: *THE RESORT TO AGGRESSION:*

CHINA, ETHIOPIA, SPAIN, 1933–1936

BISSON, THOMAS A. *Japan in China.* New York: Macmillan, 1938

BRENAN, GERALD. *The Spanish Labyrinth: an Account of the Social and Political Background of the Civil War.* New York: Macmillan, 1943

CHAMBERLIN, WILLIAM H. *Japan over Asia.* Rev. ed.
Boston: Little, Brown, 1939

CHURCHILL, WINSTON S. *While England Slept: a Survey of World Affairs*, 1932–1938. New York: Putnam's, 1938

—— *Step by Step*, 1936–1939. New York: Putnam's, 1939

GOETTE, JOHN. *Japan Fights for Asia*
New York: Harcourt, Brace, 1943

GREW, JOSEPH C. *Ten Years in Japan*
New York: Simon and Schuster, 1943

GRISWOLD, A. W. *The Far Eastern Policy of the United States*
New York: Harcourt, Brace, 1938

HUDSON, MANLEY O. *The Verdict of the League: China and Japan in Manchuria.* Boston: World Peace Foundation, 1933

HORRABIN, JAMES F. *An Atlas of Current Affairs.* 7th ed.
New York: Knopf, 1940

LATTIMORE, OWEN. *Manchuria: Cradle of Conflict.* Rev. ed.
New York: Macmillan, 1935

MADARIAGA, SALVADOR DE. *Spain*
New York: Creative Age Press, 1943

PEERS, E. ALLISON. *The Spanish Tragedy, 1930–1936. Dictatorship, Republic, Chaos.* New York: Oxford University Press, 1936

— *Spain in Eclipse, 1937–1943*
London: Methuen, 1943

REMER, CHARLES F. *Foreign Investments in China*
New York: Macmillan, 1933

SCHUMPETER, E. B. (ed.). *The Industrialization of Japan and Manchukuo,*
1930–1940. New York: Macmillan, 1940

SLOCOMBE, GEORGE. *The Dangerous Sea: the Mediterranean and its Future*
New York: Macmillan, 1937

WHITE, THEODORE, and JACOBY, ANALEE. *Thunder out of China*
New York: William Sloane Associates, 1946

CHAPTER XXXII: *THE FAILURE OF APPEASEMENT:*

AUSTRIA, ALBANIA, CZECHOSLOVAKIA, 1936–1939

BALL, MARGARET M. *Post-War German-Austrian Relations. The Anschluss Movement.* Stanford: Stanford University Press, 1938

DE MENDELSSOHN, PETER. *Design for Aggression*
New York: Harper, 1947

Events Leading up to World War II: Chronological History, 1931–1944
Washington: Government Printing Office, 1945

JORDAN, W. M. *Great Britain, France, and the German Problem,* 1918–1939
New York: Oxford University Press, 1944

KERNER, ROBERT J. (ed.). *Czechoslovakia: Twenty Years of Independence*
Berkeley: University of California Press, 1940

MACARTNEY, C. A. *Problems of the Danube Basin*
New York: Macmillan, 1942

SCHMITT, BERNADOTTE E. *From Versailles to Munich*
Chicago: University of Chicago Press, 1938

SCHUMAN, FREDERICK L. *Europe on the Eve*
New York: Knopf, 1939

SCHUMAN, FREDERICK L. *Night over Europe: the Diplomacy of Nemesis,* 1939–1940. New York: Knopf, 1941

SCOTT, JOHN. *Europe in Revolution,* 1938–1945
Boston: Houghton Mifflin, 1945

WOLFERS, ARNOLD. *Britain and France between Two Wars: Conflicting Strategies of Peace since Versailles*
New York: Harcourt, Brace, 1940

⤜⤜ PART IX ⤛⤛

WORLD WAR II: 1939–1945

Histories of the War

Chronology of the Second World War
New York: Royal Institute of International Affairs, 1947

COMMAGER, HENRY STEELE (ed.). *The Story of the Second World War*
Boston: Little, Brown, 1945

GORDON, DAVID L. and DANGERFIELD, ROYDEN. *The Hidden Weapon: The Story of Economic Warfare*
New York: Harper, 1947

MC INNIS, EDGAR. *The War.* 5 vols.
New York: Oxford University Press, 1940–1945

MILLER, FRANCIS T., and others. *History of World War II*
New York: Winston, 1945

MILLIS, WALTER (ed.). *The War Reports of General Marshall, General Arnold, Admiral King*
Philadelphia: Lippincott, 1947

MORISON, SAMUEL ELIOT. *History of United States Naval Operations in World War II*
Boston: Little, Brown, 1947–

SHUGG, ROGER W., DE WEERD, H. A. *World War II*
Washington: Infantry Journal, 1946

CHAPTER XXXIII: *FROM THE INVASION OF POLAND*
TO THE FALL OF FRANCE

SEPTEMBER, 1939–JUNE, 1940

AGHION, RAOUL. *The Fighting French.* New York: Holt, 1943

BROWN, FRANCIS, and MANDITCH, LUCAS. *The War in Maps: an Atlas of the New York Times Maps*
New York: Oxford University Press, 1946

CHURCHILL, WINSTON S. *Blood, Sweat and Tears*
New York: Putnam's, 1941

DE GAULLE, CHARLES. *The Speeches of General de Gaulle, June, 1940–December, 1942.* New York: Oxford University Press, 1944

DIVINE, ARTHUR D. *Navies in Exile.* New York: Dutton, 1944

DRAPER, THEODORE. *The Six Weeks War: France, May 10–June 25, 1940*
New York: Viking, 1944

HOLBORN, LOUISE W. *War and Peace Aims of the United Nations, September 1, 1939–December 31, 1942*
Boston: World Peace Foundation, 1943

LEE, ASHER. *The German Air Force.* New York: Harper, 1946

LORRAINE, JACQUES. *Behind the Battle of France*
New York: Oxford University Press, 1943

MARCHAL, LEON. *Vichy: Two Years of Deception*
New York: Macmillan, 1943

STEMBRIDGE, JASPER H. *The Oxford War Atlas.* Vols. 1–4
New York: Oxford University Press, 1941–

WATTS, FRANKLIN, and AUSUBEL, NATHAN. *Voices of History: Great Speeches and Papers of the Year.* Issued annually.
New York: F. Watts, 1942–43. Gramercy, 1944–

CHAPTER XXXIV: *FROM THE FALL OF FRANCE*

TO THE GERMAN ATTACK ON RUSSIA

JUNE, 1940–JUNE, 1941

BARTIMEUS. *East of Malta, West of Suez*
Boston: Little, Brown, 1944

CLIFFORD, ALEXANDER C. *The Conquest of North Africa, 1940–1943*
Boston: Little, Brown, 1943

ELLIOTT, WILLIAM Y., and HALL, DUNCAN. *The British Commonwealth at War.* New York: Knopf, 1943

HAYES, C. J. H. *Wartime Mission in Spain, 1942–1945*
New York: Macmillan, 1945

HODSON, J. L. *British Merchantmen at War: the Official Story of the Merchant Navy, 1939–1944.* New York: Ziff-Davis, 1945

HOLLIS, EVERETT. *Unconditional Surrender*
New York: Howell Soskin, 1945

KAHN, ALFRED E. *Great Britain and the World Economy*
New York: Columbia University Press, 1946

KARIG, WALTER, and others. *Battle Report: the Atlantic War*, 1939–1945
New York: Rinehart, 1946

KERR, WALTER B. *The Russian Army: Its Men, Its Leaders, and Its Battles*
New York: Knopf, 1944

STALIN, JOSEPH V. *The Great Patriotic War of the Soviet Union*
New York: International Publishers, 1945

STETTINIUS, EDWARD R., JR. *Lend-Lease, Weapon for Victory*
New York: Macmillan, 1944

ST. JOHN, ROBERT. *From the Land of Silent People*
New York: Doubleday, Doran, 1942

WERTH, ALEXANDER. *Leningrad*. New York: Knopf, 1944

WHITE, D. FEDOTOFF. *The Growth of the Red Army*
Princeton: Princeton University Press, 1944

Chapter XXXV: *THE WAR BECOMES GLOBAL*

JUNE, 1941—DECEMBER, 1942

ALSOP, STEWART, and BRADEN, THOMAS. *Sub Rosa: the Office of Strategic Services and American Espionage*
New York: Reynal and Hitchcock, 1946

ANDERSON, ROBERT E. *The Merchant Marine and World Frontiers*
New York: Cornell Maritime Press, 1945

CANT, GILBERT. *America's Navy in World War II*. Rev. ed.
New York: John Day, 1943

GOODMAN, JACK. *While You Were Gone: a Report on Wartime Life in the United States*. New York: Simon and Schuster, 1945

HAILEY, FOSTER. *Pacific Battle Line: the First Two Desperate Years*
New York: Macmillan, 1944

KARIG, WALTER, and KELLEY, WELBOURN. *Battle Report: Pearl Harbor to Coral Sea*. New York: Farrar and Rinehart, 1944

LANGER, WILLIAM L. *Our Vichy Gamble*
New York: Knopf, 1947

MOORHEAD, ALAN. *The End in Africa*. New York: Harper, 1943

PRATT, FLETCHER. *The Navy's War.* New York: Harper, 1944

SILL, VAN RENSSALAER. *American Miracle: The Story of War Construction around the World*
New York: Odyssey, 1947

TAN PEI-YING. *The Building of the Burma Road*
New York: McGraw-Hill, 1945

CHAPTER XXXVI: *THE TURNING OF THE TIDE*

JANUARY, 1943—JUNE, 1944

BUTCHER, HARRY C. *My Three Years with Eisenhower . . .* 1942–1945
New York: Simon and Schuster, 1946

DAVIS, KENNETH S. *Soldier of Democracy: a Biography of Dwight Eisenhower.* New York: Doubleday, Doran, 1945

EISENHOWER, DWIGHT D. *Eisenhower's Own Story of the War*
New York: Arco, 1946

FRYE, WILLIAM. *Marshall: Citizen-Soldier*
Indianapolis: Bobbs-Merrill, 1947

LEIGH, RANDOLPH. *Forty-eight Million Tons to Eisenhower*
Washington: The Infantry Journal, 1945

MARSHALL, GEORGE C. *The Winning of the War in Europe and the Pacific.* Biennial Report of the Chief of Staff of the United States Army, July 1, 1943—June 30, 1945. New York: Simon and Schuster, 1945

MILLER, FRANCIS T. *Eisenhower, Man and Soldier*
Philadelphia: Winston, 1944

MOOREHEAD, ALAN. *Montgomery: A Biography*
New York: Coward McCann, 1947

PARRY, ALBERT. *Russian Cavalcade*
New York: Ives Washburn, 1944

ROLO, CHARLES J. *Wingate's Raiders: an Account of the Fabulous Campaigns behind the Japanese Lines in Burma*
New York: Viking, 1944

SNOW, EDGAR. *People on our Side.* New York: Random House, 1944

WERTH, ALEXANDER. *The Year of Stalingrad.* New York: Knopf, 1947

Chapter XXXVII: *THE LIBERATION OF EUROPE*

JUNE, 1944–MAY, 1945

BARNES, G. M. *Weapons of World War II*
New York: Van Nostrand, 1947
BERNADOTTE, COUNT FOLKE. *The Curtain Falls*
New York: Knopf, 1945
DE GUINGAND, SIR FRANCIS, *Operation Victory*
New York: Scribners, 1947
GLUECK, SHELDON. *The Nuremberg Trial and Aggressive War*
New York: Knopf, 1946
LEMKIN, RAPHAEL. *Axis Rule in Occupied Europe: Laws of Occupation*
New York: Carnegie Endowment for International Peace, 1944
MACARTNEY, M. H. H. *The Rebuilding of Italy*
New York: Macmillan, 1946
MERRIAM, ROBERT E. *Dark December*
Chicago: Ziff-Davis, 1947
MILLIS, WALTER. *The Last Phase: the Allied Victory in Western Europe, June 6, 1944–May 8, 1945*
Boston: Houghton Mifflin Company, 1946
Occupied Europe: German Exploitation and its Postwar Consequences
London: Royal Institute of International Affairs, 1944
TREVOR-ROPER, H. R. *The Last Days of Hitler*
New York: Macmillan, 1947

Chapter XXXVIII: *THE PACIFIC OFFENSIVE*

BISSON, T. A. *Japan's War Economy*. New York: Macmillan, 1945
CANT, GILBERT. *The Great Pacific Victory*. New York: John Day, 1946
JENSEN, OLIVER. *Carrier War*. New York: Pocket Books, 1945
POTTER, ROBERT D. *The Atomic Revolution*. New York: McBride, 1946
PRATT, FLETCHER. *Fleet against Japan*. New York: Harper, 1946
PULESTON, W. D. *The Influence of Sea Power in World War II*.
New Haven: Yale University Press, 1947
Victory in Burma
New York: British Information Service, 1945

PART X

The Contemporary World

AUSUBEL, NATHAN (ed.). *Voices of History: 1945–1946*
    New York: Gramercy, 1946

BRASSEY'S NAVAL ANNUAL, 1946, edited by H. G. Thursfield
    New York: Macmillan, 1947

COALE, ANSLEY J. *The Problem of Reducing Vulnerability to Atomic Bombs.* Princeton: Princeton University Press, 1947

Current History (Monthly), edited by D. G. Redmond
    Philadelphia: Events Publishing Co., 1946–

Foreign Affairs (Quarterly)
    New York: Council on Foreign Relations, 1922–

Jane's All the World's Aircraft, edited by Leonard Bridgman
    New York: Macmillan, 1946

KIRK, DUDLEY. *Europe's Population in the Interwar Years*
    New York: League of Nations, 1947

MANNHEIM, KARL. *Diagnosis of Our Time*
    New York: Oxford University Press, 1944

POTTER, ROBERT D. *The Atomic Revolution*
    New York: McBride, 1946

Statesman's Year-Book, edited by M. Epstein
    New York: Macmillan, 1946–

STOCKING, GEORGE W., and WATKINS, MYRON W. *Cartels in Action*
    New York: Twentieth Century Fund, 1946

KAFKA, ROGER and PEPPERBURG, ROY L. *Warships of the World: Victory Edition.* New York: Cornell Maritime Press, 1947

PATTERSON, E. M. *An Introduction to World Economics*
    New York: Macmillan, 1947

The World Today (Monthly)
    New York: The Royal Institute of International Affairs. New Series,
    1945–

ZACHAROFF, LUCIEN. *The World's Wings*
    New York: Duell, Sloan and Pearce, 1946

Chapter XXXIX: *THE UNITED NATIONS*

DEAN, VERA M. *The Four Cornerstones of Peace: the Aims and Achievements of the United Nations Conferences*
New York: McGraw-Hill, 1946

DOLIVET, LOUIS (ed.). *The United Nations: a Handbook on the New World Organization.* New York: Farrar and Rinehart, 1946

FINER, HERMAN. *The United Nations Economic and Social Council*
Boston: World Peace Foundation, 1946

HUDSON, MANLEY O. *International Tribunals: Past and Future*
Washington: Carnegie Endowment for International Peace, 1945

HUXLEY, JULIAN. *UNESCO: Its Purpose and Philosophy*
New York: Public Affairs Press, 1947

PRICE, JOHN. *The International Labor Movement*
New York: Oxford University Press, 1945

ROYAL INSTITUTE OF INTERNATIONAL AFFAIRS. *United Nations Documents,*
1941–1945. New York: Royal Institute of International Affairs, 1946

UNITED NATIONS. *Report of the Secretary-General on the Work of Organization.* New York: United Nations, 1946

Chapter XL: *THE PEACE TREATIES*

CIANFARRA, CAMILLE. *The Vatican and the War*
New York: Dutton, 1944

Department of State Bulletin. Vol. XVI, no. 413
Washington: Government Printing Office, 1947

SCHECHTMAN, JOSEPH B. *European Population Transfers,* 1939–1945
New York: Oxford University Press, 1946

SOUTHARD, FRANK A. *The Finances of European Liberation*
New York: Columbia University Press, 1946

VALKENBURG, SAMUEL VAN. *Peace Atlas of Europe*
New York: Duell, Sloan and Pearce, 1946

WELLES, SUMNER. *An Intelligent American's Guide to the Peace*
New York: Dryden Press, 1945

—— *Where Are We Heading?* New York: Harper, 1946

CHAPTER XLI: *THE UNITED STATES IN THE ROLE*

OF A WORLD POWER

American Year Book, edited by William M. Schuyler
New York: Thomas Nelson & Sons, 1946

BAXTER, JAMES PHINNEY. *Scientists Against Time*
Boston: Little, Brown, 1946

Department of State Bulletin Vol. XIV *et sqq.*
Washington: Government Printing Office, 1945–

DEWHURST, J. FREDERIC, and ASSOCIATES. *America's Needs and Resources*
New York: Twentieth Century Fund, 1947

GUNTHER, JOHN. *Inside U.S.A.*
New York: Harper, 1947

KOOP, THEODORE. *Weapon of Silence* [Censorship]
Chicago: University of Chicago Press, 1946

Military Affairs (Quarterly)
Baltimore: American Military Institute

NELSON, OTTO LAUREN. *National Security and the General Staff*
Washington: Infantry Journal, 1946

The South American Handbook
New York: Trade and Travel Publications, 1946–

United States Naval Institute Proceedings (Monthly)
Annapolis: United States Naval Institute, 1946–

WHITAKER, ARTHUR P. (ed.). *Inter-American Affairs* (Annual)
New York: Columbia University Press, 1941–

WILSON, CHARLES MORROW. *Oil Across the World: the Saga of American
Pipelines.* New York: Longmans, Green, 1946

CHAPTER XLII: *THE BRITISH EMPIRE UNDER*

RECONSTRUCTION

EVANS, TREVOR. *Bevin of Britain.* New York: Norton, 1946

FISHER, A. G. B. *International Implications of Full Employment in Great
Britain.* New York: Royal Institute of International Affairs, 1946

KAHN, ALFRED E. *Great Britain in the World Economy*
New York: Columbia University Press, 1946

MAC KAY, R. A. (ed.). *Newfoundland: Economic, Diplomatic and Strategic Studies*. New York: Oxford University Press, 1946
SOLJAK, PHILIP. *New Zealand, Pacific Pioneer*
New York: Macmillan, 1946

CHAPTER XLIII: *THE UNION OF SOVIET SOCIALIST REPUBLICS*

BAYKOV, ALEXANDER. *Soviet Foreign Trade*
Princeton: Princeton University Press, 1946
CASEY, ROBERT PIERCE. *Religion in Russia*
New York: Harper, 1946
CHASE, THOMAS G. *The Story of Lithuania*
New York: Stratford Books, 1946
GREGORY, JAMES S., and SHAVE, D. W. *The U.S.S.R.* [Geographical Survey]
New York: Wiley, 1946
LORIMER, FRANK. *The Population of the Soviet Union*
New York: Columbia University Press, 1946
MANDEL, WILLIAM. *A Guide to the Soviet Union*
New York: Dial Press, 1946
SOMERVILLE, JOHN. *Soviet Philosophy*
New York: Columbia University Press, 1946
TIMASHEFF, NICHOLAS. *The Great Retreat. The Growth and Decline of Communism in Russia*. New York: Dutton, 1946

CHAPTER XLIV: *THE EUROPEAN STATES AFTER WORLD WAR II*

BEUKEMA, HERMAN; GEER, WILLIAM, and associates. *Contemporary Foreign Governments*. New edition. New York: Rinehart, 1946
FITZGERALD, WALTER. *The New Europe*. New York: Harper, 1946
GRINDROD, MURIEL. *The New Italy 1943–1947*
New York: Royal Institute of International Affairs, 1947
HUGHES, JOHN E. *Report from Spain*
New York: Holt, 1947

KING, WILLIAM B. and O'BRIEN, FRANK. *The Balkans: Frontier of Two Worlds*. New York: Knopf, 1947

ROUCEK, JOSEPH S. (ed.). *Governments and Politics Abroad* New York: Funk and Wagnalls, 1947

— (ed.). *Central-Eastern Europe: Crucible of World Wars* New York: Prentice-Hall, 1946

SCHECHTMAN, JOSEPH B. *European Population Transfers* New York: Oxford University Press, 1946

CHAPTER XLV: *THE MEDITERRANEAN AREA AND THE NEAR EAST*

ANTONIUS, GEORGE. *The Arab Awakening* New York: Putnam's, 1946

Department of State Bulletin. Supplement. Aid to Greece and Turkey. Vol. XVI, no. 409 A. Washington: Government Printing Office, 1947

GOMME, A. W. *Greece*. The World Today series New York: Oxford University Press, 1945

HAAS, WILLIAM S. *Iran* New York: Columbia University Press, 1946

HOURANI, A. H. *Syria and Lebanon* New York: Royal Institute of International Affairs, 1946

LONGRIGG, STEPHEN H. *A Short History of Eritrea* New York: Oxford University Press, 1946

MC NEILL, WILLIAM H. *The Greek Dilemma: War and Aftermath* Philadelphia: Lippincott, 1947

Middle East Journal. Washington, D.C. 1946—

PARKES, JAMES. *The Jewish Problem in the Modern World* New York: Oxford University Press, 1946

ROYAL INSTITUTE OF INTERNATIONAL AFFAIRS, *Great Britain and Palestine* New York: Royal Institute of International Affairs, 1945

STARK, FREYA. *The Arab Island: the Middle East* New York: Knopf, 1945

TWITCHELL, K. S. *Saudi Arabia* Princeton: Princeton University Press, 1947

CHAPTER XLVI: *ASIA*

COUPLAND, SIR REGINALD. *India: A Restatement*
New York: Oxford University Press, 1946

BOEKE, J. H. *The Evolution of the Netherlands Indies Economy*
New York: Institute of Pacific Relations, 1946

CHIH TSANG. *China's Postwar Markets*
New York: Institute of Pacific Relations, 1945

GRADJDANZEV, ANDREW J. *Modern Korea*
New York: John Day, 1944

JOSEPH, FRANKLIN H. *Far East Report* [American Pacific Bases]
Boston: Christopher, 1946

KATO, MASUO. *The Lost War.* New York: Knopf, 1946

LANG, OLGA. *Chinese Family and Society*
New Haven: Yale University Press, 1946

LASKER, BRUNO. *Asia on the Move*
New York: Holt, 1945

Occupation of Japan: Policy and Progress. Publications of the Department
of State. Washington: Government Printing Office, 1947

ROBSON, R. W. (ed.). *Pacific Islands Handbook*, 1944
New York: Macmillan, 1945

ROBEQUAIN, CHARLES. *The Economic Development of French Indo-China*
New York: Oxford University Press, 1944

TA CHEN. *Population in Modern China*
Chicago: University of Chicago Press, 1946

TAYLOR, EDMOND. *Richer by Asia*
Boston: Houghton Mifflin, 1947

PART XI

WESTERN CULTURE IN THE TWENTIETH CENTURY

DAMPIER, W. C. D. *A History of Science and its Relations with Philosophy and Religion.* Rev. ed. New York: Macmillan, 1942

JOAD, C. E. M. *Guide to Modern Thought.* New York: Stokes, 1933

LONDON, KURT. *Backgrounds of Conflict: Ideas and Forms in World Politics.* New York: Macmillan, 1945

ODUM, HOWARD W. *Understanding Society.* New York: Macmillan, 1947

READ, HERBERT. *Art and Society.* New York: Macmillan, 1937

ROSEN, S. MC KEE, and LAURA F. *Technology and Society*
New York: Macmillan, 1941

NORTHROP, F. S. C. *The Meeting of East and West*
New York: Macmillan, 1946

CHAPTER XLVII: *SCIENCE AND TECHNOLOGY*

BAITSELL, GEORGE (ed.). *Science in Progress* (Annual series)
New Haven: Yale University Press, 1941–

EDDINGTON, A. S. *The Nature of the Physical World*
New York: Macmillan, 1928

LIEBER, LILLIAN R., and HUGH. *The Einstein Theory of Relativity*
New York: Farrar and Rinehart, 1945

FENTON, CARROLL LANE, and ADAMS, MILDRED. *The Story of the Great Geologists.* Garden City: Doubleday, Doran, 1945

GOLDMAN, FRANZ. *Public Medical Care*
New York: Columbia University Press, 1945

HOGBEN, LAUNCELOT T. *Science for the Citizen.* New York: Knopf, 1938

—— *Mathematics for the Million*
New York: Norton, 1940

JEANS, SIR JAMES. *The Universe Around Us*
New York: Macmillan, 1944

KAEMPFFERT, WALDEMAR. *Science Today and Tomorrow* (Annual series)
New York: Viking, 1944–

MC MILLEN, WHEELER. *New Riches from the Soil: the Progress of Chemurgy.* New York: Van Nostrand, 1946

O'NEILL, JOHN J. *You and the Universe: What Science Reveals*
New York: Ives Washburn, 1946

SMYTH, HENRY D. *Atomic Energy for Military Purposes*
Princeton: Princeton University Press, 1946

WARD, HAROLD. *New Worlds in Medicine*
New York: McBride, 1946

WINSLOW, C-E. A. *The Conquest of Epidemic Disease*
Princeton: Princeton University Press, 1943

CHAPTER XLVIII: *ARCHITECTURE, ART, AND MUSIC*

BENOIT-LEVY, JEAN. *The Art of the Motion Picture*
New York: Coward McCann, 1946

CHENEY, SHELDON. *The Story of Modern Art.* New York: Viking, 1941

EISENSTEIN, SERGEI. *The Film Sense*
New York: Harcourt Brace, 1947

FAURE, ELIE. *History of Art: Modern Art*
Garden City: Garden City Publishing Co., 1937

FINNEY, THEODORE M. *A History of Music.* New rev. ed.
New York: Harcourt Brace, 1947

GLOAG, JOHN. *Industrial Art Explained*
New York: Macmillan, 1947

LONDON, KURT. *The Seven Soviet Arts*
London: Faber and Faber, 1937

MARTYNOV, IVAN. *Shostakovich: the Man and his Work*
New York: Philosophical Library, 1947

MORRISON, HUGH. *Louis Sullivan: Prophet of Modern Architecture*
New York: Norton, 1935

SALAZAR, ADOLFO. *Music in Our Time*
New York: Norton, 1946

SLONIMSKY, NICOLAS. *Music Since 1900*
New York: Norton, 1943

VALINTINER, W. R. *Origins of Modern Sculpture*
New York: Wittenborn, 1946

WRIGHT, FRANK LLOYD. *Frank Lloyd Wright on Architecture: Selected Writings*, 1894–1940. New York: Duell, Sloan and Pearce, 1941

CHAPTER XLIX: *LITERATURE*

BAILEY, J. O. *Pilgrims Through Space and Time*
New York: Argus Books, 1947

COLUM, MARY. *From These Roots: the Ideas that Have Made Modern Literature*. New York: Columbia University Press, 1944

CROCE, BENEDETTO. *European Literature in the Nineteenth Century*
London: Chapman, 1924

GREGORY, HORACE, and ZATURENSKA, MARYA. *A History of American Poetry*, 1900–1940. New York: Harcourt, Brace, 1946

KUNITZ, S. J., and HAYCRAFT, HOWARD (eds.). *Twentieth Century Authors*
New York: Wilson, 1942

LAVRIN, JANKO. *An Introduction to the Russian Novel*
New York: Whittlesley House, 1947

MARBLE, ANNIE RUSSELL. *Nobel Prize Winners in Literature*, 1901–1931
New York: Appleton, 1932

MULLER, HERBERT T. *Modern Fiction: a Study in Values*
New York: Funk and Wagnalls, 1937

MENNINGER, K. A. *The Human Mind*. New York: Knopf, 1930

PRITCHETT, V. S. *The Living Novel*
New York: Reynal and Hitchcock, 1947

SMITH, HORATIO (ed.). *Columbia Dictionary of Modern European Literature*. New York: Columbia University Press, 1947

SNELL, GEORGE. *The Shapers of American Fiction*
New York: Dutton, 1947

TINDALL, WILLIAM YORK. *Forces in Modern British Literature*, 1885–1946
New York: Knopf, 1947

CHAPTER L: *PHILOSOPHY AND RELIGION*

AUBREY, E. E. *Present Theological Tendencies*
New York: Harper, 1936

BEARD, CHARLES. *The Unique Function of American Education in Democracy*. Washington: National Education Association, 1937

CHILDS, HARWOOD L. *Propaganda and Dictatorship*
Princeton: Princeton University Press, 1936

COLE, G. D. H. *What Marx Really Meant.* New York: Knopf, 1934

JURJI, EDWARD J. *The Great Religions of the Modern World*
Princeton: Princeton University Press, 1946

KANDEL, I. L. *Comparative Education.* Boston: Houghton Mifflin, 1933

KNELLER, G. F. *The Educational Philosophy of National Socialism*
New Haven: Yale University Press, 1941

KROEBER, A. L. *Configurations of Culture Growth*
Berkeley: University of California Press, 1944

LOWNDES, GEORGE A. N. *The Silent Revolution: Public Education in England and Wales.* New York: Oxford University Press, 1939

LATOURETTE, KENNETH SCOTT. *History of the Expansion of Christianity*
7 volumes. Volumes VI and VII. New York: Harper, 1937–1945

NORTHROP, F. S. C. *The Meeting of East and West*
New York: Macmillan, 1946

ROUCEK, JOSEPH S. (ed.). *Twentieth Century Political Thought*
New York: Philosophical Library, 1946

SCHNEIDER, HERBERT W. *A History of American Philosophy*
New York: Columbia University Press, 1946

SPENGLER, OSWALD. *The Decline of the West*
New York: Knopf, 1939

TOYNBEE, ARNOLD J. *A Study of History.* Abridged ed. by D. C. Somervell
New York: Oxford University Press, 1947

VALENTINE, P. F. (ed.). *Twentieth Century Education*
New York: Philosophical Library, 1946

INDEX

AALAND Islands, 228, 626

Abdul Hamid II, Sultan of Turkey, 85, 102

Abstractionism, in modern art, 679, 681

Abyssinia. *See* Ethiopia

Accident Insurance Law, German, 47

Acoustical torpedoes, in World War II, 482

Addis Ababa, 488

Aden, 21, 639, 642

Adler, Alfred, 694

Adowa, battle of (1896), 14, 79

Aehrenthal, Alois von, Austrian foreign minister, 85, 86

Afghanistan, 14, 43, 56; after World War I, 335

Africa, partitioning of (1890–1899), 14; racial problems, 33, 35; British supremacy in, after World War II, 601–603

Age of steam, 11

Agrarian problem, in eastern Europe, 328–332

Agricultural Research Council, British, 600

Agriculture, in Great Britain, 19, 600–601; in United States, 244; improved methods in, 671–672

Aguinaldo, Emilio, 378

Air power, in World War II, 512–514, 530. *See also* Luftwaffe

Air Transport Command, in World War II, 513

Aisne river, 134

Alaska, 584; bought by United States, 335

Albania, 184, 632, 633; principality created, 103; Italy occupies (1939), 408, 456–457; in World War II, 486

Albert canal, 472

Alcan highway, 276, 499, 584

Aleutian islands, 259, 379

Alexander, King of Yugoslavia, 397

Alexander II, Czar of Russia, 66, 335

Alexandra, Czarina of Russia, 293

Alexandria, Egypt, 501–502

Alfonso XIII, King of Spain, 445

Algeciras, convention of (1906), 644

Algeria, France occupies (1830), 51, 52; after World War II, 643

Algiers, Allies capture (1942), 502

Allied Control Council, Berlin, 568

All-India Union, 646

All-Russian Congress of Soviets, 302, 303

Alsace-Lorraine, 57, 58, 169, 184, 393; Germany acquires, 39; returned to France, 192

American Expeditionary Force, in World War I, 142, 146, 158

Amritsar massacre (1919), 341

Andersen, Hans Christian, 100

Anglo-American Blockade Committee, World War II, 511

Anglo-French Entente (1904), 23, 54

Anglo-Japanese Alliance (1902), 254, 273

Angola, 97

Ankara, 101, 333

Annam, 14, 52, 350; proclaims independence, 650

Anti-Comintern Pact, Germany, Italy, Japan (1936), 317

Antisemitism, in Nazi Germany, 414–415, 527. *See also* Jews

Antwerp, falls to Allies (1944), 518

Appeasement, policy of, in democratic nations, 449–450

Arabia, 635; German influence in, 43; rise of modern, 638–640. *See also* Saudi Arabia

Arabian Nights, 6

Arabs, seek independence, 201

Architecture, development of modern, 675–677

Ardahan, 636

Argentine Republic, 252, 282–283

Armament, expansion of European, in nineteenth century, 117, 119; Washington Naval Conference (1922), 257, 259, 270, 358, 439; London Naval Conference (1930), 259; American attitude on, 270–272; race for, after 1933, 437–440; control of, by United Nations, 549–551

Armenians, in Soviet Russia, 322

Arnhem, 518

Arras, 143, 146

Asia, in Middle Ages, 4–6; European concessions and conquests (1890–1899), 14–16; United States and (1898–1939), 254–260; Russian expansion in, 335–338. *See also* countries by name

Asia Minor, division of, after World War I, 200–201. *See also* Near East

Asquith, Herbert, British prime minister, 27, 28–29, 30

Assembly, of United Nations, 546, 550

Athenia, Germans sink, 469

Athens, Germans occupy (1941), 486

Index

Exchange, international, after World War I, 426

Export-import trade. *See* Foreign trade

Expressionism, in modern art, 678–680

Extraordinary Commission for the Repression of Counterrevolution, Sabotage, and Speculation, Soviet secret police, 327

F.F.I. *See* French Forces of the Interior

Factory system. *See* Industrial Revolution

Fair Employment Practices Act, American, 577

Falkenhayn, General von, 137

Falkland Islands, 21; battle of (1914), 152

Falla, Manuel de, 684

Far East, foreign powers in (1898–1930), 254–257. *See also* Asia and individual countries

Farrell, General Edelmiro J., 282

Fascist Grand Council, 405, 406

Fascist Party, rise of, in Italy, 402–403; political system, 403–406; economic program, 406–408

Fashoda Affair (1898), 14, 54, 113

Federal Bureau of Investigation, 250

Federal Bureau of Reclamation, 245

Federal Home Loan Bank, 572

Federal Housing Administration, 572

Federal Power Commission, 245

Federal Public Housing Authority, 572

Federation of Indo-China, 650

Feudalism, decline of, 7

Fighting French, 643

Figl, Leopold, 629

Fiji Islands, 381

Finland, 210, 269; independence recognized (1920), 198, 199; land reforms, 329; Russo-Finnish War (1939), 466; accepts armistice (1944), 518–519; peace treaty (1946), 565–567; after World War II, 626

Finns, in Soviet Russia, 322

First Army, American, 518; French, 518

Fisher, Vardis, 699

Fiume, 404

Five-Year Plans, of Soviet Union, 309–313, 608

Flanders, 8; in World War I, 161; battle of (1940), 472, 473

Flemings, 623

Florence, falls to Allies (1944), 518

Foch, Ferdinand, supreme commander in World War I, 132, 146

Food, increased production of, 671–673

Food administration, World War I, 141

Food and Agricultural Organization, United Nations, 552

Foodstuffs, British imports of, 19–20

Fordney-McCumber Tariff Act (1922), 208, 265

Foreign trade, British, 19–21, 37, 109–110, 594–598; German, 22, 37–38, 114; Russian, prior to World War I, 65; Italian, 76; Austro-Hungarian, 84; Spanish, 96; Belgo-Dutch, 98; French, 114; in World War I, 162–164; after World War I, 264–266; American, 264–265, 266; Canadian, 274; Latin American, 281, 284; Netherlands Indies, 352; Japanese, 363–364; in Great Depression, 433

Formosa, 16, 357; Japan captures, 255, 363

Four-Year Plan, Nazis introduce (1936), 415

Fourteen Points, Wilson's, 171, 183, 190–191

Fourth French Republic, 620–623

France, colonial expansion, 8, 51–52, 113–114; imperialism (1890–1899), 14, 17; British entente with (1904), 23; member of Triple Entente, 23, 41, 43, 56, 70, 86, 126, 127; war with Germany (1870–1871), 39, 53, 105; resources, 50–53; problem of population, 52–53; defense, 53–58; quest for allies prior to World War I, 53–56; accord with Russia (1894), 54; insecurity of, 56–58; Third Republic, 58–60; social justice, 58–63; church and state separated, 60–61; rise of Socialist Party, 62–63; foreign trade, 114; in World War I, 127–129, 132, 134, 136–137, 143, 145, 146, 149; army and armament (1914), 168–169; war debt, 206, 207, 210–211, 212–213; advocates immobility after 1918, 261–262; in eastern Europe (1920–1930), 332; (1919–1939), 393–395; political feuds and factions, 395–398; decline of prestige (1933–1939), 398–400; growth of urban population, 423–425; policy of appeasement, 449–450; declares war on Germany (1939), 464, 465–466, 467–469; fall of (1940), 470–475; Allies liberate (1944), 515–518; after World War II, 620–623; colonial empire after World War II, 642–643, 650

France, Anatole, 692

Franchise, extension of British, 24

Francis I, Emperor of Austria (previously Holy Roman Emperor Francis II), 83

Francis Ferdinand, Archduke, assassination of, 93, 121, 125

Francis Joseph, Emperor of Austria, 90–91, 194

Franco, Francisco, 397, 447, 633–634

Franco-Prussian War, 39, 53, 105

Franco-Russian accord (1935), 399

Franco-Russian Alliance, 23, 54

Frankfort, Assembly of (1848–1849), 44

Free trade, British, in nineteenth century, 25, 37, 108

Free Trade Party, British, 27

French Canadians, 276–277

French Equatorial Africa, 52

French Forces of the Interior, 516, 517

French Indo-China. *See* Indo-China

French National Committee of Liberation, 643

French Revolution, 18, 71, 106, 148

French West Africa, 14, 52, 113

Freud, Sigmund, 670, 694

Functionalism, in modern architecture, 676

G.I. BILL of Rights, 570

Gabès, 503

Galapagos Islands, American bases established on, 499

Galicia, 91

Gallipoli, in World War I, 161

Galsworthy, John, 690

Gama, Vasco da, 7

Gandhi, Mohandas K., 341, 342

Garibaldi, Giuseppe, 78

Gaspari, Alcide de, Italian premier, 632

Gauguin, Paul, 678–679

Gaulle, General Charles de, 473, 620

General Confederation of Labor, French, 396, 399

General Motors Corporation, 574

General Munitions Board, in World War I, 141

Geneva Protocol (1924), 262

Genghis Khan, 6

Gentile, Giovanni, philosopher of Fascism, 705

George V, of England, 29, 389

George II, King of the Hellenes, 636

George Washington Bridge, 676

Georgians, in Soviet Russia, 322

Georgiev, Kimon, 559

German East Africa, 14, 161, 194, 385

German Evangelical Church, 717

German High Seas Fleet, 151, 152, 153

German Samoa, 194

German South West Africa, 14, 161, 194, 385

Germany, imperialism (1890–1899), 14, 17; naval program (1898–1900), 21–22, 23; trade rivalry with Britain, 22, 109; organization and expansion, 36–38; growth of national pride, 39; defense, 39–43; preparations for war, 41–42, 57; Triple Alliance, 41, 53, 80; penetration of Balkans, 42–43; social justice, 43–49; authoritarian bureaucracy, 44–46; Prussian influence, 44–45; rise of Socialist Party, 46–49; Reinsurance Treaty, 53; Three Emperors' League, 53; Dual Alliance, 53, 86, 254; expansion of, in nineteenth century, 114, 115; foreign trade, 114, 163, 266; enters World War I, 127–131; military strategy, 131–134; land operations, 134–137, 144–147; proposes peace parley (1916), 137–138; submarine warfare in World War I, 139–140, 143–144, 155–158, 479; diplomacy prior to World War I, 149–150; naval operations (1914–1918), 151–154; War Guilt Thesis, 168–170; disarmament (1919–1920), 188–194; reparations bill, 202–206; defaults on reparations payments, 209–212; United States ends war with, 221–222; admitted to League of Nations, 224, 225–226, 227; resigns from League of Nations, 271; rise of Hitler, 410–413; Nazi revolution, 413–415; national economy under Nazis, 415–417; revival of militarism, 417–419; growth of urban population, 423–425; rearmament of, 449; annexes Austria, 453–456; dismembers Czechoslovakia, 457–460; invades Poland (1939), 463–464; nonaggression pact with Soviets (1939), 464; invades Denmark and Norway (1940), 469–470; invades France (1940), 470–475; battle of Britain (1940–1941), 476–479; battle of the Atlantic (1941), 479–483; Balkan campaign (1940–1941), 486–487; Mediterranean campaign, 487–489, 501–502, 503–505; growing tension with Russia, 489–490; Russian campaign, 491–495, 507–509; Normandy invasion, 515–518; battle for, 518, 519–520; surrenders to Allies (1945), 520; Allied occupation, 525; reconstruction, 567–568, 626–628

Gibraltar, 21, 642

Gilbert Islands, 381; United States captures (1943), 532

Giolitti, Giovanni, 80, 82